TWELVE AMERICAN PLAYS

Alternate Edition

TWELVE AMERICAN PLAYS

Alternate Edition

EDITED BY

Richard Corbin

AND

Miriam Balf

New York

CHARLES SCRIBNER'S SONS

1113151719 K/P 201816141210

Printed in the United States of America
Library of Congress Catalog Card Number 72–1901
SBN 684–13002–5 (paper)

PREFACE

This book offers a selection of memorable plays written by American playwrights during the last half century. Each was chosen primarily for its dramatic quality and the relevance of its theme and story to the lives and interests of today's students.

We have included significant plays from each decade, beginning in 1922 with Eugene O'Neill's expressionistic play "*The Hairy Ape*," and ending in 1965 with *Day of Absence*, a comedy with elements of the Absurd written by the black playwright Douglas Turner Ward. We have struck a balance between comedy and drama by selecting six serious plays and six comedies. A musical play is included among the comedies because the form is probably the most distinctive American contribution to the tradition of world drama. Among the serious plays, we have included one television drama because such a script seems a more logical choice today than a motion picture script which has an almost identical format.

Represented in this anthology are the various types of dramatic writing: tragedy, comedy, melodrama, farce, satire, fantasy, social and political problem plays, and the "Theater of the Absurd." These selections are varied enough to touch on most of the dramatic styles: romanticism, realism, expressionism, symbolism, and theatricalism (or non-realism).

The introduction, "How to Read a Play," is addressed to the student and is designed to improve his reading and understanding of plays. In this section there is a discussion of the uniqueness of the play form, as contrasted with other literary types, with specific suggestions for gaining maximum enjoyment from the staging of plays in the theater of one's mind.

Since plays are not written in a vacuum, the brief "History of the Theater" is a quick summary for student and teacher to highlight the main dramatic trends for each of the decades represented.

Before each play there is a brief discussion of its style and other information to heighten the enjoyment of reading it. Following each play are concise questions and suggestions for discussion and writing, intended to provoke thought about the play, to supplement but not to interfere with the teacher's own ideas for handling the play. In the discussion sections, professional critical comment illuminates the themes, the techniques, the characterizations and the philosophical implications of each play.

Included in the Appendix are a glossary of technical stage terms for those who are interested, brief biographies of the playwrights represented, and a list of additional important plays for supplementary reading.

Because of space limitations and the difficulties in obtaining permission, and also because some modern plays are less appealing to young people, there are some outstanding plays and playwrights we could not include in this anthology. We regret we could not include Arthur Miller's *Death of a Salesman*, and we suggest that students might make this play part of their supplementary reading.

These are plays for people everywhere, of any age, who are probing for meanings, for perspectives and for lasting values.

For the great wealth of American dramatic criticism which provided us with the ideas, the controversies, and the stimulating differences of opinion that we have quoted and used so liberally, we thank the men of the theater —both its creators and its critics—who write so perceptively and so provocatively.

And for invaluable help with the difficulties of manuscript preparation, we would like to thank Mildred A. Busch, Harriet Davis, and Selma Michael.

May 1972

RICHARD CORBIN
MIRIAM BALF

CONTENTS

Preface v

How to Read a Play ix

About the American Theater in the Twentieth Century xiii

PLAYS

Arsenic and Old Lace / JOSEPH KESSELRING 3

The Little Foxes / LILLIAN HELLMAN 51

The Rainmaker / RICHARD NASH 91

Our Town / THORNTON WILDER 139

The Teahouse of the August Moon / JOHN PATRICK 171

There Shall Be No Night / ROBERT SHERWOOD 213

The King and I / RICHARD RODGERS AND OSCAR HAMMERSTEIN II 259

Requiem for a Heavyweight / ROD SERLING 299

Harvey / MARY CHASE 329

"The Hairy Ape" / EUGENE O'NEILL 369

The Glass Menagerie / TENNESSEE WILLIAMS 399

Day of Absence / DOUGLAS TURNER WARD 439

Notes on the Playwrights 461

Glossary of Theater Terms 469

Other Important American Plays 473

How to Read a Play

A play in printed form is not a finished product like a novel or a short story; it is a blueprint for a stage production. In it the playwright tells the artists and technicians of the theater what to say and do on stage. Just as a builder can read the architect's blueprint of a house and know where the windows and doors should be, so in the theater the director, the actors, the set designer, the costume designer, the lighting designer and all the other technical crews backstage "collaborate" with the playwright to bring his "blueprint" or "play" to life. The printed script of a play, therefore, is not an end in itself but only the beginning of a collaboration between the playwright and all the "middlemen" of the theater which culminates in a "smash hit" or a "flop" on opening night.

You, as a reader of plays, should try to become all of these people who work to bring a play to life on the stage, though of course the stage is in your mind. You should try to see the actors walking across the stage and gesturing, and you must understand the reason for each move they make and each line they speak. This is the trick, the visualization and creation—the seeing as you read.

SETTING THE SCENE

Perhaps you have not had the opportunity to see many professional stage productions, but you have undoubtedly watched plays on television and in motion pictures and are very much aware of the importance of setting. When you read a play, study the opening stage directions carefully and then set up the stage in your mind.

For example, in *The Little Foxes*, the playwright tells you "the room is good-looking, the furniture expensive, but it reflects no particular taste. Everything is of the best and that is all." What might this tell you about the family living there? How would this room differ from the prosperous ranch in *The Rainmaker*? The difference in the furnishings of these two rooms will explain much about the differences in the two families.

You must put thought and imagination into your reading. Use any clue you can find in the script and all your own experience and knowledge of life to help you visualize and project on your stage what the playwright planned.

BRINGING THE CHARACTERS TO LIFE

You next put people on your stage—not just "characters," but living, breathing people. Who are they? What do they look like? How do they behave? Most important, *why* do they behave as they do? A playwright rarely tells you at the start everything you need to know to visualize a person or to understand the subtleties of his nature. You get to know his characters bit by bit, revelation by revelation, just as you do people in real life, so that by the end of the play you could probably predict what each would do in any real life situation.

Sometimes, in the early stage directions, a playwright may describe his characters fully. In *The Glass Menagerie*, though, Tennessee Williams doesn't describe Amanda at all. But when she begins to talk, we learn a great deal about her, right from her opening, "We can't say grace until you come to the table!" until her final "Go then! Go to the moon—you selfish dreamer!"

Sometimes we learn about characters by what other people say about them. In *Harvey,* Myrtle complains people are always saying, "That's Myrtle Mae Simmons. Her uncle is Elwood P. Dowd—the biggest screwball in town." This line of hers tells us something not only about Elwood but also about the speaker, Myrtle, and the townspeople who passed the original judgment.

Finally, people are revealed by their actions—by what they do. In the two hours it takes to stage a play, you frequently learn to know the characters better than your own friends or family. Why? Because the playwright begins shortly before a crisis facing his *main* characters. In times of crisis, people are likely to reveal themselves as they actually are. Also, the playwright cuts away all the unessential trivia of life that might blur our understanding. He carefully *selects* only the incidents that develop the story, compressing much of the irrelevant chitchat of daily living into pointed dialogue and action.

STRUCTURING THE STORY

The primary difference between a play and any other form of story telling is that a play is structured for performance. This means that the playwright must so mold and shape his material that he captures and holds the total attention of his audience from the time the curtain rises till the play ends.

The basic factor in holding audience attention is the element of *conflict.* If the *protagonist* (the hero or main character) has a goal which it is vital for him to attain, and if his *antagonist* (often known as the "villain") has a conflicting goal, you have conflict. Without it there is no drama. The moment conflict erupts on a stage between two forces, the audience is interested. If the antagonist then places obstacles or *complications* between the main character and the attainment of his goal, the audience becomes involved.

The protagonist can be involved in a conflict with another person (the *antagonist*), or he can be involved in a different type of conflict with the elements or his environment. In such a conflict, the antagonist could be fire, flood, drought or earthquake—any natural force outside of man. These are modern day versions of ancient Greek myths that tell of conflicts between man and his gods—or man fighting against the unalterable fate the gods seem to be inflicting upon him.

There is still a third kind of conflict that you are more likely to find in modern plays—man battling forces within himself: a Nobel Award scientist deciding whether or not to go to war to help defend his country (*There Shall Be No Night*), a young man struggling to free himself from his past (*Glass Menagerie*), a washed-up fighter struggling to keep his dignity (*Requiem for a Heavyweight*). These are instances of internal conflict, of people fighting against their inner torments, their desires, their frustrations.

But conflict alone doesn't make a play. A playwright must develop the conflict by means of a *plot,* that is, by presenting his series of incidents, or *complications* for the protagonist, in a carefully structured order of mounting *suspense* until we reach the highest point of interest or crisis in the play (the *climax*).

Up to the climax, the main question of the *rising action* or suspense is what will happen to the protagonist. After the climax or crisis or turning point, the main question of the play is what will the protagonist do about his crisis. This is called the *falling* action. The main character's final actions to solve his problem make the *resolution* of the play.

The important factor in a good play is the growth of the main character. He has to have some *scene of recognition* at the end in which he learns something about himself from his experiences. In some forms of modern playwriting, especially in the "Theater of the Absurd," the characters learn nothing. It is the audience who learns and the recognition scene is theirs.

HEARING THE CHARACTERS TALK

Watching or reading a play, you can often sense what the characters are about to do before they do it. How can you explain what is in the character's mind when he himself may not yet know? The only clues you have are what the character is doing, what the character is saying, and the manner in which he says it. The dialogue in a play and the way the actor speaks his lines reveal a great deal about him.

But what the character is thinking may be something quite different from what he says. For example, in *Requiem for a Heavyweight,* the fight manager says to his aging, washed-up fighter when he gets to the dressing room after a one-sided beating, "Bum night, kid. Just a bum night all the way around. There'll be others." And the dazed fighter answers, "Sure. Others." Though neither says what is really in his mind—that this is the end—the audience knows without question that it is.

We learn about characters on a stage not only through how they think and what they say, but through the rhythm in which they say it. In *The King and I,* the King speaks in short staccato bursts of dialogue fitting a highly excitable, imperious man. How is Anna's rhythm different and what does it reveal about her? In *The Rainmaker,* Starbuck speaks in the dynamic rhythm of an advertising pitch man. Contrast Lizzie's even speech with his.

A play is also written for the eye. You can get so caught up in reading the dialogue that you overlook what would instantly be seen in the theater, since the stage is a visual art. When a playwright writes into his directions "a pause," "a silence," or a description of some other stage business that tells the actor what to say or do, you must consider these matters carefully. In the funeral scene in the last act of *Our Town,* the mourners never speak, but once they have left, Dr. Gibbs, who has lingered, brings some fresh flowers from the new grave to the old, then stands for a moment in silence.

A piece of stage business often speaks more eloquently than the most emotion-packed line. And whether this business is written into the play in brackets or suggested, you must be alert to the pauses, the silences, the action. For this is the punctuation that gives dialogue depth and meaning.

Theater at its best is a total experience. For a brief hour or two, you can put your own problems aside while you sit in the darkened theater, transported to a different world. As the world of the play unfolds, the lives of the characters stand revealed. In them you begin to recognize truths about yourself, your friends, and your family.

Even when the characters on the stage are strange and alien to you—a con man out West making rain, a gentleman drinker with an invisible companion—their response to crisis often casts unexpected light into the dark corners of your own life.

As long as man wants to find out more about his neighbor, the world around him, and the world inside himself, he will continue to go to the theater. Or, if theaters are not easily available, he will continue to read plays, turning the lights up and raising the curtain on the stage of his mind.

About the American Theater in the Twentieth Century

The repertoire of the American theater at the dawn of the twentieth century ranged generally from sentiment to rip-roaring melodrama, flavored by an occasional nineteenth-century heroic romance of European origin. American producers were more interested in the realism of stage settings than they were in the advent of realistic writing sparked by Ibsen, Chekhov and Strindberg on modern European stages.

The American theater came of age after the First World War when Eugene O'Neill and the growing "Little Theater" movement in this country turned to this new realism. Spurred by the growth on the East Coast of the American university theaters and of art theaters like the Provincetown Players, the Washington Square Players and Eva Le Gallienne's Civic Repertory Theater, modern American drama was now on its way.

The post-war prosperity brought with it a tremendous sense of freedom and individuality. The drama of the twenties was distinguished not only by its quantity but by its endless experimentation in form, its wide range of themes, and the emergence of a whole galaxy of playwrights including Rice, Howard, Kaufman, Anderson, Barry, Sherwood and Behrman, who were to dominate the stage for the next twenty years.

In 1929, the stock market crash ushered in the depression decade of the 1930's. The esthetic revolt of the stage in the twenties became a social revolt in the thirties. With the financial struggle at home and rising fascism abroad, the theater began to stress social significance. The same playwrights who had written with cynical sophistication in the twenties were now committed to social causes.

Clifford Odets sought for answers in the bourgeois world of the Bronx, Robert Sherwood wrote about his "lost generation," and Lillian Hellman, in *The Little Foxes*, went back to an earlier society to show the effects of ruthless greed. Thornton Wilder rose above daily struggles in *Our Town* in his search for eternal truths.

Except for the Theater Guild, all of the little theater movements of the twenties succumbed to the depression. In their place arose new producing organizations: the Group Theater, the Playwrights Company, the Mercury Theater of Orson Welles, the Labor stages, Communist theater groups and from 1935 to 1939 the exciting Federal Theater, a WPA project to help unemployed theater artists.

Pearl Harbor in December 1941 changed the face of the American theater once more. During the years of the Second World War, plays like Robert Sherwood's *There Shall Be No Night* reflected a new interest in man's psychological and emotional reaction to the problems of war.

Sharing the stage with the largely melodramatic and realistic war plays were the escapist comedies like *Arsenic and Old Lace* and *Harvey*. The post-war period in 1945 brought a new interest in violence and emotion. But the exaltation and ferment of the twenties and thirties had given way to a mood of grim resignation. The plays dealt with loneliness, sadness, weariness and defeat, but according to the playwrights, society was no longer to blame; the fault lay now in the individual.

Except for the work of two newcomers, Arthur Miller and Tennessee Williams, the forties were distinguished chiefly by the exuberant mushrooming of a new type of musical play, beginning with Rodgers and Hammerstein's *Oklahoma* in 1943.

The fifties saw the political expansion of Communism, and the congressional purges of suspected Red sympathizers. The result was a period of national anxiety and conformity. At a time when many Americans were afraid to speak out, the American theater came to a vital resurgent life, with plays like *The Crucible* and *The Diary of Anne Frank*, in a fight for freedom of the individual conscience.

In addition to this creative rebirth on Broadway, two new movements were highly significant in the fifties; the first was the growth of the "Theater of the Absurd." Introduced by foreign playwrights, this exciting new technique was developed by young Americans in off-Broadway one-act plays like Edward Albee's *The Sandbox*. The second movement was the spread of theater throughout America on college and university stages and in community theaters like the Tyrone Guthrie Theater in Minneapolis.

The sixties was marked by the emergence of a new force in the theater—black playwrights writing about black people, as in Douglas Turner Ward's *Day of Absence*. Starting off-Broadway, this vital movement spread rapidly to Harlem, to Broadway, to the college campuses, to the community theater.

So the American theater, which reached its maturity in the twenties in the experimentation of the "Little Theaters" on the East Coast, is still experimenting in the sixties and seventies. But now the vast continent of America has become the new "Broadway."

TWELVE AMERICAN PLAYS

Alternate Edition

Arsenic and Old Lace

{1941}

JOSEPH KESSELRING

CHARACTERS
(In Order of Appearance)

ABBY BREWSTER	MORTIMER BREWSTER
REV. DR. HARPER	MR. GIBBS
TEDDY BREWSTER	JONATHAN BREWSTER
OFFICER BROPHY	DR. EINSTEIN
OFFICER KLEIN	OFFICER O'HARA
MARTHA BREWSTER	LIEUTENANT ROONEY
ELAINE HARPER	MR. WITHERSPOON

$\mathcal{W}$hen *Arsenic and Old Lace* opened on Broadway in 1941 to packed houses rocking with laughter, drama columns were filled with controversy about whether or not murder and insanity are proper topics for comedy.

Actually, Joseph Kesselring had written his "madcap murder farce" originally as serious melodrama, but during rehearsals its mood changed to that of farce. The producers, realizing that the multiple-murders in the play might be difficult for an audience to accept, converted it into a melodramatic farce.

Although farce aims at laughs, and melodrama at thrills, both farce and melodrama gain their effects by much the same techniques: by concentration on situation rather than on character; by action that is fast and physical; by characters who are types rather than individuals; and above all, by constant exaggeration of character and event. People in the audience must never be given time to think or they will realize that it is all nonsense.

Arsenic and Old Lace ran for nearly four years and grossed more than four million dollars. It ran in London as long as in New York, and has since played all over the world. The play has been turned into both a successful movie and a television production. It continues to be a staple in high school and university theaters.

Arsenic and Old Lace

ACT ONE

SCENE: *It is late afternoon in September. The time is the present. The living room of the old Brewster home in Brooklyn, N.Y., is just as Victorian as the two sisters,* ABBY *and* MARTHA BREWSTER, *who occupy the house with their nephew,* TEDDY.
There is a staircase leading to the upper floor, broken by a landing with a window looking out on the front porch. At the top of the stairs, a balcony with a door leading to bedrooms and an archway beyond which are stairs to the top floor. There is a large window, a long window seat below it. A door leads to the cellar, another to the kitchen, and the main door of the house, which opens onto the porch. When the curtain rises, ABBY BREWSTER, *a plump little darling in her late sixties, is presiding at the tea table. The table is lighted by candles. Seated in armchair at her left is the* REV. DR. HARPER, *and on her right, standing, her nephew,* TEDDY, *whose costume includes a frock coat and pince-nez attached to a black ribbon.* TEDDY *is in his forties and has a large black mustache, and his manner and make-up suggest Theodore Roosevelt.*

ABBY. Yes, indeed, my sister Martha and I have been talking all week about your sermon last Sunday. It's really wonderful, Dr. Harper—in only two short years you've taken on the spirit of Brooklyn.

HARPER. That's very gratifying, Miss Brewster.

ABBY. You see, living here next to the church all our lives, we've seen so many ministers come and go. The spirit of Brooklyn we always say is friendliness—and your sermons are not so much sermons as friendly talks.

TEDDY. Personally, I've always enjoyed my talks with Cardinal Gibbons—or have I met him yet?

ABBY. No dear, not yet. [*Changing the subject.*] Are the biscuits good?

TEDDY. [*He sits on sofa.*] Bully!

ABBY. Won't you have another biscuit, Dr. Harper?

HARPER. Oh, no, I'm afraid I'll have no appetite for dinner now. I always eat too many of your biscuits just to taste that lovely jam.

ABBY. But you haven't tried the quince. We always put a little apple in with it to take the tartness out.

HARPER. No, thank you.

ABBY. We'll send you over a jar.

HARPER. No, no. You keep it here so I can be sure of having your biscuits with it.

ABBY. I do hope they don't make us use that imitation flour again. I mean with this war trouble. It may not be very charitable of me, but I've almost come to the conclusion that this Mr. Hitler isn't a Christian.

HARPER. [*With a sigh.*] If only Europe were on another planet!

TEDDY. [*Sharply.*] Europe, sir?

HARPER. Yes, Teddy.

TEDDY. Point your gun the other way!

HARPER. Gun?

ABBY. [*Trying to calm him.*] Teddy.

TEDDY. To the West! There's your danger! There's your enemy! Japan!

HARPER. Why, yes—yes, of course.

ABBY. Teddy!

TEDDY. No, Aunt Abby! Not so much talk about Europe and more about the canal!

ABBY. Well, let's not talk about war. Will you have another cup of tea, dear?

TEDDY. No, thank you, Aunt Abby.

ABBY. Dr. Harper?

HARPER. No, thank you. I must admit, Miss Abby, that war and violence seem far removed from these surroundings.

ABBY. It is peaceful here, isn't it?

HARPER. Yes—peaceful. The virtues of another day—they're all here in this house. The gentle virtues that went out with candlelight and good manners and low taxes.

ABBY. [Glancing about her contentedly.] It's one of the oldest houses in Brooklyn. It's just as it was when Grandfather Brewster built and furnished it—except for the electricity—and we use it as little as possible. It was Mortimer who persuaded us to put it in.

HARPER. [Beginning to freeze.] Yes, I can understand that. Your nephew Mortimer seems to live only by electric light.

ABBY. The poor boy has to work so late. I understand he's taking Elaine with him to the theatre again tonight. Teddy, your brother Mortimer will be here a little later.

TEDDY. [Baring his teeth in a broad grin.] Dee-lighted!

ABBY. [To Harper.] We're so happy it's Elaine Mortimer takes to the theatre with him.

HARPER. Well, it's a new experience for me to wait up until three o'clock in the morning for my daughter to be brought home.

ABBY. Oh, Dr. Harper, I hope you don't disapprove of Mortimer.

HARPER. Well—

ABBY. We'd feel so guilty if you did—sister Martha and I. I mean since it was here in our home that your daughter met Mortimer.

HARPER. Of course, Miss Abby. And so I'll say immediately that I believe Mortimer himself to be quite a worthy gentleman. But I must also admit that I have watched the growing intimacy between him and my daughter with some trepidation. For one reason, Miss Abby.

ABBY. You mean his stomach, Dr. Harper?

HARPER. Stomach?

ABBY. His dyspepsia—he's bothered with it so, poor boy.

HARPER. No, Miss Abby, I'll be frank with you. I'm speaking of your nephew's unfortunate connection with the theatre.

ABBY. The theatre! Oh, no, Dr. Harper! Mortimer writes for a New York newspaper.

HARPER. I know, Miss Abby, I know. But a dramatic critic is constantly exposed to the theatre, and I don't doubt but what some of them do develop an interest in it.

ABBY. Well, not Mortimer. You need have no fear of that. Why, Mortimer hates the theatre.

HARPER. Really?

ABBY. Oh, yes! He writes awful things about the theatre. But you can't blame him, poor boy. He was so happy writing about real estate, which he really knew something about, and then they just made him take this terrible night position.

HARPER. My! My!

ABBY. But, as he says, the theatre can't last much longer anyway and in the meantime it's a living. [Complacently.] Yes, I think if we give the theatre another year or two, perhaps . . . [A knock on door.] Well, now, who do you suppose that is? [They all rise as ABBY goes to door; TEDDY starts for door at same time, but ABBY stops him.] No, thank you, Teddy. I'll go. [She opens door to admit two COPS, OFFICERS BROPHY and KLEIN.] Come in, Mr. Brophy.

BROPHY. Hello, Miss Brewster.

ABBY. How are you, Mr. Klein?

KLEIN. Very well, Miss Brewster.

[The COPS cross to TEDDY who is standing near desk, and salute him. TEDDY returns salute.]

TEDDY. What news have you brought me?

BROPHY. Colonel, we have nothing to report.

TEDDY. Splendid! Thank you, gentlemen! At ease!

[COPS relax; ABBY has closed door, and turns to them.]

ABBY. You know Dr. Harper.

KLEIN. Sure! Hello, Dr. Harper.

BROPHY. [Turns to ABBY, doffing cap.] We've come for the toys for the Christmas Fund.

ABBY. Oh, yes.

HARPER. [Standing below table.] That's a splendid work you men do—fixing up discarded toys to give poor children a happier Christmas.

KLEIN. It gives us something to do when we have to sit around the station. You get tired playing cards and then you start cleaning your gun, and the first thing you know you've shot yourself in the foot. [KLEIN *drifts around to window seat.*]

ABBY. [*Crossing to* TEDDY.] Teddy, go upstairs and get that big box from your Aunt Martha's room. [TEDDY *crosses upstage toward stairs.* ABBY *speaks to* BROPHY.] How is Mrs. Brophy today? Mrs. Brophy has been quite ill, Dr. Harper.

BROPHY. [*To* HARPER.] Penumonia!

HARPER. I'm sorry to hear that.

TEDDY. [*Reaching first landing on stairs where he stops and draws an imaginary sword; shouting.*] CHARGE! [*He charges up stairs and exits off balcony. The others pay no attention to this.*]

BROPHY. Oh, she's better now. A little weak still—

ABBY. [*Starting toward kitchen.*] I'm going to get you some beef broth to take to her.

BROPHY. Don't bother, Miss Abby! You've done so much for her already.

ABBY. [*At kitchen door.*] We made it this morning. Sister Martha is taking some to poor Mr. Benitzky right now. I won't be a minute. Sit down and be comfortable, all of you. [*She exits into kitchen.*]

[HARPER *sits again.* BROPHY *crosses to table and addresses the other two.*]

BROPHY. She shouldn't go to all that trouble.

KLEIN. Listen, try to stop her or her sister from doing something nice—and for nothing! They don't even care how you vote. [*He sits on window seat.*]

HARPER. When I received my call to Brooklyn and moved next door my wife wasn't well. When she died and for months before—well, if I know what pure kindness and absolute generosity are, it's because I've known the Brewster sisters.

[*At this moment* TEDDY *steps out on balcony and blows a bugle call. They all look.*]

BROPHY. [*Stepping upstage; remonstrating.*] Colonel, you promised not to do that.

TEDDY. But I have to call a Cabinet meeting to get the release of those supplies. [TEDDY *wheels and exits.*]

BROPHY. He used to do that in the middle of the night. The neighbors raised cain

with us. They're a little afraid of him, anyway.

HARPER. Oh, he's quite harmless.

KLEIN. Suppose he does think he's Teddy Roosevelt. There's a lot worse people he could think he was.

BROPHY. Damn shame—a nice family like this hatching a cuckoo.

KLEIN. Well, his father—the old girls' brother—was some sort of a genius, wasn't he? And their father—Teddy's grandfather —seems to me I've heard he was a little crazy too.

BROPHY. Yeah—he was crazy like a fox. He made a million dollars.

HARPER. Really? Here in Brooklyn?

BROPHY. Yeah. Patent medicine. He was a kind of a quack of some sort. Old Sergeant Edwards remembers him. He used the house here as a sort of clinic—tried 'em out on people.

KLEIN. Yeah, I hear he used to make mistakes occasionally, too.

BROPHY. The department never bothered him much because he was pretty useful on autopsies sometimes. Especially poison cases.

KLEIN. Well, whatever he did he left his daughters fixed for life. Thank God for that—

BROPHY. Not that they ever spend any of it on themselves.

HARPER. Yes, I'm well acquainted with their charities.

KLEIN. You don't know a tenth of it. When I was with the Missing Persons Bureau I was trying to trace an old man that we never did find—[*Rises.*]—do you know there's a renting agency that's got this house down on its list for furnished rooms? They don't rent rooms—but you can bet that anybody who comes here lookin' for a room goes away with a good meal and probably a few dollars in their kick.

BROPHY. It's just their way of digging up people to do some good to.

[MARTHA BREWSTER *enters.* MARTHA *is also a sweet elderly woman with Victorian charm. She is dressed in the old-fashioned manner of* ABBY, *but with a high lace collar that covers her neck.* MEN *all rise.*]

MARTHA [*At door.*] Well, now, isn't this nice? [*Closes door.*]

BROPHY. [*Crosses to* MARTHA.] Good afternoon, Miss Brewster.

MARTHA. How do you do, Mr. Brophy? Dr. Harper. Mr. Klein.

KLEIN. How are you, Miss Brewster? We dropped in to get the Christmas toys.

MARTHA. Oh, yes, Teddy's Army and Navy. They wear out. They're all packed. [*She turns to stairs.* BROPHY *stops her.*]

BROPHY. The Colonel's upstairs after them—it seems the Cabinet has to O.K. it.

MARTHA. Yes, of course. I hope Mrs. Brophy's better?

BROPHY. She's doin' fine, ma'am. Your sister's getting some soup for me to take to her.

MARTHA. Oh, yes, we made it this morning. I just took some to a poor man who broke ever so many bones.

ABBY. [*Enters from kitchen carrying a covered pail.*] Oh, you're back, Martha. How was Mr. Benitzky?

MARTHA. Well, dear, it's pretty serious, I'm afraid. The doctor was there. He's going to amputate in the morning.

ABBY. [*Hopefully.*] Can we be present?

MARTHA. [*Disappointment.*] No. I asked him but he says it's against the rules of the hospital. [MARTHA *crosses to sideboard, puts pail down. Then puts cape and hat on small table.*]

[TEDDY *enters on balcony with large cardboard box and comes downstairs to desk, putting box on stool.* KLEIN *crosses to toy box, while* HARPER *speaks.*]

HARPER. You couldn't be of any service —and you must spare yourselves something.

ABBY. [*To* BROPHY.] Here's the broth, Mr. Brophy. Be sure it's good and hot.

BROPHY. Yes, ma'am.

KLEIN. This is fine—it'll make a lot of kids happy. [*Lifts out toy soldier.*] That O'Malley boy is nuts about soldiers.

TEDDY. That's General Miles. I've retired him. [KLEIN *removes ship.*] What's this! The *Oregon!*

MARTHA. Teddy, dear, put it back.

TEDDY. But the *Oregon* goes to Australia.

ABBY. Now, Teddy—

TEDDY. No, I've given my word to Fighting Bob Evans.

MARTHA. But, Teddy—

KLEIN. What's the difference what kid gets it—Bobby Evans, Izzy Cohen? [*Crosses to door with box, opens door.*

BROPHY *follows.*] We'll run along, ma'am, and thank you very much.

ABBY. Not at all. [*The* COPS *stop in doorway, salute* TEDDY *and exit.* ABBY *crosses and shuts door as she speaks.* TEDDY *starts upstairs.*] Good-by.

HARPER. [*Crosses to sofa, gets hat.*] I must be getting home.

ABBY. Before you go, Dr. Harper—

TEDDY. [*Has reached stair landing.*] CHARGE! [*He dashes upstairs. At top he stops and with a sweeping gesture over the balcony rail, invites all to follow him as he speaks.*] Charge the blockhouse! [*He dashes through door, closing it after him.*]

[HARPER *looks after him.* MARTHA *is fooling with a pin on her dress.* ABBY *stands to the right of* HARPER.]

HARPER. The blockhouse?

MARTHA. The stairs are always San Juan Hill.

HARPER. Have you ever tried to persuade him that he wasn't Teddy Roosevelt.

ABBY. Oh, no!

MARTHA. He's so happy being Teddy Roosevelt.

ABBY. Once, a long time ago [*She walks across to* MARTHA.], remember, Martha? We thought if he would be George Washington it might be a change for him—

MARTHA. But he stayed under his bed for days and just wouldn't be anybody.

ABBY. And we'd so much rather he'd be Mr. Roosevelt than nobody.

HARPER. Well, if he's happy—and what's more important you're happy—[*He takes blue-backed legal paper from inside side pocket.*] you'll see that he signs these.

MARTHA. What are they?

ABBY. Dr. Harper has made all arrangements for Teddy to go to Happy Dale Sanitarium after we pass on.

MARTHA. But why should Teddy sign any papers now?

HARPER. It's better to have it all settled. If the Lord should take you away suddenly perhaps we couldn't persuade Teddy to commit himself and that would mean an unpleasant legal procedure. Mr. Witherspoon understands they're to be filed away until the time comes to use them.

MARTHA. Mr. Witherspoon? Who's he?

HARPER. He's the superintendent of Happy Dale.

ABBY. [*To* MARTHA.] Dr. Harper has arranged for him to drop in tomorrow or the next day to meet Teddy.

HARPER. [*Going to door and opening it.*] I'd better be running along or Elaine will be over here looking for me.

ABBY. [*Calls out after him.*] Give our love to Elaine—and Dr. Harper, please don't think harshly of Mortimer because he's a dramatic critic. Somebody has to do those things. [ABBY *closes door, comes back into room.*]

MARTHA. [*At sideboard, puts legal papers on it; notices tea things on table.*] Did you just have tea? Isn't it rather late?

ABBY. [*As one who has a secret.*] Yes—and dinner's going to be late too.

[TEDDY *enters on balcony, starts downstairs to first landing.* MARTHA *steps to* ABBY.]

MARTHA. So? Why?

ABBY. Teddy! [TEDDY *stops on landing.*] Good news for you. You're going to Panama and dig another lock for the canal.

TEDDY. Dee-lighted! That's bully! Just bully! I shall prepare at once for the journey. [*He turns to go upstairs, stops as if puzzled, hurries back to landing, cries CHARGE! and rushes up and off.*]

MARTHA. [*Elated.*] Abby! While I was out?

ABBY. [*Taking* MARTHA's *hand.*] Yes, dear! I just couldn't wait for you. I didn't know when you'd be back and Dr. Harper was coming.

MARTHA. But all by yourself?

ABBY. Oh, I got along fine!

MARTHA. I'll run right downstairs and see. [*She starts happily for cellar door.*]

ABBY. Oh, no, there wasn't time, and I was all alone.

MARTHA. [*Looks around room toward kitchen.*] Well—

ABBY. [*Coyly.*] Martha—just look in the window seat. [MARTHA *almost skips to window seat, and just as she gets there a knock is heard on door. She stops. They both look toward door.* ABBY *hurries to door and opens it.* ELAINE HARPER *enters.* ELAINE *is an attractive girl in her twenties; she looks surprisingly smart for a minister's daughter.*] Oh, it's Elaine. [*Opens door.*] Come in, dear.

ELAINE. Good afternoon, Miss Abby. Good afternoon, Miss Martha. I thought Father was here.

MARTHA. [*Stepping to left of table.*] He just this minute left. Didn't you meet him?

ELAINE. [*Pointing to window.*] No, I took the short cut through the cemetery. Mortimer hasn't come yet?

ABBY. No, dear.

ELAINE. Oh? He asked me to meet him here. Do you mind if I wait?

MARTHA. Not at all.

ABBY. Why don't you sit down, dear?

MARTHA. But we really must speak to Mortimer about doing this to you.

ELAINE. [*Sits in chair.*] Doing what?

MARTHA. Well, he was brought up to know better. When a gentleman is taking a young lady out he should call for her at her house.

ELAINE. [*To both.*] Oh, there's something about calling for a girl at a parsonage that discourages any man who doesn't embroider.

ABBY. He's done this too often—we're going to speak to him.

ELAINE. Oh, please don't. After young men whose idea of night life was to take me to prayer meeting, it's wonderful to go to the theatre almost every night of my life.

MARTHA. It's comforting for us too, because if Mortimer has to see some of those plays he has to see—at least he's sitting next to a minister's daughter. [MARTHA *steps to back of table.*]

[ABBY *crosses to back of table, starts putting tea things on tray.* ELAINE *and* MARTHA *help.*]

ABBY. My goodness, Elaine, what must you think of us—not having tea cleared away by this time. [*She picks up tray and exits to kitchen.*]

[MARTHA *blows out one candle and takes it to sideboard.* ELAINE *blows out other, takes it to sideboard.*]

MARTHA. [*As* ABBY *exits.*] Now don't bother with anything in the kitchen until Mortimer comes, and then I'll help you. [*To* ELAINE.] Mortimer should be here any minute now.

ELAINE. Yes. Father must have been surprised not to find me at home. I'd better run over and say good night to him. [*She crosses to door.*]

MARTHA. It's a shame you missed him, dear.

ELAINE. [*Opening door.*] If Mortimer comes you tell him I'll be right back. [*She has opened door, but sees* MORTIMER *just outside.*] Hello, Mort!

MORTIMER. [*Entering.*] Hello, Elaine. [*As he passes her going toward* MARTHA, *thus placing himself between* ELAINE *and* MARTHA, *he reaches back and pats* ELAINE *on the fanny . . . then embraces* MARTHA.] Hello, Aunt Martha.

MARTHA. [*Exiting to kitchen, calling as she goes.*] Abby, Mortimer's here!

[ELAINE *slowly closes door.*]

MORTIMER. [*Turning.*] Were you going somewhere?

ELAINE. I was just going over to tell Father not to wait up for me.

MORTIMER. I didn't know that was still being done, even in Brooklyn. [*He throws his hat on sofa.*]

[ABBY *enters from kitchen.* MARTHA *follows, stays in doorway.*]

ABBY. [*Crosses to* MORTIMER.] Hello, Mortimer.

MORTIMER. [*Embraces and kisses her.*] Hello, Aunt Abby.

ABBY. How are you, dear?

MORTIMER. All right. And you look well. You haven't changed much since yesterday.

ABBY. Oh, my goodness, it was yesterday, wasn't it? We're seeing a great deal of you lately. [*She crosses and starts to sit in chair.*] Well, come, sit down. Sit down.

MARTHA. [*Stops her from sitting.*] Abby —haven't we something to do in the kitchen?

ABBY. Huh?

MARTHA. You know—the tea things.

ABBY. [*Suddenly seeing* MORTIMER *and* ELAINE, *and catching on.*] Oh, yes! Yes! The tea things— [*She backs toward kitchen.*] Well—you two just make yourselves at home. Just—

MARTHA. —make yourselves at home. [*They exit through kitchen door,* ABBY *closing door.*]

ELAINE. [*Stepping to* MORTIMER, *ready to be kissed.*] Well, can't you take a hint?

MORTIMER. [*Complaining.*] No . . . that was pretty obvious. A lack of inventiveness, I should say.

ELAINE. [*Only slightly annoyed as she crosses to table, and puts handbag on it.*] Yes—that's exactly what you'd say.

MORTIMER. [*At desk, fishing various pieces of note paper from his pockets, and separating dollar bills that are mixed in with papers.*] Where do you want to go for dinner?

ELAINE. [*Opening bag, looking in hand mirror.*] I don't care. I'm not very hungry.

MORTIMER. Well, I just had breakfast. Suppose we wait until after the show?

ELAINE. But that'll make it pretty late, won't it?

MORTIMER. Not with the little stinker we're seeing tonight. From what I've heard about it we'll be at Blake's by ten o'clock.

ELAINE. You ought to be fair to these plays.

MORTIMER. Are these plays fair to me?

ELAINE. *I've* never seen you walk out on a musical.

MORTIMER. That musical isn't opening tonight.

ELAINE. [*Disappointed.*] No?

MORTIMER. Darling, you'll have to learn the rules. With a musical there are always four changes of title and three postponements. They liked it in New Haven but it needs a lot of work.

ELAINE. Oh, I was hoping it was a musical.

MORTIMER. You have such a light mind.

ELAINE. Not a bit. Musicals somehow have a humanizing effect on you. [*He gives her a look.*] After a serious play we join the proletariat in the subway and I listen to a lecture on the drama. After a musical you bring me home in a taxi [*Turning away.*] and you make a few passes.

MORTIMER. Now wait a minute, darling, that's a very inaccurate piece of reporting.

ELAINE. [*Leaning against end of table.*] Oh, I will admit that after the Behrman play you told me I had authentic beauty— and that's a hell of a thing to say to a girl. It wasn't until after our first musical you told me I had nice legs. And I have too.

MORTIMER. [*Stares at her legs a moment, then walks over and kisses her.*] For a minister's daughter you know a lot about life. Where'd you learn it?

ELAINE. [*Casually.*] In the choir loft.

MORTIMER. I'll explain that to you sometime, darling—the close connection between eroticism and religion.

ELAINE. Religion never gets as high as the choir loft. [*Crosses below table, gathers up bag.*] Which reminds me, I better tell Father please not to wait up for me tonight.

MORTIMER. [*Almost to himself.*] I've never been able to rationalize it.

ELAINE. What?

MORTIMER. My falling in love with a girl who lives in Brooklyn.

ELAINE. Falling in love? You're not stooping to the articulate, are you?

MORTIMER. [*Ignoring this.*] The only way I can regain my self-respect is to keep you in New York.

ELAINE. [*A few steps toward him.*] Did you say keep?

MORTIMER. No, no. I've come to the conclusion that you're holding out for the legalities.

ELAINE. [*Crossing to him as he backs away.*] I can afford to be a good girl for quite a few years yet.

MORTIMER. [*Stops and embraces her.*] And I can't wait that long. Where could we be married in a hurry—say tonight?

ELAINE. I'm afraid Father will insist on officiating.

MORTIMER. [*Turning away from her.*] Oh, God! I'll bet your father could make even the marriage service sound pedestrian.

ELAINE. Are you by any chance writing a review of it?

MORTIMER. Forgive me, darling. It's an occupational disease. [*She smiles at him lovingly and walks toward him. He meets her halfway and they forget themselves for a moment in a sentimental embrace and kiss. When they come out of it, he turns away from her quickly.*] I may give that play tonight a good notice.

ELAINE. Now, darling, don't pretend that you love me that much.

MORTIMER. [*Looks at her with polite lechery, then starts toward her.*] Be sure to tell your father not to wait up tonight.

ELAINE. [*Aware that she can't trust either of them, and backing upstage.*] I think tonight I'd better tell him to wait up.

MORTIMER. [*Following her.*] I'll telephone Winchell to publish the banns.

ELAINE. [*Backing.*] Nevertheless—

MORTIMER. All right, everything formal and legal. But not later than next month.

ELAINE. [*Runs into his arms.*] Darling! I'll talk it over with Father and set the date.

MORTIMER. No—we'll have to see what's in rehearsal. There'll be a lot of other first nights in October.

[TEDDY *enters from balcony and comes downstairs dressed in tropical clothes and a solar topee. At foot of stairs he sees* MORTIMER, *crosses to him and shakes hands.*]

TEDDY. Hello, Mortimer!

MORTIMER. [*Gravely.*] How are you, Mr. President?

TEDDY. Bully, thank you. Just bully! What news have you brought me?

MORTIMER. Just this, Mr. President—the country is squarely behind you.

TEDDY. [*Beaming.*] Yes, I know. Isn't it wonderful? [*He shakes* MORTIMER'S *hand again.*] Well, good-by. [*He crosses to* ELAINE *and shakes hands with her.*] Good-by. [*He goes to cellar door.*]

ELAINE. Where are you off to, Teddy?

TEDDY. Panama. [*He exits through cellar door, shutting it.* ELAINE *looks at* MORTIMER *inquiringly.*]

MORTIMER. Panama's the cellar. He digs locks for the canal down there.

[ELAINE *takes his arm and they stroll to the table.*]

ELAINE. You're so sweet with him—and he's very fond of you.

MORTIMER. Well, Teddy was always my favorite brother.

ELAINE. [*Stopping and turning to him.*] Favorite? Were there more of you?

MORTIMER. There's another brother—Jonathan.

ELAINE. I never heard of him. Your aunts never mention him.

MORTIMER. No, we don't like to talk about Jonathan. He left Brooklyn very early—by request. Jonathan was the kind of boy who liked to cut worms in two—with his teeth.

ELAINE. What became of him?

MORTIMER. I don't know. He wanted to become a surgeon like Grandfather but he wouldn't go to medical school first and his practice got him into trouble.

ABBY. [*Enters from kitchen.*] Aren't you two going to be late for the theatre?

MORTIMER. [*His arm around* ELAINE'S *neck; looks at his wrist watch.*] We're skipping dinner. We won't have to start for half an hour.

ABBY. [*Backing away.*] Well, then I'll leave you two alone together again.

ELAINE. Don't bother, darling. [*Moving in front of* MORTIMER.] I'm going to run over to speak to Father. [*To* MORTIMER.]

Before I go out with you he likes to pray over me a little. [*She runs to door and opens it, keeping her hand on outside doorknob.*] I'll be right back—I'll cut through the cemetery.

MORTIMER. [*Crosses to her, puts his hand on her.*] If the prayer isn't too long, I'd have time to lead you beside distilled waters.

[ELAINE *laughs and exits.* MORTIMER *shuts door.*]

ABBY. [*Happily.*] Mortimer, that's the first time I've ever heard you quote the Bible. We knew Elaine would be a good influence for you.

MORTIMER. [*Laughs, then turns to* ABBY.] Oh, by the way—I'm going to marry her.

ABBY. What? Oh, darling! [*She runs and embraces him. Then she dashes toward kitchen doors as* MORTIMER *crosses to window and looks out.*] Martha, Martha! [MARTHA *enters from kitchen.*] Come right in here. I've got the most wonderful news for you—Mortimer and Elaine are going to be married.

MARTHA. Married? Oh, Mortimer! [*She runs over to* MORTIMER, *who is looking out window, embraces and kisses him.* ABBY *comes to his left. He has his arms around both of them.*]

ABBY. We hoped it would happen just like this.

MARTHA. Well, Elaine must be the happiest girl in the world.

MORTIMER. [*Pulls curtain back, looks out window.*] Happy! Just look at her leaping over those gravestones. [*As he looks out window* MORTIMER's *attention is suddenly drawn to something.*] Say! What's that?

MARTHA [*Looking out over his shoulder.*] What's what, dear?

MORTIMER. See that statue there. That's a horundinida carnina.

MARTHA. Oh, no, dear—that's Emma B. Stout ascending to heaven.

MORTIMER. No, no—standing on Mrs. Stout's left ear. That bird—that's a red-crested swallow. I've only seen one of those before in my life.

ABBY. [*Crosses around above table and pushes chair into table.*] I don't know how you can be thinking about a bird now—what with Elaine and the engagement and everything.

MORTIMER. It's a vanishing species. [*He turns away from window.*] Thoreau was very fond of them. [*He crosses to desk to look through various drawers and papers.*] By the way, I left a large envelope around here last week. It was one of the chapters of my book on Thoreau. Have you seen it?

MARTHA. [*Pushing armchair into table.*] Well, if you left it here it must be here somewhere.

ABBY. When are you going to be married? What are your plans? There must be something more you can tell us about Elaine.

MORTIMER. Elaine? Oh, yes, Elaine thought it was brilliant. [*He crosses to sideboard, looks through cupboards and drawers.*]

MARTHA. What was, dear?

MORTIMER. My chapter on Thoreau. [*He finds a bundle of papers in a drawer and takes them to table and looks through them.*]

ABBY. Well, when Elaine comes back I think we ought to have a little celebration. We must drink to your happiness. Martha, isn't there some of that Lady Baltimore cake left?

[*During last few speeches* MARTHA *has picked up pail from sideboard and her cape, hat and gloves from table.*]

MARTHA. Oh, yes!

ABBY. And I'll open a bottle of wine.

MARTHA. [*As she exits to kitchen.*] Oh, and to think it happened in this room!

MORTIMER. [*Has finished looking through papers, is gazing around room.*] Now where could I have put that?

ABBY. Well, with your fiancée sitting beside you tonight, I do hope the play will be something you can enjoy for once. It may be something romantic. What's the name of it?

MORTIMER. *Murder Will Out.*

ABBY. Oh dear! [*She disappears into kitchen as* MORTIMER *goes on talking.*]

MORTIMER. When the curtain goes up the first thing you'll see will be a dead body. [*He lifts window seat and sees one. Not believing it, he drops window seat again and starts downstage. He suddenly stops, then goes back, throws window seat open and stares in. He goes slightly mad for a moment. He backs away, then hears* ABBY *humming on her way into the room. He drops window seat again and holds it down, staring around the room.* ABBY *enters carrying a silencer and tablecloth which she puts on armchair, then picks up bundle of papers and returns them to drawer in sideboard.* MORTIMER *speaks in a somewhat strained voice.*] Aunt Abby!

ABBY. [*At sideboard.*] Yes, dear?

MORTIMER. You were going to make plans for Teddy to go to that . . . sanitarium—Happy Dale—

ABBY. [*Bringing legal papers from sideboard to* MORTIMER.] Yes, dear, it's all arranged. Dr. Harper was here today and brought the papers for Teddy to sign. Here they are.

MORTIMER. [*Takes them from her.*] He's got to sign them right away.

ABBY. [*Arranging silencer on table;* MARTHA *enters from kitchen door with table silver and plates on a tray, and sets tray on sideboard.*] That's what Dr. Harper thinks. Then there won't be any legal difficulties after we pass on.

MORTIMER. He's got to sign them this minute! He's down in the cellar—get him up here right away.

MARTHA. [*Unfolding tablecloth.*] There's no such hurry as that.

ABBY. No. When Teddy starts working on the canal you can't get his mind on anything else.

MORTIMER. Teddy's got to go to Happy Dale now—tonight.

MARTHA. Oh, no, dear, that's not until after we're gone.

MORTIMER. Right away, I tell you! Right away!

ABBY. [*Turning to* MORTIMER.] Why, Mortimer, how can you say such a thing? Why, as long as we live we'll never be separated from Teddy.

MORTIMER. [*Trying to be calm.*] Listen, darlings, I'm frightfully sorry, but I've got some shocking news for you. [*The* AUNTS *stop work and look at him with some interest.*] Now we've all got to try and keep our heads. You know we've sort of humored Teddy because we thought he was harmless.

MARTHA. Why he *is* harmless!

MORTIMER. He *was* harmless. That's why he has to go to Happy Dale. Why he has to be confined.

ABBY. [*Stepping to* MORTIMER.] Mortimer, why have you suddenly turned against Teddy? Your own brother?

MORTIMER. You've got to know sometime. It might as well be now. Teddy's —killed a man!

MARTHA. Nonsense, dear.

MORTIMER. [*Rises and points to window seat.*] There's a body in the window seat!

ABBY. Yes, dear, we know.

MORTIMER. [*Does a double-take as* ABBY *and* MARTHA *busy themselves again at table.*] You *know*?

MARTHA. Of course, dear, but it has nothing to do with Teddy. [*Gets tray from sideboard—arranges silver and plates on table.*]

ABBY. Now, Mortimer, just forget about it—forget you ever saw the gentleman.

MORTIMER. *Forget?*

ABBY. We never dreamed you'd peek.

MORTIMER. But who is he?

ABBY. His name's Hoskins—Adam Hoskins. That's really all I know about him—except that he's a Methodist.

MORTIMER. That's all you know about him? Well, what's he doing here? What happened to him?

MARTHA. He died.

MORTIMER. Aunt Martha, men don't just get into window seats and die.

ABBY. No, he died first.

MORTIMER. Well, how?

ABBY. Oh, Mortimer, don't be so inquisitive. The gentleman died because he drank some wine with poison in it.

MORTIMER. How did the poison get in the wine?

MARTHA. Well, we put it in wine because it's less noticeable—when it's in tea it has a distinct odor.

MORTIMER. *You* put it in the wine?

ABBY. Yes. And I put Mr. Hoskins in the window seat because Dr. Harper was coming.

MORTIMER. So you knew what you'd done! You didn't want Dr. Harper to see the body!

ABBY. Well, not at tea—that wouldn't have been very nice. Now, Mortimer, you know the whole thing, just forget about it. I do think Martha and I have the right to our own little secrets. [*She crosses to sideboard to get two goblets from cupboard as* MARTHA *comes to table from sideboard with salt dish and pepper shaker.*]

MARTHA. And don't you tell Elaine! [*She*

gets third goblet from sideboard, then turns to ABBY *who takes tray from sideboard.*] Oh, Abby, while I was out I dropped in on Mrs. Schultz. She's much better but she would like us to take Junior to the movies again.

ABBY. Well, we must do that tomorrow or next day.

MARTHA. Yes, but this time we'll go where we want to go. [*She starts for kitchen door.* ABBY *follows.*] Junior's not going to drag me into one of those scary pictures. [*They exit into kitchen as* MORTIMER *wheels around and looks after them.* ABBY *shuts door.*]

MORTIMER. [*Dazed, looks around the room; his eyes come to rest on phone on desk; he crosses to it and dials a number; into phone.*] City desk! . . . Hello, Al. Do you know who this is? . . . That's right. Say, Al, when I left the office, I told you where I was going, remember? Well, where did I say? . . . Uh-huh. Well, it would take me about half an hour to get to Brooklyn. What time have you got? [*He looks at his watch.*] That's right, I must be here. [*He hangs up, sits for a moment, then suddenly leaps off stool toward kitchen.*] Aunt Abby! Aunt Martha! Come in here! [*The two* AUNTS *bustle in.* MARTHA *has tray with plates, cups, saucers and soup cups.*] What are we going to do? What are we going to do?

MARTHA. What are we going to do about what, dear?

MORTIMER. [*Pointing to window seat.*] There's a body in there.

ABBY. Yes—Mr. Hoskins.

MORTIMER. Well, good heavens, I can't turn you over to the police! But what am I going to do?

MARTHA. Well, for one thing, dear, stop being so excited.

ABBY. And for pity's sake stop worrying. We told you to forget the whole thing.

MORTIMER. Forget! My dear Aunt Abby, can't I make you realize that something has to be done?

ABBY. [*A little sharply.*] Now, Mortimer, you behave yourself. You're too old to be flying off the handle like this.

MORTIMER. But Mr. Hotchkiss—

ABBY. [*On her way to sideboard, stops and turns to* MORTIMER.] Hoskins, dear. [*She continues on her way to sideboard and gets napkins and rings from drawer.*

MARTHA *puts her tray, with cups and plates, on table.* MORTIMER *continues speaking through this.*]

MORTIMER. Well, whatever his name is, you can't leave him there.

MARTHA. We don't intend to, dear.

ABBY. [*Crossing to table with napkins and rings.*] No, Teddy's down in the cellar now digging the lock.

MORTIMER. You mean you're going to bury Mr. Hotchkiss in the cellar?

MARTHA. [*Stepping to him.*] Oh, yes, dear—that's what we did with the others.

MORTIMER. [*Walking away.*] No! You can't bury Mr.—[*Double-take; turns back to them.*]—others?

ABBY. The other gentlemen.

MORTIMER. When you say others—do you mean—others? More than one others?

MARTHA. Oh, yes, dear. Let me see, this is eleven. [*To* ABBY.] Isn't it, Abby?

ABBY. No, dear, this makes twelve.

[MORTIMER *backs away from them, stunned, toward phone stool at desk.*]

MARTHA. Oh, I think you're wrong, Abby. This is only eleven.

ABBY. No, dear, because I remember when Mr. Hoskins first came in, it occurred to me that he would make just an even dozen.

MARTHA. Well, you really shouldn't count the first one.

ABBY. Oh, *I* was counting the first one. So that makes it twelve.

[*Phone rings.* MORTIMER, *in a daze turns toward it and without picking up receiver, speaks.*]

MORTIMER. Hello! [*He comes to, picks up receiver.*] Hello. Oh, hello, Al. My, it's good to hear your voice.

ABBY. [*Still holding out for a "twelve" count.*] Well, anyway, they're all down in the cellar—

MORTIMER. [*To* AUNTS.] Ssshhh—[*Into phone, as* AUNTS *cross to sideboard and put candelabras from top to bottom shelf.*] Oh, no, Al, I'm sober as a lark. I just called you because I was feeling a little Pirandello—Piran—you wouldn't know, Al. Look, I'm glad you called. Get hold of George right away. He's got to review the play tonight. I can't make it. No, Al, you're wrong. I'll tell you all about it tomorrow. Well, George has got to cover the play tonight! This is my department and I'm running it! You get ahold of George! [*He hangs up and sits a moment trying to collect himself.*] Now let's see, where were we? [*He suddenly leaps from stool.*] TWELVE!

MARTHA. Yes, Abby thinks we ought to count the first one and that makes twelve. [*She goes back to sideboard.*]

MORTIMER. [*Placing a chair; then takes* MARTHA'S *hand, leads her to chair and sets her in it.*] All right—now—who was the first one?

ABBY. [*Crossing from above table to* MORTIMER.] Mr. Midgely. He was a Baptist.

MARTHA. Of course, I still think we can't claim full credit for him because he just died.

ABBY. Martha means without any help from us. You see, Mr. Midgely came here looking for a room—

MARTHA. It was right after you moved to New York.

ABBY. And it didn't seem right for that lovely room to be going to waste when there were so many people who needed it—

MARTHA. He was such a lonely old man. . . .

ABBY. All his kith and kin were dead and it left him so forlorn and unhappy—

MARTHA. We felt so sorry for him.

ABBY. And then when his heart attack came—and he sat dead in that chair [*Pointing to armchair.*] looking so peaceful—remember, Martha—we made up our minds then and there that if we could help other lonely old men to that same peace—we would!

MORTIMER. [*All ears.*] He dropped dead right in that chair! How awful for you!

MARTHA. Oh, no, dear. Why, it was rather like old times. Your grandfather always used to have a cadaver or two around the house. You see, Teddy had been digging in Panama and he thought Mr. Midgely was a yellow fever victim.

ABBY. That meant he had to be buried immediately.

MARTHA. So we all took him down to Panama and put him in the lock. [*She rises, puts her arm around* ABBY.] Now that's why we told you not to worry about it because we know exactly what's to be done.

MORTIMER. And that's how all this

started—that man walking in here and dropping dead.

ABBY. Of course, we realized we couldn't depend on that happening again. So—

MARTHA. [*Crosses to* MORTIMER.] You remember those jars of poison that have been up on the shelves in Grandfather's laboratory all these years—?

ABBY. You know your Aunt Martha's knack for mixing things. You've eaten enough of her piccalilli.

MARTHA. Well, dear, for a gallon of elderberry wine I take one teaspoonful of arsenic, then add a half teaspoonful of strychnine and then just a pinch of cyanide.

MORTIMER. [*Appraisingly.*] Should have quite a kick.

ABBY. Yes! As a matter of fact one of our gentlemen found time to say "How delicious!"

MARTHA. Well, I'll have to get things started in the kitchen.

ABBY. [*To* MORTIMER.] I wish you could stay for dinner.

MARTHA. I'm trying out a new recipe.

MORTIMER. I couldn't eat a thing.

[MARTHA *goes out to kitchen.*]

ABBY .[*Calling after* MARTHA.] I'll come and help you, dear. [*She pushes chair into table.*] Well, I feel so much better now. Oh, you have to wait for Elaine, don't you? [*She smiles.*] How happy you must be. [*She goes to kitchen doorway.*] Well, dear, I'll leave you alone with your thoughts. [*She exits, shutting door.*]

[*The shutting of the door wakes* MORTIMER *from his trance. He crosses to window seat, kneels down, raises cover, looks in. Not believing, he lowers cover, rubs his eyes, raises cover again. This time he really sees Mr. Hoskins. Closes window seat hastily, rises, steps back. Runs over and closes drapes over window. Backs up to table. Sees water glass on table, picks it up, raises it to lips, suddenly remembers that poisoned wine comes in glasses, puts it down quickly. Crosses to cellar door, opens it.* ELAINE *enters; he closes cellar door with a bang. As* ELAINE *puts her bag on top of desk he looks at her, and it dawns on him that he knows her. He speaks with faint surprise.*]

MORTIMER. Oh, it's you.

ELAINE. [*Crosses to him, takes his hand.*] Don't be cross, darling! Father could see that I was excited—so I told him about us and that made it hard for me to get away. But listen, darling—he's not going to wait up for me tonight.

MORTIMER. [*Looking at window seat.*] You run along home, Elaine, and I'll call you up tomorrow.

ELAINE. Tomorrow!

MORTIMER. [*Irritated.*] You know I always call you up every day or two.

ELAINE. But we're going to the theatre tonight.

MORTIMER. No—no we're not!

ELAINE. Well, why not?

MORTIMER. [*Turning to her.*] Elaine, something's come up.

ELAINE. What, darling? Mortimer—you've lost your job!

MORTIMER. No—no—I haven't lost my job. I'm just not covering that play tonight. [*Pushing her.*] Now you run along home, Elaine.

ELAINE. But I've got to know what's happened. Certainly you can tell me.

MORTIMER. No, dear, I can't.

ELAINE. But if we're going to be married—

MORTIMER. Married?

ELAINE. Have you forgotten that not fifteen minutes ago you proposed to me?

MORTIMER. [*Vaguely.*] I did? Oh—yes! Well, as far as I know that's still on. [*Urging her to go again.*] Now you run along home, Elaine. I've got to do something.

ELAINE. Listen, you can't propose to me one minute and throw me out of the house the next.

MORTIMER. [*Pleading.*] I'm not throwing you out of the house, darling. Will you get out of here?

ELAINE. No, I won't get out of here. [MORTIMER *crosses toward kitchen.* ELAINE *crosses below to window seat.*] Not until I've had some kind of explanation. [ELAINE *is about to sit on window seat.* MORTIMER *grabs her by the hand. Phone rings.*]

MORTIMER. Elaine! [*He goes to phone, dragging* ELAINE *with him.*] Hello! Oh, hello, Al. Hold on a minute, will you? All right, it's important! But it can wait a minute, can't it? Hold on! [*He puts receiver on desk. Takes* ELAINE's *bag from top of desk and hands it to her. Then takes her by hand and leads her to door and opens it.*] Look, Elaine, you're a sweet girl and I love you. But I have something on my mind now and I want you to go home and wait until I call you.

ELAINE. [*In doorway.*] Don't try to be masterful.

MORTIMER. [*Annoyed to the point of being literate.*] When we're married and I have problems to face I hope you're less tedious and uninspired!

ELAINE. And when we're married *if* we're married—I hope I find you adequate! [*She exits.* MORTIMER *runs out on porch after her.*]

MORTIMER. Elaine! Elaine! [*He runs back in, shutting door, crosses and kneels on window seat to open window. Suddenly remembers contents of window seat and leaps off it. Dashes into kitchen but remembers Al is on phone, reenters immediately and crosses to phone.*] Hello, Al? Hello . . . hello . . . [*He pushes hook down and starts to dial when doorbell rings. He thinks it's the phone.* ABBY *enters from kitchen.*] Hello. Hello, Al?

ABBY. [*Crossing to door and opening it.*] That's the doorbell, dear, not the telephone. [MORTIMER *pushes hook down . . . dials.* MR. GIBBS *steps in doorway.*] How do you do? Come in.

GIBBS. I understand you have a room to rent.

[MARTHA *enters from kitchen. Puts Lazy Susan on sideboard, then goes to table.*]

ABBY. Yes. Won't you step in?

GIBBS. [*Stepping into room.*] Are you the lady of the house?

ABBY. Yes, I'm Miss Brewster. And this is my sister, another Miss Brewster.

GIBBS. My name is Gibbs.

ABBY. [*Easing him to chair.*] Oh, won't you sit down? I'm sorry we were just setting the table for dinner.

MORTIMER. [*Into phone.*] Hello—let me talk to Al again. City desk. AL!! CITY DESK! WHAT? I'm sorry, wrong number. [*He hangs up and starts dialing again as* GIBBS *looks at him.* GIBBS *turns to* ABBY.]

GIBBS. May I see the room?

MARTHA. Why don't you sit down a minute and let's get acquainted.

GIBBS. That won't do much good if I don't like the room.

ABBY. Is Brooklyn your home?

GIBBS. Haven't got a home. Live in a hotel. Don't like it.

MORTIMER. [Into phone.] Hello. City desk.

MARTHA. Are your family Brooklyn people?

GIBBS. Haven't got any family.

ABBY. [Another victim.] All alone in the world?

GIBBS. Yep.

ABBY. Well, Martha— [MARTHA goes happily to sideboard, gets bottle of wine from cupboard and a wineglass, and sets them on table. ABBY eases GIBBS into chair and continues speaking to him.] Well, you've come to just the right house. Do sit down.

MORTIMER. [Into phone.] Hello, Al? Mort. We got cut off. Al, I can't cover the play tonight—that's all there is to it, I can't!

MARTHA. What church do you go to? There's an Episcopal church practically next door. [Her gesture toward window brings her to window seat and she sits.]

GIBBS. I'm Presbyterian. Used to be.

MORTIMER. [Into phone.] What's George doing in Bermuda? [Rises and gets loud.] Certainly I told him he could go to Bermuda—it's my department, isn't it? Well, you've got to get somebody. Who else is there around the office? [He sits on second chair.]

GIBBS. [Annoyed; rises and walks in front of table.] Is there always this much noise?

MARTHA. Oh, he doesn't live with us. [ABBY sits.]

MORTIMER. [Into phone.] There must be somebody around the place. Look, Al, how about the office boy? You know, the bright one—the one we don't like? Well, you look around the office, I'll hold on.

GIBBS. I'd really like to see the room.

ABBY. It's upstairs. Won't you try a glass of our wine before we start up?

GIBBS. Never touch it.

MARTHA. We make this ourselves. It's elderberry wine.

GIBBS. [To MARTHA.] Elderberry wine. Hmmph. Haven't tasted elderberry wine since I was a boy. Thank you. [He pulls armchair around and sits as ABBY uncorks bottle and starts to pour wine.]

MORTIMER. [Into phone.] Well, there must be some printers around. Look, Al,

the fellow who sets my copy. He ought to know about what I'd write. His name is Joe. He's the third machine from the left. But, Al, he might turn out to be another Burns Mantle!

GIBBS. [To MARTHA.] Do you have your own elderberry bushes?

MARTHA. No, but the cemetery is full of them.

MORTIMER. [Into phone.] No, I'm not drinking, but I'm going to start now.

GIBBS. Do you serve meals?

ABBY. We might, but first just see whether you like our wine.

[MORTIMER hangs up, puts phone on top of desk. He sees wine on table. Goes to sideboard, gets glass, brings it to table and pours drink. GIBBS has his glass in hand and is getting ready to drink.]

MARTHA. [Sees MORTIMER pouring wine.] Mortimer! Eh eh eh eh! [GIBBS stops and looks at MARTHA. MORTIMER pays no attention.] Eh eh eh eh!

[As MORTIMER raises glass to lips ABBY reaches up and pulls his arm down.]

ABBY. Mortimer. Not that. [MORTIMER, still dumb, puts his glass down on table. Then he suddenly sees GIBBS who has just got glass to his lips and is about to drink. He points across table at GIBBS and gives a wild cry. GIBBS looks at him, putting his glass down. MORTIMER, still pointing at GIBBS, goes around table toward him. GIBBS, seeing a madman, rises slowly and backs toward door, then turns and runs for it, MORTIMER following him. GIBBS opens door and MORTIMER pushes him out, closing door after him. Then he turns and leans on door in exhausted relief. Meantime, MARTHA has risen and crossed to armchair, while ABBY has risen and crossed to the center of the room.]

ABBY. [Greatly disappointed.] Now you've spoiled everything. [She goes to sofa and sits.]

[MARTHA sits in armchair. MORTIMER looks from one to the other . . . then speaks to ABBY.]

MORTIMER. You can't do things like that. I don't know how to explain this to you, but it's not only against the law. It's wrong! [To MARTHA.] It's not a nice thing to do. [MARTHA turns away from him as ABBY has just done.] People wouldn't understand. [*Points to door after* GIBBS.] *He* wouldn't understand.

MARTHA. Abby, we shouldn't have told Mortimer!

MORTIMER. What I mean is—well, this has developed into a very bad habit.

ABBY. [*Rises.*] Mortimer, we don't try to stop you from doing things you like to do. I don't see why you should interfere with us.

[*Phone rings.* MORTIMER *answers.* MARTHA *rises.*]

MORTIMER. Hello? [*It's* AL *again.*] All right, I'll see the first act and I'll pan the hell out of it. But look, Al, you've got to do something for me. Get hold of O'Brien —our lawyer, the head of our legal department. Have him meet me at the theatre. Now, don't let me down. O.K. I'm starting now. [*He hangs up and turns to* AUNTS.] Look, I've got to go to the theatre. I can't get out of it. But before I go will you promise me something?

MARTHA. We'd have to know what it was first.

MORTIMER. I love you very much and I know you love me. You know I'd do anything in the world for you and I want you to do just this little thing for me.

ABBY. What do you want us to do?

MORTIMER. Don't *do* anything. I mean don't do *anything*. Don't let anyone in this house—and leave Mr. Hoskins right where he is.

MARTHA. Why?

MORTIMER. I want time to think—and I've got quite a little to think about. You know I wouldn't want anything to happen to you.

ABBY. Well, what on earth could happen to us?

MORTIMER. [*Beside himself.*] Anyway— you'll do this for me, won't you?

MARTHA. Well—we were planning on holding services before dinner.

MORTIMER. Services!

MARTHA. [*A little indignant.*] Certainly. You don't think we'd bury Mr. Hoskins without a full Methodist service, do you? Why he was a Methodist.

MORTIMER. But can't that wait until I get back?

ABBY. Oh, then you could join us.

MORTIMER. [*Going crazy himself.*] Yes! Yes!

ABBY. Oh, Mortimer, you'll enjoy the services—especially the hymns. [*To* MARTHA.] Remember how beautifully Mortimer used to sing in the choir before his voice changed?

MORTIMER. And remember, you're not going to let anyone in this house while I'm gone—it's a promise!

MARTHA. Well—

ABBY. Oh, Martha, we can do that now that Mortimer's co-operating with us. [*To* MORTIMER.] Well, all right, Mortimer.

[MORTIMER *heaves a sight of relief. Crosses to sofa and gets his hat. Then on his way to opening door, he speaks.*]

MORTIMER. Have you got some paper? I'll get back just as soon as I can. [*Taking legal papers from coat pocket as he crosses.*] There's a man I've got to see.

[ABBY *has gone to desk for stationery. She hands it to* MORTIMER.]

ABBY. Here's some stationery. Will this do?

MORTIMER. [*Taking stationery.*] That'll be fine. I can save time if I write my review on the way to the theatre. [*He exits.*]

[*The* AUNTS *stare after him.* MARTHA *crosses and closes door.* ABBY *goes to sideboard and brings two candelabras to table, then matches from sideboard—lights candles.*]

MARTHA. Mortimer didn't seem quite himself today.

ABBY. [*Lighting candles.*] Well, that's only natural—I think I know why.

MARTHA. [*Lighting floor lamp.*] Why?

ABBY. He's just become engaged to be married. I suppose that always makes a man nervous.

MARTHA. [*During this speech she goes to first landing and closes drapes over window, then comes downstairs and turns off remote switch.*] Well, I'm so happy for Elaine—and their honeymoon ought to give Mortimer a real vacation. I don't think he got much rest this summer.

ABBY. Well, at least he didn't go kiting off to China or Spain.

MARTHA. I could never understand why he wanted to go to those places.

ABBY. Well, I think to Mortimer, the theatre has always seemed pretty small potatoes. He needs something big to criticize—something like the human race. [*She sets the candelabras on the table.*]

MARTHA. Oh, Abby, if Mortimer's coming back for the services for Mr. Hoskins, we'll need another hynmnal. There's one in my room. [*She starts upstairs.*]

ABBY. You know, dear, it's really my turn to read the services, but since you weren't here when Mr. Hoskins came I want you to do it.

MARTHA. [*Pleased.*] That's very nice of you, dear—but, are you sure you want me to?

ABBY. It's only fair.

MARTHA. Well, I think I'll wear my black bombazine and Mother's old brooch. [*She starts up again when doorbell rings.*]

ABBY. [*Crossing as far as desk.*] I'll go, dear.

MARTHA. [*Hushed.*] We promised Mortimer we wouldn't let anyone in.

ABBY. [*Trying to peer through curtained window in door.*] Who do you suppose it is?

MARTHA. Wait a minute, I'll look. [*She turns to landing window and peeks out the curtains.*] It's two men—and I've never seen them before.

ABBY. Are you sure?

MARTHA. There's a car at the curb—they must have come in that.

ABBY. Let me look! [*She hurries upstairs. There is a knock on door.* ABBY *peeks out the curtains.*]

MARTHA. Do you recognize them?

ABBY. They're strangers to me.

MARTHA. We'll just have to pretend we're not at home. [*The two of them huddle back in corner of landing.*]

[*Another knock at the door, the knob is turned, and door swings slowly open. A tall man walks in, looking about the room. He has assurance and ease, as though the room were familiar to him. There is something sinister about the man—something that brings a slight chill in his presence. It is in his walk, his bearing, and his strange resemblance to Boris Karloff. From stair landing* ABBY *and* MARTHA *watch him, almost afraid to speak. Having completed his survey of the room, the man turns and addresses someone outside the front door.*]

JONATHAN. Come in, Doctor. [DR. EINSTEIN *enters. He is somewhat ratty in appearance. His face wears the benevolent smirk of a man who lives in a pleasant haze of alcohol. There is something about him that suggests the unfrocked priest. He stands just inside the door, timid but expectant.*] This is the home of my youth. As a boy I couldn't wait to escape from this place—now I'm glad to escape back into it.

EINSTEIN. [*Shutting door, his back to* AUNTS.] Yah, Chonny, it's a fine hide-out.

JONATHAN. The family must still live here. There's something so unmistakably Brewster about the Brewsters. I hope there's a fatted calf awaiting the return of the prodigal.

EINSTEIN. Yah. I'm hungry. [*He suddenly sees the fatted calf in the form of the two glasses of wine on table.*] Look, Chonny, drinks! [*He runs over to the table.*]

JONATHAN. As though we were expected. A good omen.

[*They raise glasses to their lips as* ABBY *steps down a couple of stairs and speaks.*]

ABBY. Who are you? What are you doing here?

[*They both put glasses down.* EINSTEIN *picks up his hat from armchair, ready to run for it.* JONATHAN *turns to* ABBY.]

JONATHAN. Why, Aunt Abby! Aunt Martha! It's Jonathan.

MARTHA. [*Frightened.*] You get out of here.

JONATHAN. [*Crossing to* AUNTS.] I'm Jonathan—your nephew, Jonathan.

ABBY. Oh, no, you're not. You're nothing like Jonathan, so don't pretend you are! You just get out of here!

JONATHAN. [*Coming closer.*] But I am Jonathan. And this [*Indicating* EINSTEIN.] is Dr. Einstein.

ABBY. And he's not Dr. Einstein either.

JONATHAN. Not Dr. Albert Einstein—Dr. Herman Einstein.

ABBY. [*Down another step.*] Who are you? You're not our nephew, Jonathan.

JONATHAN. [*Peering at* ABBY's *outstretched hand.*] I see you're still wearing the lovely garnet ring that Grandma Brewster bought in England. [ABBY *gasps, looks at ring.*] And you, Aunt Martha, still the high collar—to hide the scar where Grandfather's acid burned you.

[MARTHA's *hand goes to her throat. The* AUNTS *look at* JONATHAN.

MARTHA *comes down a few steps to behind* ABBY.]

MARTHA. His voice is like Jonathan's.

ABBY. [*Stepping down to stage floor.*] Have you been in an accident?

JONATHAN. [*His hand goes to side of his face.*] No—[*He clouds.*]—my face—Dr. Einstein is responsible for that. He's a plastic surgeon. He changes people's faces.

MARTHA. [*Comes down to* ABBY.] But I've seen that face before. [*To* ABBY.] Abby, remember when we took the little Schultz boy to the movies and I was so frightened? It was that face!

[JONATHAN *grows tense and looks toward* EINSTEIN. EINSTEIN *addresses* AUNTS.]

EINSTEIN. Easy, Chonny—easy! [*To* AUNTS.] Don't worry, ladies. The last five years I give Chonny three new faces. I give him another one right away. This last face—well, I saw that picture too—just before I operate. And I was intoxicated.

JONATHAN. [*With a growing and dangerous intensity as he walks toward* EINSTEIN.] You see, Doctor—you see what you've done to me. Even my own family—

EINSTEIN. [*To calm him.*] Chonny—you're home—in this lovely house— [*To* AUNTS.] How often he tells me about Brooklyn—about this house—about his aunts that he lofes so much. [*To* JONATHAN.] They know you, Chonny. [*To* ABBY, *as he leads her toward* JONATHAN.] You know it's Jonathan. Speak to him. Tell him so. [*He drifts beyond table.*]

ABBY. Well—Jonathan—it's been a long time—what have you been doing all these years?

MARTHA. Yes, Jonathan, where have you been?

JONATHAN. [*Recovering his composure.*] Oh, England, South Africa, Australia—the last five years Chicago. Dr. Einstein and I were in business there together.

ABBY. Oh, we were in Chicago for the World's Fair.

MARTHA. [*For want of something to say.*] Yes—we found Chicago awfully warm.

EINSTEIN. Yah—it got hot for us too.

JONATHAN. [*Turning on the charm as he crosses above* ABBY, *placing himself between the* AUNTS.] Well, it's wonderful to be in Brooklyn again. And you—Abby —Martha—you don't look a day older. Just

as I remembered you—sweet—charming— hospitable. [*The* AUNTS *don't react too well to this charm.*] And dear Teddy— [*He indicates with his hand a lad of eight or ten.*]—did he get into politics? [*He turns to* EINSTEIN.] My little brother, doctor, was determined to become President.

ABBY. Oh, Teddy's fine! Just fine! And Mortimer's well too.

JONATHAN. [*A bit of a sneer.*] I know about Mortimer. I've seen his picture at the head of his column. He's evidently fulfilled all the promise of his early nasty nature.

ABBY. [*Defensively.*] We're very fond of Mortimer.

[*There is a slight pause. Then* MARTHA *speaks uneasily as she gestures toward door.*]

MARTHA. Well, Jonathan, it's very nice to have seen you again.

JONATHAN. [*Expanding.*] Bless you, Aunt Martha. [*Crosses and sits in chair.*] It's good to be home again.

[*The* AUNTS *look at each other with dismay.*]

ABBY. Well, Martha, we mustn't let what's on the stove boil over. [*She starts to kitchen, then sees* MARTHA *isn't following. She crosses back and tugs at* MARTHA, *then crosses toward kitchen again.* MARTHA *follows, then speaks to* JONATHAN.]

MARTHA. Yes, if you'll excuse us for a minute, Jonathan. Unless you're in a hurry to go somewhere.

[JONATHAN *looks at her balefully.* MARTHA *walks around table, takes bottle of wine and puts it back in sideboard, then exits with* ABBY. ABBY, *who has been waiting in kitchen doorway for* MARTHA, *closes door after them.* EINSTEIN *crosses to behind* JONATHAN.]

EINSTEIN. Well, Chonny, where do we go from here? We got to think fast. The police. The police have got pictures of that face. I got to operate on you right away. We got to find some place for that —and we got to find a place for Mr. Spenalzo too.

JONATHAN. Don't waste any worry on that rat.

EINSTEIN. But, Chonny, we got a hot stiff on our hands.

JONATHAN. [*Flinging hat onto sofa.*] Forget Mr. Spenalzo.

EINSTEIN. But you can't leave a dead body in the rumble seat. You shouldn't have killed him, Chonny. He's a nice fellow—he gives us a lift—and what happens?

JONATHAN. [Remembering bitterly.] He said I looked like Boris Karloff! [He starts for EINSTEIN.] That's your work, Doctor. You did that to me!

EINSTEIN. [He's backed away from table.] Now, Chonny—we find a place somewhere—I fix you up quick!

JONATHAN. Tonight!

EINSTEIN. Chonny—I got to eat first. I'm hungry—I'm weak.

[The AUNTS enter from kitchen. ABBY comes to JONATHAN. MARTHA remains in kitchen doorway.]

ABBY. Jonathan—we're glad that you remembered us and took the trouble to come in and say hello. But you were never happy in this house and we were never happy while you were in it—so, we've just come in to say good-by.

JONATHAN. [Takes a menacing step toward ABBY; then decides to try the charm again.] Aunt Abby, I can't say that your feeling toward me comes as a surprise. I've spent a great many hours regretting the many heartaches I must have given you as a boy.

ABBY. You were quite a trial to us, Jonathan.

JONATHAN. But my great disappointment is for Dr. Einstein. [EINSTEIN is a little surprised.] I promised him that no matter how rushed we were in passing through Brooklyn, I'd take the time to bring him here for one of Aunt Martha's homecooked dinners.

MARTHA. [Rises to this a bit.] Oh . . .

ABBY. I'm sorry. I'm afraid there wouldn't be enough.

MARTHA. Abby, it's a pretty good-sized pot roast.

JONATHAN. Pot roast!

MARTHA. I think the least we can do is to—

JONATHAN. Thank you, Aunt Martha! We'll stay to dinner.

ABBY. [Backing to kitchen door and not at all pleased.] Well, we'll hurry it along.

MARTHA. Yes! [She exits into kitchen.]

ABBY. [Stopping in doorway.] Oh, Jonathan, if you want to freshen up—why don't you use the washroom in Grandfather's old laboratory?

JONATHAN. [Crossing to her.] Is that still there?

ABBY. Oh, yes. Just as he left it. Well, I'll help Martha get things started—since we're all in a hurry. [She exits into kitchen.]

EINSTEIN. Well, we get a meal anyway.

JONATHAN. Grandfather's laboratory! [Looks upstairs.] And just as it was. Doctor, a perfect operating room.

EINSTEIN. Too bad we can't use it.

JONATHAN. After you've finished with me— Why, we could make a fortune here. The laboratory—that large ward in the attic—ten beds, Doctor—and Brooklyn is crying for your talents.

EINSTEIN. Vy vork yourself up, Chonny? Anyway, for Brooklyn I think we're a year too late.

JONATHAN. You don't know this town, Doctor. Practically everybody in Brooklyn needs a new face.

EINSTEIN. But so many of the old faces are locked up.

JONATHAN. A very small percentage—and the boys in Brooklyn are famous for paying generously to stay out of jail.

EINSTEIN. Take it easy, Chonny. Your aunts—they don't want us here.

JONATHAN. We're here for dinner, aren't we?

EINSTEIN. Yah—but after dinner?

JONATHAN. [Crossing to sofa.] Leave it to me, Doctor. I'll handle it. Why, this house'll be our headquarters for years.

EINSTEIN. Oh, that would be beautiful, Chonny! This nice quiet house. Those aunts of yours—what sweet ladies. I love them already. I get the bags, yah?

JONATHAN. [Stopping him.] Doctor! We must wait until we're invited.

EINSTEIN. But you chust said that—

JONATHAN. We'll be invited.

EINSTEIN. And if they say no—?

JONATHAN. Doctor—two helpless old women—? [He sits on sofa.]

EINSTEIN. [Takes bottle flask from hip pocket and unscrews cork as he crosses to window seat.] It's like comes true a beautiful dream— Only I hope you're not dreaming. [He stretches out on window seat, taking a swig from bottle.] It's so peaceful.

JONATHAN. [Stretched out on sofa.] That's what makes this house so perfect for us—it's so peaceful.

[TEDDY *enters from cellar, blows a terrific blast on his bugle, as* JONATHAN *sits up.* TEDDY *marches to stairs and on up to first landing as the two men look at his tropical garb with some astonishment.*]

TEDDY. CHARGE! [*He rushes up the stairs and off.*]

[JONATHAN *watches him from foot of stairs.* EINSTEIN, *sitting on window seat, takes a hasty swig from his flask.*]

ACT TWO

SCENE: *The same. Later that night.* JONATHAN, *with an after-dinner cigar, is occupying armchair left of table, completely at his ease.* ABBY *and* MARTHA, *seated on window seat, are giving him a nervous attention in the attitude of people who wish their guests would go home.* EINSTEIN *is relaxed and happy in chair right of table. Dinner dishes have been cleared. There is a red cloth on the table, with a saucer to serve as ash tray for* JONATHAN. *The room is in order. All doors are closed, as are drapes over windows.*

JONATHAN. Yes, Aunties, those five years in Chicago were amongst the busiest and happiest of my life.

EINSTEIN. And from Chicago we go to South Bend, Indiana. [*He shakes his head as though he wishes they hadn't.*]

JONATHAN. [*Gives him a look.*] They wouldn't be interested in our experience in Indiana.

ABBY. Well, Jonathan, you've led a very interesting life, I'm sure—but we really shouldn't have allowed you to talk so late. [*She starts to rise.* JONATHAN *seats her just by the tone of his voice.*]

JONATHAN. My meeting Dr. Einstein in London, I might say, changed the whole course of my life. You remember I had been in South Africa, in the diamond business—then Amsterdam, the diamond market. I wanted to go back to South Africa—and Dr. Einstein made it possible for me.

EINSTEIN. A good job, Chonny. [*To* AUNTS.] When we take off the bandages—his face look so different, the nurse had to introduce me.

JONATHAN. I loved that face. I still carry the picture with me. [*He produces snapshot-size picture from inside coat pocket, looks at it a moment, then hands it to* MARTHA. *She looks at it and hands it to* ABBY.]

ABBY. This looks more the way you used to look, but still I wouldn't know you.

JONATHAN. I think we'll go back to that face, Doctor.

EINSTEIN. Yah, it's safe now.

ABBY. [*Rising.*] Well, I know you both want to get to—where you're going.

JONATHAN. [*Relaxing even more.*] My dear aunts—I'm so full of that delicious dinner I'm unable to move a muscle.

EINSTEIN. [*Relaxing too.*] Yah, it's nice here.

MARTHA. [*Rises.*] After all—it's very late and—

[TEDDY *enters on balcony wearing his solar topee, carrying a book, open, and another topee.*]

TEDDY. [*Descending stairs.*] I found it! I found it!

JONATHAN. What did you find, Teddy?

TEDDY. The story of my life—my biography. Here's the picture I was telling you about, General. [*He lays open book on table showing picture to* EINSTEIN.] Here we are, both of us. "President Roosevelt and General Goethals at Culebra Cut." That's me, General, and that's you.

EINSTEIN. [*Looks at picture.*] My, how I've changed.

TEDDY. [*Looks at* EINSTEIN, *a little puzzled, but makes adjustment.*] Well, you see that picture hasn't been taken yet. We haven't even started work on Culebra Cut. We're still digging locks. And now, General, we will both go to Panama and inspect the new lock. [*Hands him topee.*]

ABBY. No, Teddy—not to Panama.

EINSTEIN. We go some other time. Panama's a long way off.

TEDDY. Nonsense, it's just down in the cellar.

JONATHAN. The cellar?

MARTHA. We let him dig the Panama Canal in the cellar.

TEDDY. [*Severely.*] General Goethals, as President of the United States, Commander in Chief of the Army and Navy and the man who gave you this job, I demand that you accompany me on the inspection of the new lock.

JONATHAN. Teddy! I think it's time you went to bed.

TEDDY. I beg your pardon! [*He walks to* JONATHAN, *putting on his pince-nez as he crosses.*] Who are you?

JONATHAN. I'm Woodrow Wilson. Go to bed.

TEDDY. No—you're not Wilson. But your face is familiar. Let me see— You're not anyone I know now. Perhaps later— On my hunting trip to Africa—yes, you look like someone I might meet in the jungle.

[JONATHAN *stiffens.* ABBY *crosses in front of* TEDDY, *getting between him and* JONATHAN.]

ABBY. It's your brother, Jonathan, dear.

MARTHA. [*Rising.*] He's had his face changed.

TEDDY. So that's it—a nature faker!

ABBY. And perhaps you had better go to bed, Teddy—Jonathan and his friend have to go back to their hotel.

JONATHAN. [*Rising.*] General Goethals [*To* EINSTEIN.], inspect the canal.

EINSTEIN. [*Rising.*] All right, Mr. President. We go to Panama.

TEDDY. Bully! Bully! [*He crosses to cellar door, opens it.*] Follow me, General. [EINSTEIN *goes up to left of* TEDDY; TEDDY *taps solar topee in* EINSTEIN's *hand, then taps his own head.*] It's down south you know. [*He exits downstairs.*]

[EINSTEIN *puts on topee, which is too large for him. Then turns in cellar doorway.*]

EINSTEIN. Well—bon voyage. [*He exits, closing door.*]

JONATHAN. Aunt Abby, I must correct your misapprehension. You spoke of our hotel. We have no hotel. We came directly here—

MARTHA. Well, there's a very nice little hotel just three blocks down the—

JONATHAN. [*Cutting her off.*] Aunt Martha, this is my home.

ABBY. But, Jonathan, you can't stay here. We need our rooms.

JONATHAN. You need them?

ABBY. Yes, for our lodgers.

JONATHAN. [*Alarmed.*] Are there lodgers in this house?

MARTHA. Well, not just now, but we all plan to have some.

JONATHAN. [*Cutting her off again.*] Then my old room is still free.

ABBY. But, Jonathan, there's no place for Dr. Einstein.

JONATHAN. [*Crosses to table, drops cigar ashes into saucer.*] He'll share the room with me.

ABBY. No, Jonathan, I'm afraid you can't stay here.

[JONATHAN *grinds cigar out in saucer, then starts toward* AUNTS. *They back around table,* MARTHA *first.*]

JONATHAN. Dr. Einstein and I need a place to sleep. You remembered, this afternoon, that as a boy I could be disagreeable. It wouldn't be very pleasant for any of us if—

MARTHA. [*Frightened.*] Perhaps we'd better let them stay here tonight—

ABBY. Well, just overnight, Jonathan.

JONATHAN. That's settled. Now, if you'll get my room ready—

MARTHA. [*Starting upstairs,* ABBY *following.*] It only needs airing out.

ABBY. We keep it ready to show our lodgers. I think you and Dr. Einstein will find it comfortable.

[JONATHAN *follows them to first landing and leans on newel post.* AUNTS *are on balcony.*]

JONATHAN. You have a most distinguished guest in Dr. Einstein. I'm afraid you don't appreciate his skill. But you will. In a few weeks you'll see me looking like a very different Jonathan.

MARTHA. He can't operate on you here.

JONATHAN. [*Ignoring her.*] When Dr. Einstein and I get organized—when we resume practice— Oh, I forgot to tell you. We're turning Grandfather's laboratory into an operating room. We expect to be quite busy.

ABBY. Jonathan, we will not let you turn this house into a hospital.

JONATHAN. [*Laughing.*] A hospital—heavens no! It will be a beauty parlor.

EINSTEIN. [*Enters excitedly from cellar.*] Hey, Chonny, down in the cellar— [*He sees* AUNTS *and stops.*]

JONATHAN. Dr. Einstein—my dear aunts have invited us to live with them.

EINSTEIN. Oh, you fixed it?

ABBY. Well, you're sleeping here tonight.

JONATHAN. Please get our room ready immediately.

MARTHA. Well—

ABBY. For tonight.

[*They exit through arch.* JONATHAN *comes to foot of stairs.*]

EINSTEIN. Chonny, when I go down in the cellar, what do you think I find?

JONATHAN. What?

EINSTEIN. The Panama Canal.

JONATHAN. [*Disgusted.*] The Panama Canal.

EINSTEIN. It just fits Mr. Spenalzo. It's a hole Teddy dug. Six feet long and four feet wide.

JONATHAN. [*Gets the idea; opens cellar door and looks down.*] Down there!

EINSTEIN. You'd think they knew we were bringing Mr. Spenalzo along. That's hospitality.

JONATHAN. [*Closing cellar door.*] Rather a good joke on my aunts—their living in a house with a body buried in the cellar.

EINSTEIN. How do we get him in?

JONATHAN. Yes. We can't just walk him through the door. [*He sees window in wall.*] We'll drive the car up between the house and the cemetery—then when they've gone to *bed,* we'll bring Mr. Spenalzo in through the window.

EINSTEIN. [*Taking out bottle flask.*] Bed! Just think, we've got a bed tonight! [*He starts swigging.*]

JONATHAN. [*Grabbing his arm.*] Easy, Doctor. Remember you're operating tomorrow. And this time you'd better be sober.

EINSTEIN. I fix you up beautiful.

JONATHAN. And if you don't— [*Gives* EINSTEIN *shove to door.*]

ABBY. [*Entering on balcony with* MARTHA.] Jonathan! Your room is ready.

JONATHAN. Then you can go to bed. We're moving the car up behind the house.

MARTHA. It's all right where it is—until morning.

JONATHAN. [*At opened door.*] I don't want to leave it in the street—that might be against the law. [*He exits.*]

[EINSTEIN *follows him out, closing door.* ABBY *and* MARTHA *start downstairs and reach below table.*]

MARTHA. Abby, what are we going to do.

ABBY. Well, we're not going to let them stay more than one night in this house for one thing. What would the neighbors think? People coming in here with one face and going out with another.

MARTHA. What are we going to do about Mr. Hoskins?

ABBY. [*Crosses to window seat;* MARTHA *follows.*] Oh, Mr. Hoskins. It can't be very comfortable for him in there. And he's been so patient, the poor dear. Well, I think Teddy had better get Mr. Hoskins downstairs right away.

MARTHA. [*Adamant.*] Abby—I will not invite Jonathan to the funeral services.

ABBY. Oh, no. We'll wait until they've gone to bed and then come down and hold the services.

TEDDY. [*Enters from cellar, gets book from table.*] General Goethals was very pleased. He says the Canal is just the right size.

ABBY. Teddy! Teddy, there's been another yellow fever victim.

TEDDY. [*Takes off pince-nez.*] Dear me—this will be a shock to the General.

MARTHA. Then we mustn't tell him about it.

TEDDY. [*To* MARTHA.] But it's his department.

ABBY. No, we mustn't tell him, Teddy. It would just spoil his visit.

TEDDY. I'm sorry, Aunt Abby. It's out of my hands—he'll have to be told. Army regulations, you know.

ABBY. No, Teddy, we *must* keep it a secret.

MARTHA. Yes.

TEDDY. [*He loves them.*] A state secret?

ABBY. Yes, a state secret.

MARTHA. Promise?

TEDDY. [*What a silly request.*] You have the word of the President of the United States. [*Crosses his heart.*] Cross my heart and hope to die. [*He spits.*] Now let's see— [*Puts pince-nez on, then puts arms around both* AUNTS.] how are we going to keep it a secret?

ABBY. Well, Teddy, you go back down in the cellar and when I turn out the lights —when it's all dark—you come up and take the poor man down to the Canal. [*Urging him to cellar door, which he opens.*] Now go along, Teddy.

MARTHA. And we'll come down later and hold services.

TEDDY. [*In doorway.*] You may announce the President will say a few words. [*He starts, then turns back.*] Where is the poor devil?

MARTHA. He's in the window seat.

TEDDY. It seems to be spreading. We've never had yellow fever there before. [*He exits, closing door.*]

ABBY. Martha, when Jonathan and Dr. Einstein come back, let's see if we can get them to go to bed right away.

MARTHA. Yes. Then by the time they're asleep, we'll be dressed for the funeral. [*Sudden thought.*] Abby, I've never even seen Mr. Hoskins.

ABBY. Oh, my goodness, that's right— you were out. Well, you just come right over and see him now. [*They go to window seat, ABBY first.*] He's really very nice looking—considering he's a Methodist. [*As they go to lift window seat, JONATHAN throws window open from outside with a bang. AUNTS scream and draw back. JONATHAN puts his head in through drapes.*]

JONATHAN. We're bringing—the luggage through here.

ABBY. Jonathan, your room's waiting for you. You can go right up.

[*Two dusty bags and a large instrument case are passed through window by EINSTEIN. JONATHAN puts them on floor.*]

JONATHAN. I'm afraid we don't keep Brooklyn hours—but you two run along to bed.

ABBY. Now, you must be very tired, both of you—and we don't go to bed this early.

JONATHAN. Well, you should. It's time I came home to take care of you.

MARTHA. We weren't planning to go until—

JONATHAN. [*Stronger.*] Aunt Martha, did you hear me say go to bed! [*AUNT MARTHA starts upstairs as EINSTEIN comes in through window and picks up two bags. JONATHAN takes instrument case and puts it on top of window seat.*] The instruments can go to the laboratory in the morning.

[*EINSTEIN starts upstairs. JONATHAN closes window. MARTHA is part way upstairs as EINSTEIN passes her.*] Now, then, we're all going to bed. [*He crosses as ABBY goes to light switch.*]

ABBY. I'll wait till you're up, then turn out the lights.

[*JONATHAN, going upstairs, sees EINSTEIN pausing at balcony door. MARTHA is almost up to balcony.*]

JONATHAN. Another flight, Doctor. [*To MARTHA.*] Run along, Aunt Martha. [*MARTHA hurries into doorway. EINSTEIN goes through arch to third floor. JONATHAN continues on to end of balcony. ABBY is at light switch.*] All right, Aunt Abby.

ABBY. [*Stalling; looks toward cellar door.*] I'll be right up.

JONATHAN. Now, Aunt Abby. Turn out the lights!

[*ABBY turns switch, plunging stage into darkness except for spot shining down stairway from arch. ABBY goes upstairs to her door where MARTHA is waiting. She takes a last frightened look at JONATHAN and exits. MARTHA closes door. JONATHAN goes off through arch, closing that door. A street light shines through main door on stage floor. TEDDY opens cellar door, then turns on cellar light, outlining him in doorway. He crosses to window seat and opens it—the window seat cover gives out its usual rusty squeak. He reaches in and pulls Mr. Hoskins. He gets Mr. Hoskins over his shoulder and, leaving window seat open, crosses to cellar door and goes down into cellar with Mr. Hoskins. Closes door. JONATHAN and EINSTEIN come through arch. It is dark. They light matches and listen at the aunts' door for a moment. EINSTEIN speaks.*]

EINSTEIN. All right. Chonny.

[*The matches go out. JONATHAN lights another and they come down to foot of stairs.*]

JONATHAN. I'll get the window open. You go around and hand him through.

EINSTEIN. No, he's too heavy for me. You go outside and push—I stay here and pull. Then together we get him down to Panama.

JONATHAN. All right. [*He blows out match, crosses and opens door.*] I'll take a look around outside the house. When I tap on the glass, you open the window.

EINSTEIN. All right. [JONATHAN *exits, closing door.* EINSTEIN *lights match. He bumps into table and match goes out. He feels his way from there. We hear ejaculations and noise.* EINSTEIN *has fallen into window seat. In window seat he lights another match and slowly rises up to a sitting position and looks around. He blows out match and hauls himself out of window seat.*] Who left dis open? Dummkopf! [*We hear the creak of the cover as he closes it. In the darkness we hear a tap on window.* EINSTEIN *opens it. Then in a hushed voice.*] Chonny? O.K. Allez Oop. Wait—wait a minute. You lost a leg somewhere. Ach—now I got him. Come on—ugh—[*He falls on floor and there is a crash of a body and the sound of a "Sshhhh" from outside.*] That was me, Chonny. I schlipped.

JONATHAN. Be more careful.

[*Pause.*]

EINSTEIN. Well, his shoe came off. . . . All right, Chonny. I got him! [*There is a knock at door.*] Chonny! Somebody at the door! Go quick. NO. I manage here—go quick!

[*A second knock at door. A moment's silence and we hear the creak of window seat as* EINSTEIN *puts Mr. Spenalzo in Mr. Hoskins' place. A third knock, as* EINSTEIN *struggles with body. A fourth knock and then the creak of the window seat as* EINSTEIN *closes it. He scurries around to beside desk, keeping low to avoid being seen through door.* ELAINE *enters, calling softly.*]

ELAINE. Miss Abby! Miss Martha! [*In the dim path of light she calls toward balcony.*] Miss Abby! Miss Martha! [*Suddenly* JONATHAN *steps through door and closes it. The noise swings* ELAINE *around and she gasps.*] Uhhh! Who is it? Is that you, Teddy? [JONATHAN *comes toward her as she backs into chair.*] Who are you?

JONATHAN. Who are *you?*

ELAINE. I'm Elaine Harper—I live next door!

JONATHAN. Then what are you doing here?

ELAINE. I came over to see Miss Abby and Miss Martha.

JONATHAN. [*To* EINSTEIN, *without turning;* EINSTEIN *has crept to light switch after passing* JONATHAN *in dark.*] Turn on the lights, Doctor. [*The lights go on.* ELAINE *gasps as she sees* JONATHAN *and sits in chair.* JONATHAN *looks at her for a moment.*] You chose rather an untimely moment for a social call. [*He crosses toward window seat, looking for Spenalzo, but doesn't see him. He looks up, behind table. Looks out window, then comes back into the room.*]

ELAINE. [*Trying to summon courage.*] I think you'd better explain what *you're* doing here.

JONATHAN. We happen to live here.

ELAINE. You *don't* live here. I'm in this house every day and I've never seen you before. [*Frightened.*] Where are Miss Abby and Miss Martha? What have you done to them?

JONATHAN. Perhaps we'd better introduce ourselves. This— [*Indicating.*] —is Dr. Einstein.

ELAINE. [*Looks at* EINSTEIN.] Dr. Einstein? [*She turns back to* JONATHAN. EINSTEIN, *behind her back, is gesturing to* JONATHAN *the whereabouts of Spenalzo.*]

JONATHAN. A surgeon of great distinction— [*He looks under table for Spenalzo, and not finding him—*] and something of a magician.

ELAINE. And I suppose you're going to tell me you're Boris Kar——

JONATHAN. I'm Jonathan Brewster.

ELAINE. [*Drawing back almost with fright.*] Oh—you're Jonathan!

JONATHAN. I see you've heard of me.

[EINSTEIN *drifts to front of sofa.*]

ELAINE. Yes—just this afternoon for the first time.

JONATHAN. [*Stepping toward her.*] And what did they say about me?

ELAINE. Only that there was another brother named Jonathan—that's all that was said. [*Calming.*] Well, that explains everything. Now that I know who you are— [*Running to door.*] I'll be running along back home. [*The door is locked. She turns to* JONATHAN.] If you'll kindly unlock the door.

[JONATHAN *goes to her, then, before reaching her, he turns to door and unlocks it.* EINSTEIN *drifts down to chair. As* JONATHAN *opens door part way,* ELAINE *starts toward it. He turns and stops her with a gesture.*]

JONATHAN. "That explains everything"? Just what did you mean by that? Why did you come here at this time of night?

ELAINE. I thought I saw someone prowling around the house. I suppose it was you.

JONATHAN. [*Closes door and locks it, leaving key in lock.*] You thought you saw someone prowling around the house?

ELAINE. Yes—weren't you outside? Isn't that your car?

JONATHAN. You saw someone at the car?

ELAINE. Yes.

JONATHAN. [*Coming toward her as she backs away.*] What else did you see?

ELAINE. Just someone walking around the house to the car.

JONATHAN. What else did you see?

ELAINE. Just that—that's all. That's why I came over here. I wanted to tell Miss Abby to call the police. But if it was you, and that's your car, I don't need to bother Miss Abby. I'll be running along. [*She takes a step toward door. He steps in her path.*]

JONATHAN. What was the man doing at the car?

ELAINE. [*Excited.*] I don't know. You see I was on my way over here.

JONATHAN. I think you're lying.

EINSTEIN. I think she tells the truth, Chonny. We let her go now, huh?

JONATHAN. I think she's lying. Breaking into a house this time of night. I think she's dangerous. She shouldn't be allowed around loose. [*He seizes* ELAINE's *arm. She screams.*]

ELAINE. Take your hands off me—

JONATHAN. Doctor—

[*As* EINSTEIN *starts,* TEDDY *enters from cellar, shutting door. He looks at* JONATHAN, *then speaks to* EINSTEIN.]

TEDDY. [*Simply.*] It's going to be a private funeral. [*He goes upstairs to first landing.* ELAINE *crosses to desk, dragging* JONATHAN *with her.*]

ELAINE. Teddy! Teddy! Tell these men who I am.

TEDDY. [*Turns and looks at her.*] That's my daughter—Alice. [*Dashing upstairs.*] CHARGE!

ELAINE. [*Struggling to get away from* JONATHAN.] No! No! Teddy!

[JONATHAN *has* ELAINE's *arm twisted in back of her, his other hand is over her mouth.*]

JONATHAN. Doctor! Your handkerchief! [*As* EINSTEIN *hands him a handkerchief,* JONATHAN *releases his hand from* ELAINE's *mouth to take it. She screams. He puts his hand over her mouth again; spies the cellar door and speaks to* EINSTEIN.] The cellar!

[EINSTEIN *runs and opens cellar door. Then he runs back and turns off light switch, putting stage in darkness.* JONATHAN *then pushes* ELAINE *through cellar doorway.* EINSTEIN *runs back and down cellar stairs with* ELAINE. JONATHAN *shuts door, remaining on stage as the* AUNTS *enter on balcony above in their mourning clothes. Everything is in complete darkness except for street lamp.*]

ABBY. What's the matter?

MARTHA. What's happening down there? [MARTHA *shuts her door and* ABBY *puts on lights from switch on balcony. They look down at the room a moment, then come downstairs, speaking as they come.*]

ABBY. What's the matter? [*Reaching foot of stairs as she sees* JONATHAN.] What are you doing?

JONATHAN. We caught a burglar—a sneak thief. Go back to your room.

ABBY. We'll call the police.

JONATHAN. We've called the police. We'll handle this. Go back to your room. Do you hear me?

[*The doorbell rings, followed by several knocks.* ABBY *runs and opens door.* MORTIMER *enters with suitcase. At the same time,* ELAINE *runs out of cellar and into* MORTIMER's *arms.* JONATHAN *makes a grab for* ELAINE *but misses.* EINSTEIN *sneaks behind* JONATHAN.]

ELAINE. Mortimer! [*He drops suitcase.*] Where have you been?

MORTIMER. To the Nora Bayes Theatre and I should have known better. [*He sees* JONATHAN.] My God! I'm still there.

ABBY. This is your brother Jonathan— and this is Dr. Einstein.

MORTIMER. [*Surveys his* AUNTS *all dressed in black.*] I know this isn't a nightmare, but what is it?

JONATHAN. I've come back home, Mortimer.

MORTIMER. [*Looking at him, and then to* ABBY.] Who did you say this was?

ABBY. It's your brother Jonathan. He's had his face changed. Dr. Einstein performed the operation.

MORTIMER. [*Taking a closer look at* JONATHAN.] Jonathan! Jonathan, you always were a horror, but do you have to look like one?

[JONATHAN *takes a step toward him.* EINSTEIN *pulls on his sleeve.* ELAINE *and* MARTHA *draw back to desk.*]

EINSTEIN. Easy, Chonny! Easy.

JONATHAN. Mortimer, have you forgotten the things I used to do to you when we were boys? Remember the time you were tied to the bedpost—the needles under your fingernails—?

MORTIMER. By God, it is Jonathan. Yes, I remember. I remember you as the most detestable, vicious, venomous form of animal life I ever knew.

[JONATHAN *grows tense.* ABBY *steps between them.*]

ABBY. Now don't you two boys start quarrelling again the minute you've seen each other.

MORTIMER. There won't be any fight, Aunt Abby. Jonathan, you're not wanted here—get out!

JONATHAN. Dr. Einstein and I have been invited to stay.

MORTIMER. Not in this house.

ABBY. Just for tonight.

MORTIMER. I don't want him anywhere near me.

ABBY. But we did invite them for tonight, and it wouldn't be very nice to go back on our word.

MORTIMER. [*Unwillingly.*] All right, tonight. But the first thing in the morning—out! [*He picks up his suitcase.*] Where are they sleeping?

ABBY. We put them in Jonathan's old room.

MORTIMER. That's my old room. [*Starts upstairs.*] I'm sleeping in that room. I'm here to stay.

MARTHA. Oh, Mortimer, I'm so glad.

EINSTEIN. Chonny, we sleep down here.

MORTIMER. You bet your life you sleep down here.

EINSTEIN. [*To* JONATHAN.] You sleep on sofa and I sleep on the window seat.

[*At the mention of window seat,* MORTIMER *has reached the landing; after hanging his hat on hall tree, he turns and comes slowly downstairs,*

speaking as he reaches the floor and crossing over to window seat.]

MORTIMER. The window seat! Oh, well, let's not argue about it. That window seat's good enough for me for tonight. I'll sleep on the window seat. [*As* MORTIMER *crosses above table,* EINSTEIN *makes a gesture as though to stop him from going to window seat, but he's too late. He turns to* JONATHAN *as* MORTIMER *sits on window seat.*]

EINSTEIN. You know, Chonny—all this argument—it makes me think of Mr. Spenalzo.

JONATHAN. Spenalzo. [*He looks around for Spenalzo again. Realizing it would be best for them to remain downstairs, he speaks to* MORTIMER.] Well, now, Mortimer— It really isn't necessary to inconvenience you like this—we'll sleep down here.

MORTIMER. [*Rising.*] Jonathan, your sudden consideration for me is very unconvincing.

EINSTEIN. [*Goes upstairs to landing.*] Come along, Chonny. We get our things out of the room, eh?

MORTIMER. Don't bother, Doctor!

JONATHAN. By the way, Doctor, I've completely lost track of Mr. Spenalzo.

MORTIMER. Who's this Mr. Spenalzo?

EINSTEIN. [*From landing.*] Just a friend of ours Chonny's been looking for.

MORTIMER. Well, don't bring anyone else in here!

EINSTEIN. It's all right, Chonny. While we pack I tell you all about it. [*He goes on up and through arch.* JONATHAN *starts upstairs.*]

ABBY. Mortimer, you don't have to sleep down here. I can go in with Martha and you can take my room.

JONATHAN. [*He has reached the balcony.*] No trouble at all, Aunt Abby. We'll be packed in a few minutes. And then you can have the room, Mortimer. [*He exits through arch.*]

[MORTIMER *walks to sofa.* MARTHA *crosses to armchair and as* MORTIMER *speaks she picks up sport shoe belonging to Spenalzo, that* EINSTEIN *put there in blackout scene, unnoticed by anyone. She pretends to dust hem of her dress.*]

MORTIMER. You're just wasting your time—I told you I'm sleeping down here.

ELAINE. [*Leaps up from stool into* MOR-TIMER's *arms.*] Mortimer!

MORTIMER. What's the matter with you, dear?

ELAINE. [*Semi-hysterical.*] I've almost been killed.

MORTIMER. You've almost been— [*He looks quickly at the* AUNTS.] Abby! Martha!

MARTHA. No! It was Jonathan.

ABBY. He mistook her for a sneak thief.

ELAINE. No, it was more than that. He's some kind of maniac. Mortimer, I'm afraid of him.

MORTIMER. Why, darling, you're trembling. [*Seats her on sofa. To* AUNTS.] Have you got any smelling salts?

MARTHA. No, but do you think some hot tea, or coffee—?

MORTIMER. Coffee. Make some for me, too—and some sandwiches. I haven't had any dinner.

MARTHA. We'll make something for both of you.

[MORTIMER *starts to question* ELAINE *as* ABBY *takes off her hat and gloves and puts them on sideboard. Talks to* MARTHA *at the same time.*]

ABBY. Martha, we can leave our hats downstairs here, now.

MORTIMER. [*Turns and sees her.*] You weren't going out somewhere, were you? Do you know what time it is? It's after twelve. [*The word twelve rings a bell.*] TWELVE! [*He turns to* ELAINE.] Elaine, you've got to go home!

ELAINE. Whaa-t?

ABBY. Why, you wanted some sandwiches for you both. It won't take a minute. [*She exits into kitchen.*]

[MORTIMER *is looking at* ELAINE *with his back to* MARTHA. MARTHA *crosses over to him with shoe in hand by her side.*]

MARTHA. Why, don't you remember—we wanted to celebrate your engagement? [*She punctuates the word "engagement" by pointing the shoe at* MORTIMER's *back. She looks at the shoe in amazement, wondering how it ever got in her hand. She stares at it a moment (the other two do not see it, of course), then puts it on top of the table. Finally dismissing it she turns to* MORTIMER *again.*] That's what we'll do, dear. We'll make a nice supper for both of you. [*She starts out kitchen door, then*

turns back.] And we'll open a bottle of wine! [*She exits kitchen door.*]

MORTIMER. [*Vaguely.*] All right. [*Suddenly changes his mind and runs to kitchen door.*] No WINE! [*He closes the door and comes back as* ELAINE *rises from the sofa to him. She is still very upset.*]

ELAINE. Mortimer! What's going on in this house?

MORTIMER. [*Suspicious.*] What do you mean—what's going on in this house?

ELAINE. You were supposed to take me to dinner and the theatre tonight—you called it off. You asked me to marry you—I said I would—and five minutes later you threw me out of the house. Tonight, just after your brother tries to strangle me, you want to chase me home. Now, listen, Mr. Brewster—before I go home, I want to know where I stand. Do you love me?

MORTIMER. [*Taking her hands.*] I love you very much, Elaine. In fact I love you so much I can't marry you.

ELAINE. Have you suddenly gone crazy?

MORTIMER. I don't think so but it's just a matter of time. [*They both sit on sofa as* MORTIMER *begins to explain.*] You see, insanity runs in my family. [*He looks upstairs and toward kitchen.*] It practically gallops. That's why I can't marry you, dear.

ELAINE. Now wait a minute, you've got to do better than that.

MORTIMER. No, dear—there's a strange taint in the Brewster blood. If you really knew my family it's—well—it's what you'd expect if Strindberg had written *Hellzapoppin.*

ELAINE. Now just because Teddy is a little—

MORTIMER. No, it goes way back. The first Brewster—the one who came over on the *Mayflower.* You know in those days the Indians used to scalp the settlers—he used to scalp the Indians.

ELAINE. Mortimer, that's ancient history.

MORTIMER. No, the whole family . . . [*He rises and points to a picture of Grandfather over the sideboard.*] Take my grandfather—he tried his patent medicines out on dead people to be sure he wouldn't kill them.

ELAINE. He wasn't so crazy. He made a million dollars.

MORTIMER. And then there's Jonathan.

You just said he was a maniac—he tried to kill you.

ELAINE. [*Rises, crosses to him.*] But he's your brother, not you. I'm in love with you.

MORTIMER. And there's Teddy, too. You *know* Teddy. He thinks he's Roosevelt. No, dear, no Brewster should marry. I realize now that if I'd met my father in time I'd have stopped him.

ELAINE. Now, darling, all this doesn't prove *you're* crazy. Look at your aunts—they're Brewsters, aren't they?—and the sanest, sweetest people I've ever known.

MORTIMER. [*Walking to window seat, speaking as he goes.*] Well, even they have their peculiarities.

ELAINE. [*Turning.*] Yes, but what lovely peculiarities! Kindness, generosity—human sympathy—

[MORTIMER *sees* ELAINE's *back is to him. He lifts window seat to take a peek, and sees Mr. Spenalzo instead of Mr. Hoskins. He puts window seat down again and staggers to table, and leans on it.*]

MORTIMER. [*To himself.*] There's another one!

ELAINE. [*Turning to* MORTIMER.] Oh, Mortimer, there are plenty of others. You can't tell me anything about your aunts.

MORTIMER. I'm not going to. [*Crossing to her.*] Look, Elaine, you've got to go home. Something very important has just come up.

ELAINE. Up, from where? We're here alone together.

MORTIMER. I know I'm acting irrationally, but just put it down to the fact that I'm a mad Brewster.

ELAINE. If you think you're going to get out of this by pretending you're insane—you're crazy. Maybe you're not going to marry me, but I'm going to marry you. I love you, you dope.

MORTIMER. [*Urging her to door.*] Well, if you love me will you get the hell out of here!

ELAINE. Well, at least take me home, won't you? I'm afraid.

MORTIMER. Afraid! A little walk through the cemetery?

ELAINE. [*Crosses to door, then changing tactics, turns to* MORTIMER.] Mortimer, will you kiss me good night?

MORTIMER. [*Holding out arms.*] Of course, dear. [*What* MORTIMER *plans to be a desultory peck,* ELAINE *turns into a production number. He comes out of it with no loss of poise.*] Good night, dear. I'll call you up in a day or two.

ELAINE. [*Walks to door in a cold fury, opens it and turns to* MORTIMER.] You—you critic! [*She slams door after her.*]

[MORTIMER *looks at the door helplessly, then turns and stalks to the kitchen door.*]

MORTIMER. [*In doorway.*] Aunt Abby! Aunt Martha! Come in here!

ABBY. [*Offstage.*] We'll be in in a minute, dear.

MORTIMER. Come in here now! [*He stands down by window seat.*]

ABBY. [*Enters from kitchen.*] Yes, dear, what is it? Where's Elaine?

MORTIMER. I thought you promised me not to let anyone in this house while I was gone!

[*The following speeches overlap.*]

ABBY. Well, Jonathan just walked in—

MORTIMER. I don't mean Jonathan—

ABBY. And Dr. Einstein was with him—

MORTIMER. I don't mean Dr. Einstein. Who's that in the window seat?

ABBY. We told you— Mr. Hoskins.

[MORTIMER *throws open the window seat and steps back.*]

MORTIMER. It is *not* Mr. Hoskins.

[ABBY, *a little puzzled, walks to window seat and looks in; then speaks very simply.*]

ABBY. Who can that be?

MORTIMER. Are you trying to tell me you've never seen this man before?

ABBY. I certainly am. Why, this is a fine how do you do! It's getting so anybody thinks he can walk into this house.

MORTIMER. Now Aunt Abby, don't you try to get out of this. That's another one of your gentlemen!

ABBY. Mortimer, how can you say such a thing! That man's an imposter! And if he came here to be buried in our cellar he's mistaken.

MORTIMER. Oh, Aunt Abby, you admitted to me that you put Mr. Hoskins in the window seat.

ABBY. Yes, I did.

MORTIMER. Well, this man couldn't have just got the idea from Mr. Hoskins. By the way—where is Mr. Hoskins? [*He looks toward cellar door.*]

ABBY. He must have gone to Panama.

MORTIMER. Oh, you buried him?

ABBY. No, not yet. He's just down there waiting for the services, poor dear. We haven't had a minute what with Jonathan in the house. [*At the mention of* JONATHAN'*s name,* MORTIMER *closes the window seat.*] Oh, dear. We've always wanted to hold a double funeral [*Crossing to kitchen door.*] but I will not read services over a total stranger.

MORTIMER. [*Going up to her.*] A stranger! Aunt Abby, how can I believe you? There are twelve men in the cellar and you admit you poisoned them.

ABBY. Yes, I did. But you don't think I'd stoop to telling a fib. Martha! [*She exits into kitchen.*]

[*At the same time* JONATHAN *enters through the arch onto balcony and comes down quickly to foot of stairs.* He sees MORTIMER *and crosses to him.*]

JONATHAN. Oh, Mortimer—I'd like to have a word with you.

MORTIMER. [*Standing up to him.*] A word's about all you'll have time for, Jonathan, because I've decided you and your doctor friend are going to have to get out of this house just as quickly as possible.

JONATHAN. [*Smoothly.*] I'm glad you recognize the fact that you and I can't live under the same roof—but you've arrived at the wrong solution. Take your suitcase and get out! [*He starts to walk by* MORTIMER, *anxious to get to the window seat, but* MORTIMER *makes a big sweep around table and comes back to him.*]

MORTIMER. Jonathan! You're beginning to bore me. You've played your one-night stand in Brooklyn—move on!

JONATHAN. My dear Mortimer, just because you've graduated from the back fence to the typewriter, don't think you've grown up. . . . [*He takes a sudden step around* MORTIMER *and gets to the window seat and sits.*] I'm staying, and you're leaving—and I mean now!

MORTIMER. [*Crossing to him.*] If you think I can be frightened—if you think there's anything I fear—

JONATHAN. [*He rises, they stand facing each other.*] I've lived a strange life, Mortimer. But it's taught me one thing—to be afraid of nothing! [*They glare at each other with equal courage when* ABBY *marches in from kitchen, followed by* MARTHA.]

ABBY. Martha, just look and see what's in that window seat.

[*Both* MEN *throw themselves on the window seat simultaneously.*]

MORTIMER. ⎫
JONATHAN. ⎬ Now, Aunt Abby!

[MORTIMER *turns his head slowly to* JONATHAN, *light dawning on his face. He rises with smiling assurance.*]

MORTIMER. Jonathan, let Aunt Martha see what's in the window seat. [JONATHAN *freezes dangerously.* MORTIMER *crosses to* ABBY.] Aunt Abby, I owe you an apology. [*He kisses her on forehead.*] I have very good news for you. Jonathan is leaving. He's taking Dr. Einstein and their cold companion with him. [JONATHAN *rises, but holds his ground.*] Jonathan, you're my brother. You're a Brewster. I'm going to give you a chance to get away and take the evidence with you—you can't ask for more than that. [JONATHAN *doesn't move.*] Very well—in that case I'll have to call the police. [MORTIMER *crosses to phone and picks it up.*]

JONATHAN. Don't reach for that telephone. Are you still giving me orders after seeing what's happened to Mr. Spenalzo?

MARTHA. Spenalzo?

ABBY. I knew he was a foreigner.

JONATHAN. Remember what happened to Mr. Spenalzo can happen to you too.

[*There is a knock on door.* ABBY *crosses and opens it and* OFFICER O'HARA *sticks his head in.*]

O'HARA. Hello, Miss Abby.

ABBY. Oh, Officer O'Hara. Is there something we can do for you?

[MORTIMER *puts phone down and drifts down to* O'HARA. JONATHAN *turns.*]

O'HARA. I saw your lights on and thought there might be sickness in the house. [*He sees* MORTIMER.] Oh, you got company—I'm sorry I disturbed you.

MORTIMER. [*Taking* O'HARA *by the arm.*] No, no, come in.

ABBY. Yes, come in.

MARTHA. [*Crossing to door.*] Come right in, Officer O'Hara. [MORTIMER *leads* O'HARA *in a couple of steps and shuts door.*] This is our nephew, Mortimer.

O'HARA. Pleased to meet you.

[JONATHAN *starts toward kitchen.*]

ABBY. [*Stopping* JONATHAN.] And this is another nephew, Jonathan.

O'HARA. [*Crosses below* MORTIMER *and gestures to* JONATHAN *with his night stick.*] Pleased to make your acquaintance. [JONATHAN *ignores him.* O'HARA *speaks to* AUNTS.] Well, it must be nice havin' your nephews visitin' you. Are they going to stay with you for a bit?

MORTIMER. I'm staying. My brother Jonathan is just leaving.

[JONATHAN *starts for stairs.* O'HARA *stops him.*]

O'HARA. I've met you here before, haven't I?

ABBY. I'm afraid not. Jonathan hasn't been home for years.

O'HARA. Your face looks familiar to me. Maybe I seen a picture of you somewheres.

JONATHAN. I don't think so. [*He hurries upstairs.*]

MORTIMER. Yes, Jonathan, I'd hurry if I were you. Your things are all packed anyway, aren't they?

O'HARA. Well, you'll be wanting to say your good-bys. I'll be running along.

MORTIMER. What's the rush? I'd like to have you stick around until my brother goes.

[JONATHAN *exits through arch.*]

O'HARA. I just dropped in to make sure everything was all right.

MORTIMER. We're going to have some coffee in a minute. Won't you join us?

ABBY. Oh, I forgot the coffee. [*She goes out to kitchen.*]

MARTHA. [*Crossing to kitchen door.*] Well, I'd better make some more sandwiches. I ought to know your appetite by this time, Officer O'Hara. [*She goes out to kitchen.*]

O'HARA. Don't bother. I'm due to ring in in a few minutes.

MORTIMER. You can have a cup of coffee with us. My brother will be gone soon. [*He leads* O'HARA *to armchair.*] Sit down.

O'HARA. Say—ain't I seen a photograph of your brother around here someplace?

MORTIMER. I don't think so. [*He sits at table.*]

O'HARA. He certainly reminds me of somebody.

MORTIMER. He looks like somebody you've probably seen in the movies.

O'HARA. I never go to the movies. I hate 'em! My mother says the movies is a bastard art.

MORTIMER. Yes, it's full of them. Your, er, mother said that?

O'HARA. Yeah. My mother was an actress —a stage actress. Perhaps you heard of her—Peaches Latour.

MORTIMER. It sounds like a name I've seen on a program. What did she play?

O'HARA. Well, her big hit was *Mutt and Jeff*. Played it for three years. I was born on tour—the third season.

MORTIMER. You were?

O'HARA. Yep. Sioux City, Iowa. I was born in the dressing room at the end of the second act, and Mother made the finale.

MORTIMER. What a trouper! There must be a good story in your mother—you know, I write about the theatre.

O'HARA. You do? Saay! You're not Mortimer Brewster, the dramatic critic!

MORTIMER. Yes.

O'HARA. Well, I certainly am glad to meet you. [*He moves his hat and stick preparatory to shaking hands with* MORTIMER. *He also picks up the sport shoe which* MARTHA *has left on the table. He looks at it just for a split second and puts it on the end of table.* MORTIMER *sees it and stares at it.*] Say, Mr. Brewster—we're in the same line of business.

MORTIMER. [*Still intent on shoe.*] We are?

O'HARA. Yeah. I'm a playwright. Oh, this being on the police force is just temporary.

MORTIMER. How long have you been on the force?

O'HARA. Twelve years. I'm collecting material for a play.

MORTIMER. I'll bet it's a honey.

O'HARA. Well, it ought to be. With all the drama I see being a cop. Mr. Brewster —you got no idea what goes on in Brooklyn.

MORTIMER. I think I have. [*He puts the shoe under his chair, then looks at his watch, then looks toward balcony.*]

O'HARA. Say, what time you got?

MORTIMER. Ten after one.

O'HARA. Gee, I gotta ring in. [*He starts for door but* MORTIMER *stops him.*]

MORTIMER. Wait a minute, O'Hara. On that play of yours—I may be able to help you. [*Sits him in chair.*]

O'HARA. [*Ecstasy.*] You would! [*Rises.*] Say, it was fate my walking in here tonight. Look—I'll tell you the plot!

[*At this point* JONATHAN *enters on the balcony followed by* DR. EINSTEIN. *They each have a bag. At the same moment* ABBY *enters from the kitchen. Helpful as the* COP *has been,* MORTIMER *does not want to listen to his plot. As he backs away from him he speaks to* JONATHAN *as they come downstairs.*]

MORTIMER. Oh, you're on your way, eh? Good! You haven't got much time, you know.

ABBY. Well, everything's just about ready. [*Sees* JONATHAN *and* EINSTEIN *at foot of stairs.*] Oh, you leaving now, Jonathan? Good-by. Good-by, Dr. Einstein. [*She sees instrument case above window seat.*] Oh, doesn't this case belong to you? [*This reminds* MORTIMER *of Mr. Spenalzo, also.*]

MORTIMER. Yes, Jonathan—you can't go without *all* of your things. [*Now to get rid of* O'HARA. *He turns to him.*] Well, O'Hara, it was nice meeting you. I'll see you again and we'll talk about your play.

O'HARA. [*Refusing to leave.*] Oh, I'm not leaving now, Mr. Brewster.

MORTIMER. Why not?

O'HARA. Well, you just offered to help me with my play, didn't you? You and me are going to write my play together.

MORTIMER. I can't do that, O'Hara— I'm not a creative writer.

O'HARA. I'll do the creating. You just put the words to it.

MORTIMER. But, O'Hara—

O'HARA. No, sir, Mr. Brewster. I ain't leaving this house till I tell you the plot. [*He crosses and sits on window seat.*]

JONATHAN. [*Starting for door.*] In that case, Mortimer . . . we'll be running along.

MORTIMER. Don't try that. You can't go yet. You've got to take *everything* with you, you know. [*He turns and sees* O'HARA *on window seat and runs to him.*] Look, O'Hara, you run along now, eh? My brother's just going—

O'HARA. I can wait. I've been waiting twelve years.

[MARTHA *enters from kitchen with a tray of coffee and sandwiches.*]

MARTHA. I'm sorry I was so long.

MORTIMER. Don't bring that in here.

O'Hara, would you join us for a bite in the kitchen?

MARTHA. The kitchen?

ABBY. [*To* MARTHA.] Jonathan's leaving.

MARTHA. Oh. Well, that's nice. Come along, Officer O'Hara. [*She exits to kitchen.*]

[O'HARA *gets to kitchen doorway as* ABBY *speaks.*]

ABBY. Sure you don't mind eating in the kitchen, Mr. O'Hara?

O'HARA. And where else would you eat?

ABBY. Good-by, Jonathan, nice to have seen you again.

[O'HARA *exits to kitchen, followed by* ABBY. MORTIMER *crosses to kitchen doorway and shuts door, then turns to* JONATHAN.]

MORTIMER. I'm glad you came back to Brooklyn, Jonathan, because it gives me a chance to throw you out—and the first one out is your boy friend, Mr. Spenalzo.

[*He lifts up window seat. As he does so,* O'HARA, *sandwich in hand, enters from kitchen.* MORTIMER *drops window seat.*]

O'HARA. Look, Mr. Brewster, we can talk in here.

MORTIMER. [*Pushing him into kitchen.*] Coming right out.

JONATHAN. I might have known you'd grow up to write a play with a policeman.

MORTIMER. [*From kitchen doorway.*] Get going now—all three of you. [*He exits, shutting door.*]

[JONATHAN *puts bag down and crosses to window seat.*]

JONATHAN. Doctor, this affair between my brother and me has got to be settled.

EINSTEIN. [*Crossing to window seat for instrument case and bringing it back to foot of stairs.*] Now, Chonny, we got trouble enough. Your brother gives us a chance to get away—what more could you ask?

JONATHAN. You don't understand. [*He lifts window seat.*] This goes back a good many years.

EINSTEIN. [*Foot of stairs.*] Now, Chonny, let's get going.

JONATHAN. [*Harshly.*] We're not going. We're going to sleep right here tonight.

EINSTEIN. With a cop in the kitchen and Mr. Spenalzo in the window seat?

JONATHAN. That's all he's got on us. [*Puts window seat down.*] We'll take Mr.

Spenalzo down and dump him in the bay, and come right back here. Then if he tries to interfere—

EINSTEIN. Now, Chonny.

JONATHAN. Doctor, you know when I make up my mind—

EINSTEIN. Yeah—when you make up your mind, you lose your head. Brooklyn ain't a good place for you.

JONATHAN. [*Peremptorily.*] Doctor!

EINSTEIN. O.K. We got to stick together. [*He crosses to bags.*] Someday we get stuck together. If we're coming back here do we got to take these with us?

JONATHAN. No. Leave them here. Hide them in the cellar. Move fast! [*He moves to bags as* EINSTEIN *goes down cellar with instrument case.*] Spenalzo can go out the same way he came in! [*He kneels on window seat and looks out. Then as he starts to lift window seat,* EINSTEIN *comes in from the cellar with some excitement.*]

EINSTEIN. Hey, Chonny, come quick!

JONATHAN. [*Crossing to him.*] What's the matter?

EINSTEIN. You know that hole in the cellar?

JONATHAN. Yes.

EINSTEIN. We got an *ace* in the hole. Come on, I show you. [*They both exit into cellar.* JONATHAN *shuts door.*]

[MORTIMER *enters from kitchen, sees their bags still there. He opens window seat and sees Spenalzo. Then he puts his head out window and yells.*]

MORTIMER. Jonathan! Jonathan! [JONATHAN *comes through cellar door unnoticed by* MORTIMER *and crosses to back of him.* EINSTEIN *comes down into center of room.*] Jonathan!

JONATHAN. [*Quietly.*] Yes, Mortimer.

MORTIMER. [*Leaping backward to table.*] Where have you two been? I thought I told you to get—

JONATHAN. We're not going.

MORTIMER. Oh, you're not? You think I'm not serious about this, eh? Do you want O'Hara to know what's in that window seat?

JONATHAN. We're staying here.

MORTIMER. [*Crossing around table to kitchen door.*] All right! You asked for it. This gets me rid of you and Officer O'Hara at the same time. [*Opens kitchen door, yells out.*] Officer O'Hara, come in here!

JONATHAN. If you tell O'Hara what's in

the window seat, I'll tell him what's down in the cellar.

[MORTIMER *closes kitchen door quickly.*]

MORTIMER. The cellar?

JONATHAN. There's an elderly gentleman down there who seems to be very dead.

MORTIMER. What were you doing down in the cellar?

EINSTEIN. What's *he* doing down in the cellar?

[O'HARA'S *voice is heard offstage.*]

O'HARA. No, thanks, ma'am. They were fine. I've had plenty.

JONATHAN. Now what are you going to say to O'Hara?

[O'HARA *walks in kitchen door.*]

O'HARA. Say, Mr. Brewster, your aunts want to hear it too. Shall I get them in here?

MORTIMER. [*Pulling him.*] No, O'Hara, you can't do that now. You've got to ring in.

[O'HARA *stops as* MORTIMER *opens the door.*]

O'HARA. The hell with ringing in. I'll get your aunts in here and tell you the plot. [*He starts for kitchen door.*]

MORTIMER. [*Grabbing him.*] No, O'Hara, not in front of all these people. We'll get together alone someplace later.

O'HARA. How about the back room at Kelly's?

MORTIMER. Fine! You go ring in, and I'll meet you at Kelly's.

JONATHAN. [*At window seat.*] Why don't you two go down in the cellar?

O'HARA. That's all right with me. [*Starts for cellar door.*] Is this the cellar?

MORTIMER. [*Grabbing him again, pushing toward door.*] Nooo! We'll go to Kelly's. But you're going to ring in on the way.

O'HARA. [*As he exits.*] All right, that'll only take a couple of minutes. [*He's gone.*]

[MORTIMER *takes his hat from hall tree and crosses to open door.*]

MORTIMER. I'll ditch this guy and be back in five minutes. I'll expect to find you gone. [*Changes his mind.*] Wait for me. [*He exits.*]

[EINSTEIN *sits at table.*]

JONATHAN. We'll wait for him, Doctor.

I've waited a great many years for a chance like this.

EINSTEIN. We got him right where we want him. Did he look guilty!

JONATHAN. [*Rising.*] Take the bags back up to our room, Doctor.

[EINSTEIN *gets bags and reaches foot of stairs with them.* ABBY *and* MARTHA *enter from kitchen.* ABBY *speaks as she enters.*]

ABBY. Have they gone? [*Sees* JONATHAN *and* EINSTEIN.] Oh—we thought we heard somebody leave.

JONATHAN. Just Mortimer, and he'll be back in a few minutes. Is there any food left in the kitchen? I think Dr. Einstein and I would enjoy a bite.

MARTHA. But you won't have time.

ABBY. No, if you're still here when Mortimer gets back he won't like it.

EINSTEIN. He'll like it. He's gotta like it.

JONATHAN. Get something for us to eat while we bury Mr. Spenalzo in the cellar.

MARTHA. [*Crossing to below table.*] Oh no!

ABBY. He can't stay in our cellar. No, Jonathan, you've got to take him with you.

JONATHAN. There's a friend of Mortimer's downstairs waiting for him.

ABBY. A friend of Mortimer's?

JONATHAN. He and Mr. Spenalzo will get along fine together. They're both dead.

MARTHA. They must mean Mr. Hoskins.

EINSTEIN. Mr. Hoskins?

JONATHAN. You know about what's downstairs?

ABBY. Of course we do, and he's no friend of Mortimer's. He's one of our gentlemen.

EINSTEIN. Your chentlemen?

MARTHA. And we won't have any strangers buried in our cellar.

JONATHAN. [*Noncomprehending.*] But Mr. Hoskins—

MARTHA. Mr. Hoskins isn't a stranger.

ABBY. Besides, there's no room for Mr. Spenalzo. The cellar's crowded already.

JONATHAN. Crowded? With what?

ABBY. There are twelve graves down there now.

[*The two men draw back in amazement.*]

JONATHAN. Twelve graves!

ABBY. That leaves very little room and we're going to need it.

JONATHAN. You mean you and Aunt Martha have murdered—?

ABBY. Murdered! Certainly not. It's one of our charities.

MARTHA. [*Indignantly.*] Why, what we've been doing is a mercy.

ABBY. [*Gesturing outside.*] So you just take your Mr. Spenalzo out of here.

JONATHAN. [*Still unable to believe.*] You've done that—here in this house— [*Points to floor.*] And you've buried them down there!

EINSTEIN. Chonny—we've been chased all over the world—they stay right here in Brooklyn and do just as good as you do.

JONATHAN. [*Facing him.*] What?

EINSTEIN. You've got twelve and they've got twelve.

JONATHAN. [*Slowly.*] I've got thirteen.

EINSTEIN. No, Chonny, twelve.

JONATHAN. Thirteen! [*Counting on fingers.*] There's Mr. Spenalzo. Then the first one in London—two in Johannesburg—one in Sydney—one in Melbourne—two in San Francisco—one in Phoenix, Arizona—

EINSTEIN. Phoenix?

JONATHAN. The filling station. The three in Chicago and the one in South Bend. That makes thirteen!

EINSTEIN. But you can't count the one in South Bend. He died of pneumonia.

JONATHAN. He wouldn't have got pneumonia if I hadn't shot him.

EINSTEIN. [*Adamant.*] No, Chonny, he died of pneumonia. He don't count.

JONATHAN. He counts with me. I say thirteen.

EINSTEIN. No, Chonny. You got twelve and they got twelve. [*Crossing to aunts.*] The old ladies are just as good as you are.

[*The two* AUNTS *smile at each other happily.* JONATHAN *turns, facing the three of them and speaks menacingly.*]

JONATHAN. Oh, they are, are they? Well, that's easily taken care of. All I need is one more, that's all—just one more.

[MORTIMER *enters hastily, closing door behind him, and turns to them with a nervous smile.*]

MORTIMER. Well, here I am!

[JONATHAN *turns and looks at him with the widening eyes of someone who has just solved a problem.*]

ACT THREE

SCENE 1

SCENE: *The scene is the same. Still later that night. The window seat is open and we see that it's empty. The armchair has been shifted to right of table. The drapes over the windows are closed. All doors except cellar are closed.* ABBY's *hymnal and black gloves are on sideboard.* MARTHA's *hymnal and gloves are on table. Otherwise the room is the same. As the curtain rises we hear a row from the cellar, through the open door. The speeches overlap in excitement and anger until the* AUNTS *appear on the stage, from cellar door.*

MARTHA. You stop doing that!

ABBY. This is our house and this is our cellar and you can't do that.

EINSTEIN. Ladies! Please! Go back upstairs where you belong.

JONATHAN. Abby! Martha! Go upstairs!

MARTHA. There's no use your doing what you're doing because it will just have to be undone.

ABBY. I tell you we won't have it and you'd better stop it right now.

MARTHA. [*Entering from cellar.*] All right! You'll find out. You'll find out whose house this is. [*She crosses to door, opens it and looks out, then closes it.*]

ABBY. [*Entering.*] I'm warning you! You'd better stop it! [*To* MARTHA.] Hasn't Mortimer come back yet?

MARTHA. No.

ABBY. It's a terrible thing to do—to bury a good Methodist with a foreigner. [*She crosses to window seat.*]

MARTHA. [*Crossing to cellar door.*] I will not have our cellar desecrated!

ABBY. [*Drops window seat.*] And we promised Mr. Hoskins a full Christian funeral. Where do you suppose Mortimer went?

MARTHA. I don't know, but he must be doing something—because he said to Jonathan, "You just wait, I'll settle this."

ABBY. [*Walking to sideboard.*] Well, he can't very well settle it while he's out of the house. That's all we want settled—what's going on down there.

[MORTIMER *enters, closes door.*]

MORTIMER. [*As one who has everything settled.*] All right. Now, where's Teddy?

[*The* AUNTS *are very much annoyed with* MORTIMER.]

ABBY. Mortimer, where have you been?

MORTIMER. I've been over to Dr. Gilchrist's. I've got his signature on Teddy's commitment papers.

MARTHA. Mortimer, what is the matter with you?

ABBY. Running around getting papers signed at a time like this!

MARTHA. Do you know what Jonathan's doing?

ABBY. He's putting Mr. Hoskins and Mr. Spelzano in together.

MORTIMER. [*To cellar door.*] Oh, he is, is he? Well, let him. [*He shuts cellar door.*] Is Teddy in his room?

MARTHA. Teddy won't be any help.

MORTIMER. When he signs these commitment papers I can tackle Jonathan.

ABBY. What have they got to do with it?

MORTIMER. You had to go and tell Jonathan about those twelve graves. If I can make Teddy responsible for those I can protect you, don't you see?

ABBY. No, I don't see. And we pay taxes to have the police protect us.

MORTIMER. [*Going upstairs.*] I'll be back down in a minute.

ABBY. [*Takes gloves and hymnal from table.*] Come, Martha. We're going for the police.

[MARTHA *gets her gloves and hymnal from sideboard. They both start to door.*]

MORTIMER. [*On landing.*] All right. [*He turns and rushes downstairs to door before they can reach it.*] The police! You can't go for the police.

MARTHA. Why can't we?

MORTIMER. [*Near door.*] Because if you tell the police about Mr. Spenalzo they'd find Mr. Hoskins too [*Crosses to* MARTHA.] and that might make them curious, and

37

they'd find out about the other twelve gentlemen.

ABBY. Mortimer, we know the police better than you do. I don't think they'd pry into our private affairs if we asked them not to.

MORTIMER. But if they found your twelve gentlemen they'd have to report to headquarters.

MARTHA. [*Pulling on her gloves.*] I'm not so sure they'd bother. They'd have to make out a very long report—and if there's one thing a policeman hates to do, it's to write.

MORTIMER. You can't depend on that. It might leak out! And you couldn't expect a judge and jury to understand.

MARTHA. Oh, Judge Cullman would.

ABBY. [*Drawing on her gloves.*] We know him very well.

MARTHA. He always comes to church to pray—just before election.

ABBY. And he's coming here to tea some day. He promised.

MARTHA. Oh, Abby, we must speak to him again about that. [*To* MORTIMER.] His wife died a few years ago and it's left him very lonely.

ABBY. Well, come along, Martha. [*She starts toward door.* MORTIMER *gets there first.*]

MORTIMER. No! You can't do this. I won't let you. You can't leave this house, and you can't have Judge Cullman to tea.

ABBY. Well, if you're not going to do something about Mr. Spenalzo, we are.

MORTIMER. I am going to do something. We may have to call the police in later, but if we do, I want to be ready for them.

MARTHA. You've got to get Jonathan out of this house!

ABBY. And Mr. Spenalzo, too!

MORTIMER. Will you please let me do this my own way? [*He starts upstairs.*] I've got to see Teddy.

ABBY. [*facing* MORTIMER *on stairs.*] If they're not out of here by morning, Mortimer, we're going to call the police.

MORTIMER. [*On balcony.*] They'll be out, I promise you that! Go to bed, will you? And for God's sake get out of those clothes—you look like Judith Anderson. [*He exits into hall, closing door.*]

[*The* AUNTS *watch him off.* MARTHA *turns to* ABBY.]

MARTHA. Well, Abby, that's a relief, isn't it?

ABBY. Yes—if Mortimer's really going to do something at last, it just means Jonathan's going to a lot of unnecessary trouble. We'd better tell him. [ABBY *starts to cellar door as* JONATHAN *comes in. They meet in front of sofa. His clothes are dirty.*] Oh, Jonathan—you might as well stop what you're doing.

JONATHAN. It's all done. Did I hear Mortimer?

ABBY. Well, it will just have to be undone. You're all going to be out of this house by morning. Mortimer's promised.

JONATHAN. Oh, are we? In that case, you and Aunt Martha can go to bed and have a pleasant night's sleep.

MARTHA. [*Always a little frightened by* JONATHAN, *starts upstairs.*] Yes. Come, Abby.

[ABBY *follows* MARTHA *upstairs.*]

JONATHAN. Good night, Aunties.

ABBY. Not good night, Jonathan. Goodby. By the time we get up you'll be out of this house. Mortimer's promised.

MARTHA. [*On balcony.*] And he has a way of doing it too!

JONATHAN. Then Mortimer is back?

ABBY. Oh, yes, he's up here talking to Teddy.

MARTHA. Good-by, Jonathan.

ABBY. Good-by, Jonathan.

JONATHAN. Perhaps you'd better say good-by to Mortimer.

ABBY. Oh, you'll see Mortimer.

JONATHAN. [*Sitting on stool.*] Yes—I'll see Mortimer.

[ABBY *and* MARTHA *exit.* JONATHAN *sits without moving. There is murder in his thought.* EINSTEIN *enters from cellar. He dusts off his trouser cuffs, lifting his leg, and we see he is wearing Spenalzo's sport shoes.*]

EINSTEIN. Whew! That's all fixed up. Smooth like a lake. Nobody'd ever know they were down there. [JONATHAN *still sits without moving.*] That bed feels good already. Forty-eight hours we didn't sleep. [*Crossing to second stair.*] Come on, Chonny, let's go up, yes?

JONATHAN. You're forgetting, Doctor.

EINSTEIN. Vat?

JONATHAN. My brother Mortimer.

EINSTEIN. Chonny—tonight? We do that tomorrow or the next day.

JONATHAN. [*Just able to control him-self.*] No, tonight! Now!

EINSTEIN. [*Down to floor.*] Chonny, please—I'm tired—and tomorrow I got to operate.

JONATHAN. Yes, you're operating tomorrow, Doctor. But tonight we take care of Mortimer.

EINSTEIN. [*Kneeling in front of* JONA-THAN, *trying to pacify him.*] But, Chonny, not tonight—we go to bed, eh?

JONATHAN. [*Rising;* EINSTEIN *straightens up too.*] Doctor, look at me. You can see it's going to be done, can't you?

EINSTEIN. [*Retreating.*] Ach, Chonny— I can see. I know dat look!

JONATHAN. It's a little too late for us to dissolve our partnership.

EINSTEIN. O.K., we do it. But the quick way. The quick twist like in London. [*He gives that London neck another twist with his hands and makes a noise suggesting strangulation.*]

JONATHAN. No, Doctor, I think this calls for something special. [*He walks toward* EINSTEIN.] I think perhaps the Melbourne method.

EINSTEIN. Chonny—no—not that. Two hours! And when it was all over, what? The fellow in London was just as dead as the fellow in Melbourne.

JONATHAN. We had to work too fast in London. There was no æsthetic satisfaction in it—but Melbourne, ah, there was something to remember.

EINSTEIN. Remember! [*He shivers.*] I vish I didn't. No Chonny—not Melbourne —not me!

JONATHAN. Yes, Doctor. Where are the instruments?

EINSTEIN. I won't do it, Chonny—I won't do it.

JONATHAN. [*Advancing on him as* EIN-STEIN *backs up.*] Get your instruments!

EINSTEIN. No, Chonny!

JONATHAN. Where are they? Oh, yes— you hid them in the cellar. Where?

EINSTEIN. I won't tell you.

JONATHAN. [*Going to cellar door.*] I'll find them, Doctor. [*He exits to cellar, closing door.*]

[TEDDY *enters on balcony and lifts his bugle to blow.* MORTIMER *dashes out and grabs his arm.* EINSTEIN *has rushed to cellar door. He stands there as* MORTIMER *and* TEDDY *speak.*]

MORTIMER. Don't do that, Mr. President.

TEDDY. I cannot sign any proclamation without consulting my Cabinet.

MORTIMER. But this must be a secret.

TEDDY. A secret proclamation? How unusual.

MORTIMER. Japan mustn't know until it's signed.

TEDDY. Japan! Those yellow devils. I'll sign it right away. [*Taking legal paper from* MORTIMER.] You have my word for it. I can let the Cabinet know later.

MORTIMER. Yes, let's go and sign it.

TEDDY. You wait here. A secret proclamation has to be signed in secret.

MORTIMER. But at once, Mr. President.

TEDDY. I'll have to put on my signing clothes. [TEDDY *exits.*]

[MORTIMER *comes downstairs.* EIN-STEIN *crosses and takes* MORTIMER'S *hat off of hall tree and hands it to him.*]

EINSTEIN. [*Anxious to get* MORTIMER *out of the house.*] Ah, you go now, eh?

MORTIMER. [*Takes hat and puts it on desk.*] No, Doctor, I'm waiting for something. Something important.

EINSTEIN. Please—you go now!

MORTIMER. Dr. Einstein, I have nothing against you personally. You seem to be a nice fellow. Take my advice and get out of this house and get just as far away as possible.

EINSTEIN. Trouble, yah! You get out.

MORTIMER. All right, don't say I didn't warn you.

EINSTEIN. I'm warning you—get away quick.

MORTIMER. Things are going to start popping around here any minute.

EINSTEIN. Listen—Chonny's in a bad mood. When he's like dis, he's a madman —things happen—terrible things.

MORTIMER. Jonathan doesn't worry me now.

EINSTEIN. Ach, himmel—don't those plays you see teach you anything?

MORTIMER. About what?

EINSTEIN. Vell, at least people in plays act like they got sense—that's more than you do.

MORTIMER. [*Interested in this observation.*] Oh, you think so, do you? You think people in plays act intelligently. I wish you had to sit through some of the ones I have to sit through. Take the little opus

I saw tonight, for instance. In this play, there's a man—he's supposed to be bright [JONATHAN *enters from cellar with instrument case, stands in doorway and listens to* MORTIMER.]—he knows he's in a house with murderers—he ought to know he's in danger—he's even been warned to get out of the house—but does he go? No, he stays there. Now I ask you, Doctor, is that what an intelligent person would do?

EINSTEIN. You're asking me?

MORTIMER. He didn't even have sense enough to be frightened, to be on guard. For instance, the murderer invites him to sit down.

EINSTEIN. [*He moves so as to keep* MORTIMER *from seeing* JONATHAN.] You mean —"Won't you sit down?"

MORTIMER. [*Reaches out and pulls armchair toward himself without turning his head from* EINSTEIN.] Believe it or not, that one was in there too.

EINSTEIN. And what did he do?

MORTIMER. [*Sitting in armchair.*] He sat down. Now mind you, this fellow's supposed to be bright. There he sits—just waiting to be trussed up. And what do you think they use to tie him with.

EINSTEIN. Vat?

MORTIMER. The curtain cord.

[JONATHAN *spies curtain cords on either side of window in wall. He crosses, stands on window seat and cuts cords with penknife.*]

EINSTEIN. Vell, why not? A good idea. Very convenient.

MORTIMER. A little too convenient. When are playwrights going to use some imagination! The curtain cord!

[JONATHAN *has got the curtain cord and is moving in slowly behind* MORTIMER.]

EINSTEIN. He didn't see him get it?

MORTIMER. See him? He sat there with his back to him. That's the kind of stuff we have to suffer through night after night. And they say the critics are killing the theatre—it's the playwrights who are killing the theatre. So there he sits—the big dope—this fellow who's supposed to be bright—just waiting to be trussed up and gagged.

[JONATHAN *drops loop of curtain cord over* MORTIMER's *shoulder and draws it taut. At the same time he throws*

other loop of cord on floor beside EINSTEIN. *Simultaneously,* EINSTEIN *leaps to* MORTIMER *and gags him with handkerchief, then takes his curtain cord and ties* MORTIMER's *legs to chair.*]

EINSTEIN. [*Finishing up the tying.*] You're right about dat fella—he vasn't very bright.

JONATHAN. Now, Mortimer, if you don't mind—we'll finish the story. [*He goes to sideboard and brings two candelabras to table and speaks as he lights them.* EINSTEIN *remains kneeling beside* MORTIMER.] Mortimer, I've been away for twenty years, but never once in all that time—my dear brother—were you out of my mind. In Melbourne one night, I dreamed of you— when I landed in San Francisco I felt a strange satisfaction—once more I was in the same country with you. [JONATHAN *has finished lighting candles. He crosses and flips light switch, darkening stage. As he crosses,* EINSTEIN *gets up and crosses to window seat.* JONATHAN *picks up instrument case at cellar doorway and sets it on table between candelabras and opens it, revealing various surgical instruments both in the bottom of case and on the inside of the cover.*] Now, Doctor, we go to work! [*He removes an instrument from the case and fingers it lovingly, as* EINSTEIN *crosses and kneels on chair left of table. He is not too happy about all this.*]

EINSTEIN. Please, Chonny, for me, the quick way!

JONATHAN. Doctor! This must really be an artistic achievement. After all, we're performing before a very distinguished critic.

EINSTEIN. Chonny!

JONATHAN. [*Flaring.*] Doctor!

EINSTEIN. [*Beaten.*] All right. Let's get it over. [*He closes drapes tightly and sits on window seat.* JONATHAN *takes three or four more instruments out of the case and fingers them. At last, having the necessary equipment laid out on the towel, he begins to put on a pair of rubber gloves.*]

EINSTEIN. I gotta have a drink. I can't do this without a drink.

[*He takes bottle from pocket. Drinks. Finds it's empty. Rises.*]

JONATHAN. Pull yourself together, Doctor.

EINSTEIN. I gotta have a drink. Ven ve valked in here this afternoon there was wine here—remember? Vere did she put that? [*He looks at sideboard and remembers. He goes to it, opens cupboard and brings bottle and two wine glasses to table top.*] Look, Chonny, we got a drink. [*He pours wine into the two glasses, emptying the bottle.* MORTIMER *watches him.*] Dat's all dere is. I split it with you. We both need a drink. [*He hands one glass to* JONATHAN, *then raises his own glass to his lips.* JONATHAN *stops him.*]

JONATHAN. One moment, Doctor—please. Where are you manners? [*He looks at* MORTIMER.] Yes, Mortimer, I realize now it was you who brought me back to Brooklyn. . . . [*He looks at wine, then draws it back and forth under his nose, smelling it. He decides that it's all right apparently, for he raises his glass—*] Doctor—to my dear dead brother—

[*As they set the glasses to their lips,* TEDDY *steps out on the balcony and blows a terrific call on his bugle.* EINSTEIN *and* JONATHAN *drop their glasses, spilling the wine.* TEDDY *turns and exits.*]

EINSTEIN. Ach Gott!

JONATHAN. Damn that idiot! [*He starts for stairs.* EINSTEIN *rushes out and intercepts him.*] He goes next! That's all—he goes next!

EINSTEIN. No, Chonny, not Teddy—that's where I shtop—not Teddy!

JONATHAN. We get to Teddy later!

EINSTEIN. We don't get to him at all.

JONATHAN. Now we've got to work fast! [*He walks back to* MORTIMER, EINSTEIN *in front of* MORTIMER.]

EINSTEIN. Yah, the quick way—eh, Chonny?

JONATHAN. Yes, Doctor, the quick way! [*He pulls a large silk handkerchief from his inside pocket and drops it around* MORTIMER's *neck.*]

[*At this point the door bursts open and* OFFICER O'HARA *comes in, very excited.*]

O'HARA. Hey! The Colonel's gotta quit blowing that horn!

JONATHAN. [*He and* EINSTEIN *are standing in front of* MORTIMER, *hiding him from* O'HARA.] It's all right, Officer. We're taking the bugle away from him.

O'HARA. There's going to be hell to pay in the morning. We promised the neighbors he wouldn't do that any more.

JONATHAN. It won't happen again, Officer. Good night.

O'HARA. I'd better speak to him myself. Where are the lights? [O'HARA *puts on lights and goes upstairs to landing, when he sees* MORTIMER.] Hey! You stood me up. I waited an hour at Kelly's for you. [*He comes downstairs and over to* MORTIMER *and looks at him, then he speaks to* JONATHAN *and* EINSTEIN.] What happened to him?

EINSTEIN. [*Thinking fast.*] He was explaining the play he saw tonight—that's what happened to the fella in the play.

O'HARA. Did they have that in the play you saw tonight? [MORTIMER *nods his head—yes.*] Gee, they practically stole that from the second act of my play—[*He starts to explain.*] Why, in my second act, just before the—[*He turns back to* MORTIMER.] I'd better begin at the beginning. It opens in my mother's dressing room, where I was born—only I ain't born yet—[MORTIMER *rubs his shoes together to attract* O'HARA's *attention.*] Huh? Oh, yeah. [O'HARA *starts to remove the gag from* MORTIMER's *mouth and then decides not to.*] No! You've got to hear the plot. [*He gets stool and brings it to right of* MORTIMER *and sits, continuing on with his "plot" as the curtain falls.*] Well, she's sitting there making up, see—when all of a sudden through the door—a man with a black mustache walks in—turns to my mother and says—"Miss Latour, will you marry me?" He doesn't know she's pregnant.

SCENE 2

SCENE: *Scene is the same. Early the next morning. Daylight is streaming through the windows. All doors are closed; all drapes are open.* MORTIMER *is still tied in his chair and seems to be in a semiconscious state.* JONATHAN *is asleep on sofa.* EINSTEIN *intoxicated, is seated with his head resting on table top.* O'HARA, *with his coat off and his collar loosened, is standing over the stool which is between him and* MORTIMER. *He has progressed to the most exciting scene of his play. There is a bottle of whisky and a water tumbler on the table along with a plate full of cigarette butts.*

O'HARA.—there she is lying unconscious across the table in her lingerie—the chink is standing over her with a hatchet—[*He takes the pose.*] I'm tied up in a chair just like you are—the place is an inferno of flames—it's on fire—when all of a sudden—through the window—in comes Mayor LaGuardia. [EINSTEIN *raises his head and looks out the window. Not seeing anyone he reaches for the bottle and pours himself another drink.* O'HARA *crosses above to him and takes the bottle.*] Hey, remember who paid for that—go easy on it.

EINSTEIN. Vell, I'm listening, ain't I? [*He crosses to* JONATHAN *on the sofa.*]

O'HARA. How do you like it so far?

EINSTEIN. Vell, it put Chonny to sleep. [O'HARA *has just finished a swig from the bottle.*]

O'HARA. Let him alone. If he ain't got no more interest than that—he don't get a drink. [EINSTEIN *takes his glass and sits on bottom stair. At the same time* O'HARA *crosses, puts stool under desk and whisky bottle on top of desk, then comes back to center and goes on with his play.*] All right. It's three days later—I been transferred and I'm under charges—that's because somebody stole my badge. [*He pantomimes through following lines.*] All right. I'm walking my beat on Staten Island—Forty-Sixth Precinct—when a guy I'm following, it turns out—is really following me. [*There is a knock on door.* EINSTEIN *goes up and looks out landing window. Leaves glass behind drape.*] Don't let anybody in. So I figure I'll outsmart him. There's a vacant house on the corner. I goes in.

EINSTEIN. It's cops!

O'HARA. I stands there in the dark and I see the door handle turn.

EINSTEIN. [*Rushing downstairs, shakes* JONATHAN *by the shoulder.*] Chonny! It's cops! Cops! [JONATHAN *doesn't move.* EINSTEIN *rushes upstairs and off through the arch.*]

[O'HARA *is going on with his story without a stop.*]

O'HARA. I pulls my guns—braces myself against the wall—and I says—"Come in." [OFFICERS BROPHY *and* KLEIN *walk in, see* O'HARA *with gun pointed at them and raise their hands. Then, recognizing their fellow officer, lower them.*] Hello, boys.

BROPHY. What the hell is going on here?

O'HARA. [*Goes to* BROPHY.] Hey, Pat, whaddya know? This is Mortimer Brewster! He's going to write my play with me. I'm just tellin' him the story.

KLEIN. [*Crossing to* MORTIMER *and untying him.*] Did you have to tie him up to make him listen?

BROPHY. Joe, you better report in at the station. The whole force is out looking for ya.

O'HARA. Did they send you here for me?

KLEIN. We didn't know you was here.

BROPHY. We came to warn the old ladies that there's hell to pay. The Colonel blew that bugle again in the middle of the night.

KLEIN. From the way the neighbors have been calling in about it you'd think the Germans had dropped a bomb on Flatbush Avenue.

[*He has finished untying* MORTIMER. *Puts cords on sideboard.*]

BROPHY. The Lieutenant's on the warpath. He says the Colonel's got to be put away someplace.

MORTIMER. [*Staggers to feet.*] Yes! Yes!

O'HARA. [*Going to* MORTIMER.] Gee, Mr. Brewster, I got to get away, so I'll just run through the third act quick.

MORTIMER. [*Staggering.*] Get away from me.

[BROPHY *gives* KLEIN *a look, goes to phone and dials.*]

KLEIN. Say, do you know what time it is? It's after eight o'clock in the morning.

O'HARA. It is? [*He follows* MORTIMER *to stairs.*] Gee, Mr. Brewster, them first two acts run a little long, but I don't see anything we can leave out.

MORTIMER. [*Almost to landing.*] You can leave it *all* out.

[BROPHY *sees* JONATHAN *on sofa.*]

BROPHY. Who the hell is this guy?

MORTIMER. [*Hanging on railing, almost to balcony.*] That's my brother.

BROPHY. Oh, the one that ran away? So he came back.

MORTIMER. Yes, he came back!

[JONATHAN *stirs as if to get up.*]

BROPHY. [*Into phone.*] This is Brophy. Get me Mac. [*To* O'HARA, *sitting on bottom stair.*] I'd better let them know we found you, Joe. [*Into phone.*] Mac? Tell the Lieutenant he can call off the big manhunt—we got him. In the Brewster home. [JONATHAN *hears this and suddenly becomes very much awake, looking up to see* KLEIN *to his left and* BROPHY *to his right.*] Do you want us to bring him in? Oh—all right, we'll hold him right here. [*He hangs up.*] The Lieutenant's on his way over.

JONATHAN. [*Rising.*] So I've been turned in, eh? [BROPHY *and* KLEIN *look at him with some interest.*] All right, you've got me! [*Turning to* MORTIMER, *who is on balcony looking down.*] And I suppose you and that stool-pigeon brother of mine will split the reward?

KLEIN. Reward?

[*Instinctively* KLEIN *and* BROPHY *both grab* JONATHAN *by an arm.*]

JONATHAN. [*Dragging cops.*] Now, I'll do some turning in! You think my aunts are sweet charming old ladies, don't you? Well, there are thirteen bodies buried in their cellar.

MORTIMER. [*As he rushes off to see* TEDDY.] Teddy! Teddy! Teddy!

KLEIN. What the hell are you talking about?

BROPHY. You'd better be careful what you're saying about your aunts—they happen to be friends of ours.

JONATHAN. [*Raving as he drags them toward cellar door.*] I'll show you! I'll prove it to you! You come to the cellar with me!

KLEIN. Wait a minute! Wait a minute!

JONATHAN. Thirteen bodies! I'll show you where they're buried.

KLEIN. [*Refusing to be kidded.*] Oh, yeah?

JONATHAN. You don't want to see what's down in the cellar?

BROPHY. [*Releases* JONATHAN'S *arm, then to* KLEIN.] Go on down in the cellar with him, Abe.

KLEIN. [*Drops* JONATHAN'S *arm, backs away a step and looks at him.*] I'm not so sure I want to be down in the cellar with him. Look at that puss. He looks like Boris Karloff. [JONATHAN, *at mention of Karloff, grabs* KLEIN *by the throat, starts choking him.*] Hey—what the hell— Hey, Pat, Get him off me.

[BROPHY *takes out rubber blackjack.*]

BROPHY. Here, what do you think you're doing! [*He socks* JONATHAN *on head.* JONATHAN *falls unconscious, face down.*]

[KLEIN, *throwing* JONATHAN'S *weight to floor, backs away, rubbing his throat.*]

KLEIN. Well, what do you know about that?

[*There is a knock on door.*]

O'HARA. Come in.

[LIEUTENANT ROONEY *bursts in, slamming door after him. He is a very tough, driving, dominating officer.*]

ROONEY. What the hell are you men doing here? I told you I was going to handle this.

KLEIN. Well, sir, we was just about to— [KLEIN'S *eyes go to* JONATHAN *and* ROONEY *sees him.*]

ROONEY. What happened? Did he put up a fight?

BROPHY. This ain't the guy that blows the bugle. This is his brother. He tried to kill Klein.

KLEIN. [*Feeling his throat.*] All I said was he looked like Boris Karloff.

ROONEY. [*His face lights up.*] Turn him over.

[*The two cops turn* JONATHAN *over on his back.* KLEIN *steps back.* ROONEY *crosses in front of* BROPHY *to take a look at* JONATHAN.]

BROPHY. We kinda think he's wanted somewhere.

ROONEY. Oh, you kinda *think* he's wanted somewhere? If you guys don't look at the circulars we hang up in the station, at least you could read *True Detective.* Certainly he's wanted. In Indiana! Escaped from the prison for the Criminal Insane! He's a lifer. For God's sake that's how he was described—he *looked* like Karloff!

KLEIN. Was there a reward mentioned?

ROONEY. Yeah—and *I'm* claiming it.

BROPHY. He was trying to get us down in the cellar.

KLEIN. He said there was thirteen bodies buried down there.

ROONEY. [*Suspicious.*] Thirteen bodies buried in the cellar? [*Deciding it's ridiculous.*] And that didn't tip you off he came out of a nuthouse!

O'HARA. I thought all along he talked kinda crazy.

[ROONEY *sees* O'HARA *for the first time. Turns to him.*]

ROONEY. Oh, it's Shakespeare! [*Crossing to him.*] Where have you been all night? And you needn't bother to tell me.

O'HARA. I've been right here, sir. Writing a play with Mortimer Brewster.

ROONEY. Yeah? Well, you're gonna have plenty of time to write that play. You're suspended! Now get back and report in.

[O'HARA *takes his coat, night stick, and cap from top of desk. Goes to door and opens it, then turns to* ROONEY.]

O'HARA. Can I come over some time and use the station typewriter?

ROONEY. No! Get out of here. [O'HARA *runs out.* ROONEY *closes door and turns to the cops.* TEDDY *enters on balcony and comes downstairs unnoticed and stands at* ROONEY'S *back.*] Take that guy somewhere else and bring him to. [*The cops bend down to pick up* JONATHAN.] See what you can find out about his accomplice. [*The cops stand up again in a questioning attitude.* ROONEY *explains.*] The guy that helped him escape. He's wanted too. No wonder Brooklyn's in the shape it's in, with the police force full of flatheads like you —falling for that kind of a story—thirteen bodies in the cellar!

TEDDY. But there are thirteen bodies in the cellar.

ROONEY. [*Turning on him.*] Who are you?

TEDDY. I'm President Roosevelt.

ROONEY. What the hell is this?

BROPHY. He's the fellow that blows the bugle.

KLEIN. Good morning, Colonel.

[*They salute* TEDDY, *who returns it.* ROONEY *finds himself saluting* TEDDY *also. He pulls his hand down in disgust.*]

ROONEY. Well, Colonel, you've blown your last bugle.

TEDDY. [*Seeing* JONATHAN *on floor.*] Dear me—another yellow fever victim?

ROONEY. Whaat?

TEDDY. All the bodies in the cellar are yellow fever victims.

[ROONEY *crosses exasperatedly to door.*]

BROPHY. No, Colonel, this is a spy we caught in the White House.

ROONEY. [*Pointing to* JONATHAN.] Will you get that guy out of here!

[COPS *pick up* JONATHAN *and drag him to kitchen.* TEDDY *follows them.* MORTIMER *enters, comes downstairs.*]

TEDDY. [*Turning back to* ROONEY.] If there's any questioning of spies, that's my department!

ROONEY. You keep out of this!

TEDDY. You're forgetting! As President, I am also head of the Secret Service.

[BROPHY *and* KLEIN *exit with* JONATHAN *into kitchen.* TEDDY *follows them briskly.* MORTIMER *has walked in.*]

MORTIMER. Captain—I'm Mortimer Brewster.

ROONEY. Are you sure?

MORTIMER. I'd like to talk to you about my brother Teddy—the one who blew the bugle.

ROONEY. Mr. Brewster, we ain't going to talk about that—he's got to be put away!

MORTIMER. I quite agree with you. In fact, it's all arranged for. I had these commitment papers signed by Dr. Gilchrist, our family physician. Teddy has signed them himself, you see—and I've signed them as next of kin.

ROONEY. Where's he going?

MORTIMER. Happy Dale.

ROONEY. All right, I don't care where he goes as long as he goes!

MORTIMER. Oh, he's going all right. But I want you to know that everything that's happened around here Teddy's responsible for. Now, those thirteen bodies in the cellar—

ROONEY. [*He's had enough of those thirteen.*] Yeah—yeah—those thirteen bodies in the cellar! It ain't enough that the neighbors are all afraid of him, and his disturbing the peace with that bugle—but can you imagine what would happen if that cockeyed story about thirteen bodies in the cellar got around? And now he's starting a yellow fever scare. Cute, ain't it?

MORTIMER. [*Greatly relieved, with an embarrassed laugh.*] Thirteen bodies. Do you think anybody would believe that story?

ROONEY. Well, you can't tell. Some people are just dumb enough. You don't know what to believe sometimes. About a year ago a crazy guy starts a murder rumor over in Greenpoint, and I had to dig up a half-acre lot, just to prove that—

[*There is a knock on door.*]

MORTIMER. Will you excuse me? [*He goes to door and admits* ELAINE *and* MR. WITHERSPOON, *an elderly, tight-lipped disciplinarian. He is carrying a briefcase.*]

ELAINE. [*Briskly.*] Good morning, Mortimer.

MORTIMER. [*Not knowing what to expect.*] Good morning, dear.

ELAINE. This is Mr. Witherspoon. He's come to meet Teddy.

MORTIMER. To meet Teddy?

ELAINE. Mr. Witherspoon's the Superintendent of Happy Dale.

MORTIMER. [*Eagerly.*] Oh, come right in. [*They shake hands.* MORTIMER *indicates* ROONEY.] This is Captain—

ROONEY. Lieutenant Rooney. I'm glad you're here, Super, because you're taking him back with you today!

WITHERSPOON. Today? I didn't know that—

ELAINE. [*Cutting in.*] Not today!

MORTIMER. Look, Elaine, I've got a lot of business to attend to, so you run along home and I'll call you up.

ELAINE. Nuts! [*She crosses to window seat and sits.*]

WITHERSPOON. I had no idea it was this immediate.

ROONEY. The papers are all signed, he goes today!

[TEDDY *backs into room from kitchen, speaking sharply in the direction whence he's come.*]

TEDDY. Complete insubordination! You men will find out I'm no mollycoddle. [*He slams door and comes down to below table.*] When the President of the United States is treated like that—what's this country coming to?

ROONEY. There's your man, Super.

MORTIMER. Just a minute! [*He crosses to* TEDDY *and speaks to him as to a child.*] Mr. President, I have very good news for you. Your term of office is over.

TEDDY. Is this March the Fourth?

MORTIMER. Practically.

TEDDY. [*Thinking.*] Let's see—OH! Now I go on my hunting trip to Africa! Well, I must get started immediately. [*He starts across the room and almost bumps into* WITHERSPOON. *He looks at him, then steps back to* MORTIMER.] Is he trying to move into the White House before I've moved out?

MORTIMER. Who, Teddy?

TEDDY. [*Indicating* WITHERSPOON.] Taft!

MORTIMER. This isn't Mr. Taft, Teddy. This is Mr. Witherspoon—he's to be your guide in Africa.

TEDDY. [*Shakes hands with* WITHERSPOON *enthusiastically.*] Bully! Bully! I'll bring down my equipment. [*He crosses to stairs.* MARTHA *and* ABBY *have entered on balcony during last speech and are coming downstairs.*] When the safari comes, tell them to wait.

[*As he passes the* AUNTS *on his way to landing, he shakes hands with each, without stopping his walk.*] Good-by, Aunt Abby. Good-by, Aunt Martha. I'm on my way to Africa—isn't it wonderful? [*He has reached the landing.*] CHARGE! [*He charges up the stairs and off.*]

[*The* AUNTS *are at foot of stairs.*]

MORTIMER. [*Coming to* AUNTS.] Good morning, darlings.

MARTHA. Oh, we have visitors.

MORTIMER. [*He indicates* ROONEY.] This is Lieutenant Rooney.

ABBY. [*Crossing, shakes hands with him.*] How do you do, Lieutenant? My, you don't look like the fussbudget the policemen say you are.

MORTIMER. Why the Lieutenant is here —You know, Teddy blew his bugle again last night.

MARTHA. Yes, we're going to speak to Teddy about that.

ROONEY. It's a little more serious than that, Miss Brewster.

MORTIMER. [*Easing* AUNTS *to* WITHERSPOON, *who is at table where he has opened his briefcase and extracted some papers.*] And you haven't met Mr. Witherspoon. He's the Superintendent of Happy Dale.

ABBY. Oh, Mr. Witherspoon—how do you do?

MARTHA. You've come to meet Teddy.

ROONEY. [*Somewhat harshly.*] He's come to *take* him.

[*The* AUNTS *turn to* ROONEY *questioningly.*]

MORTIMER. [*Making it as easy as possible.*] Aunties—the police want Teddy to go there, today.

ABBY. Oh—no!

MARTHA. [*Behind* ABBY.] Not while we're alive!

ROONEY. I'm sorry, Miss Brewster, but it has to be done. The papers are all signed and he's going along with the Superintendent.

ABBY. We won't permit it. We'll promise to take the bugle away from him.

MARTHA. We won't be separated from Teddy.

ROONEY. I'm sorry, ladies, but the law's the law! He's committed himself and he's going!

ABBY. Well, if he goes, we're going too.

MARTHA. Yes, you'll have to take us with him.

MORTIMER. [*Has an idea, crosses to* WITHERSPOON.] Well, why not?

WITHERSPOON. [*To* MORTIMER.] Well, that's sweet of them to want to, but it's impossible. You see, we can't take *sane* people at Happy Dale.

MARTHA. [*Turning to* WITHERSPOON.] Mr. Witherspoon, if you'll let us live there with Teddy, we'll see that Happy Dale is in our will—and for a very generous amount.

WITHERSPOON. Well, the Lord knows we could use the money, but—I'm afraid—

ROONEY. Now let's be sensible about this, ladies. For instance, here I am wasting my morning when I've got serious work to do. You know there are still *murders* to be solved in Brooklyn.

MORTIMER. Yes! [*Covering.*] Oh, are there?

ROONEY. It ain't only his bugle blowing and the neighbors all afraid of him, but things would just get worse. Sooner or later we'd be put to the trouble of digging up your cellar.

ABBY. Our cellar?

ROONEY. Yeah. Your nephew's been telling around that there are thirteen bodies in your cellar.

ABBY. But there are thirteen bodies in our cellar.

[ROONEY *looks disgusted.* MORTIMER *drifts quietly to front of cellar door.*]

MARTHA. If that's why you think Teddy has to go away—you come down to the cellar with us and we'll prove it to you.

ABBY. There's one—Mr. Spenalzo—who doesn't belong here and who will have to leave—but the other twelve are our gentlemen.

MORTIMER. I don't think the Lieutenant wants to go down in the cellar. He was telling me that only last year he had to dig up a half-acre lot—weren't you Lieutenant?

ROONEY. That's right.

ABBY. [*To* ROONEY.] Oh, you wouldn't have to dig here. The graves are all marked. We put flowers on them every Sunday.

ROONEY. Flowers? [*He steps toward* ABBY, *then turns to* WITHERSPOON, *indicating the* AUNTS *as he speaks.*] Superintendent—don't you think you can find room for these ladies?

WITHERSPOON. Well, I—

ABBY. [*To* ROONEY.] You come along with us, and we'll show you the graves.

ROONEY. I'll take your word for it, lady—I'm a busy man. How about it, Super?

WITHERSPOON. Well, they'd have to be committed.

MORTIMER. Teddy committed himself. Can't they commit themselves? Can't they sign the papers?

WITHERSPOON. Why, certainly.

MARTHA. [*Sits in chair at table as* WITHERSPOON *draws it out for her.*] Oh, if we can go with Teddy, we'll sign the papers. Where are they?

ABBY. [*Sitting at other side of table;* MORTIMER *helps her with chair.*] Yes, where are they?

[WITHERSPOON *opens briefcase for more papers.* KLEIN *enters from kitchen.*]

KLEIN. He's coming around, Lieutenant.

ABBY. Good morning, Mr. Klein.

MARTHA. Good morning, Mr. Klein. Are you here too?

KLEIN. Yeah. Brophy and me have got your other nephew out in the kitchen.

ROONEY. Well, sign 'em up, Superintendent. I want to get this all cleaned up. [*He crosses to kitchen door, shaking his head as he exits.*] Thirteen bodies.

[KLEIN *follows him out.* MORTIMER *is beside* ABBY, *fountain pen in hand;* WITHERSPOON *to right of* MARTHA, *also with pen.*]

WITHERSPOON. [*Handing* MARTHA *pen.*] If you'll sign right here. [MARTHA *signs.*]

MORTIMER. And you here, Aunt Abby. [ABBY *signs.*]

ABBY. I'm really looking forward to going—the neighborhood here has changed so.

MARTHA. Just think, a front lawn again. [EINSTEIN *enters through arch and comes downstairs to door carrying suitcase. He picks hat from hall tree on way down.*]

WITHERSPOON. Oh, we're overlooking something.

MARTHA. What?

WITHERSPOON. Well, we're going to need the signature of a doctor.

MORTIMER. Oh! [*He sees* EINSTEIN *about to disappear through the door.*] Dr. Einstein! Will you come over here—we'd like you to sign some papers.

EINSTEIN. Please, I must—

MORTIMER. [*Crosses to him.*] Just come right over, Doctor. At one time last night, I thought the Doctor was going to operate on me. [EINSTEIN *crosses to table.*] Just sign right here, Doctor.

[*The* DOCTOR *signs* ABBY's *paper and* MARTHA's *paper.* ROONEY *and* KLEIN *enter from kitchen.* ROONEY *crosses to desk and dials phone.* KLEIN *stands near kitchen door.*]

ABBY. Were you leaving, Doctor?

EINSTEIN. I think I must go.

MARTHA. Aren't you going to wait for Jonathan?

EINSTEIN. I don't thing we're going to the same place.

[MORTIMER *sees* ELAINE *on window seat and crosses to her.*]

MORTIMER. Hello, Elaine. I'm glad to see you. Stick around, huh?

ELAINE. Don't worry, I'm going to.

[MORTIMER *stands back of* MARTHA's *chair.* ROONEY *speaks into phone.*]

ROONEY. Hello, Mac. Rooney. We've picked up that guy that's wanted in Indiana. Now there's a description of his accomplice—it's right on the desk there—read it to me. [EINSTEIN *sees* ROONEY *at phone. He starts toward kitchen and sees* KLEIN *standing there. He comes back to table and stands there dejectedly waiting for the pinch.* ROONEY *repeats the description, given him over phone, looking blankly at* EINSTEIN *the while.*] Yeah—about

fifty-four—five foot six—hundred and forty pounds—blue eyes—talks with a German accent. Poses as a doctor. Thanks, Mac. [*He hangs up as* WITHERSPOON *crosses to him with papers in hand.*]

WITHERSPOON. It's all right, Lieutenant. The Doctor here has just completed the signatures.

[ROONEY *goes to* EINSTEIN *and shakes his hand.*]

ROONEY. Thanks, Doc. You're really doing Brooklyn a service.

[ROONEY *and* KLEIN *exit to kitchen.* EINSTEIN *stands amazed for a moment then grabs up his hat and suitcase and disappears through door. The* AUNTS *rise and cross over, looking out after him.* ABBY *shuts the door and they stand there.*]

WITHERSPOON. Mr. Brewster, you sign now as next of kin.

[*The* AUNTS *whisper to each other as* MORTIMER *signs.*]

MORTIMER. Yes, of course. Right here?

WITHERSPOON. That's fine.

MORTIMER. That makes everything complete—everything legal?

WITHERSPOON. Oh, yes.

MORTIMER. [*With relief.*] Well, Aunties, now you're safe.

WITHERSPOON. [*To* AUNTS.] When do you think you'll be ready to start?

ABBY. Well, Mr. Witherspoon, why don't you go upstairs and tell Teddy just what he can take along?

WITHERSPOON. Upstairs?

MORTIMER. I'll show you.

ABBY. [*Stopping him.*] No, Mortimer, you stay here. We want to talk to you. [*To* WITHERSPOON.] Yes, Mr. Witherspoon, just upstairs and turn to the left.

[WITHERSPOON *puts his briefcase on sofa and goes upstairs, the* AUNTS *keeping an eye on him while talking to* MORTIMER.]

MARTHA. Well, Mortimer, now that we're moving, this house really is yours.

ABBY. Yes, dear, we want you to live here now.

MORTIMER. No, Aunt Abby, this house is too full of memories.

MARTHA. But you'll need a home when you and Elaine are married.

MORTIMER. Darlings, that's very indefinite.

ELAINE. [*Rises and crosses to* MORTIMER.] It's nothing of the kind—we're going to be married right away.

[WITHERSPOON *has exited off balcony.*]

ABBY. Mortimer—Mortimer, we're really very worried about something.

MORTIMER. Now, darlings, you're going to love it at Happy Dale.

MARTHA. Oh, yes, we're very happy about the whole thing. That's just it—we don't want anything to go wrong.

ABBY. Will they investigate those signatures?

MORTIMER. Don't worry, they're not going to look up Dr. Einstein.

MARTHA. It's not his signature, dear, it's yours.

ABBY. You see, you signed as next of kin.

MORTIMER. Of course. Why not?

MARTHA. Well, dear, it's something we never wanted to tell you. But now you're a man—and it's something Elaine should know too. You see, dear—you're not really a Brewster.

[MORTIMER *stares, as does* ELAINE.]

ABBY. Your mother came to us as a cook —and you were born about three months afterward. But she was such a sweet woman—and such a good cook we didn't want to lose her—so brother married her.

MORTIMER. I'm—not—really—a—Brewster?

MARTHA. Now, don't feel badly about it, dear.

ABBY. And Elaine, it won't make any difference to you?

MORTIMER. [*Turning slowly to face* ELAINE, *his voice rising.*] Elaine! Did you hear? Do you understand? I'm a bastard!

[ELAINE *leaps into his arms. The two* AUNTS *watch them, then* MARTHA *takes a few steps.*]

MARTHA. Well, now I really must see about breakfast.

ELAINE. [*Leading* MORTIMER *to door and opening it.*] Mortimer's coming over to my house. Father's gone to Philadelphia, and Mortimer and I are going to have breakfast together.

MORTIMER. Yes, I need some coffee— I've had quite a night.

ABBY. In that case I should think you'd want to get to bed.

MORTIMER. [*With a sidelong glance at* ELAINE.] I do. [*They exit, closing door.*]

[WITHERSPOON *enters on balcony, car-*

rying two canteens. He starts downstairs when TEDDY enters carrying large canoe paddle. He is dressed in Panama outfit with pack on his back.*]

TEDDY. One moment, Witherspoon. Take this with you! [*He exits off balcony again as* WITHERSPOON *comes on downstairs to sofa. He puts canteens on sofa and leans paddle against wall.*]

[*At the same time* ROONEY *and the two* COPS *with* JONATHAN *between them enter. The cops have twisters around* JONATHAN's *wrists.*]

ROONEY. We won't need the wagon. My car's out front.

MARTHA. Oh, you leaving now, Jonathan?

ROONEY. Yeah—he's going back to Indiana. There's some people there want to take care of him for the rest of his life. Come on.

[ROONEY *opens door as the two* COPS *and* JONATHAN *go to it.*]

ABBY. Well, Jonathan, it's nice to know you have someplace to go.

MARTHA. We're leaving too.

ABBY. Yes, we're going to Happy Dale.

JONATHAN. Then this house is seeing the last of the Brewsters.

MARTHA. Unless Mortimer wants to live here.

JONATHAN. I have a suggestion to make. Why don't you turn this property over to the church?

ABBY. Well, we never thought of that.

JONATHAN. After all, it *should* be part of the cemetery.

ROONEY. All right, get going, I'm a busy man.

JONATHAN. [*Holding his ground for his one last word.*] Good-by, Aunties. Well, I can't better my record now but neither can you—at least I have that satisfaction. The score stands even, *twelve* to *twelve*. [JONATHAN *and the* COPS *exit as the* AUNTS *look out after them.*]

[WITHERSPOON *crosses above to window seat and stands quietly looking out the window. His back is to the aunts.*]

MARTHA. [*Starting toward door to close it.*] Jonathan always was a mean boy. Never could stand to see anyone get ahead of him. [*She closes door.*]

ABBY. [*Turning slowly around as she speaks.*] I wish we could show him he isn't so smart! [*Her eyes fall on* WITHER-SPOON. *She studies him.* MARTHA *turns from door and sees* ABBY's *contemplation.* ABBY *speaks sweetly.*] Mr. Witherspoon? [WITHERSPOON *turns around facing them.*] Does your family live with you at Happy Dale?

WITHERSPOON. I have no family.

ABBY. Oh—

MARTHA. [*Stepping into room.*] Well, I suppose you consider everyone at Happy Dale your family?

WITHERSPOON. I'm afraid you don't quite understand. As head of the institution, I have to keep quite aloof.

ABBY. That must make it very lonely for you.

WITHERSPOON. It does. But my duty is my duty.

ABBY. [*Turning to* MARTHA.] Well, Martha— [MARTHA *takes her cue and goes to sideboard for bottle of wine. Bottle in cupboard is empty. She puts it back and takes out full bottle from other cupboard. She brings bottle and wineglass to table.* ABBY *continues talking.*] If Mr. Witherspoon won't join us for breakfast, I think at least we should offer him a glass of elderberry wine.

WITHERSPOON. [*Severely.*] Elderberry wine?

MARTHA. We make it ourselves.

WITHERSPOON. [*Melting slightly.*] Why, yes . . . [*Severely again.*] Of course, at Happy Dale our relationship will be more formal—but here— [*He sits in chair as* MARTHA *pours wine.* ABBY *is beside* MARTHA.] You don't see much elderberry wine nowadays—I thought I'd had my last glass of it.

ABBY. Oh, no—

MARTHA. [*Handing him glass of wine.*] No, here it is.

> [WITHERSPOON *toasts the ladies and lifts glass to his lips, but the curtain falls before he does. . . .*]

For Discussion and Writing

1. How many murders were committed in *Arsenic and Old Lace*? The number has been estimated variously as twelve, thirteen, twenty-five, twenty-six—and *none* (this last figure submitted by an actor who played Mortimer). Which estimate seems most valid to you? How do you justify your conclusion?

2. Critic Richard Lockridge compared *Arsenic and Old Lace* to a three-ring circus. Discuss this description of the structure of the play, considering such questions as: How would you separate the characters into three rings? Which story thread would you assign the center ring? Which character serves as "master of ceremonies" to link all three rings? Would the various plots and subplots mean more if each was presented as a separate play?

3. No matter how fantastic the plot, most good farces *begin* plausibly with a commonplace realistic setting, ordinary, everyday characters, and behavior which appears to be perfectly normal and usual. Then somewhere in the first scene comes a wild and incredible incident. If the audience accepts this first startling event, they will find a logic in all the insanity that follows. Discuss how *Arsenic and Old Lace* employs this technique.

4. Professor Baker of the famous Harvard 47 Workshop for Playwrights once remarked, "Any crime, any perversion of the human mind is not a subject for farce, comedy, burlesque, or simple joking. No matter how you treat it, it will not be funny." Does *Arsenic and Old Lace*, in your opinion, support or refute this statement of Professor Baker's? Can you point to any other comedies to support your opinion?

5. Write in the form of a dialogue an argument between Jonathan and Dr. Einstein over Jonathan's next face. The two are in total disagreement as to who he should be next.
Or, as an alternative, write a dialogue which might take place between a corpse in the cellar and any one of the new victims.
In either of these flights of fancy, keep in mind the fact that humor grows usually from situations where the participants take themselves and their problems seriously.

The Little Foxes

{1939}

LILLIAN HELLMAN

"TAKE US THE FOXES, THE LITTLE FOXES,
THAT SPOIL THE VINES; FOR OUR VINES
HAVE TENDER GRAPES."

*For Arthur Kober and Louis Kronenberger
who have been my good friends*

CHARACTERS

(In Order of Appearance)

ADDIE	REGINA GIDDENS
CAL	WILLIAM MARSHALL
BIRDIE HUBBARD	BENJAMIN HUBBARD
OSCAR HUBBARD	ALEXANDRA GIDDENS
LEO HUBBARD	HORACE GIDDENS

*The scene of the play is the living room of the Giddens house,
in a small town in the South.*

ACT ONE: The Spring of 1900, evening.

ACT TWO: A week later, early morning.

ACT THREE: Two weeks later, late afternoon.

There has been no attempt to write Southern dialect. It is to
be understood that the accents are Southern.

One of the most important dramas written during the Depression of the 1930's was Lillian Hellman's *The Little Foxes*, which opened in February 1939.

Like most other social writers of the thirties, Miss Hellman struck at the causes of the economic upheaval. Unlike the protest plays of her contemporaries, though, *The Little Foxes* goes back to another society in embattled times—the South in the early 1900's—when a rising industrial order was exploiting the land and the people in a relentless drive for money and power.

Like all social drama, this play is a study of people in conflict with the forces of their society. From this conflict hopefully emerges an awareness of life's truer values.

Miss Hellman adapted *The Little Foxes* to film in 1941. Five years later she gave the theater *Another Part of the Forest*, a play in which she examined the same rapacious family twenty years earlier in their lives. In 1949, audiences enjoyed a powerful musical version of *The Little Foxes* called *Regina* by Marc Blitzstein (available on records).

Three decades later, the play, a classic of the American stage, continues to speak relevantly about our social problems.

The Little Foxes

ACT ONE

SCENE: *The living room of the Giddens house, in a small town in the deep South, the Spring of 1900. Upstage is a staircase leading to the second story. Upstage, right, are double doors to the dining room. When these doors are open we see a section of the dining room and the furniture. Upstage, left, is an entrance hall with a coat-rack and umbrella stand. There are large lace-curtained windows on the left wall. The room is lit by a center gas chandelier and painted china oil lamps on the tables. Against the wall is a large piano. Downstage, right, are a high couch, a large table, several chairs. Against the left back wall are a table and several chairs. Near the window there are a smaller couch and tables. The room is good-looking, the furniture expensive; but it reflects no particular taste. Everything is of the best and that is all.*

AT RISE: ADDIE, *a tall, nice-looking Negro women of about fifty-five, is closing the windows. From behind the closed dining-room doors there is the sound of voices. After a second,* CAL, *a middle-aged Negro, comes in from the entrance hall carrying a tray with glasses and a bottle of port.* ADDIE *crosses, takes the tray from him, puts it on table, begins to arrange it.*

ADDIE. [*Pointing to the bottle.*] You gone stark out of your head?

CAL. No, smart lady, I ain't. Miss Regina told me to get out that bottle. [*Points to bottle.*] That very bottle for the mighty honored guest. When Miss Regina changes orders like that you can bet your dime she got her reason.

ADDIE. [*Points to dining room.*] Go on. You'll be needed.

CAL. Miss Zan she had two helpings frozen fruit cream and she tell that honored guest, she tell him that you make the best frozen fruit cream in all the South.

ADDIE. [*Smiles, pleased.*] Did she? Well, see that Belle saves a little for her. She like it right before she go to bed. Save a few little cakes, too, she like—

[*The dining-room doors are opened and quickly closed again by* BIRDIE HUBBARD. BIRDIE *is a woman of about forty, with a pretty, well-bred, faded face. Her movements are usually nervous and timid, but now, as she comes running into the room, she is gay and excited.* CAL *turns to* BIRDIE.]

BIRDIE. Oh, Cal. [*Closes door.*] I want you to get one of the kitchen boys to run home for me. He's to look in my desk drawer and— [*To* ADDIE.] My, Addie. What a good supper! Just as good as good can be.

ADDIE. You look pretty this evening, Miss Birdie, and young.

BIRDIE. [*Laughing.*] Me, young? [*Turns back to* CAL.] Maybe you better find Simon and tell him to do it himself. He's to look in my desk, the left drawer, and bring my music album right away. Mr. Marshall is very anxious to see it because of his father and the opera in Chicago. [*To* ADDIE.] Mr. Marshall is such a polite man with his manners and very educated and cultured and I've told him all about how my mama and papa used to go to Europe for the music— [*Laughs. To* ADDIE.] Imagine going all the way to Europe just to listen to music. Wouldn't

54

that be nice, Addie? Just to sit there and listen and— [*Turns and steps to* CAL.] *Left* drawer, Cal. Tell him that twice because he forgets. And tell him not to let any of the things drop out of the album and to bring it right in here when he comes back.

[*The dining-room doors are opened and quickly closed by* OSCAR HUBBARD. *He is a man in his late forties.*]

CAL. Yes'm. But Simon he won't get it right. But I'll tell him.

BIRDIE. Left drawer, Cal, and tell him to bring the blue book and—

OSCAR. [*Sharply.*] Birdie.

BIRDIE. [*Turning nervously.*] Oh, Oscar. I was just sending Simon for my music album.

OSCAR. [*To* CAL.] Never mind about the album. Miss Birdie has changed her mind.

BIRDIE. But, really, Oscar. Really I promised Mr. Marshall. I— [CAL *looks at them, exits.*]

OSCAR. Why do you leave the dinner table and go running about like a child?

BIRDIE. [*Trying to be gay.*] But, Oscar, Mr. Marshall said most specially he *wanted* to see my album. I told him about the time Mama met Wagner, and Mrs. Wagner gave her the signed program and the big picture. Mr Marshall wants to see that. Very, very much. We had such a nice talk and—

OSCAR. [*Taking a step to her.*] You have been chattering to him like a magpie. You haven't let him be for a second. I can't think he came South to be bored with you.

BIRDIE. [*Quickly, hurt.*] He wasn't bored. I don't believe he was bored. He's a very educated, cultured gentleman. [*Her voice rises.*] I just don't believe it. You always talk like that when I'm having a nice time.

OSCAR. [*Turning to her, sharply.*] You have had too much wine. Get yourself in hand now.

BIRDIE. [*Drawing back, about to cry, shrilly.*] What am I doing? I am not doing anything. What am I doing?

OSCAR. [*Taking a step to her, tensely.*] I said get yourself in hand. Stop acting like a fool.

BIRDIE. [*Turns to him, quietly.*] I don't believe he was bored. I just don't believe it. Some people like music and like to talk about it. That's all I was doing.

[LEO HUBBARD *comes hurrying through*

the dining-room door. He is a young man of twenty, with a weak kind of good looks.]

LEO. Mama! Papa! They are coming in now.

OSCAR. [*Softly.*] Sit down, Birdie. Sit down now. [BIRDIE *sits down, bows her head as if to hide her face.*]

[*The dining-room doors are opened by* CAL. *We see people beginning to rise from the table.* REGINA GIDDENS *comes in with* WILLIAM MARSHALL. REGINA *is a handsome woman of forty.* MARSHALL *is forty-five, pleasant-looking, self-possessed. Behind them comes* ALEXANDRA GIDDENS, *a very pretty, rather delicate-looking girl of seventeen. She is followed by* BENJAMIN HUBBARD, *fifty-five, with a large jovial face and the light graceful movements that one often finds in large men.*]

REGINA. Mr. Marshall, I think you're trying to console me. Chicago may be the noisiest, dirtiest city in the world but I should still prefer it to the sound of our horses and the smell of our azaleas. I should like crowds of people, and theatres, and lovely women— *Very* lovely women, Mr. Marshall?

MARSHALL. [*Crossing to sofa.*] In Chicago? Oh, I suppose so. But I can tell you this: I've never dined there with three *such* lovely ladies.

[ADDIE *begins to pass the port.*]

BEN. Our Southern women are well favored.

LEO. [*Laughs.*] But one must go to Mobile for the ladies, sir. Very elegant worldly ladies, too.

BEN. [*Looks at him very deliberately.*] Worldly, eh? *Worldly*, did you say?

OSCAR. [*Hastily, to* LEO.] Your uncle Ben means that worldliness is not a mark of beauty in any woman.

LEO. [*Quickly.*] Of course, Uncle Ben. I didn't mean—

MARSHALL. Your port is excellent, Mrs. Giddens.

REGINA. Thank you, Mr. Marshall. We had been saving that bottle, hoping we could open it just for you.

ALEXANDRA. [*As* ADDIE *comes to her with the tray.*] Oh. May I *really*, Addie?

ADDIE. Better ask Mama.

ALEXANDRA. May I, Mama?

REGINA. [*Nods, smiles.*] In Mr. Marshall's honor.

ALEXANDRA. [*Smiles.*] Mr. Marshall, this will be the first taste of port I've ever had. [ADDIE *serves* LEO.]

MARSHALL. No one ever had their first taste of a better port. [*He lifts his glass in a toast; she lifts hers; they both drink.*] Well, I suppose it is all true, Mrs. Giddens.

REGINA. What is true?

MARSHALL. That you Southerners occupy a unique position in America. You live better than the rest of us, you eat better, you drink better. I wonder you find time, or want to find time, to do business.

BEN. A great many Southerners don't.

MARSHALL. Do all of you live here together?

REGINA. Here with me? [*Laughs.*]Oh, no. My brother Ben lives next door. My brother Oscar and his family live in the next square.

BEN. But we are a very close family. We've always *wanted* it that way.

MARSHALL. That is very pleasant. Keeping your family together to share each other's lives. My family moves around too much. My children seem never to come home. Away at school in the winter; in the summer, Europe with their mother—

REGINA. [*Eagerly.*] Oh, yes. Even down here we read about Mrs. Marshall in the society pages.

MARSHALL. I dare say. She moves about a great deal. And all of you are part of the same business? Hubbard Sons?

BEN. [*Motions to* OSCAR.] Oscar and me. [*Motions to* REGINA.] My sister's good husband is a banker.

MARSHALL. [*Looks at* REGINA, *surprised.*] Oh.

REGINA. I am so sorry that my husband isn't here to meet you. He's been very ill. He is at Johns Hopkins. But he will be home soon. We think he is getting better now.

LEO. I work for Uncle Horace. [REGINA *looks at him.*] I mean I work for Uncle Horace at his bank. I keep an eye on things while he's away.

REGINA. [*Smiles.*] Really, Leo?

BEN. [*Looks at* LEO, *then to* MARSHALL.] Modesty in the young is as excellent as it is rare. [*Looks at* LEO *again.*]

OSCAR. [*To* LEO.] Your uncle means that a young man should speak more modestly.

LEO. [*Hastily, taking a step to* BEN.] Oh, I didn't mean, sir—

MARSHALL. Oh. Mrs. Hubbard. Where's that Wagner autograph you promised to let me see? My train will be leaving soon and—

BIRDIE. The autograph? Oh. Well. Really, Mr. Marshall, I didn't mean to chatter so about it. Really I— [*Nervously, looking at* OSCAR.] You must excuse me. I didn't get it because, well, because I had—I—I had a little headache and—

OSCAR. My wife is a miserable victim of headaches.

REGINA [*Quickly.*] Mr. Marshall said at supper that he would like you to play for him, Alexandra.

ALEXANDRA. [*Who has been looking at* BIRDIE.] It's not I who play well, sir. It's my aunt. She plays just wonderfully. She's my teacher. [*Rises. Eagerly.*] May we play a duet? May we, Mama?

BIRDIE. [*Taking* ALEXANDRA'S *hand.*] Thank you, dear. But I have my headache now. I—

OSCAR. [*Sharply.*] Don't be stubborn, Birdie. Mr. Marshall wants you to play.

MARSHALL. Indeed I do. If your headache isn't—

BIRDIE. [*Hesitates, then gets up, pleased.*] But I'd like to, sir. Very much. [*She and* ALEXANDRA *go to the piano.*]

MARSHALL. It's very remarkable how you Southern aristocrats have kept together. Kept together and kept what belonged to you.

BEN. You misunderstand, sir. Southern aristocrats have *not* kept together and have *not* kept what belonged to them.

MARSHALL. [*Laughs, indicates room.*] You don't call this keeping what belongs to you?

BEN. But we are not aristocrats. [*Points to* BIRDIE *at the piano.*] Our brother's wife is the only one of us who belongs to the Southern aristocracy.

[BIRDIE *looks towards* BEN.]

MARSHALL. [*Smiles.*] My information is that you people have been here, and solidly here, for a long time.

OSCAR. And so we have. Since our great-grandfather.

BEN. [*Smiles.*] Who was *not* an aristocrat, like Birdie's.

MARSHALL. [*A little sharply.*] You make great distinctions.

BEN. Oh, they have been made for us. And maybe they are important distinctions. [*Leans forward, intimately.*] Now you take Birdie's family. When my great-grandfather came here they were the highest-tone plantation owners in this state.

LEO. [*Steps to* MARSHALL. *Proudly.*] My mother's grandfather was governor of the state before the war.

OSCAR. They owned the plantation, Lionnet. You may have heard of it, sir?

MARSHALL. [*Laughs.*] No, I've never heard of anything but brick houses on a lake, and cotton mills.

BEN. Lionnet in its day was the best cotton land in the South. It still brings us in a fair crop. [*Sits back.*] Ah, they were great days for those people—even when I can remember. They had the best of everything. [BIRDIE *turns to them.*] Cloth from Paris, trips to Europe, horses you can't raise any more, niggers to lift their fingers—

BIRDIE. [*Suddenly.*] We were good to our people. Everybody knew that. We were better to them than—

[MARSHALL *looks up at* BIRDIE.]

REGINA. Why, Birdie. You aren't playing.

BEN. But when the war comes these fine gentleman ride off and leave the cotton, *and* the women, to rot.

BIRDIE. My father was killed in the war. He was a fine soldier, Mr. Marshall. A fine man.

REGINA. Oh, certainly, Birdie. A famous soldier.

BEN. [*To* BIRDIE.]But that isn't the tale I am telling Mr. Marshall. [*To* MARSHALL.] Well, sir, the war ends. [BIRDIE *goes back to piano.*] Lionnet is almost ruined, and the sons finish ruining it. And there were thousands like them. Why? [*Leans forward.*] Because the Southern aristocrat can adapt himself to nothing. Too high-tone to try.

MARSHALL. Sometimes it is difficult to learn new ways. [BIRDIE *and* ALEXANDRA *begin to play.* MARSHALL *leans forward, listening.*]

BEN. Perhaps, perhaps. [*He sees that* MARSHALL *is listening to the music. Irritated, he turns to* BIRDIE *and* ALEXANDRA *at the piano, then back to* MARSHALL.] You're right, Mr. Marshall. It is difficult to learn new ways. But maybe that's why it's profitable. *Our* grandfather and *our* father learned the new ways and learned how to make them pay. They work. [*Smiles nastily.*] *They* are in trade. Hubbard Sons, Merchandise. Others, Birdie's family, for example, look down on them. [*Settles back in chair.*] To make a long story short, Lionnet now belongs to *us.* [BIRDIE *stops playing.*] Twenty years ago we took over their land, their cotton, and their daughter. [BIRDIE *rises and stands stiffly by the piano.* MARSHALL, *who has been watching her, rises.*]

MARSHALL. May I bring you a glass of port, Mrs. Hubbard?

BIRDIE. [*Softly.*] No, thank you, sir. You are most polite.

REGINA. [*Sharply, to* BEN.] You are boring Mr. Marshall with these ancient family tales.

BEN. I hope not. I hope not. I am trying to make an important point— [*Bows to* MARSHALL.] for our future business partner.

OSCAR. [*To* MARSHALL.] My brother always says that it's folks like us who have struggled and fought to bring to our land some of the prosperity of your land.

BEN. Some people call that patriotism.

REGINA. [*Laughs gaily.*] I hope you don't find my brothers too obvious, Mr. Marshall. I'm afraid they mean that this is the time for the ladies to leave the gentlemen to talk business.

MARSHALL. [*Hastily.*] Not at all. We settled everything this afternoon. [MARSHALL *looks at his watch.*] I have only a few minutes before I must leave for the train. [*Smiles at her.*] And I insist they be spent with you.

REGINA. *And* with another glass of port.

MARSHALL. Thank you.

BEN. [*To* REGINA.] I am a plain man and I am trying to say a plain thing. A man ain't only in business for what he can get out of it. It's got to give him something here. [*Puts hand to his breast.*] That's every bit as true for the nigger picking cotton for a silver quarter, as it is for you and me. [REGINA *gives* MARSHALL *a glass of port.*] If it don't give him something here, then he don't pick the cotton right. Money isn't all. Not by three shots.

MARSHALL. Really? Well, I always thought it was a great deal.

REGINA. And so did I, Mr. Marshall.

MARSHALL. [*Leans forward. Pleasantly, but with meaning.*] Now you don't have to convince me that you are the right people for the deal. I wouldn't be here if you hadn't convinced me six months ago. You want the mill here, and I want it here. It isn't my business to find out *why* you want it.

BEN. To bring the machine to the cotton, and not the cotton to the machine.

MARSHALL. [*Amused.*] You have a turn for neat phrases, Hubbard. Well, however grand your reasons are, mine are simple: I want to make money and I believe I'll make it on you. [*As* BEN *starts to speak, he smiles.*] Mind you, I have no objections to more high-minded reasons. They are mighty valuable in business. It's fine to have partners who so closely follow the teachings of Christ. [*Gets up.*] And now I must leave for my train.

REGINA. I'm sorry you won't stay over with us, Mr. Marshall, but you'll come again. Any time you like.

BEN. [*Motions to* LEO, *indicating the bottle.*] Fill them up, boy, fill them up. [LEO *moves around filling the glasses as* BEN *speaks.*] Down here, sir, we have a strange custom. We drink the *last* drink for a toast. That's to prove that the Southerner is always still on his feet for the last drink. [*Picks up his glass.*] It was Henry Frick, your Mr. Henry Frick, who said, "Railroads are the Rembrandts of investments." Well, *I* say, "Southern cotton mills *will be* the Rembrandts of investment." So I give you the firm of Hubbard Sons and Marshall, Cotton Mills, and to it a long and prosperous life.

[*They all pick up their glasses,* MARSHALL *looks at them, amused. Then he, too, lifts his glass, smiles.*]

OSCAR. The children will drive you to the depot. Leo! Alexandra! You will drive Mr. Marshall down.

LEO. [*Eagerly, looks at* BEN *who nods.*] Yes, sir. [*To* MARSHALL.] Not often Uncle Ben lets *me* drive the horses. And a beautiful pair they are. [*Starts for hall.*] Come on, Zan.

ALEXANDRA. May I drive tonight, Uncle Ben, please? I'd like to and—

BEN. [*Shakes his head, laughs.*] In your evening clothes? Oh, no, my dear.

ALEXANDRA. But Leo always— [*Stops, exits quickly.*]

REGINA. I don't like to say good-bye to you, Mr. Marshall.

MARSHALL. Then we won't say good-bye. You have promised that you would come and let me show you Chicago. Do I have to make you promise again?

REGINA. [*Looks at him as he presses her hand.*] I promise again.

MARSHALL. [*Touches her hand again, then moves to* BIRDIE.] Good-bye, Mrs. Hubbard.

BIRDIE. [*Shyly, with sweetness and dignity.*] Good-bye, sir.

MARSHALL. [*As he passes* REGINA.] Remember.

REGINA. I will.

OSCAR. We'll see you to the carriage.

[MARSHALL *exits, followed by* BEN *and* OSCAR. *For a second* REGINA *and* BIRDIE *stand looking after them. Then* REGINA *throws up her arms, laughs happily.*]

REGINA. And there, Birdie, goes the man who has opened the door to our future.

BIRDIE. [*Surprised at the unaccustomed friendliness.*] What?

REGINA. [*Turning to her.*] Our future. Yours and mine, Ben's and Oscar's, the children— [*Looks at* BIRDIE's *puzzled face, laughs.*] Our future! [*Gaily.*] You were charming at supper, Birdie. Mr. Marshall certainly thought so.

BIRDIE. [*Pleased.*] Why, Regina! Do you think he did?

REGINA. Can't you tell when you're being admired?

BIRDIE. Oscar said I bored Mr. Marshall. [*Then quietly.*] But he admired *you*. He told me so.

REGINA. What did he say?

BIRDIE. He said to me, "I hope your sister-in-law will come to Chicago. Chicago will be at her feet." He said the ladies would bow to your manners and the gentlemen to your looks.

REGINA. Did he? He seems a lonely man. Imagine being lonely with all that money. I don't think he likes his wife.

BIRDIE. Not like his wife? What a thing to say.

REGINA. She's away a great deal. He said that several times. And once he made fun of her being so social and high-tone. But that fits in all right. [*Sits back, arms on back of sofa, stretches.*] Her being social, I mean. She can introduce me. It won't take long with an introduction from her.

BIRDIE. [*Bewildered.*] Introduce you? In Chicago? You mean you really might go? Oh, Regina, you can't leave here. What about Horace?

REGINA. Don't look so scared about everything, Birdie. I'm going to live in Chicago. I've always wanted to. And now there'll be plenty of money to go with.

BIRDIE. But Horace won't be able to move around. You know what the doctor wrote.

REGINA. There'll be millions, Birdie, millions. You know what I've always said when people told me we were rich? I said I think you should either be a nigger or a millionaire. In between, like us, what for? [*Laughs. Looks at* BIRDIE.] But I'm not going away tomorrow, Birdie. There's plenty of time to worry about Horace when he comes home. If he ever decides to come home.

BIRDIE. Will we be going to Chicago? I mean, Oscar and Leo and me?

REGINA. You? I shouldn't think so. [*Laughs.*] Well, we must remember tonight. It's a very important night and we mustn't forget it. We shall plan all the things we'd like to have and then we'll really have them. Make a wish, Birdie, any wish. It's bound to come true now.

[BEN *and* OSCAR *enter.*]

BIRDIE. [*Laughs.*] Well. Well, I don't know. Maybe. [REGINA *turns to look at* BEN.] Well, I guess I'd know right off what I wanted.

[OSCAR *stands by the upper window, waves to the departing carriage.*]

REGINA. [*Looks up at* BEN, *smiles. He smiles back at her.*] Well, you did it.

BEN. Looks like it might be we did.

REGINA. [*Springs up, laughs.*] Looks like it! Don't pretend. You're like a cat who's been licking the cream. [*Crosses to wine bottle.*] Now we must all have a drink to celebrate.

OSCAR. The children, Alexandra and Leo, make a very handsome couple, Regina. Marshall remarked himself what fine young folks they were. How well they looked together!

REGINA. [*Sharply.*] Yes. You said that before, Oscar.

BEN. Yes, sir, It's beginning to look as if the deal's all set. I may not be a subtle man—but— [*Turns to them. After a second.*] Now somebody ask me how I know the deal is set.

OSCAR. What do you mean, Ben?

BEN. You remember I told him that down here we drink the *last* drink for a toast?

OSCAR. [*Thoughtfully.*] Yes. I never heard that before.

BEN. Nobody's ever heard it before. God forgives those who invent what they need. I already had his signature. But we've all done business wth men whose word over a glass is better than a bond. Anyway it don't hurt to have both.

OSCAR. [*Turns to* REGINA.] You understand what Ben means?

REGINA. [*Smiles.*] Yes, Oscar. I understand. I understood immediately.

BEN. [*Looks at her admiringly.*] Did you, Regina? Well, when he lifted his glass to drink, I closed my eyes and saw the bricks going into place.

REGINA. And *I* saw a lot more than that.

BEN. Slowly, slowly. As yet we have only our hopes.

REGINA. Birdie and I have just been planning what we want. I know what I want. What will you want, Ben?

BEN. Caution. Don't count the chickens. [*Leans back, laughs.*] Well, God would allow us a little daydreaming. Good for the soul when you've worked hard enough to deserve it. [*Pauses.*] I think I'll have a stable. For a long time I've had my good eyes on Carter's in Savannah. A rich man's pleasure, the sport of kings, why not the sport of Hubbards? Why not?

REGINA. [*Smiles.*] Why not? What will you have, Oscar?

OSCAR. I don't know. [*Thoughtfully.*] The pleasure of seeing the bricks grow will be enough for me.

BEN. Oh, of course. Our *greatest* pleasure will be to see the bricks grow. But we are all entitled to a little side indulgence.

OSCAR. Yes, I suppose so. Well, then, I think we might take a few trips here and there, eh, Birdie?

BIRDIE. [*Surprised at being consulted.*] Yes, Oscar. I'd like that.

OSCAR. We might even make a regular trip to Jekyll Island. I've heard the Cornelly place is for sale. We might think about buying it. Make a nice change. Do you good, Birdie, a change of climate. Fine shooting on Jekyll, the best.

BIRDIE. I'd like—

OSCAR. [*Indulgently.*] What would you like?

BIRDIE. *Two* things. Two things I'd like most.

REGINA. Two! I should like a thousand. You are modest, Birdie.

BIRDIE. [*Warmly, delighted with the unexpected interest.*] I should like to have Lionnet back. I know you own it now, but I'd like to see it fixed up again, the way Mama and Papa had it. Every year it used to get a nice coat of paint—Papa was very particular about the paint—and the lawn was so smooth all the way down to the river, with the trims of zinnias and red-feather plush. And the figs and blue little plums and the scuppernongs— [*Smiles. Turns to* REGINA.] The organ is still there and it wouldn't cost much to fix. We could have parties for Zan, the way Mama used to have for me.

BEN. That's a pretty picture, Birdie. Might be a most pleasant way to live. [*Dismissing* BIRDIE.] What do you want, Regina?

BIRDIE. [*Very happily, not noticing that they are no longer listening to her.*] I could have a cutting garden. Just where Mama's used to be. Oh, I do think we could be happier there. Papa used to say that *nobody* had ever lost their temper at Lionnet, and *nobody* ever would. Papa would never let anybody be nasty-spoken or mean. No, sir. He just didn't like it.

BEN. What do you want, Regina?

REGINA. I'm going to Chicago. And when I'm settled there and know the right people and the right things to buy—because I certainly don't now—I shall go to Paris and buy them. [*Laughs.*] I'm going to leave you and Oscar to count the bricks.

BIRDIE. Oscar. Please let me have Lionnet back.

OSCAR. [*To* REGINA.] You are serious about moving to Chicago?

BEN. She is going to see the great world and leave us in the little one. Well, we'll come and visit you and meet all the great and be proud to think you are our sister.

REGINA. [*Gaily.*] Certainly. And you won't even have to learn to be subtle, Ben.

Stay as you are. You will be rich and the rich don't have to be subtle.

OSCAR. But what about Alexandra? She's seventeen. Old enough to be thinking about marrying.

BIRDIE. And, Oscar, I have one more wish. Just one more wish.

OSCAR. [*Turns.*] What is it, Birdie? What are you saying?

BIRDIE. I want you to stop shooting. I mean, so much. I don't like to see animals and birds killed just for the killing. You only throw them away—

BEN. [*To* REGINA.] It'll take a great deal of money to live as you're planning, Regina.

REGINA. Certainly. But there'll be plenty of money. You have estimated the profits very high.

BEN. I have—

BIRDIE. [OSCAR *is looking at her furiously.*] And you never let anybody else shoot, and the niggers need it so much to keep from starving. It's wicked to shoot food just because you like to shoot, when poor people need it so—

BEN. [*Laughs.*] I have estimated the profits very high—for myself.

REGINA. What did you say?

BIRDIE. I've always wanted to speak about it, Oscar.

OSCAR. [*Slowly, carefully.*] What are you chattering about?

BIRDIE. [*Nervously.*] I was talking about Lionnet and—and about your shooting—

OSCAR. You are exciting yourself.

REGINA. [*To* BEN.] I didn't hear you. There was so much talking.

OSCAR. [*To* BIRDIE.] You have been acting very childish, very excited, all evening.

BIRDIE. Regina asked me what I'd like.

REGINA. What did you say, Ben?

BIRDIE. Now that we'll be so rich everybody was saying what they would like, so *I* said what *I* would like, too.

BEN. I said— [*He is interrupted by* OSCAR.]

OSCAR. [*To* BIRDIE.] Very well. We've all heard you. That's enough now.

BEN. I am waiting. [*They stop.*] I am waiting for you to finish. You and Birdie. Four conversations are three too many. [BIRDIE *slowly sits down.* BEN *smiles, to* REGINA.] I said that I had, and I do, estimate the profits very high—for myself, and Oscar, of course.

REGINA. [*Slowly.*] And what does that mean?

[BEN *shrugs, looks towards* OSCAR.]

OSCAR. [*Looks at* BEN, *clears throat.*] Well, Regina, it's like this. For forty-nine per cent Marshall will put up four hundred thousand dollars. For fifty-one per cent— [*Smiles archly.*] a controlling interest, mind you, we will put up two hundred and twenty-five thousand dollars besides offering him certain benefits that our [*Looks at* BEN.] local position allows us to manage. Ben means that two hundred and twenty-five thousand dollars is a lot of money.

REGINA. I know the terms and I know it's a lot of money.

BEN. [*Nodding.*] It is.

OSCAR. Ben means that we are ready with our two-thirds of the money. Your third, Horace's I mean, doesn't seem to be ready. [*Raises his hand as* REGINA *starts to speak.*] Ben has written to Horace, I have written, and you have written. He answers. But he never mentions this business. Yet we have explained it to him in great detail, and told him the urgency. Still he never mentions it. Ben has been very patient, Regina. Naturally, you are our sister and we want you to benefit from anything we do.

REGINA. And in addition to your concern for me, you do not want control to go out of the family. [*To* BEN.] That right, Ben?

BEN. That's cynical. [*Smiles.*] Cynicism is an unpleasant way of saying the truth.

OSCAR. No need to be cynical. We'd have no trouble raising the third share, the share that you want to take.

REGINA. I am sure you could get the third share, the share you were saving for me. But that would give you a strange partner. And strange partners sometimes want a great deal. [*Smiles unpleasantly.*] But perhaps it would be wise for you to find him.

OSCAR. Now, now. Nobody says we *want* to do that. We would like to have you in and you would like to come in.

REGINA. Yes. I certainly would.

BEN. [*Laughs, puts up his hand.*] But we haven't heard from Horace.

REGINA. I've given my word that Horace will put up the money. That should be enough.

BEN. Oh, it was enough. I took your word. But I've got to have more than your word now. The contracts will be signed this week, and Marshall will want to see our money soon after. Regina, Horace has been in Baltimore for five months. I know that you've written him to come home, and that he hasn't come.

OSCAR. It's beginning to look as if he doesn't want to come home.

REGINA. Of course he wants to come home. You can't move around with heart trouble at any moment you choose. You know what doctors are like once they get their hands on a case like this—

OSCAR. They can't very well keep him from answering letters, can they? [REGINA *turns to* BEN.] They couldn't keep him from arranging for the money if he wanted to—

REGINA. Has it occurred to you that Horace is also a good business man?

BEN. Certainly. He is a shrewd trader. Always has been. The bank is proof of that.

REGINA. Then, possibly, he may be keeping silent because he doesn't think he is getting enough for his money. [*Looks at* OSCAR.] Seventy-five thousand he has to put up. That's a lot of money, too.

OSCAR. Nonsense. He knows a good thing when he hears it. He knows that we can make *twice* the profit on cotton goods manufactured *here* than can be made in the North.

BEN. That isn't what Regina means. [*Smiles.*] May I interpret you, Regina? [*To* OSCAR.] Regina is saying that Horace wants *more* than a third of our share.

OSCAR. But he's only putting up a third of the money. You put up a third and you get a third. What else *could* he expect?

REGINA. Well, *I* don't know. I don't know about these things. It would seem that if you put up a third you should only get a third. But then again, there's no law about it, is there? I should think that if you knew your money was very badly needed, well, you just might say, I want more, I want a bigger share. You boys have done that. I've heard you say so.

BEN. [*After a pause, laughs.*] So you believe he has deliberately held out? For a larger share? [*Leaning forward.*] Well, I *don't* believe it. But I *do* believe that's what *you* want. Am I right, Regina?

REGINA. Oh, I shouldn't like to be too definite. But I *could* say that I wouldn't like to persuade Horace unless he did get a larger share. I must look after his interests. It seems only natural—

OSCAR. And where would the larger share come from?

REGINA. I don't know. That's not my business. [Giggles.] But perhaps it could come off your share, Oscar.

[REGINA and BEN laugh.]

OSCAR. [Rises and wheels furiously on both of them as they laugh.] What kind of talk is this?

BEN. I haven't said a thing.

OSCAR. [To REGINA.] You are talking very big tonight.

REGINA. [Stops laughing.] Am I? Well, you should know me well enough to know that I wouldn't be asking for things I didn't think I could get.

OSCAR. Listen. I don't believe you can even get Horace to come home, much less get money from him or talk quite so big about what you want.

REGINA. Oh, I can get him home.

OSCAR. Then why haven't you?

REGINA. I thought I should fight his battles for him, before he came home. Horace is a very sick man. And even if you don't care how sick he is, I do.

BEN. Stop this foolish squabbling. How can you get him home?

REGINA. I will send Alexandra to Baltimore. She will ask him to come home. She will say that she wants him to come home, and that I want him to come home.

BIRDIE. [Suddenly.] Well, of course she wants him here, but he's sick and maybe he's happy where he is.

REGINA. [Ignores BIRDIE, to BEN.] You agree that he will come home if she asks him to, if she says that I miss him and want him—

BEN. [Looks at her, smiles.] I admire you, Regina. And I agree. That's settled now and— [Starts to rise.]

REGINA. [Quickly.] But before she brings him home, I want to know what he's going to get.

BEN. What do you want?

REGINA. Twice what you offered.

BEN. Well, you won't get it.

OSCAR. [To REGINA.] I think you've gone crazy.

REGINA. I don't want to fight, Ben—

BEN. I don't either. You won't get it. There isn't any chance of that. [Roguish-

ly.] You're holding us up, and that's not pretty, Regina, not pretty. [Holds up his hand as he sees she is about to speak.] But we need you, and I don't want to fight. Here's what I'll do: I'll give Horace forty per cent, instead of the thirty-three and a third he really should get. I'll do that, provided he is home and his money is up within two weeks. How's that?

REGINA. All right.

OSCAR. I've asked before: where is this extra share coming from?

BEN. [Pleasantly.] From you. From your share.

OSCAR. [Furiously.] From me, is it? That's just fine and dandy. That's my reward. For thirty-five years I've worked my hands to the bone for you. For thirty-five years I've done all the things you didn't want to do. And this is what I—

BEN. [Turns slowly to look at OSCAR. OSCAR breaks off.] My, my. I am being attacked tonight on all sides. First by my sister, then by my brother. And I ain't a man who likes being attacked. I can't believe that God wants the strong to parade their strength, but I don't mind doing it if it's got to be done. [Leans back in his chair.] You ought to take these things better, Oscar. I've made you money in the past. I'm going to make you more money now. You'll be a very rich man. What's the difference to any of us if a little more goes here, a little less goes there—it's all in the family. And it will stay in the family. I'll never marry. [ADDIE enters, begins to gather the glasses from the table. OSCAR turns to BEN.] So my money will go to Alexandra and Leo. They may even marry some day and— [ADDIE looks at BEN.]

BIRDIE. [Rising.] Marry—Zan and Leo—

OSCAR. [Carefully.] That would make a great difference in my feelings. If they married.

BEN. Yes, that's what I mean. Of course it would make a difference.

OSCAR. [Carefully.] Is that what you mean, Regina?

REGINA. Oh, it's too far away. We'll talk about it in a few years.

OSCAR. I want to talk about it now.

BEN. [Nods.] Naturally.

REGINA. There's a lot of things to consider. They are first cousins, and—

OSCAR. That isn't unusual. Our grandmother and grandfather were first cousins.

REGINA. [*Giggles.*] And look at us.

[BEN *giggles.*]

OSCAR. [*Angrily.*] You're both being very gay with my money.

BEN. [*Sighs.*] These quarrels. I dislike them so. [*Leans forward to* REGINA.] A marriage might be a very wise arrangement, for several reasons. And then, Oscar has given up something for you. You should try to manage something for him.

REGINA. I haven't said I was opposed to it. But Leo is a wild boy. There were those times when he took a little money from the bank and—

OSCAR. That's all past history—

REGINA. Oh, I know. And I know all young men are wild. I'm only mentioning it to show you that there are considerations—

BEN. [*Irritated because she does not understand that he is trying to keep* OSCAR *quiet.*] All right, so there are. But please assure Oscar that you will think about it very seriously.

REGINA. [*Smiles, nods.*] Very well. I assure Oscar that I will think about it seriously.

OSCAR. [*Sharply.*] That is not an answer.

REGINA. [*Rises.*] My, you're in a bad humor and you shall put me in one. I have said all that I am willing to say now. After all, Horace has to give his consent, too.

OSCAR. Horace will do what you tell him to.

REGINA. Yes, I think he will.

OSCAR. And I have your word that you will try to—

REGINA. [*Patiently.*] Yes, Oscar. You have my word that I will think about it. Now do leave me alone.

[*There is the sound of the front door being closed.*]

BIRDIE. I—Alexandra is only seventeen. She—

REGINA. [*Calling.*] Alexandra? Are you back?

ALEXANDRA. Yes, Mama.

LEO. [*Comes into the room.*] Mr. Marshall got off safe and sound. Weren't those fine clothes he had? You can always spot clothes made in a good place. Looks like maybe they were done in England. Lots of men in the North send all the way to England for their stuff.

BEN. [*To* LEO.] Were you careful driving the horses?

LEO. Oh, yes, sir. I was.

[ALEXANDRA *has come in on* BEN'S *question, hears the answer, looks angrily at* LEO.]

ALEXANDRA. It's a lovely night. You should have come, Aunt Birdie.

REGINA. Were you gracious to Mr. Marshall?

ALEXANDRA. I think so, Mama. I liked him.

REGINA. Good. And now I have great news for you. You are going to Baltimore in the morning to bring your father home.

ALEXANDRA. [*Gasps, then delighted.*] Me? Papa said I should come? That must mean— [*Turns to* ADDIE.] Addie, he must be well. Think of it, he'll be back home again. We'll bring him home.

REGINA. You are going alone, Alexandra.

ADDIE. [ALEXANDRA *has turned in surprise.*] Going alone? Going by herself? A child that age! Mr. Horace ain't going to like Zan traipsing up there by herself.

REGINA. [*Sharply.*] Go upstairs and lay out Alexandra's things.

ADDIE. He'd expect me to be along—

REGINA. I'll be up in a few minutes to tell you what to pack. [ADDIE *slowly begins to climb the steps. To* ALEXANDRA.] I should think you'd like going alone. At your age it certainly would have delighted me. You're a strange girl, Alexandra. Addie has babied you so much.

ALEXANDRA. I only thought it would be more fun if Addie and I went together.

BIRDIE. [*Timidly.*] Maybe I could go with her, Regina. I'd really like to.

REGINA. She is going alone. She is getting old enough to take some responsibilities.

OSCAR. She'd better learn now. She's almost old enough to get married. [*Jovially, to* LEO, *slapping him on shoulder.*] Eh, son?

LEO. Huh?

OSCAR. [*Annoyed with* LEO *for not understanding.*] Old enough to get married, you're thinking, eh?

LEO. Oh, yes, sir. [*Feebly.*] Lots of girls get married at Zan's age. Look at Mary Prester and Johanna and—

REGINA. Well, she's not getting married tomorrow. But she is going to Baltimore tomorrow, so let's talk about that. [*To* ALEXANDRA.] You'll be glad to have Papa home again.

ALEXANDRA. I wanted to go before, Mama. You remember that. But you said *you* couldn't go, and that *I* couldn't go alone.

REGINA. I've changed my mind. [*Too casually.*] You're to tell Papa how much you missed him, and that he must come home now—for your sake. Tell him that you *need* him home.

ALEXANDRA. Need him home? I don't understand.

REGINA. There is nothing for you to understand. You are simply to say what I have told you.

BIRDIE. [*Rises.*] He may be too sick. She couldn't do that—

ALEXANDRA. Yes, He may be too sick to travel. I couldn't make him think he had to come home for me, if he is too sick to—

REGINA. [*Looks at her, sharply, challengingly.*] You *couldn't* do what I tell you to do, Alexandra?

ALEXANDRA. [*Quietly.*] No. I couldn't. If I thought it would hurt him.

REGINA. [*After a second's silence, smiles pleasantly.*] But you are doing this for Papa's own good. [*Takes* ALEXANDRA's *hand.*] You must let me be the judge of his condition. It's the best possible cure for him to come home and be taken care of here. He mustn't stay there any longer and listen to those alarmist doctors. You are doing this entirely for his sake. Tell your papa that I want him to come home, that I miss him very much.

ALEXANDRA. [*Slowly.*] Yes, Mama.

REGINA. [*To the others. Rises.*] I must go and start getting Alexandra ready now. Why don't you all go home?

BEN. [*Rises.*] I'll attend to the railroad ticket. One of the boys will bring it over. Good night, everybody. Have a nice trip, Alexandra. The food on the train is very good. The celery is so crisp. Have a good time and act like a little lady. [*Exits.*]

REGINA. Good night, Ben. Good night, Oscar— [*Playfully.*] Don't be so glum, Oscar. It makes you look as if you had chronic indigestion.

BIRDIE. Good night, Regina.

REGINA. Good night, Birdie. [*Exits upstairs.*]

OSCAR. [*Starts for hall.*] Come along.

LEO. [*To* ALEXANDRA.] Imagine your not wanting to go! What a little fool you are.

Wish it were me. What I could do in a place like Baltimore!

ALEXANDRA. [*Angrily, looking away from him.*] Mind your business. I can guess the kind of things *you* could do.

LEO. [*Laughs.*] Oh, no, you couldn't. [*He exits.*]

REGINA. [*Calling from the top of the stairs.*] Come on, Alexandra.

BIRDIE. [*Quickly, softly.*] Zan.

ALEXANDRA. I don't understand about my going, Aunt Birdie. [*Shrugs.*] But anyway, Papa will be home again. [*Pats* BIRDIE's *arm.*] Don't worry about me. I can take care of myself. Really I can.

BIRDIE. [*Shakes her head, softly.*] That's not what I'm worried about. Zan—

ALEXANDRA. [*Comes close to her.*] What's the matter?

BIRDIE. It's about Leo—

ALEXANDRA. [*Whispering.*] He beat the horses. That's why we were late getting back. We had to wait until they cooled off. He always beats the horses as if—

BIRDIE. [*Whispering frantically, holding* ALEXANDRA's *hands.*] He's my son. My own son. But you are more to me—more to me than my own child. I love you more than anybody else—

ALEXANDRA. Don't worry about the horses. I'm sorry I told you.

BIRDIE. [*Her voice rising.*] I am *not* worrying about the horses. I am worrying about *you.* You are *not* going to marry Leo. I am not going to let them do that to you—

ALEXANDRA. Marry? To Leo? [*Laughs.*] I wouldn't marry, Aunt Birdie. I've never even thought about it—

BIRDIE. But they have thought about it. [*Wildly.*] Zan, I couldn't stand to think about such a thing. You and—

[OSCAR *has come into the doorway on* ALEXANDRA's *speech. He is standing quietly, listening.*]

ALEXANDRA. [*Laughs.*] But I'm not going to marry. And I'm certainly not going to marry Leo.

BIRDIE. Don't you understand? They'll make you. They'll make you—

ALEXANDRA. [*Takes* BIRDIE's *hands, quietly, firmly.*] That's foolish, Aunt Birdie. I'm grown now. Nobody can make me do anything.

BIRDIE. I just couldn't stand—

OSCAR. [*Sharply.*] Birdie. [BIRDIE *looks*

up, *draws quickly away from* ALEXANDRA. *She stands rigid, frightened. Quietly.*] Birdie, get your hat and coat.

ADDIE. [*Calls from upstairs.*] Come on, baby. Your mama's waiting for you, and she ain't nobody to keep waiting.

ALEXANDRA. All right. [*Then softly, embracing* BIRDIE.] Good night Aunt Birdie. [*As she passes* OSCAR.] Good night, Uncle Oscar. [BIRDIE *begins to move slowly towards the door as* ALEXANDRA *climbs the stairs.* ALEXANDRA *is almost out of view when* BIRDIE *reaches* OSCAR *in the doorway. As* BIRDIE *quickly attempts to pass him, he slaps her hard, across the face.*

BIRDIE *cries out, puts her hand to her face. On the cry,* ALEXANDRA *turns, begins to run down the stairs.*] Aunt Birdie! What happened? What happened? I—

BIRDIE. [*Softly, without turning.*] Nothing, darling. Nothing happened. [*Quickly, as if anxious to keep* ALEXANDRA *from coming close.*] Now go to bed. [OSCAR *exits.*] Nothing happened. [*Turns to* ALEXANDRA *who is holding her hand.*] I only—I only twisted my ankle. [*She goes out.* ALEXANDRA *stands on the stairs looking after her as if she were puzzled and frightened.*]

CURTAIN

ACT TWO

SCENE: *Same as Act One. A week later, morning.*

AT RISE: *The light comes from the open shutter of the right window; the other shutters are tightly closed.* ADDIE *is standing at the window, looking out. Near the dining-room doors are brooms, mops, rags, etc. After a second,* OSCAR *comes into the entrance hall, looks in the room, shivers, decides not to take his hat and coat off, comes into the room. At the sound of the door,* ADDIE *turns to see who has come in.*

ADDIE. [*Without interest.*] Oh, it's you, Mr. Oscar.

OSCAR. What is this? It's not night. What's the matter here? [*Shivers.*] Fine thing at this time of the morning. Blinds all closed. [ADDIE *begins to open shutters.*] Where's Miss Regina? It's cold in here.

ADDIE. Miss Regina ain't down yet.

OSCAR. She had any word?

ADDIE. [*Wearily.*] No, sir.

OSCAR. Wouldn't you think a girl that age could get on a train at one place and have sense enough to get off at another? Something must have happened. If Zan say she was coming last night, she's coming last night. Unless something happened. Sure fire disgrace to let a baby like that go all that way alone to bring home a sick man without—

OSCAR. You do a lot of judging around here, Addie, eh? Judging of your white folks, I mean.

ADDIE. [*Looks at him, sighs.*] I'm tired. I been up all night watching for them.

REGINA. [*Speaking from the upstairs hall.*] Who's downstairs, Addie? [*She appears in a dressing gown, peers down from the landing.* ADDIE *picks up broom, dustpan and brush and exits.*] Oh, it's you, Oscar. What are you doing here so early? I haven't been down yet. I'm not finished dressing.

OSCAR. [*Speaking up to her.*] You had any word from them?

REGINA. No.

OSCAR. Then something certainly has happened. People don't just say they are arriving on Thursday night, and they haven't come by Friday morning.

REGINA. Oh, nothing has happened. Alexandra just hasn't got sense enough to send a message.

OSCAR. If nothing's happened, then why aren't they here?

REGINA. You asked me that ten times last night. My, you do fret so, Oscar. Anything might have happened. They may have missed connections in Atlanta, the train may have been delayed—oh, a hundred things could have kept them.

OSCAR. Where's Ben?

REGINA. [*As she disappears upstairs.*]

Where should he be? At home, probably. Really, Oscar, I don't tuck him in his bed and I don't take him out of it. Have some coffee and don't worry so much.

OSCAR. Have some coffee? There isn't any coffee. [*Looks at his watch, shakes his head. After a second* CAL *enters with a large silver tray, coffee urn, small cups, newspaper.*] Oh, there you are. Is everything in this fancy house always late?

CAL. [*Looks at him surprised.*] You ain't out shooting this morning, Mr. Oscar?

OSCAR. First day I missed since I had my head cold. First day I missed in eight years.

CAL. Yes, sir. I bet you. Simon he say you had a mighty good day yesterday morning. That's what Simon say. [*Brings* OSCAR *coffee and newspaper.*]

OSCAR. Pretty good, pretty good.

CAL. [*Laughs, slyly.*] Bet you got enough bobwhite and squirrel to give every nigger in town a Jesus-party. Most of 'em ain't had no meat since the cotton picking was over. Bet they'd give anything for a little piece of that meat—

OSCAR. [*Turns his head to look at* CAL.] Cal, if I catch a nigger in this town going shooting, you know what's going to happen.

[LEO *enters.*]

CAL. [*Hastily.*] Yes, sir, Mr. Oscar. I didn't say nothing about nothing. It was Simon who told me and— Morning, Mr. Leo. You gentlemen having your breakfast with us here?

LEO. The boys in the bank don't know a thing. They haven't had any message.

[CAL *waits for an answer, gets none, shrugs, moves to door, exits.*]

OSCAR. [*Peers at* LEO.] What you doing here, son?

LEO. You told me to find out if the boys at the bank had any message from Uncle Horace or Zan—

OSCAR. I told you if they had a message to bring it here. I told you that if they didn't have a message to stay at the bank and do your work.

LEO. Oh, I guess I misunderstood.

OSCAR. You didn't misunderstand. You just were looking for any excuse to take an hour off. [LEO *pours a cup of coffee.*] You got to stop that kind of thing. You got to start settling down. You going to be a married man one of these days.

LEO. Yes, sir.

OSCAR. You also got to stop with that woman in Mobile. [*As* LEO *is about to speak.*] You're young and I haven't got no obection to outside women. That is, I haven't got no objections so long as they don't interfere with serious things. Outside women are all right in their place, but *now* isn't their place. You got to realize that.

LEO. [*Nods.*] Yes, sir. I'll tell her. She'll act all right about it.

OSCAR. Also, you got to start working harder at the bank. You got to convince your Uncle Horace you going to make a fit husband for Alexandra.

LEO. What do you think has happened to them? Supposed to be here last night— [*Laughs.*] Bet you Uncle Ben's mighty worried. Seventy-five thousand dollars worried.

OSCAR. [*Smiles happily.*] Ought to be worried. Damn well ought to be. First he don't answer the letters, then he don't come home— [*Giggles.*]

LEO. What will happen if Uncle Horace don't come home or don't—

OSCAR. Or don't put up the money? Oh, we'll get it from outside. Easy enough.

LEO. [*Surprised.*] But *you* don't want outsiders.

OSCAR. What do I care who gets my share? I been shaved already. Serve Ben right if he had to give away some of his.

LEO. Damn shame what they did to you.

OSCAR. [*Looking up the stairs.*] Don't talk so loud. Don't you worry. When I die, you'll have as much as the rest. You might have yours *and* Alexandra's. I'm not so easily licked.

LEO. I wasn't thinking of myself, Papa—

OSCAR. Well, you should be, you should be. It's every man's duty to think of himself.

LEO. You think Uncle Horace don't want to go in on this?

OSCAR. [*Giggles.*] That's my hunch. He hasn't showed any signs of loving it yet.

LEO. [*Laughs.*] But he hasn't listened to Aunt Regina yet, either. Oh, he'll go along. It's too good a thing. Why wouldn't he want to? He's got plenty and plenty to invest with. He don't even have to sell anything. Eighty-eight thousand worth of Union Pacific bonds sitting right in his safe deposit box. All he's got to do is open the box.

OSCAR. [*After a pause. Looks at his watch.*] Mighty late breakfast in this fancy house. Yes, he's had those bonds for fifteen years. Bought them when they were low and just locked them up.

LEO. Yeah. Just has to open the box and take them out. That's all. Easy as easy can be. [*Laughs.*] The things in that box! There's all those bonds, looking mighty fine. [OSCAR *slowly puts down his newspaper and turns to* LEO.] Then right next to them is a baby shoe of Zan's and a cheap old cameo on a string, and, *and—* nobody'd believe this—a piece of an old violin. Not even a whole violin. Just a piece of an old thing, a piece of a violin.

OSCAR. [*Very softly, as if he were trying to control his voice.*] A piece of a violin! What do you think of that!

LEO. Yes sirree. A lot of other crazy things, too. A poem, I guess it is, signed with his mother's name, and two old schoolbooks with notes and— [LEO *catches* OSCAR's *look. His voice trails off. He turns his head away.*]

OSCAR. [*Very softly.*] How do you know what's in the box, son?

LEO. [*Stops, draws back, frightened, realizing what he has said.*] Oh, well. Well, er. Well, one of the boys, sir. It was one of the boys at the bank. He took old Manders' keys. It was Joe Horns. He just up and took Manders' keys and, and— well, took the box out. [*Quickly.*] Then they all asked me if I wanted to see, too. So I looked a little, I guess, but then I made them close up the box quick and I told them never—

OSCAR. [*Looks at him.*] Joe Horns, you say? He opened it?

LEO. Yes, sir, yes, he did. My word of honor. [*Very nervously looking away.*] I suppose that don't excuse *me* for looking— [*Looking at* OSCAR.] but I did make him close it up and put the keys back in Manders' drawer—

OSCAR. [*Leans forward, very softly.*] Tell the truth, Leo. I am not going to be angry with you. Did you open the box yourself?

LEO. *No, sir, I didn't.* I told you I didn't. No, I—

OSCAR. [*Irritated, patient.*] I am *not* going to be angry with you. [*Watching* LEO *carefully.*] Sometimes a young fellow deserves credit for looking round him to see what's going on. Sometimes that's a good sign in a fellow your age. [OSCAR *rises.*] Many great men have made their fortune with their eyes. Did you open the box?

LEO. [*Very puzzled.*] No. I—

OSCAR. [*Moves to* LEO.] Did you open the box? It may have been—well, it may have been a good thing if you had.

LEO. [*After a long pause.*] I opened it.

OSCAR. [*Quickly.*] Is that the truth? [LEO *nods.*] Does anybody else know that you opened it? Come, Leo, don't be afraid of speaking the truth to me.

LEO. No. Nobody knew. Nobody was in the bank when I did it. But—

OSCAR. Did your Uncle Horace ever know you opened it?

LEO. [*Shakes his head.*] He only looks in it once every six months when he cuts the coupons, and sometimes Manders even does that for him. Uncle Horace don't even have the keys. Manders keeps them for him. Imagine not looking at all that. You can bet if I had the bonds, I'd watch 'em like—

OSCAR If you had them. [LEO *watches him.*] *If* you had them. Then you could have a share in the mill, you and me. A fine, big share, too. [*Pauses, shrugs.*] Well, a man can't be shot for wanting to see his son get on in the world, can he, boy?

LEO. [*Looks up, begins to understand.*] No, he can't. Natural enough. [*Laughs.*] But I haven't got the bonds and Uncle Horace has. And now he can just sit back and wait to be a millionaire.

OSCAR. [*Innocently.*] You think your Uncle Horace likes you well enough to lend you the bonds if he decides not to use them himself?

LEO. Papa, it must be that you haven't had your breakfast! [*Laughs loudly.*] Lend me the bonds! My God—

OSCAR. [*Disappointed.*] No, I suppose not. Just a fancy of mine. A loan for three months, maybe four, easy enough for us to pay it back then. Anyway, this is only April— [*Slowly counting the months on his fingers.*] and if he doesn't look at them until Fall, he wouldn't even miss them out of the box.

LEO. That's it. He wouldn't even miss them. Ah, well—

OSCAR. No, sir. Wouldn't even miss them. How could he miss them if he never looks at them? [*Sighs as* LEO *stares at him.*] Well, here we are sitting around waiting for him to come home and invest his money in something he hasn't lifted his hand to get. But I can't help thinking he's acting strange. You laugh when I say he could lend you the bonds if he's not going to use them himself. But would it hurt him?

LEO. [*Slowly looking at* OSCAR.] No. No, it wouldn't.

OSCAR. People ought to help other people. But that's not always the way it happens. [BEN *enters, hangs his coat and hat in hall. Very carefully.*] And so sometimes you got to think of yourself. [*As* LEO *stares at him,* BEN *appears in the doorway.*] Morning, Ben.

BEN. [*Coming in, carrying his newspaper.*] Fine sunny morning. Any news from the runaways?

REGINA. [*On the staircase.*] There's no news or you would have heard it. Quite a convention so early in the morning, aren't you all? [*Goes to coffee urn.*]

OSCAR. You rising mighty late these days. Is that the way they do things in Chicago society?

BEN. [*Looking at his paper.*] Old Carter died in Senateville. Eighty-one is a good time for us all, eh? What do you think has really happened to Horace, Regina?

REGINA. Nothing.

BEN. [*Too casually.*] You don't think maybe he never started from Baltimore and never intends to start?

REGINA. [*Irritated.*] Of course they've started. Didn't I have a letter from Alexandra? What is so strange about people arriving late? He has that cousin in Savannah he's so fond of. He may have stopped to see him. They'll be along today some time, very flattered that you and Oscar are so worried about them.

BEN. I'm a natural worrier. Especially when I am getting ready to close a business deal and one of my partners remains silent *and* invisible.

REGINA. [*Laughs.*] Oh, is that it? I thought you were worried about Horace's health.

OSCAR. Oh, that too. Who could help but worry? I'm worried. This is the first day I haven't shot since my head cold.

REGINA. [*Starts towards dining room.*] Then you haven't had your breakfast.

Come along. [OSCAR *and* LEO *follow her.*]

BEN. Regina. [*She turns at dining-room door.*] That cousin of Horace's has been dead for years and, in any case, the train does not go through Savannah.

REGINA. [*Laughs, continues into dining room, seats herself.*] Did he die? You're always remembering about people dying. [BEN *rises.*] Now I intend to eat my breakfast in peace, and read my newspaper.

BEN. [*Goes toward dining room as he talks.*] This is second breakfast for me. My first was bad. Celia ain't the cook she used to be. Too old to have taste any more. If she hadn't belonged to Mama, I'd send her off to the country.

[OSCAR *and* LEO *start to eat.* BEN *seats himself.*]

LEO. Uncle Horace will have some tales to tell, I bet. Baltimore is a lively town.

REGINA. [*To* CAL.] The grits isn't hot enough. Take it back.

CAL. Oh, yes'm. [*Calling into kitchen as he exits.*] Grits didn't hold the heat. Grits didn't hold the heat.

LEO. When I was at school three of the boys and myself took a train once and went over to Baltimore. It was so big we thought we were in Europe. I was just a kid then—

REGINA. I find it very pleasant [ADDIE *enters.*] to have breakfast alone. I hate chattering before I've had something hot. [CAL *closes the dining-room doors.*] Do be still, Leo.

[ADDIE *comes into the room, begins gathering up the cups, carries them to the large tray. Outside there are the sounds of voices. Quickly* ADDIE *runs into the hall. A few seconds later she appears again in the doorway, her arm around the shoulders of* HORACE GIDDENS, *supporting him.* HORACE *is a tall man of about forty-five. He has been good looking, but now his face is tired and ill. He walks stiffly, as if it were an enormous effort, and carefully, as if he were unsure of his balance.* ADDIE *takes off his overcoat and hangs it on the hall tree. She then helps him to a chair.*]

HORACE. How are you, Addie? How have you been?

ADDIE. I'm all right, Mr. Horace. I've just been worried about you.

[ALEXANDRA *enters. She is flushed and*

excited, her hat awry, her face dirty. Her arms are full of packages, but she comes quickly to ADDIE.]

ALEXANDRA. Now don't tell me how worried you were. We couldn't help it and there was no way to send a message.

ADDIE. [*Begins to take packages from* ALEXANDRA.] Yes, sir, I was mighty worried.

ALEXANDRA. We had to stop in Mobile over night. Papa— [*Looks at him.*] Papa didn't feel well. The trip was too much for him, and I made him stop and rest— [*As* ADDIE *takes the last package.*] No, don't take that. That's father's medicine. I'll hold it. It mustn't break. Now, about the stuff outside. Papa must have his wheel chair. I'll get that and the valises—

ADDIE. [*Very happy, holding* ALEXANDRA'S *arms.*] Since when you got to carry your own valises? Since when I ain't old enough to hold a bottle of medicine? [HORACE *coughs.*] You feel all right, Mr. Horace?

HORACE. [*Nods.*] Glad to be sitting down.

ALEXANDRA. [*Opening package of medicine.*] He doesn't feel all right. [ADDIE *looks at her, then at* HORACE.] He just says that. The trip was very hard on him, and now he must go right to bed.

ADDIE. [*Looking at him carefully.*] Them fancy doctors, they give you help?

HORACE. They did their best.

ALEXANDRA. [*Has become conscious of the voices in the dining room.*] I bet Mama was worried. I better tell her we're here now. [*She starts for door.*]

HORACE. Zan. [*She stops.*] Not for a minute, dear.

ALEXANDRA. Oh, Papa, you feel bad again. I knew you did. Do you want your medicine?

HORACE. No, I don't feel that way. I'm just tired, darling. Let me rest a little.

ALEXANDRA. Yes, but Mama will be mad if I don't tell her we're here.

ADDIE. They're all in there eating breakfast.

ALEXANDRA. Oh, are they all here? Why do they *always* have to be here? I was hoping Papa wouldn't have to see anybody, that it would be nice for him and quiet.

ADDIE. Then let your papa rest for a minute.

HORACE. Addie, I bet your coffee's as good as ever. They don't have such good coffee up North. [*Looks at the urn.*] Is it as good, Addie? [ADDIE *starts for coffee urn.*]

ALEXANDRA. No. Dr. Reeves said not much coffee. Just now and then. I'm the nurse now, Addie.

ADDIE. You'd be a better one if you didn't look so dirty. Now go and take a bath, Miss Grown-up. Change your linens, get out a fresh dress and give your hair a good brushing—go on—

ALEXANDRA. Will you be all right, Papa?

ADDIE. Go on.

ALEXANDRA. [*On stairs, talks as she goes up.*] The pills Papa must take once every four hours. And the bottle only when—only if he feels very bad. Now don't move until I come back and don't talk much and remember about his medicine, Addie—

ADDIE. Ring for Belle and have her help you and then I'll make you a fresh breakfast.

ALEXANDRA. [*As she disappears.*] How's Aunt Birdie? Is she here?

ADDIE. It ain't right for you to have coffee? It will hurt you?

HORACE. [*Slowly.*] Nothing can make much difference now. Get me a cup, Addie. [*She looks at him, crosses to urn, pours a cup.*] Funny. They can't make coffee up North. [ADDIE *brings him a cup.*] They don't like red pepper, either. [*He takes the cup and gulps it greedily.*] God, that's good. You remember how I used to drink it? Ten, twelve cups a day. So strong it had to stain the cup. [*Then slowly.*] Addie, before I see anybody else, I want to know why Zan came to fetch me home. She's tried to tell me, but she doesn't seem to know herself.

ADDIE. [*Turns away.*] I don't know. All I know is big things are going on. Everybody going to be high-tone rich. Big rich. You too. All because smoke's going to s a out of a building that ain't even up yet.

HORACE. I've heard about it.

ADDIE. And, er— [*Hesitates—steps to him.*] And—well, Zan, she going to marry Mr. Leo in a little while.

HORACE. [*Looks at her, then very slowly.*] What are you talking about?

ADDIE. That's right. That's the talk, God help us.

HORACE. [*Angrily.*] What's the talk?

ADDIE. I'm telling you. There's going to be a wedding— [*Angrily turns away.*] Over my dead body there is.

HORACE. [*After a second, quietly.*] Go and tell them I'm home.

ADDIE. [*Hesitates.*] Now you ain't to get excited. You're to be in your bed—

HORACE. Go on, Addie. Go and say I'm back. [ADDIE *opens dining room doors. He rises with difficulty, stands stiff, as if he were in pain, facing the dining room.*]

ADDIE. Miss Regina. They're home. They got here—

REGINA. Horace! [REGINA *quickly rises, runs into the room. Warmly.*] Horace! You've finally arrived. [*As she kisses him, the others come forward, all talking together.*]

BEN. [*In doorway, carrying a napkin.*] Well, sir, you had us all mighty worried. [*He steps forward. They shake hands.* ADDIE *exits.*]

OSCAR. You're a sight for sore eyes.

HORACE. Hello, Ben.

[LEO *enters, eating a biscuit.*]

OSCAR. And how you feel? Tip-top, I bet, because that's the way you're looking.

HORACE. [*Coldly, irritated with* OSCAR's *lie.*] Hello, Oscar. Hello, Leo, how are you?

LEO. [*Shaking hands.*] I'm fine, sir. But a lot better now that you're back.

REGINA. Now sit down. What did happen to you and where's Alexandra? I am so excited about seeing you that I almost forgot about her.

HORACE. I didn't feel good, a little weak, I guess, and we stopped over night to rest. Zan's upstairs washing off the train dirt.

REGINA. Oh, I am so sorry the trip was hard on you. I didn't think that—

HORACE. Well, it's just as if I had never been away. All of you here—

BEN. Waiting to welcome you home.

[BIRDIE *bursts in. She is wearing a flannel kimono and her face is flushed and excited.*]

BIRDIE. [*Runs to him, kisses him.*] Horace!

HORACE. [*Warmly pressing her arm.*] I was just wondering where you were, Birdie.

BIRDIE. [*Excited.*] Oh, I would have been here. I didn't know you were back until Simon said he saw the buggy. [*She draws back to look at him. Her face so-bers.*] Oh, you don't look well, Horace. No, you don't.

REGINA. [*Laughs.*] Birdie, what a thing to say—

HORACE. [*Looking at* OSCAR.] Oscar thinks I look very well.

OSCAR. [*Annoyed. Turns on* LEO.] Don't stand there holding that biscuit in your hand.

LEO. Oh, well. I'll just finish my breakfast, Uncle Horace, and then I'll give you all the news about the bank— [*He exits into the dining room.*]

OSCAR. And what is that costume you have on?

BIRDIE. [*Looking at* HORACE.] Now that you're home, you'll feel better. Plenty of good rest and we'll take such fine care of you. [*Stops.*] But where is Zan? I missed her so much.

OSCAR. I asked you what is that strange costume you're parading around in?

BIRDIE. [*Nervously, backing towards stairs.*] Me? Oh! It's my wrapper. I was so excited about Horace I just rushed out of the house—

OSCAR. Did you come across the square dressed that way? My dear Birdie, I—

HORACE. [*To* REGINA, *wearily.*] Yes, it's just like old times.

REGINA. [*Quickly to* OSCAR.] Now, no fights. This is a holiday.

BIRDIE. [*Runs quickly up the stairs.*] Zan! Zannie!

OSCAR. Birdie! [*She stops.*]

BIRDIE. Oh. Tell Zan I'll be back in a little while. [*Whispers.*] Sorry, Oscar. [*Exits.*]

REGINA. [*To* OSCAR *and* BEN.] Why don't you finish your breakfast and let Horace rest for a minute?

BEN. [*Crossing to dining room with* OSCAR.] Never leave a meal unfinished. There are too many poor people who need the food. Mighty glad to see you home, Horace. Fine to have you back. Fine to have you back.

OSCAR. [*To* LEO *as* BEN *closes dining-room doors.*] Your mother has gone crazy. Running around the streets like a woman— [*The moment* REGINA *and* HORACE *are alone, they become awkward and self-conscious.*]

REGINA. [*Laughs awkwardly.*] Well. Here we are. It's been a long time. [HORACE *smiles.*] Five months. You know,

Horace, I wanted to come and be with you in the hospital, but I didn't know where my duty was. Here, or with you. But you know how much I *wanted* to come.

HORACE. That's kind of you, Regina. There was no need to come.

REGINA. Oh, but there was. Five months lying there all by yourself, no kinfolks, no friends. Don't try to tell me you didn't have a bad time of it.

HORACE. I didn't have a bad time. [*As she shakes her head, he becomes insistent.*] No, I didn't, Regina. Oh, at first when I—when I heard the news about myself—but after I got used to that, I liked it there.

REGINA. You *liked* it? [*Coldly.*] Isn't that strange. You liked it so well you didn't want to come home?

HORACE. That's not the way to put it. [*Then, kindly, as he sees her turn her head away.*] But there I was and I got kind of used to it, kind of to like lying there and thinking. [*Smiles.*] I never had much time to think before. And time's become valuable to me.

REGINA. It sounds almost like a holiday.

HORACE. [*Laughs.*] It was, sort of. The first holiday I've had since I was a little kid.

REGINA. And here I was thinking you were in pain and—

HORACE. [*Quietly.*] I was in pain.

REGINA. And instead you were having a holiday! A holiday of thinking. Couldn't you have done that here?

HORACE. I wanted to do it before I came here. I was thinking about us.

REGINA. About us? About you and me? Thinking about you and me after all these years. [*Unpleasantly.*] You shall tell me everything you thought—some day.

HORACE. [*There is silence for a minute.*] Regina. [*She turns to him.*] Why did you send Zan to Baltimore?

REGINA. Why? Because I wanted you home. You can't make anything suspicious out of that, can you?

HORACE. I didn't mean to make anything suspicious about it. [*Hesitantly, taking her hand.*] Zan said you wanted me to come home. I was so pleased at that and touched, it made me feel good.

REGINA. [*Taking away her hand, turns.*] Touched that I should want you home?

HORACE. [*Sighs.*] I'm saying all the wrong things as usual. Let's try to get along better. There isn't so much more time. Regina, what's all this crazy talk I've been hearing about Zan and Leo? Zan and Leo marrying?

REGINA. [*Turning to him, sharply.*] Who gossips so much around here?

HORACE. [*Shocked.*] Regina!

REGINA. [*Annoyed, anxious to quiet him.*] It's some foolishness that Oscar thought up. I'll explain later. I have no intention of allowing any such arrangement. It was simply a way of keeping Oscar quiet in all this business I've been writing you about—

HORACE. [*Carefully.*] What has Zan to do with any business of Oscar's? Whatever it is, you had better put it out of Oscar's head immediately. You know what I think of Leo.

REGINA. But there's no need to talk about it now.

HORACE. There is no need to talk about it ever. Not as long as I live. [HORACE *stops, slowly turns to look at her.*] As long as I live. I've been in a hospital for five months. Yet since I've been here you have not once asked me about—about my health. [*Then gently.*] Well, I suppose they've written you. I can't live very long.

REGINA. [*Coldly.*] I've never understood why people have to talk about this kind of thing.

HORACE. [*There is a silence. Then he looks up at her, his face cold.*] You misunderstand. I don't intend to gossip about my sickness. I thought it was only fair to tell you. I was not asking for your sympathy.

REGINA. [*Sharply, turns to him.*] What do the doctors think caused your bad heart?

HORACE. What do you mean?

REGINA. They didn't think it possible, did they, that your fancy women may have—

HORACE. [*Smiles unpleasantly.*] Caused my heart to be bad? I don't think that's the best scientific theory. You don't catch heart trouble in bed.

REGINA. [*Angrily.*] I didn't think you did. I only thought you might catch a bad conscience—in bed, as you say.

HORACE. I didn't tell them about my bad conscience. Or about my fancy women.

Nor did I tell them that my wife has not wanted me in bed with her for— [*Sharply.*] How long is it, Regina? [REGINA *turns to him.*] Ten years? Did you bring me home for this, to make me feel guilty again? That means you want something. But you'll not make me feel guilty any more. My "thinking" has made a difference.

REGINA. I see that it has. [*She looks towards dining-room door. Then comes to him, her manner warm and friendly.*] It's foolish for us to fight this way. I didn't mean to be unpleasant. I was stupid.

HORACE. [*Wearily.*] God knows I didn't either. I came home wanting so much not to fight, and then all of a sudden there we were. I got hurt and—

REGINA. [*Hastily.*] It's all my fault. I didn't ask about—about your illness because I didn't want to remind you of it. Anyway I never believe doctors when they talk about— [*Brightly.*] when they talk like that.

HORACE. [*Not looking at her.*] Well, we'll try our best with each other. [*He rises.*]

REGINA. [*Quickly.*] I'll try. Honestly, I will. Horace, Horace, I know you're tired but, but—couldn't you stay down here a few minutes longer? I want Ben to tell you something.

HORACE. Tomorrow.

REGINA. I'd like to now. It's very important to me. It's very important to all of us. [*Gaily, as she moves toward dining room.*] Important to your beloved daughter. She'll be a very great heiress—

HORACE. Will she? That's nice.

REGINA. [*Opens doors.*] Ben, are you finished breakfast?

HORACE. Is this the mill business I've had so many letters about?

REGINA. [*To* BEN.] Horace would like to talk to you now.

HORACE. Horace would not like to talk to you now. I am very tired, Regina—

REGINA. [*Comes to him.*] Please. You've said we'll try our best with each other. I'll try. Really, I will. Please do this for me now. You will see what I've done while you've been away. How I watched your interests. [*Laughs gaily.*] And I've done very well too. But things can't be delayed any longer. Everything must be settled this week— [HORACE *sits down,* BEN *enters.* OSCAR *has stayed in the dining room, his*

head turned to watch them. LEO *is pretending to read the newspaper.*] Now you must tell Horace all about it. Only be quick because he is very tired and must go to bed. [HORACE *is looking up at her. His face hardens as she speaks.*] But I think your news will be better for him than all the medicine in the world.

BEN. [*Looking at* HORACE.] It could wait. Horace may not feel like talking today.

REGINA. What an old faker you are! You know it can't wait. You know it must be finished this week. You've been just as anxious for Horace to get here as I've been.

BEN. [*Very jovial.*] I suppose I have been. And why not? Horace has done Hubbard Sons many a good turn. Why shouldn't I be anxious to help him now?

REGINA. [*Laughs.*] Help him! Help him when you need him, that's what you mean.

BEN. What a woman you married, Horace. [*Laughs awkwardly when* HORACE *does not answer.*] Well, then I'll make it quick. You know what I've been telling you for years. How I've always said that every one of us little Southern business men had great things—[*Extends his arm.*] —right beyond our finger tips. It's been my dream: my dream to make those fingers grow longer. I'm a lucky man, Horace, a lucky man. To dream and to live to get what you've dreamed of. That's *my* idea of a lucky man. [*Looks at his fingers as his arm drops slowly.*] For thirty years I've cried bring the cotton mills to the cotton. [HORACE *opens medicine bottle.*] Well, finally I got up nerve to go to Marshall Company in Chicago.

HORACE. I know all this. [*He takes the medicine.* REGINA *rises, steps to him.*]

BEN. Can I get you something?

HORACE. Some water, please.

REGINA. [*Turns quickly.*] Oh, I'm sorry. Let me. [*Brings him a glass of water. He drinks as they wait in silence.*] You feel all right now?

HORACE. Yes. You wrote me. I know all that.

[OSCAR *enters from dining room.*]

REGINA. [*Triumphantly.*] But you don't know that in the last few days Ben has agreed to give us—you, I mean—a much larger share.

HORACE. Really? That's very generous of him.

BEN. [*Laughs.*] It wasn't so generous of me. It was smart of Regina.

REGINA. [*As if she were signaling* HORACE.] I explained to Ben that perhaps you hadn't answered his letters because you didn't think he was offering you enough, and that the time was getting short and you could guess how much he needed you—

HORACE. [*Smiles at her, nods.*] And I could guess that he wants to keep control in the family?

REGINA. [*To* BEN, *triumphantly.*] Exactly. [*To* HORACE.] So I did a little bargaining for you and convinced my brothers they weren't the only Hubbards who had a business sense.

HORACE. Did you have to convince them of that? How little people know about each other! [*Laughs.*] But you'll know better about Regina next time, eh, Ben? [BEN, REGINA, HORACE *laugh together.* OSCAR's *face is angry.*] Now let's see. We're getting a bigger share. [*Looking at* OSCAR.] Who's getting less?

BEN. Oscar.

HORACE. Well, Oscar, you've grown very unselfish. What's happened to you?

[LEO *enters from dining room.*]

BEN. [*Quickly, before* OSCAR *can answer.*] Oscar doesn't mind. Not worth fighting about now, eh, Oscar?

OSCAR. [*Angrily.*] I'll get mine in the end. You can be sure of that. I've got my son's future to think about.

HORACE. [*Sharply.*] Leo? Oh, I see. [*Puts his head back, laughs.* REGINA *looks at him nervously.*] I am beginning to see. Everybody will get theirs.

BEN. I knew you'd see it. Seventy-five thousand, and that seventy-five thousand will make you a million.

REGINA. [*Steps to table, leaning forward.*] It will, Horace, it will.

HORACE. I believe you. [*After a second.*] Now I can understand Oscar's self-sacrifice, but what did you have to promise Marshall Company beside the money you're putting up?

BEN. They wouldn't take promises. They wanted guarantees.

HORACE. Of what?

BEN. [*Nods.*] Water power. Free and plenty of it.

HORACE. You got them that, of course.

BEN. Cheap. You'd think the Governor of a great state would make his price a little higher. From pride, you know. [HORACE *smiles.* BEN *smiles.*] Cheap wages. "What do you mean by cheap wages?" I say to Marshall, "Less than Massachusetts," he says to me, "and that averages eight a week." "Eight a week! By God," I tell him, "*I'd* work for eight a week myself." Why, there ain't a mountain white or a town nigger but wouldn't give his right arm for three silver dollars every week, eh, Horace?

HORACE. Sure. And they'll take less than that when you get around to playing them off against each other. You can save a little money that way, Ben. [*Angrily.*] And make them hate each other just a little more than they do now.

REGINA. What's all this about?

BEN. [*Laughs.*] There'll be no trouble from anybody, white or black. Marshall said that to me. "What about strikes? That's all we've had in Massachusetts for the last three years." I say to him, "What's a strike? I never heard of one. Come South, Marshall. We got good folks and we don't stand for any fancy fooling."

HORACE. You're right. [*Slowly.*] Well, it looks like you made a good deal for yourselves, and for Marshall, too. [*To* BEN.] Your father used to say he made the thousands and you boys would make the millions. I think he was right. [*Rises.*]

REGINA. [*They are all looking at* HORACE. *She laughs nervously.*] Millions for *us*, too.

HORACE. Us? You and me? I don't think so. We've got enough money, Regina. We'll just sit by and watch the boys grow rich. [*They watch* HORACE *tensely as he begins to move towards the staircase. He passes* LEO, *looks at him for a second.*] How's everything at the bank, Leo?

LEO. Fine, sir. Everything is fine.

HORACE. How are all the ladies in Mobile? [HORACE *turns to* REGINA, *sharply.*] Whatever made you think I'd let Zan marry—

REGINA. Do you mean that you are turning this down? Is it possible that's what you mean?

BEN. No, that's not what he means. Turning down a fortune. Horace is tired. He'd rather talk about it tomorrow—

REGINA. We can't keep putting it off this way. Oscar must be in Chicago by the end of the week with the money and contracts.

OSCAR. [*Giggles, pleased.*] Yes, sir. Got to be there end of the week. No sense going without the money.

REGINA. [*Tensely.*] I've waited long enough for your answer. I'm not going to wait any longer.

HORACE. [*Very deliberately.*] I'm very tired now, Regina.

BEN. [*Hastily.*] Now, Horace probably has his reasons. Things he'd like explained. Tomorrow will do. I can—

REGINA. [*Turns to* BEN, *sharply.*] I want to know his reasons now! [*Turns back to* HORACE.]

HORACE. [*As he climbs the steps.*] I don't know them all myself. Let's leave it at that.

REGINA. We shall not leave it at that! We have waited for you here like children. Waited for you to come home.

HORACE. So that you could invest my money. So this is why you wanted me home? Well, I had hoped— [*Quietly.*] If you are disappointed, Regina, I'm sorry. But I must do what I think best. We'll talk about it another day.

REGINA. We'll talk about it now. Just you and me.

HORACE. [*Looks down at her. His voice is tense.*] Please, Regina. It's been a hard trip. I don't feel well. Please leave me alone now.

REGINA. [*Quietly.*] I want to talk to you, Horace. I'm coming up. [*He looks at her for a minute, then moves on again out of sight. She begins to climb the stairs.*]

BEN. [*Softly.* REGINA *turns to him as he speaks.*] Sometimes it is better to wait for the sun to rise again. [*She does not answer.*] And sometimes, as our mother used to tell you, [REGINA *starts up stairs.*] it's unwise for a good-looking woman to frown. [BEN *rises, moves towards stairs.*] Softness and a smile do more to the hearts of men— [*She disappears.* BEN *stands looking up the stairs. There is a long silence. Then, suddenly,* OSCAR *giggles.*]

OSCAR. Let us hope she'll change his mind. Let us hope. [*After a second* BEN *crosses to table, picks up his newspaper.* OSCAR *looks at* BEN. *The silence makes* LEO *uncomfortable.*]

LEO. The paper says twenty-seven cases of yellow fever in New Orleans. Guess the flood-waters caused it. [*Nobody pays attention.*] Thought they were building the levees high enough. Like the niggers always say: a man born of woman can't build nothing high enough for the Mississippi. [*Gets no answer. Gives an embarrassed laugh.*]

[*Upstairs there is the sound of voices. The voices are not loud, but* BEN, OSCAR, LEO *become conscious of them.* LEO *crosses to landing, looks up, listens.*]

OSCAR [*Pointing up.*] Now just suppose she don't change his mind? Just suppose he keeps on refusing?

BEN. [*Without conviction.*] He's tired. It was a mistake to talk to him today. He's a sick man, but he isn't a crazy one.

OSCAR. [*Giggles.*] But just suppose he is crazy. What then?

BEN. [*Puts down his paper, peers at* OSCAR.] Then we'll go outside for the money. There's plenty who would give it.

OSCAR. And plenty who will want a lot for what they give. The ones who are rich enough to give will be smart enough to want. That means we'd be working for them, don't it, Ben?

BEN. You don't have to tell me the things I told you six months ago.

OSCAR. Oh, you're right not to worry. She'll change his mind. She always has. [*There is a silence. Suddenly* REGINA's *voice becomes louder and sharper. All of them begin to listen now. Slowly* BEN *rises, goes to listen by the staircase.* OSCAR *watching him, smiles. As they listen* REGINA's *voice becomes very loud.* HORACE's *voice is no longer heard.*] Maybe. But I don't believe it. I never did believe he was going in with us.

BEN. [*Turning on him.*] What the hell do you expect me to do?

OSCAR. [*Mildly.*] Nothing. You done your almighty best. Nobody could blame you if the whole thing just dripped away right through our fingers. You can't do a thing. But there may be something I could do for us. [OSCAR *rises.*] Or, I might better say, Leo could do for us. [BEN *stops, turns, looks at* OSCAR. LEO *is staring at* OSCAR.] Ain't that true, son? Ain't it true you might be able to help your own kinfolks?

LEO. [*Nervously taking a step to him.*] Papa, I—

BEN. [*Slowly.*] How would he help us, Oscar?

OSCAR. Leo's got a friend. Leo's friend owns eighty-eight thousand dollars in Union Pacific bonds. [BEN *turns to look at* LEO.] Leo's friend don't look at the bonds much—not for five or six months at a time.

BEN. [*After a pause.*] Union Pacific. Uh, huh. Let me understand. Leo's friend would—would lend him these bonds and he—

OSCAR. [*Nods.*] Would be kind enough to lend them to us.

BEN. Leo.

LEO. [*Excited, comes to him.*] Yes, sir?

BEN. When would your friend be wanting the bonds back?

LEO. [*Very nervous.*] I don't know. I—well, I—

OSCAR. [*Sharply. Steps to him.*] You told me he won't look at them until Fall—

LEO. Oh, that's right. But I—not till Fall. Uncle Horace never—

BEN. [*Sharply.*] Be still.

OSCAR. [*Smiles at* LEO.] Your uncle doesn't wish to know your friend's name.

LEO. [*Starts to laugh.*] That's a good one. Not know his name—

OSCAR. Shut up, Leo! [LEO *turns away slowly, moves to table.* BEN *turns to* OSCAR.] He won't look at them again until September. That gives us five months. Leo will return the bonds in three months. And we'll have no trouble raising the money once the mills are going up. Will Marshall accept bonds?

[BEN *stops to listen to sudden sharp voices from above. The voices are now very angry and very loud.*]

BEN. [*Smiling.*] Why not? Why not? [*Laughs.*] Good. We are lucky. We'll take the loan from Leo's friend—I think he will make a safer partner than our sister. [*Nods towards stairs. Turns to* LEO.] How soon can you get them?

LEO. Today. Right now. They're in the safe-deposit box and—

BEN. [*Sharply.*] I don't want to know where they are.

OSCAR. [*Laughs.*] We will keep it secret from you. [*Pats* BEN's *arm.*]

BEN. [*Smiles.*] Good. Draw a check for our part. You can take the night train for Chicago. Well, Oscar, [*Holds out his hand.*] good luck to us.

OSCAR. Leo will be taken care of?

LEO. I'm entitled to Uncle Horace's share. I'd enjoy being a partner—

BEN. [*Turns to stare at him.*] You would? You can go to hell, you little— [*Starts towards* LEO.]

OSCAR. [*Nervously.*] Now, now. He didn't mean that. I only want to be sure he'll get something out of all this.

BEN. Of course. We'll take care of him. We won't have any trouble about that. I'll see you at the store.

OSCAR. [*Nods.*] That's settled then. Come on, son. [*Starts for door.*]

LEO. [*Puts out his hand.*] I didn't mean just that. I was only going to say what a great day this was for me and— [BEN IGnores *his hand.*]

BEN. Go on.

[LEO *looks at him, turns, follows* OSCAR *out.* BEN *stands where he is, thinking. Again the voices upstairs can be heard.* REGINA's *voice is high and furious.* BEN *looks up, smiles, winces at the noise.*]

ALEXANDRA. [*Upstairs.*] Mama—Mama—don't . . . [*The noise of running footsteps is heard and* ALEXANDRA *comes running down the steps, speaking as she comes.*] Uncle Ben! Uncle Ben! Please go up. Please make Mama stop. Uncle Ben, he's sick, he's so sick. How can Mama talk to him like that—please, make her stop. She'll—

BEN. Alexandra, you have a tender heart.

ALEXANDRA. [*Crying.*] Go on up, Uncle Ben, please—

[*Suddenly the voices stop. A second later there is the sound of a door being slammed.*]

BEN. Now you see. Everything is over. Don't worry. [*He starts for the door.*] Alexandra, I want you to tell your mother how sorry I am that I had to leave. And don't worry so, my dear. Married folk frequently raise their voices, unfortunately. [*He starts to put on his hat and coat as* REGINA *appears on the stairs.*]

ALEXANDRA. [*Furiously.*] How can you treat Papa like this? He's sick. He's very sick. Don't you know that? I won't let you.

REGINA. Mind your business, Alexandra. [*To* BEN. *Her voice is cold and calm.*] How much longer can you wait for the money?

BEN. [*Putting on his coat.*] He has refused? My, that's too bad.

REGINA. He will change his mind. I'll find a way to make him. What's the longest you can wait now?

BEN. I could wait until next week. But I can't wait until next week. [*He giggles, pleased at the joke.*] I could but I can't. Could and can't. Well, I must go now. I'm very late—

REGINA. [*Coming downstairs towards him.*] You're not going. I want to talk to you.

BEN. I was about to give Alexandra a message for you. I wanted to tell you that Oscar is going to Chicago tonight, so we can't be here for our usual Friday supper.

REGINA. [*Tensely.*] Oscar is going to Chi— [*Softly.*] What do you mean?

BEN. Just that. Everything is settled. He's going on to deliver to Marshall—

REGINA. [*Taking a step to him.*] I demand to know what— You are lying. You are trying to scare me. *You haven't got the money.* How could you have it? You can't have— [BEN *laughs.*] You will wait until I—

[HORACE *comes into view on the landing.*]

BEN. You are getting out of hand. Since when do I take orders from you?

REGINA. Wait, you— [BEN *stops.*] How *can* he go to Chicago? Did a ghost arrive with the money? [BEN *starts for the hall.*] I don't believe you. Come back here. [REGINA *starts after him.*] Come back here, you— [*The door slams. She stops in the doorway, staring, her fists clenched. After a pause she turns slowly.*]

HORACE. [*Very quietly.*] It's a great day when you and Ben cross swords. I've been waiting for it for years.

ALEXANDRA. Papa, Papa, please go back! You will—

HORACE. And so they don't need you, and so you will not have your millions, after all.

REGINA. [*Turns slowly.*] You hate to see anybody live now, don't you? You hate to think that I'm going to be alive and have what I want.

HORACE. I should have known you'd think that was the reason.

REGINA. Because you're going to die and you know you're going to die.

ALEXANDRA. [*Shrilly.*] Mama! Don't— Don't listen, Papa. Just don't listen. Go away—

HORACE. Not to keep you from getting what you want. Not even partly that. [*Holding to the rail.*] I'm sick of you, sick of this house, sick of my life here. I'm sick of your brothers and their dirty tricks to make a dime. There must be better ways of getting rich than cheating niggers on a pound of bacon. Why should I give you the money? [*Very angrily.*] To pound the bones of this town to make dividends for you to spend? You wreck the town, you and your brothers, *you* wreck the town and live on it. Not me. Maybe it's easy for the dying to be honest. But it's not my fault I'm dying. [ADDIE *enters, stands at door quietly.*] I'll do no more harm now. I've done enough. I'll die my own way. And I'll do it without making the world any worse. I leave that to you.

REGINA. [*Looks up at him slowly, calmly.*] I hope you die. I hope you die soon. [*Smiles.*] I'll be waiting for you to die.

ALEXANDRA. [*Shrieking.*] Papa! Don't— Don't listen— Don't—

ADDIE. Come here, Zan. Come out of this room.

[ALEXANDRA *runs quickly to* ADDIE, *who holds her.* HORACE *turns slowly and starts upstairs.*]

CURTAIN

ACT THREE

SCENE: *Same as Act One. Two weeks later. It is late afternoon and it is raining.*

AT RISE: HORACE *is sitting near the window in a wheel chair. On the table next to him is a safe-deposit box, and a small bottle of medicine.* BIRDIE *and* ALEXANDRA *are playing the piano. On a chair is a large sewing basket.*

BIRDIE. [*Counting for* ALEXANDRA.] One and two and three and four. One and two and three and four. [*Nods—turns to* HORACE.] We once played together, Horace. Remember?

HORACE. [*Has been looking out of the window.*] What, Birdie?

BIRDIE. We played together. You and me.

ALEXANDRA. *Papa* used to play?

BIRDIE. Indeed he did. [ADDIE *appears at the door in a large kitchen apron. She is wiping her hands on a towel.*] He played the fiddle and very well, too.

ALEXANDRA. [*Turns to smile at* HORACE.] I never knew—

ADDIE. Where's your mama?

ALEXANDRA. Gone to Miss Safronia's to fit her dresses.

[ADDIE *nods, starts to exit.*]

HORACE. Addie.

ADDIE. Yes, Mr. Horace.

HORACE. [*Speaks as if he had made a sudden decision.*] Tell Cal to get on his things. I want him to go an errand.

[ADDIE *nods, exits.* HORACE *moves nervously in his chair, looks out of the window.*]

ALEXANDRA. [*Who has been watching him.*] It's too bad it's been raining all day, Papa. But you can go out in the yard tomorrow. Don't be restless.

HORACE. I'm not restless, darling.

BIRDIE. I remember so well the time we played together, your papa and me. It was the first time Oscar brought me here to supper. I had never seen all the Hubbards together before, and you know what a ninny I am and how shy. [*Turns to look at* HORACE.] You said you could play the fiddle and you'd be much obliged if I'd play with you. *I* was obliged to *you*, all right, all right. [*Laughs when he does not answer her.*] Horace, you haven't heard a word I've said.

HORACE. Birdie, when did Oscar get back from Chicago?

BIRDIE. Yesterday. Hasn't he been here yet?

ALEXANDRA. [*Stops playing.*] No. Neither has Uncle Ben since—since that day.

BIRDIE. Oh, I didn't know it was *that* bad. Oscar never tells me anything—

HORACE. [*Smiles, nods.*] The Hubbards have had their great quarrel. I knew it would come some day. [*Laughs.*] It came.

ALEXANDRA. It came. It certainly came all right.

BIRDIE. [*Amazed.*] But Oscar was in such a good humor when he got home, I didn't—

HORACE. Yes, I can understand that.

[ADDIE *enters carrying a large tray with glasses, a carafe of elderberry wine and a plate of cookies, which she puts on the table.*]

ALEXANDRA. Addie! A party! What for?

ADDIE. Nothing for. I had the fresh butter, so I made the cakes, and a little elderberry does the stomach good in the rain.

BIRDIE. Isn't this nice! A party just for us. Let's play party music, Zan.

[ALEXANDRA *begins to play a gay piece.*]

ADDIE. [*To* HORACE, *wheeling his chair to center.*] Come over here, Mr. Horace, and don't be thinking so much. A glass of elderberry will do more good.

[ALEXANDRA *reaches for a cake.* BIRDIE *pours herself a glass of wine.*]

ALEXANDRA. Good cakes, Addie. It's nice here. Just us. Be nice if it could always be this way.

BIRDIE. [*Nods happily.*] Quiet and restful.

ADDIE. Well, it won't be that way long. Little while now, even sitting here, you'll hear the red bricks going into place. The next day the smoke'll be pushing out the chimneys and by church time that Sunday every human born of woman will be living on chicken. That's how Mr. Ben's been telling the story.

HORACE. [*Looks at her.*] They believe it that way?

ADDIE. Believe it? They use to believing what Mr. Ben orders. There ain't been so much talk around here since Sherman's army didn't come near.

HORACE. [*Softly.*] They are fools.

ADDIE. [*Nods, sits down with the sewing basket.*] You ain't born in the South unless you're a fool.

BIRDIE. [*Has drunk another glass of wine.*] But we didn't play together after that night. Oscar said he didn't like me to play on the piano. [*Turns to* ALEXANDRA.] You know what he said that night?

ALEXANDRA. Who?

BIRDIE. Oscar. He said that music made him nervous. He said he just sat and waited for the next note. [ALEXANDRA *laughs.*] He wasn't poking fun. He meant it. Ah, well— [*She finishes her glass, shakes her head.* HORACE *looks at her, smiles.*] Your papa don't like to admit it, but he's been mighty kind to me all these years. [*Running the back of her hand along his sleeve.*] Often he'd step in when somebody said something and once— [*She stops, turns away, her face still.*] Once he stopped Oscar from— [*She stops, turns. Quickly.*] I'm sorry I said that. Why, here I am so happy and yet I think about bad things. [*Laughs nervously.*] That's not right, now, is it? [*She pours a drink.* CAL *appears in the door. He has on an old coat and is carrying a torn umbrella.*]

ALEXANDRA. Have a cake, Cal.

CAL. [*Comes in, takes a cake.*] Yes'm. You want me, Mr. Horace?

HORACE. What time is it, Cal?

CAL. 'Bout ten minutes before it's five.

HORACE. All right. Now you walk yourself down to the bank.

CAL. It'll be closed. Nobody'll be there but Mr. Manders, Mr. Joe Horns, Mr. Leo—

HORACE. Go in the back way. They'll be at the table, going over the day's business. [*Points to the deposit box.*] See that box?

CAL. [*Nods.*] Yes, sir.

HORACE. You tell Mr. Manders that Mr. Horace says he's much obliged to him for bringing the box, it arrived all right.

CAL. [*Bewildered.*] He know you got the box. He bring it himself Wednesday. I opened the door to him and he say, "Hello, Cal, coming on to summer weather."

HORACE. You say just what I tell you. Understand?

[BIRDIE *pours another drink, stands at table.*]

CAL. No, sir. I ain't going to say I understand. I'm going down and tell a man he give you something he already know he give you, and you say "understand."

HORACE. Now, Cal.

CAL. Yes, sir. I just going to say you obliged for the box coming all right. I ain't going to understand it, but I'm going to say it.

HORACE. And tell him I want him to come over here after supper, and to bring Mr. Sol Fowler with him.

CAL. [*Nods.*] He's to come after supper and bring Mr. Sol Fowler, your attorney-at-law, with him.

HORACE. [*Smiles.*] That's right. Just walk right in the back room and say your piece. [*Slowly.*] In front of everybody.

CAL. Yes, sir. [*Mumbles to himself as he exits.*]

ALEXANDRA. [*Who has been watching* HORACE.] Is anything the matter, Papa?

HORACE. Oh, no. Nothing.

ADDIE. Miss Birdie, that elderberry going to give you a headache spell.

BIRDIE. [*Beginning to be drunk. Gaily.*] Oh, I don't think so. I don't think it will.

ALEXANDRA. [*As* HORACE *puts his hand to his throat.*] Do you want your medicine, Papa?

HORACE. No, no. I'm all right, darling.

BIRDIE. Mama used to give me elderberry wine when I was a little girl. For hiccoughs. [*Laughs.*] You know, I don't think people get hiccoughs any more. Isn't that funny? [BIRDIE *laughs.* HORACE *and* ALEXANDRA *laugh.*] I used to get hiccoughs just when I shouldn't have.

ADDIE. [*Nods.*] And nobody gets growing pains no more. That is funny. Just as if there was some style in what you get. One year an ailment's stylish and the next year it ain't.

BIRDIE. [*Turns.*] I remember. It was my first big party, at Lionnet I mean, and I was so excited, and there I was with hiccoughs and Mama laughing. [*Softly. Looking at carafe.*] Mama always laughed. [*Picks up carafe.*] A big party, a lovely dress from Mr. Worth in Paris, France, and hiccoughs. [*Pours drink.*] My brother pounding me on the back and Mama with the elderberry bottle, laughing at me. Everybody was on their way to come, and I was such a ninny, hiccoughing away. [*Drinks.*] You know, that was the first day I ever saw Oscar Hubbard. The Ballongs were selling their horses and he was going there to buy. He passed and lifted his hat —we could see him from the window— and my brother, to tease Mama, said maybe we should have invited the Hubbards to the party. He said Mama didn't like them because they kept a store, and he said that was old-fashioned of her. [*Her face lights up.*] And then, and *then,* I saw Mama angry for the first time in my life. She said that wasn't the reason. She said she was old-fashioned, but not that way.

She said she was old-fashioned enough not to like people who killed animals they couldn't use, and who made their money charging awful interest to poor, ignorant niggers and cheating them on what they bought. She was very angry, Mama was. I had never seen her face like that. And then suddenly she laughed and said, "Look, I've frightened Birdie out of the hiccoughs." [*Her head drops. Then softly.*] And so she had. They were all gone. [*Moves to sofa, sits.*]

ADDIE. Yeah, they got mighty well off cheating niggers. Well, there are people who eat the earth and eat all the people on it like in the Bible with the locusts. Then there are people who stand around and watch them eat it. [*Softly.*] Sometimes I think it ain't right to stand and watch them do it.

BIRDIE. [*Thoughtfully.*] Like I say, if we could go back to Lionnet. Everybody'd be better there. They'd be good and kind. I like people to be kind. [*Pours drink.*] Don't you, Horace; don't you like people to be kind?

HORACE. Yes, Birdie.

BIRDIE. [*Very drunk now.*] Yes, that was the first day I ever saw Oscar. Who would have thought— [*Quickly.*] You all want to know something? Well, I don't like Leo. My very own son, and I don't like him. [*Laughs, gaily.*] My, I guess I even like Oscar more.

ALEXANDRA. Why did you marry Uncle Oscar?

ADDIE. [*Sharply.*] That's no question for you to be asking.

HORACE. [*Sharply.*] Why not? She's heard enough around here to ask anything.

ALEXANDRA. Aunt Birdie, why did you marry Uncle Oscar?

BIRDIE. I don't know. I thought I liked him. He was kind to me and I thought it was because he liked me too. But that wasn't the reason— [*Wheels on ALEXANDRA.*] Ask why *he* married *me*. I can tell you that: He's told it to me often enough.

ADDIE. [*Leaning forward.*] Miss Birdie, don't—

BIRDIE. [*Speaking very rapidly, tensely.*] My family was good and the cotton on Lionnet's field was better. Ben Hubbard wanted the cotton and [*Rises.*] Oscar Hubbard married it for him. He was kind to me, then. He used to smile at me. He hasn't smiled at me since. Everybody knew that's what he married me for. [ADDIE *rises.*] Everybody but me. Stupid, stupid me.

ALEXANDRA. [*To* HORACE, *holding his hand, softly.*] I see. [*Hesitates.*] Papa, I mean—when you feel better couldn't we go away? I mean, by ourselves. Couldn't we find a way to go—

HORACE. Yes, I know what you mean. We'll try to find a way. I promise you, darling.

ADDIE. [*Moves to* BIRDIE.] Rest a bit, Miss Birdie. You get talking like this you'll get a headache and—

BIRDIE. [*Sharply, turning to her.*] I've never had a headache in my life. [*Begins to cry hysterically.*] You know it as well as I do. [*Turns to* ALEXANDRA.] I never had a headache, Zan. That's a lie they tell for me. I drink. All by myself, in my own room, by myself, I drink. Then, when they want to hide it, they say, "Birdie's got a headache again"—

ALEXANDRA. [*Comes to her quickly.*] Aunt Birdie.

BIRDIE. [*Turning away.*] Even you won't like me now. You won't like me any more.

ALEXANDRA. I love you. I'll always love you.

BIRDIE. [*Furiously.*] Well, don't. Don't love me. Because in twenty years you'll just be like me. They'll do all the same things to you. [*Begins to laugh hysterically.*] You know what? In twenty-two years I haven't had a whole day of happiness. Oh, a little, like today with you all. But never a single, whole day. I say to myself, if only I had one more *whole* day, then— [*The laugh stops.*] And that's the way you'll be. And you'll trail after them, just like me, hoping they won't be so mean that day or say something to make you feel so bad—only you'll be worse off because you haven't got my Mama to remember— [*Turns away, her head drops. She stands quietly, swaying a little, holding onto the sofa.* ALEXANDRA *leans down, puts her cheek on* BIRDIE's *arm.*]

ALEXANDRA. [*To* BIRDIE.] I guess we were all trying to make a happy day. You know, we sit around and try to pretend nothing's happened. We try to pretend we are not here. We make believe we are just by ourselves, someplace else, and it doesn't work. [*Kisses* BIRDIE's *hand.*] Come now, Aunt Birdie, I'll walk you home. You and me. [*She takes* BIRDIE's *arm. They move slowly out.*]

BIRDIE. [*Softly as they exit.*] You and me.

ADDIE. [*After a minute.*] Well. First time I ever heard Miss Birdie say a word. [HORACE *looks at her.*] Maybe it's good for her. I'm just sorry Zan had to hear it. [HORACE *moves his head as if he were uncomfortable.*] You feel bad, don't you? [*He shrugs.*]

HORACE. So you didn't want Zan to hear? It would be nice to let her stay innocent, like Birdie at her age. Let her listen now. Let her see everything. How else is she going to know that she's got to get away? I'm trying to show her that. I'm trying, but I've only got a little time left. She can even hate me when I'm dead, if she'll only learn to hate and fear this.

ADDIE. Mr. Horace—

HORACE. Pretty soon there'll be nobody to help her but you.

ADDIE. [*Crossing to him.*] What can I do?

HORACE. Take her away.

ADDIE. How can I do that? Do you think they'd let me just go away with her?

HORACE. I'll fix it so they can't stop you when you're ready to go. You'll go, Addie?

ADDIE. [*After a second, softly.*] Yes, sir. I promise. [*He touches her arm, nods.*]

HORACE. [*Quietly.*] I'm going to have Sol Fowler make me a new will. They'll make trouble, but you make Zan stand firm and Fowler'll do the rest. Addie, I'd like to leave you something for yourself. I always wanted to.

ADDIE. [*Laughs.*] Don't you do that, Mr. Horace. A nigger woman in a white man's will! I'd never get it nohow.

HORACE. I know. But upstairs in the armoire drawer there's seventeen hundred dollar bills. It's money left from my trip. It's in an envelope with your name. It's for you.

ADDIE. Seventeen hundred dollar bills! My God, Mr. Horace, I won't know how to count up that high. [*Shyly.*] It's mighty kind and good of you. I don't know what to say for thanks—

CAL. [*Appears in doorway.*] I'm back. [*No answer*] I'm back.

ADDIE. So we see.

HORACE. Well?

CAL. Nothing. I just went down and spoke my piece. Just like you told me. I say, "Mr. Horace he thank you mightily for the safe box arriving in good shape and he say you come right after supper to his house and bring Mr. Attorney-at-law Sol Fowler with you." Then I wipe my hands on my coat. Every time I ever told a lie in my whole life, I wipe my hands right after. Can't help doing it. Well, while I'm wiping my hands, Mr. Leo jump up and say to me, "What box? What you talking about?"

HORACE. [*Smiles.*] Did he?

CAL. And Mr. Leo say he got to leave a little early cause he got something to do. And then Mr. Manders say Mr. Leo should sit right down and finish up his work and stop acting like somebody made him Mr. President. So he sit down. Now, just like I told you, Mr. Manders was mighty surprised with the message because he knows right well he brought the box— [*Points to box, sighs.*] But he took it all right. Some men take everything easy and some do not.

HORACE. [*Puts his head back, laughs.*] Mr. Leo was telling the truth; he *has* got something to do. I hope Manders don't keep him too long. [*Outside there is the sound of voices.* CAL *exits.* ADDIE *crosses quickly to* HORACE, *puts basket on table, begins to wheel his chair towards the stairs. Sharply.*] No. Leave me where I am.

ADDIE. But that's Miss Regina coming back.

HORACE. [*Nods, looking at door.*] Go away, Addie.

ADDIE. [*Hesitates.*] Mr. Horace. Don't talk no more today. You don't feel well and it won't do no good—

HORACE. [*As he hears footsteps in the hall.*] Go on. [*She looks at him for a second, then picks up her sewing from table and exits as* REGINA *comes in from hall.* HORACE's *chair is now so placed that he is in front of the table with the medicine.* REGINA *stands in the hall, shakes umbrella, stands it in the corner, takes off her cloak and throws it over the banister. She stares at* HORACE.]

REGINA. [*As she takes off her gloves.*] We had agreed that you were to stay in your part of this house and I in mine. This room is *my* part of the house. Please don't come down here again.

HORACE. I won't.

REGINA. [*Crosses towards bell-cord.*] I'll get Cal to take you upstairs.

HORACE. [*Smiles.*] Before you do I want to tell you that after all, we have invested our money in Hubbard Sons and Marshall, Cotton Manufacturers.

REGINA. [*Stops, turns, stares at him.*] What are you talking about? You haven't seen Ben— When did you change your mind?

HORACE. I didn't change my mind. *I* didn't invest the money. [*Smiles.*] It was invested for me.

REGINA. [*Angrily.*] What—?

HORACE. I had eighty-eight thousand dollars' worth of Union Pacific bonds in that safe-deposit box. They are not there now. Go and look. [*As she stares at him, he points to the box.*] Go and look, Regina. [*She crosses quickly to the box, opens it.*] Those bonds are as negotiable as money.

REGINA. [*Turns back to him.*] What kind of joke are you playing now? Is this for my benefit?

HORACE. I don't look in that box very often, but three days ago, on Wednesday it was, because I had made a decision—

REGINA. I want to know what you are talking about.

HORACE. [*Sharply.*] Don't interrupt me again. Because I had made a decision, I sent for the box. The bonds were gone. Eighty-eight thousand dollars gone. [*He smiles at her.*]

REGINA. [*After a moment's silence, quietly.*] Do you think I'm crazy enough to believe what you're saying?

HORACE. [*Shrugs.*] Believe anything you like.

REGINA. [*Stares at him, slowly.*] Where did they go to?

HORACE. They are in Chicago. With Mr. Marshall, I should guess.

REGINA. What did they do? Walk to Chicago? Have you really gone crazy?

HORACE. Leo took the bonds.

REGINA. [*Turns sharply then speaks softly, without conviction.*] I don't believe it.

HORACE. [*Leans forward.*] I wasn't there but I can guess what happened. This fine gentleman, to whom you were willing to marry your daughter, took the keys and opened the box. You remember that the day of the fight Oscar went to Chicago?

Well, he went with my bonds that his son Leo had stolen for him. [*Pleasantly.*] And for Ben, of course, too.

REGINA. [*Slowly, nods.*] When did you find out the bonds were gone?

HORACE. Wednesday night.

REGINA. I thought that's what you said. Why have you waited three days to do anything? [*Suddenly laughs.*] This *will* make a fine story.

HORACE. [*Nods.*] Couldn't it?

REGINA. [*Still laughing.*] A fine story to hold over their heads. How could they be such fools? [*Turns to him.*]

HORACE. But I'm not going to hold it over their heads.

REGINA. [*The laugh stops.*] What?

HORACE. [*Turns his chair to face her.*] I'm going to let them keep the bonds—as a loan from you. An eighty-eight-thousand-dollar loan; they should be grateful to you. They will be, I think.

REGINA. [*Slowly, smiles.*] I see. You are punishing me. But I won't let you punish me. If you won't do anything, I will. Now. [*She starts for door.*]

HORACE. You won't do anything. Because you can't. [REGINA *stops.*] It won't do you any good to make trouble because I shall simply say that I lent them the bonds.

REGINA. [*Slowly.*] You would do that?

HORACE. Yes. For once in your life I am tying your hands. There is nothing for you to do. [*There is silence. Then she sits down.*]

REGINA. I see. You are going to lend them the bonds and let them keep all the profit they make on them, and there is nothing I can do about it. Is that right?

HORACE. Yes.

REGINA. [*Softly.*] Why did you say that I was making this gift?

HORACE. I was coming to that. I am going to make a new will, Regina, leaving you eighty-eight thousand dollars in Union Pacific bonds. The rest will go to Zan. It's true that your brothers have borrowed your share for a little while. After my death I advise you to talk to Ben and Oscar. They won't admit anything and Ben, I think, will be smart enough to see that he's safe. Because I knew about the theft and said nothing. Nor will I say anything as long as I live. Is that clear to you?

REGINA. [*Nods, softly, without looking*

at him.] You will not say anything as long as you live.

HORACE. That's right. And by that time they will probably have replaced your bonds, and then they'll belong to you and nobody but us will ever know what happened. [*Stops, smiles.*] They'll be around any minute to see what I am going to do. I took good care to see that word reached Leo. They'll be mighty relieved to know I'm going to do nothing and Ben will think it all a capital joke on you. And that will be the end of that. There's nothing you can do to them, nothing you can do to me.

REGINA. You hate me very much.

HORACE. No.

REGINA. Oh, I think you do. [*Puts her head back, sighs.*] Well, we haven't been very good together. Anyway, I don't hate you either. I have only contempt for you. I've always had.

HORACE. From the very first?

REGINA. I think so.

HORACE. I was in love with *you.* But why did *you* marry *me?*

REGINA. I was lonely when I was young.

HORACE. *You* were lonely?

REGINA. Not the way people usually mean. Lonely for all the things I wasn't going to get. Everybody in this house was so busy and there was so little place for what I wanted. I wanted the world. Then, and then— [*Smiles.*] Papa died and left the money to Ben and Oscar.

HORACE. And you married me?

REGINA. Yes, I thought— But I was wrong. You were a small-town clerk then. You haven't changed.

HORACE. [*Nods, smiles.*] And that wasn't what you wanted.

REGINA. No. No, it wasn't what I wanted. [*Pauses, leans back, pleasantly.*] It took me a little while to find out I had made a mistake. As for you—I don't know. It was almost as if I couldn't stand the kind of man you were— [*Smiles, softly.*] I used to lie there at night, praying you wouldn't come near—

HORACE. Really? It was as bad as that?

REGINA. [*Nods.*] Remember when I went to Doctor Sloan and I told you he said there was something the matter with me and that you shouldn't touch me any more?

HORACE. I remember.

REGINA. But you believed it. I couldn't understand that. I couldn't understand that anybody could be such a soft fool. That was when I began to despise you.

HORACE. [*Puts his hand to his throat, looks at the bottle of medicine on table.*] Why didn't you leave me?

REGINA. I told you I married you for something. It turned out it was only for this. [*Carefully.*] This wasn't what I wanted, but it was something. I never thought about it much but if I had [HORACE *puts his hand to his throat.*] I'd have known that you would die before I would. But I couldn't have known that you would get heart trouble so early and so bad. I'm lucky, Horace. I've always been lucky. [HORACE *turns slowly to the medicine.*] I'll be lucky again. [HORACE *looks at her. Then he puts his hand to his throat. Because he cannot reach the bottle he moves the chair closer. He reaches for the medicine, takes out the cork, picks up the spoon. The bottle slips and smashes on the table. He draws in his breath, gasps.*]

HORACE. Please. Tell Addie— The other bottle is upstairs. [REGINA *has not moved. She does not move now. He stares at her. Then, suddenly as if he understood, he raises his voice. It is a panic-stricken whisper, too small to be heard outside the room.*] Addie! Addie! Come— [*Stops as he hears the softness of his voice. He makes a sudden, furious spring from the chair to the stairs, taking the first few steps as if he were a desperate runner. On the fourth step he slips, gasps, grasps the rail, makes a great effort to reach the landing. When he reaches the landing, he is on his knees. His knees give way, he falls on the landing, out of view.* REGINA *has not turned during his climb up the stairs. Now she waits a second. Then she goes below the landing, speaks up.*]

REGINA. Horace. Horace. [*When there is no answer, she turns, calls.*] Addie! Cal! Come in here. [*She starts up the steps.* ADDIE *and* CAL *appear. Both run towards the stairs.*] He's had an attack. Come up here. [*They run up the steps quickly.*]

CAL. My God. Mr. Horace—

[*They cannot be seen now.*]

REGINA. [*Her voice comes from the head of the stairs.*] Be still, Cal. Bring him in here.

[*Before the footsteps and the voices have completely died away,* ALEX-

ANDRA *appears in the hall door, in her raincloak and hood. She comes into the room, begins to unfasten the cloak, suddenly looks around, sees the empty wheel chair, stares, begins to move swiftly as if to look in the dining room. At the same moment* ADDIE *runs down the stairs.* ALEXANDRA *turns and stares up at* ADDIE.]

ALEXANDRA. Addie! What?

ADDIE. [*Takes* ALEXANDRA *by the shoulders.*] I'm going for the doctor. Go upstairs. [ALEXANDRA *looks at her, then quickly breaks away and runs up the steps.* ADDIE *exits. The stage is empty for a minute. Then the front door bell begins to ring. When there is no answer, it rings again. A second later* LEO *appears in the hall, talking as he comes in.*]

LEO. [*Very nervous.*] Hello. [*Irritably.*] Never saw any use ringing a bell when a door was open. If you are going to ring a bell, then somebody should answer it. [*Gets in the room, looks around, puzzled, listens, hears no sound.*] Aunt Regina. [*He moves around restlessly.*] Addie. [*Waits.*] Where the hell— [*Crosses to the bell cord, rings it impatiently, waits, gets no answer, calls.*] Cal! Cal! [CAL *appears on the stair landing.*]

CAL. [*His voice is soft, shaken.*] Mr. Leo. Miss Regina says you stop that screaming noise.

LEO. [*Angrily.*] Where is everybody?

CAL. Mr. Horace he got an attack. He's bad. Miss Regina says you stop that noise.

LEO. Uncle Horace— What— What happened? [CAL *starts down the stairs, shakes his head, begins to move swiftly off.* LEO *looks around wildly.*] But when— You seen Mr. Oscar or Mr. Ben? [CAL *shakes his head. Moves on.* LEO *grabs him by the arm.*] Answer me, will you?

CAL. No, I ain't seen 'em. I ain't got time to answer you. I got to get things. [CAL *runs off.*]

LEO. But what's the matter with him? When did this happen— [*Calling after* CAL.] You'd think Papa'd be some place where you could find him. I been chasing him all afternoon.

[OSCAR *and* BEN *come into the room, talking excitedly.*]

OSCAR. I hope it's not a bad attack.

BEN. It's the first one he's had since he came home.

LEO. Papa, I've been looking all over town for you and Uncle Ben—

BEN. Where is he?

OSCAR. Addie said it was sudden.

BEN. [*To* LEO.] Where is he? When did it happen?

LEO. Upstairs. Will you listen to me, please? I been looking for you for—

OSCAR. [*To* BEN.] You think we should go up? [BEN, *looking up the steps, shakes his head.*]

BEN. I don't know. I don't know.

OSCAR. [*Shakes his head.*] But he was all right—

LEO. [*Yelling.*] Will you listen to me?

OSCAR. [*Sharply.*] What is the matter with you?

LEO. I been trying to tell you. I been trying to find you for an hour—

OSCAR. Tell me what?

LEO. Uncle Horace knows about the bonds. He knows about them. He's had the box since Wednesday—

BEN. [*Sharply.*] Stop shouting! What the hell are you talking about?

LEO. [*Furiously.*] I'm telling you he knows about the bonds. Ain't that clear enough—

OSCAR. [*Grabbing* LEO's *arm.*] You Goddamn fool! Stop screaming!

BEN. Now what happened? Talk quietly.

LEO. You heard me. Uncle Horace knows about the bonds. He's known since Wednesday.

BEN. [*After a second.*] How do you know that?

LEO. Because Cal comes down to Manders and says the box came O.K. and—

OSCAR. [*Trembling.*] That might not mean a thing—

LEO. [*Angrily.*] No? It might not, huh? Then he says Manders should come here tonight and bring Sol Fowler with him. I guess that don't mean a thing either.

OSCAR. [*To* BEN.] Ben— What— Do you think he's seen the—

BEN. [*Motions to the box.*] There's the box. [*Both* OSCAR *and* LEO *turn sharply.* LEO *makes a leap to the box.*] You ass. Put it down. What are you going to do with it, eat it?

LEO. I'm going to— [*Starts.*]

BEN. [*Furiously.*] Put it down. Don't touch it again. Now sit down and shut up for a minute.

OSCAR. Since Wednesday. [*To* LEO.] You

said he had it since Wednesday. Why
didn't he say something— [*To* BEN.] I don't
understand—

LEO. [*Taking a step.*] I can put it back.
I can put it back before anybody knows.

BEN. [*Who is standing at the table,
softly.*] He's had it since Wednesday. Yet
he hasn't said a word to us.

OSCAR. *Why? Why?*

LEO. What's the difference why? He
was getting ready to say plenty. He was
going to say it to Fowler tonight—

OSCAR. [*Angrily.*] Be still. [*Turns to
BEN, looks at him, waits.*]

BEN. [*After a minute.*] I don't believe
that.

LEO. [*Wildly.*] You don't believe it?
What do I care what *you* believe? I do the
dirty work and then—

BEN. [*Turning his head sharply to* LEO.]
I'm remembering that. I'm remembering
that, Leo.

OSCAR. What do you mean?

LEO. You—

BEN. [*To* OSCAR.] If you don't shut that
little fool up, I'll show you what I mean.
For some reason he knows, but he don't
say a word.

OSCAR. Maybe he didn't know that *we*—

BEN. [*Quickly.*] That *Leo*— He's no fool.
Does Manders know the bonds are missing?

LEO. How could I tell? I was half crazy.
I don't think so. Because Manders seemed
kind of puzzled and—

OSCAR. But we got to find out— [*He
breaks off as* CAL *comes into the room
carrying a kettle of hot water.*]

BEN. How is he, Cal?

CAL. I don't know, Mr. Ben. He was bad.
[*Going towards stairs.*]

OSCAR. But when did it happen?

CAL. [*Shrugs.*] He wasn't feeling bad
early. [ADDIE *comes in quickly from the
hall.*] Then there he is next thing on the
landing, fallen over, his eyes tight—

ADDIE. [*To* CAL.] Dr. Sloan's over at the
Ballongs. Hitch the buggy and go get him.
[*She takes the kettle and cloths from him,
pushes him, runs up the stairs.*] Go on.
[*She disappears.* CAL *exits.*]

BEN. Never seen Sloan anywhere when
you need him.

OSCAR. [*Softly.*] Sounds bad.

LEO. He would have told *her* about it.

Aunt Regina. He would have told his own
wife—

BEN. [*Turning to* LEO.] Yes, he might
have told her. But they weren't on such
pretty terms and maybe he didn't. Maybe
he didn't. [*Goes quickly to* LEO.] Now,
listen to me. If she doesn't know, it may
work out all right. If she does know, you're
to say he lent you the bonds.

LEO. Lent them to me! Who's going to
believe that?

BEN. Nobody.

OSCAR. [*To* LEO.] Don't you understand?
It can't do no harm to say it—

LEO. Why should I say he lent them to
me? Why not to you? [*Carefully.*] Why
not to Uncle Ben?

BEN. [*Smiles.*] Just because he didn't
lend them to me. Remember that.

LEO. But all he has to do is say he didn't
lend them to me—

BEN. [*Furiously.*] But for some reason,
he doesn't seem to be talking, does he?
[*There are footsteps above. They all
stand looking at the stairs.* REGINA
begins to come slowly down.]

BEN. What happened?

REGINA. He's had a bad attack.

OSCAR. Too bad. I'm so sorry we weren't
here when—when Horace needed us.

BEN. When *you* needed us.

REGINA. [*Looks at him.*] Yes.

BEN. How is he? Can we—can we go up?

REGINA. [*Shakes her head.*] He's not
conscious.

OSCAR. [*Pacing around.*] It's that—it's
that bad? Wouldn't you think Sloan could
be found quickly, just once, just once?

REGINA. I don't think there is much for
him to do.

BEN. Oh, don't talk like that. He's come
through attacks before. He will now.
[REGINA *sits down. After a second she
speaks softly.*]

REGINA. Well. We haven't seen each
other since the day of our fight.

BEN. [*Tenderly.*] That was nothing.
Why, you and Oscar and I used to fight
when we were kids.

OSCAR. [*Hurriedly.*] Don't you think we
should go up? Is there anything we can do
for Horace—

BEN. You don't feel well. Ah—

REGINA. [*Without looking at them.*] No,
I don't. [*Slight pause.*] Horace told me

about the bonds this afternoon. [*There is an immediate shocked silence.*]

LEO. The bonds. What do you mean? What bonds? What—

BEN. [*Looks at him furiously. Then to* REGINA.] The Union Pacific bonds? *Horace's* Union Pacific bonds?

REGINA. Yes.

OSCAR. [*Steps to her, very nervously.*] Well. Well what—what about them? What— could he say?

REGINA. He said that Leo had stolen the bonds and given them to you.

OSCAR. [*Aghast, very loudly.*] That's ridiculous, Regina, absolutely—

LEO. I don't know what you're talking about. What would I— Why—

REGINA. [*Wearily to* BEN.] Isn't it enough that he stole them from me? Do I have to listen to this in the bargain?

OSCAR. You are talking—

LEO. I didn't steal anything. I don't know why—

REGINA. [*To* BEN.] Would you ask them to stop that, please? [*There is silence for a minute.* BEN *glowers at* OSCAR *and* LEO.]

BEN. Aren't we starting at the wrong end, Regina? What did Horace tell you?

REGINA. [*Smiles at him.*] He told me that Leo had stolen the bonds.

LEO. I didn't steal—

REGINA. Please. Let me finish. Then he told me that he was going to pretend that he had lent them to you [LEO *turns sharply to* REGINA, *then looks at* OSCAR, *then looks back at* REGINA.] as a present from me— to my brothers. He said there was nothing I could do about it. He said the rest of his money would go to Alexandra. That is all. [*There is a silence.* OSCAR *coughs,* LEO *smiles slyly.*]

LEO. [*Taking a step to her.*] I told you he had lent them— I could have told you—

REGINA. [*Ignores him, smiles sadly at* BEN.] So I'm very badly off, you see. [*Carefully.*] But Horace said there was nothing I could do about it as long as he was alive to say he had lent you the bonds.

BEN. You shouldn't feel that way. It can all be explained, all be adjusted. It isn't as bad—

REGINA. So you, at least, are willing to admit that the bonds were stolen?

BEN. [OSCAR *laughs nervously.*] I admit no such thing. It's possible that Horace made up that part of the story to tease

you— [*Looks at her.*] Or perhaps to punish you. Punish you.

REGINA. [*Sadly.*] It's not a pleasant story. I feel bad, Ben, naturally. I hadn't thought—

BEN. Now you shall have the bonds safely back. That was the understanding, wasn't it, Oscar?

OSCAR. Yes.

REGINA. I'm glad to know that. [*Smiles.*] Ah, I had greater hopes—

BEN. Don't talk that way. That's foolish. [*Looks at his watch.*] I think we ought to drive out for Sloan ourselves. If we can't find him we'll go over to Senateville for Doctor Morris. And don't think I'm dismissing this other business. I'm not. We'll have it all out on a more appropriate day.

REGINA. [*Looks up, quietly.*] I don't think you had better go yet. I think you had better stay and sit down.

BEN. We'll be back with Sloan.

REGINA. Cal has gone for him. I don't want you to go.

BEN. Now don't worry and—

REGINA. You will come back in this room and sit down. I have something more to say.

BEN. [*Turns, comes towards her.*] Since when do I take orders from you?

REGINA. [*Smiles.*] You don't—yet. [*Sharply.*] Come back, Oscar. You too, Leo.

OSCAR. [*Sure of himself, laughs.*] My dear Regina—

BEN. [*Softly, pats her hand.*] Horace has already clipped your wings and very wittily. Do I have to clip them, too? [*Smiles at her.*] You'd get farther with a smile, Regina. I'm a soft man for a woman's smile.

REGINA. I'm smiling, Ben. I'm smiling because you are quite safe while Horace lives. But I don't think Horace will live. And if he doesn't live I shall want seventy-five per cent in exchange for the bonds.

BEN. [*Steps back, whistles, laughs.*] Greedy! What a greedy girl you are! You want so much of everything.

REGINA. Yes. And if I don't get what I want I am going to put all three of you in jail.

OSCAR. [*Furiously.*] You're mighty crazy. Having just admitted—

BEN. And on what evidence would you put Oscar and Leo in jail?

REGINA. [*Laughs, gaily.*] Oscar, listen

to him. He's getting ready to swear that it was you and Leo! What do you say to that? [OSCAR *turns furiously towards* BEN.] Oh, don't be angry, Oscar. I'm going to see that he goes in with you.

BEN. Try anything you like, Regina. [*Sharply.*] And now we can stop all this and say good-bye to you. [ALEXANDRA *comes slowly down the steps.*] It's his money and he's obviously willing to let us borrow it. [*More pleasantly.*] Learn to make threats when you can carry them through. For how many years have I told you a good-looking woman gets more by being soft and appealing? Mama used to tell you that. [*Looks at his watch.*] Where the hell is Sloan? [*To* OSCAR.] Take the buggy and— [*As* BEN *turns to* OSCAR, *he sees* ALEXANDRA. *She walks stiffly. She goes slowly to the lower window, her head bent. They all turn to look at her.*]

OSCAR. [*After a second, moving toward her.*] What? Alexandra— [*She does not answer. After a second,* ADDIE *comes slowly down the stairs, moving as if she were very tired. At foot of steps, she looks at* ALEXANDRA, *then turns and slowly crosses to door and exits.* REGINA *rises.* BEN *looks nervously at* ALEXANDRA, *at* REGINA.]

OSCAR. [*As* ADDIE *passes him, irritably to* ALEXANDRA.] Well, what is— [*Turns into room—sees* ADDIE *at foot of steps.*]— what's? [BEN *puts up a hand, shakes his head.*] My God, I didn't know—who *could* have known—I didn't know he was that sick. Well, well—I— [REGINA *stands quietly, her back to them.*]

BEN. [*Softly, sincerely.*] Seems like yesterday when he first came here.

OSCAR. [*Sincerely, nervously.*] Yes, that's true. [*Turns to* BEN.] The whole town loved him and respected him.

ALEXANDRA. [*Turns.*] Did you love him, Uncle Oscar?

OSCAR. Certainly, I— What a strange thing to ask! I—

ALEXANDRA. Did you love him, Uncle Ben?

BEN. [*Simply.*] He had—

ALEXANDRA. [*Suddenly starts to laugh very loudly.*] And you, Mama, did you love him, too?

REGINA. I know what you feel, Alexandra, but please try to control yourself.

ALEXANDRA. [*Still laughing.*] I'm trying, Mama. I'm trying very hard.

BEN. Grief makes some people laugh and some people cry. It's better to cry, Alexandra.

ALEXANDRA. [*The laugh has stopped. Tensely moves toward* REGINA.] What was Papa doing on the staircase?

[BEN *turns to look at* ALEXANDRA.]

REGINA. Please go and lie down, my dear. We all need time to get over shocks like this. [ALEXANDRA *does not move.* REGINA'S *voice becomes softer, more insistent.*] Please go, Alexandra.

ALEXANDRA. No, Mama. I'll wait. I've got to talk to you.

REGINA. Later. Go and rest now.

ALEXANDRA. [*Quietly.*] I'll wait, Mama. I've plenty of time.

REGINA. [*Hesitates, stares, makes a half shrug, turns back to* BEN.] As I was saying. Tomorrow morning I am going up to Judge Simmes. I shall tell him about Leo.

BEN. [*Motioning toward* ALEXANDRA.] Not in front of the child, Regina. I—

REGINA. [*Turns to him. Sharply.*] I didn't ask her to stay. Tomorrow morning I go to Judge Simmes—

OSCAR. And what proof? What proof of all this—

REGINA. [*Turns sharply.*] None. I won't need any. The bonds are missing and they are with Marshall. That will be enough. If it isn't, I'll add what's necessary.

BEN. I'm sure of that.

REGINA. [*Turns to* BEN.] You can be quite sure.

OSCAR. We'll deny—

REGINA. Deny your heads off. You couldn't find a jury that wouldn't weep for a woman whose brothers steal from her. And you couldn't find twelve men in this state you haven't cheated and hate you for it.

OSCAR. What kind of talk is this? You couldn't do anything like that! We're your own brothers. [*Points upstairs.*] How can you talk that way when upstairs not five minutes ago—

REGINA. [*Slowly.*] There are people who can never go back, who must finish what they start. I am one of those people, Oscar. [*After a slight pause.*] Where was I? [*Smiles at* BEN.] Well, they'll convict you. But I won't care much if they don't. [*Leans forward, pleasantly.*] Because by that time you'll be ruined. I shall also tell my story to Mr. Marshall, who likes me,

I think, and who will not want to be involved in your scandal. A respectable firm like Marshall and Company. The deal would be off in an hour. [*Turns to them angrily.*] And you know it. Now I don't want to hear any more from any of you. *You'll do no more bargaining in this house.* I'll take my seventy-five per cent and we'll forget the story forever. That's one way of doing it, and the way I prefer. You know me well enough to know that I don't mind taking the other way.

BEN. [*After a second, slowly.*] None of us have ever known you well enough, Regina.

REGINA. You're getting old, Ben. Your tricks aren't as smart as they used to be. [*There is no answer. She waits, then smiles.*] All right. I take it that's settled and I get what I asked for.

OSCAR. [*Furiously to* BEN.] Are you going to let her do this—

BEN. [*Turns to look at him, slowly.*] You have a suggestion?

REGINA. [*Puts her arms above her head, stretches, laughs.*] No, he hasn't. All right. Now, Leo, I have forgotten that you ever saw the bonds. [*Archly, to* BEN *and* OSCAR.] And as long as you boys both behave yourselves, I've forgotten that we ever talked about them. You can draw up the necessary papers tomorrow. [BEN *laughs.* LEO *stares at him, starts for door. Exits.* OSCAR *moves towards door angrily.* REGINA *looks at* BEN, *nods, laughs with him. For a second,* OSCAR *stands in the door, looking back at them. Then he exits.*]

REGINA. You're a good loser, Ben. I like that.

BEN. [*He picks up his coat, then turns to her.*] Well, I say to myself, what's the good? You and I aren't like Oscar. We're not sour people. I think that comes from a good digestion. Then, too, one loses today and wins tomorrow. I say to myself, years of planning and I get what I want. Then I don't get it. But I'm not discouraged. The century's turning, the world is open. Open for people like you and me. Ready for us, waiting for us. After all this is just the beginning. There are hundreds of Hubbards sitting in rooms like this throughout the country. All their names aren't Hubbard, but they are all Hubbards and they will own this country some day. We'll get along.

REGINA. [*Smiles.*] I think so.

BEN. Then, too, I say to myself, things may change. [*Looks at* ALEXANDRA.] I agree with Alexandra. What is a man in a wheel chair doing on a staircase? I ask myself that.

REGINA. [*Looks up at him.*] And what do you answer?

BEN. I have no answer. But maybe some day I will. Maybe never, but maybe some day. [*Smiles. Pats her arm.*] When I do, I'll let you know. [*Goes towards hall.*]

REGINA. When you do, write me. I will be in Chicago. [*Gaily.*] Ah, Ben, if Papa had only left me his money.

BEN. I'll see you tomorrow.

REGINA. Oh, yes. Certainly. You'll be sort of working for me now.

BEN. [*As he passes* ALEXANDRA, *smiles.*] Alexandra, you're turning out to be a right interesting girl. [*Looks at* REGINA.] Well, good night all. [*He exits.*]

REGINA. [*Sits quietly for a second, stretches, turns to look at* ALEXANDRA.] What do you want to talk to me about, Alexandra?

ALEXANDRA. [*Slowly.*] I've changed my mind. I don't want to talk. There's nothing to talk about now.

REGINA. You're acting very strange. Not like yourself. You've had a bad shock today. I know that. And you loved Papa, but you must have expected this to come some day. You knew how sick he was.

ALEXANDRA. I knew. We all knew.

REGINA. It will be good for you to get away from here. Good for me, too. Time heals most wounds, Alexandra. You're young, you shall have all the things I wanted. I'll make the world for you the way I wanted it to be for me. [*Uncomfortably.*] Don't sit there staring. You've been around Birdie so much you're getting just like her.

ALEXANDRA. [*Nods.*] Funny. That's what Aunt Birdie said today.

REGINA. [*Nods.*] Be good for you to get away from all this.

[ADDIE *enters.*]

ADDIE. Cal is back, Miss Regina. He says Dr. Sloan will be coming in a few minutes.

REGINA. We'll go in a few weeks. A few weeks! That means two or three Saturdays, two or three Sundays. [*Sighs.*] Well, I'm very tired. I shall go to bed. I don't want any supper. Put the lights out and lock up.

[ADDIE *moves to the piano lamp, turns it out.*] You go to your room, Alexandra. Addie will bring you something hot. You look very tired. [*Rises. To* ADDIE.] Call me when Dr. Sloan gets here. I don't want to see anybody else. I don't want any condolence calls tonight. The whole town will be over.

ALEXANDRA. Mama, I'm not coming with you. I'm not going to Chicago.

REGINA. [*Turns to her.*] You're very upset, Alexandra.

ALEXANDRA. [*Quietly.*] I mean what I say. With all my heart.

REGINA. We'll talk about it tomorrow. The morning will make a difference.

ALEXANDRA. It won't make any difference. And there isn't anything to talk about. I am going away from you. Because I want to. Because I know Papa would want me to.

REGINA. [*Puzzled, careful, polite.*] You *know* your papa wanted you to go away from me?

ALEXANDRA. Yes.

REGINA. [*Softly.*] And if I say no?

ALEXANDRA. [*Looks at her.*] Say it, Mama, say it. And see what happens.

REGINA. [*Softly, after a pause.*] And if I make you stay?

ALEXANDRA. That would be foolish. It wouldn't work in the end.

REGINA. You're very serious about it, aren't you? [*Crosses to stairs.*] Well, you'll change your mind in a few days.

ALEXANDRA. You only change your mind when you want to. And I won't want to.

REGINA. [*Going up the steps.*] Alexandra, I've come to the end of my rope. Somewhere there has to be what I want, too. Life goes too fast. Do what you want; think what you want; go where you want. I'd like to keep you with me, but I won't make you stay. Too many people used to make me do too many things. No, I won't make you stay.

ALEXANDRA. You couldn't, Mama, because I want to leave here. As I've never wanted anything in my life before. Because now I understand what Papa was trying to tell me. [*Pause.*] All in one day: Addie said there were people who ate the earth and other people who stood around and watched them do it. And just now Uncle Ben said the same thing. Really, he said the same thing. [*Tensely.*] Well, tell him for me, Mama, I'm not going to stand around and watch you do it. Tell him I'll be fighting as hard as he'll be fighting [*Rises.*] some place where people don't just stand around and watch.

REGINA. Well, you have spirit, after all. I used to think you were all sugar water. We don't have to be bad friends. I don't want us to be bad friends, Alexandra. [*Starts, stops, turns to* ALEXANDRA.] Would you like to come and talk to me, Alexandra? Would you—would you like to sleep in my room tonight?

ALEXANDRA. [*Takes a step towards her.*] Are you afraid, Mama? [*Regina does not answer. She moves slowly out of sight.* ADDIE *comes to* ALEXANDRA, *presses her arm.*]

THE CURTAIN FALLS

For Discussion and Writing

1. *The Little Foxes* has frequently been called a masterpiece of dramatic construction. Discuss the various techniques in this play that merit such description.

What are the various threads or story lines woven into the structure of *The Little Foxes?* What is the binding or unifying device?

Where does the play surprise you with reversals of what you expect to happen? Do these reversals grow out of the plot or out of the characters? Point to scenes in the play that support your opinion.

2. What tricks or contrived devices does Miss Hellman make bold use of in *The Little Foxes?* Discuss your reactions as to whether these devices hurt or help the play.

3. Discuss whether, in your opinion, the theme of *The Little Foxes* calls for the use of violence and evil, or are violence and evil used for their own sake? Can you think of any way to carry out the theme in a less horrifying fashion?

4. In *The Little Foxes,* why does the playwright have the Hubbards use the word "nigger"? What does this tell you about their characters?

5. Since *The Little Foxes* was a social drama written during the economic turbulence of the Depression, there was considerable difference among viewers as to its true significance, namely:

Was the Hubbard family a symbol of the capitalist system?

Was the play a morality play attacking the vices of greed and avarice in all humans?

Was it just a play about one particular family with no universal implications at all?

Discuss which of these interpretations you believe most valid.

6. Early in Act III, Addie says, "Well, there are people who eat the earth and eat all the people on it like in the Bible with the locusts. Then there are people who stand around and watch them eat it. Sometimes I think it ain't right to stand and watch them do it."

The idea in this quotation is repeated later by Ben and by Alexandra. Find their speeches and discuss how they help to reveal the theme of the play. Divide the characters in this play into the "locusts," the "watchers," and the "fighters."

7. Miss Hellman had once contemplated a sequel to *The Little Foxes* to be set twenty years later. Choose either of the two following incidents and write it as a scene occurring in such a sequel.

A gathering of the Hubbard clan at the funeral of Birdie.

A meeting between Regina and her daughter who have not seen each other for the twenty-year span. This can be a chance meeting or a planned one. It can take place anywhere you choose with any characters you want to add.

The Rainmaker

{1954}

N. RICHARD NASH

CHARACTERS

(In Order of Appearance)

H. C. CURRY	FILE
NOAH CURRY	SHERIFF THOMAS
JIM CURRY	BILL STARBUCK
LIZZIE CURRY	

SCENES

*The play takes place in a Western state on a summer
day in a time of drought*

ACT ONE: Day

ACT TWO: That evening

ACT THREE: Later the same night

$\mathcal{F}$or fifteen long years, Richard Nash worked on *The Rainmaker*, first as an outline for the libretto of a musical, then as a full length play, and finally as the outline for a novel. When none of these received attention, he rewrote the work as a television drama which was successfully produced.

In 1954, *The Rainmaker* opened on Broadway, not as a musical, but as the stage play included in this volume. Since then, it has been turned into a motion picture, revised for amateur theaters, translated into thirty languages, published in drama magazines and anthologies. It finally found its way back to Broadway as the musical *110 in the Shade* in 1964.

The play is a "romantic comedy," which is perhaps best defined as a play that introduces both an element of the imaginative into the ordinary affairs of life and a heightened emotional mood that guarantees a happy ending. No matter how strongly we feel that in real life things couldn't possibly work out this way, we willingly suspend our usual scepticism during the course of a "romantic comedy."

Foreword

When drought hits the lush grasslands of the richly fertile West, they are green no more and the dying is a palpable thing. What happens to verdure and vegetation, to cattle and livestock can be read in the coldly statistical little bulletin freely issued by the Department of Agriculture. What happens to the people of the West—beyond the calculable and terrible phenomena of sudden poverty and loss of substance—is an incalculable and febrile kind of desperation. Rain will never come again; the earth will be sere forever; and in all of heaven there is no promise of remedy.

Yet, men of wisdom like H. C. Curry know to be patient with heaven. They know that the earth will not thirst forever; they know that one day they will again awaken to a green morning. Young people like Lizzie, his daughter, cannot know this as certainly as he does. Bright as she is, she cannot know. She can only count the shooting stars, and hope.

The play is set in such a drought-beset region in the moment when Lizzie's hope is faltering. Because the hopes of Lizzie and H. C., of Jim and Starbuck and File are finally brought to blessing, because the people of the play are deserving and filled with love of one another—and most important, because it is not always that the hopes of deserving, loving human beings *are* blessed—this play is a comedy and a romance. It must never be forgotten that it is a romance, never for an instant by the director, the actors, the scenic designer or the least-sung usher in the theatre.

In this regard there must be, without eschewing truth, a kind of romantic beauty in the relationships of all the characters with one another. Especially so in the Curry family, even when Noah is laying down the stern law of a rigid God who, to Noah, looks rather like an irate Certified Public Accountant. There must be love in the house, or somewhere a benign promise.

This same felicity in the sets. True, the Curry ranch house—the living and dining rooms, the kitchen—is a place where people scratch their heads and take their shoes off, where woodwork has to be scrubbed and pots scoured. But more important, it is a place where beauty is made out of affection and all manner of gentleness. The tack room, if seen realistically, might be a dust bin attractive only to the termites and the rodents of the night. But if the designer sees it romantically—as Lizzie might see it, with all its memorabilia of childhood—it will tell the hopeful promise intended. Or File's office—it is not an office really, although File's roll-top desk is there and his old-fashioned telephone—it is File's secret hiding place from the world, the island where he errantly believes he can bring balm to his loneliness.

Despite the mention of many playing areas, it is essential that this be a one-set play. The center stage area should be the house—the living room or "parlor" as they called it in those days, combined with dining and kitchen areas into one large playing space, taking up perhaps half the stage. Down right, File's office, approximately a quarter of the stage—and down left, the tack room, the remaining quarter. It is essential that it be a one-set play —not for reasons of production economy, although economies will fortuitously flow from it—but because the designer can best serve the unity intended if the visual effects seem to be closely related and unified. And in the same regard—to avoid time separations as well as spatial ones—there must be no lowering of a curtain between scenes—merely a dimming of light in one area and a lift in light in another.

If there is incidental music in the play, it should sing on the romantic instruments and forswear brass and tympani. It should lament on strings and woodwinds and promise sweet melody.

Perhaps the best rule of thumb in direction, acting, scenery, music is this oversimplification: Let us not use the panoramic lenses. Let us focus closely, but through a romantically gauzed lens, on the face of Lizzie's loneliness, and on her hope. Life can be seen deeply through small lenses. And truthfully even through gauze.

The Rainmaker

ACT ONE

The lights come up slowly to reveal the center area of the stage which is the interior of the CURRY *house. The* CURRY *ranch is a prosperous one and the house is a place where gentle, kindly people who have an uneducated but profoundly true sense of beauty have lived in love of one another. It is strongly masculine in its basic structure—brick and hand-hewn beams and such—but it shows* LIZZIE'S *hand in many of its appointments. We see a comfortable kitchen on the left; the rest of the downstairs living area is a combination of living and dining room. One of the earliest telephones on the wall; a gramophone with a horn; a primitive radio, a crystal set which, when operated, sets up a fearful screech of static. There are stairs to the bedrooms; a rear door to the ranch proper and to the barn and tack room; and a larger, more imposing front door to the private road that leads to the main highway.*

It is early morning of a scorching, drought-ridden day. Already the blazing sun has taken over the house.

When the lights are up we see H. C. CURRY *making breakfast. He is in his mid-fifties, powerfully set, capable, a good man to take store in. But he's not all prosaic efficiency—there is deep vision in him.*

A moment, then his oldest son, NOAH, *comes in from outdoors.* NOAH *is somewhat like his father, without* H.C.'s *imagination. As a matter of fact, he has little imagination at all—a somewhat self-righteous man, rigidly opinionated.*

NOAH. That you, Pop?

H.C. Yeah. Mornin', Noah.

NOAH. I heard somebody fussin' around in the kitchen—I was hopin' it was Lizzie.

H.C. She was so dead beat after her trip I figured I'd let her sleep.

NOAH. Yeah. I heard her walkin' her room last night until hell knows when. [*Looking at his pocket watch.*] Gettin' late. Maybe I better wake her up.

[*He starts for the stairs.*]

H.C. No, don't do that, Noah. She must of had a pretty rough time. Let her sleep it off.

NOAH. Well, if she had a rough time—it was your idea. . . . I was sure hopin' she'd cook breakfast. [*Then, quickly, with a half smile, so as not to offend* H.C.] But I guess if we didn't croak after a week of your cookin', we can live through another meal.

[NOAH *goes to the radio and fiddles with it. It screeches.*]

H.C. Noah, Jimmy just fixed that thing—don't you go breakin' it again.

NOAH. If that kid's gonna waste his money on a darnfool crystal set—why can't we get some good out of it? Can't hear a thing.

H.C. What do you want to hear?

NOAH. Thought somebody'd say somethin' about the drought.

H.C. Only one thing to say. No rain.

NOAH. [*Switching off the set.*] And no sign of it, neither. [*He goes to the calendar alongside of which hangs a pencil on a string.*] Well, cross out another day.

H.C. Noah, I wish you wouldn't do that—you and that damn calendar. Why'n't you stop countin'? When it rains, it rains!

NOAH. I'd sure like to take it easy like you and Jim. You know what I seen this mornin'? Three more calves down and out—and a couple of heifers! And you know what I had to do? I had to give Sandy and Frank their time.

H.C. [*Disturbed.*] You mean you fired them?

NOAH. No—I just laid 'em off—till the drought's over.

H.C. You shouldn't of done that, Noah.

NOAH. Listen, Pop—if you want to take over the bookkeepin', you're welcome to it. [*Taking two large black ledgers off the desk.*] Here's the books—you can have 'em!

H.C. [*With a smile.*] Now, I wouldn't do that to you, Noah. You'd be lost without Accounts Receivable and Debit and Credit. [*As* NOAH *bridles.*] Don't get mad, Noah. What I mean is—I can't make head or tail out of your new-style system!

NOAH. All right then. Let's stick to the deal—the rest of you do the dreamin', I'll do the figurin'.

H.C. Yeah, but we said figures—not people.

NOAH. People are figures! Sandy and Frank are *red* figures! I don't like to lay nobody off any more'n you do—but it's gotta be done!

H.C. How do you want your eggs?

NOAH. What's the best way you can't ruin 'em?

H.C. Raw.

NOAH. I'll take 'em raw.

[NOAH *goes into the kitchen and comes back quickly with a couple of eggs. Almost simultaneously,* JIM CURRY *comes racing downstairs.* JIM *is the youngest in the family, in his early twenties—but he's big and broad-shouldered and looks older until he opens his mouth, and then he's a child. He has been convinced that he isn't very bright and this is his great cross. He is filled with inchoate longing. At the moment he is agog with excitement, as he nearly always is; but right now his frenzy has to do with universal catastrophe.*]

JIM. Mornin'! Mornin', Pop!

H.C. and NOAH. Mornin', Jimmy . . . Mornin'.

JIM. Pop! Pop, it's like I said yesterday—just like I told you!

H.C. What'd you tell me, Jim?

JIM. I said to you like this, I said: "Pop the whole world's gonna blow up!" I said: "The world's gonna get all s-w-o-l-e up—and bust right in our faces!"

H.C. You sure of that, Jimmy?

JIM. You bet I'm sure! And I ain't the only one thinks that way! Last night—at the dance—Gil Demby and the boys, they say to me: "Jim, whatta you think of this drought?" And I says to them: "The world's gonna blow up! It's gonna get all swole up and bust in our faces!" And you know what? They all said: "Jim Curry, you hit it right on the head!"

H.C. [*Gently, affectionately.*] They were kiddin' you, Jimmy.

JIM. No, they weren't! Gil Demby—he's been to college—and he said it's all got to do with the sun! You gotta understand, Pop—you see, the sun—it's got a lot of spots on it. And them spots is growin'. And one of these days them spots is gonna get so big the sun won't be able to shine through. And then, brother—bang!

NOAH. You keep thinkin' about that you're gonna miss your breakfast.

JIM. Yeah. Ain't no good thinkin' about it—it just gets me all upset. [*Noticing* NOAH's *food.*] Holy mackerel, Noah—them eggs is raw!

NOAH. What of it?

JIM. What's the matter—you sick?

NOAH. No, I ain't sick.

JIM. You sure must be sick if you're eatin' raw eggs.

H.C. He's all right, Jim. He just don't like my cookin'.

JIM. Why? You cook better'n Lizzie. I like the way you cook, Pop. Everything slides down nice and greasy.

H.C. [*Wryly accepting the dubious compliment.*] Thanks, Jim. How do you want your eggs?

JIM. Oh, any old way.

H.C. How many?

JIM. [*Casually.*] I guess five or six-ll do.

NOAH. He ain't so hungry today.

[JIM *has already begun to gorge on bread and jam.*]

NOAH. Jimmy . . .

JIM. [*Bolting his food—not looking up.*] Huh?

NOAH. Jimmy, if you'll come up for a minute, I got somethin' to say to you.

JIM. What?

NOAH. Last night . . . You coulda got yourself into a hatful of trouble.

JIM. [*Embarrassed to discuss it in front of his father.*] Do we have to talk about it now?

H.C. What kind of trouble, Noah?

NOAH. [*Distastefully.*] A certain girl named Snookie.

H.C. Oh—was Snookie at the dance?

NOAH. Was she at the dance? You'da thought nobody *else* was there! She comes drivin' up in a brand-new five-cylinder Essex car! And her hair is so bleach-blonde . . .

JIM. It ain't bleached!

NOAH. Don't tell me! Gil Demby says she comes into the store and buys a pint of peroxide every month.

JIM. What's that? I use peroxide for a cut finger.

NOAH. If she got cut that often she'd bleed to death.

JIM. You just don't like her 'cause she smokes cigarettes.

NOAH. Right in front of people!

H.C. [*Quietly.*] What happened, Jim?

NOAH. I'll tell you what happened. Along about nine-thirty I look around. No Jim—and no Snookie. That dumb kid—he walked outta that barn dance without even tippin' his hat. And he went off with that hot-pants girl.

JIM. I didn't go off with her—I went off by myself. I walked outside and I was lookin' at that Essex. And pretty soon she comes out and she's kinda starin' me up and down. And I says to her: "How many cylinders has this Essex got?" And she says: "Five." And then she says to me: "How tall are you?" And I says: "Six." And before you know it we're ridin' in the Essex and she's got that car racin' forty miles an hour. Man, it was fast!

NOAH. Everything about her is fast.

JIM. [*Rearing.*] Whatta you mean by that, Noah?

NOAH. Just what I said! [*To* H.C.] When the dance was over—when we were all supposed to go pick Lizzie up at the depot—I had to go lookin' for him. And you know where he was? He was sittin' in that girl's car—parked outside of Demby's store—and the two of them—I never seen such carryin's on! They were so twisted up together, I couldn't tell where he left off and Snookie began. If I hadn't of come along, hell knows what would of happened.

JIM. [*Tragically.*] Yeah . . . hell knows . . . I could of come home with her little red hat.

H.C. With her what?

NOAH. She wears a little red hat.

H.C. Well, why would you come home with her little red hat?

JIM. Nothin'—nothin'.

NOAH. Go on—tell him.

JIM. Noah—you quit it!

NOAH. Well, I'll tell him. She always wears this little red hat. And last night, Dumbo Hopkinson says to her: "Snookie, you gonna wear that little red hat all your life?" And she giggles and says: "Well, I hope not, Dumbo! I'm gonna give it to some handsome fella—when, as and if!" [*As* H.C. *smiles.*] It ain't funny, Pop! [*To* JIM.] Do you know what trouble you can get yourself into with a girl like that? A dumb kid like you—why, pretty soon she's got you hog-tied and you have to marry her!

JIM. Why don't you let me alone?

NOAH. [*Outraged.*] Did you hear that, Pop?

H.C. Maybe it's a good idea, Noah.

NOAH. What's a good idea?

H.C. To let him alone.

JIM. Maybe it is!

NOAH. [*Hurt; in high dudgeon.*] All right! If you want me to let you alone—kid, you're alone!

JIM. [*Withdrawing a little.*] I don't know what you're gettin' so mad about.

NOAH. You don't, huh? You think I like lookin' out for you? Well, I don't! Taggin' after me all your life! "How do I tie my shoelaces? How do I do long division?" Well, if you don't want me to give you no advice—if you think you're so smart, you just go and get along by yourself!

JIM. I ain't sayin' I'm so smart. Heck, I don't mind you tellin' me how to do and how to figure things out . . .

NOAH. [*Bitingly.*] Thanks!

JIM. What I mean—I appreciate it [*Bellowing.*] I just wish you wouldn' holler!

H.C. All right—that's enough, boys! [*A

moment. H.C. *goes to the thermometer.*]
A hundred and one degrees.

NOAH. If only it'd cool off at night.

JIM. I don't mind a hot night. [*Longingly.*] Somethin' about a hot night . . . Gets you kind of—well—all stirred up inside. . . . Why don't Lizzie come down and make our breakfast, Pop?

H.C. Let her sleep. She didn't sleep much last night.

JIM. Yeah. Gets off the train—comes home—and starts cleanin' up her bedroom in the middle of the night. Hell, there was no need for that. I cleaned her room up real nice.

H.C. [*Quietly.*] Jimmy, when some girls ain't happy, they cry. . . . Lizzie works.

JIM. Yeah. Well, what are we gonna do about her?

H.C. [*Worriedly.*] I don't know.

JIM. We gotta do *somethin'*, Pop. We gotta at least talk to her. Mention!

H.C. Who's gonna mention it to her?

JIM. Well . . . you're her father.

H.C. I don't see bein' her father's got everything to do with it. I could say you're her brothers.

NOAH. I told you, Pop—I'm not gonna mention it to her.

JIM. Me neither. I'm not gonna mention.

H.C. Stop sayin' exactly what Noah's sayin'. Speak for yourself.

JIM. I say what Noah is sayin' because I agree with him. When I don't, I spit in his eye.

H.C. Then why won't you talk with her?

JIM. Because if we do, she'll think we're tryin' to get rid of her.

H.C. She'll sure think the same if *I* do it.

NOAH. Maybe.

JIM. May *be.*

H.C. So there you are!

JIM. But you're her father and comes a time when a father's gotta mention.

H.C. I can't! I can't just speak up and say: "Lizzie, you gotta get married!" She knows she's gotta get married. We all know it.

NOAH. Well then—seems there's no point to mention anything.

[LIZZIE CURRY *comes down the stairs. At first glance, she seems a woman who can cope with all the aspects of her life. She has the world of materiality under control; she is a good housekeeper; pots and pans, needles and thread—when she touches them, they serve. She knows well where she fits in the family—she is daughter, sister, mother, child—and she enjoys the manifold elements of her position. She has a sure ownership of her own morality, for the tenets of right and wrong are friendly to her—and she is comfortably forthright in living by them. A strong and integral woman in every life function—except one. Here she is, twenty-seven years old, and no man outside the family has loved her or found her beautiful. And yet, ironically, it is this one unfulfilled part of* LIZZIE *that is the most potentially beautiful facet of the woman, this yearning for romance, this courageous searching for it in the desert of her existence. . . . But she is at great pains to conceal these hungers—by an open display of good humor, by laughter at herself—and by behaving, in a western world of men, as if she were as much a man as any of them.* LIZZIE, *the Tomboy. But if some day a man should find her, he will find no tomboy but a full and ready woman, willing to give herself with the totality of her rich being.*]

LIZZIE. Morning, Pop—Noah—Jimmy.

H.C. Mornin', honey.

NOAH and JIM. Mornin', Lizzie . . . Hi, Liz.

LIZZIE. Sure good to be home again.

H.C. Just what the boys were sayin'—sure good to have Lizzie home again.

LIZZIE. No sign of rain yet, is there?

H.C. Not a cloud nowhere.

LIZZIE. I dreamed we had a rain—a great big rain!

H.C. Did you, Lizzie?

LIZZIE. Thunderstorm! Rain coming down in sheets! Lightning flashed—thunder rolled up and down the canyon like a kid with a big drum! I looked up and I laughed and yelled . . . ! [*With a laugh.*] Oooh, it was wonderful!

NOAH. Drought's drought—and a dream's a dream.

LIZZIE. But it was a nice dream, Noah—and nearly as good as rain.

NOAH. Near ain't rain!

H.C. It's too bad we picked you up at

the depot so late last night, Lizzie. Didn't have much time to talk about your trip.

NOAH. Looks like it perked you up real good. Yeah, you were lookin' all dragged out by the heat. What was it like in Sweetriver?

LIZZIE. Hotter'n hell.

[POP and JIM laugh.]

NOAH. I don't see nothin' funny in her talkin' like a cowhand.

LIZZIE. Sorry, Noah. That's about all the conversation I've heard for a week.

H.C. How's Uncle Ned, Lizzie? And Aunt Ivy?

JIM. And how's all them boys?

LIZZIE. [Muscularly.] Big.

H.C. If they take after Aunt Ivy I bet they talked your ear off.

LIZZIE. No, they take after Uncle Ned. They just grunt.

NOAH. Who got to be the best-lookin' of the boys, Lizzie?

LIZZIE. Oh—I guess Pete.

H.C. Never could get those boys straight. Which one is Pete?

LIZZIE. He's the one with the yellow hair.

NOAH. [Quickly.] Yella hair's nice in a man!

JIM. It's honest!

LIZZIE. Oh, Pete was honest all right.

JIM. The way you said that I bet you liked him the best.

LIZZIE. Oh, I'm crazy about Pete—he asked me to marry him.

[A moment.]

H.C. Is that true, Lizzie?

JIM. [Agog.] He did? What did you tell him?

LIZZIE. I told him I would—as soon as he graduates from grammar school.

[Silence.]

JIM. Grammar school! Is he that dumb?

LIZZIE. No . . . [With a laugh.] He's only nine years old. [Seeing the stricken look on their faces.] Pop—let's not beat around the bush. I know why you sent me to Sweetriver. Because Uncle Ned's got six boys. Three of them are old enough to get married—and so am I. Well, I'm sorry you went to all that expense—the railroad ticket—all those new clothes—the trip didn't work. Noah, you can write it in the books—in red ink.

H.C. What happened at Sweetriver, Lizzie?

LIZZIE. [Emptily.] Nothing—just nothing at all.

H.C. What did you do? Where'd you go?

LIZZIE. Well, the first three or four days I was there—I stayed in my room most of the time.

NOAH. What'd you do that for?

LIZZIE. Because I was embarrassed!

NOAH. Embarrassed about what?

LIZZIE. Noah, use your head! I knew what I was there for—and the whole family knew it too. And I couldn't stand the way they were looking me over. So I'd go downstairs for my meals—and rush right back to my room. I packed—I unpacked—I washed my hair a dozen times—I read the Sears, Roebuck catalog from cover to cover. And finally I said to myself: "Lizzie Curry, snap out of this!" Well, it was a Saturday night—and they were all going to a rodeo dance. So I got myself all decked out in my highest heels and my lowest cut dress. And I walked down to that supper table and all those boys looked at me as if I was stark naked. And then for the longest while there wasn't a sound at the table except for Uncle Ned slupping his soup. And then suddenly—like a gunshot—I heard Ned Junior say: "Lizzie, how much do you weigh?"

H.C. What'd you say to that?

LIZZIE. [Squaring off.] I said, "I weigh a hundred and nineteen pounds, my teeth are all my own and I stand seventeen hands high."

NOAH. That wasn't very smart of you, Lizzie. He was just tryin' to open the conversation.

LIZZIE. [Wryly.] Well, I guess I closed it. . . . Then, about ten minutes later little Pete came hurrying in to the supper table. He was carrying a geography book and he said: "Hey, Pop—where's Madagascar?" Well, everybody ventured an opinion and they were all dead wrong. And suddenly I felt I had to make a good impression and I heard my own voice talking as if it didn't belong to me. I said: "It's an island in the Indian Ocean off the coast of Africa right opposite Mozambique." [With a wail.] Can I help it if I was good in geography?

H.C. What happened?

LIZZIE. Nothing. Not a doggone thing. Everything was so quiet it sounded like the end of the world. Then I heard Ned

Junior's voice: "Lizzie, you fixin' to be a schoolmarm?"

H.C. Oh, no!

LIZZIE. Yes. And suddenly I felt like I was way back at the high school dance—and nobody dancing with me. And I had a sick feeling that I was wearing eyeglasses again the way I used to. And I knew from that minute on that it was no go. So I didn't go to the rodeo dance with them—I stayed home and made up poems about what was on sale at Sears, Roebuck's.

H.C. You and little Pete?

LIZZIE. Yes . . . And the day I left Sweetriver little Pete was bawling. And he said: "You're the beautifulest girl that ever was!"

H.C. And he's right! You are!

LIZZIE. [More pain than pleasure.] Oh, Pop, please . . . !

H.C. We see you that way—he saw you that way . . .

LIZZIE. But not his big brothers!

H.C. Because you didn't show yourself right.

LIZZIE. I tried, Pop—I tried!

H.C. No, you didn't! You hid behind your books. You hid behind your glasses that you don't even wear no more. You're afraid of bein' beautiful.

LIZZIE. [In an outburst.] I'm afraid to think I am when I know I'm not!

[Her intensity stops the discussion. Then:]

H.C. Lizzie . . . ?

LIZZIE. Yes?

H.C. Me and the boys—we put our heads together—and we thought we'd mention somethin' to you.

LIZZIE. What?

H.C. [Uncomfortably, to NOAH.] You want to tell her about it, Noah?

NOAH. Nope. It's your idea, Pop.

H.C. Well, the boys and me—after we get some work done—we figure to ride into Three Point this afternoon.

LIZZIE. Well?

H.C. We're goin' to the sheriff's office and gonna talk to his deputy.

LIZZIE. [Alert now.] File?

H.C. Yes—File.

LIZZIE. Pop, that's the craziest idea . . .

H.C. I'm just gonna invite him to supper, Lizzie.

LIZZIE. If you do, I won't be here.

H.C. I can invite a fella to supper in my own house, can't I?

LIZZIE. I don't want you to go out and lasso a husband for me!

H.C. I won't do anything of the kind. I won't even say your name. We'll start talkin' about a poker game maybe—and then we'll get around to supper—and before you know it, he'll be sittin' in that chair.

LIZZIE. No!

H.C. Lizzie, we're goin'—no matter what you say!

NOAH. Hold on, Pop. I'm against this. But if Lizzie says it's okay to go down there and talk to File—I'll go right along with you. But one thing—we won't do it if Lizzie says no.

LIZZIE. And that's what I say—no!

H.C. Don't listen to Noah! Every time you and Jim have to scratch your back, you turn and ask Noah.

LIZZIE. Because he's the only sensible one around here, Pop. The three of us—we get carried away and then—

H.C. [Interrupting hotly.] For once in your life—get carried away! It won't hurt you—not a bit!

NOAH. That's the dumbest advice I ever heard.

H.C. Noah, any time something comes up that you can't figure on paper—you say it's dumb! What's so dumb about it?

NOAH. It's a matter of pride!

H.C. What the hell is pride anyway?

NOAH. Well, if you don't know what it is, I ain't gonna try to tell you. But me and Lizzie—we know what it is. Don't we, Lizzie?

[As LIZZIE turns away, H.C. sees her rejection of "pride" as a reason for not going through with the plan. Now he confronts her with the question.]

H.C. Is that why you say no, Lizzie? Pride?

LIZZIE. [Avoiding the confrontation.] Pop, if you want to invite somebody to supper—go ahead—but not File!

H.C. For Pete sake, why not?

LIZZIE. Because File—he doesn't even know I'm on earth!

H.C. [With a quiet smile.] He knows, Lizzie—he knows.

LIZZIE. No, he doesn't. Whenever we ride into town, File's got a great big hello for you and Noah and Jim—but he's got nothing for me. He just barely sneaks his hat off his head—and that's all. He makes a *point* of ignoring me.

H.C. [*Quietly.*] When a man makes a *point* of ignorin' you, he ain't ignorin' you at all. [*As she looks at him quickly.*] How about it, Lizzie? File for supper?

LIZZIE. [*In an outburst.*] No—I don't like him!—no!—no!

H.C. If you don't really like him—one no is enough. . . . And you can say it quiet.

LIZZIE. [*Controlling herself—quietly, deliberately.*] All right— I don't like him. I don't like the way he tucks his thumbs in his belt—and I don't like the way he always seems to be thinking deep thoughts.

H.C. [*Secretly amused.*] I thought you liked people with deep thoughts.

LIZZIE. Not File.

H.C. [*Gently—soberly.*] Lizzie—when you were a kid—if I ever thought you were lyin'—I'd say to you: "Honest in truth?" And then you'd never lie. Well, I'm sayin' it now . . . You don't like File—honest in truth?

LIZZIE. [*Flustered.*] Oh, Pop, that's silly!

H.C. I asked you a question. Honest in truth?

LIZZIE. [*Chattering evasively.*] Pop, that's a silly childish game and all you'll get is a silly childish answer and I refuse —I simply refuse to—to . . . [*But suddenly she puts the brakes on. In an outburst.*] Oh, for God sake, go on and invite him!

H.C. [*With a whooping shout.*] O-kaaay! Come on, boys! [*At the doorway.*] You go ahead and cook a great supper, Lizzie!

[*The men hurry out. For an instant, LIZZIE is unnerved, alarmed at what she has let herself in for. Then suddenly, her spirits rising with expectancy, she goes about clearing the breakfast dishes. When LIZZIE is happy she dances as she works. LIZZIE is dancing. The lights fade.*]

[*The lights come up to disclose the inside of the SHERIFF's office. There is an ancient roll-top desk with an old-style telephone on it. On the wall, a bulletin board with various "Wanted" posters featuring the faces of criminals. A door leading to a washroom which, with its Franklin stove and homemade ice box, serves as File's kitchen. His bed is a well-worn* leather couch in the corner of the office proper. The walls are warmly stained knotty pine. The office is empty a moment, then FILE enters, followed by SHERIFF THOMAS. FILE's thumbs, as LIZZIE described them, are tucked in his belt. He is a lean man, reticent, intelligent, in his late thirties. He smiles wryly at the world and at himself. Perhaps he is a little bitter; if so, his bitterness is leavened by a mischievous humor. He and the SHERIFF are deep in argument. Actually, it is the SHERIFF who is arguing; FILE is detached, humoring the SHERIFF's argument. The men are obviously fond of each other.*]

SHERIFF. I won't *charge* you nothin' for it, File.

FILE. [*With a smile.*] That's nice of you, Sheriff—but right now I don't want no dog.

SHERIFF. How do you know you don't want him until you see him?

FILE. Well, I seen dogs before.

SHERIFF. Not this one—he's different. I tell you, File—you see this little fella and you'll reach out and wanta hug him to death.

FILE. [*Humoring him.*] Think I will, huh?

SHERIFF. Yes, you will. You know what he does? There's five little puppies in that litter, but him—he's the smartest. When my wife feeds those other puppies, they stampede to the first bowl she fills. But not him. He lets them fight and scrounge for the *first* bowl—and he eats every speck out of the other four. Now whattaya think of that?

FILE. I think he's gonna bust right open.

SHERIFF. No, he ain't. I'll tell you another thing. He's real lovin'. If you're sittin' in your bare feet, he'll come over and lick your big toe. And pretty soon, there he is —dead asleep—right across your feet. How about it, File?

FILE. [*Hesitating.*] Well . . . that sounds real homey—but I'll do without him.

SHERIFF. File, you make me disgusted. It ain't right for you to shack up all by yourself—with a coffee pot and a leather sofa. Especially once you been married. When you lose your wife, the nights get damn cold. And you gotta have somethin' warm up against your backside.

FILE. Well, last night was a hundred and four degrees.

SHERIFF. All right—if you don't want the dog—if you're the kind of fella that don't like animals . . .

FILE. [*Amused.*] I like animals, Sheriff.

SHERIFF. If you liked animals, you'd have animals.

FILE. Oh, I've had 'em.

SHERIFF. [*Disbelievingly.*] I'll bet! What kind?

FILE. Well, back in Pedleyville—I went out and got myself a raccoon.

SHERIFF. A racoon ain't a dog!

FILE. [*With a smile.*] No—I guess it ain't. But I liked him. He was awful clean. You give him a banana, and he'd wash it ten times. He was a crazy little fella—made me laugh.

SHERIFF. Yeah? Whatever happened to him?

FILE. I don't know. One day he took to the woods and never came back, the little bastard.

SHERIFF. [*Triumphantly.*] There! See? Now can you figure a *dog* doin' that? No, sir! I tell you, File, if you never had a dog . . .

FILE. Oh, I had a dog.

SHERIFF. [*Defensively.*] When did you have a dog?

FILE. When I was a kid.

SHERIFF. [*Testing for the truth of it.*] What kind of dog was it?

FILE. Mongrel. Just a kid's kind.

SHERIFF. What'd you call him?

FILE. Dog.

SHERIFF. No, I mean what was his name?

FILE. Dog!

SHERIFF. [*Exasperated.*] Didn't you have no name for him?

FILE. Dog! That was his name—Dog!

SHERIFF. That ain't no fittin' name for a dog!

FILE. I don't see why not!

SHERIFF. [*Shocked.*] You don't see why not?

FILE. Nope. He always came when I called him.

SHERIFF. [*Almost apoplectic.*] Hell, man, you couldn't of liked him much if you didn't even give him a name.

FILE. Oh, I liked him a lot, Sheriff. Gave him everything he wanted. Let him break it up—rip things to pieces. Took

good care of him too—better than he took care of himself.

SHERIFF. Why? What happened to him?

FILE. Dumb little mutt ran under a buckboard.

SHERIFF. Well, hell—you figure everything's gonna run away—or get run over?

FILE. [*With a smile.*] Oh, I dunno . . . I just don't want a dog, Sheriff. Not that I ain't obliged.

SHERIFF. All right . . . Maybe you'll change your mind.

FILE. I don't think so.

SHERIFF. Stubborn bastard . . . Well, I guess I'll have a look around—see what's doin'.

FILE. [*As the* SHERIFF *goes to the door.*] Yeah . . . Sleeps on your feet, does he?

SHERIFF. [*Laughing.*] Right on my feet! Right on my big old stinkin' feet! See you later, File.

[*He goes out.* FILE *stretches and, as he does, he notes a rip under his sleeve. He goes to the desk, pulls out an old cigar box, opens it and takes out a needle and thread from his makeshift sewing kit. He threads the needle and starts to mend the rip when the telephone rings. He lets the needle and thread dangle from his shirt as he answers the phone.*]

FILE. Hello . . . No, Sheriff Thomas just left. I'll take it—I'm his deputy. Name of what? Tornado Johnson? Yeah, I got it. What's he wanted for? [*Writing on a pad.*] Is he armed? I say is he got a gun? All right . . . Yeah, send us a picture as soon as you get it.

[*As he hangs up, the three* CURRY *men enter. They are embarrassed about their errand, and, although they have plotted a plan of action, they're nervous about its outcome.* NOAH *is sullenly against this whole maneuver.*]

FILE. Hey, H.C. Hey, boys.

H.C., NOAH and JIM. Hey, File . . . Hey, File . . . Hey, File.

FILE. Ridin' over, you boys seen any sign of rain?

NOAH. Not a spit.

FILE. [*With a trace of a smile, but not unkindly.*] What's it like in Sweetriver?

NOAH. [*Tensing a little.*] How'd we know? We ain't been to Sweetriver.

FILE. Sheriff says that Lizzie's been to Sweetriver.

FILE. [*Quietly.*] Well, I won't be over at your place, Jim.

JIM. [*Riled—to* H.C.] You said for me to be friendly. Well, I'm tryin' but he don't want to be friendly.

FILE. [*Evenly.*] I want to be friendly, Jim—but I don't want to be married.

[*A flash of tense silence.*]

JIM. [*Exploding.*] Who says we're invitin' you over for Lizzie? You take that back!

FILE. Won't take nothin' back, Jim.

JIM. Then take somethin' else.

[JIM's *fist flashes out but* FILE *is too quick for him. He parries the single blow and levels off one of his own. It connect squarely with* JIM's *eye and* JIM *goes down. The fight is over that quickly.*]

NOAH. [*Tensely, to* FILE.] If I didn't think he had it comin', I'd wipe you up good and clean!

FILE. He had it comin'.

[*An instant.* NOAH *is the most humiliated of all of them.*]

NOAH. [*To* H.C. *more than to* FILE.] I guess we all did. [*To* JIM.] Come on, turtlehead, let's go home.

[NOAH *goes out quickly, followed by* JIM. *But* H.C. *remains with* FILE. *Silence.* FILE *speaks quietly.*]

FILE. I shouldn't of hit him, H.C.

H.C. Oh, that's all right. Only thing is—you know you lost that fight.

FILE. What?

H.C. Yeah. It wouldn't of hurt you to come to supper. It mighta done you some good.

FILE. We weren't talkin' about supper!

H.C. [*Meeting the confrontation squarely.*] That's right. We were talkin' about Lizzie. And she mighta done you some good too.

FILE. I can mend my own shirts.

H.C. Seems to me you need a lot more mendin' than shirts.

FILE. What do you mean by that?

H.C. Just what I said. You need mendin'.

[H.C. *starts for the door.*]

FILE. Wait a minute, H.C.! You don't drop a word like that and just leave it.

H.C. All right—what'd you hit him for?

FILE. He threw a punch.

H.C. Yeah—and you ducked it fine. He wouldn't of thrown another one—we'da stopped him. What'd you hit him for?

FILE. I'm sorry! I got angry!

H.C. That's the point—why? We come around here and say we like you enough to have you in our family. Is that an insult?

FILE. I don't like people interferin'.

H.C. Interferin' with what?

FILE. I'm doin' all right—by myself!

H.C. You ain't doin' all right! A fella who won't make friends with nobody—who locks himself in against a whole town that wants to like him—he ain't doin' all right! And if he says he is, he's a liar!

FILE. Take it easy, H.C.

H.C. I said a liar and I mean it! You talk about yourself as bein' a widower. And, because we all got respect for your feelin's, we all say: "Okay, if he wants us to call him widower, that's what we'll call him." But you ain't a widower—and everybody in this town knows it!

FILE. [*Losing his temper.*] I am a widower! My wife died six years ago—back in Pedleyville!

H.C. Your wife didn't die, File—she ran out on you! And you're a divorced man. But we'll all go on calling you a widower as long as you want us to. Hell, it don't hurt us none—to us it's only a little lie. But to you . . . ! A fella who shuts himself up with that lie—he needs mendin'! [*A moment.*] Want to throw any more punches?

[FILE *slowly turns away from him.* H.C. *goes out. Brooding,* FILE *goes back to his desk. He resumes the mending of his shirt but his mind is not on it; his thoughts are turned inward. The lights fade.*]

[*The lights come up on the* CURRY *house again.* LIZZIE *is just finishing the supper preparations. She works competently, quickly, bubbling with excitement. A quick survey of the kitchen—everything is fine. Now she has to dress. She hurries to the dining room and notices there are only four chairs around the table. She shoves two chairs apart, gets another one and pushes it up against the table to make the fifth. The sight of five chairs instead of the customary four is exhilarating to her. Singing, she hurries toward the stairs. At this moment,* NOAH *comes in. He is in low, dis-*

gruntled spirits—but seeing LIZZIE, he tries to smile.]

LIZZIE. You all back so soon? [*Chattering excitedly.*] Now don't walk heavy because the lemon cake will fall! You told File six o'clock, I hope.

NOAH. Uh—we didn't tell him no exact time.

LIZZIE. [*In a spate of words.*] Now that's real smart! Suppose he comes at seven and all the cooking goes dry? I got the prettiest lemon cake in the oven—and a steak and kidney pie as big as that table. Oh, look at me—I better change my dress or I'll get caught looking a mess!

[*As she starts up the stairs he tries to stop her.*]

NOAH. Lizzie . . .

[*Just then the phone rings.*]

LIZZIE. Answer the telephone, will you, Noah?

[LIZZIE *rushes upstairs. The phone rings again and* NOAH *answers it.*]

NOAH. Hello!

[JIM *enters. He has an effulgent black eye.*]

NOAH. [*Into phone—annoyed at the instrument.*] Hello—hello! No, this ain't Jim—it's Noah. Who's this? [*To* JIM—*darkly.*] It's Snookie Maguire.

JIM. Hot dog!

[*He catapults across the room and reaches for the receiver. But* NOAH, *with one hand over the mouthpiece, withholds the receiver from* JIM *with his other hand.*]

NOAH. What exactly do you mean—hot dog?

JIM. [*Lamely.*] Just hot dog, Noah.

NOAH. What are you gonna say to her?

JIM. I don't know what she's gonna say to me.

NOAH. Well, watch out.

JIM. [*Into phone—he coos lovingly.*] Hello . . . Hello, Snookie . . . Oh, I'm fine —I'm just fine and dandy! How are you? Fine and dandy? Well, I'm sure glad you're fine and dandy too!

NOAH. [*Muttering disgustedly.*] Fine-and-dandy-my-big-foot!

JIM. [*So sweetly!*] I was gonna telephone you, Snookie. But you telephoned me, di'n't you? Ain't that the prettiest co-incidence?

NOAH. [*Nauseated.*] Jimmy, for Pete sake!

JIM. [*Into phone.*] What? . . . You mean it, Snookie? You mean it? Gee, I sure hope you mean it!

NOAH. What's all that you mean it about?

JIM. [*To* NOAH—*in raptures.*] She says: "It's a hot night and the moon looks like the yoke of an egg—and the Essex is sayin', 'Chug-chug, where's little Jimmy?' "

NOAH. Well, you tell her chug-chug, little Jimmy's gonna sit home on his little fat bottom!

JIM. Now wait a minute, Noah . . . !

NOAH. Don't say wait a minute! If you wanta get mixed up with poison, you go right ahead! But I wash my hands!

JIM. [*Unhappily—into phone.*] Hello, Snookie . . . I just can't tonight . . . [*Confused.*] Well, I don't know why exactly. Anyway, I can't talk now . . . Oh, Snookie —[*Longingly.*]—are you still wearin' your little red hat? [*Relieved.*] That's fine, Snookie—you take care of that! . . . Goodbye, Snookie.

[*He hangs up.*]

NOAH. See that? What'd I tell you! You go out with her once and she starts chasin' you.

JIM. Well, I don't see what's wrong with that, Noah.

NOAH. [*Shocked.*] You don't?

JIM. No! She wants a date with me she calls me on the phone. Lizzie wants a date with File—we go down and try and fetch him.

NOAH. Well, if you remember, I didn't approve of goin' down to see File neither.

JIM. Why not? People want to get together—they oughta get together. It don't matter how, does it?

NOAH. Now, you ask yourself if it don't really matter—go on and ask yourself, Jimmy.

JIM. [*Suddenly lost when he has to figure it out for himself.*] Well, maybe it does . . . Holy mackerel, I sure wish I could figure things out. [*At the radio.*] You think I could get Kansas City this time of the night?

NOAH. I don't think you could get Kansas City any time of the day or night!

JIM. Yeah? Well, maybe I got it and I didn't know it! Last night—when everybody went to bed, I couldn't sleep. So I come downstairs and I fiddled with that crystal set and suddenly I hear a sound like the prettiest music. And I says to myself: "Sonofagun, I got Kansas City!"

NOAH. Static—that's all—just static.

JIM. I knew you'd say that, Noah. And I figured the answer to it: If it feels like Kansas City, it is Kansas City!

NOAH. Then why don't you make it feel like Africa?

JIM. On that little crystal set? [*A moment. Then, longingly.*] I sure wish I could get *somethin'!*

[H.C. *comes in.*]

H.C. Where's Lizzie? Did you tell her?

NOAH. No—she ran upstairs to get dressed.

[LIZZIE *comes hurrying down the stairs. She is all dressed up and in a flurry of anticipation.*]

LIZZIE. Well, folks, how do I look?

H.C. Beautiful.

LIZZIE. You know, Pop—I really think I am!—if you don't look too close! [*Exuberantly.*] When do you suppose File will get here? I ought to know some time we can start eating!

H.C. [*Quietly.*] We can start any time you say.

LIZZIE. Any time? [*She looks at him quickly—and quickly gets the point. Then, pretending that life goes on unchanged, even pretending to see some advantage in* FILE's *not coming, she rattles on with studied casualness.*] Well, you better wash up—and we can have more room at the table and . . . [*She has gone to the table to remove* FILE's *fifth chair, but she cannot bring herself to do it.*] . . . File's not coming . . .

H.C. No.

LIZZIE. I see.

JIM. [*Quickly.*] Not that he didn't want to come! He wanted to—a lot!

LIZZIE. He did, huh?

JIM. Sure! Pop said: "Come to supper tonight, File." And when Pop said that—[*Quickly, to* H.C.]—did you notice how his face kinda—well—it lighted up? Did you notice that?

H.C. [*Lamely.*] Yeah.

JIM. And then File said: "Sure—sure I'll come! Glad to come!" And then suddenly he remembered.

LIZZIE. [*Quietly—not at all taken in.*] What did he remember, Jimmy?

JIM. Well, he remembered there's some kind of outlaw runnin' around. And he

figured—bein' Sheriff's deputy—he better stick around and pay attention to his job. Business before pleasure. [*Pleased with himself.*] That's just what he said—business before pleasure. Yessir, File was real friendly!

LIZZIE. Friendly, huh? What happened to your eye?

JIM. It kinda swole up on me.

NOAH. File hit him.

LIZZIE. You mean you fought to get him to come here?

JIM. It was only a little fight, Lizzie.

LIZZIE. [*Trying to laugh.*] Why didn't you make it a big one—a riot! Why didn't you all just pile on and slug him!

JIM. Lizzie, you're seein' this all wrong.

LIZZIE. I'm seeing it the way it happened! He said: "She might be a pretty good cook—and it might be a good supper —but she's plain! She's as plain as old shoes!"

H.C. He didn't say anything like that!

JIM. He didn't say nothin' about shoes!

H.C. Lizzie—we made a mess of it.

NOAH. If you'da taken my advice there wouldn't of been a mess.

H.C. [*Annoyed.*] Noah, you're always right!

NOAH. I said don't go down and talk to File—nobody listened. I said don't send her to Sweetriver—nobody listened. So what happens? Disappointments!

H.C. We gotta take a risk, Noah.

NOAH. No, we don't! We gotta figure things out so there ain't no risk! We gotta see things the way they are! [*Angry, unhappy.*] Hell, I'm tired of talkin' like this! I don't like to say no to everything. And I don't like to be right all the time! But for God's sake . . . !

H.C. Well, Noah, I'm stumped. If you were Lizzie's father, what would you do?

NOAH. Who says we gotta do anything? We been pushin' her around—tryin' to marry her off! What if she don't get married? Is that the end of everything? She's got a home! She's got a family—she's got bed and board and clothes on her back and plenty to eat!

LIZZIE. That's right. From now on we listen to Noah.

H.C. No! Don't you dare listen to him!

NOAH. Why not? She's got everything she needs!

H.C. You mean she's got everything you

can tote up in your bookkeepin' books! But she ain't got what'll make her happy!

JIM. And she ain't gonna get it! [*As they all look at him in surprise.*] Because she's goin' at it all wrong!

LIZZIE. How, Jimmy? How am I going at it wrong?

JIM. Because you don't talk to a man the way you oughta! You talk too serious! And if there's anything scares hell out of a fella it's a serious-talkin' girl!

H.C. Well, that's the way Lizzie is—and she can't be anything else.

JIM. Yes, she can! She's as smart as any of them girls down at the Ladies' Social Club. She can go down to the Social on Wednesday nights—and she can giggle and flirt as good as any of them.

H.C. What do you want her to turn into —Lily Ann Beasley?

JIM. Lily Ann Beasley gets any man she goes for. Why, I saw her walk up to Phil Mackie one mornin'—and she wiggled her hips like a cocker spaniel and she said: "Phil Mackie, how many toes have you got?" And he said, "Well, naturally—I got ten." And she said, "Why, that's just the right number of toes for a big strong man to have!" And pretty soon he was cooked! He started followin' her around—and she got him so nervous, he bust right out with the shingles.

LIZZIE. Well, if she wants Phil Mackie she can have him—shingles and all.

JIM. And how about that livestock fella from Chicago . . . ?

LIZZIE. Jimmy! Can I treat a man the way she treated him? [*Imitating Lily Ann.*] "My—a polka-dot tie! I just adore a man with a polka-dot tie! Those little round dots go right to my heart!"

JIM. Yeah—and that poor fella—the blood rushed out of his face and I thought he'd keel right over in the horse trough.

LIZZIE. I don't want a man to keel over. I want him to stand up straight—and I want to stand up straight *to* him. Without having to trick him. [*With a cry.*] Isn't that possible with a man? Isn't it *possible?*

NOAH. [*Quietly.*] No, it ain't.

H.C. Yes, it is, Lizzie!

NOAH. No! For once in his life, Jim said somethin' sensible. [*Confronting* LIZZIE *quietly.*] If it's a man you want, you gotta get him the *way a man gets got!*

LIZZIE. If that's the way a man gets got, I don't want any of them!

H.C. Lizzie . . .

LIZZIE. No! To hell with File! To hell with all of them!

NOAH. Don't use that language!

LIZZIE. Hell—hell—hell! To hell with all of them!

[*It is an outcry straight from the heart—rebellious but aching—and they can do nothing to help her. Suddenly, the outside door swings open, screaming on its hinges, whacking the wall like a pistol shot. Everybody turns to the door but all they can see is a vista of sky—no one is there.*]

NOAH. Who opened that door?

JIM. Musta been the wind!

[BILL STARBUCK *steps into the doorway. He is a big man, lithe, agile— a loud braggart, a gentle dreamer. He carries a short hickory stick—it is his weapon, his magic wand, his pride of manhood. He hear's* JIM's *line about the wind.*]

STARBUCK. Wind? Did you say wind? There's not a breath of wind anywhere in the world!

NOAH. Who are you?

STARBUCK. The name's Starbuck! Starbuck is the name! [*He espies* LIZZIE *and his whole manner changes. He doffs his hat and his bow is part gallantry, part irony.*] Lady of the house—hello!

LIZZIE. [*Involuntarily.*] Hello.

STARBUCK. That's a mighty nice dress— it oughta go to a party.

LIZZIE. [*Not charmed.*] Don't you knock on a door before you come in?

STARBUCK. If I'da knocked any harder, I'da broken the door down.

H.C. What is it? What can we do for you?

STARBUCK. You're askin' the wrong question. The question is what can I do for you?

NOAH. I don't remember we called for anybody to do anything.

STARBUCK. You should have, Mister— you sure should have! You need a lot of help. You're in a parcel of trouble. You lost twelve steers on the north range and sixty-two in the gully. The calves are starvin' and the heifers are down on their knees.

JIM. You know a heckuva lot about our herd!

STARBUCK. [*Noticing* JIM'S *black eye.*] Man, that sure is a shiner! [*To* H.C.] Your ranch, Mister?

NOAH. He owns it—I run it.

STARBUCK. [*To* NOAH.] Well, I guess I'll talk to *you.* You got a look of business about you, Mister. You got your feet apart —and you stand solid on the ground. And I know while you're standin' that way, everything's in its right place—and the earth ain't gonna dare to move! That's the kind of a man I like to talk to! Well, what are you gonna do about them cattle?

NOAH. If you know we lost the cattle, you oughta know what killed them. Drought! Ever hear of it?

STARBUCK. Hear of it! That's *all* I hear! Wherever I go, there's drought ahead of me. But when I leave—behind me there's rain—*rain!*

LIZZIE. I think this man's crazy!

STARBUCK. Sure! That's what I am! Crazy! I woke up this mornin'—I looked at the world and I said to myself: The world's gone completely out of its mind. And the only thing that can set it straight is a first-class, A-number-one lunatic! Well, here I am, folks—crazy as a bedbug! Did I introduce myself? The name is Starbuck —*Rainmaker!*

H.C. [*Doubtfully.*] I've heard about rainmakers.

NOAH. I read about a rainmaker—I think it was Idaho.

STARBUCK. What'd you read, Mister?

NOAH. I can't remember whether they locked him up or ran him out of town.

STARBUCK. Might be they strung him up on a sycamore tree.

NOAH. Look, fella, the idea is—we don't believe in rainmakers.

STARBUCK. What do you believe in, Mister—dyin' cattle?

JIM. You really mean you can bring rain?

LIZZIE. He talks too fast—he can't bring anything.

JIM. I asked him. Can you bring rain?

STARBUCK. It's been done, brother—it's been done!

JIM. [*Excitedly.*] Where? How?

STARBUCK. [*With a flourish of his stick.*] How? Sodium chloride! Pitch it up high—

right up to the clouds. Electrify the cold front. Neutralize the warm front. Barometricize the tropopause. Magnetize occlusions in the sky.

LIZZIE. [*Confronting him quietly.*] In other words—bunk!

[*Realizing he will have to contend with* LIZZIE *and* NOAH, *he suddenly and shrewdly reverses his field—he agrees with her.*]

STARBUCK. Lady, you're right! You know why that sounds like bunk? Because it *is* bunk! Bunk and hokey pokey! And I tell you, I'd be ashamed to use any of those methods.

JIM. What method do you use?

STARBUCK. My method's like my name— it's all my own. You want to hear my deal?

LIZZIE. We're not interested.

NOAH. Not one bit!

H.C. What is it?

NOAH. Pop, you're not listenin' to this man . . . ?

H.C. [*Quietly to* STARBUCK.] Any charge for listenin'?

STARBUCK. No charge—free!

H.C. Go ahead. What's the deal?

STARBUCK. One hundred dollars in advance—and inside of twenty-four hours you'll have rain!

JIM. [*In a dither.*] You mean it! Real rain?

STARBUCK. Rain is rain, brother! It comes from the sky. It's a wetness known as water. Aqua pura. Mammals drink it, fish swim in it, little boys wade in it, and birds flap their wings and sing like sunrise. Water! I recommend it!

JIM. [*Convinced.*] Pay him the hundred, Noah!

LIZZIE. Noah, don't be a chump!

NOAH. Me?—don't worry—I won't!

JIM. We got the drought, Noah! It's rain, Lizzie—we need it!

LIZZIE. We won't get a drop of it! Not from him!

H.C. [*Quietly.*] How would you do it, Starbuck?

STARBUCK. Now don't ask me no questions.

LIZZIE. Why? It's a fair question! How will you do it?

STARBUCK. What do you care how I do it, sister, as long as it's done? But I'll tell you how I'll do it. I'll lift this stick and take a long swipe at the sky and let down a shower of hailstones as big as cantaloupes. I'll shout out some good old Nebraska cusswords and you turn around and there's a lake where your corral used to be. Or I'll just sing a little tune maybe and it'll sound so pretty and sound so sad you'll weep and your old man will weep and the sky will get all misty-like and shed the prettiest tears you ever did see. How'll I do it? Girl, I'll just do it!

NOAH. Where'd you ever bring rain before?

LIZZIE. What town? What state?

STARBUCK. Sister, the last place I brought rain is now called Starbuck—they named it after me! Dry? I tell you, those people didn't have enough damp to blink their eyes. So I get out my big wheel and my rolling drum and my yella hat with three little feathers in it. I look up at the sky and I say: "Cumulus!" I say: "Cumulo-nimbus! Nimbulo-cumulus!" And pretty soon —way up there—there's a teeny little cloud lookin' like a white-washed chicken house. And then I look up and there's a herd of white buffalo stampedin' across the sky. And then, sister-of-all-good-people, down comes the rain! Rain in buckets, rain in barrels, fillin' the lowlands, floodin' the gullies. And the land is as green as the valley of Adam. And when I rode out of there I looked behind me and I see the prettiest colors in the sky—green, blue, purple, gold—colors to make you cry. And me? I'm ridin' right through that rainbow —Well, how about it? Is it a deal?

H.C. Well . . .

LIZZIE. [Seeing her father's indecision.] Pop—no! He's a liar and a con man!

H.C. [Reluctantly.] Yep, that's what he is all right—a liar and a con man!

STARBUCK. Hurts me to hear you say that, Mister! Well, so long to you—so long for a sorry night!

[He starts for the door.]

H.C. Wait a minute!

STARBUCK. You said I was a con man!

H.C. You're a liar and a con man—but I didn't say I wouldn't take your deal!

LIZZIE. Pop . . .

H.C. [Quickly, to LIZZIE.] I didn't say I would, neither!

NOAH. Pop, you ain't gonna throw away a hundred bucks!

H.C. It's my hundred, Noah!

NOAH. How do I write it in the books?

H.C. Write it as a gamble, Noah! I've lost more'n that in poker on a Saturday night!

LIZZIE. You get an even chance in poker!

H.C. Lizzie, I knew an old fella once— and he had the asthma. He went to every doctor and still he coughed and still he wheezed. Then one day a liar and a con man come along and took the old man for fifty dollars and a gold-plated watch. But a funny thing . . . ! After that con man left, the old boy never coughed one minute until the day he was kicked by a palomino!

LIZZIE. That's a crazy reason!

STARBUCK. I'll give you better reasons, Lizzie-girl! You gotta take my deal because once in your life you gotta take a chance on a con man. You gotta take my deal because there's dyin' calves that might pick up and live. Because a hundred bucks is only a hundred bucks—but rain in a dry season is a sight to behold. You gotta take my deal because it's gonna be a hot night— and the world goes crazy on a hot night— and maybe that's what a hot night is for.

H.C. [Suddenly.] Starbuck, you got you a deal!

STARBUCK. [With a quick smile.] Tell you: I knew I had a deal the minute I walked into this house!

JIM. How'd you know that?

STARBUCK. I see four of you and five places set for supper. And I says to myself: Starbuck, your name's written right on that chair!

H.C. [With a laugh.] Let's eat!

[STARBUCK. tosses his hat up on the rack, throws his leg over the back of one of the dining chairs and in one movement—before the others can approach it—he is seated at the table. As the others sit down to supper . . .]

END OF ACT ONE

ACT TWO

Inside the CURRY *house, a short while after supper.* NOAH *is paying* STARBUCK *his fee, counting out the money on the dining table.* H.C. *is watching quietly;* JIM, *with keyed excitement.* LIZZIE *is clearing the supper dishes, hostile to the whole situation.*

NOAH. [*Fuming as he counts out the bills.*] Seventy—eighty—eighty-five . . . ! I'm against this, Pop.

H.C. [*Quietly.*] Keep countin', Noah.

NOAH. Ninety—ninety-five—one hundred. There's your hundred bucks.

STARBUCK. Thank you, Noah.

NOAH. Don't thank me—thank him. [*Going to his ledger.*] I'm writin' that down in my book. One hundred dollars—thrown away.

STARBUCK. No—don't write that, Noah. Write it like this. Say: On August the twenty-seventh, a man come stompin' through our doorway. We bid him time of night, we fed him a supper fit for a king and we gave him one hundred honest notes on the fair government of the United States of America. And in return for that hospitality he did us one small favor—he brought rain! [*With a smile.*] You got that? Write it!

NOAH. I don't see no rain yet.

STARBUCK. I still got twenty-three hours to bring it.

NOAH. Well, you better get busy.

JIM. [*Eagerly.*] Yeah, Starbuck, you better knuckle down.

STARBUCK. Now let's not get nervous. Rain, my friends, rain comes to the man that ain't nervous! [*Getting down to work.*] Now, what kind of rain would you like?

JIM. You mean we can choose our kind?

STARBUCK. Sure, you can choose your kind. And brother, there's all kinds! There's mizzle and there's drizzle—but you wouldn't want that. I generally give that away as a free sample. There's trickle and there's sprinkle! But that's for the little flower gardens of little pink old ladies. There's April showers that I can bring in April—but I can sometimes bring 'em in May. There's rain with thunder and rain with hail! There's flash floods—and storms that roll down the shoulder of the mountain. But the biggest of all—that's deluge!

[*Modestly.*] But don't ask me for deluge—that takes a bit of doin'.

JIM. What kind do we get for a hundred bucks?

STARBUCK. You choose it and I'll bring it.

LIZZIE. He brags so loud he gives me a pain in the neck.

STARBUCK. Look, folks, if you all act like she does, it's gonna make it mighty tough for me to do my job! Because when there's suspicions around, it's a d-r-y season!

LIZZIE. I don't doubt it.

STARBUCK. Well, she don't believe in me. How about the rest of you?

NOAH. What do you mean believe in you? We certainly don't!

STARBUCK. Then I changed my mind! I don't want your money—take it back!

[*In a temper he slams the money on the table. They are stunned.*]

H.C. Noah—please. We made a bargain—it's settled. Now be a good sport.

NOAH. [*Exasperated.*] Good sport? What's he expect me to say?

STARBUCK. I'll explain it to you, Noah. Makin' rain—it takes a lot of confidence. And if you have doubt about me—I get doubts about myself.

NOAH. Oh, I see! If you don't bring rain, you're gonna blame it on us. We didn't have confidence. Well, I'll tell you how far my confidence goes. We're losin' cattle. So I figure we'll lose a hundred bucks—that's no more than the price of a well-fed steer. And maybe—one chance in a million, thanks to you bein' *lucky*—there'll be rain and we'll *save* a few cattle. But believe in you?—not a word!

LIZZIE. You can steal our money—but that's *all* you can steal.

STARBUCK. [*In a temper.*] That's not the right attitude!

JIM. [*Manfully.*] I got the right attitude—take back your dough!

STARBUCK. No! What if I need some help?

JIM. I'll help you—so will Pop!

STARBUCK. But not him!

NOAH. Darn right I won't!

H.C. [*Shrewdly.*] Look, Noah—suppose he takes the hundred bucks. You gotta account for it in the books *some* way. Well, if there's a Chinaman's chance you can account for it as profitable investment . . . ?

NOAH. [*To* STARBUCK.] What kind of help?

STARBUCK. Nothin' you can't do. How about you, lady? Any confidence?

LIZZIE. No confidence.

JIM. We don't need her, Starbuck—here's your dough. [*As* STARBUCK *takes it.*] Now—what's the first step?

STARBUCK. Well, what I'm gonna ask you to do—it ain't gonna make sense. But what's sensible about a flash of lightnin'? What's sensible about cyclones, blizzards, flood and hurricane?

JIM. Nothin'!

STARBUCK. Right! Now—what I want you to do: [*He hurries to the window and points out.*] You see that little old wagon of mine? On that wagon I got me a big bass drum. Somebody's gotta beat that drum!

NOAH. Beat it? What for?

STARBUCK. Don't ask questions!

JIM. [*He has caught on to the rules of the game.*] And don't get sensible!

STARBUCK. That's right, Jimmy! Who's gonna beat that drum?

JIM. [*The stalwart.*] Me—I'll beat it!

STARBUCK. Jim, you're gonna be my first lieutenant. Now go on out there and every time you get the feelin' for it, you beat that drum—three times—boom—boom—boom—low, like thunder . . . Got it?

JIM. Got it! Every time I get the feelin'?

STARBUCK. That's it.

JIM. [*Eagerly.*] When do I start?

STARBUCK. Mister, you've started!

[JIM *goes out quickly and* STARBUCK *turns to* H.C.]

STARBUCK. Mister H.C., I want you to pay close attention. In that wagon I got a bucket of white paint. Now it ain't ordinary white paint—it's special—it's electromagnetized, oxygenated, *de*chromated white. Now I want you to go out there and paint a great big white arrow pointin' away from the house. That's so the house don't get struck by lightnin'.

H.C. [*With a wry smile*] That sounds reasonable.

STARBUCK. [*Pretending to talk to himself, but his eye on* NOAH.] Now . . . it's too bad you ain't got a mule on the place.

NOAH. [*Muttering.*] We got a mule.

STARBUCK. You have? That's great—that's just dandy! Noah, get a length of strong rope and go out there and tie that mule's hind legs together.

NOAH. What? Tie the hind legs of a mule? What the hell for?

STARBUCK. [*Hurt.*] Please—now, please —you gotta do like I ask you.

NOAH. I ain't gonna do it!

H.C. Come on, Noah—you promised.

NOAH. I'll be damned! Tie the hind legs of a mule!

[*In a huff,* NOAH *hurries outdoors.* H.C. *starts to follow him when* LIZZIE's *voice stops him.*]

LIZZIE. Pop—wait! [*As* H.C. *stops, she turns to him, livid with rage.*] Pop—I'm ashamed of you! I've been standing here —keeping my mouth shut—wondering how far you'd let this man go in making a fool of you!

H.C. [*Quietly.*] He can't make me any more a fool than I make out of myself.

LIZZIE. You're making a big fool of yourself! Where's your common sense?

H.C. Common sense? Why, that didn't do us no good—we're in trouble. Maybe we better throw our common sense away.

LIZZIE. For Pete sake, hang on to a little of it!

H.C. You mean go along with this fella halfway, huh? Well, I can't do that. I gotta take a chance on him—the whole chance— without fear of gettin' hurt or gettin' cheated or gettin' laughed at. . . . As far as he'll take me. [*To* STARBUCK—*confronting him levelly.*] A white arrow, did you say?

STARBUCK. [*A moment. Then, meeting his glance, his response to* H.C. *is serious, even respectful.*] A white arrow, H.C.

H.C. I'll paint it.

STARBUCK. [*With the faintest touch of desperation.*] Dammit, Mister, you're gonna get your money's worth if it's the last thing I do!

H.C. [*Quietly—almost gently.*] Don't get nervous, Boy.

STARBUCK. I ain't—not a bit of it!

H.C. That's fine. Confidence!

[H.C. *goes out. From outdoors, we hear the first deep, pompous sound of the bass drum—boom—boom—boom!*]

STARBUCK. [*Calling to* JIM.] Attaboy, Jim—you beat that drum! Make it rumble!

JIM'S VOICE. [*In the spirit of things.*] Make it rum-bullll!

[*The drum sounds off again.* LIZZIE, *fuming with anger, whirls on* STARBUCK.]

LIZZIE. Well! I'll bet you feel real proud of yourself!

STARBUCK. [*Smiling evenly.*] Kinda proud, sure.

LIZZIE. [*Raging.*] You're not satisfied to steal our money! You have to make jackasses out of us! Why'd you send them out on those fool errands? Why? What for?

STARBUCK. Maybe I thought it was necessary.

LIZZIE. You know good and well it wasn't necessary—you know it!

STARBUCK. Maybe I sent them out so's I could talk to you alone!

LIZZIE. [*Off balance.*] What?

STARBUCK. You heard me.

LIZZIE. [*Her rage mounting.*] Then why didn't you just say it straight out: Lizzie, I want to talk to you—alone—man to man!

STARBUCK. [*Quietly.*] Man to man, Lizzie?

LIZZIE. [*Bitingly.*] Excuse me—I made a mistake—you're not a man!

[STARBUCK *tenses, then controls his anger.*]

STARBUCK. Lizzie, can I ask you a little question?

LIZZIE. No!

STARBUCK. I'll ask it anyway. Why are you fussin' at the buttons on your dress?

LIZZIE. Fussing at the . . . ! I'm not!

[*And she stops doing it.*]

STARBUCK. [*Evenly, gently.*] Let 'em alone. They're all buttoned up fine—as tight as they'll ever get. . . . And it's a nice dress too. Brand new, ain't it? You expectin' somebody?

LIZZIE. None of your business.

STARBUCK. A woman gets all decked out—she must be expectin' her beau. Where is he? It's gettin' kinda late.

LIZZIE. [*Breaking out.*] I'm not expecting anybody!

STARBUCK. [*Quietly.*] Oh, I see. You were—but now you ain't. Stand you up?

LIZZIE. Mr. Starbuck, you've got more gall . . . !

[*And she starts for the stairs. But he grabs her arm.*]

STARBUCK. Wait a minute!

LIZZIE. Let go of me!

STARBUCK. [*Tensely.*] The question I really wanted to ask you before—it didn't have nothing' to do with buttons. It's this: The minute I walked into your house—before I hardly said a word—you didn't like me! Why?

LIZZIE. I said let go!

STARBUCK. [*Letting her go.*] You didn't like me—why? Why'd you go up on your hind legs like a frightened mare?

LIZZIE. I wasn't frightened!

STARBUCK. Yes, you were!

LIZZIE. Of you? Of what?

STARBUCK. I don't know! Mares get scared by lots of things—fire—lightning—the smell of blood!

LIZZIE. I wasn't scared, Mr. Starbuck. You paraded yourself in here—and you took over the place. I don't like to be taken by a con man.

STARBUCK. [*Lashing out.*] Wait a minute! I'm sick and tired of this! I'm tired of you queerin' my work, callin' me out of my name!

LIZZIE. I called you what you are—a big-mouthed liar and a fake!

STARBUCK. [*With mounting intensity.*] How do you know I'm a liar? How do you know I'm a fake? Maybe I *can* bring rain! Maybe when I was born God whispered a special word in my ear! Maybe He said: "Bill Starbuck, you ain't gonna have much in this world—you ain't gonna have no money, no fancy spurs, no white horse with a golden saddle! You ain't gonna have no wife and no kids—no green little house to come home to! But Bill Starbuck—wherever you go—you'll bring rain!" Maybe that's my one and only blessing!

LIZZIE. There's no such blessing in the world!

STARBUCK. I seen even better blessings, Lizzie-girl! I got a brother who's a doctor. You don't have to tell him where you ache or where you pain. He just comes in and lays his hand on your heart and pretty soon you're breathin' sweet again. And I got another brother who can sing—and when he's singin', that song is there—and never leaves you! [*With an outcry.*] I used to think—

why ain't *I* blessed like Fred or Arny? Why am I just a nothin' man, with nothin' special to my name? And then one summer comes the drought—and Fred can't heal it away and Arny can't sing it away. But me —I got down to the hollow and I look up and I say: "Rain! Dammit! *Please*—bring rain!" And the rain came! And I knew—I knew I was one of the family! [*Suddenly quiet, angry with himself.*] That's a story. You don't have to believe it if you don't want to.

[*A moment. She is affected by the story—but she won't let herself be. She pulls herself together with some effort.*]

LIZZIE. I don't believe it.

STARBUCK. You're like Noah. You don't believe in anything.

LIZZIE. That's not true.

STARBUCK. Yes, it is. You're scared to believe in anything. You put the fancy dress on—and the beau don't come. So you're scared that nothin'll ever come. You got no faith.

LIZZIE. [*Crying out.*] I've got as much as anyone!

STARBUCK. You don't even know what faith is. And I'm gonna tell you. It's believin' you see white when your eyes tell you black. It's knowin'—with your heart!

LIZZIE. And I know you're a fake.

STARBUCK. [*In sudden commiseration.*] Lizzie, I'm sad about you. You don't believe in nothin'—not even in yourself! You don't even believe you're a woman. And if you *don't*—you're *not!*

[*He turns on his heel and goes outdoors.* LIZZIE *stands there, still hearing his words. She is deeply perturbed by them. The heat seems unbearable. From outdoors, the sound of the drum —boom—boom—boom.*]

LIZZIE. [*Upset—weakly.*] Jimmy—please! Please—quit that!

[*But he doesn't hear her. The drum continues. She rushes upstairs as the lights fade.*]

[*The lights come up inside the* SHERIFF's *office. The room is dimly illuminated by the gooseneck lamp on* FILE's *desk and by the brilliant moonlight streaming through the window.* FILE *is lying on his leather couch staring unseeingly up at the ceiling. At last he gets up and stretches. He*

is unhappy and uncomfortable. He takes up a cardboard, fans himself once or twice and throws down the cardboard. The door opens and the SHERIFF *comes in.*]

FILE. Anything doin'?

SHERIFF. Not a thing—so I ran home for a while. . . . Any calls?

FILE. [*Looking at a paper on his desk.*] The Gannoways had their baby . . . Peak's Junction called and said that Tornado Johnson fella was seen ridin' our way. Old lady Keeley called and said she heard thunder.

SHERIFF. How can she? She's deaf as a post.

FILE. I thought I heard it too. But it was too regular.

[*Far in the distance, the sound of* JIM's *drum.*]

SHERIFF. There it is! . . . Sure ain't thunder.

FILE. Lots of electricity in the air. My hair's full of it.

SHERIFF. Mine too. Even in my clothes. My wife says when she walks around, it sounds like she's walkin' in taffety. I says: "You been naggin' for a new silk dress— now I won't have to buy it for you!"

[*The* SHERIFF *howls uproariously at his own joke.* FILE *doesn't smile—he is far away, preoccupied.*]

SHERIFF. What's the matter, File? Where'd you go off to?

FILE. What? Oh—I'm right here.

SHERIFF. [*Watching him closely.*] Phil Mackie says the Curry boys came by.

FILE. Oh, yes—I forgot.

SHERIFF. Anything important?

FILE. No.

SHERIFF. Phil says he saw Jim Curry come out of here wearin' a black eye.

FILE. He did, huh?

SHERIFF. Yeah—and he wasn't wearin' it when he came in. . . . What happened?

FILE. [*With a flare of temper.*] Tell Phil Mackie to mind his own damn business!

SHERIFF. [*Surprised—after a hurt instant.*] And me to mind mine?

FILE. I'm sorry, Sheriff. [*A moody moment, then:*] Sheriff . . . I been thinkin' . . . I changed my mind.

SHERIFF. About what?

FILE. That dog you were talkin' about.

SHERIFF. You did, huh?

FILE. Yes. If the offer still holds, I'll take him off your hands.

SHERIFF. [*Embarrassed.*] Well, I'll tell you, File—you said you didn't want him. And Little Bobby Easterfield come over . . .

FILE. [*Hiding his disappointment—interrupting.*] Oh, I see. . . . Well, that's all right—it don't have to be that particular puppy.

SHERIFF. My wife gave the others away too—this mornin' . . . I'm sorry, File.

FILE. No—forget it.

SHERIFF. What made you change your mind about the dog, File?

FILE. [*Evasively.*] Oh, I don't know. . . .

SHERIFF. Didn't have anything to do with the Currys, did it?

FILE. [*With an even greater flare of temper.*] Now what the hell would my wantin' a dog have to do with the Currys, for God's sake!

SHERIFF. [*Equally angry.*] File, what's the matter with you? What is it? What's the matter with you?

FILE. I don't know . . . Heat, I guess . . . Mind if I take an hour off?

SHERIFF. Take two hours—take three!

FILE. [*Trying to smile.*] No—an hour'll do me fine.

[*He starts for the door.*]

SHERIFF. If I need you where'll you be?

FILE. [*Evasively.*] Oh—'round about. So long, Sheriff . . .

[FILE *goes out. The* SHERIFF's *eyes follow him with a sober glance. The lights fade.*]

[*The lights come up inside the living room which is momentarily unoccupied. From outdoors we hear the sound of* JIM's *drum.* H.C. *comes in through the back door, carrying a whitewash brush and a pail of white paint. His face is daubed with whitewash as are his clothes. Bent nearly double from having been painting the arrow, he absent-mindedly sets the paint pail and the brush down on the floor. Abruptly he realizes that the paint bucket will leave a mark and he snatches up the bucket and sets it outdoors. Re-entering quickly he looks at the floor now marked with paint. He scurries guiltily into the kitchen, grabs a towel and rushes back to clean up the mess. About to apply the spotless towel to the floor he realizes*

one doesn't get paint on a clean towel. He tosses the towel away, pulls out his shirt tail and kneels, applying the shirt tail to the floor. NOAH *enters, unheard.* NOAH *has had discourteous treatment by the recalcitrant mule; he is limping. He stops at the sight of his father and watches* H.C. *Then:*]

NOAH. He said paint the ground, not the floor.

H.C. [*Startled.*] I ain't paintin' the floor —I'm cleanin' it.

[*He rises and* NOAH *gets a good look at him.*]

NOAH. Your face is all over whitewash.

H.C. Yep—I reckon it is.

NOAH. So's your shirt.

H.C. Yep.

NOAH. To look at you, you'd think you never painted nothin' in your life.

H.C. [*Sheepishly.*] I didn't see the bush.

NOAH. What bush?

H.C. [*Annoyed.*] I was paintin' backward in the dark and suddenly there was that damn bush—and I bumped—and the paint slopped all over everything!

[NOAH *crosses the room away from his father.* H.C. *notices that* NOAH *is limping.*]

H.C. What you limpin' about?

NOAH. Mule.

H.C. Kick you? [*As* NOAH *grunts.*] Bad?

NOAH. [*Annoyed.*] Bad or good, a mule's kick is a mule's kick.

[NOAH *sits at the table, working at his ledgers. Suddenly, from outdoors, louder than ever: Boom—boom—boom!* NOAH *goes to the window and calls cholerically.*]

NOAH. Jimmy, for Pete sake—come in here and quit beatin' that drum!

[*The drumbeat stops.* H.C. *smiles.*]

H.C. I think he enjoys it.

NOAH. Sure. He's got the easiest job of all of us.

H.C. Well, he's the lieutenant.

[JIM *enters, carrying the biggest bass drum in the world. He just stands there in the doorway, grinning. They stare at him. He beats the drum once, with a flourish, just for the hell of it.*]

NOAH. Jimmy, you quit that!

JIM. He said for me to beat it every time I get the feelin'.

H.C. [*Tolerantly.*] Well, Jimmy, if you

can try to resist the feelin' we'll all appreciate it.

JIM. Holy mackerel, Pop, your face is all over whitewash.

H.C. [*Feigning surprise.*] It is, is it?

JIM. Yeah—so's your shirt.

H.C. Well, whattaya know?

JIM. Whyn't you wash up? You look foolish.

H.C. You don't look so bright yourself, totin' that drum.

JIM. What am I gonna do with it?

NOAH. [*Exasperated.*] For the love of Mike, don't be so dumb!

JIM. [*Hurt and angry.*] Don't call me that, Noah!

[*Silence He sets down the drum.*]

H.C. I didn't notice—anybody see a cloud?

NOAH. Not a wisp of a one! And don't you expect it!

JIM. I wouldn't be so sure about that, Noah.

NOAH. You wouldn't—I would!

JIM. I think he *is* gonna bring rain! Because I been lookin' in his wagon. Boy, he's got all kinds of wheels and flags and a bugle and firecrackers . . .

NOAH. And all kinds of stuff that a con man would have—but nothin' that's got anything to do with rain!

JIM. You're wrong, Noah. Look at this book.

[*He pulls a small book out of his pocket.*]

H.C. What's that, Jimmy?

JIM. I found this in his wagon. And I says to him, what's this? And he says: "You can have it—with my compliments!"

NOAH. Well, what is it?

JIM. [*Excitedly.*] It's all about the weather! And you know what? I figure it's some kind of magic.

[NOAH *groans.*]

H.C. What's it say?

JIM. Listen! [*Reading with difficulty.*] "Icy cirrus in the ascendant over aqueous cumulus. Prognostication fine if cirrus unchanged to rainy altostratus." [*Eagerly.*] How's that?

NOAH. That's fine!

JIM. You know what that means?

NOAH. No. Do you ?

JIM. I figure you don't have to know what it means—all you have to do is know how to say it!

NOAH. Like abracadabra.

JIM. What?

NOAH. Like . . Never mind.

JIM. [*Resolutely.*] I'm gonna study this book. Because I figure if this fella really knows how to bring rain, he knows it from this book. And after he goes—if *we* got the book—we won't never have to worry about rain no more.

H.C. That's real foresight, Jimmy.

JIM. I'm sure glad he gave it to me. You know what he did? He wrote in it. [*Reading the flyleaf.*] "To Jimmy Curry—who understands this book every bit as good as I do." [*Modestly.*] Of course I *don't*—but I think it's real nice of him to write it.

[JIM *takes the cushion off a chest that is by the window. He opens the chest.*]

H.C. What are you doin' in Lizzie's linen chest?

JIM. He asked me could he spend the night in the tack room and I said yes. So I figured I'd get him some bedding.

NOAH. You're stretchin' yourself to make him cozy, ain't you?

JIM. Why not? I like him!

H.C. Funny—me too.

NOAH. [*Disgustedly.*] Both of you! He's certainly pullin' the wool over *your* eyes!

JIM. I'm out there with the drum—waitin' for the feelin' to come—and he comes over and we had a great talk, the two of us!

NOAH. What'd he try to sell you *this* time?

JIM. [*In fervent defense of* STARBUCK.] Nothin'! He didn't try to sell me nothin'. He just come over—and I'm lookin' up at the sky—and he says: "What are you thinkin' about, Jim?" Real serious—like he gives a damn. "What are you thinkin' about, Jim?"

H.C. And what'd you tell him?

JIM. [*Importantly.*] I said: "Not much."

H.C. Well, that's a good start to a conversation.

JIM. And then before I know it, I'm tellin' him everything about myself. I'm tellin' him how I never got good marks in school—I never could figure about the Revolution and the Silva War—but I could tell the goddamndest stories. And I'm tellin' him about Lizzie and about how

Noah snores at night. And I even told him about Snookie.

NOAH. Yeah?

JIM. Yeah! I says to him: "What do you think of a girl that wears loud clothes and puts lip rouge on her mouth and always goes around in a little red hat? Is she fast?" And you know what he said? [*Triumphantly.*] He said: "Never judge a heifer by the flick of her tail!"

H.C. [*Suppressing a smile.*] Sounds like sensible advice.

JIM. I think so! And then he says: "What do you think of the world?" And I say to him: "It's gonna get all *swole* up and bust right in our faces! And you know what he told me? [*This, to him, is the most wonderful part.*] He said: "It's happened before—and it can happen again!"

NOAH. He's crazy.

JIM. No, he ain't! He said there's been stars that that happened to! They just went brrrroom! and blew up in the sky! And if it can happen to them, it can happen to us. Now I never knew that—I just made that up right outta my own head.

NOAH. There! I told you he'd sell you a bill of goods.

JIM. [*Angrily.*] Noah, I understand that crack. You mean he was tryin' to make me feel smart—and I ain't.

NOAH. Oh, shut up!

JIM. No, I won't shut up.

NOAH. What the hell's got into you?

JIM. I just thought of somethin', Noah. You know the only time I feel real dumb?

NOAH. When?

JIM. When I'm talkin' to you! Now why the hell *is* that Noah?

[LIZZIE *comes down the stairs.*]

H.C. Lizzie—I thought you went to bed.

LIZZIE. It's roasting up there.

H.C. We oughta get one of those electric fans.

[STARBUCK *appears at the open door.* LIZZIE *sees him.*]

LIZZIE. It's not only the heat. Jimmy and his drum.

[*The telephone rings.* NOAH *answers it.*]

NOAH. Hello . . . Who? . . . No—he's not here.

[*And summarily, he hangs up.*]

JIM. Who was that?

NOAH. Who else would have all that gall?

JIM. Snookie! Noah, that call was for me!

NOAH. Well?

JIM. [*Angry.*] Why'd you hang up on her?

NOAH. Save you the trouble.

JIM. [*Raging to the point of tears.*] You didn't even ask me.

NOAH. I didn't think it was necessary.

JIM. If she calls me on the phone, you don't have to tell her I ain't here. I can do it myself.

NOAH. How can you yourself tell her you ain't here? Talk sense!

JIM. Maybe it don't make sense but you damn well know what I mean.

NOAH. [*Incensed.*] Listen, Jimmy! If you want to get yourself in hot water—if you want me to wash my hands of you—all you have to do is lift that phone and call her right back.

STARBUCK. [*With studied casualness.*] He's right, Jimmy. That's all you have to do.

NOAH. Stay out of this!

STARBUCK. I'm just agreeing with you, Noah. [*To* JIM.] You can call her right back.

[*A moment of painful indecision on* JIM's *part. He looks at* STARBUCK *and at* NOAH *who is standing squarely in front of the telephone.*]

STARBUCK. [*With quiet, urgent encouragement.*] Go on, kid.

JIM. I—I don't have her telephone number.

STARBUCK. All you have to do is call the operator. I'm sure there ain't that many phones in Three Point.

JIM. [*Miserably—more plea than anger.*] Let me alone, Starbuck!

STARBUCK. Go on!

[JIM *turns away.* STARBUCK *wheels around to* H.C.]

STARBUCK. H.C., a word from you might be a lot of help.

H.C. [*Quietly.*] He'll work it out, Starbuck.

STARBUCK. [*Seeing that* H.C. *won't interfere, he moves quickly to* LIZZIE.] Lizzie! Tell Jimmy to make the call!

LIZZIE. [*With difficulty.*] Starbuck, we'll all thank you not to interfere in our family.

STARBUCK. [*Squelched.*] Sorry . . . Guess I'm a damn fool!

[*Quickly, he turns on his heel and*

goes out to the tack room. There is a
heavy silence in the room. LIZZIE
notices the bedding.]
LIZZIE. What are these sheets doing
here?
H.C. [Indicating STARBUCK.] For him.
Jimmy was going to take them out to the
tack room—if it's all right.
LIZZIE. It's all right. Go on Jimmy.
JIM. I don't want to now!
[And deeply upset, ashamed to face
STARBUCK, ashamed to stay with the
others, he hurries upstairs.]
LIZZIE. [Quietly.] You shouldn't have
done that, Noah.
NOAH. [Guiltily—unhappily.] Some-
body's gotta do it.
LIZZIE. I think you liked doing it.
NOAH. No, I didn't! [In a hurt outburst.]
For Pete sake—somebody take this family
off my hands. I don't want to run it.
H.C. You don't have to run the family,
Noah—only the ranch.
NOAH. They're both tied up together.
And if you don't like the way I do
things . . .
H.C. [Interrupting.] That ain't so, Noah!
There's some things you do real good!
NOAH. [In a pained outburst.] Then why
don't you give me a little credit once in a
while? I'm tryin' to keep this family goin'.
I'm tryin' to keep it from breakin' its heart
on one foolishness after another. And what
do I get for it? Nothin' but black looks
and complaints! [Passionately.] Why?
H.C. Because you're tryin' to run the
family the way you run the ranch.
NOAH. There's no other way.
H.C. Noah, that's a terrible mistake.
When I was your age I had my nose
pressed to the grindstone—just like you—
and I couldn't see what was goin' on
around me. Your mother used to say: "Let
up, Harry—stop and catch your breath."
Well, after she died I had to take her
advice—on account of you three kids. And
I turned around to enjoy my family.
[Quietly, urgently.] And I found out a
good thing, Noah. If you let 'em live—
people pay off better than cattle.
NOAH. [In low anger.] Don't be so proud
of the way you let us live, Pop. [Pointing
to LIZZIE.] Just look at her—and don't be
so damn proud of yourself.
H.C. [Angry and apprehensive.] What
do you mean by that, Noah?

NOAH. Never mind! You think about it!
[In cold fury, NOAH goes out. Long
silence. When H.C. speaks to LIZZIE
he doesn't look at her. There is heavy
worry in his voice.]
H.C. What does he mean, Lizzie?
LIZZIE. [Evasively.] I don't know. . . .
Don't pay any attention to him, Pop.
[She is itchy, restless. Her mood is
mercurial, changing quickly between
her yearning to find something new to
to do with herself—and her need to
hide this yearning . . . perhaps by
laughing at herself, by laughing at the
world, by laughing at nothing at all.]
LIZZIE. I don't know whether I'm hungry or thirsty. You like something to eat?
H.C. No, thanks. Noah's hinting that I
made some big mistake with you, Lizzie.
Did I?
LIZZIE. [With surface laughter, with
bravura.] Of course not. I'm perfect!
Everybody knows I'm perfect! A very nice
girl—good housekeeper, bright mind, very
honest! So damn honest it kills me! How
about a sandwich?
H.C. [Puzzled by her mood. More definitely than before.] No, thanks.
LIZZIE. "You gotta get a man like a man
gets got!" That's what Noah said. [Laugh-
ing.] Now isn't that stupid? Why, it's not
even good English!
H.C. [Soberly.] Don't think about that,
Lizzie.
LIZZIE. [Protesting too much.] Think
about it? Why, I wouldn't give it a second
thought! [Abruptly.] Pop, do you know
what that Starbuck man said to me?
H.C. [Quietly.] What, Lizzie?
LIZZIE. No—why repeat it? A man like
that—if you go repeating what people like
that have to say . . . ! [Abruptly.] Why
doesn't it rain? What we need is a flood—
[With sudden false gaiety.]—a great big
flood—end of the world—ta-ta-goo'bye!
[Abruptly serious.] Pop, can a woman take
lessons in being a woman?
H.C. You don't have to take lessons. You
are one.
LIZZIE. [Here it is—the outcry.] Starbuck says I'm not! ! ! !
[A split second of surprise on H.C.'s
part.]
H.C. If Starbuck don't see the woman
in you, he's blind.
LIZZIE. Is File blind? Are they all blind?

[*Then, with deepening pain.*] Pop, I'm sick and tired of *me*. I want to get out of *me* for a while—be somebody else.

H.C. Go down to the Social Club and be Lily Ann Beasley—is that you want to be?

LIZZIE. Lily Ann Beasley knows how to get along.

H.C. Then you better call her on the telephone—ask her to let you join up.

LIZZIE. [*Defiantly.*] I will! You see if I don't! And I'm going to buy myself a lot of new dresses—cut way down to here! And I'll get myself some bright lip rouge —and paint my mouth so it looks like I'm always whistling!

H.C. Fine! Go ahead! Look like a silly little jackass!

LIZZIE. It won't be *me* looking silly— it'll be somebody else. You've got to hide what you are. You can't be honest.

H.C. [*Angrily.*] You wouldn't know how to be anything else.

LIZZIE. Oh, wouldn't I? Wouldn't I? You think it's hard? It's easy! Watch me—it's easy—look at this!

[*She crosses the room, swinging her hips voluptuously. When she speaks it is with a silly, giggling voice—imitating Lily Ann.*]

LIZZIE. [*To an imaginary man.*] Why, hello, Gil Demby—how goodie-good-lookin' you are! Such curly blond hair, such pearly white teeth! C'n I count your teeth? One— two—three—four—nah-nah, mustn't bite! And all those muscle-ie muscles! Ooh, just hard as stone, that's what they are, hard as stone! Oh, dear, don't tickle—don't tickle— or little Lizzie's gonna roll right over and dee-I-die!

[*She is giggling uproariously. As she continues this makeshow, she carries herself into convulsions of laughter. And H.C., seeing that she has unintentionally satirized the very thing she proposes to emulate, joins her laughter. While this has been going on, they haven't noticed that FILE has appeared in the open doorway—and has witnessed most of LIZZIE's improvisation.*]

FILE. Good evening.

[*The laughter in the room stops. LIZZIE stands stock still in mortification.*]

H.C. Hello, File. Come in.

FILE. Kinda late. I hope I'm not disturbin' you.

H.C. No—no! We were just—well, I don't know *what* we were doin'—but come on in!

FILE. [*Entering. Quietly.*] Hello, Lizzie.

LIZZIE. Hello, File.

FILE. No—uh—no let-up in the drought, is there?

LIZZIE. Nope. None—at all.

FILE. [*Uncomfortably—to* H.C.] H.C., I got to thinkin' about the little fuss I had with Jimmy and—about his eye and—well —I wanted to apologize. I'm sorry.

H.C. [*With a hidden smile.*] You said that this afternoon, File.

FILE. But I didn't say it to Jim.

H.C. That's true—you didn't. [*With a quick look at* LIZZIE.] He's upstairs—I'll send him down.

[*And quickly* H.C. *starts up the stairs. But* LIZZIE, *seeing it is her father's plan to leave her alone with* FILE, *takes a quick step toward the stairs and, all innocence, calls up to* JIM.]

LIZZIE. Oh, Jim—Jimmy—can you come down for a minute?

H.C. [*With studied casualness.*] That's all right, Lizzie—I was goin' up anyway.

[*And giving her no choice, he disappears from sight.* LIZZIE *and* FILE *are both aware of* H.C.'s *maneuver. They are both painfully embarrassed, unable to meet one another's glance.*]

LIZZIE. [*Just to fill the silence.*] Would you—do you care for a cup of coffee?

FILE. No, thank you—I already had my supper.

LIZZIE. [*Embarrassed at the mention of "supper".*] Yes—yes; of course.

FILE. I didn't mean to mention supper . . . sorry I said it.

LIZZIE. Lemonade?

FILE. No, thank you.

LIZZIE. [*In agony—talking compulsively.*] I make lemonade with limes. I guess if you make it with limes you can't really call it *lemon*-ade, can you?

FILE. [*Generously—to put her at ease.*] You can if you want to. No law against it.

LIZZIE. But it's really *lime*-ade, isn't it?

FILE. Yep—that's what it is. Limeade.

LIZZIE. [*Taking his mannish tone.*] That's what it is, all right!

[*An impasse—nothing more to talk about. At last* JIM *appears. He comes*

down the steps quickly—and he is all
grins that FILE is visiting.]

JIM. You call me, Lizzie? . . . Hey, File.

FILE. Hell, Jim . . . My, that's a bad eye.
I came around to say I'm sorry.

JIM. [Delighted to have FILE here, he
is all forgiveness. Expansively.] Oh, don't
think nothin' of it, File! Bygones is bygones!

FILE. Glad to hear you talk that way.

JIM. Sure—sure.

[An awkward silence. JIM's grin fills
the whole room. He looks from one
to the other, not knowing what to say,
not knowing how to get out.]

JIM. [Abruptly.] Well—well! File's here,
huh? [Silence. On a burst of enthusiasm.]
Yessir—he certain'y is!

[And, in sheer happy animal spirits,
he gives one loud whack at the drum
—and races outdoors. He leaves a
vacuum behind him.]

FILE. Was that Jim's drum I been
hearin'?

LIZZIE. Yes.

FILE. [With a dry smile.] Didn't know
he was musical.

LIZZIE. [Smiling at his tiny little joke.]
Uh—wouldn't you like to sit down—or
something?

FILE. No, thank you . . . [Referring to
the absent JIM. and H.C.] I guess they both
knew I was lyin'.

LIZZIE. Lying? About what?

FILE. I didn't come around to apologize
to Jim.

LIZZIE. What did you come for, File?

FILE. To get something off my chest.
[His difficulties increasing.] This afternoon
—your father—he —uh—[Diving in.] Well,
there's a wrong impression goin' on in the
town—that I'm a widower. Well, I'm not.

LIZZIE. [Quietly—trying to ease things
for him.] I know that, File.

FILE. I know you know it—but I gotta
say it. [Blurting it out.] I'm a divorced
man.

LIZZIE. You don't have to talk about it
if you don't . . .

FILE. [Interrupting roughly.] Yes, I do!
I came to tell the truth. To your father—
and to the whole town. I've been denyin'
that I'm a divorced man—well, now I admit it. That's all I want to say—[Angrily.]—
and that squares me with everybody.

LIZZIE. [Soberly.] Does it?

FILE. Yes, it does! And from here on in—
if I want to live alone—all by myself—it's
nobody's business but my own!

[He has said what he thinks he came
to say. And having said it, he turns
on his heel and starts to beat a hasty
retreat. But LIZZIE stops him.]

LIZZIE. [Sharply.] Wait a minute! [As he
turns.] You're dead wrong!

FILE. Wrong? How?

LIZZIE. [Hotly.] It's everybody's business!

FILE. How do you figure that, Lizzie?

LIZZIE. Because you owe something to
people.

FILE. I don't owe anything to anybody.

LIZZIE. Yes, you do!

FILE. What?

LIZZIE. [Inarticulate—upset.] I don't
know—friendship. If somebody holds out
his hand toward you, you've got to reach—
and take it.

FILE. What do you mean I've got to?

LIZZIE. [In an outburst.] Got to! There
are too many people alone . . . ! And if
you're lucky enough for somebody to want
you—for a friend—[With a cry.] It's an
obligation!

[Stillness. He is deeply disturbed by
what she has said; even more disturbed by her impassioned manner.]

FILE. This . . . this ain't somethin' the
two of us can settle by just talkin' for a
minute.

LIZZIE. [Tremulously.] No, it isn't.

FILE. It'll take some time.

LIZZIE. Yes.

[A spell has been woven between
them. Suddenly it is broken by NOAH's
entrance. Coming in by way of the
front door, he is surprised to see
FILE.]

NOAH. Oh, you here, File?

FILE. Yeah, I guess I'm here.

NOAH. [Looking for an excuse to
leave.] Uh—just comin' in for my feed
book.

[He gets one of his ledgers and goes
out the front door. It looks as though
the charmed moment is lost between
them.]

FILE. [Going to the door.] Well.

LIZZIE. [Afraid he will leave.] What
were we saying?

FILE. What were you sayin'?

LIZZIE. [Snatching for a subject that will

keep him here.] I—you were telling me about your divorce.

FILE. No—I wasn't . . . [*Then, studying her, he changes his mind.*] . . . but I will. [*As he moves a step back into the room.*] She walked out on me.

LIZZIE. I'm sorry.

FILE. Yes—with a schoolteacher. He was from Louisville.

LIZZIE. [*Helping him get it said.*] Kentucky? [*As he nods.*] Was she—I guess she was beautiful . . . ?

FILE. Yes, she was.

LIZZIE. [*Her hopes dashed.*] That's what I was afr—[*Catching herself.*]—that's what I thought.

FILE. Black hair.

LIZZIE. [*Drearily, with an abortive little movement to her un-black hair.*] Yes . . . black hair's pretty, all right.

FILE. I always used to think: If a woman's got pitch-black hair, she's already halfway to bein' a beauty.

LIZZIE. [*Agreeing—but without heart.*] Oh, yes—at least halfway.

FILE. And she had black eyes too—and I guess that did the other half. [*Suddenly, intensely—like a dam bursting.*] With a schoolteacher, dammit! Ran off with a schoolteacher!

LIZZIE. What was *he* like?

FILE. [*With angry intensity.*] He had weak hands and nearsighted eyes! And he always looked like he was about ready to faint. And she ran off with *him!* And there I was . . . [*A cry of pain and rage.*] I'll never understand it!

LIZZIE. [*Gently.*] Maybe the teacher needed her and you didn't.

FILE. Sure I needed her!

LIZZIE. Did you tell her her so?

FILE. [*Raging.*] No, I didn't! Why should I?

LIZZIE. [*Astounded.*] Why *should* you? Why *didn't* you?

FILE. Look here! There's one thing I learned. *Be independent!* If you don't *ask* for things—if you don't let on you *need* things—pretty soon you *don't* need 'em.

LIZZIE. [*Desperately.*] There are some things you *always* need.

FILE. [*Doggedly.*] I won't ask for anything.

LIZZIE. But if you *had* asked her, she might have stayed.

FILE. I know darn well she mighta

stayed. The night she left she said to me: "File, tell me not to go! Tell me don't go!"

LIZZIE. [*In wild astonishment.*] And you didn't?

FILE. I tried—I couldn't!

LIZZIE. Oh, pride . . . !

FILE. Look, if a woman wants to go, let her go! If you have to hold her back— *it's no good!*

LIZZIE. File, if you had to do it over again . . .

FILE. [*Interrupting, intensely.*] I still wouldn't ask her to stay!

LIZZIE. [*In a rage against him.*] Just two words—"don't go!"—you wouldn't say them?

FILE. It's not the words! It's beggin'— and I won't beg!

LIZZIE. You're a fool!

[*It's a slap in the face. A dreadful moment for an overly proud, stubborn man. A dreadful moment for* LIZZIE. *It's a time for drastic measures—or he will go. Having failed with* FILE *on an honest, serious level, she seizes upon flighty falsity as a mode of behavior. Precipitously, she becomes Lily Ann Beasley, the flibbertigibbet.*]

LIZZIE. [*Chattering with false, desperate laughter.*] Whatever am I doing? Getting so serious with you, File! I shoulda known better—because whenever I do, I put my foot in it. Because bein' serious—that's not my nature. I'm really a happy-go-lucky girl —just like any other girl and I—would you like some grapes?

FILE. [*Quietly.*] No, thank you.

LIZZIE. [*Giddily.*] They're very good. And so purply and pretty. We had some right after supper. Oh, I wish you'd been here to supper. I made such a nice supper. I'm a good cook—and I just love cookin'. I think there's only one thing I like better than cookin'. I'll bet you can't guess what that is! [*As he is silent.*] Go on—guess!

FILE. [*Puzzled at her changed manner.*] I don't know.

LIZZIE. Readin' a book! I love to read! Do you read very much?

FILE. [*Watching her as if she were a strange specimen.*] No. Only legal circulars —from Washington.

LIZZIE. [*Seizing on any straw to engage him in the nonsensical chit-chat.*] Oh,

Washington! I just got through readin' a book about him! What a great man! Don't you think Washington was a great man?

FILE. [*Drily.*] Father of our country.

LIZZIE. Yes—exactly! And when you think of all he went through! All that sufferin'! Valley Forge—and all those bleedin' feet! When you *think* of it!

FILE. I don't think about it much.

LIZZIE. And why should you? A busy man like you! [*More Lily Ann Beasley than ever.*] Oh, my, what a nice tie! I just die for men in black silk bow ties!

FILE. [*Quietly—getting angry.*] It ain't silk—it's celluloid!

LIZZIE. No! I can't believe it! It looks so real—it looks so real!

FILE. [*Significantly—like a blow.*] It ain't real—it's fake!

LIZZIE. [*Unable to stop herself.*] And when you smile you've got the strongest white teeth!

FILE. [*Angrily.*] Quit that!

LIZZIE. [*Stunned.*] What . . . ?

FILE. [*Raging.*] Quit it! Stop sashayin' around like a dumb little flirt!

LIZZIE. [*With a moan.*] Oh, no . . .

FILE. Silk tie—strong white teeth! What do you take me for? And what do you take yourself for?

LIZZIE. [*In flight, in despair.*] I was trying to—trying to . . .

FILE. Don't be so damn ridiculous! Be yourself!

[*Saying which, he leaves quickly. Alone,* LIZZIE *is at her wits' end—humiliated, ready to take flight from everything, mostly from herself.* H.C. *enters.*]

H.C. What happened, Lizzie?

[JIM *rushes in.*]

JIM. What'd he do—run out on you? What happened?

[NOAH *comes hurrying in from outdoors.*]

NOAH. I never seen a man run so fast! Where'd he go?

LIZZIE. [*Berserk—to all of them.*] My God, were you watching a show? Did you think it was lantern slides?

H.C. I'm sorry, Lizzie—we couldn't help bein' interested.

JIM. What'd he say?

NOAH. What'd *you* say?

LIZZIE. I didn't say anything! Not one sensible thing. I couldn't even talk to him!

H.C. But you were talkin'!

LIZZIE. No! I was sashaying around like Lily Ann Beasley! I was making a fool of myself! Why can't I ever *talk* to anybody?

H.C. Lizzie, don't blame youself! If *you* couldn't talk to *him*—I'm sure File couldn't talk to you either. It wasn't only your fault.

NOAH. [*Savagely.*] No! It wasn't her fault—and it wasn't File's fault [*Squaring off at his father.*] And you know damn well whose fault it was!

H.C. You mean it was mine, Noah?

NOAH. You bet it was yours!

LIZZIE. [*Seeing a fight—trying to head it off.*] Noah—Pop . . .

H.C. No! He's got to explain that!

[*At this point* STARBUCK *appears at the doorway. He leans against door frame, silent, listening.*]

NOAH. [*Accepting* H.C.'s *challenge.*] I'll explain it, all right. You been building up a rosy dream for her—and she's got no right to hope for it.

H.C. She's got a right to hope for anything.

NOAH. No! She's gotta face the facts—and you gotta help her face them! Stop tellin' her lies!

H.C. I never told her a lie in my life!

NOAH. You told her nothin' *but* lies. When she was a kid with eyeglasses you told her she's the smartest girl in the world. When she started growin' up you told her she was beautiful. And that's the worst lie of all. Because you know—deep down in your heart—you know—she's not beautiful. *She's plain!*

JIM. Noah, you quit that!

NOAH. [*Whirling on* JIM.] And you go right along with him. Every time Lizzie admits she's plain you tell her she's a ravin' beauty. [*Whipping around to* LIZZIE.] But you better listen to me! I'm the only one around here that loves you enough to tell you the truth! You're plain!

JIM. [*Violently.*] Goddamn it, Noah—you quit it!

NOAH. [*Brutally—to* LIZZIE.] Go look at yourself in the mirror—you're plain!

JIM. Noah!

[*Saying which,* JIM *hurls himself at his brother. But the instant he gets to him,* NOAH *strikes out with a tough fist. It catches* JIM *hard and he goes reeling. He returns with murder in his eye but* NOAH *slaps him across the face, grabs the boy and forces him back toward the table. Meanwhile, a frenetic outburst from* H.C. *and* LIZZIE.]

H.C. *and* LIZZIE. Noah—Jim—stop it! Stop it, both of you—stop it!

[*Simultaneously,* STARBUCK *rushes forward and breaks the two men apart. Out of* NOAH's *grip,* JIM *goes berserk, bent on killing* NOAH. *But* STARBUCK *holds him off.*]

JIM. [*Through tears and rage.*] Let me go, Starbuck—let me go!

STARBUCK. Quit it, you damn fool—quit it!

JIM. [*With a cry.*] Let go!

STARBUCK. Get outside! [*Letting him go.*] Now go on—get outside!

JIM. [*Weeping.*] Sure—I'll get outside! I'll get outside and never come back!

[*And in an outburst of tears, he rushes outdoors.*]

NOAH. The next time that kid goes at me, I'll—I'll . . .

STARBUCK. The next time he goes at you, I'll see he has fightin' lessons!

NOAH. Look, you—clear out of here!

STARBUCK. No, I won't clear out! And while I'm here, you're gonna quit callin' that kid a dumbbell—because he's not. He can take a lousy little bulletin that comes from the weather bureau—and he can see magic in it. He can hear thunder in a drum—and you wouldn't understand that —because it's not in your books!

NOAH. I said clear out!

STARBUCK. [*He cannot be stopped.*] And while I'm here, don't you ever call her plain. Because you don't know what's plain and what's beautiful. You don't know what beautiful is.

NOAH. Starbuck, this is family—it's not your fight!

STARBUCK. Yes, it is! I been fightin' fellas like you all my life. And I always lose. But this time—by God, this time . . . !

[*He reins himself in, then hurries outdoors. We hear his voice calling "Jim! —Jim!" A long silence.* NOAH *breaks the stillness with quiet deliberateness.*]

NOAH. [*To* LIZZIE *and* H.C.] I'm sorry I hit Jim—and I'll tell him so. But I ain't sorry for a single word I said to her.

H.C. [*Angry.*] Noah, that's enough!

NOAH. [*Intensely.*] No, it ain't enough! [*To* LIZZIE.] Lizzie, you better think about what I said. Nobody's gonna come ridin' up here on a white horse. Nobody's gonna snatch you up in his arms and marry you, You're gonna be an old maid! And the sooner you face it, the sooner you'll stop breakin' your heart.

[*He goes upstairs. Silence.*]

LIZZIE. [*Dully—half to herself.*] Old maid . . .

H.C. Lizzie, forget it. Forget everything he said.

LIZZIE. No . . . he's right.

H.C. [*With a plea.*] Lizzie . . .

LIZZIE. He's right, Pop. I've known it a long time. But it wasn't so bad until he put a name to it. Old maid. [*With a cry of despair.*] Why is it so much worse when you put a name to it?

H.C. Lizzie, you gotta believe me . . .

LIZZIE. I don't believe you, Pop. You've been lying to me—and I've been lying to myself!

H.C. Lizzie, honey—please . . .

LIZZIE. Don't—don't! I've got to see things the way they are. And the way they will be. I've got to start thinking of myself as a spinster. Jim will get married. And one of these days, even Noah will get married. I'll be the visiting aunt. I'll bring presents to their children—to be sure I'm welcome. And Noah will say: "Junior, be kind to your Aunt Lizzie—her nerves aren't so good." And Jim's wife will say: "She's been visiting here a whole week now—when'll she ever go?" [*With an outcry.*] Go where, for God's sake—go where?

H.C. [*In pain for her.*] Lizzie, you'll always have a home. This house'll be yours.

LIZZIE. [*Hysterically.*] House—house—house!

H.C. [*Trying to calm, to comfort her.*] Lizzie, stop it!

LIZZIE. [*Inconsolable.*] My skin's hot all over. When I touch it, it's cold.

H.C. Lizzie . . .

LIZZIE. I'm all tied up! My clothes are tyin' me up! I can't move in my clothes!

H.C. Lizzie . . .

LIZZIE. Help me, Pop—tell me what to do! Help me!

H.C. Lizzie—Lizzie . . . !

[*Abruptly, without thinking—in a frantic movement—she snatches up the bed linens off the linen trunk—and races outdoors. The lights fade.*] [*Brightest moonlight—moonlight alone —illuminates the inside of the tack room. It is a rough, picturesque room— a junk room really—at the rear of the house. A slanting ceiling with huge hand-hewn beams; large casement windows which give such a vast expanse of bluest night sky that we feel we are more outdoors than in; a wagon wheel against a wall; leather goods—saddles, horse traces and the like; a wagon seat made into a bench, with faded homemade pillows to fit it; an old castaway cot against the wall. It is a room altogether accidental, yet altogether romantic. . . .* STARBUCK *is preparing to go to bed. He takes off his boots and his neckerchief, then he stands in the center of the room, not moving, thinking intently. He hurries to the door, closes it and barricades it with the wagonseat bench. He moves to the windows and tries to open them but they are nailed shut. It's stifling in here. He takes his shirt off and sits on the edge of the cot, suffering the heat. He waves his shirt around to make a breeze. Then he decides to forego caution—and removes the barricade, opening the door. He lies down on the cot. The stillness is a palpable thing, and the heat. As he relaxes, as he slips back into his solitude, a lonely little humming comes from him. It grows in volume and occasionally we hear the words of the song. Suddenly he hears a sound and sits bolt upright.*]

STARBUCK. Who's that? [*He rises tautly.*] Who's there?

[LIZZIE *stands in the doorway, trying not to look into the room. She is carrying the bed linens. She knocks on the door frame.*]

LIZZIE. [*Trying to sound calm.*] It's me —Lizzie.

[STARBUCK *starts to put on his shirt. An awkward motion. Then* LIZZIE, *without entering the room, hands the bedding across the threshold.*]

LIZZIE. Here.

STARBUCK. What's that?

LIZZIE. Bed linens—take them.

STARBUCK. Is that what you came out for?

LIZZIE. [*After a painful moment.*] No . . . I came out because . . .

[*She finds it too difficult to continue.*]

STARBUCK. [*Gently.*] Go on, Lizzie.

LIZZIE. I came out to thank you for what you said to Noah.

STARBUCK. I meant every word of it.

LIZZIE. What you said about Jim—I'm sure you meant that.

STARBUCK. What I said about you.

LIZZIE. I don't believe you.

STARBUCK. Then what are you thankin' me for. What's the matter, Lizzie? You afraid that if you stop bein' sore at me you'll like me a little?

LIZZIE. No . . .

[*And she starts to go.*]

STARBUCK. [*Stopping her.*] Then stay and talk to me! [*As she hesitates.*] It's lonely out here and I don't think I'll sleep much—not in a strange place.

LIZZIE. Then I guess you never sleep. Running from one strange place to another.

STARBUCK. [*With a smile.*] Not runnin' —travelin'.

LIZZIE. Well, if that's the kind of life you like . . .

STARBUCK. Oh, it's not what a man likes —it's what he's got to do. Now what would a fella in my business be doin' stayin' in the same place? Rain's nice—but it ain't nice all the time.

LIZZIE. [*Relaxing a bit.*] No, I guess not.

STARBUCK. People got no use for me— except maybe once in a lifetime. And when my work's done, they're glad to see me go.

LIZZIE. [*Caught by the loneliness in his voice.*] I never thought of it that way.

STARBUCK. Why would you? You never thought of me as a real rainmaker—not until just now.

LIZZIE. I still don't think it!

[*Now she starts to go more determinedly than before.* STARBUCK *stops her physically this time.*]

STARBUCK. Lizzie—wait! Why don't you

let yourself think of me the way you *want* to?

LIZZIE. [*Unnerved.*] What do you mean?

STARBUCK. Think like Lizzie, not like Noah.

LIZZIE. I don't know what you're talking about.

STARBUCK. What are you scared of?

LIZZIE. You! I don't trust you!

STARBUCK. Why? What don't you trust about me?

LIZZIE. Everything! The way you talk, the way you brag—why even your name.

STARBUCK. What's wrong with my name?

LIZZIE. It sounds fake! It sounds like you made it up!

STARBUCK. You're darn right! I did make it up.

LIZZIE. There! Of course!

STARBUCK. Why not? You know what name I was born with? Smith! Smith, for the love of Mike, *Smith!* Now what kind of a handle is that for a fella like me? I needed a name that had the whole sky in it! And the power of a man! Star—buck! Now there's a name—and it's mine.

LIZZIE. No, it's not. You were born Smith —and that's your name.

STARBUCK. You're wrong, Lizzie. The name you choose for yourself is more your own than the name you were born with. And if I was you I'd sure choose another name than Lizzie.

LIZZIE. Thank you—I'm very pleased with it.

STARBUCK. Oh, no you ain't. You ain't pleased with anything about yourself. And I'm sure you ain't pleased with "Lizzie."

LIZZIE. I don't ask *you* to be pleased with it, Starbuck. *I am.*

STARBUCK. Lizzie? Why, it don't *stand* for anything.

LIZZIE. It stands for me! *Me!* I'm not the Queen of Sheba—I'm not Lady Godiva— I'm not Cinderella at the Ball.

STARBUCK. Would you like to be?

LIZZIE. Starbuck, you're ridiculous!

STARBUCK. What's ridiculous about it? Dream you're somebody—*be* somebody! But Lizzie? That's nobody! So many millions of wonderful women with wonderful names! [*In an orgy of delight.*] Leonora, Desdemona, Carolina, Pauline, Annabella,

Florinda, Natasha, Diane! [*Then, with a pathetic little lift of his shoulders.*] Lizzie.

LIZZIE. Good night, Starbuck!

STARBUCK. [*With a sudden inspiration.*] Just a minute, Lizzie—just one little half of a minute. I got the greatest name for you —the greatest name—just listen. [*Then, like a love lyric.*] Melisande.

LIZZIE. [*Flatly.*] I don't like it.

STARBUCK. That's because you don't know anything about her. But when I tell you who she was—lady, when I tell you who she was!

LIZZIE. Who?

STARBUCK. [*Improvising.*] She was the most beautiful . . . ! She was the beautiful wife of King Hamlet! Ever hear of him?

LIZZIE. [*Giving him rope.*] Go on! Go on!

STARBUCK. He was the fella who sailed across the ocean and brought back the Golden Fleece! And you know why he did that? Because Melisande begged him for it! I tell you, that Melisande—she was so beautiful and her hair was so long and curly—every time he looked at her he just fell right down and died. And this King Hamlet, he'd do anything for her—anything she wanted. So when she said: "Hamlet, I got a terrible hankerin' for a soft Golden Fleece," he just naturally sailed right off to find it. And when he came back —all bleedin' and torn—he went and laid that Fleece of Gold right down at her pretty white feet. And she took that fur piece and she wrapped it around her pink naked shoulders and she said: "I got the Golden Fleece—and I'll never be cold no more." . . . Melisande! What a woman. What a *name!*

LIZZIE. [*Quietly.*] Starbuck, you silly jackass. You take a lot of stories—that I've read in a hundred different places—and you roll them up into one big fat ridiculous lie!

STARBUCK. [*Angry, hurt.*] I wasn't lyin' —I was dreamin'!

LIZZIE. It's the same thing!

STARBUCK. [*With growing anger.*] If you think it's the same thing then I take it back about your name! Lizzie—it's just right for you. I'll tell you another name that would suit you—Noah! Because you and your brother—you've got no dream.

LIZZIE. [*With an outcry.*] You think all

dreams have to be your kind? Golden Fleece and thunder on the mountain! But there are other dreams, Starbuck! Little quiet ones that come to a woman when she's shining the silverware and putting moth flakes in the closet.

STARBUCK. Like what?

LIZZIE. [*Crying.*] Like a man's voice saying: "Lizzie, is my blue suit pressed?" And the same man saying: "Scratch between my shoulder blades." And kids laughing and teasing and setting up a racket. And how it feels to say the word "Husband!" . . . There are all kinds of dreams, Mr. Starbuck. Mine are small ones—like my name—Lizzie. But they're *real* like my name—real! So you can have yours—and I'll have mine!

[*Unable to control her tears, she starts to run away. This time he grabs her fully, holding her close.*]

STARBUCK. Lizzie . . .

LIZZIE. Please . . .

STARBUCK. I'm sorry, Lizzie! I'm sorry!

LIZZIE. It's all right—let me go!

STARBUCK. I hope your dreams come true, Lizzie—I hope they do!

LIZZIE. They won't—they never will!

STARBUCK. Believe in yourself and they will!

LIZZIE. I've got nothing to believe in.

STARBUCK. You're a woman! Believe in that!

LIZZIE. How can I when nobody else will?

STARBUCK. *You* gotta believe it first! [*Quickly.*] Let me ask you, Lizzie—are you pretty?

LIZZIE. [*With a wail.*] No—I'm plain!

STARBUCK. There! You see? You don't know you're a woman!

LIZZIE. I am a woman! A plain one!

STARBUCK. There's no such thing as a plain woman! Every real woman is pretty! They're all pretty in a different way—but they're all pretty!

LIZZIE. Not me! When I look in the looking glass . . .

STARBUCK. Don't let Noah be your lookin' glass!

LIZZIE. He's not. My looking glass is right on the wall.

STARBUCK. It's in the wrong place. It's gotta be inside you.

LIZZIE. No . . .

STARBUCK. Don't be afraid—*look!* You'll

see a pretty woman, Lizzie. Lizzie, you gotta be your own lookin' glass. And then one day the lookin' glass will be the man who loves you. It'll be his eyes, maybe. And you'll look in the mirror and you'll be more than pretty—you'll be beautiful!

LIZZIE. [*Crying out.*] It'll never happen!

STARBUCK. Make it happen! Lizzie, why don't you think "pretty" and take down your hair?

[*He reaches for her hair.*]

LIZZIE. [*In panic.*] No!

STARBUCK. Please, Lizzie!

[*He is taking the pins out of her hair.*]

LIZZIE. No—no . . .

STARBUCK. Nobody sees you, Lizzie—nobody but me! [*Taking her in his arms.*] Now close your eyes, Lizzie—close them! [*As she obeys.*] Now—say: "I'm pretty!"

LIZZIE. [*Trying.*] I'm—I'm—I can't!

STARBUCK. Say it! Say it, Lizzie!

LIZZIE. I'm . . . pretty.

STARBUCK. Say it again!

LIZZIE. [*With a little cry.*] Pretty!

STARBUCK. Say it—mean it!

LIZZIE. [*Exalted.*] I'm pretty! I'm pretty! I'm pretty!

[*He kisses her. A long kiss and she clings to him, passionately, the bonds of her spinsterhood breaking away. The kiss over, she collapses on the cot, sobbing.*]

LIZZIE. [*Through the sobs.*] Why did you do that?

STARBUCK. [*Going beside her on the cot.*] Because when you said you were pretty, it was true!

[*Her sobs are louder, more heart-rending because, for the first time, she is happy.*]

STARBUCK. Lizzie—look at me!

LIZZIE. I can't!

STARBUCK. [*Turning her to him.*] Stop cryin' and look at me! Look at my eyes! What do you see?

LIZZIE. [*Gazing through her tears.*] I can't *believe* what I see!

STARBUCK. Tell me what you see!

LIZZIE. [*With a sob of happiness.*] Oh, is it me? Is it really me?

[*Now she goes to him with all her giving.*]

END OF ACT TWO

ACT THREE

The lights come up inside the house to reveal H.C. *at the telephone.*

H.C. [*Into phone.*] Thank you, Howard —I'm sorry I woke you up. . . . Well, if you hear from Jimmy, you call me right away, will you? No, nothin's wrong. . . . Thank you.

[*He hangs up and paces worriedly.* NOAH *comes down the stairs wearing his bathrobe. He has been unable to sleep a wink.*]

NOAH. [*Grumpily.*] Jimmy get home yet?

H.C. Nope.

NOAH. That dopey kid. It's near two o'clock.

H.C. Go back to sleep, Noah. Don't worry about him.

NOAH. I ain't worryin' about him. I don't give a damn what happens to him.

H.C. Okay—fine.

NOAH. Maybe he's at the Hopkinsons. . . . I'll call them.

H.C. I called them all. Nobody seen him.

NOAH. If you'da seen my side of this, it wouldn't of happened.

H.C. I see your side, Noah—I just ain't *on* your side.

NOAH. [*Angrily.*] Nobody is!

H.C. Cheer up, Noah. For a fella who's got nobody on his side you sure have twisted those kids around your little finger. If you tell Jim he's a puppy dog, he starts to bark. If you call Lizzie a monkey, she scratches.

[*At this instant,* JIM *stands in the doorway. He looks very cocky, very self-satisfied, ten feet taller than before. He is smoking an enormous cigar with an air of aloof grandeur. He struts majestically into the room.*]

JIM. Good e-ve-ning!

NOAH. Where the hell you been?

JIM. [*With a lordly gesture.*] Out—out—out!

NOAH. What's wrong with you? Are you drunk?

JIM. [*With an air of superiority.*] No, Big Brother, I ain't drunk. But if I cared to be drunk, I'd be google-eyed!

H.C. [*Secretly amused.*] Where'd you get the stogie, Jim?

JIM. It ain't a stogie. It's a Havana Panatela. Eighty-fi' cents. And it's a present.

NOAH. Who the hell gave it to you?

JIM. I-the-hell gave it to me! For bein' a big boy. Write it on the books, Noah. In big red numbers.

NOAH. You didn't tell us where you been.

JIM. I don't have to—but I will. I been out with my favorite girl—[*He takes a little red hat out of his pocket, unfolds it and slaps it on his head.*]—Snookie!

NOAH. You crazy, dumb little . . .

JIM. [*Warningly—with an even smile.*] Uh-uh-uh-uh! Don't say dumb no more, Noah. Or I shall take this eighty-fi' cent Havana Panatela and I shall squash it right in your mean old face.

H.C. What happened, Jimmy?

NOAH. Can't you see what happened? He went ridin' with Snookie Maguire and she got him all hot up and then, by God, she trapped him. And she gave him her little red hat for a consolation prize.

JIM. Big Brother, you got it all wrong.

NOAH. Don't lie to me, Jimmy Curry! The minute I stopped lookin' after you, you got yourself in trouble.

JIM. Noah, when I tell you what *really* happened, you're gonna split your britches! We went ridin'—yep, that's right. We opened that Essex up and we went forty million miles an hour. And then we stopped that car and we got out and we sat down under a great big tree. And we could look through the branches and see the sky all full of stars—*damn*, it was full of stars. And I turned around and I kissed her. I kissed her once, I kissed her a hundred times. I kissed her *real!* And while I was doin' that, I knew I could carry her anywhere—right straight to the moon. But all the time, I kept thinkin': "Noah's gonna come along and he's gonna say 'Whoa!' He's gonna say: 'Jim, you're dumb! You're so dumb you ain't got sense enough to say whoa to yourself—so I'm sayin' it for you—Whoa!'" But Noah didn't show up—and I kept right on kissin'. And then somethin' happened. *She* was cryin' and *I* was cryin' and I

127

thought any minute now we'll be right up there on the moon. And then—then!—without Noah bein' there—all by my smart little self—*I said whoa!*

H.C. Yippeeeeee!

JIM. [*Formally.*] Thank you, Pop—your yipee is accepted.

NOAH. I don't believe a word of it. Why'd she give you the hat?

JIM. For the same reason I give her my elk's tooth! We're engaged!

NOAH. So I was right. She did trap you.

JIM. [*Warningly.*] Noah, I see I'm gonna have to give you this Havana Panatela.

H.C. Don't listen to him, Jimmy. Congratulations.

JIM. [*Touched.*] Thanks, Pop—thank you very kindly. [*Suddenly elated.*] I gotta tell Lizzie! Where's Lizzie?

NOAH. Where the Sam Hill do you think she is? She's asleep.

JIM. [*Hurrying to the stairs.*] Well, then, I'll wake her up!

H.C. Wait, Jimmy . . . Lizzie's not up there.

JIM. Where is she?

[*A moment.*]

NOAH. Where is she, Pop?

H.C. She's out in the tack room.

NOAH. You mean with Starbuck?

H.C. Yes.

JIM. Man, that's great! [*Pulling another cigar out of his pocket.*] I got another cigar for Lizzie.

NOAH. [*Quietly to* H.C.] Wait a minute. You mean you let her walk in on that fella when he's sleepin'?

H.C. I don't think she just walked in on him, Noah. I'm sure she knocked on the door first.

JIM. Sure—Lizzie's real polite.

NOAH. Pop! You didn't even try to stop her?

H.C. No, I didn't! You called her an old maid. You took away the last little bit of hope she ever had. And when you left, she lifted up those bed linens and ran out. I didn't ask her where she was goin'—but I'm glad she went. Because if she lost her hope in here—maybe she'll find it out there.

NOAH. That was in your mind the minute you laid eyes on that fella.

H.C. If it was in my mind, I didn't know it.

NOAH. That's why you let him stay.

JIM. We let him stay because he's a rainmaker.

NOAH. It's got nothin' to do with him bein' a rainmaker! [*To* H.C.] You knew he was a fake the minute he opened his mouth. But you gave him a hundred bucks —you let him order us around—you gave him the run of the whole ranch. Why? Was it for rain? No! It was for Lizzie!

H.C. You put it awful cut and dried, Noah.

NOAH. It's the truth! [*Deeply affected.*] And I don't see how you could do that, Pop!

H.C. Noah, you got a sound in your voice makes me feel I oughta be ashamed. Well, I'm not.

NOAH. If you're not ashamed of sellin' your daughter short, then you lost your self-respect.

JIM. What the hell *is* self-respect anyway?

NOAH. You shut up!

JIM. I'll never shut up no more! I think it's great them bein' out there together. They might get real serious about each other. And before you know it, I got me a new brother. Boy, I'd swap him for you any day!

NOAH. You won't have to swap him for anybody. Because he ain't the marryin' kind—not that faker.

JIM. I bet he is the marryin' kind—I bet he is! Hey, Pop, what do you figure a rainmaker makes?

NOAH. [*Exploding.*] Rain!

JIM. No—I mean money! I guess there ain't no scale of wages to go by. A hundred here—a hundred there. Pop, you reckon a fella can support a wife makin' rain around the country?

H.C. [*Soberly.*] Don't let's be beforehand, Jimmy.

[*Suddenly there, on the threshold,* FILE *and the* SHERIFF. FILE *knocks on the door frame.*]

FILE. Mind if we come in, H.C.?

H.C. Hello, File . . . Hey, Sheriff—come on in.

NOAH *and* JIM. Hey, File . . . Hey, Sheriff.

H.C. Kinda late to be visitin', ain't it, Sheriff?

SHERIFF. Well, we're not exactly visitin' H.C.

FILE. How's Lizzie?

H.C. Fine, boy, fine. [*With a trace of puzzled amusement.*] You just seen her a little while ago.

FILE. [*With a little embarrassment.*] Yeah—I know.

H.C. You and the Sheriff come callin' on Lizzie?

FILE. [*Quickly.*] No—no.

H.C. What can I do for you?

FILE. I'll tell you, H.C. We been gettin' a lot of phone calls from Pedleyville and Peak's Junction and all down the state line. They been lookin' for a fella—well, he's a kinda con man. Name of Tornado Johnson. . . . [*But he can't get his mind off* LIZZIE.] She asleep?

H.C. [*Baiting him goodnaturedly.*] Who —Lizzie?

FILE. Well, I reckon she is . . . You get any wind of him?

H.C. Who?

FILE. [*Irritably.*] Tornado Johnson.

H.C. Nope.

FILE. [*Referring to a slip of paper.*] Tornado Johnson—alias Bill Harmony— alias Bill Smith.

H.C. I never met anybody call himself by any of those names.

FILE. Well, a fella that's got three aliases can easy have four. Anybody else come around here?

H.C. [*Smiling.*] Only you, File.

FILE. [*Looking toward the stairs.*] Kind of a hot night to be asleep, ain't it?

H.C. Lizzie's a good sleeper.

FILE. Yeah . . . must be.

SHERIFF. No Tornado Johnson, huh?

H.C. Nope.

SHERIFF. Seems a little fishy.

JIM. How do you mean fishy?

SHERIFF. Well, Pedleyville and the Junction and Three Point—we all kinda figured this together and—uh . . .

[*Embarrassed, he looks at* FILE.]

FILE. Look, H.C., we know it ain't like you to protect a criminal.

NOAH. [*Quickly.*] Really a criminal, huh?

FILE. [*Uncomfortably.*] Well, he's wanted!

H.C. What's he wanted for, File?

FILE. [*Referring to his notes again—but not actually reading them.*] He's wanted in the state of Kansas. He sold four hundred tickets to a great big Rain Festival. Well, there wasn't no rain—so there couldn't be no festival. In a small town in

Nebraska he drummed up a lot of excitement about what he called a Spectacular Eclipse of the Sun—and he peddled a thousand pair of smoked eyeglasses to see it with. No eclipse. In the month of February he sold six hundred wooden poles— fifteen dollars apiece. He called them Tornado Rods. Claimed that if that town ever got hit by a tornado the wind would just blow through there like a gentle spring breeze—and not hurt a thing. Well, when he left, the town got hit by every blow you can imagine—windstorm, hailstorm, cyclone and hurricane. Blew the Tornado Rods off the roof and blew the town off the map!

JIM. How about a tornado? Did it ever get hit by a tornado?

FILE. No, it didn't.

JIM. Well, that's all he guaranteed— that it wouldn't get hit by a tornado. And it didn't!

H.C. Don't sound like a criminal to me, File.

FILE. [*As* H.C. *shakes his head.*] Does sound like a con man, don't he, H.C.?

H.C. Maybe.

SHERIFF. Anyway, we got orders to lock him up—and we'd sure appreciate some help.

H.C. Sorry I can't help you, Sheriff.

FILE. I got a feelin' you can. They say this fella carries a great big bass drum wherever he goes. Whose drum is that?

JIM. It's mine. I'm figurin' to be a drummer.

FILE. What do *you* figure to be, H.C.— a whitewash painter?

H.C. Maybe.

FILE. Must be some reason you painted that big white arrow on the ground.

H.C. It's my ground, File.

FILE. [*Taking a step toward the window.*] Yeah—it's your ground all right. But whose wagon is that?

[*Silence.*]

SHERIFF. Let's go have a look at that wagon, File.

[FILE *and the* SHERIFF *quickly go out.*]

NOAH. [*In an outburst, to* H.C.] Why'd you do that? Why the hell did you do that?

H.C. [*Upset.*] I don't know.

NOAH. I heard it said that the dry heat makes some people go crazy in their heads!

H.C. You think I'm crazy, Noah?

H.C. Yeah.

FILE. What's it like?

NOAH. Dry.

FILE. How'd Lizzie like it in Sweetriver?

NOAH. [*Sensing that their legs are being pulled.*] Fine—she liked it fine!

JIM. Yeah—she liked it fine! Three barn dances, a rodeo, a summer fair and larkin' all over the place.

[*He laughs loudly.* NOAH *squirms as he realizes that* FILE *sees through them. And* H.C. *feels queasy. Then, jumping in.*]

H.C. How's your poker, File?

FILE. My what?

H.C. Poker.

FILE. Oh, I don't like poker much.

JIM. You don't? Don't you like Spit in the Ocean?

FILE. Not much.

H.C. We figured to ask you to play some cards.

FILE. I gave cards up a long time. H.C.

JIM. [*Stymied.*] You did, huh?

FILE. Mm-hm.

[*Silence. An impasse. Suddenly* JIM *sees the needle hanging down from* FILE's *shirt.*]

JIM. File, what's that hangin' down from your shirt?

FILE. [*A little self-consciously.*] Kinda looks like a needle.

H.C. It sure does.

JIM. What's the matter—your shirt tore?

FILE. Looks like it.

JIM. Fix it yourself, do you?

FILE. Sure do.

JIM. [*Clucking in sympathy.*] Tch-tch-tch-tch-tch-tch.

FILE. [*Suppressing the smile.*] Oh, I wouldn't say that, Jim. I been fixin' my own shirts ever since I became a widower back in Pedleyville.

JIM. Lizzie fixes all my shirts.

FILE. Well, it sure is nice to have a sister.

JIM. [*Significantly.*] Or somethin'!

FILE. That's right.

[*Silence. Another impasse.*]

JIM. [*Abruptly.*] Yessir! Sure is great what a great time Lizzie had in Sweetriver!

H.C. Great!

FILE. Did—uh—did Lizzie come back by herself?

NOAH. [*Tensing.*] Sure! She went by herself, didn't she?

FILE. [*With a dry smile.*] That don't mean nothin'. I rode down to Leverstown to buy myself a mare. I went by myself but I came back with a mare!

JIM. [*Getting to the point; starting to lose his temper.*] Well, she didn't go to buy nothin'! Get it, File—nothin'!

FILE. [*Evenly.*] Don't get ornery, Jim. I just asked a friendly question.

NOAH. [*To* JIM—*with hidden warning.*] Sure! Just a friendly question—don't get ornery.

H.C. [*Baiting the trap for* FILE.] I always say to Jim—the reason you ain't got no real friends is 'cause you're ornery! You just don't know how to make friends!

JIM. [*Hurt and angry.*] Sure I do—sure I do!

H.C. No, you don't! [*Meaningfully.*] Do you ever ask a fella out to have a drink? No! Do you ever say to a fella: Come on home and have some supper?

JIM. [*Suddenly remembering the objective; not sure how to spring the trap.*] I guess you're right. I'm sorry, File. Didn't mean to get ornery. Come on out and have a drink.

NOAH. [*Reflexively.*] Supper!

JIM. [*Quickly, realizing his error.*] Yeah —come on home and have some supper.

FILE. [*Aware of the trap.*] Guess I'll say no to the supper, boys. [*With a flash of mischief.*] But I'll be glad to go out and have a drink with you.

NOAH. We don't have time for a drink. But we been figurin' to ask you to supper one of these days.

FILE. Be glad to come—one of these days.

H.C. How about tonight?

FILE. Don't have the time tonight. Seems there's some kind of outlaw comin' this way. Fella named Tornado Johnson. Have to stick around.

NOAH. You don't know he'll come this way, do you?

FILE. They say he's Three Point bound.

H.C. But you don't know he'll be here tonight.

FILE. I don't know he won't he here tonight.

JIM. Why, he might be down at Pedleyville or Peak's Junction. He might even be over at our place.

NOAH. I think somethin's wrong with you, Pop! Why didn't you tell them—straight out: "The fella you're lookin' for is in the tack room with my daughter"?

H.C. Because he's with my daughter!

NOAH. [*With angry resolve.*] All right! I didn't tell them you were lyin'. I kept my mouth shut—I stood by you. But I ain't standin' by you any more!

[*He starts for the door.*]

H.C. Where you goin', Noah?

NOAH. I'm goin' out to the tack room and bring her in.

H.C. Noah, wait!

NOAH. And I'm gonna bring him in too!

H.C. He's a quick fella, Noah—and you're a little slow on your feet!

[NOAH *rushes to the sideboard, opens a drawer and brings out a gun.*]

NOAH. I'll be quicker with this!

H.C. [*Angry.*] Put that down!

NOAH. You want Lizzie out there with him! You heard what they said about him. He's a swindler and a crook and a four-flusher and I don't know what else.

H.C. I'll tell you what else, Noah—he's a man!

JIM. Pop's right! Gettin' married is gettin' married!

H.C. Jimmy, you always say the smart thing at a dumb time!

JIM. Well, I'm all for her gettin' married—I don't care who the fella is.

NOAH. Is that the way you think, Pop?

H.C. You know it's not the way I think.

NOAH. Then I'm goin'.

H.C. I said stay here.

NOAH. [*Raging.*] It ain't right, Pop—it ain't right!

H.C. [*Exploding.*] Noah, you're so full of what's right you can't see what's *good!* It's good for a girl to get married, sure—but maybe you were right when you said she won't ever have that! Well, she's gotta have somethin'! [*With desperate resolution.*] *Lizzie has got to have somethin'!* Even if it's only one minute—with a man talkin' quiet and his hand touchin' her face.

JIM. Sure—let's give her a minute.

H.C. Shut up! [*To* NOAH.] And if you go out there and shorten the time they have together—if you put one little dark shadow over the brightest time of Lizzie's life—I swear I'll come out after you with a whip! [*Quietly.*] Now you give me that gun!

[*A taut moment during which* NOAH *and* H.C. *confront each other in open hostility.* NOAH *is too righteously proud to give the gun to his father, yet not strong enough to defy him. At last, to give in without entirely losing face, he puts the gun down on the table.* H.C. *turns away; so does* NOAH. *The lights fade.*]

[*The lights come up inside the tack room.* STARBUCK *and* LIZZIE *are sitting on the floor, leaning against the back of the wagonseat bench. They are quite intimately close, looking out through the open door at the bright expanse of sky. Lizzie has the shine of moonlight over her face and this glow, meeting her inner radiance, makes her almost beautiful.*]

STARBUCK. And I always walk so fast and ride so far I never have time to stop and ask myself no question.

LIZZIE. If you did stop, what question would you ask?

STARBUCK. Well . . . I guess I'd say: "Big Man, where you goin'?"

LIZZIE [*Quietly.*] Big Man, where *are* you going?

STARBUCK. [*After an indecisive moment.*] I don't know.

LIZZIE. Where do you want to *get* to?

STARBUCK. [*Inarticulate for the first time.*] I—I want to touch somethin'. Somethin' big—to send shivers down my spine!

LIZZIE. Yes . . . I get shivers just thinking about it.

STARBUCK. But every time I get near anything big like that, I blink my eyes and it's gone. [*With a little revolt.*] Why *is* that? Why is it the things you want are only there for the blinkin' of an eye? Why don't nothin' *stay?*

LIZZIE. [*Quietly.*] Some things stay forever.

STARBUCK. Like what?

LIZZIE. [*A little abashed.*] Never mind.

STARBUCK. You gotta tell me! Please!

LIZZIE. You fall in love with somebody —not *me*, I don't expect it'll be me—just *somebody*. And get married and have kids. And if you do, you'll live forever.

STARBUCK. [*Yearning.*] I'd sure like to live forever. [*As they look at each other intently.*] I reckon I better kiss you again. [*He kisses her and they are close for a moment.*] Didn't anybody ever kiss you before I did, Lizzie?

LIZZIE. [*With a wan smile.*] Yes—once.

STARBUCK. When was that?

LIZZIE. I was about twelve, I guess. I didn't know then whether I was pretty or plain—I just didn't think about it. There was a boy with freckles and red hair—and I thought he was the beginning of the world. But he never paid me any mind. Then one day he was standing around with a lot of other boys and they were whispering and cutting up. And suddenly, he shot over to me and kissed me hard, right on the mouth! And for a minute I was so stirred up and so happy . . . ! But then he ran back to the other kids and I heard him say: "I'll kiss anything on a dare—even your old man's pig!" So I ran home and up the back stairs and I locked my door and looked at myself in the mirror —and from that day on I knew I was plain.

STARBUCK. Are you plain, Lizzie?

LIZZIE. [*Looking at him, smiling.*] No— I'm beautiful.

STARBUCK. You are—and don't you ever forget it!

LIZZIE. [*A little sadly; reconciled to his ultimate going.*] I'll try to remember— everything—you ever said.

[STARBUCK *rises restively. Somehow he is deeply disturbed, lonely. He walks to the door, his back to* LIZZIE, *and looks out at the night. There is searching in his face, and yearning. At last it comes out in a little outcry.*]

STARBUCK. Lizzie, I want to live forever!

LIZZIE. [*Full of compassion.*] I hope you do—wherever you are—I hope you do!

STARBUCK. You don't say that as if you think I'll ever get what I'm after.

LIZZIE. [*Gently.*] I don't *know* what you're after.

STARBUCK. I'm after a clap of lightnin'! I want things to be as pretty when I *get* them as they are when I'm *thinkin'* about them!

LIZZIE. [*Hurt. He seems to disparage the moment of realization they've had together.*] I think they're prettier when you get them. I think when you get something you've been dreaming about—oh, it's so beautiful!

STARBUCK. I wasn't talkin' about us, Lizzie.

LIZZIE. Weren't you?

STARBUCK. No—I'm talkin' about everything. Nothin's as pretty in your hands as it was in your head. There ain't no world near as good as the world I got up here. [*Angrily tapping his forehead.*] Why?

LIZZIE. I don't know. Maybe it's because you don't take time to see it. Always on the go—here, there, nowhere. Running away . . . keeping your own company. Maybe if you'd keep company with the *world* . . .

STARBUCK. [*Doubtfully.*] I'd learn to love it?

LIZZIE. You might—if you saw it *real*. Some nights I'm in the kitchen washing the dishes. And Pop's playing poker with the boys. Well, I'll watch him real close. And at first I'll just see an ordinary middle-aged man—not very interesting to look at. And then, minute by minute, I'll see little things I never saw in him before. Good things and bad things—queer little habits I never noticed he had—and ways of talking I never paid any mind to. And suddenly I know who he is—and I love him so much I could cry! And I want to thank God I took the time to see him *real*.

STARBUCK. [*Breaking out.*] Well, I ain't got the time.

LIZZIE. Then you ain't got no world— except the one you make up in your head. So you better just be satisfied with that.

STARBUCK. No!

LIZZIE. I'm sorry. I didn't mean to hurt you.

[*A long moment. When at last he speaks, it is with painful difficulty.*]

STARBUCK. Lizzie . . . I got somethin' to tell you . . . You were right . . . I'm a liar and a con man and a fake. [*A moment. The words tear out of him.*] I never made rain in my life! Not a single raindrop! Nowhere! Not anywhere at all!

LIZZIE. [*In a compassionate whisper.*] I know. . . .

STARBUCK. All my life—wantin' to make a miracle! . . . Nothin'! . . . I'm a great big blowhard!

LIZZIE. [*Gently.*] No . . . You're all dreams. And it's no good to live in your dreams.

STARBUCK. [*With desperation.*] It's no good to live outside them either!

LIZZIE. Somewhere between the two . . . !

STARBUCK. Yes! [*After a moment.*] The two of us maybe. . . .

LIZZIE. [*Forcing herself to believe it might work.*] . . . Yes!

STARBUCK. Lizzie! Lizzie, would you like me to stick around for a while?

LIZZIE. [*Unable to stand the joy of it.*] Did I hear you right?

STARBUCK. Not for good, understand—just for a few days!

LIZZIE. You're—you're not fooling me, are you, Starbuck?

STARBUCK. No—I mean it!

LIZZIE. [*Crying.*] Would you stay? Would you?

STARBUCK. A few days—yes!

LIZZIE. [*Her happiness bursting.*] Oh! Oh, goodness! Oh!

STARBUCK. Lizzie . . .

LIZZIE. I can't stand it—I just can't stand it!

STARBUCK. [*Taking her in his arms.*] Lizzie . . .

LIZZIE. You look up at the sky and you cry for a star. You know you'll never get it. And then one night you look down—and there it is—shining in your hand!

[*Half laughing, half crying, she goes into his arms again as the lights fade.*]

[*The lights come up inside the house where* H.C., NOAH *and* JIM *are waiting for things to come to pass.* NOAH *is at work at his books.* JIM *is looking out the window. A restless tension in the room.*]

H.C. [*To* JIM.] Any sign of rain?

JIM. No—nothin'.

NOAH. You may as well stop lookin' for it.

JIM. Reckon I ought to beat the drum again?

NOAH. What for?

JIM. [*Abashedly.*] Oh, I forgot. [*With sudden anger.*] Look at them—look at what that Sheriff's doin'!

H.C. What?

JIM. They're ransackin' his wagon—gettin' it all messed up.

NOAH. Well, they got a right.

JIM. No, they ain't! Why, he had everything so neat in there—big wheels and books . . . Why, he's been collectin' those things for years! I an't gonna let them hurt none of that stuff!

[*Unhappily—anxious for action, anxious to come to* STARBUCK'S *rescue in*

some harmless way—he rushes out the front door.*]

NOAH. Damn fool. [*Writing in his ledger.*] How much did he say that panatela cost?

H.C. Eighty-five cents.

NOAH. He coulda had a whole box of Sweet Caporals for a dime!

[LIZZIE *enters through the rear door. The moonlight still glows on her.* NOAH *and* H.C. *turn, their eyes fixed on the girl.* LIZZIE *looks from one to another, trying to contain the rhapsody in her.*]

NOAH. Where's Starbuck?

LIZZIE. In the tack room. [*To* H.C.] He wanted to come in and talk to you, Pop—but I said let me do it first.

NOAH. What's he want to talk about?

LIZZIE. Well—I—we . . . [*Unable to speak in front of* NOAH, *she shifts nervously to:*] You know—I think I saw a wisp of a cloud.

NOAH. You're seein' things!

LIZZIE. [*Her happiness bursting forth.*] No! The smallest wisp of a cloud—floating across the moon—no bigger than a mare's tail.

NOAH. You're talkin' like him.

LIZZIE. Yes—I am—yes!

NOAH. Whyn't you comb your hair?

LIZZIE. [*With an excited laugh.*] I like it this way! I'm going to wear it this way all my life! I'm going to throw away my pins! [*Taking a handful of pins out of her pocket she tosses them high in the air.*] There! I've got no more pins! [*Then, in a rush to her father.*] But I've got something else!

H.C. [*Quietly.*] What, Lizzie?

LIZZIE. Pop . . . Oh, Pop, I've got me a beau!

H.C. [*Heavily, trying to smile.*] Have you, honey?

LIZZIE. Not an always beau—but a beau for meanwhile! Until he goes! He says he'll go in a few days—but anything can happen in a few days—anything can happen, can't it, Pop?

H.C. Yes . . . it sure can.

LIZZIE. [*Ecstatically.*] Oh, Pop, the world's turned clear around!

NOAH. Why don't you tell her, Pop?

LIZZIE. Tell me what?

H.C. [*With difficulty.*] Lizzie, you were

right about that fella. He's a liar and a con man.

LIZZIE. [*With a cry.*] But there's nothing bad about him, Pop! He's so good—and so alone—he's so terribly alone!

NOAH. That's what he deserves to be.

LIZZIE. No—nobody ought to be that. And I'll see that he's not any more. I'll be with him every minute he wants me.

NOAH. [*Going to the window—not unkindly.*] Lizzie—come here.

LIZZIE. [*Instantly apprehensive.*] What?

NOAH. I'm sorry, but you better look out this window.

[*She crosses to the window and looks out. A moment of bewilderment and dread.*]

LIZZIE. What are they here for? What are they doing on his wagon? [*As* NOAH *turns away.*] Pop!

H.C. They're gettin' evidence against him, Lizzie. The Sheriff's here to lock him up.

LIZZIE. No!

[*Suddenly she starts for the back door but* NOAH *stops her.*]

NOAH. Stay here, Lizzie!

LIZZIE. Let me go, Noah! [*In a panic, to* H.C.] They've got no right to arrest him!

H.C. I'm afraid they have.

NOAH. He cheated and swindled everywhere he went.

LIZZIE. Pop, we've got to help him!

H.C. [*Painfully.*] Lizzie, quit it! There's nothin' we can do for him!

LIZZIE. Not for him—for me! I love him!

NOAH. You're out of your mind! He'll be gone in a day or two. He'll never even remember he saw you.

LIZZIE. No—that's not true!

H.C. [*Quietly.*] You think he'd marry you, Lizzie?

LIZZIE. I don't know . . .

NOAH. Well, you won't marry *him*, I'll tell you that! You're as different as mornin' and night. He's opposite to everything you are.

LIZZIE. Opposites go to each other.

NOAH. And they wind up apart.

LIZZIE. [*Desperately.*] I'll pull him *to* me! I'll change him—I'll make him settle down! I'll make him see the world like the world is!

NOAH. Will you make him see *you* like *you* are?

LIZZIE. He does see me like I am!

NOAH. What'd he do? Tell you you're beautiful? Tell you you're a princess—straight out of a fairy tale?

LIZZIE. [*With an outcry of fright—because he has struck home.*] Let me alone!

NOAH. He did, didn't he?

H.C. [*With a violent shout.*] Stop it, Noah! [*A moment. He goes to* LIZZIE *and talks to her quietly.*] Lizzie—listen to me. There's some truth in what Noah says . . .

LIZZIE. No—

H.C. Not all truth—but some. Noah's right when he says you two ain't matched.

LIZZIE. But we are!

H.C. No, you're not! You're only matched if you see life the same way. Take Noah. He sees life the way it is—but he sees it small and he sees it mean. You see life the way it is—but you see it big and beautiful!

LIZZIE. So does Starbuck!

H.C. No. He don't see life at all. He only sees somethin' he made up in his mind. And I'm sure you ain't Lizzie to him—I'm sure he just dreamed you up in his head.

LIZZIE. No! He sees me as real as you do!

H.C. Do you believe that, Lizzie? [*As she doesn't answer.*] Do you think he sees you real, Lizzie? Answer me!

LIZZIE. [*With great effort.*]Yes . . . he does.

H.C. [*With an effort—pulling himself together.*] All right—then you better help him get away. Go out the back door and . . .

NOAH. You're not gonna let her do that, Pop!

H.C. Yes, I am!

NOAH. Pop, it's a terrible mistake!

H.C. [*Exploding.*] Don't you think I know that? But if she don't make this mistake, she'll make a bigger one. She'll stay at home and turn sensible the way you want her to be. She'll follow your rules and jump through your hoop—and pretty soon we'll have another Noah in this house. And then she won't be plain—she'll be downright ugly! [*Whirling to her.*] Now go on, Lizzie!

[*She starts for the door but* NOAH *grabs her as she tries to get by.*]

NOAH. No! I won't let you!

LIZZIE. Noah, please!

H.C. Let her go, Noah!

NOAH. You're not goin'—no!

[H.C. *rushes between them and vio-*

lently tears them apart. But NOAH
stands there, barring the door. LIZZIE,
*in a wild flight, starts for the other
door. But just as she reaches it, the*
SHERIFF, FILE *and* JIM *enter, block-
ing the doorway. A taut moment.*]
FILE. Well . . . you awake?
LIZZIE. Hello, File.
FILE. They said you were asleep.
LIZZIE. Did they? [*Trying to get past
him.*] Excuse me.
FILE. [*Blocking her path.*] Where you
goin', Lizzie?
LIZZIE. [*Afraid of giving* STARBUCK
away.] Nowhere. Outside.
FILE. [*Suspiciously.*] Wait a minute,
Lizzie! What are you in such a rush for?
LIZZIE. [*Confused.*] I—I just wanted to
see what you two were doing out there—
on that wagon!
FILE. Well, we came in now. So you
don't have to go out.
SHERIFF. [*Shrewdly—quickly.*] Unless
there's some other reason for you goin'?
LIZZIE. No—no.
SHERIFF. [*To the others—his eye on*
LIZZIE.] I guess we got what we came for.
He's got a half-dozen Tornado Rods out
there and a boxful of smoked eyeglasses
like this. [*He holds up a pair of glasses.*]
All right, H.C.—where is he?
H.C. Do your own work, Sheriff.
FILE. H.C., I don't want this family
mixed up in trouble. Tell us where he is—
please!
JIM. He left about an hour ago.
SHERIFF. Where'd he go?
JIM. Pedleyville.
FILE. How'd he go? His wagon's still
here.
H.C. He took Jim's roan.
JIM. Yeah—he took my roan.
FILE. I think you're lyin'—all of you!
[*With sudden enraged exasperation.*] What
the hell's goin' on here anyway? I ask you
questions and you tell me a pack of lies!
And for what? A stranger! A man who
don't mean anything to you! [*Abruptly he
goes still as the thought assails him.*] Or
does he? [*As he feels the tautness of the
silence, his attention slowly, slowly turns
to* LIZZIE. *Slowly, slowly he crosses the
room and places himself squarely facing
her.*] Maybe *you* better answer that question, Lizzie.

[*It is too much for her. She takes a
quick step away, in flight—but* FILE
grabs her.]
FILE. No—wait a minute! They said you
were asleep—but you weren't! Why did
they lie about that? Where were you,
Lizzie?
LIZZIE. [*Painfully.*] It has nothing to do
with you!
FILE. [*Impulsively—with deep feeling.*]
It's got a lot to do with me! Tell me!
LIZZIE. Let me go!
FILE. [*Angry—pleading.*] Lizzie . . . !
[*Suddenly we hear the voice of* STAR-
BUCK. *He is outdoors, approaching,
singing at the top of his voice. A
quick, sharp stir in the room.*]
LIZZIE. [*Shouting desperately.*] Star-
buck—go away!—run!
[*His singing continues, closer.*]
SHERIFF. File—get the other side of the
door!
LIZZIE. [*Wildly as the singing conti-
nues.*] Starbuck—run!
[STARBUCK *enters through the open
door. His pace is so rapid that he
comes full into the room, still singing.*
FILE *slams the door shut behind him.
The instant* STARBUCK *takes in the
room, his song stops. His body goes
tense, alert.*]
LIZZIE. [*With a wail.*] I told you to run!
STARBUCK. What's goin' on?
SHERIFF. Smith? Johnson? Starbuck?
STARBUCK. What do you want?
SHERIFF. Sheriff. You're under arrest.
[STARBUCK *makes one move toward
the door but* FILE *steps in his way,
gun in hand.*]
FILE. Don't go for that door!
[STARBUCK *holds his position.* LIZZIE
rushes to him with a cry.]
LIZZIE. If you hadn't been singing, you'd
have heard me!
STARBUCK. [*With an attempt at bravura.*]
I never regret singin'! [*Then, turning away
from her.*] All right, Sheriff—let's go!
[*As* FILE *goes toward him with handcuffs,* STARBUCK *reaches out his two
hands, seemingly for the bracelets,
then suddenly brings them down
simultaneously on* FILE'S *wrists. The
gun and handcuffs clatter to the floor.
As the* SHERIFF *moves toward the
men,* STARBUCK *shoves* FILE *up against*

the SHERIFF, *reaches for* NOAH's *gun on the table and holds it ready.*]

STARBUCK. Keep clear, boys!

[*He reaches for* FILE's *gun on the floor and pockets it. Then he quickly and deftly dispossesses the* SHERIFF *of his own holstered gun. He pockets that one too.*]

LIZZIE. Starbuck, get out of here—hurry up!

STARBUCK. [*Desperately.*] Lizzie—just a minute! It's as lonely as dyin' out there—will you come with me?

LIZZIE. [*Dumfounded—unable to handle the sudden offer.*] Starbuck . . .

STARBUCK. I'm talkin' to you, Lizzie! And there's no time! Come on!

[*She takes a step toward him—tentative, frightened. Suddenly, out of the tense stillness—*FILE's *voice! The words he was never able to say tear out of him in a tortured cry.*]

FILE. Lizzie—don't go!

[*She turns and looks at him, stunned, unable to believe it is* FILE's *voice.*]

LIZZIE. What's . . . that . . . ?

FILE. I said don't go!

LIZZIE. Oh, what'll I do?

STARBUCK. Hurry up, Lizzie—please!

[*Caught between the two men,* LIZZIE *glances wildly around the room.*]

LIZZIE. Pop, what am I going to do?

H.C. Whatever you do, remember you been asked! You don't never have to go through life a woman who ain't been asked!

STARBUCK. I'm sure askin'! Lizzie, listen! You're beautiful now, but you come with me and you'll be so beautiful, you'll light up the world!

LIZZIE. [*Frightened.*] No—don't say that!

STARBUCK. [*He cannot be stopped.*] You'll never be Lizzie no more—you'll be—you'll be Melisande!

LIZZIE. [*With a cry that is part lament, part relief.*] Oh, Starbuck, you said the wrong thing! I've got to be *Lizzie!* Melisande's a name for one night—but Lizzie can do me my whole life long!

STARBUCK. Come on!

LIZZIE. I can't!

[*She turns away from him.*]

STARBUCK. Lizzie!

[*Too late. Her decision has been made.* STARBUCK *tries to hide the deep desperation. He tries to smile, to be the braggart again. He addresses the* CURRY *men with a bravura shout.*]

STARBUCK. Well, boys! I'm sorry about the rain—but then I didn't stay my full time. So there's your hundred dollars! [*He tosses the bundle of money on the table.*] Another day maybe—in a dry season! So long, folks!

[*And he's out in a streak of dust.* FILE *and the* SHERIFF *make a beeline for the door but* LIZZIE *stops* FILE.]

LIZZIE. File—wait!

FILE. He'll get away!

LIZZIE. Let him get away—please let him!

FILE. We can't do that, Lizzie!

LIZZIE. Then give him a little time—give him some time!

NOAH. Don't listen to her, File! Go after him! He's a con man. He had us beatin' a drum, paintin' arrows and tyin' the hind legs of a mule. And never a sign of rain. We still got the drought.

LIZZIE. Not me! I don't have the drought—not any more! I've had rain!

JIM. And he gave us back our money!

LIZZIE. Please, File . . .

SHERIFF. [*As* FILE *doesn't move.*] File, what's wrong with you?

FILE. [*With a glance at* LIZZIE.] I don't know—but when I do go after him, I'm goin' awful slow. [*Looking at her closely.*] Somethin' about you—you sure have changed.

JIM. She's got her hair down.

FILE. It's more than her hair, I'd say. But whatever it is . . .

[*He takes a few steps toward her. They look at each other closely. He smiles—the first full, radiant smile we've seen on his face. And the warmth of it shines on* LIZZIE—*and she starts to smile too . . . Suddenly a sound in the distance—a quick, low rumble.*]

NOAH. [*Hearing the sound; not watching* JIM.] Jimmy, for Pete's sake, stop beatin' that drum!

JIM. I ain't beatin' no drum!

[*They all look at* JIM. *He is yards away from* STARBUCK's *drum. Another rumble is heard.*]

H.C. [*Unable to believe what he hears.*]

That sounds like . . . [*With a shout.*] It's thunder!
[*A streak of lightning flashes the lights, dimming the room and electrifying it at the same time.*]
JIM. Lightning!
H.C. *Light—ning!*
FILE. Look at it! It's gonna rain!
JIM. He said twenty-four hours—he said twenty-four hours!
[*More lightning, more thunder.*]
LIZZIE. [*In highest exaltation.*] It's going to rain! Rain!

[*Suddenly the door bursts open and* STARBUCK *stands on the threshold— with a look of glory on his face.*]
STARBUCK. Rain, folks—it's gonna rain! Rain, Lizzie—for the first time in my life— rain! [*Hurrying to the table.*] Gimme my hundred dollars! [*He takes his money and hurtles to the door. In the doorway, he pauses only long enough to wave to* LIZZIE.] So long—beautiful!
[*And he races out.*]

END OF ACT THREE

For Discussion and Writing

1. *The Rainmaker* has been called a "Western without shooting." What conventions of the "Western" do you recognize in this play?

2. British playwright Christopher Fry has written, "When I set about writing a comedy the idea presents itself to me first of all as a tragedy . . . If the characters . . . were not qualified for tragedy, there would be no comedy."
   Discuss the various characters in *The Rainmaker* who qualify for tragedy, pointing to lines or scenes in the play that support your opinion. What do these people share in common that makes the play a comedy?

3. Theater critic Alan S. Downer claims that the triumph of Bill Starbuck represents the "triumph of the immature and irresponsible."
   Compare your reactions with your classmates to this statement. Why in so many plays today is the romantic hero portrayed either as an alcoholic, a dope addict, or a ne'er-do-well con man, outside the pale of the social structure? Could he be labeled an anti-hero? What is an anti-hero?

4. Bill Starbuck, rainmaker and con man, claims he can produce miracles. Nobody believes him, yet his presence in the house actually brings about not one "miracle," but four. Identify these four miracles and discuss how each one restores faith in something or someone to a character in the play.

5. Richard Nash says, "At the end of the play, when Lizzie must choose between a romantic escape and the world of reality, she chooses reality."
   In your opinion, why did Lizzie make such a choice? If you had been in her position, would you have made the same choice.

6. Choose one of the following situations and try your hand at writing an original dramatic dialogue based on it.

   Write the supper table conversation that might take place between Act I and Act II with Starbuck as the guest seated in the chair set for the absent File.

   Write a conversation that could take place one year later between Lizzie and Jim's girl, Snookie, on how their husbands proposed.

Our Town

{1938}

THORNTON WILDER

CHARACTERS

(In Order of Appearance)

STAGE MANAGER	MR. WEBB
DR. GIBBS	WOMAN IN THE BALCONY
JOE CROWELL	MAN IN THE AUDITORIUM
HOWIE NEWSOME	LADY IN THE BOX
MRS. GIBBS	SIMON STIMSON
MRS. WEBB	MRS. SOAMES
GEORGE GIBBS	CONSTABLE WARREN
REBECCA GIBBS	SI CROWELL
WALLY WEBB	THREE BASEBALL PLAYERS
EMILY WEBB	SAM CRAIG
PROFESSOR WILLARD	JOE STODDARD

The entire play takes place in Grover's Corners, New Hampshire.

*W*hen *Our Town* opened on Broadway in February 1938, audiences were deeply moved by the nostalgic spell of a little New England town of the early 1900's created on a bare stage set against steampipes criss-crossing the rough brick wall of the theater. When the play had opened originally in Princeton and Boston with conventional staging and sets to unenthusiastic audiences and critics, the playwright persuaded his producer to throw out the scenery and the furniture—all except a few chairs, a table and a couple of ladders to represent upstairs bedrooms—and bring into New York a non-realistic, frankly theatrical play.

Thornton Wilder believed that instead of pretending the stage is someone's living room, the playwright should admit that it is just a stage and give the audience freedom to use its imagination to go back and forth in time and space.

Our Town has been produced in London, in Germany as *Unsere Kleine Stadt,* and in France as *Notre Petite Ville.* It has been revived at New York's City Center, turned into a successful film, been done on television (once even as a musical). College theaters, community theaters, and summer stock rediscover *Our Town* every year. And perhaps no other modern play has been more frequently produced by high school acting groups.

Our Town

ACT ONE

No curtain.
No scenery.
The audience, arriving, sees an empty stage in half-light.
Presently the STAGE MANAGER, *hat on and pipe in mouth, enters and begins placing a table and three chairs downstage left, and a table and three chairs downstage right. He also places a low bench at the corner of what will be the Webb house, left.*
"Left" and "right" are from the point of view of the actor facing the audience. "Up" is toward the back wall.
As the house lights go down he has finished setting the stage and leaning against the right proscenium pillar watches the late arrivals in the audience.
When the auditorium is in complete darkness he speaks:

STAGE MANAGER. This play is called "Our Town." It was written by Thornton Wilder; produced and directed by A. . . . (or: produced by A. . . . ; directed by B. . . .). In it you will see Miss C. . . .; Miss D. . . . ; Miss E. . . . ; and Mr. F. . . . ; Mr. G. . . . ; Mr. H. . . . ; and many others. The name of the town is Grover's Corners, New Hampshire—just across the Massachusetts line: latitude 42 degrees 40 minutes; longitude 70 degrees 37 minutes. The First Act shows a day in our town. The day is May 7, 1901. The time is just before dawn.

[*A rooster crows.*]

The sky is beginning to show some streaks of light over in the East there, behind our mount'in.

The morning star always gets wonderful bright the minute before it has to go, —doesn't it?

[*He stares at it for a moment, then goes upstage.*]

Well, I'd better show you how our town lies.

[*That is: parallel with the back wall.*] is Main Street. Way back there is the railway station; tracks go that way. Polish Town's across the tracks, and some Canuck families.

[*Toward the left.*]

Over there is the Congregational Church; across the street's the Presbyterian.

Methodist and Unitarian are over there. Baptist is down in the holla' by the river. Catholic Church is over beyond the tracks. Here's the Town Hall and Post Office combined; jail's in the basement.

Bryan once made a speech from these very steps here.

Along here's a row of stores. Hitching posts and horse blocks in front of them. First automobile's going to come along in about five years—belonged to Banker Cartwright, our richest citizen . . . lives in the big white house up on the hill.

Here's the grocery store and here's Mr. Morgan's drugstore. Most everybody in town manages to look into those two stores once a day.

Public School's over yonder. High School's still farther over. Quarter of nine mornings, noontimes, and three o'clock afternoons, the hull town can hear the yelling and screaming from those schoolyards.

[*He approaches the table and chairs downstage right.*]

This is our doctor's house,—Doc Gibbs'. This is the back door.

[*Two arched trellises, covered with vines and flowers, are pushed out, one by each proscenium pillar.*]

There's some scenery for those who think they have to have scenery.
This is Mrs. Gibbs' garden. Corn . . . peas . . . beans . . . hollyhocks . . heliotrope . . . and a lot of burdock.
[*Crosses the stage.*]
In those days our newspaper come out twice a week—the Grover's Corners *Sentinel*—and this is Editor Webb's house. And this is Mrs. Webb's garden.
Just like Mrs. Gibbs', only it's got a lot of sunflowers, too.
[*He looks upward, center stage.*]
Right here . . .'s a big butternut tree.
[*He returns to his place by the right proscenium pillar and looks at the audience for a minute.*]
Nice town, y'know what I mean?
Nobody very remarkable ever come out of it, s'far as we know.
The earliest tombstones in the cemetery up there on the mountain say 1670-1680—they're Grovers and Cartwrights and Gibbses and Herseys—same names as are around here now.
Well, as I said: it's about dawn.
The only lights on in town are in a cottage over by the tracks where a Polish mother's just had twins. And in the Joe Crowell house, where Joe Junior's getting up so as to deliver the paper. And in the depot, where Shorty Hawkins is gettin' ready to flag the 5:45 for Boston.
[*A train whistle is heard. The* STAGE MANAGER *takes out his watch and nods.*]
Naturally, out in the country—all around—there's been lights on for some time, what with milkin's and so on. But town people sleep late.
So—another day's begun.
There's Doc Gibbs comin' down Main Street now, comin' back from that baby case. And here's his wife comin' downstairs to get breakfast.
[MRS. GIBBS, *a plump, pleasant woman in the middle thirties, comes "downstairs" right. She pulls up an imaginary window shade in her kitchen and starts to make a fire in her stove.*]
Doc Gibbs died in 1930. The new hospital's named after him.
Mrs. Gibbs died first—long time ago, in fact. She went out to visit her daughter, Rebecca, who married an insurance man in Canton, Ohio, and died there—pneumonia—but her body was brought back here. She's up in the cemetery there now—in with a whole mess of Gibbses and Herseys—she was Julia Hersey 'fore she married Doc Gibbs in the Congregational Church over there.
In our town we like to know the facts about everybody.
There's Mrs. Webb, coming downstairs to get her breakfast, too.—That's Doc Gibbs. Got that call at half past one this morning. And there comes Joe Crowell, Jr., delivering Mr. Webb's *Sentinel*.
[DR. GIBBS *has been coming along Main Street from the left. At the point where he would turn to approach his house, he stops, sets down his—imaginary—black bag, takes off his hat, and rubs his face with fatigue, using an enormous handkerchief.*
MRS. WEBB, *a thin, serious, crisp woman, has entered her kitchen, left, tying on an apron. She goes through the motions of putting wood into a stove, lighting it, and preparing breakfast.*
Suddenly,* JOE CROWELL, JR., *eleven, starts down Main Street from the right, hurling imaginary newspapers into doorways.*]
JOE CROWELL, JR. Morning, Doc Gibbs.
DR. GIBBS. Morning, Joe.
JOE CROWELL, JR. Somebody been sick, Doc?
DR. GIBBS. No. Just some twins born over in Polish Town.
JOE CROWELL, JR. Do you want your paper now?
DR. GIBBS. Yes, I'll take it.—Anything serious goin' on in the world since Wednesday?
JOE CROWELL, JR. Yessir. My schoolteacher, Miss Foster, 's getting married to a fella over in Concord.
DR. GIBBS. I declare.—How do you boys feel about that?
JOE CROWELL, JR. Well, of course, it's none of my business—but I think if a person starts out to be a teacher, she ought to stay one.
DR. GIBBS. How's your knee, Joe?
JOE CROWELL, JR. Fine, Doc, I never think about it at all. Only like you said, it always tells me when it's going to rain.
DR. GIBBS What's it telling you today? Goin' to rain?

JOE CROWELL, JR. No, sir.

DR. GIBBS. Sure?

JOE CROWELL, JR. Yessir.

DR. GIBBS. Knee ever make a mistake?

JOE CROWELL, JR. No, sir.

[JOE *goes off.* DR. GIBBS *stands reading his paper.*]

STAGE MANAGER. Want to tell you something about that boy Joe Crowell there. Joe was awful bright—graduated from high school here, head of his class. So he got a scholarship to Massachusetts Tech. Graduated head of his class there, too. It was all wrote up in the Boston paper at the time. Goin' to be a great engineer, Joe was. But the war broke out and he died in France. —All that education for nothing.

HOWIE NEWSOME. [*Off left.*] Giddap, Bessie! What's the matter with you today?

STAGE MANAGER. Here comes Howie Newsome, deliverin' the milk.

[HOWIE NEWSOME, *about thirty, in overalls, comes along Main Street from left, walking beside an invisible horse and wagon and carrying an imaginary rack with milk bottles. The sound of clinking milk bottles is heard. He leaves some bottles at Mrs. Webb's trellis, then, crossing the stage to Mrs. Gibbs', he stops center to talk to Dr. Gibbs.*]

HOWIE NEWSOME. Morning, Doc.

DR. GIBBS. Morning, Howie.

HOWIE NEWSOME. Somebody sick?

DR. GIBBS. Pair of twins over to Mrs. Goruslawski's.

HOWIE NEWSOME. Twins, eh? This town's gettin' bigger every year.

DR. GIBBS. Goin' to rain, Howie?

HOWIE NEWSOME. No, no. Fine day— that'll burn through. Come on, Bessie.

DR. GIBBS. Hello Bessie. [*He strokes the horse, which has remained up center.*] How old is she, Howie?

HOWIE NEWSOME. Going on seventeen. Bessie's all mixed up about the route ever since the Lockharts stopped takin' their quart of milk every day. She wants to leave 'em a quart just the same—keeps scolding me the hull trip.

[*He reaches Mrs. Gibbs' back door. She is waiting for him.*]

MRS. GIBBS. Good morning, Howie.

HOWIE NEWSOME. Morning, Mrs. Gibbs. Doc's just comin' down the street.

MRS. GIBBS. Is he? Seems like you're late today.

HOWIE NEWSOME. Yes. Somep'n went wrong with the separator. Don't know what 'twas. [*He passes Dr. Gibbs up center.*] Doc!

DR. GIBBS Howie!

MRS. GIBBS. [*Calling upstairs.*] Children! Children! Time to get up.

HOWIE NEWSOME. Come on, Bessie! [*He goes off right.*]

MRS. GIBBS. George! Rebecca!

[DR. GIBBS *arrives at his back door and passes through the trellis into his house.*]

MRS. GIBBS. Everything all right, Frank?

DR. GIBBS. Yes. I declare—easy as kittens.

MRS. GIBBS. Bacon'll be ready in a minute. Set down and drink your coffee. You can catch a couple hours' sleep this morning, can't you?

DR. GIBBS. Hm! . . . Mrs. Wentworth's coming at eleven. Guess I know what it's about, too. Her stummick ain't what it ought to be.

MRS. GIBBS. All told, you won't get more'n three hours' sleep. Frank Gibbs, I don't know what's goin' to become of you. I do wish I could get you to go away someplace and take a rest. I think it would do you good.

MRS. WEBB. Emileee! Time to get up! Wally! Seven o'clock!

MRS. GIBBS. I declare, you got to speak to George. Seems like something's come over him lately. He's no help to me at all. I can't even get him to cut me some wood.

DR. GIBBS. [*Washing and drying his hands at the sink.* MRS. GIBBS *is busy at the stove.*] Is he sassy to you?

MRS. GIBBS. No. He just whines! All he thinks about is that baseball—George! Rebecca! You'll be late for school.

DR. GIBBS. M-m-m . . .

MRS. GIBBS. George!

DR. GIBBS. George, look sharp!

GEORGE'S VOICE. Yes, Pa!

DR. GIBBS. [*As he goes off the stage.*] Don't you hear your mother calling you? I guess Ill go upstairs and get forty winks.

MRS. WEBB. Walleee! Emileee! You'll be late for school! Walleee! You wash yourself good or I'll come up and do it myself.

REBECCA GIBBS' VOICE. Ma! What dress shall I wear?

MRS. GIBBS. Don't make a noise. Your father's been out all night and needs his sleep. I washed and ironed the blue gingham for you special.

REBECCA. Ma, I hate that dress.

MRS. GIBBS. Oh, hush-up-with-you.

REBECCA. Every day I go to school dressed like a sick turkey.

MRS. GIBBS. Now, Rebecca, you always look *very* nice.

REBECCA. Mama, George's throwing soap at me.

MRS. GIBBS. I'll come and slap the both of you,—that's what I'll do.

[*A factory whistle sounds.*
The CHILDREN *dash in and take their places at the tables. Right,* GEORGE, *about sixteen, and* REBECCA, *eleven. Left,* EMILY *and* WALLY, *same ages. They carry strapped schoolbooks.*]

STAGE MANAGER. We've got a factory in our town too—hear it? Makes blankets. Cartwrights own it and it brung 'em a fortune.

MRS. WEBB. Children! Now I won't have it. Breakfast is just as good as any other meal and I won't have you gobbling like wolves. It'll stunt your growth,—that's a fact. Put away your book, Wally.

WALLY. Aw, Ma! By ten o'clock I got to know all about Canada.

MRS. WEBB. You know the rule's well as I do—no books at table. As for me, I'd rather have my children healthy than bright.

EMILY. I'm both, Mama: you know I am. I'm the brightest girl in school for my age. I have a wonderful memory.

MRS. WEBB. Eat your breakfast.

WALLY. I'm bright, too, when I'm looking at my stamp collection.

MRS. GIBBS. I'll speak to your father about it when he's rested. Seems to me twenty-five cents a week's enough for a boy your age. I declare I don't know how you spend it all.

GEORGE. Aw, Ma,—I gotta lotta things to buy.

MRS. GIBBS. Strawberry phosphates—that's what you spend it on.

GEORGE. I don't see how Rebecca comes to have so much money. She has more'n a dollar.

REBECCA. [*Spoon in mouth, dreamily.*] I've been saving it up gradual.

MRS. GIBBS. Well, dear, I think it's a good thing to spend some every now and then.

REBECCA. Mama, do you know what I love most in the world—do you?—Money.

MRS. GIBBS. Eat your breakfast.

THE CHILDREN. Mama, there's first bell.—I gotta hurry.—I don't want any more.—I gotta hurry.

[*The* CHILDREN *rise, seize their books and dash out through the trellises. They meet, down center, and chattering, walk to Main Street, then turn left.*
The STAGE MANAGER *goes off, unobtrusively, right.*]

MRS. WEBB. Walk fast, but you don't have to run. Wally, pull up your pants at the knee. Stand up straight, Emily.

MRS. GIBBS. Tell Miss Foster I send her my best congratulations—can you remember that?

REBECCA. Yes, Ma.

MRS. GIBBS. You look real nice, Rebecca. Pick up your feet.

ALL. Good-by.

[MRS. GIBBS *fills her apron with food for the chickens and comes down to the footlights.*]

MRS. GIBBS. Here, chick, chick, chick. No, go away, you. Go away. Here, chick, chick, chick. What's the matter with *you?* Fight, fight, fight,—that's all you do. Hm . . . *you* don't belong to me. Where'd you come from? [*She shakes her apron.*] Oh, don't be so scared. Nobody's going to hurt you.

[MRS. WEBB *is sitting on the bench by her trellis, stringing beans.*]

Good morning, Myrtle. How's your cold?

MRS. WEBB. Well, I still get that tickling feeling in my throat. I told Charles I didn't know as I'd go to choir practice tonight. Wouldn't be any use.

MRS. GIBBS. Have you tried singing over your voice?

MRS. WEBB. Yes, but somehow I can't do that and stay on the key. While I'm resting myself I thought I'd string some of these beans.

MRS. GIBBS. [*Rolling up her sleeves as she crosses the stage for a chat.*] Let me help you. Beans have been good this year.

MRS. WEBB. I've decided to put up forty quarts if it kills me. The children say they hate 'em, but I notice they're able to get 'em down all winter.

[*Pause. Brief sound of chickens cackling.*]

MRS. GIBBS. Now, Myrtle. I've got to tell you something, because if I don't tell somebody I'll burst.

MRS. WEBB. Why, Julia Gibbs!

MRS. GIBBS. Here, give me some more of those beans. Myrtle, did one of those secondhand-furniture men from Boston come to see you last Friday?

MRS. WEBB. No-o.

MRS. GIBBS. Well, he called on me. First I thought he was a patient wantin' to see Dr. Gibbs. 'N he wormed his way into my parlor, and, Myrtle Webb, he offered me three hundred and fifty dollars for Grandmother Wentworth's highboy, as I'm sitting here!

MRS. WEBB. Why, Julia Gibbs!

MRS. GIBBS. He did! That old thing! Why, it was so big I didn't know where to put it and I almost give it to Cousin Hester Wilcox.

MRS. WEBB. Well, you're going to take it, aren't you?

MRS. GIBBS. I don't know.

MRS. WEBB. You don't know—three hundred and fifty dollars! What's come over you?

MRS. GIBBS. Well, if I could get the Doctor to take the money and go away someplace on a real trip, I'd sell it like that.—Y'know, Myrtle, it's been the dream of my life to see Paris, France.—Oh, I don't know. It sounds crazy, I suppose, but for years I've been promising myself that if we ever had the chance—

MRS. WEBB. How does the Doctor feel about it?

MRS. GIBBS. Well, I did beat about the bush a little and said that if I got a legacy —that's the way I put it—I'd make him take me somewhere.

MRS. WEBB. M-m-m . . . What did he say?

MRS. GIBBS. You know how he is. I haven't heard a serious word out of him since I've known him. No, he said, it might make him discontented with Grover's Corners to go traipsin' about Europe; better let well enough alone, he says. Every two years he makes a trip to the battlefields of the Civil War and that's enough treat for anybody, he says.

MRS. WEBB. Well, Mr. Webb just *admires* the way Dr. Gibbs knows everything about the Civil War. Mr. Webb's a good mind to give up Napoleon and move over to the Civil War, only Dr. Gibbs being one of the greatest experts in the country just makes him despair.

MRS. GIBBS. It's a fact! Dr. Gibbs is never so happy as when he's at Antietam or Gettysburg. The times I've walked over those hills, Myrtle, stopping at every bush and pacing it all out, like we were going to buy it.

MRS. WEBB. Well, if that secondhand man's really serious about buyin' it, Julia, you sell it. And then you'll get to see Paris, all right. Just keep droppin' hints from time to time—that's how I got to see the Atlantic Ocean, y'know.

MRS. GIBBS. Oh, I'm sorry I mentioned it. Only it seems to me that once in your life before you die you ought to see a country where they don't talk in English and don't even want to.

[*The* STAGE MANAGER *enters briskly from the right. He tips his hat to the ladies, who nod their heads.*]

STAGE MANAGER. Thank you, ladies.

[MRS. GIBBS *and* MRS. WEBB *gather up their things, return into their homes and disappear.*]

Now we're going to skip a few hours. But first we want a little more information about the town, kind of a scientific account, you might say. So I've asked Professor Willard of our State University to sketch in a few details of our past history here. Is Professor Willard here?

[PROFESSOR WILLARD, *a rural savant, pince-nez on a wide satin ribbon, enters from the right with some notes in his hand.*]

May I introduce Professor Willard of our State University. A few brief notes, thank you, Professor, —unfortunately our time is limited.

PROFESSOR WILLARD. Grover's Corners . . . let me see . . . Grover's Corners lies on the old Pleistocene granite of the Appalachian range. I may say it's some of the oldest land in the world. We're very proud of that. A shelf of Devonian basalt crosses it with vestiges of Mesozoic shale, and some sandstone outcroppings; but that's all

more recent: two hunderd, three hundred million years old.
Some highly interesting fossils have been found . . . I may say: unique fossils . . . two miles out of town, in Silas Peckham's cow pasture. They can be seen at the museum in our University at any time—that is, at any reasonable time. Shall I read some of Professor Gruber's notes on the meteorological situation—mean precipitation, et cetera?

STAGE MANAGER. Afraid we won't have time for that, Professor. We might have a few words on the history of man here.

PROFESSOR WILLARD. Yes . . . anthropological data: Early Amerindian stock. Cotahatchee tribes . . . no evidence before the tenth century of this era . . . hm . . . now entirely disappeared . . . possible traces in three families. Migration toward the end of the seventeenth century of English brachiocephalic blue-eyed stock . . . for the most part. Since then some Slav and Mediterranean—

STAGE MANAGER. And the population, Professor Willard?

PROFESSOR WILLARD. Within the town limits, 2,640.

STAGE MANAGER. Just a moment, Professor. [*He whispers into the professor's ear.*]

PROFESSOR WILLARD. Oh, yes, indeed?— The population, *at the moment,* is 2,642. The Postal District brings in 507 more, making a total of 3,149.—Mortality and birth rates: constant.—By MacPherson's gauge: 6,032.

STAGE MANAGER. Thank you very much, Professor. We're all very much obliged to you, I'm sure.

PROFESSOR WILLARD. Not at all, sir; not at all.

STAGE MANAGER. This way, Professor, and thank you again.

[*Exit* PROFESSOR WILLARD.]
Now the political and social report: Editor Webb.—Oh, Mr. Webb?

[MRS. WEBB *appears at her back door.*]

MRS. WEBB. He'll be here in a minute. . . . He just cut his hand while he was eatin' an apple.

STAGE MANAGER. Thank you, Mrs. Webb.

MRS. WEBB. Charles! Everybody's waitin'. [*Exit* MRS. WEBB.]

STAGE MANAGER. Mr. Webb is Publisher and Editor of the Grover's Corners *Sentinel.* That's our local paper, y'know.

[MR. WEBB *enters from his house, pulling on his coat. His finger is bound in a handkerchief.*]

MR. WEBB. Well . . . I don't have to tell you that we're run here by a Board of Selectmen.—All males vote at the age of twenty-one. Women vote indirect. We're lower middle class: sprinkling of professional men . . . ten per cent illiterate laborers. Politically, we're eighty-six per cent Republicans; six per cent Democrats; four per cent Socialists; rest, indifferent. Religiously, we're eighty-five per cent Protestants; twelve per cent Catholics; rest, indifferent.

STAGE MANAGER. Have you any comments, Mr. Webb?

MR. WEBB. Very ordinary town, if you ask me. Little better behaved than most. Probably a lot duller.
But our young people here seem to like it well enough. Ninety per cent of 'em graduating from high school settle down right here to live—even when they've been away to college.

STAGE MANAGER. Now, is there anyone in the audience who would like to ask Editor Webb anything about the town?

WOMAN IN THE BALCONY. Is there much drinking in Grover's Corners?

MR. WEBB. Well, ma'am, I wouldn't know what you'd call *much.* Satiddy nights the farmhands meet down in Ellery Greenough's stable and holler some. We've got one or two town drunks, but they're always having remorses every time an evangelist comes to town. No, ma'am, I'd say likker ain't a regular thing in the home here, except in the medicine chest. Right good for snake bite, y'know—always was.

BELLIGERENT MAN AT BACK OF AUDITORIUM. Is there no one in town aware of—

STAGE MANAGER. Come forward, will you, where we can all hear you—What were you saying?

BELLIGERENT MAN. Is there no one in town aware of social injustice and industrial inequality?

MR. WEBB. Oh, yes, everybody is—somethin' terrible. Seems like they spend most of their time talking about who's rich and who's poor.

BELLIGERENT MAN. Then why don't

they do something about it? [*He withdraws without waiting for an answer.*]

MR. WEBB. Well, I dunno. . . . I guess we're all hunting like everybody else for a way the diligent and sensible can rise to the top and the lazy and quarrelsome can sink to the bottom. But it ain't easy to find. Meanwhile, we do all we can to help those that can't help themselves and those that can we leave alone.—Are there any other questions?

LADY IN A BOX. Oh, Mr. Webb? Mr. Webb, is there any culture or love of beauty in Grover's Corners?

MR. WEBB. Well, ma'am, there ain't much—not in the sense you mean. Come to think of it, there's some girls that play the piano at High School Commencement; but they ain't happy about it. No, ma'am, there isn't much culture; but maybe this is the place to tell you that we've got a lot of pleasures of a kind here: we like the sun comin' up over the mountain in the morning, and we all notice a good deal about the birds. We pay a lot of attention to them. And we watch the change of the seasons; yes, everybody knows about them. But those other things—you're right, ma'am,—there ain't much.—*Robinson Crusoe* and the Bible; and Handel's "Largo," we all know that; and Whistler's "Mother" —those are just about as far as we go.

LADY IN BOX. So I thought. Thank you, Mr. Webb.

STAGE MANAGER. Thank you, Mr. Webb. [MR. WEBB *retires.*] Now, we'll go back to the town. It's early afternoon. All 2,642 have had their dinners and all the dishes have been washed.

[MR. WEBB, *having removed his coat, returns and starts pushing a lawn mower to and fro beside his house.*] There's an early-afternoon calm in our town: a buzzin' and a hummin' from the school buildings; only a few buggies on Main Street—the horses dozing at the hitching posts; you all remember what it's like. Doc Gibbs is in his office, tapping people and making them say "ah." Mr. Webb's cuttin' his lawn over there; one man in ten thinks it's a privilege to push his own lawn mower.

No, sir. It's later than I thought. There are the children coming home from school already.

[*Shrill girls' voices are heard, off left.* EMILY *comes along Main Street, carrying some books. There are some signs that she is imagining herself to be a lady of startling elegance.*]

EMILY. I can't, Lois. I've got to go home and help my mother. I promised.

MR. WEBB. Emily, walk simply. Who do you think you are today?

EMILY. Papa, you're terrible. One minute you tell me to stand up straight and the next minute you call me names. I just don't listen to you. [*She gives him an abrupt kiss.*]

MR. WEBB. Golly, I never got a kiss from such a great lady before.

[*He goes out of sight.* EMILY *leans over and picks some flowers by the gate of her house.*

GEORGE GIBBS *comes careening down Main Street. He is throwing a ball up to dizzying heights, and waiting to catch it again. This sometimes requires his taking six steps backward. He bumps into an* OLD LADY *invisible to us.*]

GEORGE. Excuse me, Mrs. Forrest.

STAGE MANAGER. [*As Mrs. Forrest.*] Go out and play in the fields, young man. You got no business playing baseball on Main Street.

GEORGE. Awfully sorry, Mrs. Forrest.— Hello, Emily.

EMILY. H'lo.

GEORGE. You made a fine speech in class.

EMILY. Well . . . I was really ready to make a speech about the Monroe Doctrine, but at the last minute Miss Corcoran made me talk about the Louisiana Purchase instead. I worked an awful long time on both of them.

GEORGE. Gee, it's funny, Emily. From my window up there I can just see your head nights when you're doing your homework over in your room.

EMILY. Why, can you?

GEORGE. You certainly do stick to it, Emily. I don't see how you can sit still that long. I guess you like school.

EMILY. Well, I always feel it's something you have to go through.

GEORGE. Yeah.

EMILY. I don't mind it really. It passes the time.

GEORGE. Yeah.—Emily, what do you think? We might work out a kinda telegraph from your window to mine; and once in a while you could give me a kinda hint or two about one of those algebra problems. I don't mean the answers, Emily, of course not . . . just some little hint . . .

EMILY. Oh, I think *hints* are allowed.— So—ah—if you get stuck, George, you whistle to me; and I'll give you some hints.

GEORGE. Emily, you're just naturally bright, I guess.

EMILY. I figure that it's just the way a person's born.

GEORGE. Yeah. But, you see, I want to be a farmer, and my Uncle Luke says whenever I'm ready I can come over and work on his farm and if I'm any good I can just gradually have it.

EMILY. You mean the house and everything?

[*Enter* MRS. WEBB *with a large bowl and sits on the bench by her trellis.*]

GEORGE. Yeah. Well, thanks . . . I better be getting out to the baseball field. Thanks for the talk, Emily.—Good afternoon, Mrs. Webb.

MRS. WEBB. Good afternoon, George.

GEORGE. So long, Emily.

EMILY. So long, George.

MRS. WEBB. Emily, come and help me string these beans for the winter. George Gibbs let himself have a real conversation, didn't he? Why, he's growing up. How old would George be?

EMILY. I don't know.

MRS. WEBB. Let's see. He must be almost sixteen.

EMILY. Mama, I made a speech in class today and I was very good.

MRS. WEBB. You must recite it to your father at supper. What was it about?

EMILY. The Louisiana Purchase. It was like silk off a spool. I'm going to make speeches all my life.—Mama, are these big enough?

MRS. WEBB. Try and get them a little bigger if you can.

EMILY. Mama, will you answer me a question, serious?

MRS. WEBB. Seriously, dear—not serious.

EMILY. Seriously,—will you?

MRS. WEBB. Of course, I will.

EMILY. Mama, am I good looking?

MRS. WEBB. Yes, of course you are. All my children have got good features; I'd be ashamed if they hadn't.

EMILY. Oh, Mama, that's not what I mean. What I mean is: am I *pretty?*

MRS. WEBB. I've already told you, yes. Now that's enough of that. You have a nice young pretty face. I never heard of such foolishness.

EMILY. Oh, Mama, you never tell us the truth about anything.

MRS. WEBB. I *am* telling you the truth.

EMILY. Mama, were *you* pretty?

MRS. WEBB. Yes, I was, if I do say it. I was the prettiest girl in town next to Mamie Cartwright.

EMILY. But, Mama, you've got to say *some*thing about me. Am I pretty enough . . . to get anybody . . . to get people interested in me?

MRS. WEBB. Emily, you make me tired. Now stop it. You're pretty enough for all normal purposes.—Come along now and bring that bowl with you.

EMILY. Oh, Mama, you're no help at all.

STAGE MANAGER. Thank you. Thank you! That'll do. We'll have to interrupt again here. Thank you, Mrs. Webb; thank you, Emily.

[MRS. WEBB *and* EMILY *withdraw.*]

There are some more things we want to explore about this town.

[*He comes to the center of the stage. During the following speech the lights gradually dim to darkness, leaving only a spot on him.*]

I think this is a good time to tell you that the Cartwright interests have just begun building a new bank in Grover's Corners—had to go to Vermont for the marble, sorry to say. And they've asked a friend of mine what they should put in the cornerstone for people to dig up . . . a thousand years from now. . . . Of course, they've put in a copy of the *New York Times* and a copy of Mr. Webb's *Sentinel.* . . . We're kind of interested in this because some scientific fellas have found a way of painting all that reading matter with a glue—a silicate glue—that'll make it keep a thousand—two thousand years.

We're putting in a Bible . . . and the Constitution of the United States—and a copy of William Shakespeare's plays. What do you say, folks? What do you think?

Y'know—Babylon once had two million people in it, and all we know about 'em is the names of the kings and some copies of wheat contracts . . . and contracts for the sale of slaves. Yet every night all those families sat down to supper, and the father came home from his work, and the smoke went up the chimney,—same as here. And even in Greece and Rome, all we know about the *real* life of the people is what we can piece together out of the joking poems and the comedies they wrote for the theatre back then.

So I'm going to have a copy of this play put in the cornerstone and the people a thousand years from now'll know a few simple facts about us—more than Treaty of Versailles and the Lindbergh flight. See what I mean?

So—people a thousand years from now —this is the way we were in the provinces north of New York at the beginning of the twentieth century.—This is the way we were: in our growing up and in our marrying and in our living and in our dying.

[*A choir partially concealed in the orchestra pit has begun singing "Blessed Be the Tie That Binds."* SIMON STIMSON *stands directing them. Two ladders have been pushed onto the stage; they serve as indication of the second story in the Gibbs and Webb houses.* GEORGE *and* EMILY *mount them, and apply themselves to their schoolwork.* DR. GIBBS *has entered and is seated in his kitchen reading.*]

Well—good deal of time's gone by. It's evening.

You can hear choir practice going on in the Congregational Church.

The children are at home doing their schoolwork.

The day's running down like a tired clock.

SIMON STIMSON. Now look here, everybody. Music come into the world to give pleasure.—Softer! Softer! Get it out of your heads that music's only good when it's loud. You leave loudness to the Methodists. You couldn't beat 'em, even if you wanted to. Now again. Tenors!

GEORGE. Hssst! Emily!

EMILY. Hello.

GEORGE. Hello!

EMILY. I can't work at all. The moonlight's so *terrible.*

GEORGE. Emily, did you get the third problem?

EMILY. Which?

GEORGE. The *third?*

EMILY. Why, yes, George—that's the easiest of them all.

GEORGE. I don't see it. Emily, can you give me a hint?

EMILY. I'll tell you one thing: the answer's in yards.

GEORGE. ! ! ! In yards? How do you mean?

EMILY. In *square* yards.

GEORGE. Oh . . . in square yards.

EMILY. Yes, George, don't you see?

GEORGE. Yeah.

EMILY. In square yards of *wallpaper.*

GEORGE. Wallpaper,—oh, I see. Thanks a lot, Emily.

EMILY. You're welcome. My, isn't the moonlight *terrible?* And choir practice going on.—I think if you hold your breath you can hear the train all the way to Contoocook. Hear it?

GEORGE. M-m-m—What do you know!

EMILY. Well, I guess I better go back and try to work.

GEORGE. Good night, Emily. And thanks.

EMILY. Good night, George.

SIMON STIMSON. Before I forget it: how many of you will be able to come in Tuesday afternoon and sing at Fred Hersey's wedding?—show your hands. That'll be fine; that'll be right nice. We'll do the same music we did for Jane Trowbridge's last month.

—Now we'll do: "Art Thou Weary; Art Thou Languid?" It's a question, ladies and gentlemen, make it talk. Ready.

DR. GIBBS. Oh, George, can you come down a minute?

GEORGE. Yes, Pa. [*He descends the ladder.*]

DR. GIBBS. Make yourself comfortable, George; I'll only keep you a minute. George, how old are you?

GEORGE. I? I'm sixteen, almost seventeen.

DR. GIBBS. What do you want to do after school's over?

GEORGE. Why, you know, Pa. I want to be a farmer on Uncle Luke's farm.

DR. GIBBS. You'll be willing, will you, to get up early and milk and feed the stock . . . and you'll be able to hoe and hay all day?

GEORGE. Sure, I will. What are you . . . what do you mean, Pa?

DR. GIBBS. Well, George, while I was in my office today I heard a funny sound . . .

and what do you think it was? It was your mother chopping wood. There you see your mother—getting up early; cooking meals all day long; washing and ironing;— and still she has to go out in the back yard and chop wood. I suppose she just got tired of asking you. She just gave up and decided it was easier to do it herself. And you eat her meals, and put on the clothes she keeps nice for you, and you run off and play baseball,—like she's some hired girl we keep around the house but that we don't like very much. Well, I knew all I had to do was call your attention to it. Here's a handkerchief, son. George, I've decided to raise your spending money twenty-five cents a week. Not, of course, for chopping wood for your mother, because that's a present you give her, but because you're getting older—and I imagine there are lots of things you must find to do with it.

GEORGE. Thanks, Pa.

DR. GIBBS. Let's see—tomorrow's your payday. You can count on it—Hmm. Probably Rebecca'll feel she ought to have some more too. Wonder what could have happened to your mother. Choir practice never was as late as this before.

GEORGE. It's only half past eight, Pa.

DR. GIBBS. I don't know why she's in that old choir. She hasn't any more voice than an old crow. . . . Traipsin' around the streets at this hour of the night . . . Just about time you retired, don't you think?

GEORGE. Yes, Pa.

[GEORGE *mounts to his place on the ladder.*
Laughter and good nights can be heard on stage left and presently MRS. GIBBS, MRS. SOAMES *and* MRS. WEBB *come down Main Street. When they arrive at the corner of the stage they stop.*]

MRS. SOAMES. Good night, Martha. Good night, Mr. Foster.

MRS. WEBB. I'll tell Mr. Webb; I *know* he'll want to put it in the paper.

MRS. GIBBS. My, it's late!

MRS. SOAMES. Good night, Irma.

MRS. GIBBS. Real nice choir practice, wa'n't it? Myrtle Webb! Look at that moon, will you! Tsk-tsk-tsk. Potato weather, for sure.

[*They are silent a moment, gazing up at the moon.*]

MRS. SOAMES. Naturally I didn't want to say a word about it in front of those others, but now we're alone—really, it's the worst scandal that ever was in this town!

MRS. GIBBS. What?

MRS. SOAMES. Simon Stimson!

MRS. GIBBS. Now, Louella!

MRS. SOAMES. But, Julia! To have the organist of a church *drink* and *drunk* year after year. You know he was drunk tonight.

MRS. GIBBS. Now, Louella! We all know about Mr. Stimson, and we all know about the troubles he's been through, and Dr. Ferguson knows too, and if Dr. Ferguson keeps him on there in his job the only thing the rest of us can do is just not to notice it.

MRS. SOAMES. *Not to notice it!* But it's getting worse.

MRS. WEBB. No, it isn't, Louella. It's getting better. I've been in that choir twice as long as you have. It doesn't happen anywhere near so often. . . . My, I hate to go to bed on a night like this.—I better hurry. Those children'll be sitting up till all hours. Good night, Louella.

[*They all exchange good nights. She hurries downstage, enters her house and disappears.*]

MRS. GIBBS. Can you get home safe, Louella?

MRS. SOAMES. It's as bright as day. I can see Mr. Soames scowling at the window now. You'd think we'd been to a dance the way the menfolk carry on.

[*More good nights.* MRS. GIBBS *arrives at her home and passes through the trellis into the kitchen.*]

MRS. GIBBS. Well, we had a real good time.

DR. GIBBS. You're late enough.

MRS. GIBBS. Why, Frank, it ain't any later n' usual.

DR. GIBBS. And you stopping at the corner to gossip with a lot of hens.

MRS. GIBBS. Now, Frank, don't be grouchy. Come out and smell the heliotrope in the moonlight.

[*They stroll out arm in arm along the footlights.*]

Isn't that wonderful? What did you do all the time I was away?

DR. GIBBS. Oh, I read—as usual. What were the girls gossiping about tonight?

MRS. GIBBS. Well, believe me, Frank—there is something to gossip about.

DR. GIBBS. Hmm! Simon Stimson far gone, was he?

MRS. GIBBS. Worst I've ever seen him. How'll that end, Frank? Dr. Ferguson can't forgive him forever.

DR. GIBBS. I guess I know more about Simon Stimson's affairs than anybody in this town. Some people ain't made for small-town life. I don't know how that'll end; but there's nothing we can do but just leave it alone. Come, get in.

MRS. GIBBS. No, not yet . . . Frank, I'm worried about you.

DR. GIBBS. What are you worried about?

MRS. GIBBS. I think it's my duty to make plans for you to get a real rest and change. And if I get that legacy, well, I'm going to insist on it.

DR. GIBBS. Now, Julia, there's no sense in going over that again.

MRS. GIBBS. Frank, you're just *unreasonable!*

DR. GIBBS. [*Starting into the house.*] Come on, Julia, it's getting late. First thing you know you'll catch cold. I gave George a piece of my mind tonight. I reckon you'll have your wood chopped for a while anyway. No, no, start getting upstairs.

MRS. GIBBS. Oh, dear. There's always so many things to pick up, seems like. You know, Frank, Mrs. Fairchild always locks her front door every night. All those people up that part of town do.

DR. GIBBS. [*Blowing out the lamp.*] They're all getting citified, that's the trouble with them. They haven't got nothing fit to burgle and everybody knows it.

[*They disappear.*

REBECCA *climbs up the ladder beside* GEORGE.]

GEORGE. Get out, Rebecca. There's only room for one at this window. You're always spoiling everything.

REBECCA. Well, let me look just a minute.

GEORGE. Use your own window.

REBECCA. I did, but there's no moon there. . . . George, do you know what I think, do you? I think maybe the moon's getting nearer and nearer and there'll be a big 'splosion.

GEORGE. Rebecca, you don't know anything. If the moon were getting nearer, the guys that sit up all night with tele-scopes would see it first and they'd tell about it, and it'd be in all the newspapers.

REBECCA. George, is the moon shining on South America, Canada and half the whole world?

GEORGE. Well—prob'ly is.

[*The* STAGE MANAGER *strolls on. Pause. The sound of crickets is heard.*]

STAGE MANAGER. Nine thirty. Most of the lights are out. No, there's Constable Warren trying a few doors on Main Street. And here comes Editor Webb, after putting his newspaper to bed.

[MR. WARREN, *an elderly policeman, comes along Main Street from the right*, MR. WEBB *from the left.*]

MR. WEBB. Good evening, Bill.

CONSTABLE WARREN. Evenin', Mr. Webb.

MR. WEBB. Quite a moon!

CONSTABLE WARREN. Yepp.

MR. WEBB. All quiet tonight?

CONSTABLE WARREN. Simon Stimson is rollin' around a little. Just saw his wife movin' out to hunt for him so I looked the other way—there he is now.

[SIMON STIMSON *comes down Main Street from the left, only a trace of unsteadiness in his walk.*]

MR. WEBB. Good evening, Simon . . . Town seems to have settled down for the night pretty well. . . .

[SIMON STIMSON *comes up to him and pauses a moment and stares at him, swaying slightly.*]

Good evening . . . Yes, most of the town's settled down for the night, Simon. . . . I guess we better do the same. Can I walk along a ways with you?

[SIMON STIMSON *continues on his way without a word and disappears at the right.*]

Good night.

CONSTABLE WARREN. I don't know how that's goin' to end, Mr. Webb.

MR. WEBB. Well, he's seen a peck of trouble, one thing after another. . . . Oh, Bill . . . if you see my boy smoking cigarettes, just give him a word, will you? He thinks a lot of you, Bill.

CONSTABLE WARREN. I don't think he smokes no cigarettes, Mr. Webb. Leastways, not more'n two or three a year.

MR. WEBB. Hm . . . I hope not.—Well good night, Bill.

CONSTABLE WARREN. Good night, Mr Webb. [*Exit.*]

MR. WEBB. Who's that up there? Is that you, Myrtle?

EMILY. No, it's me, Papa.

MR. WEBB. Why aren't you in bed?

EMILY. I don't know. I just can't sleep yet, Papa. The moonlight's so won-derful. And the smell of Mrs. Gibbs' heliotrope. Can you smell it?

MR. WEBB. Hm . . . Yes. Haven't any troubles on your mind, have you, Emily?

EMILY. *Troubles*, Papa? *No.*

MR. WEBB. Well, enjoy yourself, but don't let your mother catch you. Good night, Emily.

EMILY. Good night, Papa.

[MR. WEBB *crosses into the house, whistling "Blessed Be the Tie That Binds" and disappears.*]

REBECCA. I never told you about that letter Jane Crofut got from her minister when she was sick. He wrote Jane a letter and on the envelope the address was like this: It said: Jane Crofut; The Crofut Farm; Grover's Corners; Sutton County; New Hampshire; United States of America.

GEORGE. What's funny about that?

REBECCA. But listen, it's not finished: the United States of America; Continent of North America; Western Hemisphere; the Earth; the Solar System; the Universe; the Mind of God—that's what it said on the envelope.

GEORGE. What do you know!

REBECCA. And the postman brought it just the same.

GEORGE. What do you know!

STAGE MANAGER. That's the end of the First Act, friends. You can go and smoke now, those that smoke.

A C T   T W O

The tables and chairs of the two kitchens are still on the stage.
The ladders and the small bench have been withdrawn.
The STAGE MANAGER has been at his accustomed place watching the audience return to its seats.

STAGE MANAGER. Three years have gone by.

Yes, the sun's come up over a thousand times.

Summers and winters have cracked the mountains a little more and the rains have brought down some of the dirt.

Some babies that weren't even born before have begun talking regular sentences already; and a number of people who thought they were right young and spry have noticed that they can't bound up a flight of stairs like they used to, without their heart fluttering a little.

All that can happen in a thousand days. Nature's been pushing and contriving in other ways, too: a number of young people fell in love and got married.

Yes, the mountain got bit away a few fractions of an inch; millions of gallons of water went by the mill; and here and there a new home was set up under a roof.

Almost everybody in the world gets married,—you know what I mean? In our town there aren't hardly any exceptions. Most everybody in the world climbs into their graves married.

The First Act was called the Daily Life. This act is called Love and Marriage. There's another act coming after this: I recokon you can guess what that's about. So:

It's three years later. It's 1904.

It's July 7th, just after High School Commencement.

That's the time most of our young people jump up and get married.

Soon as they've passed their last examinations in solid geometry and Cicero's Orations, looks like they suddenly feel themselves fit to be married.

It's early morning. Only this time it's been raining. It's been pouring and thundering.

Mrs. Gibbs' garden, and Mrs. Webb's here: drenched.

All those bean poles and pea vines: drenched.

All yesterday over there on Main Street, the rain looked like curtains being blown along.

Hm . . . it may begin again any minute. There! You can hear the 5:45 for Boston. [MRS. GIBBS *and* MRS. WEBB *enter their kitchen and start the day as in the First Act.*] And there's Mrs. Gibbs and Mrs. Webb come down to make breakfast, just as though it were an ordinary day. I don't have to point out to the women in my audience that those ladies they see before them, both of those ladies cooked three meals a day—one of 'em for twenty years, the other for forty—and no summer vacation. They brought up two children apiece, washed, cleaned the house,—and *never a nervous breakdown.*

It's like what one of those Middle West poets said: You've got to love life to have life, and you've got to have life to love life. . . . It's what they call a vicious circle.

HOWIE NEWSOME. [*Off stage left.*] Giddap, Bessie!

STAGE MANAGER. Here comes Howie Newsome delivering the milk. And there's Si Crowell delivering the papers like his brother before him.

[SI CROWELL *has entered hurling imaginary newspapers into doorways;* HOWIE NEWSOME *has come along Main Street with Bessie.*]

SI CROWELL. Morning, Howie.

HOWIE NEWSOME. Morning, Si.—Anything in the papers I ought to know?

SI CROWELL. Nothing much, except we're losing about the best baseball pitcher Grover's Corners ever had—George Gibbs.

HOWIE NEWSOME. Reckon he is.

SI CROWELL. He could hit and run bases, too.

HOWIE NEWSOME. Yep. Mighty fine ball player.—Whoa! Bessie! I guess I can stop and talk if I've a mind to!

SI CROWELL. I don't see how he could give up a thing like that just to get married. Would you, Howie?

HOWIE NEWSOME. Can't tell, Si. Never had no talent that way.

[CONSTABLE WARREN *enters. They exchange good mornings.*] You're up early, Bill.

CONSTABLE WARREN. Seein' if there's anything I can do to prevent a flood. River's been risin' all night.

HOWIE NEWSOME. Si Crowell's all worked up here about George Gibbs' retiring from baseball.

CONSTABLE WARREN. Yes, sir; that's the way it goes. Back in '84 we had a player, Si—even George Gibbs couldn't touch him. Name of Hank Todd. Went down to Maine and become a parson. Wonderful ball player.—Howie, how does the weather look to you?

HOWIE NEWSOME. Oh, 'tain't bad. Think maybe it'll clear up for good.

[CONSTABLE WARREN *and* SI CROWELL *continue on their way.*

HOWIE NEWSOME *brings the milk first to Mrs. Gibbs' house. She meets him by the trellis.*]

MRS. GIBBS. Good morning, Howie. Do you think it's going to rain again?

HOWIE NEWSOME. Morning, Mrs. Gibbs. It rained so heavy, I think maybe it'll clear up.

MRS. GIBBS. Certainly hope it will.

HOWIE NEWSOME. How much did you want today?

MRS. GIBBS. I'm going to have a houseful of relations, Howie. Looks to me like I'll need three-a-milk and two-a-cream.

HOWIE NEWSOME. My wife says to tell you we hope they'll be very happy, Mrs. Gibbs. Know they *will.*

MRS. GIBBS. Thanks a lot, Howie. Tell your wife I hope she gits there to the wedding.

HOWIE NEWSOME. Yes, she'll be there; she'll be there if she kin.

[HOWIE NEWSOME *crosses to Mrs. Webb's house.*] Morning, Mrs. Webb.

MRS. WEBB. Oh, good morning, Mr. Newsome. I told you four quarts of milk, but I hope you can spare me another.

HOWIE NEWSOME. Yes'm . . . and the two of cream.

MRS. WEBB. Will it start raining again, Mr. Newsome?

HOWIE NEWSOME. Well. Just sayin' to Mrs. Gibbs as how it may lighten up. Mrs. Newsome told me to tell you as how we hope they'll both be very happy, Mrs. Webb. Know they *will.*

MRS. WEBB. Thank you, and thank Mrs. Newsome and we're counting on seeing you at the wedding.

HOWIE NEWSOME. Yes, Mrs. Webb. We hope to git there. Couldn't miss that. Come on, Bessie. [*Exit* HOWIE NEWSOME.]

[DR. GIBBS *descends in shirt sleeves, and sits down at his breakfast table.*]

DR. GIBBS. Well, Ma, the day has come. You're losin' one of your chicks.

MRS. GIBBS. Frank Gibbs, don't you say another word. I feel like crying every minute. Sit down and drink your coffee.

DR. GIBBS. The groom's up shaving himself—only there ain't an awful lot to shave. Whistling and singing, like he's glad to leave us.—Every now and then he says "I do" to the mirror but it don't sound convincing to me.

MRS. GIBBS. I declare, Frank, I don't know how he'll get along. I've arranged his clothes and seen to it he's put warm things on,—Frank! they're too *young*. Emily won't think of such things. He'll catch his death of cold within a week.

DR. GIBBS. I was remembering my wedding morning, Julia.

MRS. GIBBS. Now don't start, Frank Gibbs.

DR. GIBBS. I was the scaredest young fella in the State of New Hampshire. I thought I'd make a mistake for sure. And when I saw you comin' down that aisle I thought you were the prettiest girl I'd ever seen, but the only trouble was that I'd never seen you before. There I was in the Congregational Church marryin' a total stranger.

MRS. GIBBS. And how do you think I felt! —Frank, weddings are perfectly awful things. Farces,—that's what they are! [*She puts a plate before him.*] Here, I've made something for you.

DR. GIBBS. Why, Julia Hersey—French toast!

MRS. GIBBS. 'Tain't hard to make and I had to do *some*thing.

[*Pause.* DR. GIBBS *pours on the syrup.*]

DR. GIBBS. How'd you sleep last night, Julia?

MRS. GIBBS. Well, I heard a lot of the hours struck off.

DR. GIBBS. Ye-e-s! I get a shock every time I think of George setting out to be a family man—that great gangling thing!— I tell you Julia, there's nothing so terrifying in the world as a *son*. The relation of father and son is the darndest, awkwardest—

MRS. GIBB. Well, mother and daughter's no picnic, let me tell you.

DR. GIBBS. They'll have a lot of troubles, I suppose, but that's none of our business.

Everybody has a right to their own troubles.

MRS. GIBBS. [*At the table, drinking her coffee, meditatively.*] Yes . . . people are meant to go through life two by two. 'Tain't natural to be lonesome.

[*Pause.* DR. GIBBS *starts laughing.*]

DR. GIBBS. Julia, do you know one of the things I was scared of when I married you?

MRS. GIBB. Oh, go along with you!

DR. GIBBS. I was afraid we wouldn't have material for conversation more'n'd last us a few weeks.

[*Both laugh.*]

I was afraid we'd run out and eat our meals in silence, that's a fact.—Well, you and I been conversing for twenty years now without any noticeable barren spells.

MRS. GIBBS Well,—good weather, bad weather—'tain't very choice, but I always find something to say. [*She goes to the foot of the stairs.*] Did you hear Rebecca stirring around upstairs?

DR. GIBBS. No. Only day of the year Rebecca hasn't been managing everybody's business up there. She's hiding in her room.—I got the impression she's crying.

MRS. GIBBS. Lord's sakes!—This has got to stop.—Rebecca! Rebecca! Come and get your breakfast.

[GEORGE *comes rattling down the stairs, very brisk.*]

GEORGE. Good morning, everybody. Only five more hours to live.

[*Makes the gesture of cutting his throat, and a loud "k-k-k," and starts through the trellis.*]

MRS. GIBBS. George Gibbs, where are you going?

GEORGE. Just stepping across the grass to see my girl.

MRS. GIBBS. Now, George! You put on your overshoes. It's raining torrents. You don't go out of this house without you're prepared for it.

GEORGE. Aw, Ma. It's just a *step*!

MRS. GIBBS George! You'll catch your death of cold and cough all through the service.

DR. GIBBS. George, do as your mother tells you!

[DR. GIBBS *goes upstairs.*

GEORGE *returns reluctantly to the kitchen and pantomimes putting on overshoes.*]

MRS. GIBBS. From tomorrow on you can kill yourself in all weathers, but while you're in my house you'll live wisely, thank you.—Maybe Mrs. Webb isn't used to callers at seven in the morning.—Here, take a cup of coffee first.

GEORGE. Be back in a minute. [*He crosses the stage, leaping over the puddles.*] Good morning, Mother Webb.

MRS. WEBB. Goodness! You frightened me!—Now, George, you can come in a minute out of the wet, but you know I can't ask you in.

GEORGE. Why not—?

MRS. WEBB. George, you know's well as I do: the groom can't see his bride on his wedding day, not until he sees her in church.

GEORGE. Aw!—that's just a superstition. —Good morning, Mr. Webb.

[*Enter* MR. WEBB.]

MR. WEBB. Good morning, George.

GEORGE. Mr. Webb, you don't believe in that superstition, do you?

MR. WEBB. There's a lot of common sense in some superstitions, George. [*He sits at the table, facing right.*]

MRS. WEBB. Millions have folla'd it, George, and you don't want to be the first to fly in the face of custom.

GEORGE. How is Emily?

MRS. WEBB. She hasn't waked up yet. I haven't heard a sound out of her.

GEORGE. Emily's *asleep*!!!

MRS. WEBB. No wonder! We were up 'til all hours, sewing and packing. Now I'll tell you what I'll do; you set down here a minute with Mr. Webb and drink this cup of coffee; and I'll go upstairs and see she doesn't come down and surprise you. There's some bacon, too; but don't be long about it. [*Exit* MRS. WEBB.]

[*Embarrassed silence.*

MR. WEBB *dunks doughnuts in his coffee.*

More silence.]

MR. WEBB. [*Suddenly and loudly.*] Well, George, how are you?

GEORGE. [*Startled, choking over his coffee.*] Oh, fine, I'm fine. [*Pause.*] Mr. Webb, what sense could there be in a superstition like that?

MR. WEBB. Well, you see,—on her wedding morning a girl's head's apt to be full of . . . clothes and one thing and another.

Don't you think that's probably it?

GEORGE. Ye-e-s. I never thought of that.

MR. WEBB. A girl's apt to be a mite nervous on her wedding day. [*Pause.*]

GEORGE. I wish a fellow could get married without all that marching up and down.

MR. WEBB. Every man that's ever lived has felt that way about it, George; but it hasn't been any use. It's the womenfolk who've built up weddings, my boy. For a while now the women have it all their own. A man looks pretty small at a wedding, George. All those good women standing shoulder to shoulder making sure that the knot's tied in a mighty public way.

GEORGE. But . . . you *believe* in it, don't you, Mr. Webb?

MR. WEBB. [*With alacrity.*] Oh, yes; oh, yes. Don't you misunderstand me, my boy. Marriage is a wonderful thing,—wonderful thing. And don't you forget that, George.

GEORGE. No, sir.—Mr. Webb, how old were you when you got married?

MR. WEBB. Well, you see: I'd been to college and I'd taken a little time to get settled. But Mrs. Webb—she wasn't much older than what Emily is. Oh, age hasn't much to do with it, George,—not compared with . . . uh . . . other things.

GEORGE. What were you going to say, Mr. Webb?

MR. WEBB. Oh, I don't know.—Was I going to say something? [*Pause.*] George, I was thinking the other night of some advice my father gave me when I got married. Charles, he said, Charles, start out early showing who's boss, he said. Best thing to do is to give an order, even if it don't make sense; just so she'll learn to obey. And he said: if anything about your wife irritates you—her conversation, or anything—just get up and leave the house. That'll make it clear to her, he said. And, oh, yes! he said never, *never* let your wife know how much money you have, never.

GEORGE. Well, Mr. Webb . . . I don't think I could . . .

MR. WEBB. So I took the opposite of my father's advice and I've been happy ever since. And let that be a lesson to you, George, never to ask advice on personal matters.—George, are you going to raise chickens on your farm?

GEORGE. What?

MR. WEBB. Are you going to raise chickens on your farm?

GEORGE. Uncle Luke's never been much interested, but I thought—

MR. WEBB. A book came into my office the other day, George, on the Philo System of raising chickens. I want you to read it. I'm thinking of beginning in a small way in the back yard, and I'm going to put an incubator in the cellar—

[*Enter* MRS. WEBB.]

MRS. WEBB. Charles, are you talking about that old incubator again? I thought you two'd be talking about things worth while.

MR. WEBB. [*Bitingly.*] Well, Myrtle, if you want to give the boy some good advice, I'll go upstairs and leave you alone with him.

MRS. WEBB. [*Pulling* GEORGE *up.*] George, Emily's got to come downstairs and eat her breakfast. She sends you her love but she doesn't want to lay eyes on you. Good-by.

GEORGE. Good-by. [GEORGE *crosses the stage to his own home, bewildered and crestfallen. He slowly dodges a puddle and disappears into his house.*]

MR. WEBB. Myrtle, I guess you don't know about that older supersition.

MRS. WEBB. What do you mean, Charles?

MR. WEBB. Since the cave men: no bridegroom should see his father-in-law on the day of the wedding, or near it. Now remember that.

[*Both leave the stage.*]

STAGE MANAGER. Thank you very much, Mr. and Mrs. Webb.—Now I have to interrupt again here. You see, we want to know how all this began—this wedding, this plan to spend a lifetime together. I'm awfully interested in how big things like that begin.

You know how it is: you're twenty-one or twenty-two and you make some decisions; then whissh! you're seventy: you've been a lawyer for fifty years, and that white-haired lady at your side has eaten over fifty thousand meals with you.

How do such things begin?

George and Emily are going to show you now the conversation they had when they first knew that . . . that . . . as the saying goes . . . they were meant for one another.

But before they do it I want you to try and remember what it was like to have been very young.

And particularly the days when you were first in love; when you were like a person sleepwalking, and you didn't quite see the street you were in, and didn't quite hear everything that was said to you. You're just a little bit crazy. Will you remember that, please?

Now they'll be coming out of high school at three o'clock. George has just been elected President of the Junior Class, and as it's June, that means he'll be President of the Senior Class all next year. And Emily's just been elected Secretary and Treasurer.

I don't have to tell you how important that is.

[*He places a board across the backs of two chairs, which he takes from those at the Gibbs family's table. He brings two high stools from the wings and places them behind the board. Persons sitting on the stools will be facing the audience. This is the counter of Mr. Morgan's drugstore. The sounds of young people's voices are heard off left.*]

Yepp,—there they are coming down Main Street now.

[EMILY, *carrying an armful of—imaginary—schoolbooks, comes along Main Street from the left.*]

EMILY. I can't, Louise. I've got to go home. Good-by. Oh, Ernestine! Ernestine! Can you come over tonight and do Latin? Isn't that Cicero the worst thing—! Tell your mother you *have* to. G'by. G'by, Helen. G'by, Fred.

[GEORGE, *also carrying books, catches up with her.*]

GEORGE. Can I carry your books home for you, Emily?

EMILY. [*Coolly.*] Why . . . uh . . . Thank you. It isn't far. [*She gives them to him.*]

GEORGE. Excuse me a minute, Emily.— Say, Bob, if I'm a little late, start practice anyway. And give Herb some long high ones.

EMILY. Good-by, Lizzy.

GEORGE. Good-by, Lizzy.—I'm awfully glad you were elected, too, Emily.

EMILY. Thank you.

[*They have been standing on Main Street, almost against the back wall. They take the first steps toward the audience when* GEORGE *stops and says.*]

GEORGE. Emily, why are you mad at me?

EMILY. I'm not mad at you.

GEORGE. You've been treating me so funny lately.

EMILY. Well, since you ask me, I might as well say it right out, George,— [*She catches sight of a teacher passing.*] Goodby, Miss Corcoran.

GEORGE. Good-by, Miss Corcoran.—Wha—what is it?

EMILY. [*Not scoldingly; finding it difficult to say.*] I don't like the whole change that's come over you in the last year. I'm sorry if that hurts your feelings, but I've got to—tell the truth and shame the devil.

GEORGE. A *change?*—Wha—what do you mean?

EMILY. Well, up to a year ago I used to like you a lot. And I used to watch you as you did everything . . . because we'd been friends so long . . . and then you began spending all your time at *baseball* . . . and you never stopped to speak to anybody any more. Not even to your own family you didn't . . . and, George, it's a fact, you've got awful conceited and stuck-up, and all the girls say so. They may not say so to your face, but that's what they say about you behind your back, and it hurts me to hear them say it, but I've got to agree with them a little. I'm sorry if it hurts your feelings . . . but I can't be sorry I said it.

GEORGE. I . . . I'm glad you said it, Emily. I never thought that such a thing was happening to me. I guess it's hard for a fella not to have faults creep into his character.

[*They take a step or two in silence, then stand still in misery.*]

EMILY. I always expect a man to be perfect and I think he should be.

GEORGE. Oh . . . I don't think it's possible to be perfect, Emily.

EMILY. Well, my *father* is, and as far as I can see *your* father is. There's no reason on earth why you shouldn't be, too.

GEORGE. Well, I feel it's the other way round. That men aren't naturally good; but girls are.

EMILY. Well, you might as well know right now that I'm not perfect. It's not as easy for a girl to be perfect as a man, because we girls are more—more—nervous.—Now I'm sorry I said all that about you. I don't know what made me say it.

GEORGE. Emily,—

EMILY. Now I can see it's not the truth at all. And I suddenly feel that it isn't important, anyway.

GEORGE. Emily . . . would you like an ice-cream soda, or something, before you go home?

EMILY. Well, thank you. . . . I would.

[*They advance toward the audience and make an abrupt right turn, opening the door of Morgan's drugstore. Under strong emotion,* EMILY *keeps her face down.* GEORGE *speaks to some passers-by.*]

GEORGE. Hello, Stew,—how are you?—Good afternoon, Mrs. Slocum.

[*The* STAGE MANAGER, *wearing spectacles and assuming the role of Mr. Morgan, enters abruptly from the right and stands between the audience and the counter of his soda fountain.*]

STAGE MANAGER. Hello, George. Hello, Emily.—What'll you have?—Why, Emily Webb,—what you been crying about?

GEORGE. [*He gropes for an explanation.*] She . . . she just got an awful scare, Mr. Morgan. She almost got run over by that hardware-store wagon. Everybody says that Tom Huckins drives like a crazy man.

STAGE MANAGER. [*Drawing a drink of water.*] Well, now! You take a drink of water, Emily. You look all shook up. I tell you, you've got to look both ways before you cross Main Street these days. Gets worse every year.—What'll you have?

EMILY. I'll have a strawberry phosphate, thank you, Mr. Morgan.

GEORGE. No, no, Emily. Have an ice-cream soda with me. Two strawberry ice-cream sodas, Mr. Morgan.

STAGE MANAGER. [*Working the faucets.*] Two strawberry ice-cream sodas, yes sir. Yes, sir. There are a hundred and twenty-five horses in Grover's Corners this minute I'm talking to you. State Inspector was in here yesterday. And now they're bringing in these auto-mo-biles, the best thing to do is to just stay home. Why, I can remember when a dog could go to sleep all day in the middle of Main Street and nothing come along to disturb him. [*He sets the imaginary glasses before them.*] There they are. Enjoy 'em. [*He sees a customer, right.*] Yes, Mrs. Ellis. What can I do for you? [*He goes out right.*]

EMILY. They're so expensive.

GEORGE. No, no,—don't you think of that. We're celebrating our election. And then do you know what else I'm celebrating?

EMILY. N-no.

GEORGE. I'm celebrating because I've got a friend who tells me all the things that ought to be told me.

EMILY. George, *please* don't think of that. I don't know why I said it. It's not true. You're—

GEORGE. No, Emily, you stick to it. I'm glad you spoke to me like you did. But you'll *see*: I'm going to change so quick— you bet I'm going to change. And, Emily, I want to ask you a favor.

EMILY. What?

GEORGE. Emily, if I go away to State Agriculture College next year, will you write me a letter once in a while?

EMILY. I certainly will. I certainly will, George . . .

[*Pause. They start sipping the sodas through the straws.*]

It certainly seems like being away three years you'd get out of touch with things. Maybe letters from Grover's Corners wouldn't be so interesting after a while. Grover's Corners isn't a very important place when you think of all—New Hampshire; but I think it's a very nice town.

GEORGE. The day wouldn't come when I wouldn't want to know everything that's happening here. I know *that's* true, Emily.

EMILY. Well, I'll try to make my letters interesting.

[*Pause.*]

GEORGE. Y'know. Emily, whenever I meet a farmer I ask him if he thinks it's important to go to Agriculture School to be a good farmer.

EMILE. Why, George—

GEORGE. Yeah, and some of them say it's even a waste of time. You can get all those things, anyway, out of the pamphlets the government sends out. And Uncle Luke's getting old,—he's about ready for me to start in taking over his farm tomorrow, if I could.

EMILY. My!

GEORGE. And, like you say, being gone all that time . . . in other places and meeting other people . . . Gosh, if anything like that can happen I don't want to go away. I guess new people aren't any better than old ones. I'll bet they almost never are. Emily . . . I feel that you're as good a friend as I've got. I don't need to go and meet the people in other towns.

EMILY. But, George, maybe it's very important for you to go and learn all that about—cattle judging and soils and those things. . . . Of course, I don't know.

GEORGE. [*After a pause, very seriously.*] Emily, I'm going to make up my mind right now. I won't go. I'll tell Pa about it tonight.

EMILY. Why, George, I don't see why you have to decide right now. It's a whole year away.

GEORGE. Emily, I'm glad you spoke to me about that . . . that fault in my character. What you said was right; but there was *one* thing wrong in it, and that was when you said that for a year I wasn't noticing people, and . . . you, for instance. Why, you say you were watching me when I did everything . . . I was doing the same about you all the time. Why, sure,—I always thought about you as one of the chief people I thought about. I always made sure where you were sitting on the bleachers, and who you were with, and for three days now I've been trying to walk home with you; but something's always got in the way. Yesterday I was standing over against the wall waiting for you, and you walked home with *Miss Corcoran.*

EMILY. George! . . . Life's awful funny! How could I have known that? Why, I thought—

GEORGE. Listen, Emily, I'm going to tell you why I'm not going to Agriculture School. I think that once you've found a person that you're very fond of . . . I mean a person who's fond of you, too, and likes you enough to be interested in your character . . . Well, I think that's just as important as college is, and even more so. That's what I think.

EMILY. I think it's awfully important, too.

GEORGE. Emily.

EMILY. Y-yes, George.

GEORGE. Emily, if I *do* improve and

make a big change . . . would you be . . .
I mean: *could* you be . . .

EMILY. I . . . I am now; I always have
been.

GEORGE. [*Pause.*] So I guess this is an
important talk we've been having.

EMILY. Yes . . . yes.

GEORGE. [*Takes a deep breath and
straightens his back.*] Wait just a minute
and I'll walk you home. [*With mounting
alarm he digs into his pockets for the
money.*]

[*The* STAGE MANAGER *enters, right.*
GEORGE, *deeply embarrassed, but direct, says to him.*]

Mr. Morgan, I'll have to go home and get
the money to pay you for this. It'll only
take me a minute.

STAGE MANAGER. [*Pretending to be af-
fronted.*] What's that? George Gibbs, do
you mean to tell me—!

GEORGE. Yes, but I had reasons, Mr.
Morgan.—Look, here's my gold watch to
keep until I come back with the money.

STAGE MANAGER. That's all right. Keep
your watch. I'll trust you.

GEORGE. I'll be back in five minutes.

STAGE MANAGER. I'll trust you ten years,
George,—not a day over.—Got all over your
shock, Emily?

EMILY. Yes, thank you, Mr. Morgan. It
was nothing.

GEORGE. [*Taking up the books from the
counter.*] I'm ready.

[*They walk in grave silence across
the stage and pass through the trellis
at the Webbs' back door and disappear.
The* STAGE MANAGER *watches them
go out, then turns to the audience,
removing his spectacles.*]

STAGE MANAGER. Well,— [*He claps his
hands as a signal.*]
Now we're ready to get on with the wedding.

[*He stands waiting while the set is
prepared for the next scene.
STAGEHANDS remove the chairs, tables
and trellises from the Gibbs and
Webb houses.
They arrange the pews for the church
in the center of the stage. The congregation will sit facing the back
wall. The aisle of the church starts at
the center of the back wall and comes
toward the audience.*

*A small platform is placed against the
back wall on which the* STAGE MAN-
AGER *will stand later, playing the
minister. The image of a stained-glass
window is cast from a lantern slide
upon the back wall.
When all is ready the* STAGE MANAGER
*strolls to the center of the stage, down
front, and, musingly, addresses the
audience.*]

There are a lot of things to be said about
a wedding; there are a lot of thoughts
that go on during a wedding.

We can't get them all into one wedding,
naturally, and especially not into a wedding at Grover's Corners, where they're
awfully plain and short.

In this wedding I play the minister. That
gives me the right to say a few more
things about it.

For a while now, the play gets pretty
serious.

Y'see, some churches say that marriage is
a sacrament. I don't quite know what that
means, but I can guess. Like Mrs. Gibbs
said a few minutes ago: People were made
to live two-by-two.

This is a good wedding, but people are
so put together that even at a good wedding there's a lot of confusion way down
deep in people's minds and we thought
that that ought to be in our play, too.

The real hero of this scene isn't on the
stage at all, and you know who that is.
It's like what one of those European fellas
said: every child born into the world is
nature's attempt to make a perfect human
being. Well, we've seen nature pushing
and contriving for some time now. We all
know that nature's interested in quantity;
but I think she's interested in quality,
too,—that's why I'm in the ministry.

And don't forget all the other witnesses at
this wedding,—the ancestors. Millions of
them. Most of them set out to live two-by-
two, also. Millions of them.

Well, that's all my sermon. 'Twasn't very
long, anyway.

[*The organ starts playing Handel's
"Largo."
The congregation streams into the
church and sits in silence.
Church bells are heard.
MRS. GIBBS sits in the front row, the
first seat on the aisle, the right sec-
tion; next to her are REBECCA and*

DR. GIBBS. *Across the aisle* MRS. WEBB, WALLY *and* MR. WEBB. *A small choir takes its place, facing the audience under the stained-glass window.*

MRS. WEBB, *on the way to her place, turns back and speaks to the audience.*]

MRS. WEBB. I don't know why on earth I should be crying. I suppose there's nothing to cry about. It came over me at breakfast this morning; there was Emily eating her breakfast as she's done for seventeen years and now she's going off to eat it in someone else's house. I suppose that's it.

And Emily! She suddenly said: I can't eat another mouthful, and she put her head down on the table and *she* cried. [*She starts toward her seat in the church, but turns back and adds.*] Oh, I've got to say it: you know, there's something downright cruel about sending our girls out into marriage this way.

I hope some of her girl friends have told her a thing or two. It's cruel, I know, but I couldn't bring myself to say anything. I went into it blind as a bat myself. [*In half-amused exasperation.*] The whole world's wrong, that's what's the matter. There they come. [*She hurries to her place in the pew.*]

[GEORGE *starts to come down the right aisle of the theatre, through the audience.*

Suddenly THREE MEMBERS *of his baseball team appear by the right proscenium pillar and start whistling and catcalling to him. They are dressed for the ball field.*]

THE BASEBALL PLAYERS. Eh, George, George! Hast—yaow! Look at him, fellas—he looks scared to death. Yaow! George, don't look so innocent, you old geezer. We know what you're thinking. Don't disgrace the team, big boy. Whoo-oo-oo.

STAGE MANAGER. All right! All right! That'll do. That's enough of that. [*Smiling, he pushes them off the stage. They lean back to shout a few more catcalls.*] There used to be an awful lot of that kind of thing at weddings in the old days,—Rome, and later. We're more civilized now,—so they say.

[*The choir starts singing "Love Divine, All Love Excelling—."* GEORGE *has reached the stage. He stares at*

the congregation a moment, then takes a few steps of withdrawal, toward the right proscenium pillar. His mother, from the front row, seems to have felt his confusion. She leaves her seat and comes down the aisle quickly to him.*]

MRS. GIBBS. George! George! What's the matter?

GEORGE. Ma, I don't want to grow old. Why's everybody pushing me so?

MRS. GIBBS. Why, George . . . you wanted it.

GEORGE. No. Ma, listen to me—

MRS. GIBBS. No, no, George,—you're a man now.

GEORGE. Listen, Ma,—for the last time I ask you . . . All I want to do is to be a fella—

MRS. GIBBS. George! If anyone should hear you! Now stop. Why, I'm ashamed of you!

GEORGE. [*He comes to himself and looks over the scene.*] What? Where's Emily?

MRS. GIBBS. [*Relieved.*] George! You gave me such a turn.

GEORGE. Cheer up, Ma. I'm getting married.

MRS. GIBBS. Let me catch my breath a minute.

GEORGE. [*Comforting her.*] Now, Ma, you save Thursday nights. Emily and I are coming over to dinner every Thursday night . . . you'll see. Ma, what are you crying for? Come on; we've got to get ready for this.

[MRS. GIBBS, *mastering her emotion, fixes his tie and whispers to him.*

In the meantime, EMILY, *in white and wearing her wedding veil, has come through the audience and mounted onto the stage. She too draws back, frightened, when she sees the congregation in the church. The choir begins: "Blessed Be the Tie That Binds."*]

EMILY. I never felt so alone in my whole life. And George over there, looking so . . . ! I *hate* him. I wish I were dead. Papa! Papa!

MR. WEBB. [*Leaves his seat in the pews and comes toward her anxiously.*] Emily! Emily! Now don't get upset. . . .

EMILY. But, Papa,—I don't want to get married. . . .

MR. WEBB. Sh—sh—Emily. Everything's all right.

EMILY. Why can't I stay for a while just as I am? Let's go away,—

MR. WEBB. No, no, Emily. Now stop and think a minute.

EMILY. Don't you remember that you used to say,—all the time you used to say—all the time: that I was *your* girl! There must be lots of places we can go to. I'll work for you. I could keep house.

MR. WEBB. Sh . . . You mustn't think of such things. You're just nervous, Emily. [*He turns and calls.*] George! George! Will you come here a minute? [*He leads her toward George.*] Why you're marrying the best young fellow in the world. George is a fine fellow.

EMILY. But Papa,—

[MRS. GIBBS. *returns unobtrusively to her seat.*

MR. WEBB *has one arm around his daughter. He places his hand on* GEORGE'S *shoulder.*]

MR. WEBB. I'm giving away my daughter, George. Do you think you can take care of her?

GEORGE. Mr. Webb, I want to . . . I want to try. Emily, I'm going to do my best. I love you, Emily. I need you.

EMILY. Well, if you love me, help me. All I want is someone to love me.

GEORGE. I will, Emily. Emily. I'll try.

EMILY. And I mean for *ever*. Do you hear? For ever and ever.

[*They fall into each other's arms. The March from* Lohengrin *is heard. The* STAGE MANAGER, *as* CLERGYMAN, *stands on the box, up center.*]

MR. WEBB. Come, they're waiting for us. Now you know it'll be all right. Come, quick.

[GEORGE *slips away and takes his place beside the* STAGE MANAGER-CLERGYMAN.

EMILY *proceeds up the aisle on her father's arm.*]

STAGE MANAGER. Do you, George, take this woman, Emily, to be your wedded wife, to have . . .

[MRS. SOAMES *has been sitting in the last row of the congregation. She now turns to her neighbors and speaks in a shrill voice. Her chatter drowns out the rest of the clergyman's words.*

MRS. SOAMES. Perfectly lovely wedding! Loveliest wedding I ever saw. Oh, I do love a good wedding, don't you? Doesn't she make a lovely bride?

GEORGE. I do.

STAGE MANAGER. Do you, Emily, take this man, George, to be your wedded husband,—

[*Again his further words are covered by those of* MRS. SOAMES.]

MRS. SOAMES. Don't know *when* I've seen such a lovely wedding. But I always cry. Don't know why it is, but I always cry. I just like to see young people happy, don't you? Oh, I think it's lovely.

[*The ring. The kiss. The stage is suddenly arrested into silent tableau. The* STAGE MANAGER, *his eyes on the distance, as though to himself.*]

STAGE MANAGER. I've married over two hundred couples in my day. Do I believe in it? I don't know. M . . . marries N . . . millions of them. The cottage, the go-cart, the Sunday-afternoon drives in the Ford, the first rheumatism, the grandchildren, the second rheumatism, the deathbed, the reading of the will,— [*He now looks at the audience for the first time, with a warm smile that removes any sense of cynicism from the next line.*] Once in a thousand times it's interesting. —Well, let's have Mendelssohn's "Wedding March"!

[*The organ picks up the March. The* BRIDE *and* GROOM *come down the aisle, radiant, but trying to be very dignified.*]

MRS. SOAMES. Aren't they a lovely couple? Oh, I've never been to such a nice wedding. I'm sure they'll be happy. I always say: *happiness,* that's the great thing! The important thing is to be happy.

[*The* BRIDE *and* GROOM *reach the steps leading into the audience. A bright light is thrown upon them. They descend into the auditorium and run up the aisle joyously.*]

STAGE MANAGER. That's all the Second Act, folks. Ten minutes' intermission.

CURTAIN

ACT THREE

During the intermission the audience has seen the STAGEHANDS *arranging the stage. On the right-hand side, a little right of the center, ten or twelve ordinary chairs have been placed in three openly spaced rows facing the audience.*

These are graves in the cemetery.

Toward the end of the intermission the ACTORS *enter and take their places. The front row contains: toward the center of the stage, an empty chair; then* MRS. GIBBS; SIMON STIMSON.

The second row contains, among others, MRS. SOAMES.

The third row has WALLY WEBB.

The dead do not turn their heads or their eyes to right or left, but they sit in a quiet without stiffness. When they speak their tone is matter-of-fact, without sentimentality and, above all, without lugubriousness.

The STAGE MANAGER *takes his accustomed place and waits for the house lights to go down.*

STAGE MANAGER. This time nine years have gone by, friends—summer, 1913.

Gradual changes in Grover's Corners. Horses are getting rarer. Farmers coming into town in Fords.

Everybody locks their house doors now at night. Ain't been any burglars in town yet, but everybody's heard about 'em.

You'd be surprised, though—on the whole, things don't change much around here.

This is certainly an important part of Grover's Corners. It's on a hilltop—a windy hilltop—lots of sky, lots of clouds,—often lots of sun and moon and stars.

You come up here, on a fine afternoon and you can see range on range of hills—awful blue they are—up there by Lake Sunapee and Lake Winnipesauke . . . and way up, if you've got a glass, you can see the White Mountains and Mt. Washington —where North Conway and Conway is. And, of course, our favorite mountain, Mt. Monadnock, 's right here—and all these towns that lie around it: Jaffrey, 'n East Jaffrey, 'n Peterborough, 'n Dublin; and [*Then pointing down in the audience.*] there, quite a ways down, is Grover's Corners.

Yes, beautiful spot up here. Mountain laurel and li-lacks. I often wonder why people like to be buried in Woodlawn and Brooklyn when they might pass the same time up here in New Hampshire.

Over there—[*Pointing to stage left.*] are the old stones,—1670, 1680. Strong-minded people that come a long way to be independent. Summer people walk around there laughing at the funny words on the tombstones . . . it don't do any harm. And genealogists come up from Boston—get paid by city people for looking up their ancestors. They want to make sure they're Daughters of the American Revolution and of the *Mayflower*. . . . Well, I guess that don't do any harm, either. Wherever you come near the human race, there's layers and layers of nonsense. . . .

Over there are some Civil War veterans. Iron flags on their graves . . . New Hampshire boys . . . had a notion that the Union ought to be kept together, though they'd never seen more than fifty miles of it themselves. All they knew was the name, friends—the United States of America. The United States of America. And they went and died about it.

This here is the new part of the cemetery. Here's your friend Mrs. Gibbs. 'N let me see—Here's Mr. Stimson, organist at the Congregational Church. And Mrs. Soames who enjoyed the wedding so—you remember? Oh, and a lot of others. And Editor Webb's boy, Wallace, whose appendix burst while he was on a Boy Scout trip to Crawford Notch.

Yes, an awful lot of sorrow has sort of quieted up here. People just wild with grief have brought their relatives up to this hill. We all know how it is . . . and then time . . . and sunny days . . . and rainy days . . . 'n snow . . . We're all glad they're in a beautiful place and we're coming up here ourselves when our fit's over.

Now there are some things we all know, but we don't take'm out and look at'm very often. We all know that *something* is eternal. And it ain't houses and it ain't names, and it ain't earth, and it ain't even the stars . . . everybody knows in their bones that *something* is eternal, and that something has to do with human beings. All the greatest people ever lived have ben telling us that for five thousands years and yet you'd be surprised how people are always losing hold of it. There's something way down deep that's eternal about every human being. [*Pause.*] You know as well as I do that the dead don't stay interested in us living people for very long. Gradually, gradually, they lose hold of the earth . . . and the ambitions they had . . . and the pleasures they had . . . and the things they suffered . . . and the people they loved.

They get weaned away from earth—that's the way I put it,—weaned away.

And they stay here while the earth part of 'em burns away, burns out; and all that time they slowly get indifferent to what's goin' on in Grover's Corners.

They're waitin'. They're waitin' for something that they feel is comin'. Something important, and great. Aren't they waitin' for the eternal part in them to come out clear?

Some of the things they're going to say maybe'll hurt your feelings—but that's the way it is: mother'n daughter . . . husband 'n wife . . . enemy 'n enemy . . . money 'n miser . . . all those terribly important things kind of grow pale around here. And what's left when memory's gone, and your identity, Mrs. Smith? [*He looks at the audience a minute, then turns to the stage.*] Well! There are some *living* people. There's Joe Stoddard, our undertaker, supervising a new-made grave. And here comes a Grover's Corners boy, that left town to go out West.

[JOE STODDARD *has hovered about in the background.* SAM CRAIG *enters left, wiping his forehead from the exertion. He carries an umbrella and strolls front.*]

SAM CRAIG. Good afternoon, Joe Stoddard.

JOE STODDARD. Good afternoon, good afternoon. Let me see now: do I know you?

SAM CRAIG. I'm Sam Craig.

JOE STODDARD. Gracious sakes' alive! Of all people! I should'a knowed you'd be back for the funeral. You've been away a long time, Sam.

SAM CRAIG. Yes, I've been away over twelve years. I'm in business out in Buffalo now, Joe. But I was in the East when I got news of my cousin's death, so I thought I'd combine things a little and come and see the old home. You look well.

JOE STODDARD. Yes, yes, can't complain. Very sad, our journey today, Samuel.

SAM CRAIG. Yes.

JOE STODDARD. Yes, yes. I always say I hate to supervise when a young person is taken. They'll be here in a few minutes now. I had to come here early today— my son's supervisin' at the home.

SAM CRAIG. [*Reading stones.*] Old Farmer McCarty, I used to do chores for him—after school. He had the lumbago.

JOE STODDARD. Yes, we brought Farmer McCarty here a number of years ago now.

SAM CRAIG. [*Staring at Mrs. Gibbs' knees.*] Why, this is my Aunt Julia . . . I'd forgotten that she'd . . . of course, of course.

JOE STODDARD. Yes, Doc Gibbs lost his wife two-three years ago . . . about this time. And today's another pretty bad blow for him, too.

MRS. GIBBS. [*To Simon Stimson: in an even voice.*] That's my sister Carey's boy, Sam . . . Sam Craig.

SIMON STIMSON. I'm always uncomfortable when *they're* around.

MRS. GIBBS. Simon.

SAM CRAIG. Do they choose their own verses much, Joe?

JOE STODDARD. No . . . not usual. Mostly the bereaved pick a verse.

SAM CRAIG. Doesn't sound like Aunt Julia. There aren't many of those Hersey sisters left now. Let me see: where are . . . I wanted to look at my father's and mother's . . .

JOE STODDARD. Over there with the Craigs . . . Avenue F.

SAM CRAIG. [*Reading Simon Stimson's epitaph.*] He was organist at church, he?—Hm, drank a lot, we used to say.

JOE STODDARD. Nobody was supposed to know about it. He'd seen a peck of trouble. [*Behind his hand.*] Took his own life, y' know?

SAM CRAIG. Oh, did he?

JOE STODDARD. Hung himself in the attic. They tried to hush it up, but of course it got around. He chose his own epy-taph. You can see it there. It ain't a verse exactly.

SAM CRAIG. Why, it's just some notes of music—what is it?

JOE STODDARD. Oh, I wouldn't know. It was wrote up in the Boston papers at the time.

SAM CRAIG. Joe, what did she die of?

JOE STODDARD. Who?

SAM CRAIG. My cousin.

JOE STODDARD. Oh, didn't you know? Had some trrouble bringing a baby into the world. 'Twas her second, though. There's a little boy 'bout four years old.

SAM CRAIG. [Opening his umbrella.] The grave's going to be over there?

JOE STODDARD. Yes, there ain't much more room over here among the Gibbses, so they're opening up a whole new Gibbs section over by Avenue B. You'll excuse me now. I see they're comin'. [From left to center, at the back of the stage, comes a procession. FOUR MEN carry a casket, invisible to us. All the rest are under umbrellas. One can vaguely see: DR. GIBBS, GEORGE, the WEBBS, etc. They gather about a grave in the back center of the stage, a little to the left of center.]

MRS. SOAMES. Who is it, Julia?

MRS. GIBBS. [Without raising her eyes.] My daughter-in-law, Emily Webb.

MRS. SOAMES. [A little surprised, but no emotion.] Well, I declare! The road up here must have been awful muddy. What did she die of, Julia?

MRS. GIBBS. In childbirth.

MRS. SOAMES. Childbirth. [Almost with a laugh.] I'd forgotten all about that. My, wasn't life awful—[With a sigh.] and wonderful.

SIMON STIMSON. [With a sideways glance.] Wonderful, was it?

MRS. GIBBS. Simon! Now, remember!

MRS. SOAMES. I remember Emily's wedding. Wasn't it a lovely wedding! And I remember her reading the class poem at Graduation Exercises. Emily was one of the brightest girls ever graduated from High School. I've heard Principal Wilkins say so time after time. I called on them at their new farm, just before I died. Perfectly beautiful farm.

A WOMAN FROM AMONG THE DEAD. It's on the same road we lived on.

A MAN AMONG THE DEAD. Yepp, right smart farm.

[They subside. The group by the grave starts singing "Blessed Be the Tie that Binds."]

A WOMAN FROM AMONG THE DEAD. I always liked that hymn. I was hopin' they'd sing a hymn.

[Pause. Suddenly EMILY appears from among the umbrellas. She is wearing a white dress. Her hair is down her back and tied by a white ribbon like a little girl. She comes slowly, gazing wonderingly at the dead, a little dazed.

She stops halfway and smiles faintly. After looking at the mourners for a moment, she walks slowly to the vacant chair beside Mrs. Gibbs and sits down.]

EMILY. [To them all, quietly, smiling.] Hello.

MRS. SOAMES. Hello, Emily.

MAN AMONG THE DEAD. Hello, M's Gibbs.

EMILY. [Warmly.] Hello, Mother Gibbs.

MRS. GIBBS. Emily.

EMILY. Hello. [With surprise.] It's raining. [Her eyes drift back to the funeral company.]

MRS. GIBBS. Yes . . . They'll be gone soon, dear. Just rest yourself.

EMILY. It seems thousands and thousands of years since I . . . Papa remembered that that was my favorite hymn. Oh, I wish I'd been here a long time. I don't like being new here.—How do you do, Mr. Stimson?

SIMON STIMSON. How do you do, Emily. [EMILY continues to look about her with a wondering smile; as though to shut out from her mind the thought of the funeral company she starts speaking to Mrs. Gibbs with a touch of nervousness.]

EMILY. Mother Gibbs, George and I have made that farm into just the best place you ever saw. We thought of you all the time. We wanted to show you the new barn and a great long ce-ment drinking fountain for the stock. We bought that out of the money you left us.

MRS. GIBBS. I did?

EMILY. Don't you remember, Mother

Gibbs—the legacy you left us? Why, it was over three hundred and fifty dollars.

MRS. GIBBS. Yes, yes, Emily.

EMILY. Well, there's a patent device on the drinking fountain so that it never over-flows, Mother Gibbs, and it never sinks below a certain mark they have there. It's fine. [*Her voice trails off and her eyes return to the funeral group.*] It won't be the same to George without me, but it's a lovely farm. [*Suddenly she looks directly at Mrs. Gibbs.*] Live people don't under-stand, do they?

MRS. GIBBS. No, dear—not very much.

EMILY. They're sort of shut up in little boxes, aren't they? I feel as though I knew them last a thousand years ago . . . My boy is spending the day at Mrs. Carter's. [*She sees* MR. CARTER *among the dead.*] Oh, Mr. Carter, my little boy is spending the day at your house.

MR. CARTER. Is he?

EMILY. Yes, he loves it there.—Mother Gibbs, we have a Ford, too. Never gives any trouble. I don't drive, though. Mother Gibbs, when does this feeling go away?—Of being . . . one of *them?* How long does it . . . ?

MRS. GIBBS. Sh! dear. Just wait and be patient.

EMILY. [*With a sigh.*] I know.—Look, they're finished. They're going.

MRS. GIBBS. Sh—.

[*The umbrellas leave the stage.* DR. GIBBS *has come over to his wife's grave and stands before it a moment.* EMILY *looks up at his face.* MRS. GIBBS *does not raise her eyes.*]

EMILY. Look! Father Gibbs is bringing some of my flowers to you. He looks just like George, doesn't he? Oh, Mother Gibbs, I never realized before how troubled and how . . . how in the dark live persons are. Look at him. I loved him so. From morn-ing till night, that's all they are—troubled.

[DR. GIBBS *goes off.*]

THE DEAD. Little cooler than it was.— Yes, that rain's cooled it off a little. Those northeast winds always do the same thing, don't they? If it isn't a rain, it's a three-day blow.—

[*A patient calm falls on the stage. The* STAGE MANAGER *appears at his proscenium pillar, smoking.* EMILY *sits up abruptly with an idea.*]

EMILY. But, Mother Gibbs, one can go back; one can go back there again . . . into living. I feel it. I know it. Why just then for a moment I was thinking about . . . about the farm . . . and for a minute I *was* there, and my baby was on my lap as plain as day.

MRS. GIBBS. Yes, of course you can.

EMILY. I can go back there and live all those days over again . . . why not?

MRS. GIBBS. All I can say is, Emily, don't.

EMILY. [*She appeals urgently to the stage manager.*] But it's true, isn't it? I can go and live . . . back there . . . again.

STAGE MANAGER. Yes, some have tried— but they soon come back here.

MRS. GIBBS. Don't do it, Emily.

MRS. SOAMES. Emily, don't. It's not what you think it'd be.

EMILY. But I won't live over a sad day. I'll choose a happy one—I'll choose the day I first knew that I loved George. Why should that be painful?

[THEY *are silent. Her question turns to the stage manager.*]

STAGE MANAGER. You not only live it; but you watch yourself living it.

EMILY. Yes?

STAGE MANAGER. And as you watch it, you see the thing that they—down there— never know. You see the future. You know what's going to happen afterwards.

EMILY. But is that—painful? Why?

MRS. GIBBS. That's not the only reason why you shouldn't do it, Emily. When you've been here longer you'll see that our life here is to forget all that, and think only of what's ahead, and be ready for what's ahead. When you've been here longer you'll understand.

EMILY. [*Softly.*] But, Mother Gibbs, how can I *ever* forget that life? It's all I know. It's all I had.

MRS. SOAMES. Oh, Emily. It isn't wise. Really, it isn't.

EMILY. But it's a thing I must know for myself. I'll choose a happy day, anyway.

MRS. GIBBS. *No!*—At least, choose an un-important day. Choose the least important day in your life. It will be important enough.

EMILY. [*To herself.*] Then it can't be since I was married; or since the baby was born. [*To the stage manager, eagerly.*] I can choose a birthday at least, can't I?—I choose my twelfth birthday.

STAGE MANAGER. All right. February

11th, 1899. A Tuesday.—Do you want any special time of day?

EMILY. Oh, I want the whole day.

STAGE MANAGER. We'll begin at dawn. You remember it had been snowing for several days; but it had stopped the night before, and they had begun clearing the roads. The sun's coming up.

EMILY. [*With a cry; rising.*] There's Main Street . . . why, that's Mr. Morgan's drugstore before he changed it! . . . And there's the livery stable.

[*The stage at no time in this act has been very dark; but now the left half of the stage gradually becomes very bright—the brightness of a crisp winter morning.*

EMILY *walks toward Main Street.*]

STAGE MANAGER. Yes, it's 1899. This is fourteen years ago.

EMILY. Oh, that's the town I knew as a little girl. And, *look*, there's the old white fence that used to be around our house. Oh, I'd forgotten that! Oh, I love it so! Are they inside?

STAGE MANAGER. Yes, your mother'll be coming downstairs in a minute to make breakfast.

EMILY. [*Softly.*] Will she?

STAGE MANAGER. And you remember: your father had been away for several days; he came back on the early-morning train.

EMILY. No . . . ?

STAGE MANAGER. He'd been back to his college to make a speech—in western New York, at Clinton.

EMILY. Look! There's Howie Newsome. There's our policeman. But he's *dead;* he *died.*

[*The voices of* HOWIE NEWSOME, CONSTABLE WARREN *and* JOE CROWELL, JR., *are heard at the left of the stage.* EMILY *listens in delight.*]

HOWIE NEWSOME. Whoa, Bessie!—Bessie! 'Morning, Bill.

CONSTABLE WARREN. Morning, Howie.

HOWIE NEWSOME. You're up early.

CONSTABLE WARREN. Been rescuin' a party; darn near froze to death, down by Polish Town thar. Got drunk and lay out in the snowdrifts. Thought he was in bed when I shook'm.

EMILY. Why, there's Joe Crowell. . . .

JOE CROWELL. Good morning, Mr. Warren, 'Morning, Howie.

[MRS. WEBB *has appeared in her kitchen, but* EMILY *does not see her until she calls.*]

MRS. WEBB. Chil-*dren!* Wally! Emily! . . . Time to get up.

EMILY. Mama, I'm here! Oh! how young Mama looks! I didn't know Mama was ever that young.

MRS. WEBB. You can come and dress by the kitchen fire, if you like; but hurry.

[HOWIE NEWSOME *has entered along Main Street and brings the milk to Mrs. Webb's door.*]

Good morning, Mr. Newsome. Whhh—it's cold.

HOWIE NEWSOME. Ten below by my barn, Mrs. Webb.

MRS. WEBB. Think of it! Keep yourself wrapped up. [*She takes her bottles in, shuddering.*]

EMILY. [*With an effort.*] Mama, I can't find my blue ribbon anywhere.

MRS. WEBB. Just open your eyes, dear, that's all. I laid it out for you special—on the dresser, there. If it were a snake it would bite you.

EMILY. Yes, yes . . .

[*She puts her hand on her heart.* MR. WEBB *comes along Main Street, where he meets* CONSTABLE WARREN. *Their movements and voices are increasingly lively in the sharp air.*]

MR. WEBB. Good morning, Bill.

CONSTABLE WARREN. Good morning, Mr. Webb. You're up early.

MR. WEBB. Yes, just been back to my old college in New York State. Been any trouble here?

CONSTABLE WARREN. Well, I was called up this morning' to rescue a Polish fella—darn near froze to death he was.

MR. WEBB. We must get it in the paper.

CONSTABLE WARREN. 'Twasn't much.

EMILY. [*Whispers.*] Papa.

[MR. WEBB *shakes the snow off his feet and enters his house.* CONSTABLE WARREN *goes off, right.*]

MR. WEBB. Good morning, Mother.

MRS. WEBB. How did it go, Charles?

MR. WEBB. Oh, fine, I guess. I told'm a few things.—Everything all right here?

MRS. WEBB. Yes—can't think of anything that's happened, special. Been right cold.

Howie Newsome says it's ten below over to his barn.

MR. WEBB. Yes, well, it's colder than that at Hamilton College. Students' ears are falling off. It ain't Christian.—Paper have any mistakes in it?

MRS. WEBB. None that I noticed. Coffee's ready when you want it. [*He starts upstairs.*] Charles! Don't forget; it's Emily's birthday. Did you remember to get her something?

MR. WEBB. [*Patting his pocket.*] Yes, I've got something here. [*Calling up the stairs.*] Where's my girl? Where's my birthday girl? [*He goes off left.*]

MRS. WEBB. Don't interrupt her now, Charles. You can see her at breakfast. She's slow enough as it is. Hurry up, children! It's seven o'clock. Now, I don't want to call you again.

EMILY. [*Softly, more in wonder than in grief.*] I can't bear it. They're so young and beautiful. Why did they ever have to get old? Mama, I'm here. I'm grown up. I love you all, everything.—I can't look at everything hard enough.

[*She looks questioningly at the* STAGE MANAGER, *saying or suggesting: "Can I go in?" He nods briefly. She crosses to the inner door to the kitchen, left of her mother, and as though entering the room, says, suggesting the voice of a girl of twelve.*]

Good morning, Mama.

MRS. WEBB. [*Crossing to embrace and kiss her; in her characteristic matter-of-fact manner.*] Well, now, dear, a very happy birthday to my girl and many happy returns. There are some surprises waiting for you on the kitchen table.

EMILY. Oh, Mama, you *shouldn't* have. [*She throws an anguished glance at the stage manager.*] I can't—I can't.

MRS. WEBB. [*Facing the audience, over her stove.*] But birthday or no birthday, I want you to eat your breakfast good and slow. I want you to grow up and be a good strong girl.

That in the blue paper is from your Aunt Carrie; and I reckon you can guess who brought the post-card album. I found it on the doorstep when I brought in the milk—George Gibbs . . . must have come over in the cold pretty early . . . right nice of him.

EMILY. [*To herself.*] Oh, George! I'd forgotten that. . . .

MRS. WEBB. Chew that bacon good and slow. It'll help keep you warm on a cold day.

EMILY. [*With mounting urgency.*] Oh, Mama, just look at me one minute as though you really saw me. Mama, fourteen years have gone by. I'm dead. You're a grandmother, Mama. I married George Gibbs, Mama. Wally's dead, too. Mama, his appendix burst on a camping trip to North Conway. We felt just terrible about it—don't you remember? But, just for a moment now we're all together. Mama, just for a moment we're happy. *Let's look at one another.*

MRS. WEBB. That in the yellow paper is something I found in the attic among your grandmother's things. You're old enough to wear it now, and I thought you'd like it.

EMILY. And this is from you. Why, Mama, it's just lovely and it's just what I wanted. It's beautiful! [*She flings her arms around her mother's neck. Her* MOTHER *goes on with her cooking, but is pleased.*]

MRS. WEBB. Well, I hoped you'd like it. Hunted all over. Your Aunt Norah couldn't find one in Concord, so I had to send all the way to Boston. [*Laughing.*] Wally has something for you, too. He made it at manual-training class and he's very proud of it. Be sure you make a big fuss about it.—Your father has a surprise for you, too; don't know what it is myself. Sh—here he comes.

MR. WEBB. [*Off stage.*] Where's my girl? Where's my birthday girl?

EMILY. [*In a loud voice to the stage manager.*] I can't. I can't go on. It goes so fast. We don't have time to look at one another. [*She breaks down sobbing.*]

[*The lights dim on the left half of the stage.* MRS. WEBB *disappears.*]

I didn't realize. So all that was going on and we never noticed. Take me back—up the hill—to my grave. But first: Wait! One more look.

Good-by, Good-by, world. Good-by, Grover's Corners . . . Mama and Papa. Good-by to clocks ticking . . . and Mama's sunflowers. And food and coffee. And new-ironed dresses and hot baths . . . and sleeping and waking up. Oh, earth, you're too wonderful for anybody to realize you. [*She looks toward the stage manager and asks abruptly, through her tears.*] Do any human beings ever realize life while they live it?—every, every minute?

STAGE MANAGER. No. [*Pause.*] The saints and poets, maybe—they do some.

EMILY. I'm ready to go back. [*She returns to her chair beside Mrs. Gibbs.*] [*Pause.*]

MRS. GIBBS. Were you happy?

EMILY. No . . . I should have listened to you. That's all human beings are! Just blind people.

MRS. GIBBS. Look, it's clearing up. The stars are coming out.

EMILY. Oh, Mr. Stimson, I should have listened to them.

SIMON STIMSON. [*With mounting violence; bitingly.*] Yes, now you know. Now you know! That's what it was to be alive. To move about in a cloud of ignorance; to go up and down trampling on the feelings of those . . . of those about you. To spend and waste time as though you had a million years. To be always at the mercy of one self-centered passion, or another. Now you know—that's the happy existence you wanted to go back to. Ignorance and blindness.

MRS. GIBBS. [*Spiritedly.*] Simon Stimson, that ain't the whole truth and you know it. Emily, look at that star. I forget its name.

A MAN AMONG THE DEAD. My boy Joel was a sailor,—knew 'em all. He'd set on the porch evenings and tell 'em all by name. Yes, sir, wonderful!

ANOTHER MAN AMONG THE DEAD. A star's mighty good company.

A WOMAN AMONG THE DEAD. Yes. Yes, 'tis.

SIMON STIMSON. Here's one of *them* coming.

THE DEAD. That's funny. 'Tain't no time for one of them to be here.—Goodness sakes.

EMILY. Mother Gibbs, it's George.

MRS. GIBBS. Sh, dear. Just rest yourself.

EMILY. It's George.

[GEORGE *enters from the left, and slowly comes toward them.*]

A MAN FROM AMONG THE DEAD. And my boy, Joel, who knew the stars—he used to say it took millions of years for that speck o' light to git to the earth. Don't seem like a body could believe it, but that's what he used to say—millions of years.

[GEORGE *sinks to his knees then falls full length at Emily's feet.*]

A WOMAN AMONG THE DEAD. Goodness! That ain't no way to behave!

MRS. SOAMES. He ought to be home.

EMILY. Mother Gibbs?

MRS. GIBBS. Yes, Emily?

EMILY. They don't understand, do they?

MRS. GIBB. No, dear. They don't understand.

[*The* STAGE MANAGER *appears at the right, one hand on a dark curtain which he slowly draws across the scene.*

In the distance a clock is heard striking the hour very faintly.]

STAGE MANAGER. Most everybody's asleep in Grover's Corners. There are a few lights on: Shorty Hawkins, down at the depot, has just watched the Albany train go by. And at the livery stable somebody's setting up late and talking.—Yes, it's clearing up. There are the stars—doing their old, old crisscross journeys in the sky. Scholars haven't settled the matter yet, but they seem to think there are no living beings up there. Just chalk . . . or fire. Only this one is straining away, straining away all the time to make something of itself. The strain's so bad that every sixteen hours everybody lies down and gets a rest. [*He winds his watch.*]

Hm. . . . Eleven o'clock in Grover's Corners.—You get a good rest, too. Good night.

THE END

For Discussion and Writing

1. *Our Town* has no heroes, no villains, not even a plotted conflict in the ordinary sense. It is "neither heroic, shocking, sensational, exotic, nor even unfamiliar."

What, in your opinion, accounts for the enormous power of this play to reach people everywhere?

2. The idea for *Our Town* was suggested by the poem called "Lucinda Matlock" in Edgar Lee Masters' *Spoon River Anthology*.

Wilder quotes the last two lines of this poem in his play. Read the poem aloud and discuss what else in this poem might have inspired the playwright.

3. How did Thornton Wilder use each of the following to achieve universality:
   a. Characters (Are they individuals or symbols? Or both?)
   b. Stage Manager
   c. Use of the stage
   d. Manipulation of time
   e. Speeches

4. Thornton Wilder has one theme to which he always returns—the joy of life—"the belief that the cause of man's unhappiness is not his failue to achieve or sustain greatness, but his failure to delight in the beauty of ordinary existence."

How does the action in the play prove the truth of this theme? Why do you agree or disagree with such a philosophy? Could there be "delight in the beauty of ordinary existence" for the slum-dweller? The soldier in the foxhole?

5. In the film version of *Our Town*, Thornton Wilder authorized a revised ending in which Emily does not die. Her death, funeral, and visit back to earth all take place in her mind during the birth of her child.

Wilder wrote to the film producer, "Let her live. The idea will have been imparted anyway."

Discuss your reaction to the change in endings and to the author's comment on it. Why do you think Mr. Wilder feels the theme will get across whether Emily lives or dies?

6. Be the stage manager for an introduction to the town or street where you grew up. Write the speech in a style and with local color appropriate to your neighborhood.

Or write the scene that might have occurred if Emily had chosen to come back to a different day in her life.

The Teahouse
of the August Moon

{1953}

JOHN PATRICK

ADAPTED FROM THE NOVEL BY VERN SNEIDER

CHARACTERS

(In Order of Appearance)

SAKINI	MR. SUMATA
SERGEANT GREGOVICH	MR. SUMATA'S FATHER
COL. WAINWRIGHT PURDY III	MR. SEIKO
CAPTAIN FISBY	MISS HIGA JIGA
OLD WOMAN	MR. KEORA
OLD WOMAN'S DAUGHTER	MR. OSHIRA
THE DAUGHTER'S CHILDREN	VILLAGERS
LADY ASTOR	LADIES' LEAGUE FOR
ANCIENT MAN	DEMOCRATIC ACTION
MR. HOKAIDA	LOTUS BLOSSOM
MR. OMURA	CAPTAIN MCLEAN

ACT ONE

Scene 1: Okinawa. Colonel Purdy's Office, GHQ. *Scene 2:* Outside Captain Fisby's Quarters, GHQ. *Scene 3:* Tobiki Village.

ACT TWO

Scene 1: Tobiki Village. *Scene 2:* Colonel Purdy's Office, GHQ. *Scene 3:* Captain Fisby's Office, Tobiki. *Scene 4:* Tobiki Village.

ACT THREE

Scene 1: The Teahouse of the August Moon. *Scene 2:* Captain Fisby's Office, Tobiki. *Scene 3:* The Teahouse of the August Moon.

Teahouse of the August Moon by John Patrick. Copyright 1952 by John Patrick. Reprinted by permission of Coward, McCann & Geoghegan, Inc.
NOTICE: This play is the sole property of the author and is fully protected by copyright. It may not be acted either by professionals or by amateurs without written consent. Public readings and radio or television broadcasts are likewise forbidden. All inquiries concerning rights, including stock and amateur rights should be addressed to the author's agency, International Famous Agency, Inc., 1301 Avenue of the Americas, New York, New York 10019.
Words from the song "Deep in the Heart of Texas" by June Hershey and Don Swander are reprinted by permission of Melody Lane Publications, Inc.

The historic events that were the source of John Patrick's *The Teahouse of the August Moon* took place on Okinawa April 1, 1945. The inhabitants of that small island, some 2000 miles south of Japan, had developed through the centuries a subtle technique of passive resistance to both invading Chinese and Japanese War Lords. Now they faced a new kind of occupying force—the Americans, who arrived with little experience in the grueling business of military government.

Vern Sneider, assigned to our Army of Occupation, found that John Hersey's novel, *A Bell for Adano*, was more helpful to its beleaguered officials than the manuals sent from Washington. To help future officials facing similar problems, he wrote a novel based on his experiences.

John Patrick, who wrote the stage adaptation of this novel, chose to write a satiric comedy. Satire and farce both deal with the ludicrous, but satire exposes the ludicrous in things we cherish in order to criticize the pretensions and shortcomings in our lives, whereas farce is concerned only with getting laughs. In satire, the audience is conscious of the serious comment behind the humor.

The play made a clean sweep of the top three drama awards in 1953 (Pulitzer Prize, New York Drama Critics Award, Antoinette Perry "Tony" Award) plus many others. It has delighted audiences in London, Vienna, West Berlin, Mexico City, Tokyo—even Okinawa itself.

The Teahouse of the August Moon

ACT ONE

SCENE 1

Directly behind the house curtain is a second curtain consisting of four panels of split bamboo. Each of these sections can be raised and lowered individually.

AT RISE: As the house lights dim, the Oriental strains from a stringed instrument can be heard playing softly in the background. A pool of light picks up SAKINI *standing framed against the bamboo backing. He wears a pair of tattered shorts and a native shirt. His shoes, the gift of a G.I., are several sizes too large. His socks are also too large and hang in wrinkles over his ankles. He is an Okinawan who might be any age between thirty and sixty. In repose his face betrays age, but the illusion is shattered quickly by his smile of childlike candor.*

With hands together in prayer-like supplication, he walks down to the footlights and bows to the audience center in solemn ritual. Then he bows from the waist—to the left and to the right. Straightening up, he examines the audience seated before him with open curiosity. The music ceases. As it ceases, SAKINI *begins to work his jaws vigorously.*

SAKINI. Tootie-fruitie.

[*He takes the gum from his mouth and, wrapping it carefully in a piece of paper, puts it in a matchbox and restores it to a pocket in his shirt.*] Most generous gift of American sergeant. [*He resumes his original posture of dignity.*]

Lovely ladies, kind gentlemen:

Please to introduce myself.

Sakini by name.

Interpreter by profession.

Education by ancient dictionary.

Okinawan by whim of gods.

History of Okinawa reveal distinguished record of conquerors.

We have honor to be subjugated in fourteenth century by Chinese pirates.

In sixteenth century by English missionaries.

In eighteenth century by Japanese war lords.

And in twentieth century by American Marines.

Okinawa very fortunate.

Culture brought to us. . . . Not have to leave home for it.

Learn many things.

Most important that rest of world not like Okinawa.

World filled with delightful variation.

Illustration.

In Okinawa . . . no locks on doors.

Bad manners not to trust neighbors.

In America . . . lock and key big industry.

Conclusion?

Bad manners good business.

In Okinawa . . . wash self in public bath with nude lady quite proper.

Picture of nude lady in private home . . . quite improper.

In America . . . statue of nude lady in park win prize.

But nude lady in flesh in park win penalty.

Conclusion?

Pornography question of geography.

But Okinawans most eager to be educated by conquerors.

Deep desire to improve friction.
Not easy to learn.
Sometimes painful.
But pain makes man think.
Thought makes man wise.
Wisdom makes life endurable.
So . . .

[*He crosses back to the left of the first of the panels.*]

We tell little story to demonstrate splendid example of benevolent assimilation of democracy by Okinawa.

[*He claps his hands, signaling the stagehand to raise the first of the four panels. Flush against the curtain is revealed a sign nailed onto a denuded palm stump. It points toward the other side of the stage and reads:* COL. WAINRIGHT PURDY III.]

Boss by name of Colonel Purdy—Three. Number three after name indicate he is a son of a son of a son.

[*He steps to the next panel and claps again. The screen rolls up revealing a laundry line tied to a second denuded stump. As these panels are raised the background is revealed in sections. It includes a jeep parked against a pile of empty gasoline drums, trees ripped of foliage by recent gunfire—all creating an impression of general destruction. There are several articles of wearing apparel hanging on the laundry line, foremost of which is a pair of khaki pants size forty.*]

Colonel Purdy, Three, displays splendid example of cleanliness for native population to follow. But native population cannot follow. Native not *have* two pairs of pants.

[*He then claps for the next screen to rise, revealing more of the laundry. To the extreme right is seen the outside of Colonel Purdy's Quonset office. Nailed on the post holding the other end of the line is a sign reading:* OFFICERS' LAUNDRY ONLY.]

Colonel Purdy put up many signs. This exceedingly civilized. Make it very easy for uncivilized to know what *not* to do. Here laundry of officer not to fraternize with laundry of enlisted man.

[SAKINI *now signals for the last panel to be raised, revealing the inside of the hut. Colonel Purdy's vacant desk is beside the door. A sign denotes*

his proprietorship. Another sign admonishes the visitor to THINK! *The office is small and sparse. A bulletin board for "Daily Orders" hangs on the upstage wall. Against this wall is the desk of Sergeant Gregovich. Behind a sign denoting his rating sits the* SERGEANT. *His posture is frozen— as if awaiting a signal to come to life.* SAKINI *crosses down center to explain to his audience.*]

This gentleman honorable Sergeant Gregovich—assistant to Colonel Purdy. Not son of a son of a son.

[*He turns toward the* SERGEANT.]

Play has begun, Sergeant.

[GREGOVICH *now comes to life. He begins to chew his gum vigorously and to look about the office. He rises and crosses down to Colonel Purdy's desk. He gets down on his hands and knees in front of the desk and reaches under it.*]

Oh, you know what he is doing? Explanation. Colonel Purdy great student of history. Every month wife of Colonel Purdy send him magazine called *Adventure Magazine*. Cover has picture of pirate with black patch over eye. Everybody try to steal magazine. Colonel hide under desk so he can read first.

[GREGOVICH *rises triumphantly with the magazine.*]

But Sergeant always find. Smart mouse.

[GREGOVICH *returns to his desk and buries himself behind the pages of the magazine. At this point* COLONEL PURDY *himself enters from the left. As his laundry has indicated, he is a man of proportions. The worries of the world in general and the Army of Occupation in particular weigh heavily on his shoulders. He stops to glance at the nearest official sign. He takes out a small notebook to make an entry.* Sakini's *presence is not recognized until indicated.*]

This gentleman exalted boss—Colonel Purdy, Three. Subject of sovereign American city of Pottawattamie, Michigan.

[COLONEL PURDY *hiccups and taps his chest.*]

Also subject to indignity of indigestion. Colonel Purdy explain this by saying—

PURDY. [*Clears his throat and says to himself.*] An occupational disorder of the

Army of Occupation. [*He taps his chest again and puts the notebook away.*]

SAKINI. Colonel Purdy very wise man. Always hit nail on head. Every morning, look at sky—[COLONEL PURDY *puts his hands on his hips and glances skyward.*] And make prophecy.

PURDY. It's not going to rain today.

SAKINI. And you know what? Not rain. Of course, not rain here this time of year in whole history of Okinawa. But Colonel not make mistake. [COLONEL PURDY *goes down the laundry line and stops to button the top of a pair of shorts.*] Colonel Purdy gentleman of propriety. [PURDY *goes back to count articles of clothing.*] And precision. Always count laundry.

PURDY. [*Counts aloud.*]Un—deux—trois.

SAKINI. Explanation. Army teach Colonel French for invasion of Europe. Then send to Okinawa instead.

PURDY. . . . quatre—cinq—six—sept. [*He beams with satisfaction.*]

SAKINI. Very good. Colonel count in French and not notice one pair shorts missing in Okinawa.

PURDY. [*His expression quickly changes.*] What? [*He goes down the line and counts again in English.*] One, two, three, four, five, six, seven! [*He inhales deeply for an explosion.*]

SAKINI. [*Rushes down to the footlights.*] Oh—ladies please close ears unless want to hear unladylike oath. [*He puts his hands over his own ears.*]

PURDY. [*Explodes.*] Damitohell! Damitohell! Damitohell!

SAKINI. Now Colonel yell loud for Sakini. But Sakini hide. Pretend to be asleep. [*He promptly curls up on the ground beside the office, with his back to the* COLONEL.]

PURDY. Sakini! [SAKINI *snores.* PURDY *strides over to tower above him.*] Sakini!

SAKINI. [*Rises quickly.*] Oh—oh. Good morning, boss. You sure surprise me.

PURDY. *Where* is the boy that does my laundry!

SAKINI. Bring laundry back and go home to sleep, boss.

PURDY. I want you to find out why my laundry comes back every week with one piece missing!

SAKINI. Gets lost, boss.

PURDY. I *know* it gets lost. What I want to find out is *how* it gets lost.

SAKINI. Very simple. Boy takes laundry to top of mountain stream and throws in water. Then runs down hill fast as dickens to catch laundry at bottom. Sometimes not run fast enough.

PURDY. [*Heaves a martyr's sigh.*] No wonder you people were subjugated by the Japanese. If you're not sleeping you're running away from work. Where is your "get-up-and-go"?

SAKINI. Guess "get-up-and-go" went. [SAKINI *starts to sit on the ground.*]

PURDY. Well, get up and go over to the mess and see if Captain Fisby has arrived. If he has, tell him to report to me at once. Hurry! [*As* SAKINI *starts across the stage* PURDY *looks with annoyance at the G.I. socks that hang down over Sakini's ankles.*] Sakini!

SAKINI. [*Stops.*] Yes, boss?

PURDY. You're a civilian employee in the pay of the United States Army. And should dress accordingly. *Pull Your Socks Up!*

SAKINI. Yes, boss. [*He leans over and pulls up his socks—not a great improvement.*] Anything else, boss?

PURDY. That will be all. [SAKINI *ambles across the stage so slowly that the* COLONEL *explodes in exasperation.*] Is that as *fast* as you can walk!

SAKINI. Oh no, boss. But if walk any faster—socks fall down. [*As* SAKINI *exits,* COLONEL PURDY *closes his eyes and counts to ten in vehement French.* PURDY *remains arrested in this position.* SAKINI *re-enters downstage. He signals the closing of the panels left, shutting out the* COLONEL.]

SAKINI. Introduction now over. Kindly direct attention to office. [*He leans out toward the footlights and calls across stage.*] Oh, Honorable Sergeant—ready now to continue. [SERGEANT GREGOVICH *again comes to life. He glances out the office door and quickly hides the Adventure Magazine. He stands at attention as* COLONEL PURDY *enters.* SAKINI *exits into the wings.*]

GREGOVICH. Good morning, sir.

PURDY. At ease. [COLONEL PURDY *sits down behind his desk and begins searching through the papers on it.*] I'm thinking of getting rid of that interpreter. He doesn't set a good example.

GREGOVICH. We've got to have someone around that speaks the language, sir.

PURDY. You're quite right, Sergeant. You're quite right. It isn't often I make a mistake, but when I do—

GREGOVICH. It's a beaut?

PURDY. [*Stiffly.*] I wasn't going to say that. I was going to say—I admit it.

GREGOVICH. Sorry, sir.

PURDY. We've got a new officer reporting this morning. He's been transferred to us from "Psychological Warfare." [*Benevolently.*] I don't suppose you happen to know who *they* are?

GREGOVICH. Aren't they something at the rear of the Rear Echelon?

PURDY. They're just the cream of the Army's geniuses. They're just the brains behind the fighting heart. Every man jack of them has a mind like a steel trap. And we are lucky to be getting one of their officers.

GREGOVICH. I'll watch my step, sir.

PURDY. While we're waiting for Captain Fisby, I want you to make a note of some new signs I want painted.

GREGOVICH. [*Takes up a pad.*] The painter hasn't finished the ones you ordered yesterday, sir.

PURDY. There's only one answer to that. Put on another sign painter. Now. I noticed the men were dancing with each other in the canteen the other night.

GREGOVICH. Yes, sir. [*He writes on his pad.*] "No dancing allowed."

PURDY. [*Annoyed.*] I didn't say that, Gregovich! I don't object to the men dancing. I want them to enjoy themselves. But it doesn't set a good example for the natives to see noncoms dancing with enlisted men. So have a sign posted saying, "Sergeants Are Forbidden to Dance with Privates."

GREGOVICH. Yes, sir.

PURDY. Have another sign put up beside that clear pool of water just below the falls—"For Officers Only."

GREGOVICH. Where will the men bathe, sir?

PURDY. There is another pool just below it they can use.

GREGOVICH. If you'll pardon me, sir— they're not going to like that. They'll be bathing in water the officers have already bathed in.

PURDY. That's a valid objection, Gregovich. We don't want to do anything unreasonable. [*He concentrates for a mo-ment.*] How far is the second pool below the first?

GREGOVICH. About three hundred yards.

PURDY. [*Satisfied.*] Then it's quite all right. Water purifies itself every two hundred feet.

GREGOVICH. Do you think that will satisfy the men, sir?

PURDY. I don't see why it shouldn't. It satisfies science. Well, you might as well take those memos to the sign painter now.

GREGOVICH. Yes, sir.

[*He goes out. As soon as he is gone,* COLONEL PURDY *moves around to the front of his desk and feels under it for his* Adventure Magazine. *When he fails to find it, he kneels down on all fours to peer under the desk.* SAKINI *enters and looks around. He steps over and taps the nearest part of Colonel Purdy—his ample rear end.*]

SAKINI. Sakini here, boss.

PURDY. [*Glances around indignantly.*] Don't *ever* put your finger on an officer!

SAKINI. Not right, boss?

PURDY. No! If you want to announce your presence—knock! [*He peers under the desk again.*] Can't you natives learn anything about custom? [SAKINI *stands unhappily a moment, then leans forward and knocks gently on the* COLONEL. PURDY *rises in wrath.*] What do you think you're doing?

SAKINI. Not know, boss. Do what you ask.

PURDY. [*Moves behind his desk.*] Everything in this Godforsaken country conspires to annoy me. [*He turns to* SAKINI.] Well, where is Captain Fisby?

SAKINI. [*Points out the door.*] He come now. I run ahead. [*He points to ankles.*] Socks fall down.

[*He then steps back to allow* CAPTAIN FISBY *to enter.* CAPTAIN FISBY *is in his late twenties, nice-looking and rather on the earnest side. He is nervous and eager to make a good impression. He salutes smartly.*]

CAPTAIN FISBY. Captain Fisby reporting, sir.

PURDY. [*Returns the salute.*] Welcome to Team 147, Captain. [*He puts out his hand.*]

FISBY. [*Shakes hands.*] Thank you, sir.

PURDY. I can't tell you how glad I am

to have you, Captain. Frankly, we're so desperate for officer personnel I'd be glad to see you even if you had two heads. [SAKINI *breaks into gales of laughter.* PURDY *turns to him icily.*] That will be all, Sakini. You can wait outside.

SAKINI. [*Bows.*] I sit by door. Not sleep! [*He exits.*]

PURDY. Sit down, Captain, sit down. [FISBY *sits facing* PURDY.] Have you unpacked?

FISBY. [*Proudly.*] Yes sir! I got in last night and unpacked at once.

PURDY. Well, that's too bad, because you'll have to pack again. I'm sending you to Tobiki at once. We need a man of your caliber up there right away. [*He laughs with forced heartiness.*]

FISBY. [*Forces a laugh in return.*] Thank you.

PURDY. I'm informed, Captain, that you requested this transfer from "Psychological Warfare" to *my* outfit. May I say that I am honored.

FISBY. Well—in all fairness, sir—I think I should tell you . . . the information is only partly true.

PURDY. [*Pause.*] You *didn't* request this transfer to me?

FISBY. I was *requested* to request it, sir.

PURDY. Oh. [*He blinks to aid his digestion of this information.*] May I ask why?

FISBY. Well, my propaganda to undermine enemy morale always seemed to undermine the staff's morale instead, sir.

PURDY. *How* did you get into "Psychological Warfare" in the *first* place?

FISBY. I had been requested to request a transfer.

PURDY. From what?

FISBY. Paymaster General's office.

PURDY. What was your duty there?

FISBY. I was in charge of the payroll computation machine until—until—[*He flounders unhappily.*]

PURDY. Until *what?*

FISBY. Well, sir, machines have always been my mortal enemies. I don't think they're inanimate at all. I think they're full of malice and ill will. They—

PURDY. I *asked* you what happened, Captain.

FISBY. Well, this computation machine made a mistake of a quarter of a million dollars on the payroll. Unfortunately,

the men were paid *before* the mistake was discovered.

PURDY. What did they do to you?

FISBY. For a while I was given a job licking envelopes.

PURDY. Then you asked for a transfer?

FISBY. No, sir, I developed an allergy to glue.

PURDY. How many outfits in this man's army have you been in, Captain?

FISBY. How many are there, sir?

PURDY. Never mind. I admit disappointment but not defeat. I'd thought you were given to me in recognition of my work here. Frankly, I expect to be made a general soon, and I want that star for my wife's crown. Naturally, that's very hush-hush.

FISBY. [*Nods.*] Naturally. Maybe I just wasn't cut out to be a soldier.

PURDY. Captain, none of us was cut out to be a soldier. But we do the job. We adjust. We adapt. We roll with the punch and bring victory home in our teeth. Do you know what *I* was before the war?

FISBY. [*Hesitates unhappily.*] A football coach?

PURDY. I was the Purdy Paper Box Company of Pottawattamie. What did I know about foreigners? But my job is to teach these natives the meaning of democracy, and they're going to learn democracy if I have to shoot every one of them.

FISBY. I'm sure your wife wouldn't want her star that way, sir.

PURDY. What did you do before the war?

FISBY. I was an associate professor at Muncie.

PURDY. What did you teach?

FISBY. The humanities.

PURDY. Captain, you are finally getting a job you're qualified by training to handle—teaching these natives how to act human.

FISBY. The humanities isn't quite that, sir.

PURDY. If you can teach one thing you can teach another. Your job at Tobiki will be to teach the natives democracy and make them self-supporting. Establish some sort of industry up there.

FISBY. Is there a general plan?

PURDY. There is a specific plan. [*He ex-*

tends a document the size of a telephone book.] Washington has drawn up full instructions pertaining to the welfare and recovery of these natives villages. *This* is Plan B. Consider it your *Bible,* Captain.

FISBY. I'll study it carefully, sir. There might be some questions I'd like to ask you.

PURDY. [*Points to Plan B.*] Washington has anticipated all your questions.

FISBY. But I was thinking—

PURDY. You don't even have to think, Captain. This document relieves you of that responsibility.

FISBY. But in dealing with the natives, sir—

PURDY. [*Interrupts.*] It's all covered in Section Four: "Orienting the Oriental." How is your Luchuan?

FISBY. I don't know, sir. What is it?

PURDY. It's the native dialect. Well, I can see you'll need an interpreter. [*His eyes light up and he slaps his desk.*] I have just the man for you! [*He turns and calls out the door.*] Sakini!

FISBY. I could study the dialect, sir.

PURDY. No need. We won the war. I'll give you my own interpreter.

FISBY. Oh, I wouldn't want to deprive you of—

PURDY. I insist.

[SAKINI *enters. He bows—and then remembers. He leans forward and politely knocks on the desk.*]

SAKINI. Sakini present. Socks up. Not sleeping.

PURDY. Sakini, this is Captain Fisby.

FISBY. Hello, Sakini.

SAKINI. [*Bows, then turns to* PURDY.] We meet already. [*He smiles in comradeship.*] You forget, boss?

PURDY. [*Covers his face, counts to ten, then looks up.*] I am assigning you to Captain Fisby. He's going to take charge of a village at the top of Okinawa—a village called Tobiki.

SAKINI. Oh! Tobiki very nice place, boss. But not at top of Okinawa. At bottom.

PURDY. Don't tell me where the villages under my command are located. I happen to have looked at the map.

SAKINI. So sorry, boss. But I happen to get born in Tobiki. Is at bottom.

PURDY. [*Whips a map out of his desk.*] Then it's time you learned where you

were born. I also happen to give a course in map reading.

SAKINI. [*Looks at map.*] So sorry, boss. But map upside down.

FISBY. [*Looks at map.*] He's right.

PURDY. [*Looks at map—turns it around.*] Why in hell doesn't the Army learn how to draw a map properly! [*Turns to* SAKINI.] That will be all, Sakini. Find Sergeant Gregovich and have him assign a jeep to Captain Fisby. Then load supplies and the captain's gear in the jeep. You will be leaving at once. I'll send rice rations later.

SAKINI. [*Takes the colonel's hand and pumps it.*] Oh, thank you, boss. You very kind to send me home. I mention you in prayer to gods. [*He turns to* FISBY.] I wait at jeep for you, Captain. [*He starts to run, then slows down quickly.*] Very happy, sir. Socks up. [*He goes out.* PURDY *turns wearily to* FISBY.]

PURDY. I sometimes think we Occupation Teams have it tougher than combat troops. [*He quickly holds up a protesting hand.*] Granted they have it rough for a while. But we have the killing daily grind, with no glory in it.

FISBY. Yes, sir, I know what you mean. Life itself is a battlefield with its own obscure heroes.

PURDY. [*Looks at* FISBY *with surprise.*] I consider that poetry, Captain.

FISBY. I'm afraid it's just prose, sir. And it isn't mine, it's Victor Hugo's.

PURDY. [*Corrected.*] Oh, yes. Victor Hugo! How I loved *Tale of Two Cities.*

FISBY. Isn't that Dickens, sir?

PURDY. I guess I was thinking of the movie. Well! To get back to Tobiki. Your first job when you get there will be to establish a municipal government and build a school.

FISBY. A school?

PURDY. It's all in Plan B. I'll see that cement and lumber are sent down to you. Plan B calls for the schoolhouse to be pentagon-shaped.

FISBY. If you say so, sir.

PURDY. When the school is built, you will organize a Ladies' League for Democratic Action. You will deliver a series of lectures on democracy as outlined in the outline. Captain, this is a chance for you to make a name for yourself.

FISBY. I will, sir. You see, I feel that I've

personally delayed victory at least a year, and I have to vindicate myself.

PURDY. That's the kind of talk I like to hear from my officers. Well, I won't detain you then. [*He rises.*] My only order to you is: Put that village on the map.

FISBY. Yes, sir.

PURDY. Send me a bimonthly Progress Report—in triplicate.

FISBY. Yes, sir.

PURDY. Don't duplicate your work.

FISBY. No, sir.

PURDY. Fire those natives with the Spirit of Occupation.

FISBY. Yes, sir.

PURDY. And remember—that the eyes of Washington are on our Occupation Teams. And the eyes of the world are on Washington.

FISBY. I'll keep the eyes in mind, sir.

PURDY. Good-bye, Captain. [FISBY *salutes smartly and goes out.* PURDY *stands for a moment, moved by the vastness of the canvas. Then he turns to his desk.*] Where the hell is my *Adventure Magazine!*

THE SCENE BLACKS OUT QUICKLY

SCENE 2

SCENE: *Outside Captain Fisby's quarters.*
TIME: *A few minutes later.*
AT RISE: CAPTAIN FISBY *and* SAKINI *enter from left and cross before the panels, all of which are now down.*

SAKINI. Everything all ready, boss. We go to Tobiki now?

FISBY. I guess so. Well, wish me luck, Sakini. I'm going out to spread the gospel of Plan B.

SAKINI. You already lucky, boss. You got me.

FISBY. [*Smiles.*] Thanks . . . do you know the road?

SAKINI. No road, boss—just path for wagon cart and goat.

FISBY. Will a jeep make it?

SAKINI. We find out, boss.

FISBY. Naturally. How long will it take us?

SAKINI. Oh—not know until we arrive, boss.

FISBY. Naturally. Well, we might as well get started. I'll drive and you give directions.

SAKINI. Oh, very happy to go home.

FISBY. Where is the jeep?

SAKINI. Right here, boss.

[*He turns and claps his hands. The panels go up. The laundry line has been removed and the jeep pulled down center. The jeep is piled with Fisby's belongings. Perched high on the top of this pyramid sits a very old and very wrinkled* NATIVE WOMAN. SAKINI *pays no attention to her as he goes around the jeep test-kicking*

the tires. And the OLD WOMAN *sits disinterested and aloof from what goes on below her.*]

FISBY. Hey, wait a minute! What's she doing up there? [*He points to her. The* OLD WOMAN *sits with hands folded serenely, looking straight ahead.*]

SAKINI. She nice old lady hear we go to Tobiki village. She think she go along to visit grandson.

FISBY. Oh, she does. Well, you explain that I'm very sorry but she'll have to take a bus.

SAKINI. No buses to Tobiki. People very poor—can only travel on generosity.

FISBY. I'm sorry, but it's against regulations.

SAKINI. She not fall off, boss. She tied on.

FISBY. Well, untie her and get her down. She'll just have to find some other way to visit her grandson.

SAKINI. Her grandson mayor of Tobiki village. You make him lose face if you kick old grandmother off jeep.

FISBY. She's the mayor's grandmother?

SAKINI. Oh yes, boss.

FISBY. Well, since she's already tied on, I guess we can take her. [*He looks at the bundles.]* Are all those *mine?*

SAKINI. Oh, no. Most of bundles belong to old lady. She think she visit three or four months so she bring own bed and cooking pots.

FISBY. Well, tell her to yell out if she sees any low branches coming. [*He starts to get in.*] Let's get started.

SAKINI. Oh, can't go yet, boss.

FISBY. Why not?

SAKINI. Old lady's daughter not here.

FISBY. [*Glances at watch.*] We can't wait for a lot of good-byes, Sakini!

SAKINI. [*Looking behind* FISBY.] Oh, she come now—right on dot you bet.

[CAPTAIN FISBY *turns to witness a squat young* NATIVE WOMAN *come on pushing a wheelbarrow loaded with bundles. She stops long enough to bow low to* FISBY—*then begins to tie bundles onto the jeep.*]

FISBY. Sakini, can't the old lady leave some of that stuff behind?

SAKINI. Not her things, boss. Belong to daughter.

FISBY. Wait a minute. Is the daughter planning on going with us, too?

SAKINI. Old lady very old. Who take care of her on trip?

FISBY. Well, I—[*The* DAUGHTER *takes the wheelbarrow and hurries off.*] Hey—you come back. Sakini—tell her to come back. We can't carry any more bundles.

SAKINI. [*Calmly.*] Oh, she not go to get bundles, boss. She go to get children.

FISBY. Come here, Sakini. Now look—this sort of thing is always happening to me and I have to put a stop to it some place. This time I'm determined to succeed. It's not that I don't *want* to take them. But you can see for yourself, *there's no room left for kids!*

SAKINI. But daughter not go without children and old lady not go without daughter. And if old lady not go, mayor of Tobiki be mad at you.

[*Turns to see the* DAUGHTER *hurry back with three children in tow. They all bow politely to* FISBY. *Their mother then piles them on the hood of the jeep.*]

FISBY. For Pete's sake, Sakini, how does she expect me to see how to drive!

SAKINI. Old lady got very good eyesight. She sit on top and tell us when to turn.

[*At this point one of the* CHILDREN *climbs off the hood and points offstage.*]

CHILD. A! Wasureta!

DAUGHTER. Wasureta? Nanisa?

CHILD. Fija dayo.

[*The* CHILD *dashes offstage.*]

FISBY. Now, where's *he* going?

SAKINI. [*To* DAUGHTER.] Doshtano?

DAUGHTER. Fija turete kurendes!

SAKINI. [*To* FISBY.] He go to get goat.

FISBY. A goat!

SAKINI. Can't go and leave poor goat behind.

DAUGHTER. [*Waves gaily to the* OLD WOMAN *on top of the jeep.*] Okasan daijobu! [*She climbs the pyramid of bundles to settle beside her.*]

FISBY. Well, right here is where we start seeing who's going to lose face. No goat is going to travel on this jeep.

SAKINI. You not like goats, boss?

FISBY. It has nothing to do with whether I like goats or not. I'm positive the colonel wouldn't like it.

SAKINI. But children not go without goat, mother not go without children, old lady not go without daughter—

FISBY. [*Repeats with* SAKINI.] —and if old lady not go, the mayor of Tobiki be mad at you! [FISBY *sees the goat being led on by the* SMALL BOY.] Oh, no!

SAKINI. Everybody here, boss. Goat not got children. Goat unmarried lady goat.

FISBY. All right, all right. Put it on the hood with the kids. [*The goat is placed on the hood and held by the* CHILDREN.] We've got to get started or we'll never get off the ground.

SAKINI. All ready to go, boss. You get in now. Nobody else going.

[*But before* FISBY *can climb in an* OLD MAN *comes hurrying in and, without looking to the right or left, climbs on the back of the jeep and settles down.*]

FISBY. Now who the hell is he?

SAKINI. [*Looks at* OLD MAN.] Now who the hell is he? [*Back to* FISBY.] Not know, boss, never see before.

FISBY. Is he a relation of theirs?

SAKINI. [*To the woman on top of the jeep.*] Kore dare?

MOTHER. Mitakoto nai hito desu.

SAKINI. She say she never see him before, boss.

FISBY. Well, ask him what he's doing here!

SAKINI. [*Goes to the* OLD MAN.] Ojisan, doshtano?

OLD MAN. Washimo notte ikuyo.

SAKINI. He say he see people going somewhere on trip and he think maybe he like to go somewhere, too.

FISBY. Tell him to get off and get off quick!

SAKINI. Dame dayo, ojisan, orina, orina!

OLD MAN. [*Angrily.*] Fija noserunnera washimo noruyo!

SAKINI. He say why not take him? You take goat. He say maybe you think he not as good as goat?

FISBY. Look, Sakini, explain to him that the eyes of the world are on Washington and the eyes of Washington are on me. I can't be responsible for—

[*But before this can be translated,*

COLONEL PURDY *stalks on and comes to an abrupt halt.*]

PURDY. Captain Fisby!

FISBY. Yes, sir.

PURDY. What in the name of Occupation do you think you're doing!

FISBY. It's hard to explain, sir. . . . I, ah . . . ah . . .

[*As he founders, the* OLD LADY *on top of the bundles comes to life. She looks down and screams shrilly.*]

OLD LADY. Yakamashii oyajijana, hayo iko, iko!

PURDY. What is *she* saying?

SAKINI. She say . . . tell fat old man to shut up so we can get started! [*As* COLONEL PURDY'S *jaw drops, the panels drop also.*]

BLACKOUT

SCENE 3

SCENE: *Tobiki village.* TIME: *Ten days later.*
AT RISE: *All the bamboo panels are down.* SAKINI *walks in front of them to the center of the stage from the wings.*

SAKINI [*Bows.*]
Distance from Headquarters to Tobiki village by map . . . two inches.
By horse . . . three days.
By foot . . . four days.
By jeep . . . ten days.
Explanation:
Captain want to go to Tobiki.
Children want to go ocean. Never see ocean.
We see ocean.
Captain want to go to Tobiki.
Old lady's daughter want to visit Awasi.
We go Awasi.
Old lady make second mistake.
Captain demand we go Tobiki.
Ancient man have cousin Yatoda.
We go Yatoda.
Damn fool old lady not know one road from another.
Now we arrive Tobiki.
Tobiki welcome rice and democracy.
[*He claps his hands for the panels to be raised, then walks into the scene. The destitute village of Tobiki is revealed with its sagging huts and its ragged villagers grouped in the*

square just outside of Captain Fisby's office. This is a small bamboo structure with a thatched roof. It has a makeshift desk and field telephone. There is a cot crowded against the upper wall. FISBY, his glasses on, sits studying Plan B. He puts the document down, and, taking off his glasses, calls to SAKINI.]

FISBY. Sakini!

SAKINI. Right here, boss. Not asleep, boss.

FISBY. Good. According to Plan B, my first job here is to hold a public meeting.

SAKINI. Public waiting in public square . . . eager to meet new boss, boss.

FISBY. Good. Now, Plan B calls for a lecture on the ABC's of democracy. [*He turns to* SAKINI.] Make sure they understand that I come as a friend of the people. That we intend to lift the yoke of oppression from their shoulders.

SAKINI. Oh, they like that, boss. This their favorite speech.

FISBY. What do you mean, their favorite speech?

SAKINI. Oh, Japanese say same things

when they come, boss. Then take everything.

FISBY. Well, we're not here to *take* anything.

SAKINI. They got nothing left to take away, boss.

FISBY. [*Annoyed.*] Well, if they *did* have, we wouldn't take it. We're here to *give* them something.

SAKINI. Oh, not get angry, boss. We not mind. After eight centuries we get used to it. When friends come now, we hide things quick as the dickens.

FISBY. [*Rises, a little upset.*] Well, I guess it's up to me to convince them we really are friends. Let's meet the villagers. [*He picks up his papers.*] And let them meet Plan B.

[*As they step out the door to the office, the villagers rise and bow respectfully in unison.* FISBY *surveys them.*]

SAKINI. [*Introducing* FISBY.] Amerikano Taisho-san, Captain Fisby.

FISBY. [*Bows in return.*] Well, we might as well get started, Sakini. [*He finds a box and stands on it. He glances into Plan B and clear his throat.*] Citizens of Tobiki village. I—

SAKINI. [*Interrupts him.*] Sorry, boss. Can't begin lecture yet.

FISBY. Why not?

SAKINI. Not good manners. People bring you gifts. You must accept gifts first.

FISBY. But I'm here to bring gifts from my government to them.

SAKINI. Very rude to make people feel poor, boss.

FISBY. I don't want to make anyone feel poor, but—

SAKINI. You make them lose face if you refuse boss. They not accept democracy from you.

FISBY. All right. All right, then. Say to them that I'll accept their gifts in the name of the United States Occupation Forces.

SAKINI. [*Turns to the* VILLAGERS.] Soreja noratte okuyo!

[MR. HOKAIDA, *an enormous villager in tattered peasant clothes, steps forward.*]

MR. HOKAIDA. [*Bows diffidently and offers his present to* FISBY.] Amerika-san, korewo dozo.

SAKINI. This Mr. Hokaida, boss. He give you fine present.

FISBY. Thank you. Than you very much. [*He takes it and turns to* SAKINI *puzzled.*] What is it?

SAKINI. You not know?

FISBY. No.

SAKINI. Oh, where you been all your life, boss?

FISBY. Living without one of these, I guess.

SAKINI. Is very splendid cricket cage, boss.

FISBY. What's it used for?

SAKINI. Keep cricket in.

FISBY. Why?

SAKINI. So Fortune smile on you. Cricket very good luck.

FISBY. But there's no cricket in it.

SAKINI. Bad luck to give cricket. You must catch your own fortune. No one can get it for you.

FISBY. [*Considers this.*] Thank him and tell him I'll keep my eye out for a cricket.

SAKINI. Ya, arigato. [MR. HOKAIDA *bows away as an* ANCIENT NATIVE *steps forward and bows.*] This Mr. Omura. He bring you gift of chopsticks.

MR. OMURA. Korede mainichi gochiso wo, dozo.

SAKINI. He say: May only food of gods touch your lips.

[*As* FISBY *bows,* MR. SUMATA, *a nervous citizen in a torn straw hat, pushes his way toward* SAKINI.]

MR. SUMATA. Sugu modotte kuruyo!

SAKINI. Doshtandes?

MR. SUMATA. Ima sugu presento motte kuruyo. [*He turns and runs hurriedly off stage right.*]

FISBY. What was that?

SAKINI. That Mr. Sumata. He have present at home for you. He say not go away until he get.

[*A rather handsome young Tobikian,* MR. SEIKO, *now steps forward and extends a pair of wooden sandals.*]

MR. SEIKO. Dozo korewo chakini.

SAKINI. This Mr. Seiko. He brings you geta.

FISBY. Geta?

SAKINI. Wooden sandals. Very comfortable for tired feet. He say: May you walk in prosperity.

FISBY. Tell him I shall walk in the—the

cool—meadow—of—of pleasant memories. Is that all right?

SAKINI. Oh, that's very pretty, boss. [*He turns to* MR. SEIKO.] Ya, arigato, Seikosan.

MR. SEIKO. [*Beams, bows, and backs away.*] Iya, kosi no itari desu.

SAKINI. He say you do him honor. [*Here a chunky, flat-faced, aggressive* YOUNG WOMAN *with heavy glasses pushes forward with her present.*] Oh, this Miss Higa Jiga—unmarried lady. She bring you three eggs.

FISBY. Tell her I shall eat them for breakfast. [*He bows to her.*]

SAKINI. Captain-san, daisuki desu.

MISS HIGA JIGA. Kame no tamago desu. [*She bows away.*]

SAKINI. She say she hope you enjoy turtle eggs.

FISBY. [*Grins and bows to her.*] She'll never know.

SAKINI. You very big success. They sure like you already. [*Another* VILLAGER *steps forward and offers a gift.*] This Mr. Keora. He bring you another cricket cage. Minus cricket.

FISBY. Say to him—that my prospects of good fortune are doubled. [*He looks rather pleased with himself.*]

SAKINI. Kagowa futatsu de, un wa bai!

MR. KEORA. Hoho! Naka naka shiteki desna! [*He bows away.*]

SAKINI. He say you are inspired poet.

FISBY. [*Modestly.*] It's all in getting the hang of it.

SAKINI. [*Introducing the next citizen, a very* OLD MAN *leaning on a stick.*] This old man Mr. Oshira. He bring you fine lacquered cup he make himself.

FISBY. Tell him I'm forever in his debt for such a beautiful gift.

OSHIRA. You are most welcome, Captain.

FISBY. [*Turns to him in surprise.*] You speak English!

SAKINI. Mr. Oshira teach me English when I am little boy in Tobiki.

OSHIRA. In my youth I work in Manila. How is Mr. McKinley?

FISBY. [*Puzzled for a moment.*] Who? Oh—President McKinley. I'm afraid someone shot him.

OSHIRA. I am sad.

FISBY. It was a long time ago.

OSHIRA. Yes, a long time. [*He indicates the cup.*] May August moon fill your cup.

FISBY. May I ask, why an August moon?

OSHIRA. All moons good, but August moon little older, little wiser.

FISBY. Did Sakini say you made this cup yourself?

OSHIRA. Oh, yes. I learned from my father before me who learned from his father before him. Is our heritage.

SAKINI. Look, boss, this cup thin as paper, carved from one block of wood. Then painted many times with red lacquer.

FISBY. And did you paint the gold fish inside?

OSHIRA. [*Nods.*] It is imperfect.

SAKINI. When Mr. Oshira little boy, he work ten years to learn how to paint gold fish exactly like his papa paint.

FISBY. It's just beautiful! Can you still make things like this?

OSHIRA. One does not forget.

FISBY. Sakini, here's an industry we can start right away. This is a lost art. [*Turns to* OSHIRA.] Is there any way we could mass-produce these?

OSHIRA. Mass-produce?

FISBY. You know—set up machines and turn them out by the gross.

OSHIRA. [*Shakes his head.*] I take pride in making one cup at time, Captain. How can I take pride in work of machine?

FISBY. How many of these could you turn out in a day?

OSHIRA. If I work hard, maybe one or two a week.

FISBY. [*Disappointed.*] Well, it's a start. Make as many as you can. We'll send them up to the American Post Exchange and sell them as fast as you can turn them out.

OSHIRA. I shall do my best. The swiftness of my youth has deserted me, sir. [*He bows and moves back.*] But I shall make fewer mistakes.

FISBY. [*Excitedly.*] Sakini, tell Mr. Omura to make up a batch of chopsticks. Have everybody get to work making cricket cages, wooden sandals and—[*Pointing.*]—these straw hats. We'll put this village in the souvenir business.

SAKINI. We all make money, boss?

FISBY. If they can turn out enough of these things, I guarantee the recovery of Tobiki village. Tell them.

SAKINI. Kore dondon tskuru yoni . . . [*There is a general exchange of chatter and approval.*] They say they make everything, fast as the dickens, boss.

FISBY. Good. We're in business. Now ask them if they'd mind postponing the rest of the gifts until later. I'd like to tell them what *we're* planning for *them*.

SAKINI. Sa, sono hanashi shiyo.

CITIZENS. No agerumono naiyo! Hanashi wo kiko.

SAKINI. They say sure. They got no more presents anyhow.

FISBY. Good. First I want to tell them about the school we're going to build for their children. All set to translate?

SAKINI. All set.

FISBY. All right. [*He consults Plan B.*] Plan B says the direct approach is most effective. This is it. [*He steps back up on a box and looks forcefully at his listeners. Then he points a dramatic finger at them.*] Do you want to be ignorant?

SAKINI. [*Also points a finger.*] Issho bakaja dame daro?

[*The* CITIZENS *make a noise that sounds like "Hai."*]

FISBY. What did they say?

SAKINI. They say "Yes."

FISBY. What do you mean, "yes"? They *want* to be ignorant?

SAKINI. No, boss. But in Luchuan "yes" means "no." They say "yes," they *not* want to be ignorant.

FISBY. Oh. [*He turns back to his rapt audience and assumes his forensic posture.*] Do you want your *children* to be ignorant?

SAKINI. Issho kodomotachi mo bakaja dame daro?

[*The* VILLAGERS *respond quickly with a noise that sounds like "Lie."*]

FISBY. What did they say then?

SAKINI. They say "No."

FISBY. "No" they do, or "No," they don't?

SAKINI. Yes, they not want no ignorant children.

FISBY. Good. [*He turns back to the* VILLAGERS.] Then this is what my government is planning to do for you. First there will be daily issues of rice for everyone.

SAKINI. Mazu kome no hykyu!

[*The* VILLAGERS *cheer.*]

FISBY. We will build a fine new school here for your children. [*Then recalling Colonel Purdy's dictum.*] Pentagon-shaped.

SAKINI. Gakko taterundayo katachi wa—[*He flounders.*] Ah—Pentagon.

[*The* CITIZENS *look at each other, puzzled.*]

MISS HIGA JIGA. Nandesutte?

SAKINI. Pentagon.

MISS HIGA JIGA. Sore wa nandesuka?

SAKINI. They say what is Pentagon? Never hear before.

FISBY. Never heard of the *Pentagon!*

SAKINI. No, boss.

FISBY. Well, they certainly do need a school here. The Pentagon is—is— [*He looks down at their eager faces.*] Well, it really means five-sided.

SAKINI. Kabega itsutsusa, ii, ni, san, yon, go. [*Holds up five fingers. There is a burst of laughter from the* CITIZENS.]

MISS HIGA JIGA. [*Giggling.*] Ara, gokakuno kodomo nante arimasenyo.

SAKINI. They say no children in Tobiki got five sides.

FISBY. The *school* will be five-sided—like a building in Washington.

SAKINI. [*Explains.*] Chigauyo, chigauyo, onaji mono arundes yo, Washington ni. [*There is a decided reaction of approval.* SAKINI *turns back to* FISBY.] They very impressed.

FISBY. [*Continuing.*] Everyone will learn about democracy.

SAKINI. Mazu minshu shugi bera-bera bera-bera.

MISS HIGA JIGA. Minshu shugi bera-bera bera-bera?

SAKINI. They say: Explain what is democracy. They know what rice is.

FISBY. Oh. [*He scratches his head.*] Well, it's a system of self-determination. It's—it's the right to make the wrong choice.

SAKINI. Machigattemo iindayo.

[*They look up blankly, silently.*]

FISBY. I don't think we're getting the point over. Explain that if I don't like the way Uncle Sam treats me, I can write the President himself and tell him so.

SAKINI. Daitoryo ni tegami kaitemo iinosa.

[*The* VILLAGERS *all laugh heartily.*]

MISS HIGA JIGA. Masaka soonakoto!

SAKINI. [*Triumphantly.*] They say: But do you *send* the letters?

FISBY. Let's get on with the lecture. [*He turns back to the citizens and reads from Plan B.*] Tell them hereafter all men will be free and equal. . . .

SAKINI. Subete, jiyuu, to byodo, de ar, de ar.

FISBY. [*Increases his tempo and volume.*] Without discrimination . . .

SAKINI. [*Taking* FISBY's *tone.*] Sabetsu, taigu—haishi de ar.

FISBY. The will of the majority will rule!

SAKINI. Subete minna de kime, de ar!

FISBY. [*Finishing with a flourish.*] And Tobiki village will take its place in the brotherhood of democratic peoples the world over!

SAKINI. [*Rising to new demagogic heights.*] Koshite, Tobiki, jiyuu. Okinawa, byodo sabetsu, taigu—haishi, jiyuu, byodo de ar, de ar. [*A great burst of applause greets Sakini's performance. He turns to* FISBY.] We going over big, boss.

FISBY. [*Agrees with a nod.*] Now to get this village organized. Is the mayor here?

SAKINI. [*Points.*] Mr. Omura is mayor, boss. [MR. OMURA *steps forward.*] He only one in Tobiki with white coat.

FISBY. [*Glances at the worn, ragged coat.*] It looks to me as if you'll have to get a new coat or a new mayor soon.

SAKINI. Better keep mayor, boss. Impossible to get white coat.

FISBY. Well, since we've got a mayor, we only have to find a Chief of Agriculture and a Chief of Police. That's going to present a problem.

SAKINI. No problem, boss. You just look over gifts and see who give you best gift. Then you give him best job.

FISBY. Sakini, that is *not* the democratic way. The people themselves must choose the man best qualified. Tell them they are to elect their own Chief of Agriculture.

SAKINI. Sah! Senkyo desu. Mazu Chief of Agriculture.

WOMEN VILLAGERS [*Push* MR. SEIKO *forward shouting.*] Seiko-san, Seiko-san ga ii, Seiko-san!

SAKINI. They say they elect Mr. Seiko. He best qualified for agriculture.

FISBY. He's an experienced farmer?

SAKINI. No, boss. He's artist. He draw lovely picture of golden wheat stalk with pretty green butterfly.

FISBY. Drawing pictures of wheat doesn't make him a wheat expert.

SAKINI. Wheat not grow here anyhow, boss. Only sweet potatoes.

FISBY. All right, all right! If he's their choice.

SEIKO. Ano! Watashimo shiroi koto wo.

SAKINI. He say do he get white coat like the mayor?

FISBY. Tell him I'll get him a helmet that says "Chief of Agriculture" on it.

SAKINI. Yoshi, yoshi, kammuri ageru-yo. [SEIKO *bows and backs away.*]

FISBY. Next we want to elect a Chief of Police.

SAKINI. Kondowa Chief of Police!

VILLAGERS. [*Clamor and push the fat* MR. HOKAIDA *forward.*] Hokaida-san. Soda, soda. Hokaida-san.

FISBY. What are *his* qualifications for office?

SAKINI. People afraid of him. He champion wrestler.

[MR. HOKAIDA *flexes his muscles.*]

FISBY. Well, no one can say this isn't self-determination.

MR. HOKAIDA. Washime ano kammuri wo.

SAKINI. He say do he get helmet too?

FISBY. [*Nods.*] I'll requisition another helmet.

SAKINI. Agemasuyo.

MR. HOKAIDA. [*Bows smiling.*] Ya, doomo.

FISBY. Now for the ladies. We intend to organize a Ladies' League for Democratic Action. We'll want to elect a League President.

SAKINI. Oh, ladies never vote before—they like that. [*He turns to the* LADIES.] Kondowa Ladies' League for Democratic Action!

[*This announcement is greeted by excited chatter. The* LADIES *push* MISS JIGA *forward.*]

LADIES. Higa-Jiga-san—Higa-Jiga-san!

SAKINI. They say they elect Miss Higa Jiga. They think she make classy president.

MISS HIGA JIGA. [*Points to her head.*] Ano, watashi nimo ano booshio . . .

FISBY. [*Laughs.*] All right, I'll see that she gets a helmet, too. Now ask them if they have any question they'd like to ask *me.*

SAKINI. Sa, nanka kikitai koto ga attara

OLD WOMAN. Sakini-san, ima nanji kainai

SAKINI. They say they like to know what time is it?

FISBY. [*Puzzled.*] Time? [*Glances at his watch.*] Quarter of five, why?

SAKINI. They say they got to hurry then They not like to miss sunset. This is time of day they sit in pine grove, sip tea and watch sun go down.

FISBY. All right, thank them and tell them they can go have tea in the pine grove.

SAKINI. Ya, minna kaette mo iiyo.

[*They bow and, chattering happily among themselves, go off right.* FISBY *gathers up his gifts.*]

FISBY. How do you think we did, Sakini?

SAKINI. They co-operate, boss. Future look very rosy.

FISBY. Where do you think I can find a cricket?

SAKINI. One come along. May have one in house now and not know it.

FIGBY. Well, I'll take these things in and get started on my Progress Report. [*He goes to the office hut.*]

SAKINI. I take a little snooze then. Public speaking very exhausting.

FISBY. [*As he goes inside.*] I think I handled it pretty well.

[*He sits down at his desk. He examines his gifts and then, putting on his glasses, begins to study Plan B again. After a moment,* MR. SUMATA *enters from the right. He carries a couple of battered suitcases. He is followed by* LOTUS BLOSSOM, *a petite and lovely geisha girl in traditional costume. When they are about center stage, young* MR. SEIKO *runs up after the geisha girl. She turns to him.*]

SEIKO. Ano, chotto . . .

LOTUS BLOSSOM. Ara! Nani?

SUMATA. [*Steps in front of* SEIKO *and points an angry finger under his nose.*] Dame, dame, atchi ike. [SEIKO *bows head and retreats.* MR. SUMATA *then turns to* SAKINI.] Amerika-san doko?

SAKINI. [*Indicates the office.*] Asco.

SUMATA. [*Indicates geisha girl.*] Kore tsurete kitandayo.

SAKINI. Oh? Do-sunno?

SUMATA. Kore Taisho-san ni agetainja. [*He bows and goes off quickly, almost running. The* GEISHA *remains with* SAKINI. SAKINI *smiles and steps inside the office. He stands behind* FISBY.]

SAKINI. You busy, boss?

FISBY. [*Without turning around to him.*] Yes, but what is it?

SAKINI. Mr. Sumata leave present for you, boss.

FISBY. Put it on the shelf where it'll be out of the way.

SAKINI. [*Glances back ouside.*] Not able to do, boss. Present get mad.

FISBY. [*Turns around.*] What's this about, Sakini?

SAKINI. [*Motions to the* GEISHA, *who steps inside smiling. She bows.*] Here you are, boss.

FISBY. [*Rising.*] Who is *she*!

SAKINI. Souvenir.

FISBY. What are you talking about?

SAKINI. Present from Mr. Sumata.

FISBY. Wait a minute. Is he kidding? I can't accept a human present.

SAKINI. Oh, human present very lovely. Introducing Lotus Blossom, geisha girl first class. [*He turns to* LOTUS BLOSSOM.] Amerika-san no Captain Fisby.

LOTUS BLOSSOM. [*Smiling happily.*] Ara, ii otokomaene! Watashi sukidawa.

SAKINI. She say she very happy to belong to handsome captain. She say she serve you well.

FISBY. She's not going to serve me at all. You get that Mr. Sumata and tell him I'm returning his present.

SAKINI. Impossible to do, boss. Mr. Sumata leave present and go up mountains to visit cousin. He say good-bye and wish you much success in Tobiki.

LOTUS BLOSSOM. [*Sweetly.*] Watashi ko-koni sumun desho?

SAKINI. She say, where do you want her to stay, boss?

FISBY. You tell her I don't care where she stays. She can't stay here.

SAKINI. [*Shocked.*] Where she go then? She got no home. Mr. Sumata already gone away.

FISBY. Well, find her a place for the time being.

SAKINI. [*Grins.*] Plenty of room in my house, boss. Just me and my grandpapa.

FISBY. No, I can't do that. Sit her over on that box until I can think where to put her.

SAKINI. You can put her in business, boss.

FISBY. You keep a civil tongue in your head, Sakini.

LOTUS BLOSSOM. [*Comes over to* FISBY, *whom she has been watching with great interest.*] Okimono to ozohri motte kima-sune.

SAKINI. She like to put on your sandals

and kimono for you. She trained to please you, boss.

FISBY. I know what she's trained to do. And I don't need any translation. [*He sits down at his desk again.*] Sakini . . . take my supplies out of the shack and bring them over here. We'll set her up there where I can keep an eye on her.

SAKINI. Not very democratic, boss. You make her lose face if she not make you comfortable, boss. She think she bad geisha girl.

FISBY. You tell her . . . I've got some face to save, too . . . so she can just forget this Oriental hanky-panky.

SAKINI. Anta irantesa!

LOTUS BLOSSOM. [*Waves him away.*] Ara, nani ittennoyo. Imasara ikettatte ikarenai desho.

FISBY. Well, what did she say?

SAKINI. She say for me to go on home to grandpapa . . . she first-class geisha girl . . . she know her business. Good night, boss.

[FISBY *stands eyeing* LOTUS BLOSSOM *as* SAKINI *goes out. The lights go down quickly. During the brief blackout, the two center panels are lowered, shutting out the village street. The office of Colonel Purdy is swung into place in the last panel right. The lights come up on* PURDY *twisting the bell on his field telephone.*]

PURDY. What do you mean . . . there's no answer? Well, keep trying. I'm not the kind of a man to take "no answer" for an answer.

[*The lights come up on the opposite side of the stage in Fisby's office.* FISBY *is holding onto his jacket buttons.* LOTUS BLOSSOM *stands in front of him holding out his robe. She is gently persistent and puzzled at his reticence.*]

FISBY. It's *not* a kimono . . . it's a bathrobe. And I don't *want* to put it on.

LOTUS BLOSSOM. [*Reaches to unbutton his jacket.*] Sa! Shizukani shimasho ne.

FISBY. No, it's against regulations. [*Phone rings. He takes the robe away from* LOTUS BLOSSOM *and sits on it. Then he picks up the phone.*] Hello!

PURDY. [*Jumps.*] You don't have to shout. I can hear you. This is Colonel Purdy.

FISBY. [*Leaps to his feet and pushes* LOTUS BLOSSOM *behind him as if to hide her.*] Yes, sir.

PURDY. Just thought I'd check up on you. How are things going?

[LOTUS BLOSSOM *begins to fan her master.*]

FISBY. Well, everything seems to be under control at the moment.

[*He sits down and takes out a cigarette.* LOTUS BLOSSOM *promptly lights it for him.*]

PURDY. Anything *I* can do for you?

FISBY. [*Pauses.*] I can't think of anything, sir.

PURDY. I realize it's bound to get lonely for you down there . . . so you know what I'm going to do, my boy?

FISBY. [LOTUS BLOSSOM *gets the geta and kneels before him.* FISBY *watches her apprehensively and asks . . .*] What are you going to do?

PURDY. I'll tell you. I'm going to send you some of my old *Adventure Magazines.*

FISBY. [*As* LOTUS BLOSSOM *starts to take off his shoes.*] No. no. I don't want them. [*Into the phone.*] I mean . . . yes . . . thank you. [*He rises and twists about trying to pull his foot away from* LOTUS BLOSSOM.] I'd like something to read.

PURDY. How are you getting along with the natives?

FISBY. [*His leg over the chair.*] The problem here, sir, is a very old one. It seems to be a question of who's going to lose face.

PURDY. I understand. As Mrs. Purdy says, "East is East and West is West, and there can be no Twain." But you're making progress?

FISBY. Nothing I'd like to put on paper, sir.

[LOTUS BLOSSOM *gets his shoes off and slips the sandals on.*]

PURDY. Well, when things get moving down there, send in a detailed Progress Report.

FISBY. If that's what you want, sir.

[LOTUS BLOSSOM *recovers the robe. She reaches out to unbutton his jacket.*]

PURDY. You'll find these people lack the capacity for sustained endeavor. Don't hesitate to build a fire under them.

FISBY. [*Struggling to keep his jacket on.*] That won't be necessary, sir.

PURDY. Don't forget . . . the eyes of Washington are on you, Fisby.

FISBY. [As LOTUS BLOSSOM *tries to pull his jacket over his head.*] I hope not, sir.

PURDY. [*Ponders.*] Fisby, it just occurred to me. Have you given any thought to physical education?

FISBY. If I may say so, sir . . . [LOTUS BLOSSOM *gets one arm out.*] I consider the suggestion . . . [*He hugs the other sleeve.*] a masterpiece of timeliness. [*He gets down on one knee.*]

PURDY. Thank you, my boy. [*Pauses.*] Could you use a deck of cards? Hello? Hello, Fisby . . . you're getting weak.

[*As* FISBY *looks back at the telephone and nods in complete agreement, the two scenes black out simultaneously. The panels fall. A spot picks up* SAKINI *as he steps from the wings.*]

SAKINI. Discreet place to stop now and sip soothing cup of jasmine tea.

Conclusion?

Not yet.

Continuation shortly.

Lotus Blossom not lose face!

[*He bows.*]

THE CURTAIN FALLS

ACT TWO

SCENE 1

SCENE: *Tobiki village.* TIME: *A few days later.*

AT RISE: *All the panels are down.* SAKINI *enters from the wings and crosses down to the footlights center. He bows to the audience.*

SAKINI.

Lovely ladies, kind gentlemen:

Most traveled person in history of world is summer sun.

Each day must visit each man no matter where he live on globe.

Always welcome visitor.

Not bring gossip.

Not stay too long.

Not depart leaving bad taste of rude comment.

But summer sun never tell topside of world what bottomside like.

So bottomside must speak for self.

We continue with little story of Tobiki.

Center of industry.

Seat of democracy.

[*He beams.*]

Home of geisha girl.

[*He goes to the right proscenium arch as all the panels are raised, revealing the empty street outside of Fisby's office.* FISBY *enters, starts across stage,* SAKINI *falling in step behind him.*]

Was wondering what happened to you, boss?

FISBY. [*Stops.*] I went down to inspect the sweet-potato fields. Sakini, no one was there. The potatoes were piled up, but no one was working.

SAKINI. Very hot day, boss.

FISBY. But I can't find my Chief of Agriculture. Or the Mayor, or the Chief of Police. Where is everybody?

SAKINI. Lotus Blossom leave belongings over at Awasi—got no way to bring things here. So—everybody take wheelbarrow to help move Lotus Blossom to Tobiki.

FISBY. And has she got so many things that it takes my entire staff to move her to this village?

SAKINI. No, boss, but Chief of Police not trust Chief of Agriculture, and Mayor not trust Mr. Oshira, so all go.

FISBY. Mr. Oshira? That old man!

SAKINI. He's old, boss, but not dead.

FISBY. A fine way for officials to behave! You tell them I want to see them the moment they come back. [*He starts for his office.*] A fine thing!

SAKINI. Nothing to worry about, boss. They not beat your time. You own Lotus Blossom.

FISBY. I do *not* own her. It's not a question of—of— [*He sits down at his desk.*]

Well, this sort of nonsense isn't going to stop my work. [*He shifts the papers on his desk.*] I intend to get started on that schoolhouse today. We've got the materials, so all we need now is some good carpenters. [*He turns to* SAKINI, *who has followed him inside.*] Who is the best carpenter in the village?

SAKINI. Mr. Sumata.

FISBY. Fine. Get hold of him. Wait a minute! Isn't he the joker who gave me Lotus Blossom?

SAKINI. Mr. Sumata has finger in lots of pies, boss.

FISBY. Well, since he's vanished, who is the next best carpenter?

SAKINI. Father of Mr. Sumata.

FISBY. Where is he?

SAKINI. Go on vacation with Mr. Sumata.

FISBY. [*Beginning to get annoyed.*] Well, who is the *third* best carpenter then?

SAKINI. No more, boss. Only Sumata and son. They have what you call monopoly.

FISBY. There's something fishy about their disappearing.

[MISS HIGA JIGA, *wearing a red helmet with flowers, followed by several other* LADIES, *comes storming across the stage to the office door.* SAKINI *hears them and goes to the door.*]

MISS HIGA JIGA [*Angrily.*] Watashitachi sabetsu taigu desyo!

FISBY. [*Goes to the door also.*] What's the matter with her?

SAKINI. Miss Higa Jiga say do you know what we got in this village, boss? Discrimination.

FISBY. [*Wearily.*] Where?

[SAKINI *turns to* MISS HIGA JIGA.]

MISS HIGA JIGA. [*Indignantly.*] Watashitachi hykyu matte itara clarku ga kite clarku ga anata desuka ma dozo kochirae watashitachi nijikan mo machi mashita yo.

SAKINI. She says that Ladies' League for Democratic Action wait in line for rice rations. Along come Lotus Blossom and ration clerks say, "Oh, how do you do. Oh, please don't stand in line. You come inside and have cup of tea." Then clerks shut up warehouse and leave Ladies' League waiting in sun two hours.

FISBY. It's things like this that undermine the democratic ideal. You tell Miss

Higa Jiga I intend to do something about it. [*He storms into his office.*]

SAKINI. [*Turns to* MISS HIGA JIGA.] Nantoka shimasuyo.

FISBY. I can see right now we're going to have to get rid of the disrupting factor in our recovery. [*He picks up the field telephone and twists the handle.*] Get me Major McEvoy at Awasi.

SAKINI. [*Follows* FISBY *inside.*] What are you going to do, boss?

FISBY. This village isn't big enough for Plan B and a geisha girl.

SAKINI. Oh, boss, Tobiki never have geisha girl before. We like very much.

FISBY. She has to go. [*Then into the telephone.*] Major McEvoy? Captain Fisby at Tobiki. I have a request from one of my people to transfer to your village. Yes, it's a female citizen. Profession? Well . . . [*He looks at* SAKINI.]

SAKINI. Oh, please not send her away, boss. Not democratic.

FISBY. As a matter of fact her name *is* Lotus Blossom. *How* did *you* know? What do you mean, what am I trying to put over on you? Oh, you did? [*He hangs up. Then he glares at* SAKINI.]

SAKINI. [*With great innocence.*] He knows Lotus Blossom, boss?

FISBY. Very well. She was at Awasi and damn near wrecked his whole plan for recovery. She's been booted out of every village by every commander on the island.

SAKINI. Oh, poor little Lotus Blossom.

FISBY. Poor little Lotus Blossom my eye. She upsets every village she's in.

SAKINI. Not her fault she beautiful, boss.

FISBY. No wonder that Mr. Sumata disappeared. The major paid him a hundred yen to get her out of his village.

SAKINI. [*Eagerly.*] You keep her now boss?

FISBY. I have to. [*He points a finger at* SAKINI.] Well, she's not going to get away with causing dissension in *my* village!

[MISS HIGA JIGA, *weary of waiting outside, storms in.*]

MISS HIGA JIGA. Doshte itadakemasno Daitoryo ni tegami wo kakimasawayo.

FISBY. [*Pleads.*] Tell her to go away.

SAKINI. She say she waiting for some democratic action. She say if she don' get it, she thinks she write this Uncle Sam you talk about.

FISBY. Now, look. I don't want com

plaints going into Headquarters. Tell her discrimination is being eliminated.

SAKINI. Sabetsu yamemasyo.

MISS HIGA JIGA. Yamenakutemo iinoyo, watashitachi nimo wakete itadakeba.

SAKINI. Miss Higa Jiga say please not eliminate discrimination. She say just give her some too.

FISBY. And just what does she means by that?

SAKINI. She say Lotus Blossom unfair competition.

FISBY. Granted.

SAKINI. She say you promise everybody going to be equal.

FISBY. I intend to keep my word.

SAKINI. Well, she say she can't be equal unless she has everything Lotus Blossom has.

FISBY. What Lotus Blossom's got, the Government doesn't issue.

SAKINI. [Taking a piece of paper which MISS HIGA JIGA waves.] She make list, boss. Shall I read, boss?

FISBY. Go ahead.

SAKINI. She wants you to get her and ladies in League following items: A. Red stuff to put on lips like geisha. B. Stuff that smell pretty—

FISBY. Now, just wait a minute. What would H.Q. think if I requisitioned lipstick!

SAKINI. [Hands list back to MISS HIGA JIGA.] Dame desuyo.

MISS HIGA JIGA. Jaa Daitoryo ni tegami wo dashimaswa.

SAKINI. She say she sorry, but now she guess she just have to write this letter to Uncle Samuel after all.

FISBY. [Throws up his hands.] All right. All right! Tell her I'll call up the post exchange at Awasi and see if they have any shaving powder and toilet water.

SAKINI. Ya, katte agemasuyo.

MISS HIGA JIGA. [Beams.] Ano wasure naidene bobby pin.

SAKINI. She say, not forget bobby pins or hair.

FISBY. I think I might have been happier in the submarine command.

MISS HIGA JIGA. [Stops as she is about to go.] Mohitotsu onegai watashitachi mo mina geisha ni.

SAKINI. She say one more thing. Can you get Lotus Blossom to teach Ladies' League all to be geisha girls?

FISBY. [Leaps to his feet.] Teach the innocent women of this village to be—No! [MISS HIGA JIGA shrugs and goes outside. As FISBY sinks back at his desk, MISS HIGA JIGA talks excitedly to the WOMEN gathered outside. They run off giggling. FISBY sits at his desk and picks up Plan B.] Plan B! [He thumbs through its pages.] Let's just see if Washington anticipated this.

[He buries his chin in his hands. SAKINI sits quietly watching him. Outside in the village street, LOTUS BLOSSOM enters and starts daintily toward the office. She has only gotten halfway when SEIKO overtakes her.]

SEIKO. [Panting.] Ano, chotto.

LOTUS BLOSSOM. [Stops and looks at him archly.] Nani?

SEIKO. [Takes a chrysanthemum bud from his waist.] Ano korewo dozo.

LOTUS BLOSSOM. [Takes it indifferently.] Ara, so arigato.

SEIKO. [Strikes his heart passionately.] Boku no, kono, hato, o.

LOTUS BLOSSOM. [Flicks her finger.] Anato no hahto? Ara shinzo ne.

SEIKO. [Disembowels himself with an imaginary knife.] Harakitte shinimas.

LOTUS BLOSSOM. [Yawns.] Imagoro sonnano hayaranai noyo.

SEIKO. [Points toward Fisby's office.] Soka Amerika-san ga iinoka?

LOTUS BLOSSOM. [Haughtily.] Nandeste! Sonnakoto yokeina osowa.

SEIKO. [Laughs derisively.] Nanda rashamon janaika.

LOTUS BLOSSOM. [Backs him up with an angry finger.] Watashimo kotoni kansho shinaideyo.

SEIKO. [Bows his head.] Gomen nasai iisugi deshta.

LOTUS BLOSSOM. [Points away.] Atchi, itte. [SEIKO sighs, turns and plods off toward the sweet-potato fields, crushed and dejected. LOTUS BLOSSOM tidies her hair and continues to the office. She calls in coyly.] Fuisbee-san!

SAKINI. [Rises and looks out the door.] Oh, what do you think, boss? Lotus Blossom back. She come to see you.

FISBY. And high time. [He turns to face the door as LOTUS BLOSSOM enters and bows.] Where have you been all day? Never mind, I know—upsetting the agricultural horse cart.

LOTUS BLOSSOM. Fu-san no kao nikkori nasaruto totemo kawaii wa.

SAKINI. She say sun burst through the clouds now that you smile on her.

FISBY. I'm not smiling. [*She hands him Seiko's chrysanthemum bud.*]

SAKINI. Oh, boss, you know what she give you?

FISBY. The works.

SAKINI. When lady give gentleman chrysanthemum bud, in Okinawa that means her heart is ready to unfold.

FISBY. Well, this is one bud that's not going to flower.

LOTUS BLOSSOM. [*Offering a box she has brought.*] Kore otsukemono yo Dozo.

SAKINI. She say, you like to eat some tsukemono? Tsukemono nice thing to eat between meals.

FISBY. No.

LOTUS BLOSSOM. [*Takes geta and kneels beside him.*] Dozo ohaki osobase.

FISBY. Tell her to *leave my feet* alone.

LOTUS BLOSSOM. [*Studies* FISBY.] Kasa kaburu. Nisshabyo nanoyo.

SAKINI. She worried about you, boss. She say, when you go in hot sun, should wear *kasa*—that straw hat—on head.

FISBY. Tell her never mind about my feet or my head. I want her to stop interfering with the recovery program. To stop causing rebellion and making the men—ah—ah—discontented.

SAKINI. [*Turns to* LOTUS BLOSSOM.] Jama shicha dame dayo.

LOTUS BLOSSOM. [*Smiles.*] Fu-san ocha ikaga?

SAKINI. She say: You want some tea?

FISBY. [*Throwing himself down on his cot.*] No.

LOTUS BLOSSOM. Shami demo hikimashoka?

SAKINI. She say: You want some music?

FISBY. No.

LOTUS BLOSSOM. [*Giggles.*] Ara Fu-santara yaiteruno.

SAKINI. She say: You jealous, boss?

FISBY. [*Mirthlessly.*] Ha!

LOTUS BLOSSOM. Honto ni doshita no?

SAKINI. She say: You want to tell her your troubles, boss?

FISBY. Why should I tell her my troubles?

SAKINI. She geisha girl, that's her *business,* boss.

FISBY. Some business.

LOTUS BLOSSOM. Shoga naiwane. Mah soshite irasshai yo.

SAKINI. She say she hear about lack of co-operation here. She feel very bad. She say she want to help because you best boss she ever had. You not make her work and you not take money from her.

FISBY. [*Sits up on his cot.*] Did the other men who owned her . . . hire her out and then take money from her?

SAKINI. Oh, sure.

FISBY. Well, where I come from we have a name for men who—who—do *that* sort of thing.

SAKINI. You have geisha business in America, too?

FISBY. [*Rises.*] No! Sakini, you give her to understand I have no intention of putting her to—to work.

SAKINI. Why not, boss? She pay all her dues to Geisha Guild. She member in good standing.

FISBY. You mean they've got a union for this sort of thing?

SAKINI. Geisha girl have to be protected, boss. Must keep up rates.

FISBY. This is the most immoral thing I've ever heard of. Haven't you people any sense of shame?

SAKINI. We bad not to be ashamed, boss?

FISBY. Obviously, there is a fundamental difference between us that can't be reconciled. I don't say that where I come from there's no such thing as prostitution. But, by God, we don't have unions, set rates and collect dues!

SAKINI. But geisha girl not prostitute, boss.

FISBY. At least we have the decency— [*He stops.*] What do you mean, geisha girls aren't prostitutes? Everybody knows what they do.

SAKINI. Then everybody wrong, boss.

FISBY. Well, what do they get paid for then?

SAKINI. Hard to explain fundamental difference. Poor man like to feel rich. Rich man like to feel wise. Sad man like to feel happy. All go to geisha house and tell troubles to geisha girl. She listen politely and say, "Oh, that's too bad." She very pretty. She make tea, she sing, she dance, and pretty soon troubles go away. Is not worth something, boss?

FISBY. And that's *all* they do?

SAKINI. Very ancient and honorable profession.

FISBY. Look, Sakini, I apologize. I guess I jumped the gun. And I'm glad you explained. It sort of puts a new light on things. [*He turns to* LOTUS BLOSSOM *and grins.*]

LOTUS BLOSSOM. Ara, kyuni nikkorisite, mada okotteru no.

SAKINI. She say: Why are you smiling at her all of a sudden? You mad or something?

FISBY. Tell her that I'm a dope. That I have a coconut for a head.

SAKINI. No use, boss. She not believe.

FISBY. Then will you ask her if she'd be kind enough to give geisha lessons to the Ladies' League for Democratic Action?

SAKINI. Odori ya shami Ladies' League ni oshiete?

LOTUS BLOSSOM. Er iiwa, demo kumiai-aga kowaiwane.

SAKINI. She say Geisha Guild closed shop, but she teach if you not report her.

[*At this point the men of the village come across the square and stop before the office.* LOTUS FLOWER *goes to the door. Immediately there are ohs and ahs from the men.*]

FISBY. What is that?

SAKINI. Sound like Okinawan wolf call, boss.

FISBY. Well, let's find out. [*He goes outside to face the group, followed by* SAKINI.] Ask what's the matter.

SAKINI. Doshtano?

MR. KEORA. Minna gakko nanka yori chaya ga ii soda.

SAKINI. They say they just held meeting in democratic fashion and majority agree on resolution. They want you to build them cha ya.

FISBY. A what?

SAKINI. Cha ya. That's teahouse, boss.

FISBY. A teahouse?

SAKINI. Yes, boss. They say now that this village have geisha girl just like big city, they should have teahouse like big city too.

FISBY. But I can't build them a teahouse . . . I have no authority to do that.

SAKINI. But you tell them will of majority is law. You going to break law?

FISBY. They're going to get a school . . . that's enough.

SAKINI. But majority too old to go to school . . . they want teahouse.

FISBY. There is no provision in Plan B for a teahouse.

LOTUS BLOSSOM. Ano . . . ochaya sae tatereba mondai naija nai no.

SAKINI. Lotus Blossom say teahouse in Tobiki make recovery program work. Everybody make geta and cricket cages like crazy so they can spend money at teahouse.

FISBY. I haven't got any materials to build a teahouse.

SAKINI. Zairyo ga naiyo.

LOTUS BLOSSOM. Ara, kinoo renga ya zaimoku takusan kite orimashitayo.

SAKINI. She say Army truck come yesterday and leave beautiful brick and lovely paint.

FISBY. For the new *schoolhouse*. Tell them . . . it just can't be done.

SAKINI. Dame, dame, dame desuyo!

[FISBY *looks down into the disappointed faces of the* VILLAGERS.]

VILLAGER. Achara-san, iijiwaru dane.

SAKINI. They say you very mean to them after *all* the nice presents they give you.

FISBY. I'm sorry.

SAKINI. They very sorry too, boss. You know why?

FISBY. I think I do.

SAKINI. No, boss. When you leave here . . . Tobiki be forgotten village. Not have park, not have statue . . . not even lovely jail. Tobiki like to be proud. Teahouse give them face.

FISBY. It's going to be a fine schoolhouse. Five sides.

OSHIRA. May I speak, Captain-san?

FISBY. Of course, Mr. Oshira.

OSHIRA. There are lovely teahouses in the big cities. But the men of Tobiki have never been inside them. We are too poor and our clothes are too ragged. All of my life I have dreamed of visiting a teahouse where paper lanterns cast a light in the lotus pond and bamboo bells hanging in the pines tinkle as the breezes brush them. But this picture is only in my heart . . . I may never see it. I am an old man, sir. I shall die soon. It is evil for the soul to depart this world laden with envy or regret. Give us our teahouse, sir. Free my soul for death.

FISBY. [*Unhappily.*] But . . . we haven't got any carpenters!

SAKINI. [*Calls over the heads of the group.*] Oi! Daiku-san! Daiku-san! [MR. SUMATA *and* HIS FATHER *come trotting across the stage carrying their carpenter boxes.* SAKINI *turns to* FISBY.] Oh, what you think? Mr. Sumata and his papa just come down from mountains!

FISBY. [*Gives* SAKINI *a penetrating but defeated look.*] All right. All right! I haven't got a chance. I guess Uncle Sam is going into the teahouse business.

[*He turns and goes back into his office, followed by* LOTUS BLOSSOM.

He picks up Plan B. SAKINI *announces the decision from the steps.*]

SAKINI. Cha ya, tatete iiyo!

[*There is an outburst of cheers from the* VILLAGERS. *It sounds very much like* "Fisby-san, Banzai, Uncle Sam, Banzai!" *Inside* FISBY *begins tearing up Plan B.* LOTUS BLOSSOM *kneels before him, geta in hand.* FISBY *extends his feet and smiles down at her. The cheering outside continues. As the panels descend—*]

THE SCENE BLACKS OUT QUICKLY

SCENE 2

SCENE: *Colonel Purdy's office.* TIME: *A few weeks later.*
AT RISE: *The right panel is lifted. A light picks up* COLONEL PURDY. *He sits at his desk fuming over a report. The rest of the stage remains dark. He calls* GREGOVICH *on his office inter-com.*

PURDY. Gregovich!

GREGOVICH'S VOICE. Yes, sir?

PURDY. Get me Captain Fisby at To-biki.

GREGOVICH. Yes, sir.

[*The extreme left panel rises leaving the intervening panels lowered.* FISBY *sits with his feet propped up on his desk. He is wearing his bathrobe "kimono."* LOTUS BLOSSOM *stands at his side fanning him. Over the scene, the sound of hammering and sawing can be heard. Over this the phone can be heard to ring.* FISBY *lifts the receiver.*]

FISBY. Captain Fisby.

PURDY. Colonel Purdy.

FISBY. [*Over noise.*] Who?

PURDY. Colonel Purdy!

FISBY. I can't hear you. Hold on a minute. [*He turns to* LOTUS BLOSSOM.] See if you can stop that hammering on the teahouse for a minute.

[*He goes through the motions.* LOTUS BLOSSOM *nods understandingly and goes out.*]

PURDY. What's going on down there, Fisby?

FISBY. [*As the noises cease.*] Now, who is it?

PURDY. Colonel Purdy.

FISBY. [*Wraps his robe about his legs quickly.*] Oh, good afternoon, Colonel.

PURDY. I want to talk to you about your Progress Report.

FISBY. I sent it in.

PURDY. I have it. I have it right in front of me. I've read it twice. Now, suppose *you* tell me what it says.

FISBY. What would you like to have me explain, sir?

PURDY. I'd like you to explain why there's nothing in here about the schoolhouse. Didn't you get the lumber?

FISBY. [*Uneasily.*] Yes, sir . . . it's being used right now. But we'll need some more, I'm afraid.

PURDY. I sent ample, according to specifications. How big a structure are you building?

FISBY. Well . . . we ought to consider expansion. Populations increase.

PURDY. We don't need to consider expansion. Our troops will be out of here by the next generation. Which brings me to another point. [*He refers to the report.*] What's this about six kids being born last week?

FISBY. Well, there wasn't much else to fill the Progress Report, sir.

PURDY. Then you've failed at your indoctrination. Don't you know yet that births are entered under "Population Increases"? They are not considered progress.

FISBY. But they weren't children, sir. They were kids . . . goats.

PURDY. There must be something wrong with this connection. It sounded just as if you said "goats."

FISBY. I did, sir. Kids . . . goats. You see, we're trying to increase the livestock herd down here. I thought . . .

PURDY. Goats! I don't care what you thought. Look here, Fisby. Suppose some congressman flew in to inspect our team. How would I explain such a report?

FISBY. Well, goats will breed, sir. Congress can't stop that. And I've been concerned with . . .

PURDY. The population of civilians alone concerns us. I want to know exactly what progress you've made as outlined in Plan B.

FISBY. Well . . . I'm getting along fine with the people.

PURDY. In other words, nothing. Listen to me. Do you realize what Major McEvoy has accomplished in his village?

FISBY. No, sir.

PURDY. Well, I'll tell you. His fourth-graders know the alphabet through "M," and his whole village can sing "God Bless America" in English.

FISBY. Yes, sir. That's real progress, sir. I wish I could say the same.

PURDY. See that you do. I don't want any rotten apples in my barrel. Now . . . I want to know exactly what you have accomplished in the five weeks you've been down there.

FISBY. Well, sir . . . I've started an industry. I'm sending our first shipment out for sale this week.

PURDY. What are you making?

FISBY. [Looks down at his feet.] Oh, getas and . . .

PURDY. Wait a minute . . . what in God's name is a geta?

FISBY. Not "a" geta . . . getas . . . you have to have two.

PURDY. Are you breeding some other kind of animal?

FISBY. You wear them on your feet, sir. Excellent for strengthening the metatarsal muscles. Then . . . I have a group busy building cricket cages. . . .

PURDY. Captain Fisby!

FISBY. Yes, sir.

PURDY. What kind of cages did you say?

FISBY. Cricket. Like in cricket on the hearth. I think we'll find a great market for them. Of course, we don't supply the crickets.

PURDY. Naturally not. Captain Fisby . . . have you been taking your salt pills?

FISBY. Yes, sir . . . I take them at cha ya . . . with my tea.

PURDY. Have you been going out in the sun without your helmet?

FISBY. I wear a kasa, sir . . it's more practical . . . wind can blow through the straw.

PURDY. I see. I see. That will be all, Captain. [He hangs up quickly.]

FISBY. Hello . . . hello . . .

[He hangs up and sits looking at the phone rather puzzled. The lights go down in his office and the panel descends. COLONEL PURDY also sits looking at the phone in his office. He calls SERGEANT GREGOVICH on the intercom.]

PURDY. Sergeant! What is the name of that psychiatrist over at Awasi?

GREGOVICH. Captain McLean?

PURDY. Get him on the phone. My man at Tobiki has gone completely off his rocker!

THE SCENE BLACKS OUT QUICKLY

SCENE 3

SCENE: *Captain Fisby's office.* TIME: *A few days later.*
AT RISE: *The office is empty as the panel rises. After a moment* CAPTAIN MC LEAN *enters. He is an intense, rather wildeyed man in his middle forties. He glances about furtively, then begins to examine the papers on Fisby's desk. He makes several notes in a notebook. He picks up Fisby's cricket cage and is examining it intently when* FISBY *enters behind him. He halts upon seeing*

MC LEAN. FISBY *is wearing his blue bathrobe, his geta and a native straw hat.*

FISBY. Well, who are you?
MC LEAN. [*Gasps in surprise.*] Oh, you startled me.
FISBY. Can I do anything for you? I'm Captain Fisby.
MC LEAN. I'm Captain McLean. There was no one here . . . so I came in.
FISBY. [*He looks at his insignia.*] Oh, medical corps. What brings you to Tobiki?
MC LEAN. Well, I'm—I'm on leave. Thought I'd spend it making some—some —ethnological studies. [*He adds quickly.*] Of the natives.
FISBY. Well, you couldn't have come to a more interesting spot. Sit down, Captain.
MC LEAN. [*Sits.*] Thank you. Would you have any objection to my spending a week or so making my studies, Captain?
FISBY. Not at all. Make yourself at home. I'll take that if it's in your way.
[*He reaches out to relieve MC LEAN of the cricket cage he still holds.*]
MC LEAN. [*Glances at the cage in his hand and laughs awkwardly.*] Oh, yes, I was just examining it.
FISBY. [*Pleased at his authority on the subject.*] It's a cricket cage.
MC LEAN. [*Pauses.*] You . . . like crickets?
FISBY. I haven't found one yet. But at least I've got the cage. I've got two . . . if you want one.
MC LEAN. Thank you, no. Thank you very much. [*He looks at* FISBY'S *attire.*] What happened to your uniform. Captain?
FISBY. It's around. I find getas and a kimono much more comfortable in this climate.
MC LEAN. But isn't that a bathrobe?
FISBY. [*Shrugs.*] It passes for a kimono. Would you like to take off your shoes, Captain?
MC LEAN. Thank you . . . no. I'll keep them on if you don't mind.
FISBY. Can I offer you some tsuke-mono? You eat these during the day between meals. [*He extends a platter.*] Tsuke-mono means fragrant things.
MC LEAN. I just had a chocolate bar, thank you. [*He rises and looks out the door.*] May I ask what you're building down the road?

FISBY. [*Proudly.*] That's my cha ya. [*He pops a few tsukemonos into his mouth.*] It's really going to be something to write home about.
MC LEAN. Cha ya?
FISBY. Well, it just so happens, Captain, that I own a geisha girl. That might sound strange to you, but you get used to these things after a while. And if you have a geisha, you've got to have a cha ya. Sure you don't want some tsukemono?
MC LEAN. I really couldn't eat a thing. [*He glances out the door again.*] May I ask what the men are doing down there wading in that irrigation ditch?
FISBY. They're not wading, they're building a lotus pond. You can't have a cha ya without a lotus pond.
MC LEAN. [*Sits opposite* FISBY.] How have you felt lately, Fisby?
FISBY. McLean, I'll tell you something. I've never been happier. I feel reckless and free. And it all happened the moment I decided not to build that damned pentagon-shaped school.
MC LEAN. That what?
FISBY. The good colonel ordered me to build a pentagon-shaped schoolhouse down here. But the people wanted a teahouse. Believe it or not, someone gave me a geisha girl. So I'm giving this village what it wants. That must all sound pretty crazy to you, Mac.
MC LEAN. Well, yes and no.
FISBY. These are wonderful people with a strange sense of beauty. And hard-working . . . when there's a purpose. You should have seen them start out day before yesterday, great bundles of things they'd made piled high on their heads. Getas, cricket cages, lacquer ware—things to sell as souvenirs up north. Don't let anyone tell you these people are lazy.
ME LEAN. Oh. I see. I see.
FISBY. No, you don't. But you'll have a chance to study them.
MC LEAN. So you're building them a teahouse.
FISBY. Next thing I'm going to do for them is find out if this land here will grow anything besides sweet potatoes. I'm going to send for fertilizers and DDT and—

MC LEAN. [*Leaps to his feet.*] Chemicals!

FISBY. Sure, why not?

MC LEAN. Do you want to poison these people?

FISBY. No, but—

MC LEAN. Now you've touched on a subject that is very close to me. For years I've planned to retire and buy a farm—raise specialties for big restaurants. So let me tell you this. Chemicals will kill all your earthworms, and earthworms aerate your soil.

FISBY. They do?

MC LEAN. Do you know an earthworm leaves castings eight times its own weight every day?

FISBY. That much!

MC LEAN. Organic gardening is the only thing. Nature's way—compost, manure, but no chemicals.

FISBY. Hey! You know a lot about this.

MC LEAN. [*Modestly.*] I should. I've subscribed to all the farm journals for years.

FISBY. Say, you could help these people out while you're here—if you would. Do you think you could take over supervision—establish a sort of experimental station for them?

MC LEAN. Well, I—no—no—I haven't time.

FISBY. Take time. This is a chance for you to put some of your theories into practice.

MC LEAN. [*Haughtily.*] They are not theories. They are proven facts.

FISBY. I'll give you a couple of men to help, and all you'd have to do is tell us how.

MC LEAN. [*Hesitates.*] Is your soil acid or alkaline?

FISBY. Gosh, I don't know.

MC LEAN. Well, that's the very first thing you have to find out. Do you have bees?

FISBY. I haven't seen any.

MC LEAN. [*Shakes his head sadly.*] People always underestimate the importance of bees for pollinating.

FISBY. [*Slaps him on the back.*] Mac, you're just the man we've needed down here. You're a genius!

MC LEAN. I'll want plenty of manure.

FISBY. You'll get it.

MC LEAN. And I'll want to plan this program scientifically. I wish I had some of my books . . . and my seed catalogues.

[*He measures from the floor.*] I've got a stack of catalogues that high.

FISBY. Why don't you make a list, and I'll get the boys over at the airstrip to fly us in seeds from the States.

MC-LEAN. [*The gardener fever possesses the doctor as he begins to make his list.*] Every spring I've made lists of seeds and never had any soil to put them in. And now . . . I could actually germinate. [*He writes.*] Corn—Golden Bantam. [*Then adds enthusiastically:*] And Country Gentleman! Hybrid.

FISBY. Why don't I just leave you with your list while I check on the lotus pond? [MC LEAN *doesn't hear him.*] Well, I'll be back for tea. We have tea in the pine grove and watch the sun go down. [*He goes out.*]

MC LEAN. [*Continues with his list reading aloud.*] Cucumbers—Extra Early Green Prolific. [*His enthusiasm mounts.*] Radishes—Crimson Giant! [*The telephone begins to ring; he ignores it as he writes.*] Tomatoes—Ponderosa Earliana. [*The telephone rings insistently.*] Watermelon! [*He closes his eyes ecstatically.*]

[*The panel rises on the opposite side of the stage revealing Colonel Purdy's office. The intervening panel remains down.* COLONEL PURDY *sits at his desk jiggling his telephone hook.*]

PURDY. What's the matter with this connection! Ring again!

MC LEAN. [*Ignores the ringing.*] Watermelon—All-American Gold Medal! [*He writes it down as the phone rings. He looks up impatiently and lifts the receiver.*] Hello!

PURDY. [*Confidentially.*] Who is this?

MC LEAN. This is Captain McLean.

PURDY. This is Colonel Purdy. Can you talk?

MC LEAN. Why not?

PURDY. I was anxious to hear your report on you-know-who.

MC LEAN. On *who?*

PURDY. *Captain Fisby!* The man I sent you down to examine.

MC LEAN. Oh. [*He weighs his problem quickly.*] Oh. Well . . . I'll have to stay down here several weeks for some . . .

PURDY. Several weeks!

MC LEAN. Rome wasn't built in a day.

PURDY. What?

MC LEAN. I said, Rome wasn't built in a day.

PURDY. [Digests this.] Well . . . you're the doctor.

MC LEAN. I'll send in a report . . . from time to time. I can tell you now I expect to work miracles down here.

PURDY. Splendid . . . splendid. Is there anything I can send? Some old Adventure Magazines or anything?

MC LEAN. There are a couple of books I'd like, but I don't think you could get them.

PURDY. [Picks up pencil.] You name them.

MC LEAN. Well . . . one is Principles of Pea Production, and the other is Do's and Don'ts of Cabbage Culture. [PURDY starts to write . . . then stops.] And do you think you could lay your hands on a soil test kit?

PURDY. [Looks at earphone.] A what?

MC LEAN. [Enunciating.] A soil test kit. I want to see if the soil is sour down here.

PURDY. Sour, did you say?

MC LEAN. Yes . . . if your soil is sour your seeds won't germinate. And I sure wish I had some bees.

PURDY. There is something wrong with this connection!

MC LEAN. I'm going to take time out here to build up the soil with manure.

PURDY. [Unbelieving.] Did you say manure?

MC LEAN. I've lost faith in chemicals. You kill all your worms. I can tell you, when you kill a worm, Colonel . . . you're killing a friend. [There is a long pause.] Hello . . . hello.

PURDY. [Puts down the phone and turns to the squawk box.] Gregovich, where is Plan B!

GREGOVICH'S VOICE. What did you want, sir?

PURDY. I want to see who I send to analyze an analyst.

THE PANELS FALL QUICKLY ON
EACH SIDE OF THE STAGE

SCENE 4

SCENE: Village square. TIME: A few weeks later.

AT RISE: The panels rise to reveal the village square and Fisby's office. Natives are seated in the square, great bundles beside them. Others arrive and sink into positions of dejection. FISBY works at his desk. SAKINI enters and looks at the VILLAGERS.

SAKINI. [To MR. KEORA.] Doshtano?

KEORA. Hitotsu mo unremasenna.

SAKINI. Oh, oh . . . too bad. [SAKINI crosses and enters Fisby's office.] Boss!

FISBY. Yes.

SAKINI. Mr. Keora and everybody back from Big Koza.

FISBY. Good. Let's see how they made out. [He steps outside followed by SAKINI. He stops as he sees his VILLAGERS sitting dejectedly before their large bundles. He turns to SAKINI.] What's the matter?

SAKINI. Mr. Keora very tired. Walk two days with bundle on back to sell straw hats to American soldiers at Big Koza. Nobody buy, so walk back. Too many damn hats now, boss.

FISBY. He couldn't sell any? [SAKINI shakes his head.] Why not?

SAKINI. [Shrugs.] Soldiers not want. Soldiers say . . . what you think we are . . . hayseed? So come home.

FISBY. [Sees old MR. OSHIRA and crosses to him. OSHIRA rises.] Mr. Oshira . . . did you take your lacquer ware to Yatoda?

OSHIRA. Oh, yes . . . but come back . . . not go again.

FISBY. But I don't understand. . . . The Navy always spends money.

OSHIRA. Sailors say, "Oh, pretty good . . . how much you want?" I say, "Twenty-five yen." They say, "Oh, too much . . . can get better in five-and-ten-cent store. Give you one nickel."

FISBY. Did you explain how many years it took you to learn how to turn out such work?

OSHIRA. [Nods.] They say, "What you want us to do, cry?"

FISBY. [Angrily.] Damn stupid morons! [He turns back to OSHIRA.] Did you tell then that each cup was handmade?

OSHIRA. They say . . . not care. They say . . . at home have big machines that turn out ten cups every minute. They say . . . take nickel or jump in lake.

FISBY. [*Unhappily.*] So you had to carry them all the way back?

SAKINI. Poor Mr. Oshira. No one want his lacquer ware.

FISBY. Well, he's wrong. He's a great artist and I'll buy everything he's made myself.

SAKINI. But you not able to buy everything from everybody in Tobiki, boss.

FISBY. [*Sits down on steps.*] Tell them that they should all be proud of their work. And that I'm proud of all of them.

SAKINI. Gokro, gokro san.

FISBY. I'll think of something . . . I'll hit on an idea to bring money to this village yet.

SAKINI. Boss . . . you stop work on teahouse now?

FISBY. No! You'll get a teahouse if I give you nothing else.

SAKINI. They sure wish they could make some money to spend at teahouse, boss. Not like to go like beggars.

FISBY. Give me a little time, Sakini.

[*As they sit around, each deep in his personal problems,* MC LEAN *enters. His uniform is gone. He is wearing his bathrobe, a straw hat and geta.*]

MC LEAN. Fisby! You're just the man I want to see. Can I have a couple of boys to help me? The damn Japanese beetles are eating up my Chinese peas.

FISBY. [*Dispiritedly.*] Sure . . . I'll get a couple for you.

MC LEAN. [*Looks around.*] What's the matter?

FISBY. There's no market for our products.

MC LEAN. Oh . . . that's too bad. What are you going to do? [*He sits down.*]

FISBY. Try to think of something.

OSHIRA. The world has left us behind.

[*The* VILLAGERS *begin to rise and pick up their handiwork.*]

SEIKO. Amerika-san no seija naiyo. Sa, sa, kaette yakezake da!

SAKINI. They say . . . tell you not your fault no one wants to buy, boss. They say guess they go home now and get drunk.

FISBY. Tell them I don't blame them. If I had anything to drink . . . I'd do the same. [*As they start to file out, both* MC LEAN *and* FISBY *have a delayed reac-*

tion. *They leap to their feet together.*] Wait a minute! [*The* VILLAGERS *stop.*] What are they going to get drunk on?

SAKINI. They got nothing but brandy.

MC LEAN. Nothing but *brandy!*

FISBY. How did they manage to get brandy?

SAKINI. We make very fine brandy here, from sweet potatoes. Been making for generations.

FISBY. You make a brandy *yourselves?*

SAKINI. Oh, yes. We make for weddings and funerals.

FISBY. [*Looks at* MC LEAN.] What does it taste like?

SAKINI. You want some, boss? [*He turns to* HOKAIDA.] Imozake, skoshi!

FISBY. Sakini, if this stuff is any good at all, we're in business. This is one thing I *know* our men will buy.

SAKINI. Oh . . . I think we not like to sell brandy. Only make for ceremony.

MC LEAN. It may not be any good anyhow. There are some things even the troops won't drink.

HOKAIDA. [*Returns with an earthen jug.*] Hai, imozake. [*He hands the jug to* FISBY.]

SAKINI. There you are, boss. You like taste now?

FISBY. I'd like to smell it first. [*He gives it a sniff and jerks his head back.*]

MC LEAN. Obviously, it has a kick.

FISBY. How old is this brandy, Sakini?

SAKINI. [*Turns to Hokaida.*] Kore itsuno?

HOKAIDA. [*Holds up seven fingers.*] Issukan mae dayo.

FISBY. Seven years old?

SAKINI. Oh, no, boss. He make last week.

FISBY. It couldn't smell like that in only a week.

SAKINI. Is village secret. You try now?

FISBY. [*Hands it to* MC LEAN.] You try it, Mac. You're a medical man.

MC LEAN. [*Backs away.*] You first.

FISBY. I insist. You're my guest.

MC LEAN. I waive the honor.

FISBY. [*Turns to* SAKINI.] Has anyone ever gone blind or died from this?

MC LEAN. He said they make it for funerals.

SAKINI. Oh, no, boss. We not blind. We not dead.

FISBY. There, you see.

MC LEAN. They've worked up an immunity over the years.

FISBY. Well, I don't want to kill any of

my countrymen. Couldn't you make some sort of test, Doc? [*As* MC LEAN *considers this, the bleat of a goat is heard offstage.* FISBY *and* MC LEAN *exchange looks and nod.*] Sakini, get Lady Astor. [*To* MC LEAN.] That's Miss Higa Jiga's goat. She asked me to give it a classy name. [SAKINI *goes to get* LADY ASTOR.] MC LEAN. I'm not sure what we'll prove. Goats have hardy stomachs.

SAKINI. [*Returns leading a goat.*] Boss, you make guinea pig of goat?

FISBY. If this passes the goat-test, it's all right. No Marine would ever admit he had a weaker stomach than a goat.

MC LEAN. May I borrow this a moment? [*He takes* MR. HOKAIDA's *red helmet and pours into it from the jug.*]

SAKINI. Lady Astor very lucky goat.

FISBY. You hold her, Sakini. Proceed, Doctor . . . in the name of science. [*The goat sniffs the contents of the helmet.*] We're either going to have an industry or goat meat for dinner.

[LADY ASTOR *begins to drink the concoction. They watch her lap up the liquor and lick her lips with relish.*]

MC LEAN. [*Stands back.*] It doesn't seem to affect her. [*Draws his fingers back and forth in front of the goat's eyes.*] Reflexes all right.

FISBY. Let's watch her a minute. The future of Tobiki and the health of the Army are at stake here. [FISBY *and* MC LEAN *and the* VILLAGERS *stand watching the goat.* LADY ASTOR *is quite content.* FISBY *rises.*] Well, here goes. [*He takes the jug and samples the contents himself.* MC LEAN *watches him. Then he, too, tests from the jug. They look at each other and grin.*] Whee! [*He dashes for his office.*]

SAKINI. [*Follows.*] What you going to do, boss?

FISBY. I am about to form the Cooperative Brewing Company of Tobiki. [FISBY *is followed by* SAKINI, MC LEAN, *and some of the* VILLAGERS. *He picks up the phone.*] Get me the Officers' Club at Awasi.

SAKINI. We going to make brandy, boss?

FISBY. I'll tell you in a minute. [*He turns back to telephone.*] Hello . . . Officers' Club, Awasi? This is Captain Fisby at Tobiki. Oh, hello, Major, how are you? Major, when I was with your unit, you could never keep a supply of liquor in the club, and I stumbled onto something and

wondered if you'd be interested. Tobiki, as you know, is the heart of the brandy industry and— [*He takes the phone away from his ear as the word brandy is shouted back at him.*] Yes . . . brandy. . . . [*He turns to* MC LEAN.] Doc, look up the word "sweet potato" and see if it has another fancier name. [*He turns back to the phone.*] Yes . . . I'm here . . . yes . . . I could get you some if you could pay their price and keep the source secret. Oh, yes, it's been made here for generations. Why, you never tasted anything like it.

MC LEAN. The Haitian word for sweet potato is *b-a-t-a-t-a.* [*He spells it out.*]

FISBY. [*Into the phone.*] You've heard of Seven Star Batata, haven't you? Well, Tobiki is where it's made. [*He turns to* MC LEAN.] The Seven Star did it.

SAKINI. Brandy much better if eight or ten days old, boss.

FISBY. We also have Eight Star and Ten Star. Well, naturally the Ten Star comes a little higher. It sells for— [*He looks at* SAKINI *desperately.* SAKINI *holds up ten fingers.*] A hundred occupation yen a gallon.

SAKINI. I mean *ten* yen, boss.

FISBY. Delivered. All right, we'll send up five gallons in about a week. It'll be delivered by our Department of Agriculture. You're welcome. [*He hangs up and turns to* SAKINI.] Sakini, if every family in Tobiki starts making brandy, how much can we turn out in a week?

SAKINI. Oh, maybe . . . forty . . . fifty gallons.

FISBY. Better aim for eighty. [*He lifts the receiver again.*] I'd like to get the naval base at Big Koza, Officers' Club, Commander Myers.

SAKINI. Maybe if everybody build private stills, Tobiki can turn out hundred gallon.

FISBY. I'll know better after I talk to the Navy. [*He speaks into the phone.*] Commander Myers? Captain Fisby at Tobiki. Commander, we've got a surplus of brandy down here and I was wondering . . . [*Again he takes the phone away from his ear as the word brandy is blasted back.*] Yes. Brandy. Ten Star Batata. Well, Lady Astor won't drink anything else. Oh . . . we could supply you with as much as you want at a hundred yen a gallon.

Fifteen gallons? Right! It will be delivered Horse Cart Special in ten days. [*He hangs up and turns to the others crowding into his office.*] Sakini, tell them to all start making brandy, and in a week or two everyone in this village is going to have more money than he ever dreamed of.

SAKINI. Ah, dondon kaseide sake tsukreba minna kanega mokaruyo!

MR. KEORA. Minna shiroi koto katte moii darone?

SAKINI. They say . . . if they work like the dickens, can they all have white coats like the mayor?

FISBY. Yes. I'll get the cloth somewhere. That's a promise. [*The telephone rings.*] Wait a minute. Hello? Well, word gets around fast. [*He picks up his order blank.*] Twenty gallons? PX, GHQ, C.O.D. O.K. [*He hangs up.*] Get to work, boys! [*As they turn to leave,* FISBY *suddenly leaps to his feet.*] Wait! [*They stand frozen as he crouches and starts toward them. He slaps his hand on the floor and then rises triumphantly.*] I got my cricket!

[*The* VILLAGERS *cheer for* FISBY.]

THE PANEL FALLS QUICKLY

ACT THREE

SCENE 1

SCENE: *Teahouse of the August Moon.* TIME: *Several weeks later.*
AT RISE: *All the panels are down.* SAKINI *steps from the wings to address the audience.*

SAKINI. [*Bows.*]
Ability of Americans for mass production equaled only by American capacity for consumption.
Fortune often comes in back door while we look out front window.
Prosperity not only smile on Tobiki.
Prosperity giggle like silly girl.
Very strange.
Things we do best . . . not wanted.
Things we think least of . . . wanted most.
No conclusion.
Tobiki now village of beautiful houses.
But loveliest of all is Teahouse of August Moon.
[*He goes off extreme left, signaling for the panels to rise. Offstage the music of string instruments can be heard playing softly. The panels go up. The ugly thatched huts are gone. In the center of the stage, exquisite in its simplicity, stands the teahouse. Small bells tinkle from its pagoda roof. Soft lights glow through the colored paper panels. Dwarf pines edge the walk leading to a small bridge. An August moon hangs in the autumn sky. The silhouette of* LOTUS BLOSSOM *is framed in the center panel by the soft back lighting. She slides the panel open*

and steps into the almost bare center room of the teahouse. She crosses and lights the lanterns hanging from the eave extensions. As she goes through this ceremony, the GUESTS *wander in. Before they enter the teahouse, they remove their shoes and rinse their fingers in the ceremonial bamboo basin. Then they enter and seat themselves on green floor mats. The* WOMEN *are dressed in silk kimonos of varying hues and the majority of the men wear spotless white suits.* LOTUS BLOSSOM *bows to them and returns through the sliding door again.* FISBY *and* MC LEAN, *followed by* SAKINI, *enter.* SAKINI *wears a white suit and the* AMERICANS *wear their bathrobes and geta. They are greeted enthusiastically by the* GUESTS.]
SAKINI. I tell Lotus Blossom you here, boss. [*He disappears through the sliding panel in the center of the teahouse.*]
FISBY. [*As they walk around inspecting the grounds.*] It's really something, isn't it?
MC LEAN. Where did they all get their white suits?
FISBY. They made them.
MC LEAN. Where'd they get the cloth?
FISBY. I got it from the naval base at

Awasi for ten gallons of brandy. It's target cloth.

MC LEAN. Those kimonos aren't target cloth.

FISBY. Parachute silk. Six gallons' worth. [LOTUS BLOSSOM *enters, followed by* SAKINI. *She hurries down to* FISBY *and bows. She extends a yellow chrysanthemum to him.*]

SAKINI. Chrysanthemum bud in full bloom, boss.

LOTUS BLOSSOM. [*She bows as* FISBY *accepts the gift.*] Hop-pee. [*Her eyes almost disappear in a great smile of pride.*]

FISBY. What did she say?

SAKINI. I try like the dickens to teach her to say "happy birthday," but she can't say "birthday," boss.

LOTUS BLOSSOM. Hop-pee.

FISBY. Well . . . I'm floored! [*He bows to her.*] Thank you, Lotus Blossom. [*To* SAKINI.] How did you know?

MC LEAN. I gave you away.

SAKINI. Everybody in village like to show appreciation, boss.

FISBY. I should have had a kimono made. When you said "formal," I thought this would do.

LOTUS BLOSSOM. Hop-pee. Hop-pee.

FISBY. And a hop-pee hop-pee to you.

GUESTS. [*Murmur in the background.*] Hayaku oiwai hajimeyo, soda, soda.

SAKINI. Everybody impatient to get on with the party, boss.

LOTUS BLOSSOM. Hop-pee. [*She indicates the center mat.*]

SAKINI. You sit down now, boss. Lotus Blossom going to dance in your honor.

FISBY. You hear that. . . . She's going to dance! [*Quickly sits downs.*] Sit down, you farmer. . . . This is in my honor.

MC LEAN. My, my! How am I going to stall Purdy so I can stay down here?

FISBY. I'll have a relapse for you. [*They turn to watch* LOTUS BLOSSOM *as she takes her position and the first notes are struck by the musicians present.* LOTUS BLOSSOM *performs for them a traditional dance of infinite grace and delicacy. She finishes, concluding her performance in front of* FISBY, *who rises and bows to her.*] What a lovely little thing you are! This belongs to you. [*He returns the chrysanthemum with a flourish.* LOTUS BLOSSOM *accepts it and seats herself quickly on a mat and hides her head.*]

SAKINI. Oh, boss . . . you know what you do!

FISBY. It called for flowers.

SAKINI. That mean you give your heart to her.

FISBY. [*Lightly.*] Well, I do. We all do. [*Turns to* MC LEAN.] Wasn't that beautiful, Mac!

MC LEAN. She can dance in my cha ya any day.

SAKINI. You sit beside Lotus Blossom now, boss. You guest of honor and referee.

FISBY. [*Starts to sit down.*] Referee! I thought this was a birthday party.

SAKINI. Lotus Blossom now putting on wrestling match for you, boss.

FISBY. *Wrestlng* match?

LOTUS BLOSSOM. [*Stands up and claps hands.*] Sa, osumo hajime mashoyo.

[*Immediately two men bring in four poles which they set up downstage center to mark a square. Each pole has colored cloth hanging from it.*]

MC LEAN. Who is wrestling? [*He sits next to* FISBY.]

SAKINI. Wrestling match between Chief of Agriculture and Chief of Police.

FISBY. [*To* LOTUS BLOSSOM.] Hokaida and Seiko? [*She nods.*]

SAKINI. Grudge fight, boss.

FISBY. Really?

SAKINI. Whoever win match get to haul sweet potatoes for Lotus Blossom.

FISBY. [*Watching the poles being set up, he indicates them to* LOTUS BLOSSOM.] Why have they wrapped colored cloth around the poles?

LOTUS BLOSSOM. Kuro wa fuyu, Ao wa haru, Akaga natsu de, Shirowa akiyo. Wakkatta?

SAKINI. She explain, boss, that black cloth remind us of winter, green cloth remind us of spring, red is the summer and white the autumn.

LOTUS BLOSSOM. [*Claps her hands.*] Osumo, osumo!

[*MR. HOKAIDA, bare except for a pair of black shorts, enters and crosses to one corner of the ring, where he squats on his heels. An outburst of approval greets his entrance. He smiles with fatuous pleasure, and makes a desperate effort to hold in his fat stomach.*]

MC CLEAN. Do his black shorts mean anything?

SAKINI. Just easy to clean.

[LOTUS BLOSSOM *claps her dainty hands again.* MR. SEIKO *enters, lean and wiry, also wearing black shorts and a sweat shirt reading U.S.S. Princeton.*]

FISBY. Where did he get *that?*

SAKINI. Sailor at naval base. Some class, eh? [MR. SEIKO *peels off the shirt to great applause and squats in the opposite corner. He glares at* HOKAIDA, *who thrusts his jaw forward.*] They waiting on you to give signal now, boss.

FISBY. Waiting on *me?*

SAKINI. Oh, yes . . . you are Honorable Referee.

LOTUS BLOSSOM. [*Hands her fan to* FISBY.] Korede aizu shite kudasai.

FISBY. What do I do with this?

SAKINI. Now you cover face with fan.

FISBY. Why?

SAKINI. That mean you not take sides. Now you go to center of ring and drop fan from face.

MC LEAN. And get the hell out in a hurry.

FISBY. How many falls?

SAKINI. No falls, boss. First one to throw other out of ring—winner. [FISBY *covers his face with the fan and walks down center. The two wrestlers crouch, poised to leap, their eyes on the fan.* FISBY *whips the fan away from his face and dashes back out of range. The protagonists circle each other slowly. Suddenly all hell breaks loose. The teahouse guests cheer their favorite. The fat* MR. HOKAIDA *picks up* MR. SEIKO *and subjects him to a series of head spins and thumpings. But he exhausts himself; and it is* SEIKO *who ends by tossing* HOKAIDA *out of the ring. A cheer rises from the guests.* FISBY *sighs with relief.*] Now the judges must decide who win.

FISBY. Decide! Is there any doubt?

[*The three judges confer. They then turn to* MR. HOKAIDA *and bow.*]

SAKINI. Mr. Hokaida! The winner . . .

[*This startling announcement is greeted with approval.* SEIKO *beats his head and wails.*]

FISBY. How *could* he be the winner! He was thrown out of the ring.

SAKINI. Maybe so, but judges all cousins of Mr. Hokaida.

FISBY. But the judges are wrong.

SAKINI. [*Confidentially.*] We know who really win . . . but this way nobody lose face.

[SEIKO *and* HOKAIDA *exit.*]

LOTUS BLOSSOM. Sa kondo wa Fu-san no ban yo.

SAKINI. Lotus Blossom say guests now wish *you* to perform.

FISBY. Perform what?

SAKINI. They like now for you and doctor to sing song or something.

FISBY. Sing!

SAKINI. Must do, boss. Bad manners to refuse.

FISBY. [*Repeats in alarm.*] Sing! [*He turns to* MC LEAN.] Get on your feet, Mac, we've got to sing something.

MC LEAN. What?

FISBY. We could sing the national anthem.

MC LEAN. No, we couldn't—I don't know the words.

FISBY. How about "Deep in the Heart of Texas"?

MC LEAN. Why not? There're no Texans here. [*They step forward.*]

FISBY. Mac, let's have some fun. [*He turns to* SAKINI.] Sakini, you tell them they must all help us. They must clap and sing "Deep in the Heart of Texas" every time *we* do.

SAKINI. [*Beaming.*] Tewo tataite Deep in the Heart of Texas. [*Demonstrates clapping.*] Koshte, Deep in the Heart of Texas.

[*The* VILLAGERS *chatter and agree with enthusiasm.* FISBY *and* MC LEAN *stand close together and begin singing. Each time they come to the designated phrase,* SAKINI *gives a signal and the* VILLAGERS *join in lustily. Lost in their eager concentration, no one observes the entrance of* COLONEL PURDY. *He looks from the "kimono"-clad figures of* FISBY *and* MC LEAN *to the assemblage. As he shouts at* FISBY, *his voice is drowned out by the chorus of "Deep in the Heart of Texas." The song continues.* PURDY *signals offstage.* GREGOVICH *enters and is instructed by* COLONEL PURDY *to end the objectionable noises.*]

GREGOVICH. Captain Fisby!

[*Again the voice coincides with the shouts of "Deep in the Heart of Texas" and is lost.* COLONEL PURDY

stalks downstage center followed by
GREGOVICH.]
PURDY. Captain Fisby! What in the
name of Occupation is going on here?
[FISBY gasps and backs away. Suddenly aware of his bathrobe, he
stoops down to cover his bare legs.

MC LEAN surrenders completely to
panic. He runs to hide behind guests.
The GUESTS, alarmed by the sudden
intrusion, scatter in all directions. In
the midst of this bedlam—]

THE PANELS ARE LOWERED

SCENE 2

SCENE: Office of Captain Fisby.
TIME: Next morning.
AT RISE: The four bamboo panels are down. SAKINI enters from
the wings right and crosses down to the footlights.

SAKINI.
[Bows.]
When present is blackest,
Future can only be brighter.
Okinawa invaded many times.
Not sink in ocean yet.
Survive Chinese.
Survive Japanese.
Survive missionaries and Americans.
Invaded by typhoon.
Invaded by locust.
Invaded by cockroach and sweet-potato
moth.
Tobiki now invaded by Honorable Colonel.
Not sink in ocean.
[He goes to the left side of the stage
and raises the panels in front of
Fisby's office. He then exits. COLONEL
PURDY is seated at Fisby's desk going
through his papers. FISBY stands be-
hind him nervously watching. MC
LEAN sits on the cot biting his nails.
He rises.]
PURDY. [Without looking up.] Sit down!
[MC LEAN sits down again. PURDY turns to
FISBY and glares at him.] Where are your
bimonthly Progress Reports?
FISBY. I—I think they should be right
here under the cricket cage, sir.
PURDY. [Takes some papers from under
the cage and glances at them.] These are
all completely blank. [He turns to FISBY.]
Fisby, you can't convince me that you've
been down here for two months doing
absolutely nothing.
FISBY. Oh, no, sir. I mean yes, sir, I
have not been doing "nothing."
PURDY. You're beginning to sound like
a native.

MC LEAN. [Rises.] The tendency is always to descend to the level of the environment, sir. It's a primary postulate of
psychology.
PURDY. [Turns on him.] Well, it's a
primary regulation of the Army to make
out reports! [Back to FISBY.] Now, I want
to know exactly what you've accomplished
here from the moment you arrived.
FISBY. Well, let me think. . . .
MC LEAN. Could I—
PURDY. Sit down! [He turns to FISBY.]
How many lectures have you delivered
to the village children on democratic
theory?
FISBY. Well, let me see.
PURDY. Four-five?
FISBY. [Thinks.] Not that many, sir.
PURDY. Three?
MC LEAN. [Hopefully.] Two?
FISBY. N-no.
PURDY. You only delivered one lecture?
FISBY. None, sir.
PURDY. Don't tell me you haven't de-
livered a single lecture!
FISBY. Yes, sir, I haven't delivered no
lecture. I mean . . . any lecture.
PURDY. Did you organize a Ladies'
League for Democratic Action?
FISBY. [Beaming.] Yes, sir. I sure did. I
did that all right!
PURDY. And how many lectures on dem-
ocratic theory have you given them?
FISBY. [Deflated again.] None, sir.
PURDY. You can't mean none. You must
mean one or two.
FISBY. No, sir, none.
PURDY. I refuse to believe it.
FISBY. I'm glad, sir.

MC LEAN. [*Rises in desperation.*] Sir, I *must* go.

PURDY. Where!

MC LEAN. My *seedlings* are wilting. I have to transplant them.

PURDY. Captain, you will pack your gear and transplant yourself to your unit at once.

MC LEAN. Yes, sir. [*He turns to* FISBY.] They'll die. It's murder. [*He goes to the door and turns sadly to* FISBY *again.*] Please take care of my beans. [*He exits.*]

PURDY. [*Turns back to* FISBY.] Now! Is the schoolhouse finished?

FISBY. [*Sighs.*] No, sir.

PURDY. *Why* isn't it finished?

FISBY. It isn't finished, sir, because it isn't started.

PURDY. I have a splitting headache, Fisby. I ask you not to provoke me needlessly. Now, where is the schoolhouse?

FISBY. I never built it.

PURDY. Don't stand there and tell me you never built it. I sent the lumber down two months ago.

FISBY. [*Impressed.*] Is it *that* long, sir?

PURDY. What did you do with the lumber I sent?

FISBY. Well, I built a teahouse.

PURDY. [*Stares at him.*] I don't suppose you have any aspirin here?

FISBY. No, sir, I haven't.

PURDY. Now, sit down. Fisby. I want to be fair. [FISBY *sits down.*] I'm a patient man. When I run into something that defies reason, I like to find the reason. [*Explodes.*] What in the name of Occupation do you mean by saying you built a *teahouse* instead of a *schoolhouse!*

FISBY. It's a little hard to explain, sir. Everybody in the village wanted one . . . and Lotus Blossom needed it for her work.

PURDY. And just what is your relationship with this woman?

FISBY. Well, she was a present. So to speak. She's a geisha girl—after a fashion.

PURDY. You built this teahouse—this place for her to ply her trade—with lumber belonging to the Army of Occupation of the United States Government?

FISBY. Well, it just seemed like lumber at the time.

PURDY. Fisby, are you operating a house of prostitution here on Government rice?

FISBY. No, sir! Geishas aren't what you think.

PURDY. Don't tell me what to think. Army Intelligence warned me I'd find something mighty peculiar going on in Tobiki.

FISBY. What's Army Intelligence got to do with it, sir?

PURDY. You're not very cunning, Fisby. With all the Occupation money on the island finding its way to this village, did you think it wouldn't come to the attention of Intelligence?

FISBY. Oh.

PURDY. Why did you do it, Fisby, why!

FISBY. Well, Lotus Blossom had to have a place to teach the Ladies' League how to become geishas and—

PURDY. Fisby! You mean to say you've turned all the decent women of this village into professional . . . [*He slumps into the chair.*] How could you sink to such depths, man!

FISBY. I was only giving in to what the majority wanted, sir.

PURDY. I don't doubt that statement—not at all. It is a sad thing that it took a war to convince me that most of the human race is degenerate. Thank God I come from a country where the air is clean, where the wind is fresh, where—

FISBY. [*Interrupts.*] For heaven's sake, sir, would you please listen to me instead of yourself! There is not a thing goes on in that teahouse that your mother couldn't watch.

PURDY. [*Leaps to his feet and points a warning finger.*] You be careful how you use my mother's name, Fisby.

FISBY. Well, *my* mother then. I swear there's nothing immoral about our teahouse.

PURDY. Then answer me this. What is bringing all that Occupation money to this particular village? There is only one thing that attracts that kind of money.

FISBY. Well, evidently there are two things.

PURDY. And if it isn't honor that you sell here, what is it?

FISBY. [*Sighs unhappily.*] We . . . make things.

PURDY. What?

FISBY. Mats . . . and hats . . . and cricket cages.

PURDY. One hundred and fifty thousand

yen finds its way to this village every month. You can't convince me that the American soldier is spending that much on "cricket cages."

FISBY. Well, naturally . . . not all of it. [*The telephone rings.* FISBY *looks at it apprehensively.*]

PURDY. Answer it.

FISBY. [*Pauses.*] It's nothing important, sir.

PURDY. It might be for me. Answer it.

FISBY. [*Airily.*] Oh, it rings all day, sir. Pay no attention.

PURDY. Then I'll answer it! [*He picks up the telephone.* FISBY *covers his face.*] Hello? *What* do you want? Who is this? Well, Commander Myers, I think you have the wrong connection. This is not a brewery. Yes . . . yes . . . yes! [*He turns to look at* FISBY.] Oh . . . I see. I see. I see. [*He hangs up. He turns to* FISBY, *who smiles weakly.*]

FISBY. It was the only thing we could make that anyone wanted to buy, sir.

PURDY. Brandy! [*Sadly.*] I don't know which is worse. Putting your country in the white slave trade or the wholesale liquor business. Congress will have to decide.

FISBY. We've the most prosperous village on the island, sir.

PURDY. This ends my Army career. I promised Mrs. Purdy I'd come out a general. You've broken a fine woman's heart, Fisby.

FISBY. You said to make the village self-supporting, sir.

PURDY. I didn't tell you to encourage lewdness and drunkenness. You've sullied the reputation of your nation and all the tears—

FISBY. All right, sir, shall I kill myself?

PURDY. Oh, don't minimize this. You don't know the enemy's genius for propaganda.

FISBY. Does anyone have to know, sir? We're doing all right.

PURDY. [*Explodes.*] Yes, they have to know! I requested an investigation myself. I've notified the Inspector General. Now I'll have to radio the whole story to Washington.

FISBY. Oh.

PURDY. [*Calmer.*] Well, what have you done with all this money you've made so dishonestly?

FISBY. Banked it in Seattle.

PURDY. Oh, that's despicable—making a personal fortune off the labor of these ignorant people.

FISBY. I haven't touched a cent for myself, sir. It's been deposited in the name of the Tobiki Cooperative. The whole village are equal partners. Share and share alike.

PURDY. [*Leaps up.*] That's *Communism!*

FISBY. Is it?

PURDY. [*Sinks down again.*] I'll be lucky to get out of this war a private. [*He is a beaten man.*] Well, there is only one thing for me to do.

FISBY. What is that, sir?

PURDY. First, you are to consider yourself under technical arrest. You will proceed to H.Q. at once to await court-martial.

FISBY. Yes, sir.

PURDY. [*Steps to the door.*] Gregovich! [*He turns back to* FISBY.] I must go on to Awasi this afternoon on an inspection tour. But before I leave, I intend to wipe this stain from our country's honor.

[SERGEANT GREGOVICH *enters and salutes.*]

GREGOVICH. You called, sir?

PURDY. I did. We have some business to attend to here before going on to Awasi.

GREGOVICH. Yes, sir. I'm glad to hear it. [*He turns to* FISBY.] May I congratulate you on what you've done to this village, sir. It's a dream.

FISBY. Thank you, Sergeant.

PURDY. It is an alcoholic dream. It is one vast distillery. I want you to take a detail and some axes and smash every still in this village.

GREGOVICH. Destroy them?

PURDY. Beyond repair. I want you to take another detail and rip down that teahouse.

GREGOVICH. But, Colonel—

PURDY. Pile the lumber beside the warehouse. That is an order. Do you understand?

GREGOVICH. Yes, sir! [*As he turns to follow orders,* FISBY *sinks into his chair and the scene blacks out quickly.*]

CURTAIN

SCENE 3

SCENE: *Teahouse of the August Moon.* TIME: *A few hours later.*
AT RISE: *All the panels are down. Behind the screens can be heard the destruction of the stills and dismantling of the teahouse.* SAKINI *comes out from the wings and crosses down to the footlights. He flinches at the sound of an ax falling on wood.*

SAKINI.
  [*Sadly.*]
Oh, no comment.
  [*He walks back into the wings as all the panels are raised simultaneously. Only the frame of the teahouse has been spared. The paper panels have disappeared, the pagoda roof is gone with its tinkling bells. There are no colored lanterns and no dwarf pines to grace the path. The bare supports stand stark and ugly. Resting at the edge of the frame is a wheelbarrow.* LOTUS BLOSSOM *is collecting the last of her possessions. She takes a brass brazier down to place in the wheelbarrow. Then she stands with her back to the audience surveying all that remains of the teahouse.* FISBY *comes on, and, seeing* LOTUS BLOSSOM, *hesitates. Then he crosses to stand beside her. He takes her hand, and the two of them stand looking at the ruins.* LOTUS BLOSSOM *walks to the center of the teahouse and sits on the bare floor.* FISBY *comes up and sits on the floor facing her. She goes through the ceremony of pouring him an imaginary cup of tea.* FISBY *accepts with mock formality. As he takes the cup and pretends to drink it,* LOTUS BLOSSOM *covers her face with her hands.* FISBY *sits watching her mutely.*]
SAKINI. [*Entering.*] Jeep all loaded, boss.
FISBY. I'll be along in a minute.
SAKINI. Oh, pretty soon have nice schoolhouse here. . .
FISBY. [*Bitterly.*] Pentagon-shaped.
SAKINI. Not be too bad. You take Lotus Blossom with you?
FISBY. No.
SAKINI. What happen to her then?
FISBY. What would have happened to her if we'd never come along?
SAKINI. Not know. Maybe someday she meet nice man and give up Geisha Guild.

FISBY. Ask her if there is anything I can do for her before I go.
SAKINI. [*Comes up to stand behind them.*] Nanika iitai?
LOTUS BLOSSOM. [*Softly.*] Fu-san, watashito kekkon shite chodai.
SAKINI. [*Scolding.*] Sonna bakana koto.
LOTUS BLOSSOM. [*Persistent.*] Iikara hayaku itte!
FISBY. What does she want?
SAKINI. Oh, that crazy Lotus Blossom. She want you to marry her.
FISBY. Why should she want to marry me?
SAKINI. She think you nicest man she ever see, boss.
FISBY. Tell her that I am clumsy, that I seem to have a gift for destruction. That I'd disillusion her as I have disillusioned her people.
SAKINI. Kokai suruyo.
LOTUS BLOSSOM. Ikitai noyo. Amerika ni. Ikitai noyo.
SAKINI. She say she think she like to go to America. There everyhobdy happy. Sit around and drink tea while machines do work.
FISBY. She wouldn't like it, Sakini. I should hate to see her wearing sweaters and sport shoes and looking like an American looking like an Oriental.
SAKINI. But she want to be an American, boss. She never see an American she not like, boss.
FISBY. Some of them wouldn't like her, Sakini. In the small town where I live, there'd be some who would make her unhappy.
SAKINI. Why, boss?
FISBY. She'd be different.
SAKINI. Dame dayo.
LOTUS BLOSSOM. [*Takes Fisby's hand.*] Sonna koto naiwa, Amerikatte minshu shugi desumono ne.
SAKINI. She say not believe that. In America everybody love everybody. Everybody help everybody; that's democracy.

FISBY. No. That's faith. Explain to her that democracy is only a method—an ideal system for people to get together. But that unfortunately . . . the people who get together . . . are not always ideal.

SAKINI. That's very hard to explain, boss. She girl in love. She just want to hear pretty things.

FISBY. Then tell her that I love what she is, and that it would be wrong to change that. To impose my way of life on her.

SAKINI. Tassha dene!

FISBY. Tell her that I shall never forget her. Nor this village. Tell her that in the autumn of my life—on the other side of the world—when an August moon rises from the east, I will remember what was beautiful in my youth, and what I was wise enough to leave beautiful.

SAKINI. Issho wasurenai kara ne. Mangetsu no yoru niwa anata o omoidashimasu.

LOTUS BLOSSOM. [Remains silent a moment.] Watashi mo Fu-san no koto issho wasurenaiwa. Fu-san no koto uta ni shite, Okinawaju ni hirome masu.

SAKINI. She say she always remember you, boss. She say she guess maybe she be what she is—first-class geisha girl. She want you to know she made up long song-story about you to sing in teahouse. And maybe hundred years from now, you be famous all over Okinawa.

FISBY. [Rises.] I'd like that.

LOTUS BLOSSOM. [Rises.] Iinoyo. Fu-san damedemo Seiko-san ga irun dakara.

SAKINI. She say, since you not marry her, maybe you suggest somebody here. [FISBY laughs.] She say that Mr. Seiko been looking at her like sick goat. She say what you think of him?

FISBY. Well, he took an awful beating just so he could carry her sweet potatoes.

LOTUS BLOSSOM. Fu-san, Seiko-san iito omouno?

SAKINI. She say you think she ought to marry him?

FISBY. I think she ought to decide for herself.

[And MR. SEIKO enters. He is dressed in his white suit and his hair is slicked down tight. He crosses to LOTUS BLOSSOM. They all turn to look at him.]

SEIKO. [Bows to LOTUS BLOSSOM.] A, boku, oshimasho.

SAKINI. [To FISBY.] Mr. Seiko tell Lotus Blossom he sure like to push her wheelbarrow for her.

LOTUS BLOSSOM. Iikara sakini itte chodai.

SAKINI. She say, oh, all right, but not to think that means she's his property.

[MR. SEIKO beams like a schoolboy and, picking up the handles of the wheelbarrow, he trots off stage with LOTUS BLOSSOM's possessions. She turns to FISBY and hands him her fan.]

LOTUS BLOSSOM. Korede aizu shite chodai. Soremade watashi dokonimo ikimasen kara.

SAKINI. She say she go now, but you still her boss. She not go until you give signal.

[FISBY takes the fan and puts it before his eyes. Without waiting for him to drop it, LOTUS BLOSSOM runs off right. When he lowers the fan, he knows she's gone. He sits down on the platform that had been the teahouse veranda.]

SAKINI. You go now, boss?

FISBY. Shortly.

SAKINI. Since you not take Lotus Blossom, maybe you take me, boss?

FISBY. Major McEvoy is coming down to take charge. You'll work with him.

SAKINI. Would rather work with you.

FISBY. You'll like Major McEvoy.

SAKINI. I'll work for you for half price, boss.

FISBY. Major McEvoy will need your help in getting this village on its feet again.

SAKINI. You very hard man to bargain with, boss. If you want, I work for rice rations only.

FISBY. No.

SAKINI. You mean you going to make me work for *nothing*, boss?

FISBY. I mean *yes*, you're *not* going to work for me at all. And you belong here.

SAKINI. You know what I think happen when Americans leave Okinawa?

FISBY. What?

SAKINI. [Grins.] I think maybe we use pentagon-shaped schoolhouse for teahouse.

[FISBY *laughs. He gives* SAKINI *a slap on the shoulder.*]

FISBY. Good-bye, Sakini, you're a rare rascal and I'll miss you.

SAKINI. Good-bye, boss. [FISBY *starts off left. He has gone halfway when* SAKINI *calls.*] Boss—

FISBY. [*Stops.*] Yes?

SAKINI. You not failure.

FISBY. [*Laughs.*] I'll tell you something, Sakini. I used to worry a lot about not being a big success. I must have felt as you people felt at always being conquered. Well, now I'm not so sure who's the conqueror and who the conquered.

SAKINI. Not understand, boss.

FISBY. It's just that I've learned from Tobiki the wisdom of gracious acceptance. I don't want to be a world leader. I'm making peace with myself somewhere between my ambitions and my limitations.

SAKINI. That's good?

FISBY. It's a step backward in the right direction. [*He throws* SAKINI *a salute.*] Take care.

[*He walks off and* SAKINI *watches him go. Then, with a sigh,* SAKINI *turns to survey the skeleton of the teahouse. The silence is broken by the stormy entrance of* COLONEL PURDY.]

PURDY. Sakini! Where is Captain Fisby?

SAKINI. [*Points.*] Just leaving, boss.

PURDY. [*Shouts.*] Fisby! Fisby! [*Gestures frantically.*] Come back here at once! [*He goes to the platform and sinks down gasping.*] I'm not in shape—too much paper work. [FISBY *returns from the left.*] Where in hell have you been, Fisby? I've been looking all over for you.

FISBY. I'm ready to leave, sir.

PURDY. You can't leave. You've got to stay here. You've got to help me, Fisby.

FISBY. Help doing what, sir?

PURDY. Pulling this village back together again. All hell has broken loose, Fisby. [*He sits down to wipe his brow.*] Where is Gregovich!

FISBY. Breaking up the last of the stills, sir.

PURDY. Oh, no! [*He holds his head.*]

FISBY. What's happened, sir?

PURDY. I radioed the report to Washington. Some fool senator misunderstood. He's using this village as an example of American "get-up-and-go" in the recovery program. The Pentagon is boasting. Congress is crowing. We're all over the papers.

FISBY. But that's wonderful, sir.

PURDY. No, it's not wonderful. A Congressional Committee is flying over to study our methods. They are bringing in photographers for a magazine spread. Today, Fisby, today!

FISBY. Oh, that's bad, sir.

PURDY. [*Wails.*] Gregovich!

FISBY. Isn't there any way to stall them off, sir? Quarantine the place or something?

PURDY. You can't quarantine a congressman. They have immunity or something. [*He takes* FISBY *by the jacket.*] Fisby, help me. I don't ask for my sake. I ask for Mrs. Purdy. I could be a brigadier yet.

[*Before* FISBY *can answer,* GREGOVICH *comes in from the left and salutes.*]

GREGOVICH. You called, sir?

PURDY. [*Hurries over to him.*] Gregovich! Gregovich! You haven't destroyed all the stills, have you, Gregovich? No, of course you haven't.

GREGOVICH. Yes, sir, I have. I carried out orders to the letter.

PURDY. [*Turns away shouting.*] Why can't someone disobey orders once in a while! What has happened to the American spirit of rebellion! [GREGOVICH *hiccups, smiles sillily and folds up on the floor.* FISBY *and* PURDY *race over to kneel beside him.*] Sunstroke?

FISBY. Potato brandy.

PURDY. Sergeant, wake up. Do you hear me? That's an order.

FISBY. I'm afraid he's passed out, sir.

PURDY. It's desertion. I need every man. Gregovich, get to your feet!

[*With* FISBY's *help he gets* GREGOVICH *to his feet.*]

GREGOVICH. Sorry, sir.

PURDY. I want to ask you some questions. Stop weaving.

GREGOVICH. *You're* weaving, sir. *I'm* perfectly still.

PURDY. You smell like a brewery.

GREGOVICH. I fell in a vat.

PURDY. You got drunk.

GREGOVICH. No, sir. I fell in a vat. Naturally, I had to open my mouth to yell for help.

PURDY. Go to the office and sober up at once.

GREGOVICH. Yes, sir. [*He salutes with a happy smile, jogs off.*]

PURDY. I'm a sinking ship . . . scuttled by my own men.

[*He sinks.* SAKINI, *who has been sitting with arms folded and a fatuous grin on his face, speaks up.*]

SAKINI. Colonel Purdy?

PURDY. Don't bother me.

SAKINI. Stills not all destroyed.

PURDY. I haven't got time to . . . What did you say?

SAKINI. We not born yesterday. Get sergeant drunk . . . and give him water barrels to break.

PURDY. Sakini, my friend, you're not just saying that to make me feel better?

SAKINI. Oh, stills all good as ever. Production not cease yet.

FISBY. [*Fondly.*] You really are a rogue, Sakini.

PURDY. No . . . he's really an American. He has get-up-and-go.

FISBY. Sakini, if everybody in the village worked together . . . how long would it take to rebuild the teahouse?

PURDY. We don't ask the impossible.

SAKINI. Oh, maybe three minutes . . . maybe five.

PURDY. That's impossible.

SAKINI. We not destroy. Just take away and hide. You watch now, boss. [*He turns and calls.*] Oi, mo iiyo, mo iiyo. [*From the wings, right and left, the* VILLAGERS *step out.*] Oi, haba, haba. [*The* VILLAGERS *respond with happy cries and dash off.*] Country that has been invaded many times soon master art of hiding things.

PURDY. You think we can pull it off, Sakini?

SAKINI. You watch now.

[*And even as he speaks, the sections of the teahouse are carried in and the swift work of putting them together progresses before our eyes. Music is heard in the background. The pagoda roof with its tinkling bells is lowered. The dwarf pines and the arched bridge are brought back. The colored panels are slipped into place and the lanterns are hung.* LOTUS BLOSSOM *comes on with flowers which she arranges.* SAKINI *snaps his fingers and the August moon is magically turned on in the sky. When the final lantern is hung,* MC LEAN *comes in. He stops. His mouth falls open.*]

PURDY. Close your mouth, Captain—haven't you ever seen a cha ya before? [*He turns back to* FISBY.] Fisby, this is a land of adventure . . . a land of jade and spices . . . of Chinese junks and river pirates. . . . Makes a man's blood pound.

FISBY. Colonel . . . I consider what you just said pure . . . [*He pauses.*] . . . poetry.

PURDY. Thank you . . . thank you, boy. [*He sighs ecstatically.*] It's the mystery of the Orient.

FISBY. It's beautiful. Simply beautiful.

PURDY. There's only one thing wrong. It needs a sign to tell people what it is. And I think we ought to put a sign up over there naming this Grace Purdy Avenue. And another sign . . .

FISBY. Colonel Purdy. Won't you have a cup of tea? [*He takes his arm. As he propels him toward the teahouse, he speaks over his shoulder to* SAKINI.] Twenty Star for the colonel, Sakini.

[*As the bamboo panels begin to descend on the teahouse,* SAKINI *steps down to the audience.*]

Little story now concluded.
History of world unfinished.
Lovely ladies . . . kind gentlemen—
Go home to ponder.
What was true at the beginning remains true.
Pain makes man think.
Thought makes man wise.
Wisdom makes life endurable.
Our play has ended.
May August moon bring gentle sleep.
[*He bows.*]

THE CURTAIN FALLS

For Discussion and Writing

1. Conventionally realistic theater maintains the illusion that life itself is taking place upon the stage and that the audience looking on through the fourth wall really isn't there.

Teahouse of the August Moon breaks with this convention in its frankly theatrical treatment. Describe some of the features of the play that mark this break with tradition.

2. *Teahouse* pokes fun at several venerable institutions, American as well as Oriental. How many of these can you identify?

3. Satire, like farce, usually deals in types rather than individual characterizations because it is the folly, not the person, that is held up to ridicule. Discuss whether this statement applies to the characterization of Colonel Purdy, Captain Fisby, Captain McLean, and Sakini.

4. Princeton University Professor Alan S. Downer has said that the American comic hero of tradition is "an apparently naive fellow whose good sense and sound moral character help him to outwit his more sophisticated or experienced opponents."

How does Captain Fisby both fit into and depart from this tradition? Consider Elwood P. Dowd from *Harvey* in terms of this tradition.

5. Eric Bentley, American drama critic, protested the award of the Pulitzer Prize to *Teahouse* on the grounds that in this play "the Orientals are better than Americans, and the implied attitude to one's own country was not such rational self-criticism but a bit of self-hatred . . . the Okinawan's are sweet-natured and wise, Americans irate and stupid."

The *New York Times* said of the play, "It demonstrates how a free people can laugh easily and healthily at themselves, even in affairs so close to national pride as military occupancy."

Justify to your classmates your agreement with one or the other of these divergent viewpoints. Or present a third position if you agree with neither of them.

6. Choose one of the following suggestions and try your hand at a piece of original satiric writing:

> Give Lotus Blossom the gift of English and write a dialogue in which she and Sakini discuss the odd behavior of Captain Fisby.

> Write a progress report on the occupation from Captain Fisby to Colonel Purdy.

In the Pentagon's Plan B (Instructions for the Welfare and Recovery of Native Villages), there is—or was—a Section Four entitled "Orienting the Oriental." On the basis of the events in the play, write your version of Section Four.

There Shall Be No Night

⦃1940⦄

ROBERT E. SHERWOOD

This play is dedicated with my love to my wife Madeline

CHARACTERS

DR. KAARLO VALKONEN	MAJOR RUTKOWSKI
MIRANDA VALKONEN	JOE BURNETT
DAVE CORWEEN	BEN GICHNER
UNCLE WALDEMAR	FRANK OLMSTEAD
GUS SHUMAN	SERGEANT GOSDEN
ERIK VALKONEN	LEMPI
KAATRI ALQUIST	ILMA
DR. ZIEMSSEN	PHOTOGRAPHER
	PHOTOGRAPHER

SCENES

    I. Living room of the Valkonens' house in Helsinki. Early October, 1938.

(Intermission)

   II. The same. Late in November, 1939.

  III. The same. The next day.

  IV. The same. January 1, 1940.

(Intermission)

   V. Dave Corween's rooms in the Hotel Kamp, in Helsinki. Late in February.

  VI. Classroom in a schoolhouse near the west shore of Viipuri Bay. A few days later.

 VII. The Valkonens' living room. A few days later.

There Shall Be No Night opened in March 1940 to a confused and disturbed America. Even though Hitler's armies were rolling across Europe in a seemingly unstoppable "blitzkrieg," the United States was still clinging to its isolationism.

Sherwood, deeply moved by an American news report broadcast from the Finnish front line on Christmas Day, 1939, wrote in a few short weeks his moving drama about Finland's heroic resistance to her invasion by Russia. The play went far beyond reporting, however, in its obvious political message, its editorial approach. *There Shall Be No Night* was an urgent call to America to abandon isolationism. The conversion of the protagonist, Dr. Valkonen, from urbane citizen of the world to fighting Finnish patriot, was really the conversion of Sherwood and his post-World War I generation from pacifism to all-out resistance of Nazi ambition and ideology.

The drama played to packed houses and received standing ovations across America and in Canada. It was awarded the Pulitzer Prize in the spring of 1941.

There Shall Be No Night

SCENE 1

*The scene is the living room of the Valkonen house in the
suburbs of Helsinki. It is afternoon of a day early in October,
1938. This is a nice, neat, old-fashioned house, with large windows, through which one sees a lovely view of the harbor and
the islands. The room is comfortably furnished. On the walls,
surprisingly, are pictures from an American house. The most
prominent is a portrait of a handsome naval officer of the 1812
era. There are a dismal portrait of a substantial magnate of the
1880s, and a number of pallid little water-colors of Louisiana
scenes. There is a charcoal drawing of a wistful looking gentleman. On the piano and on the tables are many photographs of
famous doctors—Pavlov, Freud, the Mayos, Carrel, etc. Up-stage
a large door leads into the dining room. An unseen door leads
from this into the kitchen, to the right. The main entrance,
leading from the front hall, is lower right. The piano is upper
left. Near the center of the stage is a sofa, and in front of it, on a
table, are a radio microphone and a telephone. Wire connections
for this equipment run out into the dining room, where there
are a mixer and other equipment.*

Standing at the left of this table is DR. KAARLO VALKONEN. *He
is between forty-five and fifty years old—gentle, amused, vague,
and now rather self-conscious. Beside him stands his wife,*
MIRANDA, *who is beautiful, chic, and enjoying the whole situation intensely.* KAARLO *is a native Finn;* MIRANDA *comes from
New Bedford, Massachusetts. In the foreground are two* PHO-
TOGRAPHERS *with flash cameras. They are taking pictures of the
Valkonens. Toward the right stands* DAVE CORWEEN, *an American, about thirty-five years old, formerly a newspaper foreign
correspondent, now a European representative of the Columbia
Broadcasting System.*

1ST CAMERA MAN. Now—Doctor—

KAARLO. Yes—I'm ready.

MIRANDA. Wait a minute— [*She removes* KAARLO's *glasses.*]

1ST CAMERA MAN. Smile, please— [*They* BOTH *smile. The picture is taken. The* CAMERA MEN *bow and cross to the left.*]

DAVE. Will you both sit down, please? [KAARLO *and* MIRANDA *sit on sofa.*] Dr. Valkonen, would you look as though you were talking into the mike?

KAARLO. Talking?

MIRANDA. Just say something, Kaarlo—something thrilling and profound.

DAVE. Say 1—2—3—4—5—6—7—anything.

MIRANDA. And I'll look as if I were lis-tening, fascinated.

DAVE. [*Smiles.*] That's right, Mrs. Val-konen.

1ST CAMERA MAN. Ready? [*They pose for an instant while he takes the picture. He changes negatives and takes several more pictures during* KAARLO's *speech.*]

DAVE. Can't you think of something? We want to test the microphone.

KAARLO. [*Nodding.*] Yes! I can think of something. [*He leans toward microphone.*] How do you do, my dear friends in

216

America? How are you? I am well. I hope you are likewise. And do you know that the human digestive tract or alimentary canal extends for a distance of twenty-five to thirty feet, and consists of the following main parts: the mouth, pharynx, esophagus, stomach, small intestines, caecum, large intestines, rectum and anus? Into this canal flow the secretions of the salivary glands, liver and pancreas. Don't I speak English nicely? Yes. Thank you. Is that enough? [CAMERA MEN *have finished and pack their equipment, preparing to leave.*]

DAVE. That was splendid, Doctor. Thank you very much.

2ND CAMERA MAN. Thank you, Doctor.

KAARLO. Don't mention it, gentlemen.

MIRANDA. Will we get copies of those pictures?

1ST CAMERA MAN. Oh yes, Mrs. Valkonen. We hope you will like them.

KAARLO. Thank you. [CAMERA MEN *bow and go out at right.*]

DAVE. [*Calling toward dining room.*] How was it, Gus? [GUS *appears in dining-room door. He is a young American radio mechanic.*]

GUS. It sounded fine. Just speak in that same natural way, Doctor. [MIRANDA *turns to* DAVE *with some alarm.*]

MIRANDA. Was that radio on when he was talking? [GUS *goes.*]

DAVE. Don't worry, Mrs. Valkonen. It was just a test. The voice went no farther than the next room.

MIRANDA. Now, Kaarlo—when you do speak to the American people, please don't forget yourself and go through all those disgusting organs again. People don't like to be reminded of such things.

KAARLO. But I don't know yet what I'm supposed to say. You haven't finished correcting that translation.

MIRANDA. [*Rising.*] I'll finish it now. Would you like a drink, Mr. Corween?

DAVE. Not just now, thank you.

MIRANDA. We'll all have a drink after the broadcast. [*She goes out.* KAARLO *has been looking at radio apparatus.*]

KAARLO. Wonderful business, this.

DAVE. Wonderful—and awful.

KAARLO. More complicated than the alimentary canal, eh?

DAVE. Perhaps. But less essential.

KAARLO. How does my voice get from here all the way to America? Can you explain that to me?

DAVE. No, Doctor—I can't. But I can give you the outline. The voice travels from the microphone along that wire into the next room. It goes into that box in there. That's called the mixer. From there, it goes over your own telephone line to the broadcasting station, where various things happen that I don't understand. It's then transmitted on another line under the Gulf of Finland to Geneva, where it's broadcast by short wave from the League of Nations station.

KAARLO. Really! So that's what the League of Nations is doing!

DAVE. Well, they've got to do something. They send your voice to some place on Long Island, where it's transmitted to C.B.S. in New York, and then rebroadcast from coast to coast.

KAARLO. My word! Do you think any one will listen?

DAVE. [*Laughing.*] Certainly. They'll listen to all sorts of strange things on Sunday.

KAARLO. I knew I should never have agreed to this nonsense. I'll make a fool of myself.

DAVE. Oh, please, Doctor—I didn't mean to suggest that—

KAARLO. I know you didn't. But I'm still sorry. My wife's relatives will be listening, and they will write to her and say, "Kaarlo sounds older." They live in New Bedford, Massachusetts. Have you ever been there?

DAVE. I couldn't be sure.

KAARLO. A depressing place. But good people. Terrifying—but good. All of these paintings on the wall came from the house in New Bedford. [*He points to the 1812 officer.*] There's a fine looking fellow. They must have been gayer in those days. But look at that one over there. Miranda's grandfather. Did you ever see such a brigand? That's a drawing of her father on the piano. A very sensitive face. He didn't come from New Bedford— Louisiana. I think. He painted all those watercolors—swamps, and things. Miranda loved him. He must have been very charming. But he was surely a very bad painter. [UNCLE WALDEMAR *comes in from right. He is a moody, disenchanted old man.* KAARLO *rises and crosses to him.*] Ah, Uncle Waldemar—I was afraid you were going to be late. [KAARLO *kisses* UNCLE WALDEMAR.] This is Mr. Corween, of the American radio—my uncle Mr. Sederstrum.

DAVE. How do you do?

UNCLE WALDEMAR. [*Curtly.*] How do you do? [*Crosses to his easy chair at the left.*]

KAARLO. If you would like to have some music with the broadcast, Uncle Waldemar will play. A great musician. He plays the organ in the Agricola Church.

UNCLE WALDEMAR. Thank you. But I think you can do without music.

KAARLO. Look at this machine, Uncle Waldemar. [KAARLO *goes up to couch and points to microphone.*] My voice goes in there, and then into the dining room where it gets mixed, and then to the League of Nations, and then all over America. They will all be listening, because it's Sunday. [*Turns to* DAVE.] Will they hear me even in Minnesota?

DAVE. Yes, Doctor. Even in Minnesota.

KAARLO. It makes one frightened. [*Sits down.*]

DAVE. I know it does. I've been broadcasting for nearly a year now, all over Europe, and I still get mike fright when I hear that summons, "Come in, Vienna" or "Go ahead, Prague," or wherever I happen to be. [DAVE *sits down.*]

KAARLO. You were in Prague during the crisis?

DAVE. Yes—I just came from there—Prague and Munich.

KAARLE. You saw all of it, there in Munich?

DAVE. As much as we were allowed to see.

KAARLO. When we read our papers the day after that meeting last week—we just couldn't believe it. Something had happened that we couldn't understand. Could we, Uncle Waldemar?

UNCLE WALDEMAR. I could. I knew it would be a disaster.

KAARLO. Uncle Waldemar always looks on the dark side of things. There's been too much Sibelius in his life.

UNCLE WALDEMAR. I can understand what happened at Munich because I know Germany. I've lived there—I've studied music there—I've read Goethe. He knew his own people. He stood on the heights, and he said that from his point of view all life looks like some malignant disease.

DAVE. Well, he should see it now. I can tell you I was glad when they ordered me to come up here. You don't know what it means to be in a really free country again. To read newspapers that print *news* —to sit around cafes and hear people openly criticizing their government. Why— when I saw a girl in the street who wasn't afraid to use lipstick, I wanted to go right up and kiss her.

KAARLO. Why didn't you? She'd have been flattered. Our girls here like Americans, especially those gay young college boys who come here on tours— [MIRANDA *enters with manuscript of speech.* DAVE *and* KAARLO *rise.*]

MIRANDA. Here's your speech, Kaarlo. [*She gives him his speech and crosses to* UNCLE WALDEMAR, *kissing him.*] Hello, Uncle Waldemar. I'm sorry I missed church today, but there's been so much excitement around—

UNCLE WALDEMAR. It was just the same as always.

MIRANDA. [*Crossing back to table.*] Kaarlo, you'd better read that speech over to yourself first.

KAARLO. I'll go to our room and read it to the mirror. [*Goes out right.*]

DAVE. Dr. Valkonen showed me your family portraits.

MIRANDA. Oh, did he? Did he tell you his idea—that they represent the whole cycle of modern history? Rugged heroism —that's him—developing into ruthless materialism—that's him— [*She has pointed first to the 1812 ancestor, then the 1880 one. Then she crosses to piano and picks up drawing.*] —and then degenerating into intellectual impotence and decay—that's him. [*She holds picture fondly.*] Rugged heroism—that's old great-grandfather Eustis—he fought in the navy in the war of 1812.

DAVE. Did he?

MIRANDA. Yes—and he lived to sail a clipper ship to California in the Gold Rush. He didn't get any gold, but he died happy. His son, my sainted grandfather— that's that one with the beard—bought his way out of the Civil War for three hundred dollars. Then he made a nice fortune selling shoddy uniforms to the army. He did even better after the war when he packed his carpet bag and went south. He married a beautiful daughter of the ruined aristocracy, and my father was the result. [*She holds out drawing.*] You can see he was more New Orleans than New Bedford. [DAVE *looks at picture over her shoulder.*] Sargent drew that. Fine drawing, isn't it?

DAVE. Superb.

MIRANDA. [*Crossing to piano and replacing drawing.*] Father avenged the honor of the Old South. When he came into possession of the family fortune, he went systematically to work and threw it away, squandered every penny that old whiskers there had scrounged and saved. And he had a wonderful time doing it. [*She gets cigarette from box on piano and sits down.*] He was the idol of all the head waiters in London, Paris, Monte Carlo, Vienna. He took me along with him on his travels. He used to say to me, "Mandy, this won't last forever, but while it does, we're certainly going to make the most of it."

DAVE. And how did you happen to meet Dr. Valkonen? [*Lights her cigarette.*]

UNCLE WALDEMAR. [*Amused.*] Are you going to put all this on the radio?

DAVE. Oh, no! But I'd like to write something about this visit. I try to maintain my status as a newspaper man against the day when the public will get tired of being fed through their ears.

MIRANDA. Well, Kaarlo and I met in Russia in 1914. That was when my father was coming to the end of his brilliant career as a spendthrift. Kaarlo was a medical officer in St. Petersburg—that's what they called it then. Oh, he was so handsome! Thin—dark—tragic looking. I was seventeen—I'd never seen any one like him. Of course he didn't know I was alive. Then came the war and we had to leave for America. It was the end of the world for me. I pestered him with letters regularly, and he replied—once. After the revolution, he came to America to study, and we met again, and after considerable effort on my part, we were married. And that's all there is to that.

UNCLE WALDEMAR. Then he brought her back here, his American wife, and we asked him, "Is she rich?" and he said, "No." So we said, "Kaarlo is a fool."

MIRANDA. I've told you it wasn't his fault—he was too polite to refuse. [*Turns to DAVE.*] All that was a long time ago.

I think Uncle Waldemar has forgiven me now.

DAVE. I hope I'll have the pleasure of meeting your son, Mrs. Valkonen.

MIRANDA. Oh, I hope so. We're expecting him any minute. He's been away on a holiday—working. They spend all their holidays in this country working. You've never seen such energetic people.

DAVE. I suppose your son is completely a Finn—not an American?

MIRANDA. He can't quite make up his mind what he is. But now he has his first girl friend. She'll probably settle the matter for him. [KAARLO *comes in, carrying his speech.*]

KAARLO. Well, I've gone through this, and I must say it seems too dull, even for Sunday.

DAVE. [*Looking at his watch.*] It's pretty near time. I'll see if the connection is set. [DAVE *goes into dining room.* MIRANDA *rises and goes down to* UNCLE WALDEMAR. *She arranges shawl on his lap.* KAARLO *paces up and down, reading his speech.*]

MIRANDA. How's the rheumatism, Uncle Waldemar?

UNCLE WALDEMAR. It's bad.

MIRANDA. Haven't those treatments done you any good?

UNCLE WALDEMAR. No.

MIRANDA. Never mind. We'll be going soon to Italy for a holiday and we'll take you. That will make you well. [DAVE *returns and sits at table, arranging his introductory speech.*]

UNCLE WALDEMAR. Yes—I know what those holidays are like, in Italy, or anywhere else. All Kaarlo does is visit lunatic asylums. [DAVE *picks up telephone, and looks toward* GUS *in dining room.*]

GUS'S VOICE. [*From dining room.*] Go ahead.

DAVE. [*Into telephone.*] Hello—hello. This is Dave Corween—Dave Corween.... Hello, Ed. How's everything? . . . Yes—I got here this morning. Beautiful place—lovely people—and what a relief. . . . Yes! . . . No—I don't see how there can possibly be *another* crisis this year. . . . Maybe they'll let me come home for Christmas. . . . No—it's wonderfully quiet up here. Sweden, too. Yes—I came through Stockholm yesterday. [*To* KAARLO *and* MIRANDA.] If you'll sit down, we're about ready. [*They sit on sofa by table.*] How's the world series? . . . They did, eh. . . . Yes—I'm watching the time: 43½—O.K. [*He looks at his watch.*] . . . Good-bye, Ed. MIRANDA. [*To* KAARLO.] Good luck, darling—and just remember—it doesn't really matter.

GUS's VOICE. [*From dining room.*] O.K., Dave.

DAVE. Listen!

VOICE FROM LOUD-SPEAKER. This is Station WABC in New York.

KAARLO. Great God!

MIRANDA. Did you hear that, Uncle Waldemar? It's New York!

UNCLE WALDEMAR. I heard. [DAVE *cautions them to silence.*]

VOICE FROM LOUD-SPEAKER. We now take you to the Finnish capital. Go ahead, Helsinki. [DAVE *speaks briskly into microphone, using notes typed on copy paper.*]

DAVE. Hello America—this is David Corween, in Helsinki. We're bringing you the first of a series of broadcasts from Finland, Sweden and Norway, those little countries in the far north of Europe which are at peace, and intend to remain at peace. Finland is a country with a population about equal to that of Brooklyn. Like many other small nations, it achieved its freedom twenty years ago—but, unlike some of the others, it has consolidated that freedom; it has made democracy work. It has no minority problems. Its frontiers are disputed by no one. Its people are rugged, honest, self-respecting and civilized. [KAARLO *and* MIRANDA *start to speak to one another.* DAVE *signals them to be quiet and goes right on.*] I am now speaking from the home of one of Finland's most distinguished citizens, Dr. Kaarlo Valkonen, the eminent neurologist, who has received high honors in the United States, England, the Soviet Union and other nations, and has just been awarded the Nobel Prize in medicine. In announcement of this award, the directors of the Caroline Medical Institute in Stockholm stated that Dr. Valkonen has given to mankind a new understanding of the true nature and the causes of mental diseases—and I might add that those of us who have to cover the European scene these days can appreciate how much this understanding is needed. [KAARLO *is embarrassed and pained by all this; he keeps looking at* MIRANDA, *who, however, is delighted.*] Many of you have read his book,

The Defense of Man, and to some of you now listening he is known personally, as he has lived much in America, and his wife comes from that fine old Massachusetts town, New Bedford. It gives me great pleasure to bring you an outstanding servant of humanity—Dr. Kaarlo Valkonen. [*He moves microphone over to* KAARLO *and gestures to him to begin.* MIRANDA *listens intently, waiting for mishaps.*]

KAARLO. [*Loudly.*] I never heard so much introduction. [DAVE *moves microphone back from* KAARLO *and signals him to speak more quietly.*] To tell the truth, I think the Nobel prize is premature. The work I am doing will be finished by some one else many years from now. But still— I am glad to have that prize, as it enables us to go for a holiday in France and Italy, and my wife will buy some new clothes in Paris.

MIRANDA. Read what is written! [KAARLO *looks for first time at his manuscript.*]

KAARLO. [*Reading.*] Dr. Carrel has said, "For the first time in history, a crumbling civilization is capable of discerning the causes of its decay. For the first time it has at its disposal the gigantic strength of science." And he asks, "Will we utilize this knowledge and this power?" That's a question far more important than speculating about the possible results of the Munich crisis. In fact, behind this question are the real causes of all the problems we now must face. It is no doubt well known to you that insanity is increasing at an alarming rate. Indeed, the day is within sight when the few remaining sane people are put into confinement and the lunatics are at large. Does this seem a ridiculous exaggeration? Then look about you, at the present world. You see the spectacle of a great, brilliant nation, which has contributed perhaps more than all others to scientific progress. Today, the spiritual resistance of its people has been lowered to such an extent that they are willing to discard all their moral sense, all the essential principles of justice and civilization. They glorify a theory of government which is no more than co-ordinated barbarism, under the leadership of a megalomaniac who belongs in a psychopathic ward rather than a chancellery. He seeks to create a race of moral cretins whom science has rendered strong and germless in their bodies, but feeble and servile in their minds. We now know how quickly such men can be converted into brutes. It is all very well to say, "We will go to war and crush this mighty force. Free men will always triumph over slaves." But after the war—and on into the centuries—what then? How long will these same free men possess the spiritual strength that enables them to be free? There is a problem for science to solve—and we must begin by admitting our own mistakes. Science has considered disease as mechanical phenomena, to be cured by mechanical means. And we have been remarkably successful. Examine the achievements in the fight against tuberculosis—typhoid—all the ancient plagues. You will see that the number of fatalities is steadily being reduced. Then look at the degenerative diseases—insanity, which is the degeneration of the brain—and cancer, which is degeneration of the tissues. These diseases are going up, almost in the same proportion as the others are going down. Degeneration! That is the most terrifying word in the human vocabulary today. And doctors are beginning to ask, "Is there not a suspicious connection between our victories and our defeats? Are we perhaps saving children from measles and mumps that they may grow up to be neurotics and end their days in a mad-house?" Perhaps their early battles with disease toughen them. Perhaps without that essential experience, they go into maturity without having developed adequate defenses against life. What are these defenses? St. Paul has said: "We glory in tribulation; knowing that tribulation worketh patience; and patience, experience; and experience, hope." We have been striving to eliminate tribulation, and as we have succeeded we have deprived man of his experience, and thus of his hope. We have counted too heavily upon pills and serums to protect us from our enemies, just as we count too heavily upon vast systems of concrete fortifications and big navies to guard our frontiers. Of what avail are these artificial protections if each man lacks the power of resistance within himself? I am not pleading for a return of measles and mumps. I am only saying that all of us have been trying too hard to find the easy way out—when man, to be man, needs the experience of the hard way. "There is no coming to consciousness without pain," in the words of Dr. Jung, and Science has provided no substitute for pain. You have heard it said that the days of exploration are over—that there are no more lost continents—no more Eldorados. But I promise you that the greatest of all adventures in exploration is still before us—the exploration of man himself—his mind—his spirit—the thing we call his character—the quality which has raised him above the beasts. "Know thyself," said the oracle. And after thousands of years, we still don't know. Can we learn before it is too late—before the process of man's degeneration has been completed and he is again a witless ape, groping his way back into the jungle? [*Looks up and thrusts his manuscript away.*] But why should I go on spoiling your Sunday? I want to send my greetings to New Bedford, Massachusetts. I want to send especial greetings to Minnesota, home of my dear good friends, the Mayos. Perhaps I have an especial feeling of love for Minnesota because it is so much like Finland, with many beautiful lakes, and forests of birch and pine and spruce. And I know so many fine people there, with good blood that came from Finland, and our neighboring countries of Sweden, Norway and Denmark. To them, and to all my friends in the United States of America I say, "Thank you and God bless you and good-bye." [*Turns to* MIRANDA *and shrugs as though to say, "I'm sorry but that was the best I could do."* MIRANDA *leans over and kisses him.*]

DAVE. [*Into microphone.*] Thank you, Dr. Kaarlo Valkonen. This is David Corween in Helsinki, returning you now to Columbia in New York.

KAARLO. Never will I speak to one of those damned things again.

VOICE FROM LOUD-SPEAKER. We take you now to London. . . .

MIRANDA. [*Rising.*] Darling—you were wonderful! Didn't you think it was fine, Uncle Waldemar?

UNCLE WALDEMAR. If they'll listen to that, they'll listen to anything.

DAVE. [*Rising.*] You were splendid, Doctor. A definite radio personality.

MIRANDA. There!

KAARLO. [*Pleased.*] You really think so? [GUS *comes in from dining room to clear the table of equipment.*]

MIRANDA. Of course he does. Now I'll go and mix the drinks. [*She goes off into dining room.*]

GUS. They said it came through fine. I liked it myself. And I'm going to get that book of yours, Doctor. I probably can't understand it—but I'll bet it's good.

KAARLO. Why—thank you—thank you. [*GUS goes out into dining room.*] What a charming man!

DAVE. I read your book last summer when I was resting between crises. And just the other day, when I heard I was coming up here about the Nobel Prize, I tried to get a copy in Munich. The bookseller assured me, solemnly, that there could be no such book, since he had never heard of it.

KAARLO. [*Rising.*] Of course, all my books are forbidden in Germany. I should be ashamed of myself if they weren't. [*ERIK VALKONEN comes in from the right. He is seventeen years old, but mature and calm. He is handsome and healthy; there is a kind of quiet humor in his expression. With him is his girl friend, KAATRI ALQUIST, young, pretty, also healthy, and quite serious. Each of them carries a package. KAARLO goes immediately to ERIK, kisses him.*] Erik! You're just too late for my broadcast. You missed something wonderful. Hello, Kaatri, my dear. [*KAATRI curtsies to KAARLO. ERIK hands KAARLO his package.*]

ERIK. I brought you this from Viipuri, Father.

KAARLO. Viipurin Rinkelia! I'll have it with my coffee. [*Takes KAATRI over to DAVE.*] Let me introduce Miss Kaatri Alquist, Mr. Corween of the American radio. And my son, Erik. [*KAATRI curtsies to DAVE and crosses to UNCLE WALDERMAR. After greeting her, UNCLE WALDEMAR points toward dining room, as ERIK and DAVE shake hands.*]

ERIK and DAVE. How do you do?

UNCLE WALDERMAR. Mrs. Valkonen is in the dining room. [*KAATRI goes into dining room. ERIK crosses to UNCLE WALDEMAR.*]

KAATRI'S VOICE. Hello, Mrs. Valkonen.

MIRANDA'S VOICE. Kaatri, how lovely!

ERIK. [*Kissing UNCLE WALDEMAR.*] Father says he was wonderful on the radio. Is that true?

UNCLE WALDEMAR. He only said the same things you've heard a hundred times before.

KAARLO. Erik, take this to your mother in the dining room. [*ERIK takes package from KAARLO and goes into dining room.*]

ERIK. Mother! Mother! I'm back!

MIRANDA'S VOICE. Erik, darling! Did you have a good time?

KAARLO. [*Proudly.*] Fine boy, isn't he, Mr. Corween?

DAVE. Yes, fine. It's a shame he didn't hear your broadcast. He'd have been proud of you.

KAARLO. Oh—I'm an object of contempt to my own son—because, while I talk, he *acts*. He has been working on the Mannerheim Line.

DAVE. I'm afraid I don't know where that is.

KAARLO. It's on the isthmus—on the Russian frontier. It's our own little Maginot.

MIRANDA. [*Entering from dining room with ERIK and KAATRI.*] Yes, he's a definite radio personality.·. . . [*She puts box of chocolates on piano.*] Now we're going to have some coffee, and some Parker House Punch especially for you, Mr. Corween. Go and wash, children.

KAATRI. Yes, Mrs. Valkonen. [*The two maids, ILMA and LEMPI, come in from dining room with tablecloth, coffee urn, and service for six, which they put on table.*]

ERIK. You're not going just yet, Mr. Corween?

DAVE. Oh, no.

ERIK. Thank you. [*Bows and goes out after KAATRI at right.*]

MIRANDA. [*Sitting on sofa.*] You know, whenever any one comes home, from anywhere, there has to be a present. Kaatri brought me those chocolates, and Erik brought his father some of the bread they make in Viipuri. It's the custom of the country. Charming, isn't it?

DAVE. Yes. [*Starts to sit down.*]

MIRANDA. [*Under-her breath.*] That's Uncle Waldemar's chair. Come and sit by me.

DAVE. [*Sitting on couch.*] I've noticed that here—and in Sweden, too—everybody is insufferably polite. Why, yesterday, in Stockholm, my cab side-swiped another cab, so the two drivers got out and apol-

ogized to each other. It's unnatural. [UNCLE
WALDEMAR *sits at coffee table.*]

MIRANDA. I know. I've lived here for
twenty years. I've never got used to it.
[*She is starting to pour coffee.*]

KAARLO. I used to think, Mr. Corween,
in my ignorance, that you Americans have
no national character. My wife has taught
me my error. Her character is strong
enough to resist all civilizing influences.
And sometimes I think our son has inherited too much from her. [*Sits down at
table.*]

MIRANDA. That's what Kaatri thinks.
Kaatri is the girl friend I was telling you
about. I'm afraid she disapproves of me.
I'm too shallow—too frivolous.

KAARLO. Oh, Kaatri comes from a typi-
cally Finnish military family. Her father
is a colonel and her brothers are all
brought up to be fighters. Very formidable!
Maybe she does disapprove of you, my
dear, but in her heart she wishes she could
be more like you. She wishes she could
have as much fun as we do.

MIRANDA. I'll have a good talk with her
some time.

DAVE. I'm interested in that work your
son is doing.

KAARLO. I tell him it's silly—but he won't
listen.

DAVE. It seems a sensible thing for any
one to be preparing for trouble these days.

KAARLO. Yes—eminently sensible. But
they don't know how to prepare. That's
the trouble. They build those concrete pill-
boxes, and tank traps—as if such things
could save anybody when Armageddon
comes.

MIRANDA. What does it matter, darling?
They enjoy doing the work.

KAARLO. Yes—and I suppose it's good
exercise. [ERIK *and* KAATRI *come in and
go to chairs at the left, by piano.*] Erik and
hundreds of other students spend all their
free time on the Mannerheim Line. Kaatri
there, too, with the women's organization, to do the cooking and cleaning. Oh,
they have a lot of fun—and maybe a little
romance in the long evenings, eh, Kaatri?

KAATRI. [*Giggles, then answers soberly.*]
In the evening we have discussions, Dr.
Valkonen. [ERIK *brings* KAATRI'S *cup of
coffee.*]

DAVE. And may I ask—what sort of
things do you discuss?

KAATRI. Last night we tried to arrive at
some conclusions about the consequences
of the Munich treaty.

DAVE. I'd like to know what your conclusions were?

ERIK. Just what you would probably
hear in a similar discussion in America,
Mr. Corween. We thanked heaven for the
geography which puts us so far from the
scene of action. We were grateful that we
do not live in Czechoslovakia, or the
Balkans, or even England or France.
[LEMPI *enters with punch.*]

MIRANDA. [*Looking around.*] Ah—here it
is! Here's the Parker House Punch, Mr.
Corween. The old Parker House bar was
the first place my father headed for after
the reading of the will. I can't cook anything—but I can make the best rum punch
and eggnog too. If you're ever here on
New Year's Day, I'll give you some eggnog.

DAVE. I shall not forget that invitation.
[*He is happy to be in the midst of such an
untroubled, harmonious family.*]

ERIK. You came all the way here just to
have my father broadcast?

KAARLO. You see?

DAVE. I'm ordered to travel around Scandinavia and pick up as many features as I
can.

MIRANDA. I think we should drink a
toast to our benefactor, the late Alfred
Nobel. [ALL *rise.*]

KAARLO. That's it—Nobel!

KAARLO *and* MIRANDA. God bless him!

ERIK. The dynamite king.

MIRANDA. Hush, Erik. That's not in good
taste. [UNCLE WALDEMAR *crosses and sits
at piano.* OTHERS *resume their seats.*]

KAARLO. As for me, I don't care where
the money came from. Two million marks
—forty thousand dollars.

MIRANDA. [*Reverting to New England.*]
To say nothing of the solid gold medal.

KAARLO. To think I should see that much
in a lifetime, let alone all at once.

DAVE. [*To* ERIK.] What are you studying?

ERIK. Economics—sociology.

KAARLO. And skiing. He can't make up
his mind whether he wants to be another
Karl Marx, or another Olympic champion.

DAVE. Have you been much in the Soviet Union?

ERIK. Oh, yes. We lived there when father was working with Pavlov.

DAVE. And you really believe they might invade this country?

ERIK. If there were counter revolution in Russia, anything might happen. Or the Nazis might come that way. We have to be prepared.

MIRANDA. Erik, open the chocolates. Uncle Waldemar, play something. Play something gay. This is a celebration.

UNCLE WALDEMAR. I don't feel gay.

MIRANDA. Then drink this rum punch quickly and have a few more, and you'll forget your rheumatism. [*She takes him a glass of punch.*]

DAVE. Of course, the Nazis have been highly successful in terrifying people of the Bolshevik menace. But all the times I've been in Moscow, I've never seen anything but a passionate desire to be let alone, in peace. [UNCLE WALDEMAR *starts to play a particularly gloomy selection by Sibelius.*]

KAARLO. Certainly. I know the Russians. I was a medical officer in their army and I was with them in prison camp in Germany all through 1916. And during the revolution I was right there in Leningrad on the staff of the Strelka Hospital. I treated Lenin for a sore throat! And I can tell you about these Russians: they love to plot—but they don't love to fight. And the reason they don't love to fight is that they're a little like the Italians—they're too charming—they really don't know how to hate. [*During foregoing speech the doorbell has been heard, faintly, and* LEMPI *has crossed to the right and gone out.*]

MIRANDA. Uncle Waldemar, what is that you're playing?

UNCLE WALDEMAR. Sibelius.

MIRANDA. Oh, darling, can't you play something a little less solemn? [LEMPI *returns and hands* MIRANDA *a card on a silver plate.* UNCLE WALDEMAR *stops playing.*] What is it? Oh, it's Dr. Ziemssen. Tell him to come in. [LEMPI *goes out.*]

KAARLO. [*Rising.*] Dr. Ziemssen is a neighbor of ours. [DR. ZIEMSSEN *comes in. He is a mild, scholarly, correct German of thirty-five or forty.* KAARLO *meets him at the door.*] Come in, Dr. Ziemssen. I'm delighted to see you.

ZIEMSSEN. [*Shaking* KAARLO's *hand.*] Herr Doktor. [ZIEMSSEN *goes to* MIRANDA, *who rises and holds out her hand.* ZIEMSSEN *kisses it.*]

MIRANDA. How do you do, Dr. Ziemssen?

ZIEMSSEN. Frau Valkonen.

MIRANDA. You know Miss Alquist—and my family.

ZIEMSSEN. [*Bowing to each.*] Fräulein— Herr Sederstrum—Erik.

KAARLO. And may I introduce Mr. Corween of the American radio, Dr. Ziemssen.

ZIEMSSEN. Mr. Corween! I have heard a great deal of you.

DAVE. [*Sitting.*] Well—that's unusual.

KAARLO. Please— [*Indicating a chair to* ZIEMSSEN.] Dr. Ziemssen is the German Consul General. He has heard of everybody. [KAARLO *sits down.*]

ZIEMSSEN. [*Smiles.*] Only the important people. I walked over, Herr Doktor, because I just this minute talked to Berlin on the telephone and they said they had heard your broadcast. They said it came through excellently and was highly entertaining.

DAVE. It was broadcast in Germany?

ZIEMSSEN. Oh, no. But it was heard at the government short-wave station.

KAARLO. Good God! I seem to remember that I said some things that were not for your government to hear.

ZIEMSSEN. Have no worries on that score, Herr Doktor. We are well accustomed to hearing the worst about ourselves. We have heard you frequently, Mr. Corween.

KAARLO. Don't be frightened by Dr. Ziemssen. He was an anthropologist before he became a diplomat. He is very broad minded.

MIRANDA. Will you have some American punch, Dr. Ziemssen?

ZIEMSSEN. Thank you, no.

KAARLO. Then have some coffee and I'll have another cup too—and some of that Viipurin Rinkelia that Erik brought.

ZIEMSSEN. Viipurin Rinkelia! [*Turns to* ERIK.] Erik—is the work getting on well?

ERIK. It seems to be. Of course I see only a small part of it.

ZIEMSSEN. The Finnish defenses are magnificent. No one will dare to challenge them.

ERIK. The Czechs had fine defenses, too.

ZIEMSSEN. Ah, but you are more intelligent than the Czechs. You have no Allies to betray you! [*Laughs at that pleasantry*

How do you feel about that, Mr. Corween? You were at Munich.

DAVE. I'm afraid I have no feeling about anything.

MIRANDA. Then have some more punch, Mr. Corween.

DAVE. [Laughs.] No, thank you. [To ZIEMSSEN.] If you had asked me that question a few years ago—if you had asked me any questions of cosmic significance—I could have answered without a moment's hesitation. I was the youngest genius ever to be given a by-line in The Chicago Daily News. I was on intimate terms with both God and Mammon. The wisdom of the ages was set before me, on the halfshell. All I had to do was add horseradish and eat.

ZIEMSSEN. [Smiles.] You have become a little less confident in recent years?

DAVE. Well, since then I have been de-educated, if there is such a word. I've covered Manchukuo, Ethiopia, Spain, China, Austria, Czechoslovakia. And all I can say is—I'm bewildered. But I suspect, Dr. Valkonen, that when you say the human race is in danger of going insane, you're not so much a prophet of future doom as a reporter of current fact. [Becomes conscious of fact that he is holding the floor. He smiles.] I seem to be sounding off. That punch is powerful.

MIRANDA. Good! Then have some more and tell us what it was like in Ethiopia.

DAVE. Thank you. I mustn't. I must try to find out what its like here. [To ERIK.] Do you suppose I could get permission to visit those defenses you're working on?

ERIK. I should think so. Planes from Leningrad are flying over that region all the time, so I don't believe there's much secrecy.

DAVE. I must try to get there. There might be material for a broadcast.

KAARLO. If there's anything I can do— any letters of introduction?

DAVE. [Rising.] Oh, no, thank you. I'm trained to push in anywhere. Thank you very much, Mrs. Valkonen. You've been very kind. . . .

MIRANDA. [Shaking hands with him.] And you've been very nice. I hope you'll come and see us again.

DAVE. I'll probably be back some time. [Crosses to shake hands with ERIK.] Certainly in 1940 for the Olympic games. Good-bye, Mr. Valkonen.

ERIK. Good-bye, Mr. Corween.

DAVE. [To each in turn.] Good-bye, Miss Alquist. [To UNCLE WALDEMAR.] Good-bye, sir—please don't get up. [To ZIEMSSEN.] Good-bye, sir. [Crosses to KAARLO.] Good-bye, Doctor—

KAARLO. Oh, I'll see you to the door. [They go out right. MIRANDA, KAATRI, and ZIEMSSEN sit.]

MIRANDA. Do you like him, Erik? He's nice, isn't he?

ERIK. Yes. I wish I could do work like that. To be able to wander all over the earth—and see things—without being a part of them. [KAATRI darts a worried look at ERIK. She knows he is now talking with his mother's voice.]

KAATRI. [With surprising vehemence.] I'd hate such a life!

MIRANDA. Why, Kaatri?

KAATRI. When you see too much of the world it makes you cynical. I'd never want to be that.

MIRANDA. I shouldn't either. But I've travelled all over and it hasn't made me cynical. Perhaps that's because I'm just plain stupid.

ZIEMSSEN. Ah no, Frau Valkonen. It is only because you are an American.

ERIK. A journalist like Mr. Corween has the opportunity to see the truth. Maybe the ultimate truth is the ultimate futility—

MIRANDA. [Laughing at this.] Oh, dear. That boy really should have a beard.

ERIK. Even so—I'd like to know the truth about the world. All of it! [UNCLE WALDEMAR starts to play a gay tune.]

MIRANDA. Kaatri, the next time we go to America, I'll ask your father and mother if you can go with us. Would you like that?

KAATRI. Oh, I think I should love that! [KAARLO returns and sits beside MIRANDA.]

KAARLO. I hope some of your relatives will send us a cable so we'll know how I really sounded.

MIRANDA. [Again reverting to New England.] If I know New Bedford, they'll send a postcard. . . . What's that you're playing now, Uncle Waldemar? [UNCLE WALDEMAR doesn't hear. She turns to DR. ZIEMSSEN.] What is that?

ZIEMSSEN. [Listening, appreciatively.] I believe that is Merikantor's "Tolari Ja Huotari," isn't it? [Listens for a moment.]

Yes—a delightful little Finnish folk song. [UNCLE WALDEMAR *continues to play, with tinkling variations on the theme.*] MIRANDA. Oh—I love that. [*She pats KAARLO's hand. They listen silently, happily to the music.*]

CURTAIN

SCENE 2

The same. An evening late in November, 1939. KAATRI *is sitting on couch, looking toward* ERIK, *who is at window by piano, looking out.* KAATRI *is crocheting.*

KAATRI. What are you looking at, Erik?

ERIK. [*Who obviously has to think for an instant before answering this question.*] I'm looking at the stars.

KAATRI. Oh.

ERIK. There are millions of them. They're so bright you can see them reflected on the snow.

KAATRI. I know why you're looking out the window, Erik. Many people are looking out of their windows tonight—watching for the bombers.

ERIK. [*Turning from window.*] Now, Kaatri! There are no bombers coming here.

KAATRI. That's what they said in Poland. I'm sure they kept telling themselves, "The bombers won't come. Something will happen. There'll be another Munich. There'll be a revolution in Germany. The United States will forbid Europe to have a war. *Something* is sure to happen to prevent the bombers from coming to Poland." But they did come.

ERIK. They were Nazis.

KAATRI. The Russians went into Poland, too.

ERIK. Yes, and why not? The Nazis had done the work. [*Comes over and sits near her.*] All the Russians had to do was march in and take all that territory at no cost to themselves. But—they know perfectly well if they attack us it would mean betrayal of the revolution! The suffering they might inflict on us would be insignificant compared to the murder of their own honor.

KAATRI. Honor!

ERIK. That's what my father says, and he knows them.

KAATRI. [*Putting down her crocheting.*] I don't believe they ever had any honor— Tsarists or Bolshevists either. My father knows them, too. That's why he has spent his life preparing to fight them when they invade our country.

ERIK. [*Laughs.*] Oh—Kaatri—don't let's sit here telling each other what our fathers say. We're old enough to make up our own minds, aren't we?

KAATRI. I don't know, Erik.

ERIK. You've made up your mind that we're going to be married, haven't you?

KAATRI. Yes. [*She laughs, shyly.*] But— that's different.

ERIK. I'm glad it *is* different. The trouble with old people is—they remember too much—old wars, old hates. They can't get those things out of their minds. But we have no such memories. We're free of such ugly things. If there's going to be a better future, we're the ones who are going to make it. [*Takes her hands.*] Kaatri—

KAATRI. Yes, Erik?

ERIK. Next summer I'll stop being a student. I'll be a worker! And you and will be married.

KAATRI. [*Thrilled.*] What will we live on, Erik?

ERIK. [*Heroically.*] On what I make. I won't be much—but it will be enough. I'll be your man—and you'll be my woman [*They* BOTH *draw apart, laugh, then the kiss.*]

KAATRI. We'll have a wonderful wedding, won't we, Erik?

ERIK. Yes—I suppose our families will insist on that. [*They are still in each other arms.*]

KAATRI. It will be in the Agricol Church, and there'll be lots of flowers.

ERIK. Your father will be looking ster and magnificent in his colonel's uniform And my father, in his black coat, lookin bored. And Mother behaving like a gran duchess, and Uncle Waldemar playing d da-de-dum. . . . [*Hums a bar of the Wed ding March.*] And then we'll escape fro all of them, and go home, and have sever children.

KAATRI. Erik! [*They* BOTH *laugh happily and kiss each other again.*]

ERIK. Oh, Kaatri! We'll be happy people, you and I. That's all that matters, isn't it, dearest?

KAATRI. Yes. [*Suddenly the happiness fades from her face.*] No! It isn't all that matters!

ERIK. What else is there?

KAATRI. [*Looking away from him, but still holding him close.*] There's now. . . . There's this. . . . There may be war. Next summer may never come to us.

ERIK. I tell you—we don't have to think about those things. We're young and we're free. We have only our own love, for each other. [UNCLE WALDEMAR *comes in. He carries a newspaper. Looks at them. They break apart guiltily, rise, and confront him with great embarrassment.*] Oh, please forgive me, Uncle Waldemar. We were—

UNCLE WALDEMAR. Yes.

ERIK. We were only—

UNCLE WALDEMAR. I saw what you were doing. I'm sorry to have interrupted. [*He kisses* KAATRI, *then* ERIK, *and crosses to piano.* KAATRI *sits down again.*] But there's some news here.

ERIK. What is it?

UNCLE WALDEMAR. It may be good. Our government has received a message from the United States government, from Washington. They also sent the same message to Moscow. [*Comes close to them.*] It's offering their good offices to settle the Soviet-Finnish dispute. That's what they call it—the dispute. Here's what they say. [*As he starts to read,* ERIK *sits on sofa beside* KAATRI.] "We would view with extreme regret any extension of the present area of war and the consequent further deterioration of international relations." That's what they say in Washington.

KAATRI. [*Who is holding* ERIK's *hand.*] Do you suppose the Russians will listen to that?

ERIK. Of course they'll listen.

KAATRI. Erik believes they won't attack us. What do you believe, Uncle Waldemar?

UNCLE WALDEMAR. I know they will!

KAATRI. [*To* ERIK.] There!

UNCLE WALDEMAR. Do you know what the press in Moscow is saying about us? We're "that Finnish scum"—we're "bourgeois bandits"—"Tools of British imperial-ism"—"Fascist assassins." [*Crosses to the left and flings newspaper onto piano.*] Those words are the advance guard of the Red Army!

ERIK. My father doesn't agree with you.

UNCLE WALDEMAR. And what does *he* know about it?

ERIK. As much as any one could. He understands the Russians. He was the good friend of Pavlov and Gorki, and even Lenin himself.

UNCLE WALDEMAR. All those gentlemen you mention are dead. And the revolution—that's dead, too. It's embalmed and exposed in a glass coffin in front of the Kremlin. It is respected—but dead. Now comes the true disintegration—the end of the world. Your father said—men might become again like apes, groping their way back into the jungle. Well—it has come to pass. Men are groping their way through the night. The lights are out in Berlin, Paris, London. And in Warsaw, they crawl through the ruins like rats. It will be the same here. This is war in the jungle, and the winner will be crowned "King of Beasts." [MIRANDA *comes in from the right, looking very smart in her furs and her Paris hat.* ERIK *and* KAATRI *rise.*]

ERIK. Hello, Mother. Where's Father?

MIRANDA. [*Taking off hat and coat.*] He's at the laboratory. [*Puts wraps on chair at the right.*] I went there to try to make him come home. He had a lot of dogs there—there must have been thirty or forty of them—all barking and howling. I asked him what he was doing with all those dogs, but he told me to go away. [*Kisses* KAATRI.] Kaatri—are your mother and father well?

KAATRI. My mother is well, thank you. My father is with the army in the north.

MIRANDA. But he'll surely be home for Christmas?

KAATRI. Oh, yes, Mrs. Valkonen—we hope so. [MIRANDA *has come up to* ERIK. *She kisses him.*]

UNCLE WALDEMAR. I have to go to church and practice. There's to be a great service this evening—prayers for peace.

MIRANDA. [*Sitting down on sofa.*] I know.

UNCLE WALDEMAR. The President will be there and the Cabinet and the leaders of all parties. [*Starts to cross toward door at the right.*] Tonight—prayers. Tomorrow—

guns. [*Goes out. A moment of constrained silence.*]

MIRANDA. I stopped in at the American Legation on my way home and saw Mr. Walsh. I wanted to find out if he had any news. He told me that the State Department has ordered all Americans to leave Finland at once. He was very guarded in his choice of words—but he seems to think that things are rather serious.

ERIK. So does Uncle Waldemar. But that doesn't mean anything. The American government—all governments—are being pulverized with fear by this Soviet propaganda. [*Picks up paper from piano.*] They want to pulverize us, too, so that we'll give them what they want without a struggle. It's all bluff—it's all an imitation of the Nazis.

KAATRI. But when the bluff doesn't work, suppose they go on imitating the Nazis— suppose they do attack? [MIRANDA *looks from* KAATRI *to* ERIK, *awaiting his reply.*]

ERIK. [*Without emotion.*] Then—we'll have to fight—that's all.

MIRANDA. But—how can we fight?

ERIK. To the best of our ability.

MIRANDA. And how long will that last?

ERIK. A few days—a few weeks—I don't know. [*He is looking out window.*]

MIRANDA. Erik—*Erik!* [*He turns to her.*] Would *you* fight?

ERIK. Of course I would. Everybody would!

MIRANDA. Why? What good would that do?

ERIK. It would prove that this country has a right to live.

MIRANDA. And who will derive any benefit from that proof? Are you anxious to die to get applause from the civilized world—applause and probably nothing else? The Czechs are fine, brave people— but they didn't offer any resistance to the Germans.

ERIK. They couldn't. Their resistance was stolen from them at Munich.

MIRANDA. Even so—they're better off now than the Poles, who did resist.

ERIK. That doesn't affect my feeling. I only know that if any one is going to take my freedom from me, he's going to have to pay for it.

MIRANDA. Now you're talking like a boy scout.

ERIK. I'm your son, Mother. I have the same blood in me that you have—the blood of that gentleman up there. [*Points to portrait of great-grandfather Eustis.*] He fought pirates in the Mediterranean. He fought with Jackson at New Orleans.

MIRANDA. Yes—and when he died, in honored old age, they had to pass the hat around among the neighbors to get enough to bury him. . . . [*Pointing to portrait of her grandfather.*] Whereas that unselfish hero who paid another man to take his place in the conscript army—when he died —the whole town turned out—the Chamber of Commerce, the Republican Club, the Knights of Pythias—all paying tribute to the memory of a good, substantial citizen. If you have to look to your ancestry for guidance, look to him. He was no hero. He was a despicable, slimy cheat. But he did very well. . . . You say some one will have to pay for your freedom. But who will receive the payment? Not you, when you're dead.

KAATRI. [*Fiercely.*] Don't listen to her, Erik! Don't listen to her!

MIRANDA. [*Amiably.*] Why shouldn't he listen to me, Kaatri?

KAATRI. [*With too much vehemence.*] Because you're an American! You don't understand.

MIRANDA. [*Patiently.*] I understand one thing, Kaatri. Erik is my son. I want to save his life.

KAATRI. What good is his life if it has to be spent in slavery? [*To* ERIK.] and that's what it would be if he gave in to them. Slavery for you—for all of us. Oh, I know that you Americans don't like to think of such terrible things.

ERIK. Kaatri! You mustn't say that—

MIRANDA. [*Gently.*] You may say what you please about me, Kaatri. But you can't say it about Erik. He's as loyal as you are. He was born in this house, as his father was before him.

KAATRI. Dr. Valkonen is like you. He doesn't really belong to this country. He is a great scientist. He has an international mind.

MIRANDA. And is that a bad thing?

KAATRI. Oh, no—it's a good thing—a noble thing. But for Erik—it would be weakness. I'm afraid for Erik—afraid that he belongs more to America than he does to us. Oh—I don't want to be rude, Mrs. Valkonen—to you or your country. But we're desperate people now. All the men in my family—my father, my brothers—they're all in the army now, on the frontier. It's the same with all families, rich and poor, men and women. All our lives we've had to be ready to fight, for everything we are, everything we believe in. Oh, I know—it's hard for you to understand that—or to see the *need* for it that is in our souls.

ERIK. Kaatri! Of course Mother can understand! Americans fought for that same thing—for the same reason—the same need, that was in their souls. It was Americans who taught the whole world that it was *worth* fighting for!

KAATRI. Yes. But—it's just as Dr. Valkonen says. When life becomes too easy for people, something changes in their character, something is lost. Americans now are too lucky. [*Looks straight at* MIRANDA.] In your blood is the water of those oceans that have made your country safe. But—don't try to persuade Erik that life here is as easy as it is in America. [*She is speaking passionately, desperately.*] He's a Finn, and the time has come when he must behave like one.

ERIK. Kaatri—my dearest— [*Crossing behind sofa, puts a hand on* KAATRI's *shoulder. She buries her head against him.*] Don't—don't cry. [*The word "dearest" makes an emphatic impression on* MIRANDA. *She stares at them.*]

MIRANDA. Kaatri—Kaatri—are you and Erik really in love with each other?

ERIK. Mother!

MIRANDA. Darling, I started to talk to you as though you were still a child—and I wanted first to reason with you—and then if that failed, I would *forbid* you to throw your life away for a lost cause. And then Kaarti spoke up, and you called her "dearest," and that one word stopped me short. I asked Kaatri that question because I thought the answer might help me to understand this strange, new fact—that you're not my son any more. You're a man. . . . Of course, you don't have to answer.

ERIK. [*His hand on* KAATRI's *shoulder.*] We do love each other. We are going to be married.

MIRANDA. [*After a pause, kisses* KAATRI.] Erik—Kaatri—I'm glad! I'm glad.

KAARLO'S VOICE. [*From off right.*] Erik!

[ERIK *goes to door.*] Erik! You know those litters of puppies that I separated—eight litters?

ERIK. Yes, Father.

KAARLO. [*Entering, throws an arm across* ERIK's *shoulders and leads him as he talks.*] The dogs have just come back from Rovaniemi—the ones I sent up there last year. The most wonderful results. I've tested them in every way. Out of thirty-one dogs, seven are definitely—

MIRANDA. [*Breaking in.*] Kaarlo! Kaarlo!

KAARLO. Yes, my dear. [*Slips out of his coat. To* ERIK.] Take this. [*To* MIRANDA.] I want to apologize for being a little bit irritable when you came into the laboratory—but I was excited. Those dogs. . . .

MIRANDA. Never mind about that. I have something to tell you. [*She looks questioningly from* KAATRI *to* ERIK, *who nod permission for her to speak.*]

KAARLO. [*Waiting, sits.*] Yes . . . Well?

MIRANDA. Erik and Kaatri are going to be married.

KAARLO. Erik? [*Looks at him, wonderingly, then bursts out laughing.*]

MIRANDA. [*Reproachfully.*] Kaarlo!

KAARLO. [*Still laughing.*] Forgive me—but—

MIRANDA. Don't laugh. Now, it's not funny, Kaarlo.

KAARLO. No. No.

MIRANDA. No.

KAARLO. No, I know it isn't.

MIRANDA. Darling—you should congratulate them at least.

ERIK. Oh, let him laugh, Mother. Perhaps it *is* funny.

KAARLO. No, no. [*Rises.*] I *do* congratulate you, Erik. And as for you, Kaatri— [*She rises as he goes to her.*] —you're a sweet girl and I shall be delighted to have you for a daughter-in-law. [*Kisses her.*]

KAATRI. [*Curtsying.*] Thank you, Dr. Valkonen.

KAARLO. Ever since Erik was born I've been training him to be a gentleman of taste and discrimination, and, by God, I've succeeded. [*To* ERIK.] Again I congratulate you and thank you for justifying me. It's really—it's unbelievable. *You* a bridegroom! [*He kisses him.*] But we must have some schnapps—a toast to the happy couple. And then we will all have supper.

MIRANDA. Oh darling, we're having supper later, tonight. I told the maids they could go to church. And we're all going to church, too. Come with us, Kaarlo. You must go and put on your tail coat.

KAARLO. And why must we all go to church?

MIRANDA. Oh, there's going to be a great service. The President and everybody will be there. We're going to pray that this country will be able to defend itself. [KAARLO's *amusement fades instantly.*]

KAARLO. Oh! So that's it! All day I have had the utmost difficulty persuading my assistants to attend to their duties. All they wanted to think about and talk about was would we or would we not have to fight the Soviet Union? I don't want to hear any of that talk here.

MIRANDA. Neither do I, Kaarlo. But I've had to hear it. Erik is ready to fight.

KAARLO. Erik? [*Turns coldly to* ERIK.] You're a child. It seems to me that you are deciding too suddenly that you are grown up. If you want to consider yourself engaged to be married, I have no objection—I'm delighted. But I don't want to hear that you are talking to your mother, or to any one else, about going to war.

ERIK. I'm sorry, Father—but I have to do what I think best.

KAARLO. And are you *able* to think?

MIRANDA. Oh, Kaarlo! Of course Erik knows—

KAARLO. No, Miranda. Don't interrupt. [*To* ERIK.] I repeat—in forming this heroic resolve to fight—have you used one grain of the intelligence that I know you possess?

ERIK. I hope I have.

KAARLO. Hoping is not enough. You have seen those celebrations in Red Square —all those aeroplanes, those huge tanks, those troops marching—hundreds of thousands of them?

ERIK. Yes, Father—I've seen them.

KAARLO. And yet you dare to pretend you're competent to stand up against such a force as that?

ERIK. That's why I've trained with the volunteer ski troops—and why I've worked to help make the Mannerheim Line so strong they can never break through.

KAARLO. All that nonsensical child's play on skis—

ERIK. Kaatri's brother Vaino is younger

than I am—but he's with his father's regiment at the frontier . . .

KAARLO. [*Bitterly.*] Oh! If we are at war with the Soviet Union, I shall be at the frontier, too. Surely we'll need everybody, including the aged and the decrepit.

MIRANDA. Now, really, Kaarlo, that is just simply ridiculous—

KAARLO. [*Sitting.*] I can press the trigger of a machine gun just as well as Erik. . . . So that's what we're going to pray for? Ability to imitate our enemies in the display of force. It is all nothing but a substitute for intelligent thinking.

ERIK. This is not a time for intelligent thinking! That doesn't do any good.

KAARLO. No?

ERIK. When your enemies are relying on force, you can't meet them with theories. You can't throw books at them—even good books. What else can anybody do but fight?

KAARLO. [*Bitterly.*] This is no time for intelligent thinking! So this is the climax of a century of scientific miracles. This is what the great men worked for—what *they* fought for in their laboratories. Pasteur, Koch, Ehrlich, Lister. They saved lives that we might build Mannerheim Lines in which to die. [*Church bells are heard faintly in distance.*]

MIRANDA. Now—that's enough, Kaarlo. [*Rising.*] If you don't want to go to church, you don't have to. We'll go by ourselves.

KAARLO. [*Rising.*] Oh, I'll put on my tail coat and go with you. I'll join in asking God to grant the impossible. But I reserve the right to say my own prayers. [*Goes out.* MIRANDA, *who has been putting on hat and coat, crosses to* ERIK.]

MIRANDA. We'll be ready in a few minutes. And, Erik—you must not say any more to your father about going to war.

ERIK. I'll try not to, Mother. [MIRANDA *goes out.*] Poor Father! This is a terrible thing for him—for a man of great faith, as he is. The rest of us have nothing to lose but our lives. [KAATRI *goes to* ERIK—*takes hold of him.*]

KAATRI. Erik—I love you—I do love you, and I'm sorry I said things tonight that only made you more unhappy. I wasn't much help to you.

ERIK. [*Holding her tightly.*] All you said was true, Kaatri. I'm glad you said it. I have to see things clearly. I have to see my mother and father as they are. They don't really live in this country—in this time. They live together in the future—the future as my father has imagined it—not the one that may be made by unimaginative men. They are wonderful people—both of them—wonderful and unreal. You are real. You know what we have to face—and we will face it without fear. [*Kisses her, passionately.*]

KAARLO. [*Entering.*] This coat reeks of moth balls. It will be a scandal in church.

MIRANDA. [*Offstage.*] Don't worry, Kaarlo. There'll be so much of that smell in church they won't even notice you. Have you a clean handkerchief?

KAARLO. Will you bring me one, please? [ERIK *helps* KAARLO *with his coat.*] Get your coat on, Kaatri, my dear—and you too, Erik.

ERIK. Yes, father. [ERIK *and* KAATRI *go out.* MIRANDA *enters, puts a handkerchief into* KAARLO's *coat pocket. He kisses her cheek.*]

KAARLO. Come, Miranda—we go to pray. [*They start out toward the right.*] O God, have pity, for that which we have greatly feared has come upon us. [*Switches off lights. Room is in darkness, except for moonlight from windows. Church bells can still be heard.*]

CURTAIN

SCENE 3

The same. Next afternoon.
UNCLE WALDEMAR *comes in from the right, and is surprised to see black drapes at all windows. They are now drawn apart to let the sun in. He inspects them, goes to piano, sits, starts to play.* MIRANDA *calls from dining room.*

MIRANDA'S VOICE. Uncle Waldemar!

UNCLE WALDEMAR. Yes?

MIRANDA'S VOICE. Are Kaarlo and Erik with you?

UNCLE WALDEMAR. No. [MIRANDA *comes in from dining room. She is wearing an apron and carrying a dust cloth.*]

MIRANDA. Have you seen them?

UNCLE WALDEMAR. I saw Kaarlo. I stopped at the hospital.

MIRANDA. Is he all right?

UNCLE WALDEMAR. Yes. [*Greatly relieved, she kisses him.*]

MIRANDA. And Erik?

UNCLE WALDEMAR. Oh, I don't know anything about him. I thought he was here.

MIRANDA. I haven't seen him since the church service last night. He took Kaatri home and got in very late and then he was off this morning even before I was up.

UNCLE WALDEMAR. Probably he's with Kaatri now, at the Alquists' house.

MIRANDA. Did any bombs fall in that part of the city?

UNCLE WALDEMAR. No. I passed there on my way home. There was no damage here.

MIRANDA. Was the air raid bad?

UNCLE WALDEMAR. Not nearly as bad as expected. Maybe about thirty people killed.

MIRANDA. That's what the policeman told me.

UNCLE WALDEMAR. Were the police here?

MIRANDA. Yes, I was ordered to put up those black curtains on the windows before nightfall. There must be no light from the windows. . . . Oh, I'm so glad to see you, Uncle Waldemar. I've been alone here all day . . .

UNCLE WALDEMAR. Alone? Where are Ilma and Lempi?

MIRANDA. They're gone. They're both in the Lottas. From now on all of us will have to eat my cooking. It's three o'clock in the afternoon, and I just finished making the beds. They look frightful. . . . I wish Kaarlo and Erik would come home! What was Kaarlo doing at the hospital?

UKCLE WALDEMAR. I don't know. I saw him only for a moment. He had a white coat on. [MIRANDA *starts dusting furniture.*]

MIRANDA. When he left here this morning for the hospital, he said it was a good joke—his trying to be a doctor again—when it's been fifteen years since he even gave anybody an aspirin tablet.

UNCLE WALDEMAR. [*Coming down from piano.*] Miranda—

MIRANDA. Yes, Uncle Waldemar. [*She is kneeling, dusting.*]

UNCLE WALDEMAR. [*With apparent difficulty.*] Miranda, I want to tell you that I am sorry for many things that I have said.

MIRANDA. What things?

UNCLE WALDEMAR. I've talked too much about the troubles of the world.

MIRANDA. And why should you feel you have to apologize for that?

UNCLE WALDEMAR. Because now I am deeply distressed.

MIRANDA. I know you are. We're all distressed. But there's nothing we can do about it.

UNCLE WALDEMAR. I have been a poor companion for you and Kaarlo. It wasn't so bad for Kaarlo because he paid no attention. But you have been so good and kind —to me and all of us here. You came here a stranger, and you made all of us love you.

MIRANDA. [*Harshly.*] Now, for God's sake, Uncle Waldemar, don't let's have any of that!

UNCLE WALDEMAR. But there are things on my mind, and I want to say them. You have worked so hard and so well to make this a happy home—

MIRANDA. [*Dusting sofa.*] I've never done any work in my life, and I've never wanted to.

UNCLE WALDEMAR. But you have filled this house with laughter—your own peculiar American kind of laughter. And here I have been, in the midst of all this happiness, an apostle of despair.

MIRANDA. And so you want to be forgiven for telling the truth?

UNCLE WALDEMAR. [*With bitter self-accusation.*] I should have had more philosophy! I—who lived for forty years under the tyranny of the Tsars—and then saw my country rise up from the ashes of the war and the revolution. I should have been reconciled to this. And you—you never saw anything of such real misery in your country. But now—when this came—you took it calmly. You showed wisdom.

MIRANDA. I took it calmly because I didn't know what was coming. I never believed it could happen. I don't believe it now. Look at me, dusting the furniture in the face of the enemy! Did you ever see such a confession of utter helplessness? [*She tosses dust-rag aside and sits down on sofa.*]

UNCLE WALDEMAR. You like to believe you are merely frivolous. But you're not so foreign to us solemn Finns as you think. You're a daughter of the Puritans, who would resist any oppression, undergo any sacrifice, in order to worship God in their own way. . . . I have always believed in God's mercy. I have served Him in His church. Whenever I was in doubt and fear, I would go back to the teachings of Martin Luther—to the doctrine of "The Freedom of the Christian Man." And then I would believe again that the virtues of simple faith would always triumph over intolerance. Whenever I had enough money saved, I would go to Germany, to Eisenach, to the room in the Wartburg where Luther worked. "A mighty fortress is our God." But last year when I was there I saw the Nazis. I saw old friends of mine, living in terror—some of them because they have Jewish blood—some just because they retain a sense of common decency. Even ministers of the gospel—afraid that if they preached the true devotion to God's word they would go into concentration camps. I saw men marching—marching—marching. [MIRANDA *rises and begins to dust again.*] Day and night, singing "Today we own Germany—tomorrow the whole world." They didn't know where they were marching to. They didn't care. They had been drilled and lectured down to the level where marching itself was enough. I was with one of my friends, an old musician like me, and we were looking from the windows of his house. Across the street a truckload of young Nazis had pulled up and they were wrecking the home of a Jewish dentist. They wanted to take the gold he used to put in people's teeth. They were doing it systematically, as the Germans do everything. And my friend whispered to me—for he did not dare raise his voice even in his own home—he said, "They say they are doing this to fight Bolshevism. It is a lie! For they *are* Bolshevism!" And that is the truth. . . . "Today we own Germany tomorrow the whole world." Including Russia.

MIRANDA. [*Coming close to him.*] They can't win, Uncle Waldemar.

UNCLE WALDEMAR. [*Rises and looks out window.*] Can *we* prevent them from winning? All we can do is defend ourselves to the end. And then they sweep over us to the next goal—and the next—

MIRANDA. You're a good Christian, Uncle Waldemar. You have to believe that they can't win.

UNCLE WILDEMAR. [*Passionately.*] I can believe in the coming of the anti-Christ. I can believe in the Apocalypse. "And Satan shall be loosed out of his prison, and shall go out to deceive the nations which are in the four quarters of the earth." [MIRANDA *dusts keys of piano.* ERIK *comes in at the right. He is wearing uniform of ski troops.*]

ERIK. Mother—I have to leave in a few minutes— [*He sees her face as she looks at him. A long pause.* ERIK *takes off his hat. Finally she crosses to him.*] Mother, I'm going into the north with a detachment of ski troops. I don't know just where we're being sent, but we're to assemble at the station in an hour.

MIRANDA. Is Kaatri going with you?

ERIK. No. She'll be at the station, but she doesn't know yet what they want her to do. I have to fix up my pack right away.

MIRANDA. You'll want some food for the journey. I'll get some for you. . . . [*He kisses her cheek.*] Whatever we have in the kitchen—

ERIK. Thank you, Mother. [*Goes out right.*]

MIRANDA. [*To* UNCLE WALDEMAR.] If I'd only known about this sooner, I'd have gotten some things in. I—I suppose there's some canned stuff. . . . [*She seems helpless, despairing.*]

UNCLE WALDEMAR. [*Rising.*] I'll help you look, Miranda. [*As they both go toward dining room.*] I'm sure there are plenty of good things we can find for Erik.

KAARLO's VOICE. [*From off right.*] Miranda! [MIRANDA *stops short.* UNCLE VALDEMAR *goes on out, into kitchen.*]

MIRANDA. Kaarlo?

KAARLO. [*Entering.*] Yes. Miranda—look who has come back to Helsinki! Mr. Corveen, you remember him? [DAVE *comes in and goes to* MIRANDA.]

MIRANDA. Of course.

DAVE. I'm so glad to see you again, Mrs. Valkonen.

KAARLO. I just met him. He arrived only this morning, and he was on his way to see us. [*Goes to her and kisses her.*] It was awful, not being able to telephone?—But you're all right?

MIRANDA. Yes.

KAARLO. And Erik?

MIRANDA. Yes. He's here. He—

KAARLO. But—sit down, Mr. Corween. What will you have to drink?

MIRANDA. Kaarlo—

KAARLO. [*To* DAVE.] Excuse me. Yes, my dear—

MIRANDA. Kaarlo! Erik is going into the army. He's upstairs, now, packing his things.

KAARLO. Where is he going?

MIRANDA. I don't know. Into the north somewhere. [MIRANDA *goes to* DAVE.] Do you think there will be much fighting in the north, Mr. Corween?

DAVE. You know more about the situation than I do, Mrs. Valkonen.

MIRANDA. You'll forgive me, Mr. Corween. I have something to do.

DAVE. Of course. [MIRANDA *goes out into kitchen.*] I think you'd like me to go, Dr. Valkonen.

KAARLO. No, no. Sit down. Are you going to stay here for a while in Helsinki—or is this another flying visit?

DAVE. [*Sitting.*] I don't know how long I shall stay. It—it all depends.

KAARLO. You'll be broadcasting from here?

DAVE. Oh, yes, Doctor. The American public likes to be kept in touch with all that's going on.

KAARLO. That's good. We like to keep in touch with them. [*He is making a gallant attempt to sustain polite conversation.*] We heard your broadcasts from Warsaw. They were brilliant.

DAVE. Thank you. I can't say I enjoyed them very much.

KAARLO. [*Sitting—quietly.*] It was tragic, wasn't it!

DAVE. Yes, it was. Dr. Valkonen, I know that this is no time for me to be bothering you or your wife, but—

KAARLO. You are more than welcome here, my dear friend.

DAVE. I know that, Doctor. But there's something I want to say.

KAARLO. Yes?

DAVE. I saw Jim Walsh at the American Legation.

KAARLO. Yes—yes.

DAVE. He is very fond of you and Mrs. Valkonen.

KAARLO. Thank you.

DAVE. As he should be. He asked me to beg you to leave Finland at once. [KAARLO *looks at him.*] He can arrange everything. A ship has been chartered next Tuesday from Goteborg, for New York. It is to take hundreds of American refugees. Mr. Walsh can arrange passage for you and Mrs. Valkonen. He can get you to Sweden by plane. But—he must know about it at once.

KAARLO. Well, now—that's very kind of Mr. Walsh, especially when he's so busy.

DAVE. [*Earnestly.*] I hope you will do it, Dr. Valkonen.

KAARLO. You mean—go?

DAVE. Yes—and at once.

KAARLO. I am needed here for the time being. There is a great shortage of doctors. All of the young men in all the hospitals are going to the front, for service with the army medical corps. There will be many more casualties here from air raids.

DAVE. It's not my business to say so, Doctor—but that isn't suitable work for a winner of the Nobel prize.

KAARLO. [*With great sadness.*] It is not suitable work for any member of the human race, Mr. Corween. But some one must do it.

DAVE. I realize that you're a patriotic citizen of this country—

KAARLO. I am not a patriotic citizen of this country, Mr. Corween. I hope I am aware of the fact that "patriotism" as now practised is one of the most virulent manifestations of evil.

DAVE. Yes, Doctor. That's just what I mean. You're a citizen of the world. You're of importance to the whole world, not just to these few gallant men who are going to fight and die for Finland. . . . Oh—I know it's presumptuous of me to be talking to you. But—I beg you, please, for God's sake, while you still have the chance, go to a country where you can carry on your work—your own fight—to bring men to consciousness—

KAARLO. But I shall carry on that work as long as I live, Mr. Corween—wherever I am.

DAVE. As long as you live! I'm sorry if I seem unduly emotional about it, Doctor—but—I have seen too many men of intellectual distinction forced into uniform, forced to pick up guns and shoot because they had discovered that their intelligence was impotent to cope with brutal reality. *You* may be forced into that situation, Dr. Valkonen. You who have devoted yourself to discovering the inward defenses of man. You may find yourself, crouching behind a sand-bag, shooting at an illiterate Russian peasant.

KAARLO. Yes, Mr. Corween. You know whereof you speak. And I should be the last to dispute you. Now—we feel like heroes, strong in the armor of the justice of our own cause. Soon—we may be corpses. It is all very foolish—very temporary. But, you see, I am accustomed to this sort of thing. In my youth, this country was ruled by the Romanovs. I survived that oppression. I am prepared to endure it again. Let the forces of evil engulf us. If the truth is in here, my friend— [*Taps his heart.* MIRANDA *comes in with* ERIK.]

MIRANDA. Kaarlo, Erik must go now.

DAVE. [*He knows he must get out before the possibly painful farewells are said.*] I'm afraid I must go now. [*To* ERIK.] How do you do? I—I have to get back to the hotel, to stand by for orders from New York. I'll be at the Kamp, Mrs. Valkonen, and I hope I'll see you soon again. Good-bye, Doctor. Good-bye, Mrs. Valkonen.

ERIK. Good-bye.

MIRANDA. You must come to see us often.

DAVE. Thank you, I shall. Good-bye. Good luck. [DAVE *goes out. A moment of tense silence. No one knows quite what to say.*]

KAARLO. [*To* ERIK.] You're leaving now?

ERIK. Yes, Father. We're to be at the station at five o'clock. I—I'd better go at once. I don't want to be late. [*To* MIRANDA.] Where's Uncle Waldemar?

MIRANDA. He's bringing the food for you from the kitchen. You'll be able to say good-bye to him on the way out.

KAARLO. I take it you know what you're doing—what chances you have of accomplishing anything.

ERIK. Yes, Father. I think I know about that.

KAARLO. Very well, then. There's nothing I can say to you but good-bye.

ERIK. [To KAARLO.] Father, before I go, I want you to know that I'm sorry for you. I think I understand what this is for you. It's worse for you than it is for any of us. But—if it's any consolation to you—I hope you'll remember—you have a son who at least obeys the Fourth Commandment. I honor my father and my mother. [*The emotion of this is a bit too much for* ERIK. *He hides his face in his hands.* KAARLO *leans over and kisses him tenderly.*]

KAARLO. Go on, go on, Erik. [ERIK *turns from him toward* MIRANDA.]

MIRANDA. I'll go to the door with you, darling. [*They go out.* KAARLO *is alone. He goes to a chair at the extreme left, sits down, looks out window, lost, helpless.* MIRANDA *returns and sits on couch at the right.*]

KAARLO. [*Almost angrily.*] I suppose you want to weep now? Then you'd better go to our room and get it over with.

MIRANDA. What good will it do to weep? I've never in my life understood what it is to enjoy the luxury of a good cry. [*She rises suddenly.*] I'm going to the kitchen.

KAARLO. What for?

MIRANDA. I don't know. I have to start trying to learn how to cook. [*She goes out.* KAARLO *looks after her miserably. After a moment,* UNCLE WALDEMAR *comes in.*]

UNCLE WALDEMAR. Kaarlo. . . . Kaarlo—

KAARLO. Yes.

UNCLE WALDEMAR. Dr. Ziemssen is here.

KAARLO. Dr. Ziemssen?

UNCLE WALDEMAR. He has come to say good-bye. He is going back to Germany.

KAARLO. Oh. . . . Very well, I'll see him.

UNCLE WALDEMAR. [*Going off at the right.*] Come in, Dr. Ziemssen. [DR. ZIEMSSEN *comes in. He is wearing his overcoat, carrying his hat and walking stick.* UNCLE WALDEMAR *closes door behind him.*]

KAARLO. I'm delighted you came in. Let me take your coat.

ZIEMSSEN. Thank you, no, Herr Doktor. I can stay but a short time.

KAARLO. Please sit down.

ZIEMSSEN. I know this is not an opportune moment. I saw Erik go. I saluted him —a splendid young soldier. You have good cause to be proud.

KAARLO. [*As they sit on sofa.*] Thank you, Dr. Ziemssen. I'm sorry to hear you're going. I've greatly enjoyed our discussions at the Institute. But—I can well understand that this is not the place for you under the circumstances.

ZIEMSSEN. [*Seriously.*] It is not the place for you, either, Dr. Valkonen. I advise you also to go.

KAARLO. Go?

ZIEMSSEN. Leave Finland. Leave Europe at once!

KAARLO. Why is everybody ordering me out of my home? Mr. Corween was here also telling me I must leave.

ZIEMSSEN. Mr. Corween is a remarkably well-informed man. He is aware of the inevitable outcome of this war, as you yourself must be, Herr Doktor. Oh—I have all admiration for the little Finnish Army. But two hundred thousand against ten million—

KAARLO. Yes, we will be conquered, as we have been conquered before. And then we will be ruled from Moscow—as we were formerly ruled from Petersburg. But as I was just saying to Mr. Corween, I shall continue with my experiments.

ZIEMSSEN. Dr. Valkonen—I must warn you—you are making a serious mistake!

KAARLO. Mistake?

ZIEMSSEN. You are judging this situation in terms of the past.

KAARLO. One can only judge by one's own experience.

ZIEMSSEN. Precisely. Your own experience is misleading.

KAARLO. In what way, Dr. Ziemssen?

ZIEMSSEN. That is just what I wish to tell you. You think your enemies are these —these Communists who now invade your country?

KAARLO. Yes. That is what I think.

ZIEMSSEN. The Russians think so, too, but they are wrong. *We* are your enemies, Herr Doktor. This Finnish incident is one little item in our vast scheme. We make good use of our esteemed allies of the Soviet Union. All the little communist cells, in labor movements, youth movements, in all nations—they are now working for *us*, although they may not know it. Communism is a good laxative to loosen the constricted bowels of democracy. When it has served that purpose, it will disappear down the sewer with the excrement that must be purged.

KAARLO. It seems to me, Dr. Ziemssen, you are talking with extremely undiplomatic frankness.

ZIEMSSEN. I know I can do so to you, Herr Doktor. You are a scientist. You are accustomed to face facts—even those facts which to the ordinary, dull mind are too terrible to contemplate.

KAARLO. What is it you are threatening, Doctor? What is going to happen to Finland?

ZIEMSSEN. You do not know the whole story of what happened to Poland! [KAARLO *looks at him, rises, and walks away.*] You will hear the Pope in Rome weeping publicly and proclaiming that the Polish nation will rise again. I assure you it will not rise again, because, as a nation, it is dead. The same is true of every nation that we conquer; we shall see to it that none of them will ever rise again. Today, the remnants of the Polish people are scattered all the way from the Rhine to the Pacific coast of Siberia. This is a process of annihilation. It is a studied technique, and it was not invented in Moscow. You will find the blueprints of it, not in *Das Kapital,* but in *Mein Kampf.* It is all there for you to read. It involves, first, liquidation of all leaders of thought—political, religious, economic, intellectual. [KAARLO *sits down. He seems to slump.*] Among the masses—the difficult ones are killed—the weaklings are allowed to die of starvation —the strong ones are enslaved.

KAARLO. You are an anthropologist—a man of learning, Dr. Ziemssen. Do you approve of this technique?

ZIEMSSEN. Naturally, I regret the necessity for it. But I *admit* the necessity. And so must you, Dr. Valkonen. Remember that every great state of the past in its stages of construction has required slavery. Today, the greatest world state is in process of formation. There is a great need for slave labor. And—these Finns and Scandinavians would be useful. They are strong; they have great capacity for endurance. Is that brutal—ruthless? Yes. But I am now talking to a scientist, not a snivelling sentimentalist. Vivisection has been called brutal, ruthless—but it is necessary for the survival of man. So it is necessary that

inferior races be considered merely as animals. . . . Do you believe me, Herr Doktor?

KAARLO. I believe you. Although—still talking as one scientist to another—I cannot help wondering just how you establish proof that these other races are inferior, especially when you know it is a lie.

ZIEMSSEN. Of course it is a lie, biologically. But we can prove it by the very simple expedient of asserting our own superiority—just as the Romans did before they decayed—and the Anglo-Saxons, before *they* decayed. View this objectively, Herr Doktor, and then you will be able to proceed wth your experiments. You have made important progress in an important field—conditioning men to their environment. That can be of extraordinary value to us in the future. You can help to postpone, perhaps indefinitely, the time when *we* will be conquered by decay. But, first —you must accept the theory of the new world state, for that *is* the environment of the future. If you refuse to accept, and stay here and attempt to resist destiny, you will die.

KAARLO. Where can one go to escape this world state?

ZIEMSSEN. [*Smiles.*] An intelligent question, Herr Doktor. I assure you that the United States is secure for the present. It may continue so for a long time, if the Americans refrain from interfering with us in Mexico and South America and Canada. And I believe they will refrain. They are now showing far greater intelligence in that respect than ever before. They are learning to mind their own shrinking business.

KAARLO. I appreciate your motives in warning me, Dr. Ziemssen. And I understand that all you have told me is confidential.

ZIEMSSEN. [*Laughing.*] You *are* an innocent, my friend! Nothing that I have said is confidential. You may repeat it all. And you will not be believed. There is the proof of our superiority—that our objectives are so vast that our pigmy-minded enemies simply have not the capacity to believe them. They are eager to accept the big lies we give them, because they cannot comprehend the big truth. [*Rises.*] And the big truth is this: For the first time since the whole surface of the earth became known, one dynamic race is on the march to occupy that surface and rule it! When you have absorbed that huge conception, you will find that your own theories can be adjusted to it. And now I must go. [*He extends his hand to* KAARLO.] But I advise you to make haste, Herr Doktor. Finland's only lines of communication are through Sweden and Norway. We have many means of cutting those lines. Good-bye, Herr Doktor. I said good-bye. I hope we part friends. [*He goes to door.* KAARLO *nods as he shakes hands with* DR. ZIEMSSEN.] My compliments to Frau Valkonen. Good-bye. [*He goes.*]

UNCLE WALDEMAR'S VOICE. [*Heard off-stage.*] Good-bye, Dr. Ziemssen.

ZIEMSSEN'S VOICE. Good-bye, Herr Sederstrum. I have so enjoyed your music. [KAARLO *crosses and stands behind sofa.* UNCLE WALDEMAR *enters, switches on lights, goes immediately to windows and starts closing black curtains.* KAARLO *looks toward kitchen.*]

KAARLO. Uncle Waldemar—Uncle Waldemar—

UNCLE WALDEMAR. Yes. . . . What is it? [*Having fixed windows,* UNCLE WALDEMAR *turns to* KAARLO.]

KAARLO. Get your hat and coat on.

UNCLE WALDEMAR. What for?

KAARLO. I want you to go to the American Legation and see Mr. Walsh. Tell him that Mrs. Valkonen will leave on that ship Mr. Corween told me about. I believe it sails from Goteborg on Tuesday. He must make all the necessary arrangements at once. Find out what is the earliest possible moment she can leave for Sweden. Ask him if it is safe by aeroplane.

UNCLE WALDEMAR. You're sending Miranda away—alone?

KAARLO. Yes. Be quiet. She's right there in the kitchen.

UNCLE WALDEMAR. You think you can persuade her to do this?

KAARLO. I have to persuade her, and if necessary, you will help me. You know what has happened to Poland.

UNCLE WALDEMAR. Yes, I know. But— Miranda doesn't care about those things. She doesn't believe them.

KAARLO. I didn't believe them either. . . . But—I'll find another way of persuading her. If ruthlessness is the order of this

day, then I shall be ruthless, too. I will tell her I don't want her here. She is of no use in a time like this.

UNCLE WALDEMAR. That will hurt her more deeply than the Russians ever could.

KAARLO. She will recover from that hurt. Go ahead!

UNCLE WALDEMAR. Very well. [*Starts to go, but* MIRANDA *enters. She is carrying a tray on which are a coffee pot and cups.*]

MIRANDA. Uncle Waldemar—I made some coffee. Would you like some?

UNCLE WALDEMAR. No, thank you.

MIRANDA. I tasted it. It's quite good.

UNCLE WALDEMAR. Thank you—but I have to go.

MIRANDA. Where?

UNCLE WALDEMAR. I want to have some exercise and fresh air.

MIRANDA. But you've been out all day.

UNCLE WALDEMAR. Even so—I'm going out again. [*He goes out.* MIRANDA *takes her tray over to piano and puts it down.*]

MIRANDA. Poor Uncle Waldemar—all this has upset him terribly. . . . Will you have some coffee, Kaarlo?

KAARLO. No, thank you.

MIRANDA. I wish you'd try it.

KAARLO. Later, perhaps. . . . Please sit down.

MIRANDA. What is it, Kaarlo? Do you want to talk about Erik? [*Starts to go out.*]

KAARLO. No—I do not want to talk about Erik. Please sit down. [*Sits down and looks at him, curiously.*] I wish to tell you, my dear, that the time has come for you to go home.

MIRANDA. Home? This is my home.

KAARLO. I mean—to your own country. To America.

MIRANDA. [*Amazed.*] Why?

KAARLO. Because I do not wish you to stay here. Mr. Walsh at the American Legation can make all the necessary arrangements. You will probably leave for Sweden tomorrow—perhaps even tonight. We will hear soon about that. You can then go to Boston and stay with your aunt.

MIRANDA. Will you go with me?

KAARLO. Naturally not. I am needed here. You will stay in America until this business is over.

MIRANDA. And when it *is* over? What then?

KAARLO. Why—you'll come back here,

and we'll go right on living as we've always done. I might come to America and fetch you.

MIRANDA. Supposing you were killed?

KAARLO. I—killed? I'm a doctor.

MIRANDA. And do you suppose a Russian in a bombing plane ten thousand feet up can tell the difference between an ordinary person and a winner of the Nobel prize?

KAARLO. It is out of the question that I should go. Freud left Vienna after the Nazi occupation. He went to London, and he was welcomed there, he was honored. But—he couldn't speak. He knew that if he told the truth, it would be printed, and his own people, still in Austria, would be made to suffer for it, horribly. . . . So Freud was technically free—but he was silenced. What did he then have to live for? Nothing. . . . So he died. . . . No—I will not leave. You must go alone.

MIRANDA. And if I left here—what would *I* have to live for?

KAARLO. Oh, you'll manage very well in your own great, secure, distant country. [*He has been moving about the room. Her eyes have been following him, questioning him, seeking him out, with every word, every move.*]

MIRANDA. Kaarlo! Tell me the truth. Why do you want me to go?

KAARLO. What can you do here? This is a war for the defense of Finland. It must be fought by the Finnish people. [*She is staring at him. He is avoiding her gaze.*] This country becomes an armed camp. Every one of us knows what he must do, or she must do, and is trained to do it. Are you trained for anything but wearing lovely clothes, being a charming hostess? [*She looks at him, helplessly.*] You are an intelligent woman, Miranda. Reason this out for yourself. You will see that this is a time when every one who eats bread must have worked to earn it. And, God help us, there is only one form of work that matters now—resistance—blind, dogged, desperate resistance.

MIRANDA. [*Rising, and following him.*] You've said yourself—that kind of resistance is useless. [*She is trying desperately to score a point. He is trying desperately to avoid being scored on, though ever conscious of his vulnerability.*]

KAARLO. [*Angrily.*] You don't know

what I've said. Or—if you know the words, you have less idea of their meaning than the youngest of the students who hear my lectures at the Institute. I'm not insulting your courage, Miranda. Nor your good will. I'm sure you would like to be useful. But you can't. You know you can't.

MIRANDA. You think it would be impossible for me to contribute anything—to help in any way?

KAARLO. Why do I have to tell you what you must know yourself? [MIRANDA *looks at him with a look almost of bitter hostility. She turns and walks away. Unutterably miserable, he looks after her. The artifice of his frigid superiority is beginning to crumble.*] There is no reason for you to be ashamed of this. This is not your country. It is not your war.

MIRANDA. This is the country of my husband and my son.

KAARLO. And do you think Erik and I want you to be caught in these ruins?

MIRANDA. You have no right to speak of Erik! I don't think he would be particularly happy or proud to hear that his mother has scurried to safety at the first sound of a shot fired.

KAARLO. Erik has American blood in his veins. He will understand.

MIRANDA. [*Flaming.*] Oh! So that's it! His American blood will tell him that it's perfectly reasonable for me to run away. You evidently share Kaatri's opinion of me.

KAARLO. [*Desperately.*] Don't put words into my mouth that I have not uttered—

MIRANDA. [*Turning on him, suddenly coming to him.*] Then don't be afraid to come out and say what you mean. It's obvious that you don't want me here, because I'm incompetent—I'm a parasite—I'm a nonessential. In all these years that we've been together nothing has happened to disturb the lovely serenity of our home. And now comes this great calamity. And immediately you decide that you don't want me—you don't need me.

KAARLO. I didn't say that!

MIRANDA. Then what did you say? [KAARLO *is obviously making a last effort to control himself.*]

KAARLO. Miranda! You don't understand why I want you to go!

MIRANDA. It makes no difference to me whether I understand it or not. There's one thing I do know, and you'd better now it, too: I am not going. Probably, you don't need me. You have important work to do—and I'm sure that's enough, for you. But the time may come when Erik might need me, and when that time comes, I intend to be here—

KAARLO. No, please—for God's sake—don't keep on bringing Erik into it! Wasn't t bad enough to see him going away like that, in his uniform? That poor, hopeful, defenseless child! [*He sees that he has hurt her, terribly, with that.*] Oh—I'm sorry, darling. You must see that I've been making a desperate attempt to drive you to safety with lies. It's no use. You always can make me tell the truth. The real trouble is —you've had too much confidence in me. How could you know that I was living in a dream—a beautiful wishful dream in which you played your own unsubstantial but exciting part? And now—there is war —and our son goes to fight—and I wake up to discover that reality itself is a hideous nightmare. . . . I shouldn't be talking to you like this, Miranda. I'm frightened.

MIRANDA. You can never be afraid to say anything to me, darling.

KAARLO. I have suddenly realized what and where I am. I am a man working in the apparent security of a laboratory. I am working on a theory so tentative that it may take hundreds of years of research, and generations of workers, to prove it. I am trying to defeat insanity—degeneration of the human race. . . . And then—a band of pyromaniacs enters the building in which I work. And that building is the world—the whole planet—not just Finland. They set fire to it. What can I do? Until that fire is put out, there can be no peace —no freedom from fear—no hope of progress for mankind. . . . Every day that we hold them off—will only serve to increase the terror of the vengeance which must surely descend upon us. All the pathetic survivors of this war will have to pay in torture for the heroism of the dead. And it isn't just us—not just this one little breed that wants to be free. This is a war for everybody—yes—even for the scientists who thought themselves immune behind their test tubes. [*He looks into her eyes again.*] Darling! I can stand this ordeal if I know it is only for myself. I can stand it if I know you are safe—that you are beyond their reach. . . . I love you. That is the only reality left to me. I love you. [*They are in each other's arms. For a moment, they are silent.*]

MIRANDA. Then I can stand it, too, darling, whatever it is. I can stand it as long as I know that you love me—that you do need me—that I am essential, after all. Even if I am a woman who is nothing but a woman. Even at a time when the whole life of the world is marching with men. . . . [*They hold each other closely. After a moment, she rises.*] Now come and have some coffee. [*They cross to piano. She feels coffee pot.*] It's not very warm.

KAARLO. It's no matter, darling. I'm sure it's good. [*She is pouring coffee.*]

CURTAIN

SCENE 4

The same. New Year's Day, 1940. Noon. There is a Christmas tree. There are many decorations on tree, including a wide, white ribbon on which is an inscription in Finnish. At top of tree is a star. UNCLE WALDEMAR *is at piano playing something surprisingly spirited and gay.* KAARLO *comes in. Wears uniform coat of a Colonel in the Medical Corps, but otherwise he is in civilian clothes. He is buttoning up the coat. As he glances back into a mirror, he looks rather sheepish and self-conscious.* UNCLE WALDEMAR *looks at him.*

KAARLO. Well—Uncle Waldemar—haven't you anything to say about my new uniform?

UNCLE WALDEMAR. What should I say? I've seen thousands of uniforms lately. They all look the same.

KAARLO. [*Laughs.*] I know. But—for some reason—when you see one on yourself, it seems to look better.

UNCLE WALDEMAR. [*Stops playing, rises.*] Are you trying to fool me, Kaarlo?

KAARLO. Fool you? Why should I—?

UNCLE WALDEMAR. You want me to think you are proud to be going?

KAARLO. [*Gravely.*] No, Uncle Waldemar. [*Looks off to kitchen, and then speaks confidentially.*] When Erik went—I—I thought our world had come to an end. Since then—I have been struggling to adjust myself—to find in all this tragedy some intimation of hope for the future.

UNCLE WALDEMAR. [*Tenderly.*] I know, Kaarlo.

KAARLO. This [*Indicates his uniform coat.*] represents the final stage in that attempt at adjustment. It is like the moment when a scientist knows he can no longer experiment with guinea pigs—he must now test his theories on human life itself. It is kill or cure.

UNCLE WALDEMAR. What are those ribbons you are wearing?

KAARLO. The order of St. Ann with Swords—the Cross of St. George's.

UNCLE WALDEMAR. You're going into the Mannerheim Line wearing Russian decorations?

KAARLO. Why not? I won them. Or—at any rate—they were given to me. You think I should leave them off? [MIRANDA *comes in from kitchen with a tray on which are a pitcher of eggnog and five punch glasses. She sees* KAARLO'S *coat.*]

MIRANDA. What is that you are wearing?

KAARLO. It is my uniform coat. I was just trying it on.

MIRANDA. What for? What do you want with a uniform?

KAARLO. Of course I should have one. I'm a Colonel in the Army Medical Corps.

MIRANDA. Now don't tell me you want to look impressive. Why have you suddenly got a uniform?

KAARLO. Because I have to, Miranda. I'm going to Viipuri.

MIRANDA. [*Shocked.*] When are you going?

KAARLO. This afternoon, I believe. What is that on the tray you brought in?

MIRANDA. It's eggnog. I promised Dave Corween I'd make some to celebrate New Year's. Why are they sending you to Viipuri?

KAARLO. Nobody is sending me, Miranda. I'm going because I wish to. More hospital space has to be provided there, and I want to see that the work is done efficiently.

MIRANDA. Why haven't you told me about this before? You knew about it Uncle Waldemar?

UNCLE WALDEMAR. He told me only today.

KAARLO. Now really, Miranda. This is not to be taken so seriously. I am not going very far away, and I shall probably be back within a fortnight. In fact, Dave Corween is going with me and a Polish officer named Rutkowski. Dave is to broadcast from Viipuri. That proves there's no danger. [*Starts to go out at the right.*]

MIRANDA. How do you get to Viipuri?

KAARLO. I go in style . . . in that new American ambulance that just arrived from France. [*Goes out, taking off his coat.*]

MIRANDA. [*Looking after* KAARLO.] He was afraid to tell me—wasn't he, Uncle Waldemar?

UNCLE WALDEMAR. Kaarlo always likes to avoid unpleasant subjects . . . outside his laboratory.

MIRANDA. Is there something serious happening?

UNCLE WALDEMAR. Well—you know, Miranda—there is still war. They still attack.

MIRANDA. But everything's going well for us, isn't it?

UNCLE WALDEMAR. We're alive. That's more than any one expected.

MIRANDA. Why do they want more hospitals at Viipuri? I thought there weren't many wounded.

UNCLE WALDEMAR. That is because now most of the wounded are frozen to death before they can be brought in. When warmer weather comes—the fighting will be different. They will need hospitals—especially on the isthmus. [*She considers this dreadful thought for a moment.*]

MIRANDA. [*Desperately.*] Oh, God—Uncle Waldemar. Why don't we hear from Erik? He has been gone a whole month—*why* don't we hear? [UNCLE WALDEMAR *comes to her.*]

UNCLE WALDEMAR. We know Erik is

well. Kaarlo sees every casualty list—including even those who are sick. It's just that up there in the Arctic there is not much chance of sending letters. [*Doorbell is heard.*]

MIRANDA. There's the doorbell.

UNCLE WALDEMAR. I'll go, Miranda. [UNCLE WALDEMAR *goes out.* VOICES *can be heard off right.*] How do you do, Mr. Corween?

DAVE. [*Off.*] How do you do, sir?

UNCLE WALDEMAR. [*Off.*] Happy New Year!

DAVE. [*Off.*] Happy New Year to you, sir!

UNCLE WALDEMAR. [*Off.*] Go right in.

DAVE. [*Off.*] Thank you. [DAVE *comes in, dressed for a cold journey.*]

MIRANDA. Dave! Happy New Year!

DAVE. Happy New Year, Mrs. Valkonen.

MIRANDA. [*Pointing to tray.*] I've kept my promise about the eggnog.

DAVE. I'm afraid I'm going to overtax your hospitality. There are four other boys here, all going up with the ambulance.

MIRANDA. Oh! Bring them all in.

DAVE. Thank you. [*He calls off.*] Come in, boys. Come in, Major. [MAJOR RUTKOWSKI *comes in. He is a tired, tragic young Polish officer. He is followed almost at once by* JOE BURNETT, BEN GICHNER *and* FRANK OLMSTEAD. JOE *is tall, lean, wearing a smart, new aviator's uniform;* BEN *is stout and cheerful;* FRANK, *young, sensitive and serious-minded. Both* BEN *and* FRANK *wear uniforms of the American Ambulance Corps, with Red Cross insignia on sleeves.*]

DAVE. Mrs. Valkonen—this is Major Rutkowski.

RUTKOWSKI. [*Bows.*] Madame.

MIRANDA. How do you do?

DAVE. And this is the American Expeditionary Force in Finland. Joe Burnett of Haverford, Pa.—

MIRANDA. [*Shaking hands with each in turn.*] How do you do?

DAVE. Ben Gichner of Cincinnati.

MIRANDA. I'm very glad to see you.

DAVE. And Frank Olmstead of San Francisco. Mrs. Valkonen of New Bedford.

MIRANDA. Happy New Year!

JOE. Thank you, Mrs. Valkonen.

FRANK. Thank you.

BEN. And a very happy New Year to you, Madame.

MIRANDA. I have some eggnog, gentlemen— [*Their faces light up.*] In the midst of war we still have some milk and eggs and rye whiskey and even a little cream. You start serving it, Dave—while I get some more glasses. Sit down, everybody. [*She goes out through dining room.*]

DAVE. [*Crossing.*] Come on, Joe. [JOE *and* FRANK *follow* DAVE *across.* BEN *and* RUTKOWSKI *are looking about the room.*] Now, boys, remember. No remarks about the horrors of war. I'm afraid Mrs. Valkonen feels pretty badly about her husband going.

JOE. We'll be tactful, Dave.

RUTKOWSKI. [*Quietly.*] A lovely house. This would be the house of good people in any country.

BEN. It's got a sort of nice, Victorian quality. I thought everything in Finland was moderne.

FRANK. [*Who is looking at photographs on piano.*] Look, Joe. . . . Doctor Jung, Alexis Carrel, President Masaryk—

DAVE. [*Bringing drinks across to* RUTKOWSKI *and* BEN.] Here you are, Major Rutkowski. Nourishing and stimulating—but apt to be dangerous. [FRANK *is standing by piano, playing a few bars of a swing tune.*]

MIRANDA. [*Offstage.*] Have you tried it yet?

DAVE. We were waiting for you, Mrs. Valkonen. [MIRANDA *reenters with tray holding more glasses.* BEN *and* RUTKOWSKI *rise.* DAVE *takes tray from her, goes to serving table and pours drinks for* MIRANDA *and himself.*]

MIRANDA. Here you are—here are the glasses. [*To* FRANK.] Was that you playing?

FRANK. [*Diffidently.*] I wouldn't call it playing.

MIRANDA. It is wonderful.

BEN. Come on, Dave. I think you ought to make a little speech in behalf of all of us.

DAVE. I'm not at my best without a mike and a coast-to-coast hook-up. [*Raises his glass and addresses* MIRANDA.] However, we want to tell you we're glad to be here, enjoying your gracious hospitality, and we hope that this New Year will bring you and yours health and happiness.

MIRANDA. [*As circle of men gathers about her.*] Why, that was a charming speech, Dave. I wish the same to you, all of you, and I welcome you to this house and this country. And I'd like to sing the Polish anthem and "The Star-Spangled Banner," but I don't know the words of either.

DAVE. [Laughs.] That's all right, Mrs. Valkonen. Neither do we. [All drink.]

JOE. It's magnificent.

DAVE. Mrs. Valkonen, it's better even than the Parker House Punch.

BEN. Frankly, I love it.

FRANK. So do I.

RUTKOWSKI. I've never tasted anything like it before—but I'm glad to be introduced.

MIRANDA. Thank you—thank you. [To FRANK.] Do go on playing. Help yourselves as long as it lasts. There are American cigarettes. [MIRANDA sits on sofa. FRANK goes to piano and plays.]

DAVE. Everybody admires your house, Mrs. Valkonen.

BEN. Yes. I was just saying, it has a nice, old-fashioned quality.

RUTKOWSKI. It is so graceful.

MIRANDA. I'm glad you see it with the Christmas tree. That always makes it more cheerful.

FRANK. [Stops playing.] May I ask—what is the inscription on that ribbon?

MIRANDA. It's Finnish for "Glory to God in the highest and, on earth, peace, good will to men." [A pause.] We have that on the tree every Christmas. It's a tradition in this country.

KAARLO. [Calling from off stage, right.] I'll be with you in a moment, gentlemen. I have to assemble my kit.

MIRANDA. [Calling to him.] Can I help you, Kaarlo?

KAARLO. [Off.] No, thank you, my dear. Is the eggnog good, gentlemen?

DAVE. It's superb!

BEN. We're in no hurry to leave, Doctor. We're having a fine time.

MIRANDA. Have all you gentlemen just arrived in Helsinki?

BEN. We got here yesterday, ma'am. . . . I mean, Frank Olmstead and Joe Burnett and me. We came by ship from Paris to Norway. Major Rutkowski has been here since November.

MIRANDA. Had you been in the war in Poland, Major?

RUTKOWSKI. Yes, Madame, but it lasted only three weeks. I was in the cavalry.

MIRANDA. How did you manage to get here?

RUTKOWSKI. From Riga, Madame. The survivors of my regiment were driven over the Lithuanian border. I worked my way to Helsinki intending to go on through Sweden to France to join the Polish Legion there. But—

MIRANDA. But—there was a war here, so you didn't have to look any further.

RUTKOWSKI. Yes, Madame.

MIRANDA. We used to listen to Dave when he was broadcasting from Warsaw, describing the incredible heroism during the siege. Day after day we'd hear the German official radio announcing that Warsaw had fallen and then, late at night, we'd hear the government's station, playing Chopin's "Polonaise," to let us know they were still there.

BEN. We heard it, too, in Paris. It was thrilling.

DAVE. What were you doing in Paris, Ben—if it isn't too personal a question?

BEN. I was employed there! I worked for the American Express Company. I was a travel salesman. [Turns to MIRANDA.] I've sold many tours to picturesque Scandinavia and the Baltic, but this is my first visit to these parts.

MIRANDA. We're very glad that you're here.

BEN. Thank you.

MIRANDA. And what were you doing, Mr. Burnett?

JOE. For the last two years I've been in jail—in one of General Franco's mediæval dungeons.

MIRANDA. You fought in Spain?

JOE. Yes, Mrs. Valkonen.

MIRANDA. Why, you're a hero, Mr. Burnett.

JOE. No, Mrs. Valkonen. No hero, Just a bum. I went to Spain only because I was kicked out of Princeton.

DAVE. What for?

JOE. For throwing forward passes in chapel.

BEN. All fliers are a little crazy. Now, you take Frank and me—we're sane. We're ambulance drivers. We're non-combatants, we hope. We'll have a good safe view of this country. And what I want to see most is some of those ski troops. [DAVE looks at him, sharply.] Will there be any of them around Viipuri?

JOE. They're all up in the north, aren't they?

MIRANDA. Yes. They're in the north. [*Noticing* JOE's *empty glass.*] Let me get you some more. [*She takes* JOE's *glass, rises and crosses to serving table.*]

DAVE. [*Rising.*] You won't see much action around Viipuri. The Mannerheim Line is just about as quiet as the Western Front.

MIRANDA. Dave is always reassuring—at least when he's talking to me. But I think he's less optimistic when he's broadcasting the news.

DAVE. That's only because I have to dramatize things for the radio audience. They like to be scared. In fact, every night, when I'm on the air, I have to remember that I'm in competition with a thriller program called "Renfrew of the Mounted."

FRANK. I used to listen to that program. Renfrew always gets his man. [MIRANDA *looks at* FRANK, *surprised at his first contribution to the conversation.*]

MIRANDA. Did Dave say you lived in San Francisco?

FRANK. Yes, Mrs. Valkonen.

MIRANDA. And how long have you been away from home?

FRANK. I came abroad just last summer. I was going to the Sorbonne in Paris.

MIRANDA. Oh! You're a student.

FRANK. Yes, I am. I had an exchange scholarship from my own school, Leland Stanford.

MIRANDA. You must be brilliant! What sort of things were you studying?

FRANK. Well—I particularly wanted to study French verse forms. I realize it sounds pretty ridiculous—

BEN. The terrible truth is that Frank wants to be a poet. [BEN *has to laugh at that.*]

MIRANDA. Now, really—I don't see anything to laugh at.

FRANK. Perhaps you would if you could read any of my attempts.

MIRANDA. I'd love to read some of your poetry. When I was a young girl, my greatest hero was Rupert Brooke. Maybe now that you're here—and have all this experience—maybe you'll write as he did. "Honour has come back, as a king to earth, And paid his subjects with a royal wage; and Nobleness walks in our ways again; and we have come into our heritage."

FRANK. I'm afraid I could never write like Rupert Brooke, even if I were that good. He was always singing of the heroism of war.

MIRANDA. Oh! And you see it as unheroic?

FRANK. Yes, Mrs. Valkonen. I do.

BEN. In addition to being a poet—Frank is also a rabid pacifist.

MIRANDA. I'm glad to hear it. My husband is a pacifist, too. You must talk with him while you're driving to Viipuri.

FRANK. I hope I have that privilege.

BEN. I've been a pacifist myself, in my time. I used to think, I'll never let my children grow up to get into this mass murder. But now I've got to the stage of figuring I ought to help put the murderers out of business *before* my children grow up and have to fight 'em themselves.

DAVE. Have you got any children, Ben?

BEN. No. It was all hypothetical.

MIRANDA. But you came here, to Finland. You came through mine fields and submarines, didn't you?

FRANK. Yes, we did.

MIRANDA. What made you come through all that into this little war?

FRANK. Because I'm a crazy fool, that's why.

MIRANDA. That's interesting. How many crazy fools do you suppose there are in America?

DAVE. I can name four hundred and seventy-three of my own acquaintance.

BEN. The pioneers were fools. And as for that goof Columbus—why didn't *he* stay home and mind his own business? [*He is crossing to help himself to another glass of eggnog.*]

DAVE. Go easy on that punch, Ben. You've got to drive the ambulance.

BEN. You can count on me, Dave.

MIRANDA. [*To* RUTKOWSKI.] Have you ever met any Americans before, Major?

RUTKOWSKI. No, I'm sorry, I have not.

MIRANDA. Then this will give you a faint idea.

RUTKOWSKI. I am glad of the opportunity. I have often wondered what it could be like to be an American—to believe, even for a moment, that such things as peace and security are possible. You see, we have never been permitted such belief. For us, the sun rose each morning among our enemies—and it set among our enemies. And now, it is high noon, and our enemies have joined together over our country—and we are gone.

DAVE. It isn't always so completely delightful to be an American, Major. Sometimes even we have an uncomfortable feeling of insecurity. I imagine that Pontius Pilate didn't feel entirely at peace with himself. He knew that this was a good, just man, who didn't deserve death. He was against a crown of thorns on principle. But when they cried, "Crucify Him!" all Pilate could say was, "Bring me a basin of water, so that I can wash my hands of the whole matter." [KAARLO *comes in, dressed in his uniform.* UNCLE WALDEMAR *comes after him. All guests rise.*]

KAARLO. No—please—don't get up. Gentlemen—this is my Uncle, Mr. Sederstrum.

UNCLE. WALDEMAR. How do you do? [*All greet him.* MIRANDA *is staring at* KAARLO *in his uniform. He looks at her, smiles lamely.*]

KAARLO. Now I'll have a glass of that eggnog. Then I suppose we should go?

RUTKOWSKKI. [*Looking at his watch.*] I'm afraid so.

MIRANDA. Bring a glass for Uncle Waldemar, too, Dave.

BEN. To think that I should be going to Viipuri in company with a winner of the Nobel Prize.

KAARLO. I hope we don't get lost on the way. I have no sense of direction whatever. We'll rely on Major Rutkowski to guide us. The Major has been in the Mannerheim Line. Did he tell you about it? [*This to* MIRANDA, *as he pours his eggnog.*]

MIRANDA. No. He didn't.

KAARLO. Oh—he says it's very dull there. [*Lifts his glass.*] Well, gentlemen, I beg leave to drink to you, our friends from the United States and from Poland. [*All move into a circle at the left.*]

DAVE. Thank you, Doctor.

RUTKOWSKI. And long life to the Republic of Finland!

ALL. Hear, hear!

BEN. And to you, Doctor. [*They drink.*]

KAARLO. Why, Miranda, it's good! Why don't we have this every day? [FRANK *goes to piano and starts playing "Auld Lang Syne." All sing. . . .* KAATRI *comes in at the right. She wears the Lotta uniform. She is very pale.*]

MIRANDA. Kaatri! [*She goes quickly to* KAATRI, *who is looking wildly around room at all the strangers.*]

KAATRI. Mrs. Valkonen—I had to see you—

MIRANDA. Have you heard from Erik?

KAATRI. No. But I must talk to you—

DAVE. Come on, boys. Get your coats and hats on. We'll wait outside, Mrs. Valkonen.

JOE. Certainly. [*They start to go out.*]

MIRANDA. You'll forgive me, Major Rutkowski. We'll be out in just a moment.

RUTKOWSKI. Of course. [RUTKOWSKI *goes out at the right after* DAVE, JOE, BEN *and* FRANK.]

MIRANDA. Now, Kaatri dear—what is it?

KAATRI. I've written every day to Erik. I haven't heard from him since that first letter two weeks ago. I've got to see him, Mrs. Valkonen. Don't you think they could give him a little leave?

MIRANDA. He'll surely have to leave soon, dear. The Russians have to stop attacking some time. Isn't that so, Kaarlo?

KAARLO. Of course it is. Erik's all right. In fact, he's probably enjoying himself. He likes that energetic life. Now—really—I must go. . . . [*Starts to say good-bye to* UNCLE WALDEMAR.]

KAATRI. No—please, Dr. Valkonen. There's something I have to ask you. I'm going to have a baby.

MIRANDA. [*Rising.*] Darling. [*She takes her in her arms.*]

KAARLO. Well! I'm very happy to hear it.

KAATRI. I'm not happy. I don't want it! Dr. Valkonen! What can I do to stop it? Please tell me what I can do.

MIRANDA. You're not ashamed, Kaatri? There's nothing for you to be ashamed of.

KAATRI. No—I'm not! But I don't want it. You've got to help me, Dr. Valkonen.

KAARLO. Have you told your family of this?

KAATRI. No. It wouldn't be easy for them to understand, as you do, about Erik and me.

MIRANDA. Why don't you want to have a baby, Kaatri?

KAATRI. I'm working. It would make me useless—just another person to be cared for—

MIRANDA. That's not being useless.

KAATRI. It is now! What good would it be to bring a child into a world like this?

He would have no country—no hope. *Please*, Dr. Valkonen. I'm sorry to be troubling you. But—just tell me some doctor that I can see.

KAARLO. You will see Dr. Palm. Miranda —you know him.

MIRANDA. Yes, Kaarlo.

KAARLO. You take Kaatri to see him. Tell him that this is our daughter-in-law, and her baby will be our grandchild. [KAATRI *looks at him, with terror.*] Yes, my dear, you are going to have that child.

KAATRI. [*Hysterical.*] No—no! I won't have it! [*She tries desperately to break away from them.*] I won't have a child born under a curse!

MIRANDA. Quiet, dear. Please. [*She seats* KAATRI *beside her.*]

KAATRI. [*Making another frantic attempt to get away.*] No! You won't help me. I'll find a doctor—

KAARLO. Do as my wife tells you, Kaatri! You love Erik, and he loves you. You were willing to be married to him. You have taken responsibility. The highest responsibility! You are not going to evade it.

MIRANDA. Kaatri—Kaatri! [KAATRI *submits.* KAARLO *leans over her.*]

KAARLO. Whatever happens to our country, your child will not be born under a curse. It will be born to the greatest opportunity that any child has ever known, since the beginning of time. Remember that, and be brave. . . . Now—I can't keep them waiting. Good-bye, Uncle Waldemar. I'll be back soon.

UNCLE WALDEMAR. Yes, Kaarlo. Goodbye. [*They kiss.* KAARLO *leans over and kisses* KAATRI's *head, then takes* MIRANDA's *hand. She rises, looks back, motions to* UNCLE WALDEMAR *to come to* KAATRI.]

KAARLO. Come on, darling. [*They go out at the right.* KAATRI *is crumpled up on couch.* UNCLE WALDEMAR *goes over to her, sits down beside her, and takes her in his arms.*]

UNCLE WALDEMAR. Now—don't cry, Kaatri. Pay attention to what Dr. Valkonen told you. *He* knows what he is saying. If he tells you there is good hope, you can believe him.

CURTAIN

SCENE 5

Dave Corween's room in the Hotel Kamp in Helsinki. It is evening. Upper right is a door leading to corridor. At the left is a door leading to a bedroom. The room is in pretty much of a mess. At the right, on a chair, is DAVE's *typewriter, with copy paper and carbon strewn about. At the left, large table, on which is the same broadcasting apparatus seen in first scene.* DAVE *is at microphone reading from a typescript before him.* GUS *is up-stage, left, with his earphones on.*

DAVE. In an attempt to surround the main force of the Finnish army on the Karelian Isthmus, the Russians are now making determined attacks across Viipuri Bay. The Mannerheim Line, supposedly impregnable bulwark of Finland's defense, has been shattered. The bombardment of these defenses, and of Viipuri itself, has now reached the terrible total of three hundred thousand shells a day. Looking at the ruination in Viipuri, I could not help thinking of the despairing prophecies made by H. G. Wells in *The Shape of Things to Come*. Here was the awful picture of the collapse of our Western civilization, the beginning of the Age of Frus- tration. Stores and factories, public libraries, museums, movie theatres—hospitals and schools and homes—all reduced to junk heaps. The Soviet Union is being generous in the expenditure of its ammunition, and extravagantly generous with the life blood of its men. Never again will these workers of the world arise! But in Moscow, the official propaganda bureau broadcasts constantly in Finnish, sending soothing encouragement to this beleaguered little country. Today I heard them say, and I quote, "The Red Army sends greetings to the workers of Finland. The Red Army does not destroy. That is why the workers in every country love the

Red Army." And—perhaps, in the end—"love" will conquer all. . . . This is David Corween in Helsinki, returning you now to C. B. S. in New York. [GUS *switches off radio.* DAVE *turns to* JOE.] How was that, Joe? Do you think I'm holding my own against Renfrew of the Mounted?

JOE. I think you're wasting your breath, Dave. Nobody's listening.

GUS. I don't see how they can—with the complicated hook-up we've got now. And if one of those bombs today had landed fifty yards farther west, there wouldn't be any broadcasting station here at all. Did you see those craters?

DAVE. Yes.

GUS. Boy! They must be dropping those two-ton bombs now, like they had in Spain.

DAVE. Are you going to be flying around here now to protect us, Joe?

JOE. I doubt it. I guess I'll get shipped right back to the lines.

GUS. Well, I hope they don't keep us here until it's too late to get out. I'd hate to go through Warsaw again. I think I'll go down and see if I can get a cup of coffee. Where's the sugar?

DAVE. Here. [*Hands* GUS *envelope filled with sugar that has been lying on couch.*]

GUS. [*To* JOE.] See you later.

JOE. Sure. [GUS *goes out.*] Say, Dave—when you were in Viipuri, did you see anything of Ben and Frank and Dr. Valkonen?

DAVE. Yes. They got their hospitals established there and now they're working day and night to evacuate them. Ben and Frank don't seem to be having a very good time in this war.

JOE. I guess they're in a tough spot now, with those attacks across Viipuri Bay.

DAVE. Yes, I've got to go and see Mrs. Valkonen and try to think of something encouraging to say. Last week I was up in the north. I saw some of the ski troops in action.

JOE. Did you see Mrs. Valkonen's son?

DAVE. No. But I got an idea of what he must be going through. Poor kid. I remember the first time I came here he said that Finland wouldn't be in danger unless there was a counter-revolution in Russia. He had that much faith in them. Well—it seems that the counter-revolution has come.

JOE. Something else has come. I saw something today that might interest you.

DAVE. What was it?

JOE. Maybe I oughtn't to be talking to the press.

DAVE. Now listen, Joe—have another drink.

JOE. Thanks [*Pours himself another drink.*]

DAVE. You understand, Joe. Anything you tell me will be considered strictly confidential. I'll only try to pass it on to the A.P., the U.P. and the radio audience. But the censorship will stop me, so your secrets will be sacred. [JOE *drinks.*]

JOE. Well, they sent me out reconnoitering. I wanted to know what was the greatest point of Russian concentration. I had to fly very low. The weather was closing in and the ceiling was only seven or eight hundred feet, when I was coming back. I couldn't find the field I took off from. That's why I had to fly back here to make my report to the war office.

DAVE. What did you report, Joe?

JOE. I saw some staff cars coming up to the town that seemed to be general headquarters. I didn't know the name of the town, but I identified it for them on the map. I dived to give those cars a few bursts. They were full of staff officers, all right. But they weren't Russians. They were Nazis. It gave me a thrill. All this time, in fighting the Russians, I've felt just a little bit uncomfortable—you can imagine it, Dave, after my experience with the Loyalists. You know I couldn't help saying, "God forgive them—for they know not what they do." If that's the right quotation.

DAVE. It's good enough.

JOE. But when I saw those Nazis—those arrogant bastards—and I could even see the looks on their faces—all I could think of was, "God forgive *me* if I miss this glorious opportunity." I let 'em have it. It was a beautiful sight to see 'em diving into the ditches, mussing their slick gray uniforms in the mud.

DAVE. Did you get any of them?

JOE. I'm afraid I'll never know. It was just then that the Russian planes came up. And I had to take my ship away from there.

DAVE. I thought it was about time for

the Nazis to be taking a hand in this war. No wonder the tide of battle has turned. I guess they've decided there has been enough of this nonsense of Finland's resistance. Probably they want the Russians to get busy somewhere else. [JOE *puts his glass down and stands up.*]

JOE. Is there any news from home?

DAVE. Yes. . . . This has been the biggest season in the history of Miami Beach. The University of Southern California won the national basketball championship. The Beaux Arts Ball was an outstanding success. [JOE *crosses and looks into bedroom at the left.*]

JOE. Good! Say, Dave—can I have the use of that elegant bathtub of yours?

DAVE. Certainly. There may be some hot water, and maybe not.

JOE. How are you fixed for a clean shirt and underwear and socks? [JOE *goes into bedroom.*]

DAVE. I guess Gus and I can fit you out between us. [DAVE *follows* JOE *out. There is a knock at door at the right.*] Come in! [MIRANDA *comes in. Her face is pale. She comes in quietly, closing door behind her.* DAVE *calls from off left.*] I'll be right out. [MIRANDA *looks around room, then sits down. After a moment* DAVE *comes back, and is startled to see her.*] Mrs. Valkonen! [*He closes bedroom door behind him.*]

MIRANDA. Hello, Dave. I hope I'm not disturbing you. Mr. Shuman told me I might come up—I met him in the lobby.

DAVE. Of course, Mrs. Valkonen. I apologize for the mess here. . . . Would you like anything to drink?

MIRANDA. No, thank you. I came to ask you for some help, Dave.

DAVE. Anything that I can do—

MIRANDA. I want to get my daughter-in-law out of this country.

DAVE. Your daughter-in-law? [*Sits down, near her.*]

MIRANDA. Yes. You've met her—Kaatri. She was married a few days ago to my son, Erik. They were married in the hospital, before he died.

DAVE. Oh—I'm terribly sorry.

MIRANDA. I know you're sorry, Dave. . . . Kaatri is going to have a baby. . . . She's very ill. I've made all the arrangements to get her to Norway, and then to New York. But she has to leave right away.

I need some American money, Dave. Could you lend me fifty dollars? It will be paid back.

DAVE. Will that be enough?

MIRANDA. Oh, yes—that will be plenty. And— [*She opens her handbag and takes out sheet of paper.*] —here is the name and address of my aunt in Boston. When you get back to America, just write to her and tell her where to send the money. [DAVE *takes paper and puts it down on table. Takes out his wallet.*] You see—the Finnish money is worth very little in foreign exchange now. By the time Kaatri arrives in New York, it might be completely worthless. That's why I had to have dollars. If it's inconvenient for you—I'm sure I can get it somewhere else—so please don't hesitate to—

DAVE. It's perfectly convenient, and I'm very much flattered that you came to me. [*Gives her fifty dollars.*]

MIRANDA. Thank you. We had an awful time persuading Kaatri to go. We never could have persuaded her if she weren't too ill to resist. She's strong—but there are limits. [*She puts money in her handbag.*]

DAVE. I wish you were going with her.

MIRANDA. I wish I could. I should like to be present at the birth of my grandchild. Poor Kaatri. She'll have a bad time of it, all alone there. . . . Perhaps she'll have a son, and he'll grow up a nice, respectable New Englander and go to Harvard and wonder why he has an odd name like Valkonen. . . . Erik wasn't very badly wounded. He might have pulled through if he hadn't been in such a state of terrible exhaustion. It was a lucky thing that we learned where he was and got to him. I sent word to Kaarlo. I don't know where he is—somewhere around Viipuri. [*She looks at* DAVE.] They're getting closer, aren't they, Dave?

DAVE. Yes. [MIRANDA *rises.*]

MIRANDA. I'm very grateful for that loan. I hope you will come to see Uncle Waldemar and me. We're always there.

DAVE. Thank you, Mrs. Valkonen. I— I wish to God you'd let me really *do* something.

MIRANDA. But you've done a lot, Dave. That fifty dollars—

DAVE. It's not much satisfaction to know that fifty dollars is the best I can do.

MIRANDA. It's all I want, Dave. All I can use. I was desperately anxious to get Kaatri out of the country. You can understand why. It means one little link with the future. It gives us the illusion of survival—and perhaps it isn't just an illusion. . . . Good-bye, Dave.

DAVE. Good-bye. [MIRANDA goes out.]

CURTAIN

SCENE 6

Classroom in a little country schoolhouse in eastern Finland. It is afternoon of a gloomy day, a few days after preceding scene. This schoolhouse is new and clean, designed in the most modern style. Huge, opaque glass windows would admit plenty of soft sunshine if there were any today. At center upstage is a dais. Before it is a row of pupils' desks. The size of these desks indicates that this is a classroom for little children of nine or ten. There is a blackboard with arithmetical problems. On walls are tacked rows of sketches done by pupils. Around room on walls are painted, in decorative, colored Finnish script, the first ten lines of the "Kalevala." (Of course, half of these lines are on the walls which we do not see.) On the window sills, little plants are sprouting in pots. There is a door at the extreme left, leading to another schoolroom. At one of the pupils' desks, the right one, GOSDEN is sitting solemnly playing solitaire with an old, dirty pack. He is a mild, tired Englishman, about forty years old. Wears uniform of an infantry soldier. His rifle lies on desk before him. There is a scuffle at door, left. GOSDEN leaps to his feet, picks up his rifle and aims it at door. BEN GICHNER and FRANK OLMSTEAD come in. Both carry large haversacks. Both are very cold.

GOSDEN. Who are you? [BEN *and* FRANK *raise their arms immediately.*]

BEN. Friends! We're not Russians and we're not armed.

GOSDEN. [*Lowering his rifle.*] Glad to see you. Sorry but I'm a bit jumpy these days.

BEN. That's all right, pal.

GOSDEN. Americans, eh!

BEN. That's right. What are you—English?

GOSDEN. Yes. The name is Gosden. I don't rightly know what my rank is in this army, but I call myself "Sergeant."

BEN. [*Crossing and shaking hands with* GOSDEN.] Glad to know you, Sergeant. My name is Ben Gichner—this is Frank Olmstead.

FRANK. Glad to know you. [FRANK *sits at desk at the left.*]

GOSDEN. Thank you. It's a pleasure to have your company. I was getting the wind up, all alone here. [*Sees their uniforms.*] You chaps in the Medical Corps?

BEN. Yes. Ambulance drivers. Only—we've lost our ambulance—it's frozen stiff as a goat in a snowdrift. When the Russians occupy this territory they'll come into possession of a Buick.

GOSDEN. You wouldn't have much use for it here. There haven't been many wounded since we retreated from the Mannerheim Line. Only dead and missing. [FRANK *rests head on his arms.*]

FRANK. How far are the Russians from here?

GOSDEN. I wish I knew. They've probably occupied those islands out there in Viipuri Bay. Maybe they've already reached this shore. All I can say is the last time I saw them they were coming in this direction, driving us across the ice. I've been retreating across the ice for days. I've felt like a bloody Eskimo. [*Looks about room.*] Nice little schoolhouse, this. [*Reaches in his pocket.*] Like a bit of chocolate?

FRANK. No, thanks.

BEN. [*Sitting up.*] I'll have some.

GOSDEN. [*Tossing him some candy.*] It's good for energy.

BEN. Thanks, pal.

FRANK. How long have you been in this war?

GOSDEN. I joined up in London, just after Christmas.

FRANK. Why? What did you want to come here for?

GOSDEN. [Smiles.] Are you trying to trap me into making any remarks about fighting for freedom and democracy?

FRANK. [Wearily.] No.

GOSDEN. Because I had enough of that muck when I fought in the last war!

FRANK. I'm just interested to know why anybody volunteered.

GOSDEN. Well, you might say that my case is no different from any of the others. I came because I was bored, fed up. My wife and two little children were sent to Cornwall in the evacuation. Then I lost my job. I was working in the furniture department at Harrod's—and who wants to buy furniture in war time? I couldn't join up with our own army—too old. All I could do was walk the streets looking at nothing. There was no news to read in the papers—except about heroic little Finland. On Christmas, I felt I couldn't stick it out any longer. So—I thought—why not have a go at heroic little Finland? And here I am. Where I shall be tomorrow, I really couldn't say. [RUTKOWSKI comes in from the left, followed by KAARLO, who wears a Red Cross arm band on his uniform. All men rise to attention.]

RUTKOWSKI. At ease! Are there any more men here?

GOSDEN. No, sir. Only me. I was with Captain Vertti's company, but we got separated. I didn't know just where to go next, sir, so I stopped here for a bit of a rest.

RUTKOWSKI. Has there been much shelling here?

GOSDEN. I've heard plenty of heavies, overhead, but none dropping here, sir. There's also been a lot of Bolshie planes, flying low—looking the situation over, I expect.

RUTKOWSKI. They're probably shelling the railroad line between Viipuri and Helsinki. Trying to cut off all possibilities of re-enforcement. I'm going out to find if there is any one in command here. [KAARLO is greatly interested in the school-room; crosses to the right.]

KAARLO. This schoolhouse would do well for a field ambulance station. [BEN and FRANK have sat down.]

GOSDEN. [Still standing.] Begging your pardon, sir. You couldn't find a more exposed place.

RUTKOWSKI. Yes—you might say that this is Finland—small—clean—and exposed. [With a slight shrug.] I shall be back presently, Doctor. [Goes out at the left.]

KAARLO. We'll be waiting, Major. [To GOSDEN.] I'm Dr. Valkonen. How do you do? [Somewhat to GOSDEN's surprise, KAARLO extends his hand. They shake.]

GOSDEN. Thank you, sir. My name is Gosden.

KAARLO. I gather that things here are a bit disorganized.

GOSDEN. And no wonder, sir. It's a miracle that there's any sign of an army left—the way they've been pushing us. [GOSDEN sits. KAARLO crosses to dais and looks at blackboard.]

KAARLO. You know—they must have left this school very quickly—right in the midst of an arithmetic lesson. Look—there's a multiplication problem that was never finished. The pupils were probably delighted but— [Pointing to sketches.] —they evidently had to leave without knowing which picture won first prize.

BEN. How old would the kids be in a school like this?

KAARLO. From seven to twelve I should judge. It's just a little country school. I wish you could see it when the children are here. The boys are on that side, the girls there. When the teacher comes in, the boys all rise and bow stiffly. The girls make their little curtsies. Maybe in their hearts they loathe the teacher—but they're always very polite. And all very full of moral preachments. Oh, yes. . . . You see that inscription all around the walls? That's from the Kalevala—the epic poem of Finland. It had its beginnings in the songs of our minstrels a thousand years ago. Your poet, Longfellow, knew the Kalevala and used its rhythm in Hiawatha. [Looks up, and starts to recite, at first with a sort of tender amusement, and then with increasing solemnity. His eyes travel about room as he follows inscription.]

"Let us clasp our hands together,
Let us interlock our fingers;
Let us sing a cheerful measure,

Let us use our best endeavors
While our dear ones hearken to us,
And our loved ones are instructed,
While the young are standing round
    us,
Of the rising generation,
Let them learn the words of magic,
And recall our songs and legends."
[*He is quiet for a moment, looking toward
the right. Then he turns to others.*] Every
Finnish child learns about the Kalevala—
just as Americans learn those words about
Life, Liberty and the Pursuit of Happi-
ness.

FRANK. [*Earnestly.*] Dr. Valkonen—

KAARLO. Yes, Frank?

FRANK. I've wanted to ask you a question—

KAARLO. Yes?

FRANK. About your book— [FRANK *pulls
a paper-covered book, badly dog-eared,
from his jacket pocket.*]

KAARLO. You've been carrying that
around with you?

FRANK. Yes. I bought it in Viipuri when
we first went there.

BEN. Frank is more worried about your
book, Doctor, than he is about the Russians.

FRANK [*He opens book to last page.*]
There's a lot of it I don't understand, but
what I wanted to ask you about most is
the very end.

KAARLO. What is it at the end?

FRANK. [*Reads.*] "How long, O Lord,
before we shall hear the sound of the Sev-
enth Angel of the Apocalypse? Have you
forgotten the promise of St. John? 'And
they shall see his face, and his name shall
be in their foreheads. And there shall be
no night there and they need no candle,
neither light of the sun; for the Lord
giveth them light; and they shall reign
forever and ever.' How long, O Lord,
before we shall be given to see the true
revelation?" [FRANK *closes book and looks
at* KAARLO.] Why did you conclude a
scientific work with Biblical words—and
what do you mean by the true revelation?

KAARLO. [*Simply.*] It's the revealing to
us of ourselves—of what we are—and what
we may be. [*Smiles.*] Of course—we can
all use the Book of Revelation to substan-
tiate our own theories. It's an eternally
effective device. I have heard evangelist

charlatans quote it to prove that if you
do not accept their nonsense and pay for
it, you will most surely burn in hell. But
there is something profound in those words
I quoted. That unknown Jewish mystic
who wrote that—somehow, unconsciously,
he knew that man will find the true name
of God in his own forehead, in the mysteries of his own mind. "And there shall
be no night there." That is the basis of all
the work I have done.

FRANK. And how do you feel about that
work now, Dr. Valkonen?

KAARLO. I think I've learned a great deal
in the last few months. Research work in
the field! I never dreamed I would have
such a vast laboratory, with so many spe-
cimens.

BEN. Have you arrived at any new conclusions, Doctor?

KAARLO. Not conclusions, I'm afraid.
Just—somewhat stronger suspicions. It is
wonderful to see what men are capable
of—what courage—what endurance—what
utter lack of selfishness. And what a tragedy that these heroic qualities can be
tested only by disease. That's what all this
is, you know—disease. All of this—reason-
less war—aimless revolution—it's a psychological epidemic. [*Rises. It is as though
he were lecturing to a class.*] Scientists had
seen it coming, for a long time, long before 1914, even. But we had no conception
of its extent. And now the very belief of
men that they can insulate themselves
against it is in itself a sign of lunacy. The
germs of that disease travel on the air
waves. The only defenses are still here—
behind the forehead. . . . [*Pauses and
smiles, looking particularly at* GOSDEN.]
I apologize, gentlemen, for carrying on a
conversation which must be extremely boring to you.

GOSDEN. I'm an ignorant man, sir. I
haven't read this book. I didn't even know
I was in the presence of any one who had
written a book. But—from what you've
said—I have a feeling it's all hopeless. I
shouldn't care to die believing *that.*

KAARLO. Then you won't die believing
it's hopeless. That's the point, my friend.
You have lived in faith—the light is in
you—and it is the light which gives the
strength that defeats death. It's only the
fearful—the unbelieving—those who have
sold themselves to the murderers and the

liars—they are the only ones who can really die.

FRANK. But how can you deny that the light is going out—it's going fast—everywhere?

KAARLO. [*With a growing sense of excitement.*] It is just beginning to burn with a healthy flame. I know this, because I have seen it. I have seen it in all kinds of men, of all races, and all varieties of faith. They are coming to consciousness. Look at all the millions of men now under arms, and all those that are fearful that arms may be thrust upon them. Are there any illusions of glory among any of them? None whatever! Isn't that progress?

BEN. Far be it from me to argue, Doctor—but I can't see the difference whether men go to war because of illusions of glory, or just in a spirit of grim resignation.

KAARLO. There is all the difference. Because those illusions, when shattered, leave men hollow. When men lose their illusions, they say, "Oh, what's the use? What have we got to live for?" They are devitalized by the conviction of futility. But grim resignation, as you call it, that makes a man say, "This is an evil job—but I have to do it." And when men say that, they are already beginning to ask, "But *why* do I have to do it? *Why* must this evil go on forever?" And when men start asking questions, they are not satisfied until they find the answers. That is consciousness. And for the first time in history, consciousness is not just the privilege of a few secluded philosophers. It is free for all. For the first time, individual men are fighting to know themselves. . . . Forgive me, gentlemen. I forget myself. I think I am lecturing at the Medical Institute. But— [*Pauses to listen to guns.*] —the Russians are only a short distance away. This may be my last lecture. So—please permit me to finish. . . . Listen! What you hear now—this terrible sound that fills the earth—it is the death rattle. One may say easily and dramatically that it is the death rattle of civilization. But—I choose to believe differently. I believe it is the long deferred death rattle of the primordial beast. We have within ourselves the power to conquer bestiality, not with our muscles and our swords, but with the power of the light that is in our minds.

What a thrilling challenge this is to all Science! To play its part in the ultimate triumph of evolution. To help speed the day when man becomes genuinely human, instead of the synthetic creature—part bogus angel, part actual brute—that he has imagined himself in the dark past— [*Sound of an approaching motorcycle is heard.*] Is that an aeroplane? [*All listen, tensely.*]

GOSDEN. No. It's a motorbike. [*Sound stops.*] Just a despatch rider, I expect. Maybe it's orders. [JOE BURNETT *comes in from the left.*]

JOE. Hello, Ben. Hello, Frank. Hello, Doctor Valkonen.

FRANK. Joe!

BEN. Where did *you* drop from?

JOE. I saw Major Rutkowski up the road. He said you were in here.

KAARLO. Mr. Burnett! I am delighted to see you. Are you flying on this front now?

JOE. I was—up till half an hour ago. I was shot down. First time that ever happened to me. I just managed to make a landing behind our lines. I got a motorcycle and I'm going back to headquarters to see if they have any more planes.

GOSDEN. Were you scouting the Russian lines?

JOE. Yes.

GOSDEN. How do things look?

JOE. Not too good. They're bringing up everything.

BEN. Have you been in Helsinki lately, Joe?

JOE. Yes. I was there a few days ago.

BEN. Is Dave Corween still on the job?

JOE. Yes. He's still telling bed-time stories.

KAARLO. And I hope you called at my house, Mr. Burnett? Did you see my wife?

JOE. No—I didn't. [*Braces himself and crosses to* KAARLO.] I—I don't know how to say it, Doctor Valkonen—although God knows I've said it so many times before—but—I want you to know that you have my sympathy.

KAARLO. Your sympathy? [KAARLO *looks at him with such intense questioning that* JOE *gulps.*] Why do I have your sympathy, Mr. Burnett?

JOE. You don't know about your son?

KAARLO. No. [*Looks levelly at* JOE.] He's dead?

JOE. Yes.

KAARLO. Killed in action?

JOE. I believe he died in hospital, of wounds.

KAARLO. When was this?

JOE. I don't quite know. I heard of it only from Dave. He had seen Mrs. Valkonen.

KAARLO. Is—my wife well?

JOE. Yes, Doctor. She told Dave that she had been with your son in the hospital. He was married there, to Miss Alquist, before he died. His wife has gone to America. . . . I—I didn't know, Doctor, that I should be the bearer of this news— [His voice trails off.]

GOSDEN. [Rising, and speaking with great diffidence.] I should like, sir, to be permitted to put in my word of sympathy, too.

BEN. And mine also, Doctor.

FRANK. [Rising.] Wouldn't you like us to get out of here, Doctor Valkonen?

KAARLO. No, no. Thank you. And thank you for telling me, Mr. Burnett. I imagine my wife has written me all this, but we have moved about so much that there have been no letters in weeks. I'm sorry you had to undergo this embarrassment. [RUTKOWSKI comes in. Carries a cartridge belt with a revolver in a holster.]

RUTKOWSKI. I found the commanding officer. The Russians have occupied all the islands around Uuras. They're bringing tanks over the ice, and they're going to attack in force here. The Finns are forming up to drive them back. They need more men. They seem to be organizing the defense very well. But they have no reserves. They need more men. There's no point in trying to organize a field ambulance station here, Doctor. I brought this revolver and belt for you. It was salvaged from some officer who was killed. There are rifles for you men to use. [Hands belt and holster to KAARLO, who takes out revolver and stares at it.]

FRANK. We're to fight?

RUTKOWSKI. There's no compulsion if you don't wish to go.

JOE. [Quietly.] I'll be glad to go, Major.

BEN. So will I.

RUTKOWSKI. [To JOE.] Not you, Lieutenant. If there are any planes left, we need them in the air. You will report back to headquarters at Sakkijaarvi.

JOE. [Resigned.] Very good, sir.

KAARLO. We must go now? At once?

RUTKOWSKI. We may as well wait here for a little while. There will be plenty of warning when the attack starts.

KAARLO. Then—I would like to write a letter. [Puts revolver and belt down on desk.] Perhaps you will take it with you, Mr. Burnett? There must be some way they could send it on to Helsinki.

JOE. I'll do everything I possibly can, Doctor Valkonen.

KAARLO. [To RUTKOWSKI.] If I'm not finished when you're ready to go, just call me.

RUTKOWSKI. I will, Doctor. [KAARLO goes out right, taking his fountain pen from his pocket.] Have any of you gentlemen a cigarette? [BEN hands him one.] Thank you. . . . I suppose Doctor Valkonen wants to write his valedictory.

JOE. It isn't that, Major. I just gave him the news that his son was killed.

RUTKOWSKI. Oh—when I came in—I saw his face—but I didn't know the explanation. [Lights his cigarette, being careful to mask flame with his greatcoat.]

FRANK. [With sudden vehemence.] Do you know that Doctor Valkonen believes in the teachings of Christ? He believes in them as if they were scientific facts, which can yet be proved. He says so in his book. He says you can't resist evil by building Maginot Lines and big navies. The true defenses of man are in man, himself. . . . So now—there's nothing left for that great thinker to do but take a gun and go up there and shoot. [He has crossed above desks and looks at revolver.]

BEN. And how about you, Frank? Are you going up? What does the old conscience say?

FRANK. What the hell do you think it says? How could I ever live with myself again if I didn't go? That's what happens when you expose yourself to this. Oh, God —how many times have I taken an oath that if the United States were ever again duped into going to war, I'll be a conscientious objector! Let them put me in Leavenworth. I'd rather be there. I'd consider it takes more courage to be there than in the front line. But—here's the choice—given to me now—and I haven't got the guts to say, "No—I won't fight." [He has crossed to the left and sits down on floor beside JOE. RUTKOWSKI is sitting on center desk. Others are seated at other desks.]

BEN. Why don't you put all that into a poem, Frank?

FRANK. All right, Ben—go ahead and kid me.

BEN. I don't feel in a position to kid you, Frank. I've had a few necessary changes of heart myself. Once I lost a good job because they decided I was a Red. Yes. I've spent hours arguing that the Soviet Union is the greatest sociological advance in history—the greatest force for peace on earth today. . . . Now—go ahead and kid *me!*

RUTKOWSKI. [*Bitterly.*] Nobody is responsible for his opinions now. There *are* no opinions on anything.

GOSDEN. [*To* RUTKOWSKI.] How do our positions look in the line, sir?

RUTKOWSKI. Fairly well placed.

GOSDEN. Do you think we would have any chance of holding them?

RUTKOWSKI. [*With no emotion.*] No—I don't think so.

BEN. [*With a nervous laugh.*] I take it, Major—you feel we're all condemned to death?

RUTKOWSKI. Yes. [BEN *stands up. He is whistling.*]

BEN. I can't help agreeing with you, Frank. It seems a silly way to end your life.

JOE. Any way is silly. A cousin of mine was killed—he and his girl both—driving home from a debutante party at the Ritz in New York. He was a little tight, and he didn't notice the Dead End sign—and —phft!—right into the East River!

FRANK. And is that any reason why we should fight—and die?

GOSDEN. [*To* FRANK.] Every one of us can find plenty of reasons for *not* fighting, and they're the best reasons in the world. But—the time comes when you've bloody well got to fight—and you might just as well go cheerfully.

FRANK. [*Rising to his knees.*] Cheerful! What are you, anyway? Are you so stupid you can't even *think?* You said you have a wife and two little children in England. Aren't you giving any thought to them now?

GOSDEN. [*In a choked voice.*] I'll have to ask you not to mention them. My people know what I'm doing—and why.

FRANK. [*Sinking back on his heels.*] Excuse me.

RUTKOWSKI. [*Looking off toward the left.*] Poor Doctor Valkonen. He is a philosopher. He is also, for some strange reason, an optimist. He will be better dead.

BEN. Why do you say that, Major?

RUTKOWSKI. Perhaps it is only because I am Polish. [*Looks levelly at* FRANK.] You asked this gentleman to give a thought to his wife and children in England. He can think of them happily. My wife—my baby —my father—and mother—are in Warsaw— or they were there, when the Nazis came. My wife is twenty-four years old. She is very beautiful. She is the most beautiful person I have ever known. And I have read in Cardinal Hlond's report, that he has sent to the Pope—I have read that the good-looking women and the girls in Poland have been sent into Germany to be whores. [*Rises quickly and raps at door at the right. Turns to others.*] Well!

GOSDEN. [*In a desperate effort to change subject.*] I wish I'd thought to write a line myself. I *did* think of it—but I didn't know what to say. I wish I'd written to my missus to tell her I'm going up the line in good company. [KAARLO *comes in from the right. He is sealing envelope.* BEN *slaps* GOSDEN *on the back.*]

KAARLO. Here you are, Mr. Burnett. [JOE *crosses and gets letter from* KAARLO.]

JOE. I'm sure it will be delivered safely. [*Shakes hands with* KAARLO, *and salutes* RUTKOWSKI, *who returns salute.*]

KAARLO. Thank you so much.

JOE. Good-bye, sir [GOSDEN *picks up his coat and rifle. All are now making preparations to go.* KAARLO *goes to desk to get belt and revolver and put them on.*]

GOSDEN. [*To* JOE.] Best of luck, mate.

JOE. Same to you. [GOSDEN *goes out.* JOE *is about to go.*]

BEN. Joe, if you ever get back, I wish you'd send a word to my mother. Mrs. Bessie Gichner—Cincinnati. You can get her address at the American Express Company's main office in New York. They all know me there.

JOE. [*As* BEN *goes out.*] I'll remember that, Ben . . . [*Starts out.*] If I get back—

FRANK. Hey, Joe—wait a minute. I've got a message, too! [JOE *and* FRANK *have gone out on this.* RUTKOWSKI *has been watching* KAARLO *with silent sympathy as he puts on belt.*]

RUTKOWSKI. Forgive me, Doctor Valkonen. I hadn't known of the great loss you have suffered.

KAARLO. Thank you. I had been expecting that news for a long time. I was prepared for it. My son had a good character—part Finnish, part American. He was not afraid. [*Starts to go.* RUTKOWSKI *is by door at the left.*]

RUTKOWSKI. Doctor, I think you had better take off that Red Cross arm band. [RUTKOWSKI *goes. It is now so dark that* KAARLO *is a silhouette as he rips off Red Cross arm band. Goes out. The sound of the guns increases.*]

CURTAIN

SCENE 7

The Valkonens' living room. The only noticeable difference in the room is that all autographed photographs have been removed from their frames. UNCLE WALDEMAR *is at a window, looking out. It is a beautiful, sunny day. After a moment,* DAVE *and* JOE *come in from dining room.* UNCLE WALDEMAR *turns quickly.*

UNCLE WALDEMAR. I was enjoying the beautiful day.

DAVE. It *is* beautiful. It's beginning to feel almost like spring.

UNCLE WALDEMAR. Did you have a nice lunch?

DAVE. Wonderful, thank you.

UNCLE WALDEMAR. I'll go help Miranda clear the dishes.

DAVE. We begged to be allowed to help, but were ordered out of the kitchen.

UNCLE WALDEMAR. Of course. [*Gives them a courtly bow.*] You are guests. [*Goes out.* DAVE *offers* JOE *a cigarette.*]

DAVE. An incredible display of stoicism.

JOE. God—I didn't know what to say. I never know what to say. Anything you can think of sounds so lame.

DAVE. You didn't need to say anything, Joe. She's lost everybody that she loves—and now she's in terrible danger of losing her own life. But it's a matter of principle that neither she nor any one else must ever admit that there are certain undertones of tragedy in the situation. After all the centuries, New England is still New England. You might even go so far as to say that it's still England. Keep a stiff upper lip.

JOE. How long do you figure it will take the Russians to get here?

DAVE. I don't know. But I suspect it won't be long. Berlin has given out orders that this little incident must end—and if the Russians don't hurry, there are going to be some serious tantrums in the Wilhelmstrasse.

JOE. This city might hold out for a long time, like Madrid.

DAVE. I hope not. Because if it comes to a siege, you'll see German battleships out there, doing their bit in the bombardment. I wouldn't like to be here when that happens. I saw them at Danzig when they were battering Westerplatte. I could see the Nazis, watching their own barrage. They were deriving a sexual thrill from that display of devastating power.

JOE. What happens to you when you get caught in a captured city?

DAVE. I know how to wave my little red passport. I can say "I'm an American journalist" in all languages. In Nanking, I had to say it in Japanese. Oh—I get pushed around a bit—but I always live to broadcast the final hours of another gallant little republic. . . . But what about you, Joe? Have you got a plane?

JOE. I don't know. I may be in the army now. It would be pretty humiliating to end my career in the god-damned infantry.

DAVE. [*Looking toward kitchen.*] That's what Doctor Valkonen did. [JOE *glances toward kitchen.*]

JOE. Listen, Dave—can't you get Mrs. Valkonen out of this—and the old man, too?

DAVE. I've tried—but they won't leave. They're going to wait here for whatever comes, the Russians, or the Nazis, or both. They've even planned how they'll burn the house down. That's required by Finnish tradition. It's like the scorched earth in China. Mrs. Valkonen wants to stay here and die, just as her husband did. She doesn't care what happens.

JOE. It's a pity.

DAVE. That's just what it is, Joe. A wholesale pity. Three months ago, the Soviet troops marched in. They had brass bands and truck-loads of propaganda with them. They thought it would be a grand parade through Finland, like May Day in the Red Square. So now—several hundred thousand men have been killed—millions of lives have been ruined. The cause of revolution all over the world has been set back incalculably. The Soviet Union has been reduced from the status of a great power to that of a great fraud. And the Nazis have won another bloodless victory. [MIRANDA and UNCLE WALDEMAR come in from kitchen, MIRANDA wears an apron, but her dress is, as always, very feminine and chic. DAVE and JOE rise.]

MIRANDA. Well—we've washed all the dishes and put them away neatly, and now Uncle Waldemar and I haven't a thing to do until supper. Sit down, Dave—Mr. Burnett.

JOE. I'm sorry, Mrs. Valkonen. I have to go and report for duty, whatever it is.

MIRANDA. Oh—I'm sorry. But thank you so much for coming, and bringing the letter, and telling me all about that little schoolhouse.

JOE. I—I'm glad I could get here. You've been very kind to me. I can tell you that —I won't ever forget you, or Doctor Valkonen. . . . Good-bye, Mr. Sederstrum. [Shakes hands with UNCLE WALDEMAR.] Good-bye, Dave—I'll probably be seeing you. [Shakes hands with DAVE.]

DAVE. Yes, Joe—good-bye.

JOE. And if you get home before I do, don't forget those messages for Ben's and Frank's families.

DAVE. I won't, Joe.

MIRANDA. I wish you the very best of luck, Mr. Burnett.

JOE. You needn't worry about me, Mrs. Valkonen. The beautiful part of my life is that it's so utterly worthless nobody bothers to deprive me of it. Good-bye. [Goes out at the right.]

MIRANDA. I hope he comes through all right. He's the only one left of those men who went to Viipuri with Kaarlo. . . . I suppose you'll be going soon, Dave?

DAVE. I'm not sure, Mrs. Valkonen.

There's some talk of their sending me to Stockholm. They want to investigate those peace rumors.

MIRANDA. Do you think there might be peace before the Russians get here to Helsinki?

DAVE. I hope so.

UNCLE WALDEMAR. [In a completely matter-of-fact tone.] It doesn't make much difference. Either the war continues and we suffer the fate of Poland, or peace comes, as it did at Munich, and we become another Czechoslovakia. In any case, we live only at the mercy of the enemy.

MIRANDA. You'll have a great book to write about all this—won't you, Dave? Your own personal history.

DAVE. I'm afraid that words fail me, Mrs. Valkonen. Just as they've failed the whole human race.

MIRANDA. I'd like to read your book, Dave.

DAVE. [Looks at her.] What are you going to do, Mrs. Valkonen? Are you—are you planning just to sit here and wait for them?

MIRANDA. Oh no, we have our plans all made. Get out the guns, Uncle Waldemar. [UNCLE WALDEMAR goes out right.]

DAVE. Guns?

MIRANDA. We got them at the hospital. They'd been discarded by wounded soldiers. Uncle Waldemar and I have been practicing—not shooting, of course; but just learning how to work them. When this war started, Dave—when the Russians first attacked us—the President said we would fight—even the women, and the old people, and the children would fight. We have no children here—only that one in Boston, who is unborn. But Uncle Waldemar and I are here. [UNCLE WALDEMAR returns with two army rifles and some cartridge belts.] When we see them coming from the shore down there, we'll light the fire. It's all ready, down in the cellar. Then we'll go out into the garden, behind the stone wall, with the guns and ammunition. [She takes one of the rifles and a clip of ammunition.] You see—you put the clip in like this— then you shove the bolt. [She shoves it with a snap.] After each shot, you twist it and pull it back, to throw out the empty shell. Like this . . . [She demonstrates, manipulating bolt. The shells fly out.] What do you think of that, Dave? [She *looks at 1812 portrait.*] Great-grandfather Eustis thinks it's fine! [*There is something maniacal in this statement. She puts gun against wall and picks up a parcel from piano.*] I hate to add to your burdens as a carrier of bad news, Dave. But—I have a package here, that I want you to take, and also a letter from Kaarlo—the one he wrote in the schoolhouse before he was killed. The package contains Kaarlo's signed pictures of Freud and Pavlov and Carrel and the Mayos. He was very proud of those pictures. There's also the Nobel gold medal. I want you to take the package and the letter and give them to Kaatri, to keep for her child. You have that address in Boston—my aunt, who is going to pay you back the fifty dollars I borrowed?

DAVE. Yes. I have the address.

MIRANDA. [*Looking at letter.*] Kaarlo had just heard from me about Erik's death. He wanted to comfort me, in his curious way. Do you mind if I read the letter?

DAVE. Please do, Mrs. Valkonen.

MIRANDA. [*Reading.*] "In this time of our own grief it is not easy to summon up the philosophy which has been formed from long study of the sufferings of others. But I must do it, and you must help me." You see—he wanted to make me feel that I'm stronger—wiser. "I have often read the words which Pericles spoke over the bodies of the dead, in the dark hour when the light of Athenian democracy was being extinguished by the Spartans. He told the mourning people that he could not give them any of the old words which tell how fair and noble it is to die in battle. Those empty words were old, even then, twenty-four centuries ago. But he urged them to find revival in the memory of the commonwealth which they together had achieved; and he promised them that the story of their commonwealth would never die, but would live on, far away, woven into the fabric of other men's lives. I believe that these words can be said now of our own dead, and our own commonwealth. I have always believed in the mystic truth of the resurrection. The great leaders of the mind and the spirit—Socrates, Christ, Lincoln—were all done to death that the full measure of their contribution to human experience might never be lost.

Now—the death of our son is only a fragment in the death of our country. But Erik and the others who give their lives are also giving to mankind a symbol—a little symbol, to be sure, but a clear one—of man's unconquerable aspiration to dignity and freedom and purity in the sight of God. When I made that radio speech"—you remember? . . . "I quoted from St. Paul. I repeat those words to you now, darling: 'We glory in tribulations; knowing that tribulation worketh patience; and patience, experience; and experience, hope.' There are men here from all different countries. Fine men. Those Americans who were at our house on New Year's Day—and that nice Polish officer, Major Rutkowski—they are all here. They are waiting for me now, so I must close this, with all my love." [*She folds letter and hands it to DAVE.*] There it is, Dave. Take good care of it.

DAVE. I shall, Mrs. Valkonen. But it may be a long time before I can deliver it.

MIRANDA. It will be a long time before my grandchild learns to read.

DAVE. [*After a moment's silence.*] I—I have to be going now . . . [*Goes quickly to* UNCLE WALDEMAR.] Good-bye, Mr. Sederstrum.

UNCLE WALDEMAR. [*Shaking hands with* DAVE.] Good-bye, Mr. Corween.

MIRANDA. You'll surely let us know if you're going to Stockholm?

DAVE. Oh, yes, Mrs. Valkonen.

MIRANDA. We'll miss you very much, Dave. You've really become part of our life here in Helsinki. [MIRANDA *and* DAVE *have gone out on that.* UNCLE WALDEMAR *looks after them, then sits down at piano. Still looking toward door, he starts to play the Finnish folk song heard at end of first scene. After a moment,* MIRANDA *returns. She goes to couch, and sits down where she had sat beside* KAARLO. *She listens to* UNCLE WALDEMAR's *playing. She looks to the left, where* ERIK *had been, and to right, where* KAARLO *had been. She leans backward, wearily, and looks at nothing,* UNCLE WALDEMAR *goes on playing the tinkly little tune. There is a kind of peace in this Finnish-American house.*]

CURTAIN

For Discussion and Writing

1. Robert Sherwood was always concerned about one fundamental subject—the growth of his characters and of their ideas. He said, "No play seems worth writing if, at its end, its principal characters have failed to attain, during its two hours, greater stature."

In your opinion, which of the characters in this play show growth and in what way?

2. Sherwood, whose reputation grew originally from his comedies, never really lost his feeling for humor or humanity no matter how serious his topics later became. It has been said that "his sense of humor gives him a sense of proportion."

Show how this sense of humor has helped the characterizations in *There Shall Be No Night*, and how it has also kept the most serious moments from sounding grim or stuffy.

3. *The New York Times* critic, Brooks Atkinson, once said that a number of the long speeches in *There Shall Be No Night* "represent some of the best prose writing in the modern theater."

Which speeches, in your opinion, was he referring to? What essential ideas was Sherwood setting forth in them? Discuss your reactions to these ideas. Do they still have meaning for the world today?

4. At the time, many critics found it difficult to accept this play's idealistic and optimistic belief that the day would come when man would question war and why he had to fight.

In the light of recent history, who came closer to the truth, the practical critics or the idealistic playwright? What proof can you offer to support your viewpoint.

5. Critic George Jean Nathan questioned the artistic merit of propaganda in drama which he called "soapbox theater." Based on your reading of *There Shall Be No Night*, discuss Nathan's viewpoint.

6. Using the prose style of Robert Sherwood as a model, write *one* of the following:

A Nobel Prize acceptance speech for an award in any field you choose.

A serious letter to someone back home written while you are on duty in one of the United States Armed Services or civilian programs abroad.

Whichever you choose, include only ideas and conclusions that matter to you personally.

The King and I

{1951}

RICHARD RODGERS

AND

OSCAR HAMMERSTEIN II

BASED ON THE BOOK, *Anna and the King of Siam,*
BY MARGARET LANDON

CHARACTERS

(In Order of Appearance)

CAPTAIN ORTON	LADY THIANG
LOUIS LEONOWENS	PRINCE CHULALONGKORN
ANNA LEONOWENS	PRINCESS YING YAOWALAK
THE INTERPRETER	LUN THA
THE KRALAHOME	SIR EDWARD RAMSAY
THE KING	PRINCESSES AND PRINCES,
PHRA ALACK	ROYAL DANCERS, WIVES,
TUPTIM	AMAZONS, PRIESTS AND SLAVES

*The play is divided into two acts. The action takes place in
and around the King's palace, Bangkok, Siam.*

TIME: *Early eighteen sixties.*

$\mathcal{W}$hen *The King and I* opened on Broadway in March 1951, Richard Rodgers and Oscar Hammerstein II were already the recognized leaders of a new type of musical drama. Both as a team and individually, they had turned the traditional American musical comedy into an art form now known as the musical play.

The new musical has a substantial story, genuine characters, comedy which grows out of character and situation, and integration of songs, music and dance into the dramatic action.

Literature yielded Rodgers and Hammerstein their most successful collaborations—*Carousel* from Molnar's play *Liliom*, *South Pacific* from a book of short stories by James Michener. For *The King and I*, Hammerstein dramatized Margaret Landon's novel *Anna and the King of Siam*, and Rodgers wrote some of his enchanting music using two musical styles—English-type songs for the imported English schoolteacher and oriental-sounding music for the Siamese. Jerome Robbins added a stylized ballet on how the Siamese might picture *Uncle Tom's Cabin* in the number called "The Small House of Uncle Thomas." The blend of music, dance, verse, exotic costumes and opulent scenery resulted in one of the great musical plays of our times.

The King and I

ACT ONE

SCENE 1

Deck of the Chow Phya, a ship that has sailed from Singapore, up the Gulf of Siam, and is now making its way slowly along the winding river that approaches Bangkok.
CAPTAIN ORTON, a middle-aged Englishman, is leaning on the binnacle, smoking a pipe. The deck is crowded with boxes and crates of furniture.
As soon as the curtain is up LOUIS runs on.

ORTON. Hello, laddy.

LOUIS. [*Mounting the steps of the gangway, to look out on the river.*] How near are we to Bangkok, Captain?

ORTON. See that cluster of lights jutting out into the river? That's it. That's Bangkok.

LOUIS. [*Seeing the crates and boxes.*] Oh, look! All our boxes!

ORTON. Aye, and a fair lot they are.

LOUIS. We packed everything we had in our Singapore house—furniture and everything.

ANNA. [*Offstage.*] Louis! Where are you?

LOUIS. [*Running to meet her as she enters.*] Mother! Mother, look! There's Bangkok! Do you see, Mother? That cluster of lights that sticks out into the river. You see, Mother? That's Bangkok!

ANNA. [*Laughing.*] I see, Louis. I see them. It's exciting, isn't it?

LOUIS. Will the King of Siam come down to the dock to meet us?

ANNA. The King himself? I don't think so. Kings don't as a rule.

ORTON. [*With earnest concern.*] I wonder if you know what you're facing, Ma'am—an Englishwoman here in the East . . .

LOUIS. [*Running down right, looking out toward the audience, and pointing over the imaginary rail.*] Look, Mother! Look at that boat! Look at the dragon's head in the bow, and all the men standing up, carrying torches.

ORTON. That's the Royal Barge!

LOUIS. Do you suppose that's the King, the man sitting under the gold canopy?

ORTON. That's the Kralahome. [*Explaining to ANNA.*] Sort of "Prime Minister"—the King's right-hand man, you might say.

ANNA. Do you suppose he's coming out to meet us?

ORTON. No doubt of it. They'll be waiting till we pass them. Then they'll come around our stern. [*He starts to go, then turns back.*] Ma'am . . . if I might be allowed to offer you a word of warning . . .

ANNA. What is it, Captain?

ORTON. [*Indicating the barge.*] That man has power, and he can use it *for you* or *against* you.

ANNA. [*Laughing.*] Oh.

ORTON. I think you should know.

[*He goes off. A sound comes from the river, a snarling sound in rhythm, oarsmen marking the cadence of their stroke.*]

LOUIS. Look, Mother! They're closer! [*With amazement, as he gets a better view.*] Mother! The Prime Minister is naked!

ANNA. Hush, Louis, that's not a nice word. He's not naked. [*She looks again.*] Well, he's half naked.

LOUIS. They all look rather horrible, don't they, Mother? [*He draws a little closer to her.*] Father would not have liked us to be afraid, would he?

ANNA. No, Louis. Father would not have liked us to be afraid.

262

LOUIS. Mother, does anything ever frighten you?

ANNA. Sometimes.

LOUIS. What do you do?

ANNA. I whistle.

LOUIS. Oh, that's why you whistle!

ANNA. [*Laughing.*] Yes, that's why I whistle . . . [*She sings.*]
Whenever I feel afraid
I hold my head erect
And whistle a happy tune,
So no one will suspect
    I'm afraid.

While shivering in my shoes
I strike a careless pose
And whistle a happy tune,
And no one ever knows
    I'm afraid.

The result of this deception
Is very strange to tell,
For when I fool the people I fear
I fool myself as well!

I whistle a happy tune,
And ev'ry single time
The happiness in the tune
Convinces me that I'm
    Not afraid.

Make believe you're brave
And the trick will take you far;
You may be as brave
As you make believe you are.
    [LOUIS *whistles this strain, then they both sing.*]

ANNA AND LOUIS.
You may be as brave
As you make believe you are.

LOUIS. [*After a moment's reflection.*] I think that's a very good idea, Mother. A very good idea.

ANNA. It *is* a good idea, isn't it?

LOUIS. I don't think I shall ever be afraid again.

ANNA. Good!
    [LOUIS *resumes singing the refrain.* ANNA *joins in. They do not see four Siamese slaves, naked from the waist up, with knives in their belts, come over the rail, down the gangway, and line up, center. As they are happily singing the last eight measures* ANNA *turns, sees the formidable-looking Siamese, and gasps, in terror.* LOUIS *sees them, too, and clutches his mother's arm. Then they face the men and whistle—as casually as they can.*]

ORTON. [*Coming on hurriedly, followed by two deckhands.*] Clear that away! [*The deckhands remove a trunk.*] Ma'am, I wouldn't whistle. He might think it disrespectful.

ANNA. Oh, was I whistling? Sorry, I didn't realize.
    [*The* INTERPRETER *comes over the rail and down the steps.*]

INTERPRETER. [*Rather insolently, to* ANNA.] Good evening, sir. Welcome to Siam.
    [*He turns his back on her and prostrates himself, toadlike, as do the four slaves.*]

LOUIS. He called you sir!

ANNA. Hush, dear! Hush!
    [*The* KRALAHOME *comes over the rail slowly and with terrifying majesty. He is naked from the waist up, except for several necklaces. Now he addresses the* INTERPRETER *in Siamese.*]
    [AT THIS POINT, AND THROUGHOUT THE PLAY, THE SIAMESE LANGUAGE WILL BE REPRESENTED BY CERTAIN SOUNDS MADE BY THE ORCHESTRA. SIAMESE WORDS WILL NEVER BE LITERALLY PRONOUNCED. MUSIC WILL SYMBOLIZE THEM.]

INTERPRETER. [*Turning to* ANNA, *still crouching like a toad, relaying the* KRALAHOME's *questions.*] Sir, His Excellency wishes to know—are you lady who will be schoolmistress of royal children?

ANNA. [*In a small, frightened voice.*] Yes.

INTERPRETER. Have you friends in Bangkok?

ANNA. I know no one in Bangkok at all.
    [*The* INTERPRETER *delivers her answers and the* KRALAHOME *directs him to ask further questions.*]

INTERPRETER. Are you married, sir?

ANNA. I am a widow.

INTERPRETER. What manner of man your deceased husband?

ANNA. My husband was an officer of Her Majesty's Army in . . . [*She suddenly stiffens.*] Tell your master his business with me is in my capacity of schoolteacher to the royal children. He has no right to pry into my personal affairs. [ORTON *tries to* signal a warning, but she turns to him impatiently.] Well, he hasn't, Captain Orton!

[*The* INTERPRETER *gives the* KRALA-HOME *her message. The* KRALAHOME *gives the* INTERPRETER *a kick on the shoulder which sends him sprawling out of the way.*]

LOUIS. [*To* ANNA, *pointing toward the* KRALAHOME.] I don't like that man!

KRALAHOME. In foreign country is best you like everyone—until you leave.

ANNA. [*Startled.*] Your Excellency, I had no idea you spoke English.

KRALAHOME. It is not necessary for you to know everything at once. You come with me now. Your boxes are carried to palace—later.

ANNA. No. Not to the palace. I am not living at the palace.

KRALAHOME. Who say?

ANNA. The King say . . . Says! The King has promised me twenty pounds a month and a house of my own.

KRALAHOME. King do not always remember what he promise. If I tell him he break his promise, I will make anger in him. I think it is better I make anger in him about larger matters.

ANNA. But all I want is ten minutes' audience with him.

KRALAHOME. King very busy now. New Year's celebrations just finishing. Fireworks every night. Cremation of late Queen just starting.

ANNA. Oh. You have lost your Queen. I am so sorry. When did she die?

KRALAHOME. Four years ago . . . With cremation ceremony comes also fireworks.

ANNA. And what am I to do in the meantime?

KRALAHOME. In the meantime you wait —in palace.

ANNA. [*Firmly.*] Your Excellency, I will teach in the palace, but I must have a house of my own—where I can go at the end of the day when my duties are over.

KRALAHOME. What you wish to do in evening that cannot be done in palace?

ANNA. How dare you! [*Controlling herself.*] I'm sorry, Your Excellency, but you don't understand. I came here to work. I must support myself and my young son. And I shall take nothing less than what I have been promised.

KRALAHOME. You will tell King this?

ANNA. I will tell King this.

[*The faint suggestion of a smile curls the corner of the* KRALAHOME'S *mouth.*]

KRALAHOME. It will be very interesting meeting . . . You come now? [ANNA *does not answer.*] You come now, or you can stay on boat. I do not care! [*He turns toward gangway and starts to go.*]

ORTON. [*Going to* ANNA *sympathetically.*] If ,you wish to stay on my ship and return to Singapore, Ma'am . . .

ANNA. No, thank you, Captain Orton. [*Calling to the* KRALAHOME.] Your Excellency— [*The* KRALAHOME *stops and turns.*] I will go with you. I have made a bargain, and I shall live up to my part of it. But I expect a bargain to be kept on both sides. I shall go with you, Your Excellency.

KRALAHOME. To the palace?

ANNA. [*Grimly, after a pause.*] For the time being. [*The* KRALAHOME *smiles and exits over the ship's rail.* ANNA *turns to* ORTON.] Good-bye, Captain Orton, and thank you very much for everything. [*Turning to* LOUIS, *prompting him.*] Louis!

LOUIS. [*Shaking hands.*] Good-bye, Captain.

ORTON. Good-bye, laddy.

[*As they turn from the captain,* ANNA *and* LOUIS *are confronted by the* IN-TERPRETER *and the slaves standing in a stern line, their arms folded, their faces glowering in a most unfriendly manner.* ANNA *and* LOUIS *pause, then raise their chins and whistle "a happy tune" as they walk by the men and start to climb the gangway.*]

INTERMEDIATE SCENE

A Palace corridor.
Several court dancers have their costumes adjusted and last-minute touches added to their faces by make-up experts. Excitement, haste and anxiety pervade the scene. An attendant enters

*and claps his hands. The dancers bustle off promptly, their
attendants making their exit on the opposite side.*

SCENE 2

The KING's *study in the royal palace.
As the curtain rises the* KING *is seated cross-legged on a low
table, dictating letters to* PHRA ALACK, *his secretary, and paying
only scant attention to a group of girl dancers. At length he
throws the last letter at the secretary, rises and snaps his fingers.
The secretary and the dancers retire quickly. The* KING *beckons
to someone offstage. The* KRALAHOME *enters.*

KRALAHOME. Your Majesty . . .

KING. Well, well, well?

KRALAHOME. I have been meaning to
speak to you about English schoolteacher.
She is waiting to see you.

KING. She is in Siam? How long?

KRALAHOME. Two weeks, three weeks.
She had needed disciplining, Your Majesty.
She objects to living in palace.
Talks •about house she say you promise
her.

KING. I do not recollect such promise.
Tell her I will see her. I will see her in a
moment. [*Over the* KRALAHOME's *shoulder,
the* KING *sees* LUN THA *enter, preceded
by a female palace attendant.*]
Who? Who? Who?

KRALAHOME. Your Majesty, this is Lun
Tha, emissary from court of Burma.

KING. Ah! You are here for copying of
famous Bangkok temple. [*To* KRALAHOME.]
I have give permission.

KRALAHOME. [*As* TUPTIM *is carried on,
on a palanquin, by four Amazons.*] He
brings you present from Prince of Burma.

KING. Am I to trust a ruler of Burma?
Am I to trust this present they send me,
or is she a spy?

TUPTIM. [*Rising from palanquin.*] I am
not a spy . . . My name is Tuptim. You
are pleased that I speak English? My name
is Tuptim.
[*The* KING *looks at her appraisingly.
The* KRALAHOME *signals for her to
turn around. She does so. The* KING
*walks around her slowly, darts a
brief, enigmatic look at the* KRALAHOME,
and walks off.]

KRALAHOME. King is pleased with you.
He likes you.
[*He dismisses* LUN THA *and leaves.*

Before going out, LUN THA *exchanges
a worried, helpless look with* TUPTIM.
TUPTIM *turns and looks toward where
the* KING *made his exit, bitterness and
hatred in her eyes.*]

TUPTIM. The King is pleased! [*She
sings:*]
He is pleased with me!
My lord and master
Declares he's pleased with me—
What does he mean?
What does he know of me,
This lord and master?
When he has looked at me
What has he seen?
  Something young,
  Soft and slim,
  Painted cheek,
  Tap'ring limb,
  Smiling lips
  All for him,
  Eyes that shine
  Just for him—
  So he thinks . . .
  Just for him!
Though the man may be
My lord and master,
Though he may study me
As hard as he can,
The smile beneath my smile
He'll never see.
He'll never know I love
Another man,
He'll never know
I love another man!
[*The* KING *enters.* TUPTIM *immediately
resumes her humble and obedient attitude.*]
Your Majesty wishes me to leave?

KING. I will tell you when I wish you
to leave.

KRALAHOME. [*Entering, ushering in*

ANNA, *who is followed by two Amazons.*]
Schoolteacher. [ANNA *comes before the*
KING *and curtseys.*] Madame Leonowens.

KING. You are schoolteacher?

ANNA. Yes, Your Majesty, I am schoolteacher. When can I start my work?

KING. You can start when I tell you to
start.

ANNA. There is one matter we have to
settle, Your Majesty . . .

KING. [*Interrupting her.*] You are part
of general plan I have for bringing to
Siam what is good in Western culture.
Already I have bring printing press here—
for printing.

ANNA. Yes, I know, Your Majesty.

KING. How you know?

ANNA. Before I signed our agreement,
I found out all I could about Your Majesty's ambitions for Siam.

KING. Ha! This is scientific. [*He squints
at her thoughtfully.*] You are pleased with
your apartments in palace?

ANNA. They . . . are quite comfortable,
Your Majesty. [*Exchanging a look with
the* KRALAHOME.] For the time being.
But my young son and I have found it
rather . . . confining . . . with Amazons
guarding the doors and not permitting us
to leave.

KING. Strangers cannot be allowed to
roam around palace before presentment to
King. You could look out of windows.

ANNA. Yes, Your Majesty, we have done
that. We have seen New Year celebrations,
royal cremation ceremonies, etcetera,
etcetera.

KING. What is this "etcetera"?

ANNA. According to the dictionary, it
means "and the rest," Your Majesty. All
the things you have been doing while we
were waiting. The fireworks—

KING. Best fireworks I ever see at funeral. How you like my acrobats?

ANNA. Splendid, Your Majesty. Best acrobats I have ever seen at funeral.

KING. [*Pleased.*] Ha! [*To* KRALAHOME.]
Have children prepare for presentation to
schoolteacher.

ANNA. How many children have you,
Your Majesty?

KING. I have only sixty-seven altogether.
I begin very late. But you shall not teach
all of them. You shall teach only children
of mothers who are in favor of King . . .
[LADY THIANG *has entered. She prostrates*

herself before the KING.] Ah! Lady Thiang.
Madame Leonowens, this is Lady Thiang,
head wife.

[*She immediately and quite irrele-
vantly starts to sing.*]

THIANG.
There is a happy land, far, far away,
Where saints in glory stand, bright, bright
as day.

[*Speaking.*] In the beginning God created
the heaven and the earth. [ANNA *looks
puzzled.*] Mis-son-ary.

ANNA. A missionary taught you English!

THIANG. Yes, sir. Mis-son-ary.

KING. Lady Thiang, you will help
Madame Leonowens with her schoolteach-
ing, and she in her turn shall teach you
the better English. [THIANG *prostrates herself at the feet of the* KING, *to* ANNA's *surprise and horror. The* KING *explains.*] She
is grateful to me for my kindness.

ANNA. I see. [*Getting back to the issue
she is so anxious to settle.*] Your Majesty,
in our agreement, you . . .

KING. [*Talking across* ANNA.] You, Tuptim. You already speak well the English.
[TUPTIM *rises. The* KING *turns to* ANNA,
pointing to TUPTIM.] She arrive today.
She is present to me from Burma prince.

ANNA. [*Shocked.*] She is a present?

TUPTIM. Madame, you have English
books I can read?

ANNA. Of course I have.

TUPTIM. I wish most to read book called
"The Small House of Uncle Thomas." Is
by American lady, Harriet Beecher Stowa.

KING. A woman has written a book?

ANNA. A very wonderful book, Your
Majesty. All about slavery . . .

KING. Ha! President Lingkong against
slavery, no? Me, too. Slavery very bad
thing. [ANNA *looks significantly at the
prostrate figure of* LADY THIANG. *The* KING
snaps his fingers and LADY THIANG *rises.
The* KING *paces thoughtfully, speaking
half to himelf, half to* ANNA.] I think you
will teach my wives too—those wives who
are in favor.

[*During the ensuing dialogue, small
groups of the* KING's *wives peek in
through the entrances and retreat, as
if curious to hear and see, but afraid
of the* KING's *mounting temper.*]

ANNA. I shall be most happy to teach
your wives, even though that was not
part of our agreement. . . . Speaking of

our agreement reminds me that there is one little matter, about my house . . .

KING. Also, I will allow you to help me in my foreign correspondence.

ANNA. Yes, Your Majesty. I don't think you understand about the house, Your Majesty. For the time being . . .

KING. [Wheeling around suddenly.] House? House? What is this about house?

ANNA. [Startled, then recovering.] I want my house! The house you promised me, Your Majesty.

KING. You shall live in palace. You teach in palace, you shall live in palace. If you do not live in palace, you do not teach, and you go—wherever you please. I do not care. You understand this?

ANNA. I understand, but, Your Majesty, if these are the only terms on which I . . .

KING. Enough! I have no more time to talk. Talk to other women, my women— my wives.

[He snaps his fingers at TUPTIM, who follows him obediently as he exits. As soon as the KING has left, the wives rush on from all sides, chattering excitedly. They surround ANNA, taking her gloves and her reticule, fingering her clothes. Two on the floor try to lift up her skirt.]

ANNA. For goodness' sake! What is the matter? What are they trying to do to me?

THIANG. They think you wear big skirt like that because you shaped like that.

ANNA. Well, I'm not!

[She lifts her hoop skirt, revealing pantalettes. Two wives address LADY THIANG, the orchestra, as usual, playing sounds to indicate the Siamese language.]

THIANG. They wish to know, sir, if you have children?

ANNA. [Indicating his size.] One little boy.

THIANG. [Proudly.] I have boy, too— Crown Prince Chowfa Chulalongkorn, heir to throne . . . [An earnest pleading coming into her voice.] I would be happy if you would teach children.

ANNA. I would like to very much. I came all the way here from Singapore to do so, but I really cannot . . .

THIANG. You could be great help to all here, sir.

ANNA. Lady Thiang, why do you call me "sir"?

THIANG. Because you scientific. Not lowly, like woman.

ANNA. Do you all think women are more lowly than men? [THIANG translates this to the wives, all of whom smile broadly and nod their heads, apparently quite happy with the idea of female inferiority. ANNA's voice is indignant.] Well, I don't.

THIANG. Please, sir, do not tell King. Make King angry.

ANNA. King seems to be angry already. [Thoughtfully.] That lovely girl. He said she was a present . . .

THIANG. From court of Burma. I think she love another man. If so, she will never see other man again.

ANNA. Poor child!

THIANG. Oh, no, sir! She is foolish child, to wish for another man when she has King.

ANNA. But you can't help wishing for a man, if he's the man you want.

THIANG. It is strange for schoolteacher to talk so—romantic.

ANNA. [Smiling.] Romantic! I suppose I am. I was very much in love with my husband, Tom.

THIANG. Tom.

[She translates this to the wives, who repeat after her, "Tom."]

ANNA. Once a woman has loved like that, she understands all other women who are in love . . . and she's on their side, even if she's . . . a schoolteacher. [The wives again pronounce "Tom" as if fascinated by the sound.] Yes . . . Tom.

[She opens the locket around her neck and shows it to LADY THIANG.]

THIANG. [Looking at the picture.] He was pretty in face.

ANNA. Oh, dear, yes. He was very pretty in face. [She sings:]
When I think of Tom
I think about a night
When the earth smelled of summer
And the sky was streaked with white,
And the soft mist of England
Was sleeping on a hill—
I remember this,
And I always will . . .

There are new lovers now on the same silent hill,
Looking on the same blue sea,

And I know Tom and I are a part of them all,
And they're all a part of Tom and me.
[*She is far away from them now, in another time, another place.*]

Hello, young lovers, whoever you are,
I hope your troubles are few.
All my good wishes go with you tonight—
I've been in love like you.
Be brave, young lovers, and follow your star,
Be brave and faithful and true,
Cling very close to each other tonight—
I've been in love like you.
I know how it feels to have wings on your heels,
And to fly down a street in a trance.
You fly down a street on the chance that you'll meet,
And you meet—not really by chance.
Don't cry, young lovers, whatever you do,
Don't cry because I'm alone;
All of my memories are happy tonight,
I've had a love of my own,
I've had a love of my own, like yours—
I've had a love of my own.
[*Now there is a loud crash on a gong. The* KING *enters.*]

KING. The children! The children! [*To* ANNA.] They come for presentment to schoolteacher.

ANNA. But, Your Majesty, we have not solved my problem . . .

KING. Silence! You will stand here to meet royal children. [*He indicates a place for her.*]

ANNA. [*Reluctantly accepting his order.*] Very well, Your Majesty.

KING. The Royal Princes and Princesses! [*Now, to the strains of a patrol, the royal Siamese children enter, one by one, each advancing first to the* KING *and prostrating himself before his father, then rising, moving over to* ANNA, *and greeting her in the traditional manner by taking her two hands and pressing them to his fore-head, after which he backs away across the stage, and takes his place with the wives and children who have previously entered. Each succeeding child enters at about the time that his predecessor has greeted* ANNA *and is backing across the stage. The twins enter together, and the* KING *holds up two fingers to* ANNA, *so that she is sure to observe that they are twins. There are other variations. One little girl goes straight to her father, her arms outstretched, but he sternly points to the floor. She prostrates herself in the formal manner and, very much abashed, goes on to* ANNA. *One little girl, who had been delegated to give* ANNA *a rose, forgets it the first time and has to run back to* ANNA, *disgraced by her absent-mindedness. The most impressive moment is the entrance of the Crown Prince,* CHU-LALONGKORN. *The music becomes loud and brave at this point. Then, toward the end of the patrol, the music becomes softer and ends with the smallest children coming on, the last child backing up and bowing with the others on the last beat of the music. Throughout this procession,* ANNA *has obviously fallen more and more in love with the children. She is deeply touched by their courtesy, their charm, their sweetness. After they have all bowed to her and the* KING, *she slowly moves to the center of the room. She looks back at the* KING, *who nods understandingly, and then slowly she starts to untie the ribbons of her bonnet. As she takes out the pin and lifts the bonnet off her head, one little child gasps an excited "ah," and the children with one accord all rush up to her and surround her. She leans over and hugs all those she can reach, and it is obvious that they are going to be fast friends as the curtain closes.*]

SCENE 3

In the Palace grounds.
A group of PRIESTS *chant as they walk by. From the other side the children enter singing "Home Sweet Home" as a counter-*

melody to the chant. They walk two by two, in time to the music. The PRIESTS *exit. The* KING *enters and gestures to* CHULALONGKORN *to step out of line. The* PRINCE *obeys. The other children continue offstage.*

CHULALONGKORN. Father, I shall be late for school.

KING. You wait! [*There is angry purpose in his voice and manner.*] Please to recite proverb you have learned yesterday and writing down twelve times in your copybook.

CHULALONGKORN. "A thought for the day: East or West, home is best."

KING. East, West, home best. Means house! Every day for many, many months! Always something about house! Are my children to be taught nothing more?

CHULALONGKORN. Yesterday we are taught that the world is a round ball which spins on a stick through the middle. [*He looks at the* KING *to see the effect of this outrageous statement.*] Everyone knows that the world rides on the back of a great turtle, who keeps it from running into the stars.

KING. How can it be that everyone knows one thing, if many people believe another thing?

CHULALONGKORN. Then which is true? [*Pause.*]

KING. The world is a ball with stick through it . . . I believe.

CHULALONGKORN. You believe? Does that mean you do not *know*? [*His father does not answer.*] But you must know, because you are King.

KING. Good. Some day you, too, will be King and you too will know everything.

CHULALONGKORN. But how do I learn? And when do I know that I know everything?

KING. When you are King. Now leave me. [CHULALONGKORN *goes out. The* KING *soliloquizes.*] When you are King. But *I* do not know. I am not sure. I am not sure of anything. [*He sings:*]
When I was a boy
World was better spot.
What was so was so,
What was not was not.
Now I am a man—
World have change a lot:
Some things *nearly* so,
Others *nearly* not.

There are times I almost think
I am not sure of what I absolutely know.
Very often find confusion
In conclusion I concluded long ago.
In my head are many facts
That, as a student, I have studied to
procure.
In my head are many facts
Of which I wish I was more certain I
was sure!
[*He speaks:*] Is a puzzlement! What to tell a growing son
[*He sings:*]
What, for instance, shall I say to him of
women?
Shall I educate him on the ancient lines?
Shall I tell the boy, as far as he is able,
To respect his wives and love his concubines?
Shall I tell him every one is like the other,
And the better one of two is really neither?
If I tell him this I think he won't believe
it—
And I nearly think I don't believe it either!

When my father was a king
He was a king who knew exactly what
he knew,
And his brain was not a thing
Forever swinging to and fro and fro and
to.
Shall I, then, be like my father
And be wilfully unmovable and strong?
Or is better to be right?
Or am I right when I believe I may be
wrong?

Shall I join with other nations in alliance?
If allies are weak, am I not best alone?
If allies are strong with power to protect
me,
Might they not protect me out of all I
own?
Is a danger to be trusting one another,
One will seldom want to do what other
wishes . . .
But unless some day somebody trust somebody,
There'll be nothing left on earth excepting
fishes!

There are times I almost think
Nobody sure of what he absolutely
   know.
Everybody find confusion
In conclusion he concluded long ago,
And it puzzle me to learn
That though a man may be in doubt of
   what he know,
Very quickly will he fight,
He'll fight to prove that what he does
   not know is so!

Oh-h-h-h-h-h!
Sometimes I think that people going
   mad!
Ah-h-h-h-h-h!
Sometimes I think that people not so
   bad!
But no matter what I think

I must go on living life.
As leader of my kingdom I must *go*
   forth,
Be father to my children,
And husband to each wife—
Etcetera, etcetera, and so forth.
[*His arms and eyes raised in prayer*]
If my Lord in Heaven, Buddha, show
   the way,
Every day I try to live another day.
If my Lord in Heaven, Buddha, show
   the way,
Every day I do my best—for one more
   day!
[*His arms and shoulders droop. He
speaks the last line*] But . . . is a puzzle-
ment!
[*The lights go out. The voices of the
children are heard in the darkness,
coming from the schoolroom.*]

SCENE 4

*The Schoolroom. Up center is a large stand with a map hanging
from it. This is an ancient map, showing a very large Siam
with a heroic figure of an armored king superimposed. Adjoining is a much smaller Burma, with a pathetic naked figure
representing the king of that country.*
The children are lined up singing their school song. LADY
THIANG *and* TUPTIM *stand a little apart from the group, as does*
LOUIS. CHULALONGKORN *is in the group with the children and
wives.* ANNA *conducts them with a blackboard pointer. Soon
after the curtain rises, she stops them in the middle of their song.*

ANNA. Spread out, children. [*They
obey.*] Now, that last line was "English
words are all we speak." I didn't quite
understand. I want to hear the beginnings
and ends of your words. Once again, now,
and nice big smiles because we love our
school.
   WIVES AND CHILDREN. [*Singing.*]
We work and work
From week to week
At the Royal Bangkok Academy.
And English words
Are all we speak
At the Royal Bangkok Academy.
If we pay
Attention to our teacher
And obey her every rule,
We'll be grateful for
These golden years
At our dear old school.

The Royal Bangkok Academy,
Our dear old school.
   ANNA. That's fine. Now take your places.
[*The children sit, the bigger ones on the
right, with* CHULALONGKORN *and* TUPTIM
*behind them, the little ones down center,
their backs to the audience, facing* ANNA
*who stands up center. The wives line up
on the left.*] Lady Thiang, will you start?
[ANNA *hands the pointer to* LADY
THIANG.]
   THIANG. [*Using the pointer on the map.*]
Blue is ocean. Red—Siam [*Enthusiastic
reaction from the children at Siam's great
size.*] Here is King of Siam. [*Indicating
armored figure.*] In right hand is weapon
—show how to destroy all who fight him.
[*More approval.*] Green—Burma. [LADY
THIANG *looks disapprovingly at* TUPTIM.]
Here, King of Burma. [*Indicating naked*

figure.] No clothes mean how poor is King of Burma.

[*Children giggle.*]

ANNA. Thank you, Lady Thiang. Will you take my chair? [LADY THIANG *sits.* ANNA *addresses the class.*] The map you have been looking at is an old one. Today we have a surprise. Louis— [LOUIS *rolls down an 1862 world map in Mercator projection. The children gasp.*] A new map—just arrived from England. It is a gift to us from His Majesty, your King.

WIVES AND CHILDREN. [*Bowing in unison.*] The Lord of Light.

ANNA. Er—yes—The Lord of Light.

LOUIS [*With the pointer.*] The white is Siam.

[*There is a groan of disbelief and disappointment from the children and wives.*]

CHULALONGKORN. Siam not so small!

LOUIS. Wait! Let me show you England. [*Points.*] See! It is even smaller than Siam. [*Children indicate approval.*]

ANNA. For many years, before I came here, Siam was to me that little white spot. Now I have lived here for more than a year. I have met the people of Siam. And I am learning to understand them.

A PRINCESS. You like us?

ANNA. I like you very much. Very much indeed. [*The children express their delight.* ANNA *sings.*]

It's a very ancient saying,
But a true and honest thought,
That "if you become a teacher
By your pupils you'll be taught."
As a teacher I've been learning
(You'll forgive me if I boast)
And I've now become an expert
On the subject I like most:

[*She speaks.*]

Getting to know you . . .

[*She sings.*]

Getting to know you,
Getting to know all about you,
Getting to like you,
Getting to hope you like me.
Getting to know you—
Putting it my way, but nicely,
You are precisely
My cup of tea!
Getting to know you,
Getting to feel free and easy;
When I am with you,
Getting to know what to say—

Haven't you noticed?
Suddenly I'm bright and breezy
Because of
All the beautiful and new
Things I'm learning about you,
Day by day.

[*The refrain is taken up by the wives, Amazons and children.* ANNA *teaches them handshaking, and* LADY THIANG *learns to curtsey. One wife performs a dance with a fan and* ANNA, *imitating her, dances with her. Then she dances with the children. At the finish they are all seated on the floor, giggling. She rises suddenly, remembering her duties.*] My goodness! This started out to be a lesson! Now, let's get back to work!

[*They scurry back to their places.*]

CHULALONGKORN. [*Pointing to the map.*] What is that green up there?

ANNA. That is Norway. [*Repeating precisely for the benefit of her students.*] Nor-way.

WIVES AND CHILDREN. [*Imitating the sound.*] Nor-way.

ANNA. Norway is a very cold place. It is sometimes so cold that the lakes and rivers freeze, and the water becomes so hard that you can walk on it.

A SMALL PRINCE. Walk on water?

ANNA. Yes, walk on water.

CHULALONGKORN. How is it possible? Hard water!

ANNA. It is not only hard, but very slippery, too. When people walk on it, they fall down, and slide . . . [*General reaction of skepticism.*] Not only do the lakes and rivers freeze, but the raindrops, as they fall, are changed into small white spots that look like lace! This is called snow.

TUPTIM. [*Fascinated.*] Snow?

WIVES AND CHILDREN. [*Another new word.*] Snow . . .

CHULALONGKORN. [*Not to be taken in.*] Spots of lace!

ANNA. Yes, Your Highness! The water freezes—on the way down from the sky.

CHULALONGKORN. And the raindrops turn into little stars!

[*The pupils giggle, their credulity strained too far. The class becomes disorganized.*]

ANNA. Yes, Your Highness. Some *are* shaped like stars—small, white . . .

[*Bedlam is breaking loose.*]

PRINCESS YING YAOWALAK. I do not believe such thing as snow!
[Cries of assent.]
TWINS. [Dividing the lines and gestures between them, keeping two hands together.] And I do not believe that Siam is this big— [Indicating small size.] And other country so big! [Wide gesture.]
CHULALONGKORN. Siam is biggest country in world!
[Shouts, cartwheels, pandemonium greet this popular pronouncement.]
KING. [Entering suddenly.] What? What? What? [All but ANNA and LOUIS instantly prostrate themselves. The KING stands for a moment in outraged silence.] How can schoolroom be so . . . unscientific?
ANNA. Your Majesty, we have had a little misunderstanding. I was describing snow and they refused to believe that there was such a thing.
KING. Snow?
ANNA. [Gesturing snow falling.] Snow.
[CHULALONGKORN has raised his head and noted her gesture.]
KING. [Feeling his way.] Oh, yes. From mountain top.
ANNA. From the sky.
KING. From sky to mountain top.
CHULALONGKORN. Sire . . . please . . . how does it come down from the sky?
KING. Like this. [And he makes exactly the same gesture as ANNA did, lowering his hands and wiggling his fingers the while.]
CHULALONGKORN. [Gravely.] Thank you, sire.
KING. [He snaps his fingers as if bringing the picture back to his mind.] I have see picture—Switzerland!
ANNA. That's right, Your Majesty.
KING. Land all white—with snow. [Turning to the class, with an angry challenge.] Who does not believe this? [There is complete silence.]
ANNA. Well, after all, they have never seen it, and . . .
KING. Never see? If they will know only what they see, why do we have schoolroom? [He turns to the class and crackles out a sudden command.] Rise! [They all come to their feet.] Do not ever let me hear of not believing teacher, who I have bring here at high expense—twenty pounds —each month. [All eyes turn toward ANNA

with a strange accusing look, as if she were robbing the KING.] Twenty English pounds! [He stamps his foot.] Sterling! [Not knowing what "sterling" means, but impressed by the sound as the KING shouts it, they all fall to the floor again.] Children must learn. [He turns to ANNA.] Teacher must teach! Not waste time instructing children in silly English song "Home Sweet House"—to remind me of breaking promises that I never made, etcetera, etcetera, etcetera . . .
ANNA. [Summoning all her courage.] Your Majesty . . . you did promise me a house. [He glares at her, but she does not flinch.] "A brick residence adjoining the royal palace." Those were your words in your letter.
KING. I do not remember such words.
ANNA. I remember them.
KING. I will do remembering. Who is King? I remind you—so you remember that! [He is screaming now.] I do not know of any promises. I do not know anything but that you are my servant.
ANNA. [Automatically resenting the word.] Oh, no, Your Majesty!
[There is a gasp of astonishment from those in the schoolroom.]
KING. What? What? What? I say you are my servant!
ANNA. No, Your Majesty, that's not true. I most certainly am not your servant!
CHULALONGKORN. [To LOUIS.] I would say your mother has bad manners.
LOUIS. You would, would you? Well, I'd say your father has no manners at all!
ANNA. Louis! [She takes his hand and turns to face the KING.] If you do not give me the house you promised, I shall return to England. [There is a frightened murmur from her pupils. ANNA, herself, looks surprised at her own temerity.]
PRINCESS SOMAWADI. [Running to her.] No! No! No!
PRINCE SUK SAWAT. Do not go to England.
PRINCE THONGKORN YAI. [To the KING.] We learn. We believe schoolteacher.
PRINCESS YING YAOWALAK. I believe in snow!
THIANG. [To the KING.] Do not let her go away.
KING. I let her do nothing except what is my pleasure. [To ANNA.] It is my pleas-

ure you stay here. You stay here in palace.
In palace!

ANNA. No, Your Majesty!

KING. [*Weakening a little.*] I give you
servants. I give you bigger room.

ANNA. That is not the point, Your
Majesty.

KING. Why do you wish to leave these
children, all of whom are loving you so
extraordinarily?

ANNA. I don't wish to leave them. I love
them, too . . . quite extraordinarily. But I
cannot stay in a country where a promise
has no meaning.

KING. I will hear no more about this
promise . . .

ANNA. A land where there is talk of
honor, and a wish for Siam to take her
place among the modern nations of the
world! Where there is talk of great
changes, but where everything still remains according to the wishes of the King!

KING. You will say no more!

ANNA. [*On the edge of tears.*] I will say
no more, because—because I have no more
to say. [*She starts off.*] Come, Louis.
[*He follows her out, as the wives and
children call after her: "Please don't
go, Mrs. Anna," etc. But she goes!
The* KING *stamps his foot angrily to
silence them all. Then he shouts a
dismissal.*]

KING. Out! Out! Out! [*They scurry out.
The* KING's *thoughts are confused. He,
paces up and down, then stops before the
map. His voice is low and thoughtful.*]
So big a world! Siam very small . . . Eng-
land very small . . . all people very small.
No man big enough for to be alone. No
man big enough! King? King different!
King need no one . . . nobody at all!
[*Pause.*] I think!
[*He leaves the room.*]
[*In a moment* TUPTIM *comes in. She
looks around cautiously, then sits on*

the floor with a book. LUN THA *enters,
then stops quickly, surprised to find*
TUPTIM *alone.*]

LUN THA. Where is Mrs. Anna?

TUPTIM. She will not be with us ever
again. She has quarreled with the King.

LUN THA. How can we meet if she is
not with us? Mrs. Anna was our only
friend, and . . .

TUPTIM. We cannot be seen talking like
this. Anyone can come in. Pretend you
wait for her.

LUN THA. [*Bitterly.*] If only we could
stop pretending! [*He sings.*]
We kiss in a shadow,
We hide from the moon,
Our meetings are few,
And over too soon.
We speak in a whisper,
Afraid to be heard—
When people are near
We speak not a word!
Alone in our secret,
Together we sigh
For one smiling day to be free
To kiss in the sunlight
And say to the sky:
"Behold and believe what you see!
Behold how my lover loves me!"
[*He speaks.*] Tuptim, when can we meet?
When?

TUPTIM. It is not possible. We cannot
meet alone ever—not ever.
[LADY THIANG *enters at the back, sees
the two lovers together, and goes off,
unseen by them.*]

LUN THA. [*As* TUPTIM *suddenly breaks
away.*] What is it?

TUPTIM. Someone was here! [*She looks
around fearfully.*] I had a feeling someone
was watching us . . . Please go! Please!
[*He leaves.* TUPTIM *sings sadly.*]
To kiss in the sunlight
And say to the sky:
"Behold and believe what you see!
Behold how my lover loves me!"

INTERMEDIATE SCENE

The Palace corridor.
LOUIS *and* CHULALONGKORN *enter from opposite sides. After passing each other in unfriendly silence, each repents and turns at
about the same time. Then with a common impulse, they rush
toward each other and shake hands.*

CHULALONGKORN. I am sorry we nearly fought just now.

LOUIS. I am too.

CHULALONGKORN. Are you really going away?

LOUIS. Mother plans to leave on the next sailing.

CHULALONGKORN. I am not sure my father will allow your mother to go.

LOUIS. I am not sure whether my mother will allow your father not to allow her to go.

CHULALONGKORN. Why does not your mother admit that she was wrong?

LOUIS. I don't believe that Mother thinks she was wrong.

CHULALONGKORN. It begins to look as if people do not know when they are right or wrong—even after they have grown up.

LOUIS. I have noticed that, too.

CHULALONGKORN. A puzzlement! . . . When I left my father a little while ago, I heard him talking to himself. [He shakes his head.] He seemed uncertain about many things.

LOUIS. I don't believe grownups are ever certain—they only talk as if they are certain.

CHULALONGKORN. [Singing.]
There are times I almost think
They are not sure of what they absolutely know.

LOUIS.
I believe they are confused

About conclusions they concluded long ago.

CHULALONGKORN.
If my father and your mother are not sure of what they absolutely know,
Can you tell me why they fight?

LOUIS.
They fight to prove that what they do not know is so!

CHULALONGKORN. [With the mannerisms of his father.]
Oh-h-h-h-h-h!
Sometimes I think that people going mad.

LOUIS.
Ah-h-h-h-h-h!
Sometimes I think that people not so bad.

CHULALONGKORN.
But no matter what I think,
I must go on living life
And some day as a leader I must go forth,
Be father to my children
And husband to each wife.
Etcetera, etcetera, and so forth.
[His eyes and arms uplifted.]
If my Lord in Heaven, Buddha, show the way,
Every day I try to live another day,
If my Lord in Heaven, Buddha, show the way,
Every day I do my best—for one more day.
But—

LOUIS.
Is a puzzlement.
[The two boys walk off together thoughtfully.]

SCENE 5

ANNA's *bedroom.*
ANNA *is sitting on the bed. She has started to undress, but apparently has stopped, engrossed in her thoughts. Her brows knit. She glares at an imaginary adversary. Her nostrils dilate with scorn. Then she starts to let him have it:*

ANNA.
Your servant! Your servant!
Indeed I'm not your servant
(Although you give me less than servant's pay)
I'm a free and independent employé . . . employee.
[She paces the floor indignantly, then turns back to "him".]
Because I'm a woman
You think, like every woman,

I have to be a slave or concubine—
You conceited, self-indulgent libertine—
[Again correcting her pronunciation.]
Libertine.
[Narrowing her eyes vindictively.]
How I wish I'd called him that! Right to his face!
[Turning and addressing "him" again.]
Libertine! And while we're on the subject, sire,

There are certain goings on around this place
That I wish to tell you I do not admire:

I do not like polygamy
Or even moderate bigamy
(I realize
That in your eyes
That clearly makes a prig o' me)
But I am from a civilized land called Wales,
Where men like you are kept in county gaols.

In your pursuit of pleasure, you
Have mistresses who treasure you
(They have no ken
Of other men
Beside whom they can measure you)
A flock of sheep, and you the only ram—
No wonder you're the wonder of Siam!
[*At first elated by this sally a frightened, embarrassed look comes into her eyes. She speaks.*]
I'm rather glad I *didn't* say that. . . . Not with the women right there . . . and the children.
[*She sings wistfully.*]
The children, the children,
I'll not forget the children,
No matter where I go I'll always see
Those little faces looking up at me . . .

At first, when I started to teach,
They were shy and remained out of reach,
But lately I've thought
One or two have been caught
By a word I have said
Or a sentence I've read,
And I've heard an occasional question
That implied, at the least, a suggestion
That the work I was trying to do
Was beginning to show with a few . . .

That Prince Chulalongkorn
Is very like his father,
He's stubborn—but inquisitive and smart
. . .
[*Sudden tears.*]
I must leave this place before they break my heart,
I must leave this place before they break my heart!
[*She stops, picks up the watch that is on her pillow and looks down at it.*]

Goodness! I had no idea it was so late.
[*She resumes undressing, but presently she is back at the* KING *again. She becomes motionless and squints her eyes at "him."*]
Shall I tell you what I think of you?
You're spoiled!
You're a conscientious worker
But you're spoiled.
Giving credit where it's due
There is much I like in you
But it's also very true
That you're spoiled!
[*She struts up and down, imitating him.*]
Everybody's always bowing
To the King,
Everybody has to grovel
To the King.
By your Buddha you are blessed,
By your ladies you're caressed
But the one who loves you best
Is the King!

All that bowing and kowtowing
To remind you of your royalty,
I find a most disgusting exhibition.
I wouldn't ask a Siamese *cat*
To demonstrate his loyalty
By taking that ridiculous position!

How would you like it if you were a man
Playing the part of a toad?
Crawling around on your elbows and knees,
Eating the dust in the road! . . .
Toads! Toads! All of your people are toads!
[*She sinks to her knees in scornful imitation of the "toads".*]
Yes, Your Majesty; No, Your Majesty.
Tell us how low to go, Your Majesty;
Make some more decrees, Your Majesty,
Don't let us up off our knees, Your Majesty.
Give us a kick, if it please Your Majesty,
Give us a kick if you would, Your Majesty—
[*"Taking" an imaginary kick.*]
Oh! That was good, Your Majesty! . . .
[*She pounds the floor in her temper, then lies down prone, exhausted . . .* THIANG *enters and rings the string of bells by the door twice.* ANNA *does not, at first, respond. Then, only half believing she has heard a ring, she rises on her knees.*]
ANNA. Who is it?

LADY THIANG. Mrs. Anna, it is I, Lady Thiang.

ANNA. At this hour of the night! [*Opening door.*] Come in, Lady Thiang.

LADY THIANG. Mrs. Anna, will you go to King?

ANNA. Now? Has he sent for me?

THIANG. No. But he would be glad to see you. He is deeply wounded man. No one has ever spoken to him as you did today in schoolroom.

ANNA. Lady Thiang, no one has ever behaved to *me* as His Majesty did today in the schoolroom.

THIANG. And there is more distressing thing. Our agents in Singapore have found letters to British Government from people whose greedy eyes are on Siam. They describe King as a barbarian, and suggest making Siam a protectorate.

ANNA. That is outrageous! He is many things I do not like, but he is not a barbarian.

THIANG. Then you will help him?

ANNA. You mean—advise him?

THIANG. It must not sound like advice. King cannot take advice. And if you go to him, he will not bring up subject. You must bring it up.

ANNA. I cannot go to him. It's against all my principles. Certainly not without his having *asked* for me.

THIANG. He wish to be new-blood King with Western ideas. But it is hard for him, Mrs. Anna. And there is something else—Princess Tuptim. I do not tell him—for his sake. I deal with this my own way. But for these other things, he need help, Mrs. Anna.

ANNA. He has *you.*

THIANG. I am not equal to his special needs. He could be great man. But he need special help. He need *you.*

ANNA. Lady Thiang, please don't think I am being stubborn. But I simply cannot go to him. I will not.

THIANG. What more can I say to you? [*Frustrated, she tries to think of how else to persuade* ANNA. *Presently she turns back to* ANNA *and starts to sing.*]

This is a man who thinks with his heart,
His heart is not always wise.
This is a man who stumbles and falls,
But this is a man who tries.
This is a man you'll forgive and forgive,
And help and protect, as long as you live . . .

He will not always say
What you would have him say,
But now and then he'll say
    Something wonderful.
The thoughtless things he'll do
Will hurt and worry you—
Then all at once he'll do
    Something wonderful.
He has a thousand dreams
That won't come true.
You know that he believes in them
And that's enough for you.
You'll always go along,
Defend him when he's wrong
And tell him, when he's strong
    He is wonderful.
He'll always need your love—
And so he'll get your love—
A man who needs your love
    Can be wonderful!

[*As she finishes she kneels and looks up at* ANNA *suppliantly.* ANNA *takes her hand and helps her rise. Then she crosses to the bed, picks up her jacket and starts to put it on.* THIANG, *taking this as a sign that her mission is successful, smiles gratefully and leaves* ANNA *to finish dressing.*]

INTERMEDIATE SCENE

The Palace corridor.
The KRALAHOME *enters and meets* LADY THIANG.

KRALAHOME. Did you succeed? Will she go to him?

THIANG. She will go. She knows he needs her. Tell him.

KRALAHOME. I will tell him she is *anxious* to come. I will tell him it is *she* who needs *him.*

THIANG. That also will be true. [*The*

KRALAHOME *leaves her.* THIANG *soliloquizes.*] This woman knows many things, but this I think, she does not know. . . . [*She sings.*] She'll always go along, Defend him when he's wrong

And tell him when he's strong He is wonderful. He'll always need her love And so he'll get her love A man who needs your love Can be wonderful!

SCENE 6

The KING's *study. The* KING *has been reading a large English Bible, which lies open on the floor beside a cushion arm-rest. There are some English newspapers also on the floor. The* KING *is walking up and down impatiently. He goes up and out to the terrace, looks off left, sees something, and hurries down to the Bible and resumes reading it. Presently,* ANNA *enters on the terrace.*

ANNA. [*Making a curtsey.*] Your Majesty. [*She comes into the room.*] Your Majesty. [*No answer. She looks down over his shoulder.*] Your Majesty is reading the Bible!

KING. [*Remaining on the floor.*] Mrs. Anna, I think your Moses shall have been a fool.

ANNA. Moses!

KING. Moses! Moses! Moses! I think he shall have been a fool. [*Tapping the Bible.*] Here it stands written by him that the world was created in six days. You know and I know it took many ages to create world. I think he shall have been a fool to have written so. What is your opinion?

ANNA. Your Majesty, the Bible was not written by men of science, but by men of faith. [*The* KING *considers this.*] It was their explanation of the miracle of creation, which is the same miracle—whether it took six days or many centuries.

KING. [*Rising.*] Hm. [*He is impressed by her explanation but, of course, would not say so.*] You have come to apologize?

ANNA. I am sorry, Your Majesty, but . . .

KING. Good! You apologize.

ANNA. Your Majesty, I . . .

KING. I accept!

ANNA. Your Majesty, nothing that has been said can alter the fact that in my country, anyone who makes a promise must . . .

KING. Silence! [*Pursuing his own thoughts.*] Tell me about President Ling-

kong of America. Shall Mr. Lingkong be winning this war he is fighting at present?

ANNA. No one knows, Your Majesty.

KING. Does he have enough guns and elephants for transporting same?

ANNA. [*Not quite smiling.*] I don't think they have elephants in America, Your Majesty.

KING. No elephants! Then I shall send him some. [*Handing her a notebook and pencil.*] Write letter to Mr. Lingkong.

ANNA. Now?

KING. Now! When else! Now is always best time. [*He sits on the floor.*]

ANNA. Very well, Your Majesty.

KING. [*Dictating.*] From Phra Maha Mongut, by the blessing of the highest super agency in the world of the whole Universe, the King of Siam, the Sovereign of all tributary countries adjacent and around in every direction, etcetera, etcetera, etcetera. [*Almost without a break.*] Do you not have any respect for me? [ANNA *looks up from her notebook, having no idea what he means.*] Why do you stand over my head? I cannot stand all the time. And in this country, no one's head shall be higher than King's. From now on in presence you shall so conduct yourself like all other subjects.

ANNA. You mean on the floor! I am sorry. I shall try very hard not to let my head be as high as Your Majesty's—but I simply cannot possibly grovel on the floor. I couldn't possibly work that way—or think!

KING. [*He rises and studies her before*

he speaks.] You are very difficult woman. But you will observe care that head shall never be higher than mine. If I shall sit, you shall sit. If I shall kneel, you shall kneel, etcetera, etcetera, etcetera.
[*Pause.*]
ANNA. Very well, Your Majesty.
KING. Is promise?
ANNA. Is promise.
KING. Good [*He squats down on his heels to resume dictating.* ANNA *sits on the floor nearby.*] To His Royal Presidency of the United States in America. Abra-Hom Lingkong, etcetera . . . you fix up. It has occurred to us . . . [*He stretches out prone, his chin leaning on his hand. Then he notices that* ANNA's *head is higher.*] It has occurred to us— [*He gives* ANNA *a significant look, and she reluctantly keeps her promise, lying prone, so that her head is no higher than his.*] It has occurred to us that if several pairs of young male elephants were turned loose in forests of America, after a while they would increase . . .
ANNA. [*Her head snapping up from her dictating.*] Your Majesty—just *male* elephants?
KING. [*Refusing to acknowledge his mistake.*] You put in details! [*He rises, and she does also.*] Tonight my mind is on other matters—very important matters.
ANNA. [*Knowing he is getting near the subject he really wants to talk about.*] Anything you want to discuss with me?
KING. Why should I discuss important matters with woman?
ANNA. Very well, Your Majesty. [*She curtseys.*] Then I will say good night.
KING. Good night!
[ANNA *goes up toward the terrace, then turns, to give him another chance.*]
ANNA. Your Majesty . . .
KING. [*Relieved and eager.*] What, what, what?
ANNA. [*To cue him.*] I was wondering— When the boat arrived from Singapore yesterday . . .
KING. Singapore! Ha!
ANNA. Was there any news from abroad!
KING. News! Yes, there are news! They call me barbarian.
ANNA. Who?

KING. Certain parties who would use this as excuse to steal my country. Suppose you were Queen Victoria and somebody tell you King of Siam is barbarian. Do you believe?
ANNA. Well, Your Majesty . . .
KING. You will! You will! You will! You will believe I am barbarian because there is no one to speak otherwise.
ANNA. But this is a lie!
KING. It is a *false* lie!
ANNA. What have you decided to do about it?
KING. [*After a pause.*] You guess!
ANNA. Well, if someone were sending a big lie about me to England, I would do my best to send the truth to England . . . Is that what you have decided to do, Your Majesty?
KING. Yes. That is what I have decided to do. [*To himself.*] But how? [*He crosses to her.*] Guess how I shall do this!
ANNA. Well, my guess would be that when Sir Edward Ramsay arrives here . . .
KING. Ramsay? Ramsay?
ANNA. The British diplomat.
KING. Ah, yes—on way from Singapore.
ANNA. We wrote to him last month.
KING. When he is here, I shall take opportunity of expressing my opinion of English thieves who wish to steal Siam. I shall show him who is barbarian! [*Noticing her disapproval.*] What is this face you put on?
ANNA. Well, Your Majesty, my guess is that you will not fight with Sir Edward.
KING. I will not?
ANNA. No, Your Majesty. You will entertain him and his party in an especially grand manner. In this way you will make all witnesses in your favor. They will return to England and report to the Queen that you are not a barbarian.
KING. Naturally . . . naturally! [*He paces up and down, delighted with the solution.*] This is what I shall have intended to do.
ANNA. This is the only way to get the better of the British. Stand up to them. Put your best foot forward. [*The* KING, *bewildered, holds up his foot and looks at it.*] That is an expression, Your Majesty. It means dress up in your best clothes. Show them your most intelligent men, your most beautiful women. Edward admires beautiful women.

KING. [*Suspiciously.*] Edward? You call him this?

ANNA. We are old friends. I knew him in Bombay before I was married.

KING. Ah! . . . [*Walking past her thoughtfully.*] Shall it be proper for the British dignitary to see my women with no shoes on their feet? Shall it be proper for them to put their best *bare* feet forward? No! Sir Ramsay will go back and tell Queen I am a barbarian. Why do *you* not think of this?

ANNA. [*Suddenly inspired.*] We shall dress them up European fashion.

KING. You mean dress them in . . . dresses?

[ANNA *nods. They both become increasingly excited.*]

ANNA. How many women can I have to sew for me?

KING. All women in Kingdom. How many dresses?

ANNA. That depends on how many ladies are chosen by Your Majesty.

KING. You shall tell me which of my women are most like Europeans, for dressing like same. [*He crosses quickly to the throne-table, strikes a gong and shouts.*] Wake up! Wake up, everybody! Wives! Etcetera, etcetera, etcetera! [*He returns to* ANNA.] I shall command Chinese artists to paint their faces very pale. And you shall educate them in European custom and manners for presentation.

ANNA. I wonder how much time we shall have.

KING. Sir Ramsay's gunboat last reported off Songkla. How long he take depend on how many ports he call into. Let us say we have one week.

ANNA. One week! But, Your Majesty, I don't think . . . one week!

KING. In this time whole world was created—*Moses* say! . . . Are there any details I do not think of so far?

ANNA. You must give them a fine dinner—a European dinner.

KING. I was going to.

ANNA. And a ball. With music.

KING. Music. [*His face lights up.*] And dancing!

ANNA. That's right! Dancing!

KING. Why do *you* not think of dancing?

ANNA. It was an inspired idea, Your

Majesty. [*Now, in answer to the gong, the wives enter in nightdress.* TUPTIM *is first.* THIANG *also enters, but not in nightdress.*] We can give them a theatrical performance. Tuptim has written a play, a version of Uncle Tom's Cabin.

KING. Ha! We shall give them theatrical performance. We shall show them who is barbarian! [*To the wives.*] Line up! Line up! Line up! [*They do so.*] Lady Thiang! On Saturday next, at nine o'clock post meridian, we shall give fine dinner—European dinner, for probably thirty people. [THIANG *bows.*] You are to instruct steward during week he shall make eminent European dishes for tasting. I shall taste and schoolteacher shall taste. [*The children begin coming in, accompanied by their nurses and the Amazons. They rub their eyes and yawn. The* KING *turns to* ANNA.] You say who is most like European lady for dressing like same. [ANNA *crosses to inspect the wives. The* KING *continues his orders to* THIANG.] You are to make tablecloth of finest white silk for very long table. Also instruct court musicians to learn music of Europe for dancing, etcetera. [*The* TWINS, *coming in, have gone around him and are now in front of him.*] What? What? What? Am I to be annoyed by children at this moment? [*A* NURSE, *having lost her charge, comes running around him, clapping her hands.*] Who? Who? Who? [*All drop to the floor at his angry tones. Then the object of the* NURSE's *solicitude, a very tiny boy, crawls between the* KING's *legs and crouches in front of him.*] Mrs. Anna, we must be more scientific with children! [*He walks up and down angrily.*] For the next week, the men and women of my kingdom will work without sleeping until all is ready, and for what is not done, each man and woman shall be beaten a hundred strokes. Everyone must know this, Lady Thiang. Tell this to everyone! Above all, I must not be worried by anything . . . [*There is a tremendous report that sounds like a cannon, and fireworks appear on the backdrop. Discipline is immediately abandoned, and there are shrieks and cries of fear. The children huddle together with the nurses and Amazons. The* KING *and* ANNA *run up to the terrace.*] What can this be?

[*Another terrifying report.*]

ANNA. [*Pointing to the fireworks.*] Look, Your Majesty!

KING. Fireworks! [*The children, reassured, move forward a bit to enjoy the show.*] Fireworks at this hour in the morning! No one may order fireworks but me.

KRALAHOME. [*Rushing in.*] Your Majesty—the British! The gunboat!

KING. They attack?

KRALAHOME. No! They salute, and we answer with fireworks. It is Sir Edward Ramsay and his party.

ANNA. [*Horrified.*] Now?

KRALAHOME. Now! They must have come direct from Songla. No stops.

ANNA. No stops!

KING. Tell them to go back! We are not ready!

KRALAHOME. Not ready. Your Majesty?

KING. You do not know, you do not know. I had planned best idea I ever get.

ANNA. We can still do it, Your Majesty—*you* can do it.

KING. Ha! When English arrive we will put them to bed. Tomorrow morning we shall send them on sightseeing trip.

ANNA. We shall start now, this minute. Work! Work! We have only eighteen hours, but I shall do it somehow!

KING. [*Sternly.*] *I* shall do it. You shall help me. [*Resuming his orders, energetically.*] No one shall sleep tonight or tomorrow. We shall work even when the sun shines in the middle of the day. We shall . . . [*He sees a group of priests passing on the terrace.*] Ah! Priests! [*He motions them to come in.*] First we shall ask help from Buddha. Bow to him! Bow! Bow! Bow! [*They all sink to their knees, the* KING *included, and raise their hands in prayerful attitude.* ANNA *remains standing but bows her head. The* KING *chants.*] Oh, Buddha, give us the aid of your strength and your wisdom.

ALL. [*Repeating chant.*] Oh, Buddha, give us the aid of your strength and your wisdom.

[*The* KING *sits back on his heels.*]

KING. [*Clapping his hands as orientals do to get Buddha's attention.*] And help

us to prove to the visiting English that we are extraordinary and remarkable people.

ALL. And help us to prove to the visiting English that we are extraordinary and remarkable people.

[*During the repetition, the* KING *leans forward and down in a crouch, and steals a glance at* ANNA.]

KING. Help also Mrs. Anna to keep awake for scientific sewing of dresses, even though she be only a woman and a Christian, and therefore unworthy of your interest.

[ANNA *looks up in surprise at the mention of her name, and comes to the* KING *in protest.*]

ALL. Help also Mrs. Anna to keep awake for scientific sewing of dresses, even though she be only a woman and a Christian, and therefore unworthy of your interest.

KING. [*During the repetition of the prayer, to* ANNA.] A promise is a promise! Your head cannot be higher than mine! A promise! [*Reluctantly, she sinks to a kneeling position to match his. The orchestra plays strains of "Something Wonderful".*] And, Buddha, I promise you I shall give this unworthy woman a house—a house of her own—a brick residence adjoining the royal palace, according to agreement, etcetera, etcetera, etcetera.

ALL. And, Buddha, I promise you I shall give this unworthy woman a house—a house of her own—a brick residence adjoining the royal palace, according to agreement, etcetera, etcetera, etcetera.

[*As they repeat his words, the* KING *watching to make sure that* ANNA *imitates him, sits back on his heels, then leans forward, finally stretching out, prone. They are both flat on their faces. Then he raises his head and rests his chin on his hand. She does the same. Fireworks burst through the air beyond the terrace.* ANNA *and the* KING *regard each other warily. Who is taming whom?*]

CURTAIN

ACT TWO

SCENE 1

The schoolroom.
It has been converted into a dressing room for tonight. The floor and tables are littered with dressmaking materials. The wives are all dressed in their new hoopskirts, mostly finished, but all are uncomfortable in the unaccustomed clothes. A Chinese artist is painting the face of one. Others are receiving last-minute touches from two seamstresses. The faces of the wives are powdered white.
LADY THIANG *enters. She has on a Western bodice and a penang.*

THIANG. Ladies! Ladies! Clear everything away! Quickly now!
[*The wives and seamstresses clear away the materials.*]
A WIFE. Lady Thiang, what is this costume? [*Pointing to penang.*] Here is East— [*Pointing to bodice.*] Here is West!
THIANG. Have too much work to do! Cannot move fast in swollen skirt.
ANOTHER WIFE. Lady Thiang, why must we dress like this for British?
THIANG. Whatever Mrs. Anna want us to do is wise and good, but this— [*Indicating hoopskirts.*] is a puzzlement. [*She sings.*]
To prove we're not barbarians
They dress us up like savages!
To prove we're not barbarians
We wear a funny skirt!
WIVES.
To prove we're not barbarians
They dress us up like savages!
To prove we're not barbarians
We wear a funny skirt!
THIANG.
Western people funny,
Western people funny,
Western people funny,
Of that there is no doubt.
They feel so sentimental
About the oriental,
They always try to turn us
Inside down and upside out!
WIVES.
Upside out and inside down!
THIANG.
To bruise and pinch our little toes
Our feet are cramped in leather shoes—
They'd break if we had brittle toes,
But now they only hurt!

WIVES.
To bruise and pinch our little toes
Our feet are cramped in leather shoes—
They'd break if we had brittle toes,
But now they only hurt!

Western people funny,
Western people funny,
Western people funny,
Too funny to be true!
THIANG.
They think they civilize us
Whenever they advise us
To learn to make the same mistake
That they are making too!
ALL.
They think they civilize us
Whenever they advise us
To learn to make the same mistake
That they are making too!
THEY MAKE QUITE A FEW!
ANNA. [*Entering.*] Lady Thiang, here are the napkins for dinner. Will you put them on the table?
THIANG. [*Taking them.*] Thank you.
ANNA. Thank *you.* [LADY THIANG *goes out.*] Now, ladies, turn around and let me see how you look. [*The* WIVES *spread out and turn so that* ANNA *can see their backs. The* KING *enters. They immediately prostrate themselves, the hoops flying up behind them.* ANNA *sees the horrid truth.*] Oh, my goodness gracious!
KING. What shall be trouble now?
ANNA. I forgot! They have practically no—undergarments!
KING. Undergarments! [*He claps his hands and the* WIVES *rise.*] Of what importance are undergarments at this time?
ANNA. [*Stiffly.*] Of great importance.

KING. Are *you* wearing undergarments?

ANNA. Of course, Your Majesty!

KING. [*Pointing to hoopskirt, derisively.*] That a woman has no legs is useless to pretend. Wherefore, then, swollen skirt?

ANNA. The wide skirt is symbolic. It is the circle within which a female is protected.

KING. This is necessary? Englishmen are so aggressive? I did not know.

ANNA. [*Going to the* SEAMSTRESSES, *who help her remove her smock.*] I said it was symbolic.

KING. These undergarments—they are devised in symbolic, elaborate and ornamental manner?

ANNA. Sometimes.

[*Her gown now revealed, the* WIVES *gasp their admiration.*]

KING. [*Looking at her bare shoulders.*] This is what you are going to wear?

ANNA. Why, yes. Do you like it?

KING. This is what all the other visiting ladies shall look like?

ANNA. Most of them . . . I believe.

KING. You are certain this is customary? [*Indicating her bare shoulders.*] Etcetera, etcetera, etcetera . . .

ANNA. Yes, I am certain it is customary. What is so extraordinary about bare shoulders? Your own ladies . . .

KING. Ah, yes. But is different! They do not wear so many coverings up on other parts of body, etcetera, etcetera, and therefore . . .

ANNA. [*Irritated, like any woman who, displaying a new dress, meets unexpected criticism.*] Therefore what?

KING. Is different.

ANNA. I am sorry His Majesty does not approve.

KING. I do not say I do not approve, but I do say . . .

PHRA ALACK. [*Entering, prostrating himself.*] The English—they are in palace.

[*This causes immediate confusion among the* WIVES *who huddle in a frightened group.*]

THARA. They will eat us!

ANNA. They will do nothing of the kind!

KING. [*Calling* ANNA *to him, he gives her a piece of paper.*] Herewith shall be list of subjects you shall try to bring up for talk. On such subjects I am very bril-

liant, and will make great impression. You begin with Moses.

ANNA. [*Taking the paper and crowding in some last-minute coaching.*] Now remember, Your Majesty—Courtwright is the editor of a newspaper in Singapore . . .

[*She is interrupted by the entrance of* SIR EDWARD RAMSAY, *who has wandered into the room by mistake. One* WIFE *screams in fright.*]

ANOTHER WIFE. [*Indicating* SIR EDWARD's *monocle.*] Oh, evil eye! Evil eye!

[*The* WIVES *in an uncontrollable stampede throw their hoopskirts over their heads and rush out. From the look on* SIR EDWARD's *face, it is clear that they should have been supplied with undergarments.*]

ANNA. Ladies! Ladies! Come back! Don't Come Back! Oh, dear! Edward! Oh, Your Majesty, this is dreadful!

KING. [*Furious.*] Why have you not educated these girls in English custom of spying glass?

SIR EDWARD. Ah, my monocle. Was that what frightened them? Hello, Anna, my dear.

KING. [*Before they can complete their handshake.*] Who? Who? Who?

ANNA. Your Majesty, may I present Sir Edward Ramsay?

SIR EDWARD. [*Bowing.*] Your Majesty. [*He turns to* ANNA.] How are you, Anna?

KING. I regret, sir, my ladies have not given good impression.

SIR EDWARD. On the contrary, Your Majesty, I have never received so good an impression in so short a time. You have most attractive pupils, Anna.

[*The* KING *is clearly annoyed by the intimacy between* ANNA *and* SIR EDWARD.]

ANNA. Tomorrow you must meet my younger pupils—His Majesty's children. They are making wonderful progress.

SIR EDWARD. I shall be delighted. [*To* KING.] How many children have you, Your Majesty?

KING. Seventy-seven now, but I am not married very long. Next month expecting three more.

SIR EDWARD. No problem at all about an heir to the throne, is there? [*This sally falls flat with the* KING, *so he turns to* ANNA, *but it doesn't amuse her either.*] I—er—I suppose I should apologize for wandering into this room. The rest of the party were ahead of me and . . .

ANNA. I'm so glad you decided to visit us—to visit His Majesty I mean, of course . . .

SIR EDWARD. It was your postscript to His Majesty's letter that . . .

KING. [*Turning with alert suspicion.*] Postscript?

ANNA. His Majesty was most happy when you decided to accept his invitation . . . Weren't you, Your Majesty?

KING. [*Trying to figure it out.*] I was . . . happy

KRALAHOME. [*Entering.*] Your Majesty, dinner is about to be served, and I would first like to present your guests to you in the reception room.

KING. [*Clapping his hands happily, and going off.*] Dinner, dinner, dinner!

ANNA. [*To* KRALAHOME.] You have met?

KRALAHOME. [*Bowing.*] Your Excellency. [*He goes off. A waltz is being played offstage.*]

SIR EDWARD. Anna, my dear, you're looking lovelier than ever.

ANNA. Thank you, Edward.

SIR EDWARD. Found a job to do, eh? People you can help, that's it, isn't it? Extraordinary how one gets attached to people who need one. [*Listening.*] Do you hear that? Do you know we danced to that once? [*She nods.*] Bombay. Still dance?

ANNA. Not very often.

SIR EDWARD. You should. [*He puts his arm around her waist, and they dance.*]

ANNA. Edward, I think we'd better . . .

SIR EDWARD. Are you sure you don't get homesick?

ANNA. No, Edward. I told you, I have nothing there—no one.

[*The* KING *enters and watches them.*]

EDWARD. Anna, do you remember that I once asked you to marry me—before Tom came along?

ANNA. Dear Edward . . .

KING. [*Interrupting, furiously.*] Dancing —after dinner!

SIR EDWARD. Oh, sorry, sir. I'm afraid I started talking over old times.

KING. [*Looking sternly at* ANNA.] It was my impression Mrs. Anna would be of help for seating of guests at dinner table, etcetera, etcetera, etcetera.

SIR EDWARD. In that case, we'd better be going in, Anna.

[*He moves toward her, offering his arm.*]

KING. [*Coming between them, offering his arm.*] Yes, better be going in . . . Anna.

[*She takes the* KING'S *arm, and they start off left,* SIR EDWARD *following.*]

ANNA. [*After a quick look at the paper the* KING *has given her.*] His Majesty made an interesting point about Moses the other day when he was reading the Bible. It seems he takes issue with the statement that . . .

[*They are off.*]

SCENE 2

The Palace grounds.
TUPTIM *enters and crosses the stage, looking back furtively.*
She starts guiltily as she sees LADY THIANG.

THIANG. Princess Tuptim, dinner is over. King and his English guests are on way to theater pavilion. Should you not be there to begin your play?

TUPTIM. [*Rattled.*] I came out here to memorize my lines.

THIANG. [*Stopping her as she starts to go.*] I think not, Princess. I have seen you and Lun Tha together. I do not tell King this. For *his* sake. I do not wish to hurt him. But your lover will leave Siam tonight.

TUPTIM. Tonight?

THIANG. Now go to the theater, Princess. [*TUPTIM exits.* THIANG *starts off, stops as she sees* LUN THA *enter left, looks at him with stern suspicion, then exits.* LUN THA *crosses to the other side, and calls off, in a whisper.*]

LUN THA. Tuptim!

TUPTIM. [*Entering.*] Turn back and look the other way. [LUN THA *instantly does so.*] I am here in the shadow of the wall. I will stay here until she turns the corner.

. . . She has told me you will leave Siam tonight, but I don't believe her.

LUN THA. It is true, Tuptim. They have ordered me onto the first ship that leaves for Burma, and it is tonight.

TUPTIM. [*Running to him.*] What will we do?

LUN THA. You are coming with me!

TUPTIM. I!

LUN THA. You have been a slave long enough! Secret police will all be at the theater. Meet me here, after your play. Everything is arranged.

TUPTIM. I cannot believe it.

LUN THA. I can. It will be just as I have pictured it a million times. [*He sings:*]
I have dreamed that your arms are lovely,
I have dreamed what a joy you'll be.
I have dreamed every word you'll whisper
When you're close,
    Close to me.
How you look in the glow of evening
I have dreamed, and enjoyed the view.
In these dreams I've loved you so
That by now I think I know
What it's like to be loved by you—
I will love being loved by you.

TUPTIM.
Alone and awake I've looked at the stars,
The same that smiled on you;
And time and again I've thought all
    the things
That you were thinking too.
I have dreamed that your arms are lovely,
I have dreamed what a joy you'll be.
I have dreamed every word you'll whisper
When you're close,
    Close to me.
How you look in the glow of evening
I have dreamed, and enjoyed the view,
In these dreams I've loved you so
That by now I think I know

TUPTIM AND LUN THA.
What it's like to be loved by you—
I will love being loved by you.
    [ANNA *enters.* TUPTIM *runs to her.*]

TUPTIM. Mrs. Anna!

ANNA. Tuptim, they are looking for you at the theater. I guessed you were both here. I ran out to warn you. I do think you're being rather reckless.

TUPTIM. Yes, I will go. [*She starts away, then turns back and surprises* ANNA *with a suddenly serious tone in her voice.*] I must say good-bye to you now, Mrs. Anna. [*She kneels, kisses* ANNA's *hand impulsively, and runs off.*]

ANNA. [*To* LUN THA.] Gracious! Anyone would think that she never expected to see me again.
    [*He looks at her steadily, and catching his look, she crosses him, looking after* TUPTIM.]

LUN THA. Mrs. Anna, we are leaving tonight.

ANNA. Leaving? How?

LUN THA. Don't ask me how. It is better if you don't know. We shall never forget you, Mrs. Anna. [*He kisses her hand.*] Never.

ANNA. [*As he goes.*] God bless you both! [*Alone, thoughtfully, she sings.*]
I know how it feels to have wings on your heels
And to fly down a street in a trance.
You fly down a street on the chance that you'll meet,
And you meet—not really by chance.
Don't cry, young lovers, whatever you do,
Don't cry because I'm alone.
All of my memories are happy tonight,
I've had a love of my own.
I've had a love of my own, like yours,
I've had a love of my own.
    [*She starts off as the curtain closes.*]

SCENE 3

The theater pavilion.
BALLET: *"The Small House of Uncle Thomas."*
Before a curtain two attendants carry on a drum and a gong.
The drummer takes his place. The royal singers enter ceremoniously and take their places at the opposite corner. TUPTIM *enters and stands in front of the singers.*
The curtain opens, revealing the royal dancers dressed in traditional costumes, their faces painted chalk-white.

TUPTIM. [*Speaking straight out at the audience, as if addressing the* KING *and his British visitors.*] Your Majesty, and honorable guests, I beg to put before you "Small House of Uncle Thomas."
[*A tiny cabin is brought on.*]

CHORUS.
Small house of Uncle Thomas!
Small house of Uncle Thomas!
Written by a woman,
Harriet Beecher Stow-a!

TUPTIM. House is in Kingdom of Kentucky, ruled by most wicked King in all America—Simon of Legree. [*The gong is struck. The dancers make a traditional gesture denoting terror.*] Your Majesty, I beg to put before you loving friends . . . Uncle Thomas!
[*He enters from cabin.*]

CHORUS.
Dear old Uncle Thomas.

TUPTIM.
Little Eva.
[*She enters from cabin.*]

CHORUS.
Blessed Little Eva.

TUPTIM.
Little Topsy.
[*She enters from cabin.*]

CHORUS.
Mischief-maker, Topsy.

TUPTIM.
Happy people.

CHORUS.
Very happy people.
[*The happy people dance.*]

TUPTIM. Happy people. Happy people.
[*The dance over,* TUPTIM *continues.*] Your Majesty, I beg to put before you one who is not happy—the slave, Eliza.
[ELIZA *enters from cabin.*]

CHORUS.
Poor Eliza, poor Eliza,
Poor unfortunate slave.

TUPTIM.
Eliza's lord and master
King Simon of Legree.
She hates her lord and master.
[*The gong and cymbal combine in a frightening crash, and the dancers again pantomime terror according to the traditional gesture.*]
And fears him.
[*Gong and cymbal again.*]
This King has sold her lover

To far away province of O-hee-o
Lover's name is George.

CHORUS.
George.

TUPTIM.
Baby in her arms
Also called George.

CHORUS.
George.
[ELIZA *enacts what* TUPTIM *describes.*]

TUPTIM.
Eliza say she run away and look for lover George.

CHORUS.
George.

TUPTIM.
So she bid good-bye to friends and start on her escape. "The escape."
[ELIZA *now dances and mimes "the escape."*]

CHORUS.
Run, Eliza, run, Eliza!
Run from Simon.

TUPTIM.
Poor Eliza running,
And run into a rainstorm.
[*The rainstorm is depicted by dancers waving scarves. After the "storm" is over,* ELIZA *gives her "baby" a shake to dry it off.*]
Comes a mountain.
[*The mountain is formed by three men.*]

CHORUS.
Climb, Eliza!
[*After climbing the "mountain"* ELIZA *rubs her feet.*]

TUPTIM.
Hide, Eliza!

CHORUS.
Hide, Eliza, hide from Simon!
Hide in forest.
[*The trees of the forest are dancers holding branches.*]

TUPTIM. Eliza very tired. [ELIZA *exits wearily.*] Your Majesty, I regret to put before you King Simon of Legree.
[SIMON, *wearing a terrible, three-headed masque, is borne on by attendants. His slaves prostrate themselves before him in the manner of subjects of the King of Siam.*]

CHORUS.
Because one slave has run away
Simon beating every slave.

[SIMON *dances down an aisle of quivering slaves, slashing at them with his huge sword.*]

TUPTIM. Simon clever man. He decide to hunt Eliza, not only with soldiers, but with scientific dogs who sniff and smell, and thereby discover all who run away from King.

[*Now the chase ensues. Dancers with the dog masques portray bloodhounds who "sniff and smell" and pick up poor* ELIZA's *scent.* ELIZA *runs from one side of the stage to the other always followed by the dogs, and by more of the* KING's *men in each episode, and finally by the horrible* SIMON *himself. And the pursuers keep getting closer to her.*]

CHORUS.
Run, Eliza, run!
Run, Eliza, run!

Run, Eliza, run, run.
Run from Simon, run, run!

Eliza run,
Eliza run from Simon, run!
Eliza run,
Eliza run from Simon, run!

Eliza run,
Eliza run,
Run, run!

Simon getting closer . . .
Eliza getting tired . . .
Run, Eliza,
Run from Simon,
Run, Eliza, run!

TUPTIM.
Eliza come to river,
Eliza come to river.

[*Two dancers run on with a long strip of silk which they wave to indicate a flowing river.* ELIZA *stands before the "river" in frustrated horror.*]

CHORUS.
Poor Eliza!

TUPTIM.
Who can save Eliza?

CHORUS.
Only Buddha,
Buddha, Buddha, Buddha!
Save her, Buddha,

Save her, Buddha, save her! . . .
What will Buddha do?

[*Gong. The curtains part at back revealing Buddha on a high throne.*]

TUPTIM.
Buddha make a miracle!

[*An* ANGEL *with golden wings enters.*]

Buddha send an angel down.
Angel make the wind blow cold.

[*The* ANGEL *blows on the "river" through a golden horn. The strip of silk, indicating the "river," is made to lie flat on the stage. It no longer ripples. The "river" is frozen!*]

Make the river water hard,
Hard enough to walk upon.

CHORUS.
Buddha make a miracle!
Praise to Buddha!

[ELIZA *looks down at the river, somewhat puzzled. The* ANGEL *puts away her horn, then joins* ELIZA, *takes her hand and proceeds to teach her how to slide on a frozen river.*]

TUPTIM.
Angel show her how to walk on frozen water.

[ELIZA *and the* ANGEL *now do a pas-de-deux in the manner of two skaters.* ELIZA *picks it up quickly and seems to like it.*]

Now, as token of his love,
Buddha make a new miracle.

[*As* TUPTIM *describes this new miracle, the* CHORUS *keeps singing.*]

CHORUS.
Praise to Buddha!
Praise to Buddha!

TUPTIM. Send from heaven stars and blossoms,
Look like lace upon the sky.

[*Several men enter with long poles like fishing rods, and from the lines dangle large representations of snowflakes.*]

So Eliza cross the river,
Hidden by this veil of lace.

[TUPTIM *steps down a few feet.*]

Forgot to tell you name of miracle—snow

[*Suddenly* ELIZA *looks terrified, and no wonder!*]

TUPTIM AND CHORUS.
Of a sudden she can see
Wicked Simon of Legree,
Sliding 'cross the river fast,
With his bloodhounds and his slaves!

[*Now* SIMON *and his slaves enter and* ELIZA *runs away. The* ANGEL, *too, has disappeared at the wrong moment. Now, while* SIMON *and his followers start to slide and skate on the "river," very much as* ELIZA *had, the "river" begins to be active again. The strip of silk is made to wave, and the two men carrying it lift it up and start to envelop* SIMON *and his party in its folds.*]

TUPTIM. What has happened to the river?

TUPTIM AND CHORUS.
Buddha has called out the sun,
Sun has made the water soft.
Wicked Simon and his slaves
Fall in river and are drowned.

[*This is true. The* ANGEL *has come back with a huge sun, which he holds and directs upon the river. The silk is wrapped around* SIMON *and his party, and they are dragged off in it, drowned as they can be.*]

TUPTIM. On other side of river is pretty city, Canada, where Eliza sees lovely small house—guess who live in house? [*A replica of the first cabin is brought on, but this one has snow on the roof and ice on the windowpanes.*] Uncle Thomas.

[*He enters as before.*]

CHORUS.
Dear old Uncle Thomas.

TUPTIM.
Little Eva.

[*She enters.*]

CHORUS.
Blessed Little Eva.

TUPTIM.
Little Topsy.

[*She enters.*]

CHORUS.
Mischief-maker, Topsy.

TUPTIM.
Lover George.

[*The* ANGEL *enters, but this time without wings.*]

CHORUS.
Faithful lover George.

TUPTIM.
Who is looking like angel to Eliza.

[*A chord is struck.*]

They have all escaped from
Wicked King and make happy reunion.

[*They do a brief dance.*]

Topsy glad that Simon die,
Topsy dance for joy.

[*She dances a few steps, then strikes a pose.*]

I tell you what Harriet Beecher Stowe say
That Topsy say:

[*Cymbal crash.*]

"I specks I'se de wickedest critter
In de world!"

[*Another cymbal crash.* TUPTIM *frowns, an earnest, dramatic note comes into her voice. She steps forward.*]

But I do not believe
Topsy is a wicked critter.
Because I too am glad
For death of King.
Of any King who pursues
Slave who is unhappy and tries to join her
lover!

[*The dancers look frightened.* TUP-TIM's *emotions are running away with her.*]

And, Your Majesty,
I wish to say to you . . .
Your Majesty—

[*A chord is struck.* TUPTIM *collects herself.*]

And honorable guests . . .
I will tell you end of story . . .

[*The dancers look relieved. She is back in the make-believe tale of "Uncle Thomas."*]

Is very sad ending.
Buddha has saved Eliza
But with the blessings of Buddha
Also comes sacrifice.

[*Gong. Buddha is again revealed.*]

CHORUS.
Poor Little Eva,
Poor Little Eva,
Poor unfortunate child.

[*Eva comes to center, weeping.*]

TUPTIM.
Is Buddha's wish
That Eva come to him
And thank him personally
For saving of Eliza and baby.
And so she die
And go to arms of Buddha.

[EVA, *bowing her sad adieux to the audience, turns and climbs the steps to Buddha's high throne.*]

CHORUS.
Praise to Buddha,
Praise to Buddha!

[*The music mounts in loud and up-lifting crescendo. The curtain closes on the tragic tableau. The singers and dancers perform ceremonious bows in front of the curtain.*]

SCENE 4

The KING's *study.* ANNA *is seated on a pile of books beside the throne-table. The* KING *is walking up and down, smoking a long cigar.* SIR EDWARD *is standing, center, and the* KRALAHOME *is in the shadows to his left. It is night, after the banquet.*

SIR EDWARD. The evening was a great success, Your Majesty. I enjoyed Princess Tuptim's play immensely.

KING. This play did not succeed with me. It is immoral for King to drown when pursuing slave who deceive him. [*Pacing angrily.*] Immoral! Immoral! Tuptim shall know of my displeasure.

SIR EDWARD. Your conversation at dinner was most amusing.

KING. I was forced to laugh myself. I was so funny.

SIR EDWARD. Her Majesty, Queen Victoria, will be very glad to know that we have come to such "felicity of agreement" about Siam.

KING. And very happy I am thereof. Very happy.

SIR EDWARD. I think now, with your permission, I should take my leave. [*He bows. The* KING *extends his hand in a manner clearly showing how unfamiliar he is with this Western amenity.* SIR EDWARD *shakes his hand, then bows to* ANNA.] Good-bye, Anna, my dear. It was lovely to see you again.

ANNA. Good-bye, Edward. [*He goes out, escorted by the* KRALAHOME. *The* KING *turns to* ANNA.] Well, Your Majesty . . .

KING. It is all over. [*He puts his cigar in a bowl, very glad to be rid of it.*]

ANNA. May I remove my shawl? It is a very hot night. [*She does so. This makes the* KING *vaguely uneasy. He closes his own jacket across his bare chest as if to compensate for* ANNA's *lack of modesty.*] I am so pleased about everything.

KING. [*Trying not to be too sentimental about this.*] I am aware of your interest. I wish to say you have been of great help to me in this endeavor. I wish to make gift. [*He takes a ring from his finger and holds it out to her across the table, not looking at her.*] I have hope you will accept. [*She takes it slowly and gazes at it.*] Put it on finger! [*Still stunned, she does not move or speak.*] Put it on! Put it on!

[*His voice is gruff and commanding. She obeys him, slowly putting the ring on the index finger of her left hand.*]

ANNA. Your Majesty, I do not know what to say!

KING. When one does not know what to say, it is a time to be silent! [*There is a pause. Both are embarrassed. The* KING *makes small talk.*] A white elephant has been discovered in the forests of Ayuthia.

ANNA. You regard that as a good omen, don't you?

KING. Yes. Everything going well with us.

ANNA. [*Warmly.*] Everything going well with us.

[*A gong sounds off left.*]

KING. Who, who, who?

KRALAHOME. [*Offstage.*] It is I, Your Majesty.

KING. Wait, wait, wait! [*He goes to* ANNA *with a vaguely guilty manner and amazes her by replacing her shawl around her shoulders, then he calls offstage.*] Come in! Come in!

KRALAHOME. [*Entering and bowing.*] Your Majesty . . .

KING. Well, well, well?

KRALAHOME. Secret police are here. They would make report to you.

KING. [*As* ANNA *rises.*] You will wait here.

[*He goes out.*]

ANNA. [*Deeply concerned.*] Secret police?

KRALAHOME. [*Noticing ring.*] Your finger shines.

ANNA. [*Confused, feeling compromised.*] Yes. The King. I did not know what to say. Women in my country don't accept gifts from men. Of course, he's the King . . . Actually, it places me in a rather embarrassing position. I was intending to ask him for a rise in salary. And now . . .

KRALAHOME. And now it will be difficult to ask.

ANNA. Very. [*Turns to him.*] I don't suppose you would speak to him for me—about my rise in salary, I mean.

KRALAHOME. I think I shall do this for you, because this is a strange world in which men and women can be very blind about things nearest to them.

ANNA. Thank you, Your Excellency. I don't understand what you mean, but . . .

KRALAHOME. No, but that does not matter—and I do not think he will rise your salary, anyway.

KING. [*Entering briskly.*] Ha! Good news and bad news come together. [*To* KRALAHOME.] You will please to stay up all night until we have further report on item of Tuptim.

KRALAHOME. I had intended to do so, Your Majesty.

[*He bows and goes out.*]

ANNA. [*Rising.*] Perhaps I had better go, too.

KING. No! No! No! I wish to talk with you.

ANNA. Is there something wrong with Tuptim?

KING. I do not know, nor do I consider his the most important thing I must tell you. It is of greater interest that the English think highly of me. Secret police have served coffee after dinner, and listen as they talk and report conversation of British dignitaries.

ANNA. [*Shocked.*] You have been spying on your guests?

KING. How else can one find the truth? ANNA *shakes her head disapprovingly, but he ignores this.*] It appears I have made excellent impression. It is clear they do not think me barbarian.

ANNA. This is what we intended to prove.

KING. What we intended to prove! [*Suddenly switching to the second item.*] Tuptim!

ANNA. What about her?

KING. She is missing from palace. You know something of this?

ANNA [*Frightened.*] The last time I saw her, she was at the theater pavilion.

KING. That is last time anyone has seen her. She never speaks to you of running away?

ANNA [*Evasively.*] I knew she was unhappy.

KING. Why unhappy? She is in palace of King. What is greater honor for young girl than to be in palace of King?

ANNA. Your Majesty . . . If Tuptim is caught, shall she be punished?

KING. Naturally. What would you do if you were King like me?

ANNA. I believe I would give her a chance to explain. I think I would try not to be too harsh.

KING. Hmph.

ANNA. [*Earnestly.*] Your Majesty, of what interest to you is one girl like Tuptim? She is just another woman, as a bowl of rice is just another bowl of rice, no different from any other bowl of rice.

KING. Now you understand about women! [*He picks up a book from the table.*] But British poets . . .

ANNA. [*Amused.*] You have been reading poetry, Your Majesty?

KING. Out of curiosity over strange idea of love, etcetera, etcetera. I tell you this poetry is nonsense, and a silly complication of a pleasant simplicity. [*He sings.*]
A woman is a female who is human,
Designed for pleasing man, the human male.
A human male is pleased by many women,
And all the rest you hear is fairy tale.

ANNA.
Then tell me how this fairy tale began, sir.
You cannot call it just a poet's trick.
Explain to me why many men are faithful,
And true to one wife only—

KING.
They are sick!

ANNA. [*Speaking.*] But you *do* expect *women* to be faithful.

KING. Naturally.

ANNA. Why naturally?

KING. Because it is natural. It is like old Siamese rhyme. [*He sings:*]
A girl must be like a blossom
With honey for just one man.

A man must live like honey bee
And gather all he can.

To fly from blossom to blossom
A honey bee must be free,
But blossom must not ever fly
From bee to bee to bee.

ANNA. You consider this *sensible* poetry,
Your Majesty?

KING. Certainly. But listen to this, from
your own poet Alf-red Tenny-sone. [*He
reads from the book.*]
"Now folds the lily all her sweetness up,
And slips into the bosom of the lake . . .
So fold thyself, my dearest, thou, and slip
Into my bosom . . ."
[*He looks sternly at* ANNA.] English girls
are so—acrobatic?

ANNA. [*Laughing.*] Your Majesty, I
don't know if I can ever make it clear to
you . . . We do not look on women as just
human females. They are . . . Well, take
yourself. You are not just a human male.

KING. I am King.

ANNA. Exactly. So every man is like a
King and every woman like a Queen,
when they love one another.

KING. This is a sickly idea.

ANNA. It is a beautiful idea, Your Majesty. We are brought up with it, of course,
and a young girl at her first dance . . .

KING. Young girl? They dance, too? Like
I see tonight? In arms of men not their
husbands?

ANNA. Why, yes.

KING. I would not permit.

ANNA. It's very exciting when you're
young, and you're sitting on a small gilt
chair, your eyes lowered, terrified that
you'll be a wallflower. Then you see two
black shoes—white waistcoat—a face . . .
It speaks! [*She sings:*]
We've just been introduced,
I do not know you well,
But when the music started
Something drew me to your side.
So many men and girls are in each other's
arms—
It made me think we might be
Similarly occupied.
[*The* KING *sits on his throne-table
watching* ANNA, *a new interest com-
ing into his eyes.*]
Shall we dance?
On a bright cloud of music shall we fly?
Shall we dance?

Shall we then say "good night" and mean
"good-bye"?
Or, perchance,
When the last little star has left the sky,
Shall we still be together
With our arms around each other
And shall you be my new romance?
On the clear understanding
That this kind of thing can happen,
Shall we dance?
Shall we dance? Shall we dance?
[ANNA, *carried away by her reminis-
cent mood, dances around the room
until she glides by the* KING *and
realizes that he is looking at her very
much as he might look at one of his
dancing girls. This brings her to an
abrupt stop.*]

KING. Why do you stop? You dance
pretty. Go on! Go on! Go on!

ANNA. Your Majesty, I—I didn't realize
I was—after all, I'm not a dancing girl.
In England we don't—that is, a girl would
not dance while a man is looking at her.

KING. But she will dance with strange
man, holding hands, etcetera, etcetera?

ANNA. Yes. Not always a strange man
Sometimes a very good friend.

KING. [*Pause.*] Good! We dance together. You show me. [ANNA *looks a little
uncertain.*] You teach! You teach! You
teach!
[*He holds out his hands and she
takes them.*]

ANNA. It's quite simple, the polka. You
count, "one two three *and* one two three
and one two three *and*—"

KING. One two three *and.*

ANNA. [*Singing.*]
Shall we dance?

KING.
One two three *and.*

ANNA.
On a bright cloud of music shall we fly?

KING.
One two three *and.*

ANNA.
Shall we dance?

KING.
One two three *and.*

ANNA.
Shall we then say "good night" and mean
"good-bye"?

KING.
One two three, *and.* [*He sings:*]

Or perchance.
When the last little star has leave the
sky—
ANNA.
Shall we still be together,
With our arms around each other,
And shall you be my new romance?
[KING *sings the word "romance" with
her.*]
On the clear understanding
That this kind of thing can happen,
Shall we dance? Shall we dance? Shall we
dance?
[*The orchestra continues, and* ANNA *resumes her lesson.*] One two three, *and—*
[*She leads the* KING *by his hands.*]
KING. One two three—one two three—
[*He stops.*] What is wrong? I know! I
know! I forget "And." This time I remember.
KING AND ANNA. [*Counting together as
they resume dancing.*] One two three *and,*
one two three *and,* one two three *and* . . .
ANNA. That's splendid, Your Majesty!
KING. Splendid. One two and— [*He
stops and protests petulantly.*] You have
thrown me off count! [*They start again.*]
One two three *and,* one two three *and.*
[*They circle. Suddenly he stops.*] But this
is not right!
ANNA. Yes, it is. You were doing . . .
KING. No! No No! Is not right. Not the
way I see Europeans dancing tonight.
ANNA. Yes, it was. It was just like that.
KING. No! . . . Were not holding two
hands like this.
ANNA. [*Suddenly realizing what he
means.*] Oh . . . No . . . as a matter of
fact . . .
KING. Was like this. No?
[*Looking very directly into her eyes
he advances on her slowly and puts
his hand on her waist.*]
ANNA. [*Scarcely able to speak.*] Yes.
KING. Come! One two three *and,* one
two three *and* . . . [*They dance a full refrain and dance it very well indeed,
rhythmically and with spirit, both obviously enjoying it. They stop for a moment, stand off and laugh at each other.
Then he wants more. He goes back to her
slowly.*] Good! Come! We try again. This
time I do better.
ANNA. Very well, Your Majesty.
[*They dance again, but only for a
few whirls before a gong crashes, and
the* KRALAHOME *bursts in.*]
KRALAHOME. Your Majesty . . .
[*He prostrates himself.* ANNA *and the
KING stop and separate quickly.*]
KING. [*Furious.*] Why do you burst
through my door without waiting?
KRALAHOME. We have found Tuptim.
KING. [*A pause. He folds his arms, suddenly stern. His speech is cold and deliberate.*] Where is she?
KRALAHOME. Secret police are questioning her.
ANNA. [*Terrified for* TUPTIM.] Now you
have found her, what will you do with
her?
KING. [*Now miles away from her.*] I
will do—what is usually done in such
event.
ANNA. What is that?
KING. When it happens you will know.
[TUPTIM *dashes on, falls on her knees at
ANNA's feet and clings to her skirt. Two
GUARDS run after her, two more and the
INTERPRETER take positions at the door.*]
TUPTIM. Mrs. Anna! Mrs. Anna! Do not
let them beat me! Do not let them!
[*The GUARDS silence her roughly and
drag her away from ANNA.*]
KRALAHOME. She was found on Chinese
sailing ship. See! She wears disguise of
priest.
KING. [*Shouting down at* TUPTIM's
prostrate, quivering figure.] Who gave
you this robe? Who? Who? Who?
KRALAHOME. It is believed she was running away with man who brought her here
from Burma.
KING. [*Deep humiliation in his voice.*]
Dishonor. Dishonor. Dishonor.
KRALAHOME. He was not found on boat.
KING. [*To* TUPTIM.] Where is this man?
TUPTIM. I do not know.
KING. You will tell us where we will find
him! You will tell us!
TUPTIM. I do not know.
KRALAHOME. It is believed you were
lovers with this man.
TUPTIM. I was not lovers with this man.
KING. Dishonor. We will soon have
truth of this man.
[*He signals the* GUARD. *They tear the
priest robe off her, leaving her back
bare. One of them unwinds a stout
whip.*]

TUPTIM. Mrs. Anna!

ANNA. [*Throwing herself on the man with the whip.*] Stop that! Do you hear me? Stop it!

KING. [*Coldly to* ANNA.] It would be better if you understand at once that this matter does not concern you.

ANNA. But it does. It does, dreadfully . . . because of her, and even more because of you.

KING. You waste my time.

ANNA. She's only a child. She was running away because she was unhappy. Can't you understand that? Your Majesty, I beg of you—don't throw away everything you've done. This girl hurt your vanity. She didn't hurt your heart. You haven't got a heart. You've never loved anyone. You never will.

KING. [*Pause. The* KING, *stung by* ANNA's *words, seeks a way to hurt her in return.*] I show! [*He snatches the whip from the* GUARD.] Give! Give to me!

ANNA. [*Her eyes filled with horror.*] I cannot believe you are going to do this dreadful thing.

KING. You do not believe, eh? Maybe you will believe when you hear her screaming as you run down the hall! [*Pause.*]

ANNA. I am not going to run down the hall. I am going to stay here and watch you!

KING. Hold this girl! [*The two* GUARDS *grab* TUPTIM's *arms.*] I do this all myself.

ANNA. You *are* a barbarian!

KING. Down! Down! Down! [*The* GUARDS *hold* TUPTIM *down.*] Am I King, or am I not King? Am I to be cuckold in my own palace? Am I to take orders from English schoolteacher?

ANNA. No, not orders . . .

KING. Silence! . . . [*He hands the whip to the* KRALAHOME.] I am King, as I was born to be, and Siam to be governed in my way! [*Tearing off his jacket.*] Not

English way, not French way, not Chinese way. My way! [*He flings the jacket at* ANNA *and takes back the whip from the* KRALAHOME.] Barbarian, you say. There is no barbarian worse than a weak King, and I am strong King. You hear? Strong.

[*He stands over* TUPTIM, *raises the whip, meets* ANNA's *eyes, pauses, then suddenly realizing he cannot do this in front of her, he hurls the whip from him, and in deep shame, runs from the room. After a moment of silence, the* KRALAHOME *claps his hands, and the* GUARDS *yank* TUPTIM *to her feet. They are about to drag her off when the* INTERPRETER *crawls forward and speaks to the* KRALAHOME.]

INTERPRETER. The man—the lover has been found. He is dead.

TUPTIM. Dead . . . Then I shall join him soon . . . soon.

[*The* GUARDS *drag her off. The* INTERPRETER *follows. The* KRALAHOME *turns and looks at* ANNA *scornfully.*]

ANNA. I don't understand you—you or your King. I'll never understand him.

KRALAHOME. You! You have destroyed him. You have destroyed King . . . He cannot be anything that he was before. You have taken all this away from him. You have destroyed him. [*His voice growing louder.*] You have destroyed King.

ANNA. The next boat that comes to the port of Bangkok—no matter where it goes, I shall be on it. [*She takes the ring from her finger and holds it out to him.*] Give this back to His Majesty!

[*The* KRALAHOME *takes it. This the final humiliation for his* KING *to suffer.*]

KRALAHOME. [*Shouting, with heartbroken rage.*] I wish you have never come to Siam!

ANNA. So do I! [*She sobs.*] Oh, so do I! [*She runs off.*]

INTERMEDIATE SCENE

The Palace grounds.
Townspeople and children come on, eagerly watching offstage for the approaching procession. CAPTAIN ORTON *enters and meets* PHRA ALACK.

PHRA ALACK. Captain Orton! Your ship has docked in time! We are welcoming elephant prince to Bangkok.

ORTON. White elephant, eh? So that's it. I just passed the young prince. Where is the King? I didn't see him in the procession.

PHRA ALACK. [*His face clouding.*] The King is very ill. Very ill.

[*The procession now crosses the stage. Cymbal players, banner bearers, girls carrying huge oversized heads, and finally a dragon weaves on with four pairs of human legs propelling it. Girls dressed as strange birds dance around it. Finally* CHULALONGKORN *enters, accompanied by Amazons carrying ceremonial um-*

brellas. When the PRINCE *reaches the center of the stage, the* INTERPRETER *runs on and bows before him. The* PRINCE *halts.*]

INTERPRETER. Your Highness! Go no further! Go no further!

CHULALONGKORN. What is this you say?

INTERPRETER. Your father! Your father is worse!

CHULALONGKORN. Worse?

INTERPRETER. You are to return to the palace at once.

CHULALONGKORN. [*Turning to those who are near him.*] Go on with the procession.

[*He starts off and then quickens his pace, deeply worried. The procession continues, but with all its gay spirit gone. The lights fade.*]

SCENE 5

A room in ANNA's *house. It has been dismantled except for a few pieces of furniture. There is a crate, up center, a Victorian chair, an oriental coffee table, and another chair. As the curtain rises* LADY THIANG *is seated, looking thoughtful and worried.*

CHULALONGKORN. [*Entering.*] Mother! The Prime Minister told me you were here. I think Mrs. Anna and Louis have already left for the boat.

THIANG. No, Chulalongkorn. Some of their boxes are still here. [*She indicates the crate.*] The servant said they would be back soon.

[CHULALONGKORN *walks slowly toward his mother and stands before her.*

CHULALONGKORN. Mother, what is it with my father?

THIANG. It is his heart. [*She sits.*] Also, he does not seem to want to live.

CHULALONGKORN. Mother, I am frightened because I love my father and also because if he dies, I shall be King, and I do not know how to be.

THIANG. Many men learn this after they become kings.

CHULALONGKORN. I have been thinking much on things Mrs. Anna used to tell us in classroom . . . Of slavery, etcetera, etcetera, and I think also on what she has said of religion, and how it is a good and noble concern that each man find for himself that which is right and that which is wrong.

THIANG. These are good things to remember, my son, and it will be good to remember the one who taught them.

LOUIS. [*Entering.*] Chulalongkorn!

[*They shake hands.* LOUIS *bows to* LADY THIANG.]

ANNA. [*Entering after* LOUIS.] Lady Thiang! How nice of you to come to say good-bye! I was down at the ship seeing that all my boxes were on. Captain Orton must sail with the tide.

THIANG. Mrs. Anna, I did not come only to say good-bye. I come for one who must see you. [ANNA, *guessing whom she means, turns away.*] You must go to him, Mrs. Anna . . . When he heard that you were sailing, he started to write this letter. [*She unrolls a sheet of paper she has been holding.*] All day he has been writing. It was very difficult for him, madam—very difficult. He has commanded that I bring it to you.

[ANNA *takes the letter.*]

CHULALONGKORN. Please to read it to all of us. I would like to hear what my father has said.

ANNA. [*Reading.*] "While I am lying here, I think perhaps I die. This heart, which you say I have not got, is a matter of concern. It occurs to me that there shall be nothing wrong that men shall die, for all that shall matter about man is that he shall have tried his utmost best. In looking back, I discover that you think much on those people who require that you live up to best of self. You have spoken truth to me always, and for this I have often lost my temper on you. But now I do not wish to die without saying this gratitude, etcetera, etcetera. I think it very strange that a woman shall have been most earnest help of all. But, Mrs. Anna, you must remember that you have been a very difficult woman, and much more difficult than generality." [*Tears come into* ANNA's *voice. She looks up at* THIANG.] I must go to him! [*She starts out.*] Come Louis!

[*They go, followed by* THIANG *and* CHULALONGKORN.]

INTERMEDIATE SCENE

A *Palace corridor.*
ANNA *enters, followed by* LADY THIANG, CHULALONGKORN *and* LOUIS.

THIANG. I will see if he is awake. I will tell him you are here.

[*She goes out with* CHULALONGKORN.]

LOUIS. Mother, I thought you and the King were very angry with each other.

ANNA. We were, Louis.

LOUIS. Now he's dying—does that make you better friends?

ANNA. I suppose so, Louis. We can't hurt each other any more.

LOUIS. I didn't know he hurt you.

ANNA. When two people are as different as we are, they are almost bound to hurt each other.

LOUIS. He always frightened me.

ANNA. I wish you had known him better, Louis. You could have been great friends.

[*Smiling down at him.*] In some ways he was just as young as you.

LOUIS. Was he as good a king as he could have been?

ANNA. Louis, I don't think any man has ever been as good a king as he could have been . . . but this one tried. He tried very hard.

[*Pause.* LOUIS *studies her.*]

LOUIS. You really like him, don't you Mother?

ANNA. [*Barely controlling her tears.*] Yes, Louis. I like him very much. Very much indeed. [*Looking offstage.*] We can go in now.

[*They start off as the lights fade.*]

SCENE 6

The KING's *study.*
The KING *lies on his bed, his head propped up slightly. His eyes are closed.* LADY THIANG *kneels beside him.* CHULALONGKORN *is crouched on the floor in front of her, and above the bed the* KRALAHOME *kneels and never takes his eyes from the* KING's *face. Shortly after the rise of the curtain* LOUIS *enters and bows formally toward the* KING. *He is followed by* ANNA, *who curtseys and seats herself on a pile of books at the foot of the* KING's *bed. The* KING's *eyes open. Presently he addresses* ANNA.

KING. Many months . . . Many months I do not see you, Mrs. Anna. And now I die.

ANNA. Oh, no, Your Majesty.

KING. This is not scientific, Mrs. Anna. I know if I die or do not die. You are leaving Siam? [ANNA *nods.*] When?

ANNA. Very soon, Your Majesty. In fact, I can stay only a few minutes more.

KING. You are glad for this? [ANNA *can find no answer.*] People of Siam—royal children, etcetera, are not glad, and all are in great affliction of your departure.

ANNA. I shall miss them.

KING. You shall miss them, but you shall be leaving. I too am leaving. But I am not walking onto a boat with my own feet, of my own free will. I am just . . . leaving. [*His eyes close, but he has seen where* ANNA *is sitting.*] Why is your head above mine? [ANNA *rises, and* LOUIS *removes one of the books from the pile. As* ANNA *sits again,* LOUIS *kneels beside her.*] I am not afraid of that which is happening to me. [*He whistles the melody of the "Whistling Song."* ANNA *looks at him with quick surprise. He smiles and explains.*] You teach Chulalongkorn. Chulalongkorn teach me . . . "Make believe you brave"—is good idea, always.

ANNA. You are very brave, Your Majesty. Very brave.

KING. [*Taking from his finger the ring he has given her once before.*] Here is— something belonging to you. Put it on. [*He holds it out to her.*] Put it on! Put it on! Put it on! [*Then, for the first time in his life, he puts a plea in his voice.*] Please . . . wear it. [ANNA *takes it, unable to speak, and puts it on. After a moment, the children enter, accompanied by the Amazons.* LADY THIANG *rises hastily to quiet the children. The* KING *hears them.*] My children? Tell them to come here. [*They hurry in and prostrate themselves before their father.*] Good evening, my children.

CHILDREN. [*Together.*] Good evening, my father. [*Then they rush to* ANNA, *clustering around her, hugging her, greeting her in overlapping speeches.*] Oh, Mrs. Anna. Do not go! We are happy to see you. We have missed you so much, Mrs. Anna. Will you stay, Mrs. Anna? Do not go away!

LADY THIANG. Stop! Stop this noise! Did you come to see your father or Mrs. Anna?

KING. [*He has watched the children with interest.*] It is all right, Lady Thiang. It is suitable. [*The children settle on the floor around* ANNA.] Was it not said to me that someone has written a farewell letter to Mrs. Anna?

THIANG. Princess Ying Yaowalak has composed letter to Mrs. Anna. She cannot write. She only make up words.

[PRINCESS YING YAOWALAK *stands up.*]

KING. Speak letter now. [*The* PRINCESS *is uncertain.*] Say it! Say it! Say it!

YING YAOWALAK. [*Reciting her "letter."*] Dear friend and teacher: My goodness gracious, do not go away! We are in great need of you. We are like one blind. Do not let us fall down in darkness. Continue good and sincere concern for us and lead us in right road. Your loving pupil, Princess Ying Yaowalak.

[ANNA *rises, unable to speak, rushes to the little girl and hugs her.*]

CHILDREN. Please to stay, Mrs. Anna. Do not leave us! We cannot live without you! We are afraid, Mrs. Anna. We are afraid without you.

KING. Hush, children. When you are afraid, make believe you brave. [*To* ANNA.] You tell them how you do. You tell them. Let it be last thing you teach.

CHILDREN. [*As* ANNA *looks uncertainly at the* KING.] Tell us then, Mrs. Anna. What to do when afraid? You teach us.

ANNA. [*With a great effort to control her tears, she sings.*]
Whenever I feel afraid
I hold my head erect.
    [*The children hold their heads up in imitation of her.*]
And whistle a happy tune
So no one will suspect
        I'm afraid.
While shivering in my shoes
I strike a careless pose
    [*Her eyes go to* LOUIS, *who strikes the "careless pose." All the children imitate him.*]
And whistle a happy tune
And no one ever knows
        I'm afraid.

KING. [*Speaking over the music.*] You make believe you brave, and you whistle. Whistle! [*The children look at him, not comprehending. He addresses* ANNA.] You show them!

[ANNA *whistles. The* KING *motions to the children. They all try to whistle, but cannot. Finally, something like a whistle comes from the twins. This is too much for* ANNA. *She kneels and throws her arms around them, weeping freely. The sound of a boat whistle is heard off in the distance.*]

LOUIS. [*Crossing to* ANNA *and tapping her shoulder.*] Mother . . . It's the boat! It's time!

[*The children look at her anxiously. She rises.*]

CHILDREN. Do not go, Mrs. Anna. Please do not go.

[*Pause. Then, suddenly,* ANNA *starts to remove her bonnet.*]

ANNA. Louis, please go down and ask Captain Orton to take all our boxes off the ship. And have everything put back into our house. [LOUIS *runs off eagerly. The children break into shouts of joy.*]

KING. Silence! [*At the note of anger in his voice, the children, wives,* LADY THIANG *—all fall prostrate.*] Is no reason for doing of this demonstration for schoolteacher realizing her duty, for which I pay her exorbitant monthly salary of twenty . . . five pounds! Further, this is disorganized behavior for bedroom of dying King! [*To* CHULALONGKORN, *who has remained crouching below the bed.*] Chulalongkorn! Rise! [*The boy rises.*] Mrs. Anna, you take notes. [*He hands her a notebook, and she sits on the pile of books.*] You take notes from—next King. [LADY THIANG *lifts her head as the* KING *continues to the momentarily tongue-tied* PRINCE.] Well, well, well? Suppose you are King! Is there nothing you would do?

CHULALONGKORN. [*In a small, frightened voice.*] I . . . would make proclamations.

KING. Yes, yes.

CHULALONGKORN. First, I would proclaim for coming New Year—fireworks. [*The* KING *nods his approval.*] Also boat races.

KING. Boat races? Why would you have boat races with New Year celebration?

CHULALONGKORN. I like boat races. [*His confidence is growing. He speaks a little faster.*] And, father, I would make a second proclamation.

[*He swallows hard in preparation for this one.*]

KING. Well, go on! What is second proclamation? Make it! Make it!

CHULALONGKORN. Regarding custom of bowing to King in fashion of lowly toad. [*He starts to pace, very like his father.*] I do not believe this is good thing, causing embarrassing fatigue of body, degrading experience for soul, etcetera, etcetera, etcetera. . . . This is bad thing. [*He crosses his arms defiantly.*] I believe. [*He is losing his nerve a little.*] You are angry with me, my father?

KING. Why do you ask question? If you are King you are King. You do not ask

questions of sick man—[*Glaring at* ANNA.] Nor of woman! [*Pointing an accusing finger at her.*] This proclamation against bowing I believe to be your fault!

ANNA. Oh, I hope so, Your Majesty. I do hope so.

[*Music of "He Can Be Wonderful" starts to be played here—very softly.*]

CHULALONGKORN. [*Clapping his hands twice.*] Up! Rise up!

[*A few rise. The others raise their heads, but are uncertain whether they should obey him.*]

KING. Up! Up! Up! [*They all rise quickly, wives, Amazons, children.*] Two lines, like soldiers. [*They line up.*] It has been said there shall be no bowing for showing respect of King. It has been said by one who has . . . been trained for royal government.

[*His head sinks back on the pillow, and his voice on the last word was obviously weak.*]

CHULALONGKORN. [*His voice stronger and more decisive.*] No bowing like toad. No crouching. No crawling. This does not mean, however, that you do not show respect for King. [*The* KING's *eyes close.*] You will stand with shoulders square back, and chin high . . . like this. [ANNA *turns and notices that the* KING's *eyes are closed. The* KRALAHOME, *knowing that he has died, crawls on his knees to the head of the bed, and crouches there, heartbroken, and not wishing other people to see that he is weeping.* CHULALONGKORN *continues his instructions.*] You will bow to me—the gentlemen, in this way, only bending the waist. [*As he shows them and continues speaking,* ANNA *glides to the head of the bed, and feels the* KING's *hand. Then she comes around the foot of the bed and sinks to the floor beside him, taking his hand and kissing it.*] The ladies will make dip, as in Europe. [*He starts to show them a curtsey, but cannot.*] Mother—

[LADY THIANG *crosses to the center and drops a low curtsey before the women and girls carefully imitate her, sinking to the floor as the curtain falls, a final obeisance to the dead* KING, *a gesture of allegiance to the new one.*]

CURTAIN

For Discussion and Writing

1. Musical plays now treat serious subjects and contemporary themes with a new sense of truth. What is the serious theme of *The King and I*? What song best projects this theme?

2. In what way is *The King and I* like *The Teahouse of the August Moon*? How is it different from *Teahouse*? Why do you think Anna succeeds in areas where the American Army of Occupation fails?

3. In the old musical comedy, the characters were one-dimensional heroes, heroines, and villains. Show the difference in the handling of characterization in *The King and I*.

4. Another important change in the new musical is in its treatment of comedy. In early musical comedy, the humor consisted chiefly of "dragged-in" jokes and gags and topical comment. What is the main source of humor in *The King and I*? What important functions does it serve in the play in addition to furnishing amusement?

5. In most musicals, the main plot does not tell the whole story. There is usually a subplot with characters, a conflict and a story line of its own that affects the outcome of the main story.

In *The King and I*, what is the subplot and how does it help to advance the main plot?

6. Song lyrics are used for two purposes: to reveal character, and to express peak emotional moments.

What do the song lyrics in *The King and I* reveal about Anna, the King, Lady Thiang, and Tuptim?

What peak emotional moments in *The King and I* are revealed through song? In your opinion, would dialogue be more effective?

7. Write a brief scene in dialogue which could substitute for any song in *The King and I*. Use whatever characters you need.

Or, if you prefer to try your hand at lyric writing, select a scene from any other play in this book, and in place of the scene, write the lyrics of a song (solo or duet) to be sung by the characters involved.

Requiem for a Heavyweight

{1956}

ROD SERLING

CHARACTERS

HARLAN MOUNTAIN	FOX
MC CLINTOCK	JESSEY
MAISH	BARTENDER
GRACE CARRIE	FIGHTER IN BAR
ARMY	PHOTOGRAPHER
STEVE	FIGHT ANNOUNCER
MIKE	WRESTLERS
DOC	CHAMP
PARELLI	

Reprinted by permission of the author.

Jack Palance (l.) receiving Emmy Award in March 1957 for his leading role in "Requiem for a Heavyweight," Playhouse 90 production on CBS-TV network. Desi Arnaz (r.) presented the award.

R*equiem for a Heavyweight,* the Rod Serling television script used to inaugurate the "Playhouse 90" series on CBS in 1956, proved that the newest entertainment media can present dramas that are hard-hitting and artistically satisfying.

The play's authenticity arises mainly from Serling's experience as an amateur boxer while serving as a paratrooper during World War II. The impact of the play is further intensified by Serling's conviction that "our society is a man-eat-man thing on every possible level." Its style was very much influenced by the fact that "Playhouse 90" telecast live drama only.

Live productions telecast from studios located mainly in New York tend to adopt the conventions of the Broadway theater, presenting tightly constructed plays that depend more on character than on action. This style is in direct contrast to filmed TV dramas, which are shot mainly in Hollywood in the movie convention of physical outdoor action and fluid structure.

In dealing with its unique production problems, the producers of TV drama have developed their own technical shoptalk that necessarily finds its way into the writer's script. To help you read the script of *Requiem for a Heavyweight* (and others as well) with greater understanding, here is a selection of the more commonly used terms:

TYPES OF CAMERA SHOTS

Long Shot.	Camera shoots from far off yielding total view of subject.
Close Shot.	Camera shoots close to subject yielding blown-up view of part of subject.
Tight Close Up.	Very large, blown-up view of one facet of subject.
Cover Shot.	View of entire room or background.
Film Clip.	Previously shot film footage of common subjects used often (like moving trains, boats, planes, cars, etc.). These are placed in stock in film libraries to be available to directors.

TRANSITIONS BETWEEN SCENES

Cut To.	Direct jump from one scene to another, or from one person to another. Swiftest transition.
Dissolve To.	One scene fades out while the new scene fades in so that there is an overlap of the two.
Fade Out, Fade In.	Differs from the dissolve in that there is no overlap. May or may not be a dark screen between the fade out and fade in, but there is a sense of waiting. Generally used only between major portions of the story. Slowest transition.

CAMERA MOVEMENT

Pan.	Moving the camera so that it sweeps from one angle to another without a break in order to take in a wider panorama.
Dolly.	Camera on a wheeled truck (dolly) moves smoothly into, or away from the subject with a resultant close or ·long shot focus without a break.

Requiem for a Heavyweight

ACT ONE

We open on a long angle shot looking down a bare cement corridor dimly lit by intermittent green-shaded 25 watt bulbs. This is the underbelly of a fight arena and from off stage comes the occasional roar of the crowd.

On one far wall are visible a couple of fight posters announcing the cards for that night and the weeks to come. Two men stand close to one of the posters and talk in low voices. From the far end of the corridor appear "ARMY" and a fighter named HARLAN "MOUNTAIN" MC CLINTOCK, walking slowly toward the camera, the fighter leaning heavily on the arm of ARMY.

The two men pause under one of the lights and we get our first definitive view of the fighter's face. He has a bathrobe thrown loosely over his shoulders, and his body is a mass of red welts and skin abrasions. The bridge of his nose has a red crack down the middle of it. One eye is shut, the other is swollen almost to the same point, and on his cheek is a bleeding bruise and his chest is covered with sweat. ARMY is an ex-fighter, a small man, with long arms, in his late forties. He has thinning hair that reveals two thin scars that run down toward his cheeks on either side of his temple. Beyond that his face is open, kind of pleasant, rather intelligent.

ARMY. How about it, Mount, can yuh make it? Make it okay? [*The fighter nods, wets his lips as if to say something and then can't get it out. Over their shoulders we see* MAISH, *the manager, coming down the corridor. A man steps out from the wall and detains him.*]

MAISH. [*Calls out to* ARMY.] Army, stay here with him a minute, will you? I'll be right there. [*The camera moves over for a close shot of* MAISH *and the* MAN.]

MAN. Two words, Maish. Cough up.

MAISH. [*Furtive look toward* ARMY *and the fighter.*] Will you relax? I'll get it. I'll get it. Tell him I'll get it. Tell him to phone me.

MAN. Mr. Henson's no collection agency.

MAISH. I know. I know. Tell him he'll get it.

[*With this the camera moves away leaving them talking in low unintelligible voices.* ARMY *and the fighter take a few more steps down the corri-*dor until they stand very close to the two men who stand near one of the posters. They cast a few disinterested glances at the fighter and then continue their conversation.*]

MAN NUMBER ONE. So I told him. And he said I gotta.

MAN NUMBER TWO. So what did he say?

MAN NUMBER ONE. He says I gotta.

MAN NUMBER TWO. Cut ice?

MAN NUMBER ONE. [*Shrugs.*] Wid him? Illokadisguy. Itellimstraight djaeverseeanyguywalkinaringwidabustedhand?

MAN NUMBER TWO. Whaddehsay? Cut ice?

MAN NUMBER ONE. Neh! IgottaputiminnestT-ursday.

[*At this point the camera pulls away from them so that we can no longer hear them, but see them in pantomime as they continue talking only an arm's length or so away from the*

*fighter who stands bleeding in front
of them, but totally oblivious to him.*]
We cut to
[*A shot of* MAISH *and* ARMY *appearing again at the far end of the corridor.* ARMY *now has his arms full with
a bucket, some towels, and a pair of
gloves. He starts to continue down
the corridor when* MAISH *takes his
arm and with a nod toward the
fighter still standing there . . .*]

MAISH. How is he?

ARMY. [*Shrugs.*] This wasn't his night,
that's for sure.

MAISH. You are *so* right.

[*Then the two men continue down
the corridor. They approach* MC CLINTOCK *from either side, each taking an
arm, and help him move forward.
They walk a few more feet and then
stop by the door to the dressing room
and usher him into it. A fighter and
his* MANAGER *are just coming by.*]

MANAGER. What hit him?

MAISH. Don't get impatient, Jock. That's
a fast track out there. [*Then he looks at
the young fighter, obviously ill at ease.*]
You ought to see the other guy. [*The
MANAGER hustles his fighter out. Then*
MAISH *closes the door.*]

MAISH. Not a mark on him. [*Both he
and* ARMY *help* MC CLINTOCK *on to a high
rubbing table.* ARMY *pours some water into
the bucket from a dirty sink, brings the
bucket over to the table.* MAISH *takes a
towel, dampens it and starts to wipe away
the sweat and blood.*]

MAISH. Mountain, can you hear me
okay? [*The* FIGHTER *nods.*]

MAISH. Give me some of that alum, will
yuh, Army? [ARMY *digs into his pockets
and brings out a little jar.* MAISH *dabs his
finger in it and starts to apply it to the*
FIGHTER'S *face.*]

ARMY. I don't think alum'll do it, Maish.
I think that's going to take stitches.

MAISH. [*Peers into the* FIGHTER'S *face
more intently.*] Yeah, They get wider and
wider.

ARMY. The Doc's going to be coming in
a minute anyway. He'll do it. [MC CLINTOCK *wets his lips and now he speaks for
the first time. His voice is heavy, and belabored and still short of breath.*]

MC CLINTOCK. Maish? Hey, Maish . . .

MAISH. Go easy. Go easy, we've got a
lot of time.

MC CLINTOCK. Maish—too fast. Much too
fast.

MAISH. [*Nods.*] Bum night, Kid. Just a
bum night all the way around. There'll be
others.

MC CLINTOCK. Sure. Others. [MC CLINTOCK *moves a bandaged hand awkwardly
down to his side and feels.*] Check there
will yuh, Maish? By the belt. [ARMY *hurriedly pulls the trousers down a quarter of
an inch.*]

ARMY. You've got a little rope burn
down there. It'll be okay. Rubbed a sore
there. It'll be okay.

MC CLINTOCK. Hurts. [*Then he breathes
deeply again and* MAISH *goes back to dabbing water on his face. The door opens
and the* DOCTOR *enters. This is a thin, vinegar-faced old man in his sixties with a
single-breasted, old-fashioned suit with a
vest, all the buttons buttoned. He carries a
beaten-up black bag, which he tosses on
the foot of the rubbing table.*]

DOCTOR. Mountain, haven't you got
enough yet?

MAISH. It's his eye, Doc.

DOC. I know. Just as well, Maish. If he
hadn't folded I wouldn't have let him out
for number eight. [MAISH *nods but doesn't
say anything. He pulls out the butt of a
cigar from pocket and lights it. The* DOCTOR *squints, pushes his arm away.*]

DOCTOR. Let me breathe, will you? [*He
leans over the* FIGHTER *and examines the
eye, then pushes the face to the other side
a little roughly and examines the other
bruises and cuts. Then he snaps his fingers
at* ARMY *who picks up the bag and hands
it to him.*]

DOCTOR. Where do you buy your cigars,
Maish? I'll see that they condemn the
store. [*Then he reaches in the bag and
takes out some gauze, a stick with cotton
on the end of it, and a bottle of medicine.
He starts to administer to the* FIGHTER.]

ARMY. How much longer you got, Doc?
You're out this week, ain't you?

DOCTOR. Let's see. This is Wednesday—
I leave Friday.

MAISH. [*Staring down at the* FIGHTER
and obviously making small talk.] Vacation?

DOCTOR. Vacation? Retirement. I'm the
one man in the fight business who walks

away without a wobble. Thirty-eight years, Maish. Retirement.

ARMY. [*Clucks.*] Thirty-eight years.

DOCTOR. [*Administering to the* FIGHTER *as he talks.*] Thirty-eight years. Wife says I oughta write a book, but who'd buy it?

MAISH. You've seen some good ones.

DOCTOR. Good ones and bad ones. Live ones and a couple of dead ones. [*Then he straightens up, massages his back and points down with the stick toward* MC CLINTOCK.] And almost dead ones. He's got no business in there, Maish. You hungry, is that it?

MAISH. [*Picking up the* FIGHTER's *hand and massaging it absently.*] What do you mean hungry? In 1948 he was number five. You can check that in *Ring Magazine.* I could show it to you, number five, and that was only in 1948.

DOCTOR. [*Looks at him a little quizzically.*] Only 1948. And this is 1956. And that means eight years ago. Too bad he isn't a machine, Maish. Too bad none of them are machines. [*Then he laughs softly.*] I've seen a lot of them. Thirty-eight years. When I first come in they used to lay them out in front of me. They were human beings then. They were young men. Do you know what it's like now, Maish? Army? [*He leans back over* MC-CLINTOCK *and starts to work again.*] Now it's like a guy who grades meat in a packing plant. They roll the carcasses down the line in front of him and he stamps them. Beef. Understand? [*He motions toward* MC CLINTOCK.] Just a hunk of something inanimate. That's what thirty-eight years has done. [*Then musingly.*] Thirty-eight years. And suddenly I don't have a single patient with a first and last name. A set of scars. A blood type and a record— that's all *my* patients have. Look here, Maish, I want to show you something. [MAISH *leans over.*] Look at his pupil. See? Known as sclerotic damage. Look at the tissue there. Couple of good solid rights to that eye—and you can buy him a tin cup and some pencils. [*He straightens up again, puts his things back in the bag as he says.*] Or maybe that won't have to happen. Maybe some night he'll bang his head on a bathroom door and bleed to death. Either way, Maish. It could happen either way. [*Then a long pause and a deep breath.*] No more. This

was it. Mountain and I will both retire this week. [MAISH *looks from the* FIGHTER *to the* DOCTOR *and his voice is strained.*]

MAISH. What do you mean?

DOCTOR. No more.

MAISH. He could rest up. I've got nothing scheduled for him . . .

DOCTOR. [*Interrupts.*] He can rest up the rest of his life.

MAISH. What're you talking about? He's fourteen years in this business. Suddenly he gets a cut and we've got to put him out to pasture?

DOCTOR. [*Turns to him.*] Suddenly. It doesn't go fourteen years and then suddenly. And it's never one cut. It's fourteen years of cuts. [*He stretches, hoists up the bag.*] Yep, write me a book. All about my gladiator friends. You too can become pathological in thirty-eight years of relatively easy lessons.

MAISH. [*Interrupts.*] Joker. Big joker. [DOCTOR *walks over to the door, turns the knob, then looks back at* MAISH.]

DOCTOR. Joker? [*He shakes his head, nods toward* MC CLINTOCK.] Who's laughing? [*He walks out of the room and shuts the door.* ARMY *and* MAISH *stare at each other, then both look toward* MC CLINTOCK. ARMY *goes over and starts to cut away the bandages on his hands.* MAISH *stands back a few feet smoking the cigar thoughtfully. Finally* MC CLINTOCK *sits up, closes his eyes, moves his mouth and touches his jaw gingerly.*]

MC CLINTOCK. Doc here?

ARMY. He left.

MC CLINTOCK. It hurts, Maish.

MAISH. [*Turns his back.*] I don't doubt it. [*Then* MOUNTAIN *shakes his head, reacts with pain, touches the bandage on his eye.*]

MC CLINTOCK. Deep huh, Maish?

MAISH. Enough. You could hide your wallet in there. Go lie down. Rest up a minute, and *then* take your shower. [MC-CLINTOCK *pushes his feet around heavily so that they hang over the side. Then he balances himself with his hands. His head goes up and down and he breathes deeply.*]

MC CLINTOCK. I'm coming around now. Oh Lordy, I caught it tonight, Maish. I really did. What did I do wrong?

MAISH. You aged. That was the big trouble. You aged. [MC CLINTOCK *looks at him, frowns. He tries to get some thread of meaning out of the words but none comes.*]

MC CLINTOCK. What do you mean, Maish? I aged. Don't everybody age?

MAISH. [*Nods.*] Yeah, everybody ages. Everybody grows old, kid. Go ahead. I think a shower'll do you good. Try not to get that bandage wet.

[MC CLINTOCK *gets on his feet, a little wobbly. He holds the table for support, then walks out of the room toward the shower.* ARMY *starts to pick up the dirty towels and put them in a big container alongside of the door.*]

ARMY. [*Without looking up.*] What're you going to do, Maish?

MAISH. [*Shrugs.*] I dunno. Maybe I'll cut my throat.

ARMY. Somethin's wrong, isn't there?

MAISH. Where were you when the lights went out? I just lost a boy! Get with it, Army.

ARMY. Besides that . . .

MAISH. Besides that nothing. Forget it. [*Then with a desperate attempt at a kind of composure.*] I just gotta go huntin' and peckin' around, that's all. Find somebody else. Maybe try a lightweight this trip.

ARMY. I was just wondering—

MAISH. You wanna pull out, huh, Army? A million offers, huh?

ARMY. I didn't mean . . .

MAISH. [*Interrupts.*] Don't gimme a whole Megillah. I know you're good, Army. You're the best cut man in the city. I know that. You probably could take your pick. I don't know why you haven't before.

ARMY. [*With his head down.*] Never mind about me. What about the Mountain?

MAISH. [*Reacts a little guiltily.*] I dunno. He'll find something.

ARMY. It's been fourteen years.

MAISH. Fourteen years what?

ARMY. Fourteen years fight. Then one night you get out of the ring—it's all over. And what've you got . . .

MAISH. You made a living, didn't you? You did all right. [*Then he chuckles.*] Remember how I used to tout you? "The Hero of the Argonne." I even gave you the name "Army." So don't complain,

Army. You came out of it with a name at least.

ARMY. [*In a kind of wistful voice.*] Still— a guy ought to have something to show for it besides the name. [*At this moment the sound of the shower water is heard from offstage.* ARMY *looks up toward the shower.*]

ARMY. He was good, Maish.

MAISH. [*Thoughtfully, turning toward the shower.*] One of the best. He had everything that was needed. Hands, legs, brains. He could take a cannonball in his face and you could fix him up with an aspirin. He was good all right. Oh, brother—where am I ever gonna find one like him? [*The camera pans over to the door leading to the shower. We get a shot of* MC CLINTOCK *as he comes out from the waist up. He dries himself off with a towel, then looks up.*]

MC CLINTOCK. Hey, Army. Bathrobe, huh? [*The bathrobe is thrown to him and he puts it around him. Then we pull back for a cover shot as he walks back into the room toward the table. He stands there and does a little hop and jump routine on the floor, loosening up. Throwing his shoulders and head back, breathing deeply, and moving his hands and feet.*]

MC CLINTOCK. Feel better, Maish. Lot better. Eye kind of feels funny but—I'll be okay now. Got a lot of spring yet, huh? [*He moves his feet around, shuffling ring-like. He shadow boxes a bit.*] How about it, Army? Still there, huh? [ARMY *nods, not able to say anything. He exchanges a look with* MAISH.]

MAISH. [*Finally.*] Mountain—sit down, huh? [MC CLINTOCK *stops his dancing, looks from one to the other, goes over to the rubbing table and sits down.*]

MC CLINTOCK. Sure, Maish. Sure. [*Then he waits expectantly.* MAISH *starts to say something, then he looks at* ARMY, *who turns away. Then he wets his lips.*]

MAISH. The doctor looked you over.

MC CLINTOCK. [*Grins.*] Yeah. I thought he was in here. I wasn't sure, though. [*He taps his head.*] A little groggy yet, you know.

MAISH. [*Nods.*] Yeah. Well anyway he looked you over good this time.

MC CLINTOCK. Yeah?

MAISH. He figures . . . he figures you've had it. [*Then he turns away, coughs,*

takes out a cigar and lights it. MC CLIN-
TOCK *stares at him for a long moment.*]
MC CLINTOCK. What did you say, Maish?
MAISH. The doctor says you've had it.
No more. He says you've got to leave now.
MC CLINTOCK. Leave? Leave where?
MAISH. [*Whirls around and shouts.*]
Army. Lay it out for him, will yuh? Moun-
tain, no more fights. You get it? This is
where you get off. You leave. [*There's
another moment's pause.* MC CLINTOCK
gets off the table, walks over to MAISH,
pokes at him with a forefinger.]
MC CLINTOCK. Leave? Maish, that's . . .
that's crazy.
MAISH. [*Shrugs, turns away.*] So it's
crazy. Maybe I think it's crazy, but that's
what the doctor says. Go fight the com-
mission. [*Deliberately turning his back on
MC CLINTOCK.*] Have you got everything
all cleared up here, Army? [ARMY *nods.*]
MC CLINTOCK. Maish . . .
MAISH. [*Without turning to him.*] What
do you want, Mountain?
MC CLINTOCK. What'll I do?
MAISH. What'll you do? I dunno. You
do whatever you want to do. Anything
you like. It's as easy as that.
MC CLINTOCK. I mean . . . I mean a guy's
got to do something.
MAISH. So? A guy's got to do something.
So you do something. Do anything you
like.
MC CLINTOCK. [*The words come out
hard.*] Maish, I don't know anything but
fighting. You know, fourteen years pro.
You know, Maish. I've been with you fourteen years.
MAISH. And before that?
MC CLINTOCK. [*Smiles and shrugs.*] Before that what? Who remembers?
ARMY. Why don't you go back home,
kid? You talk about it enough. The green
hills of Tennessee. Is that what you call it?
Go back home. Go back to Tennessee. The
hills are probably still green.
MC CLINTOCK. What's back there? [*He
takes a few steps toward the other two
men and looks from one to the other as he
talks.*] What's back there? I haven't been
back in all those years. I don't know anybody. Nobody'd know me. [*And then suddenly as if struck by an afterthought.*]
Maish, we could try another state, maybe?
MAISH. [*Shakes his head.*] Now *you're*
talking crazy. If you don't pass muster in

New York State, you don't pass muster
any place else. You know that.
MC CLINTOCK. Maybe some club fights.
You know, unofficial.
MAISH. Where've you been? Those kind
of club fights went out with John L. Sulli-
van. [ARMY *nods, follows* MAISH *to the
door, then turns back toward* MC CLIN-
TOCK.]
ARMY. Want me to help you dress,
Mountain?
MC CLINTOCK. [*Shakes his head.*] No.
No, I can dress myself. [*Then he looks
across at* MAISH.] Maish?
MAISH. Yeah?
MC CLINTOCK. I'm . . . I'm sorry about
tonight. I'm sorry I lost.
[*We cut to a very tight close-up of*
MAISH *as his features work and then
he has to turn his eyes away.*]
MAISH. That's okay, Mountain. Don't
give it another thought. [*He goes out and
closes the door.* ARMY *sort of hangs back
by the door.*]
ARMY. [*Finally.*] We can go over to the
hotel later on and—and talk this out, make
some plans. [MC CLINTOCK *nods and
doesn't say anything. Then* ARMY *goes out
the door.* MC CLINTOCK *stands there
numbly and motionless for a long moment.
We cut to the corridor outside the dressing room.* MAISH *is walking very slowly
down the corridor. He stops abruptly.*]
MAISH. [*Waves and hollers.*] Hey, Foxy.
Hey, Fox! [*A figure ahead of him pauses,
turns, walks back toward him. This is a
little mousey guy in a jacket with a face
like a weasel.*]
FOX. Whadda yuh say, Maish? I just
seen Slaughter on Tenth Avenue. Was
there enough left to sew together?
MAISH. Break your heart, does it?
FOX. I got my own troubles. [*And then
very confident.*] You want to see the kid
now Maish? I got him right out here. You
said you might be interested . . .
MAISH. I said I *might* be.
FOX. Maish, he's a real sweetie. Middleweight. A good fast middleweight, but
he's built like a tank and I can't get him
matched on accounta the business.
MAISH. How is the business? Did you
get that fixed up?
FOX. I was one year revoked. But you
know that was a bum rap, Maish. To
pinch a guy like me for fixing fights. It's

to laugh. I swear, it's to laugh. I couldn't fix a parking ticket. But . . . ah . . . meanwhile I got no contract with the kid because I got no license to manage, so if he could just hook up with someone—you know—a real solid guy to handle him for a bit . . .

MAISH. Foxy, don't dress it up, will ya, pal? If he's here, put him on the block. Let's take a look at him. But don't choke me with publicity.

FOX. Maish, you're a doll baby. You're an everloving doll baby. [*He turns and shouts.*] Bobby! Bobby, Mr. Loomis would like to look at ya. [*At this moment a* FIGHTER *walks down the ramp from out of the shadows and approaches them. He walks with the stiff gait of an old rooster and his face looks like the Battle of the Marne.*] Here he is, Maish. Bobby Menzey.

MAISH. [*Looks him over with the practiced eye of a veteran.*] So what's to tell, Foxy? I'd like to see him spar.

FOX. He'll spar—he'll spar. I'll get a boy lined up at the gym tomorrow.

MAISH. Tell me about him. [*The* FIGHTER *starts to say something.* MAISH *holds up his hand and points to* FOX.] Let him talk.

FOX. Like I told you before, Maish, he's a sweetheart. He's fought mostly out West.

MAISH. What's his record?

FOX. [*Wets his lips.*] Like I say, he's fought mostly out West.

MAISH. Wins and losses. Lay them out. Is that hard?

FOX. Well . . . well, his record ain't so well known, Maish. He was fighting out West.

MAISH. [*Suddenly reaches out and grabs* FOX *by the vest, pulling him toward him.*] What are you trying to pull off, Fox?

FOX. [*With a worried look toward his fighter.*] Go easy on the kid, Maish . . .

MAISH. Kid? I'd hate to have my hands in boiling water since he was a kid. [*Turns to fighter.*] What's your name?

FIGHTER. Menzey—Bobby Menzey. Maybe you heard of me.

MAISH. I heard about you yesterday. But the last time I saw you fight, your name wasn't Bobby Menzey. [*The* FIGHTER *gulps and starts to stammer.*]

FOX. [*Hurriedly.*] You've got him mixed up, Maish. Menzey. Bobby Menzey. M-E-N-Z-E-Y.

MAISH. Stop it! Correct me if I'm wrong. LaPlant, isn't it? In 1949 you were a lightweight—a real comer. Sixteen straight. Then you fought Red Johns in Syracuse. He knocked you out in the second round. Then you lost six or seven straight. After that I saw you in Detroit. That was three, four years ago. [*The* FIGHTER *looks at* FOX *helplessly.*]

FOX. [*With a huge smile.*] You got me, Maish. You really got me. I had him change his name—but that don't prove nothing about his fighting.

MAISH. It doesn't huh? It means you're trying to pass off a stumblebum on me as a comer. [*He grabs* MENZEY's *face and turns it to the light.*] Look at it. I know a bleeder when I see one. One punch and his face falls apart. And this is the sweetheart, huh? This guy will never live to see the day when he's anything else besides a poor, beat-up slob.

FIGHTER. What're you talkin' about? I'm as good as I ever was.

FOX. That's right. He's still got it, Maish. Would I try to put something over on you? [*He slaps him expansively on the arm.*] Would I? A wise one like you? Think I'm crazy or something. It's to laugh, Maish. I swear it's to laugh. Go ahead, Bobby. Box around a little for him. Go ahead. [*The* FIGHTER *starts to shadow box in front of them.* MAISH *and* ARMY *exchange a look.*]

FOX. Who does he remind you of? Baer?

MAISH. Yeah, a big brown one with a ring in his nose.

FOX. Look, Maish . . .

MAISH. Knock it off. You'd better send him back to your factory. Right now.

FOX. Maish, give me a break, will ya?

MAISH. I've given you a break. I won't split your head. That's a break. I'll see you around, Fox. [*He turns and walks past him. The* FIGHTER, *suddenly seeing his shadow against a wall, begins to shadow box.*]

FOX. [*Pushes him.*] Mud for brains! So stop already. No deal. [*The camera picks up* MAISH *as he starts up the ramp. The man steps out from the wall once again and stops him.*]

MAN. Hey, Loomis . . .

MAISH. I'll get it! I'll get it! What does

Henson need—bail money? I told you I'd get it for you. Now lay off, will ya?

MAN. Mr. Henson would like to know where you're going to get it.

MAISH. Mr. Henson'll have to guess.

MAN. Mr. Henson will take it out of your skin, Loomis. Just remember that. [*He walks up the ramp and disappears.* MAISH *watches him go and the tight, set look on his face disintegrates and suddenly he is very frightened. But he recomposes his face when he sees* ARMY *walking toward him.*]

MAISH. [*With a forced smile.*] Come on, I'll buy you a drink.

ARMY. [*Looks toward the ramp.*] Fox showing off his wares? You work fast, Maish.

MAISH. People have to eat—or are you different?

ARMY. I'm not the one drumming up trade five minutes after I get the word.

MAISH. I'm drumming it up for you, too, remember, boy scout! Fox has got a boy and he can't handle him. I've got no boy and I *can* handle him. That's simple stuff, Army. That's arithmetic. [*Then his shoulders sag.*] What difference? He was a clinker. The worst.

ARMY. What now?

MAISH. I think I'll go shadow box off a cliff. Come on. I *need* a drink.

ARMY. [*Nods toward the dressing room.*] I'll wait for the kid.

MAISH. Sure. [*Then he looks up toward the ceiling and grins.*] The kid. That's what I call him too. The kid. I think that's where we goofed. As long as they wear trunks and gloves we think they're kids. They're old men. They're the oldest. I'll see you later on, Army. [*He walks on up the ramp, pausing near the top to look at a poster which advertises the fight that night. On it is a picture of* MOUNTAIN *and his opponent and the words "Main Bout" are prominent. He takes a few steps further and looks at another poster. This one shows two big clowns in a plug for a wrestling match. He takes a few steps closer to the poster and stares at it, taps it thoughtfully with his finger.*]

[*We cut to a brief tight close-up of* ARMY *noticing this. Then we cut to a long shot as* MAISH *disappears up the ramp.*]

We dissolve to

[*A shot of a little hotel and adjoining bar as seen through its front window.*]

We dissolve through the interior

[*And get a cover shot of the entire place. This is about a twenty-foot-square dingy little bistro frequented by people in the fight business—mostly ex-fighters and ring hangers-on. On the wall are pictures of fighters going back to the 1800's. A championship belt is in a frame over the bar. Other than these the place has no pretensions. It is simply there to serve drink and make up for what is probably a loss in the hotel business alongside. At the far end of the room there's a handful of fighters, obviously in nightly clatch. One fighter is holding sway with an excited blow-by-blow from some monumental battle of years before. As we pan around the room we pick up part of his speech.*]

FIGHTER NUMBER ONE. So he comes in at me. [*He holds both his hands up.*]

FIGHTER NUMBER TWO. Yeah, yeah. Go ahead.

FIGHTER NUMBER ONE. He comes at me. I sized him up. He throws a left, I duck. He throws another left. I duck. Then he throws another left.

FIGHTER NUMBER TWO. You duck.

FIGHTER NUMBER ONE. No, I don't duck. I take it right smack dab on the jaw. I'm down. Oh, man, am I down.

[*We pan past them at this moment for a shot of* MC CLINTOCK *and* ARMY *as they enter. The bartender is a flat-nosed ex-pug who nods very briefly at them as they sit on the stools.*]

BARTENDER. How're you, Mountain? Army?

ARMY. Two beers, huh, Charlie?

BARTENDER. Two beers. [*He draws them and expertly shoots them down the bar one at a time.* ARMY *takes out some money. Three one-dollar bills, separates them, lays one on the counter.*]

BARTENDER. How'd you do, Mountain?

MC CLINTOCK. Not so good, Charlie. Almost went the route, though. Doc says I'm over the hill now.

BARTENDER. [*Clucks.*] That's too bad. [*Then philosophically.*] So—now yuh can join the Wednesday-evening sewing circle! [*He jerks with his thumb in the direction of the rear of the room. Then with a long look at* MC CLINTOCK *he takes out a bottle and says.*] Have one on the house. This is the only one in the house that ain't watered. [*He pours two healthy-sized glasses and shoves them in front of each of them, and walks back down the bar.*]

ARMY. [*Turns to* MOUNTAIN, *holds up his glass.*] To Mountain McClintock. A hundred and eleven fights.

MC CLINTOCK. He wasn't so good—but he never took a dive. [ARMY *returns the laugh, starts to drink. He takes only the barest of sips, looking over the top of his glass at* MOUNTAIN, *a sad and knowing look on his face. At this moment* ARMY *sees the reflection of* MAISH *in the mirror. He turns around.*]

ARMY. Hey, Maish. Here we are. [MAISH *walks over to them.*]

MAISH. Let's get a booth.

MC CLINTOCK. How're you doing, Maish?

MAISH. I'll tell yuh when we get to the booth. [*As they get away from the bar a drunk tipsily bangs into* MAISH, *and* MC CLINTOCK *rather firmly places him out of the way.*]

MC CLINTOCK. Watch it. That's my manager.

[*The three men go to the rear and sit in an empty booth.*]

MAISH. [*Without any preliminaries. Obviously intent on getting this over.*] What did you do with your dough, Mountain?

MC CLINTOCK. You mean . . .

MAISH. [*Impatiently.*] The dough for the fight. You got six hundred and thirty-three bucks, didn't you? Where is it?

MC CLINTOCK. It's mostly gone. I owed the hotel half of it, Maish.

MAISH. [*Wets his lips.*] What about the other half?

MC CLINTOCK. [*Very slowly.*] Well, I suppose I've got some of it . . .

MAISH. [*Excited, blurts it out.*] Look, don't get cute with me. This is Maish. I asked you a question now. Have you got any money at all? [MC CLINTOCK *reaches into his pants and pulls out a crumpled roll of bills. He lays them out one at a time on the table.*]

MC CLINTOCK. I've got some. Twenty, forty, fifty-five, fifty-six, fifty-seven, fifty-

eight bucks, Maish. [*He collects and shoves it over in a bunch to* MAISH.] Here.

MAISH. Fifty-eight bucks. [*He picks it up and looks at it. He throws it back down on the table.*]

ARMY. [*A little wisely.*] What's the matter, Maish? You in hock?

MAISH. [*Nods.*] Heavy.

ARMY. How much?

MAISH. Three thousand dollars.

ARMY. [*Whistles.*] Three thousand dollars.

MC CLINTOCK. [*Very worried.*] Gee, Maish, that's a lot of money. How're we gonna get it?

MAISH. I don't know. But I haven't got much time.

ARMY. How did you get into that kind of a crack, Maish?

MAISH. [*With side look at* MC CLINTOCK, *his tone changes.*] You don't know, huh? Mountain when you were in the hospital last month with a bum hand—remember?

ARMY. That comes off the top. What're you givin' him?

MAISH. Sure. But I brought in a specialist, didn't I? And that came out of here. [*He pats his own pocket.*] And the training camp. He wanted to go up to New Jersey, so he went up to New Jersey. How much do you think that cost me a month? A lot more than my cut, I'll tell ya.

MC CLINTOCK. Gee, Maish, I didn't know that . . .

MAISH. I'm not complaining. I'm not complaining. But the money goes, you know. And one half of your take hasn't been much lately. It doesn't cover expenses, so I've been filling up the rest of it for you. Well, now we've got to pay the fiddler, Kid. We're at the end of the line now.

MC CLINTOCK. [*His face very concerned.*] I've been thinkin', Maish, if I could get me a job—you know, something to tide us over . . .

MAISH. [*Barely listening to him.*] Sure. Sure. [*Then to* ARMY.] Jack Green's got a lightweight he's touting. Maybe we could buy a piece [*He looks up to the ceiling.*] Yeah, we could buy a piece. With what? We could get his thumb. That I could afford.

MC CLINTOCK. [*Very softly.*] Get a new boy, Maish?

ARMY. [*With a quick look at* MAISH.] Not for a while yet, Mountain, just an idea.

MC CLINTOCK. Oh. Oh. I see. [*His eyes go around the room looking at the people, the tables and the pictures, very quietly.*] I remember the first night I come in here, Maish. I remember the guy's name even. Shipsky. Morty Shipsky. I knocked him out in the first round. And you and Army stood up on the bar and you shouted . . . you shouted, "Everybody take a drink on Harlan McClintock the next champ." [*He looks from one to the other.*] Remember? That was the night you give me the name "Mountain."

ARMY. [*Quietly.*] I remember.

MC CLINTOCK. Sure. You asked me where I was from and I told you. I told you I lived in Tennessee on a mountain. And that's when . . . that's when Maish here says, "That's what we'll call ya. We'll call ya Mountain." [*He looks around the room again.*] How many nights we come in here, Maish? How many nights?

ARMY. A lot of 'em.

MC CLINTOCK. Couple of hundred, I guess? Couple of hundred nights. We could just sit and talk here by the hour about this fight or that fight, or some other fighter, or a fight we were gonna get. By the hour.

MAISH. [*A little disjointedly.*] It's the breaks that's all. It's the breaks.

MC CLINTOCK. All of a sudden I—I'm sittin' here and it becomes different. Like . . . right now even . . . I'm on the outside lookin' in. Like . . . I didn't belong with you guys any more. [*Then suddenly his face becomes a mask as realization seems to flood into it and he slowly gets up on his feet.*]

ARMY. Look, Mountain . . .

MAISH. Why don't you sit down and have another drink? It's early . . .

MC CLINTOCK. [*Shakes his head.*] I think I'll just . . . I'll just take a walk. I'll see you later. [*He turns to go and is suddenly aware of the little knot of men in the back of the room still talking about fights. He looks at them for a moment, almost winces, and then to nobody in particular says.*] That's no way. That's no way at all.

ARMY. What did you say, Mountain?

MC CLINTOCK. [*As if awakened sud-*]denly.] Nothin'. Nothin', Army. I'll see you later. [MC CLINTOCK *turns and walks down the room to the door and goes out. The* BARTENDER *comes over with a tray and places it on the table in front of* MAISH *and* ARMY.]

BARTENDER. How about you, Army? You want something? [ARMY *doesn't answer him. He is staring toward the door.* MAISH *drops a coin on the tray and makes a motion with his head for the* BARTENDER *to get lost. The* BARTENDER *walks back toward the bar.*]

MAISH. Hey, Army.

ARMY. [*Without looking at him.*] What?

MAISH. Look at me when I'm talking to yuh, will yuh? I don't like talking to a guy's neck.

ARMY. [*Reluctantly turns toward him.*] How'd you lose the dough?

MAISH. How do you think?

ARMY. You bet against him, didn't you?

MAISH. [*Not meeting his eyes.*] Something like that.

ARMY. You don't sidestep very good.

MAISH. You want it clearer, huh?

ARMY. A little bit.

MAISH. I said he wouldn't go four.

ARMY. [*Smiles a crooked little smile.*] Big disappointment, huh?

MAISH. There was another way? The minute they tell me he was matched against Gibbons I figure we should throw in the towel while he's signing the contract. Save wear and tear. Gibbons! Thirty-one fights and thirty-one wins. He's got a lit fuse in each hand. And they match him against the Mountain.

ARMY. They match him?

MAISH. Did I? I just go through the motions. Good fast brawl, they said. Couple of nice crowd-pleasers in a pier six. Harlan Mountain McClintock, ex-leading heavyweight contender. Ex is right. Very ex. Eight years ex. He's past prime, Army. I take what I can find—you know that. They say fight Gibbons, I say OK. They say Marciano. I say bring on Marciano.

ARMY. You coulda tol' 'em . . .

MAISH. Tell 'em, tell 'em, tell 'em. Tell 'em what? Tell 'em I've got a dead-weight has-been on my back? That he shouldn't fight any more? And then what do I do? Put in for a pension? [*At this moment a* MAN *walks up to the table, nods briefly at* ARMY, *and then smiles broadly at* MAISH.]

MAN. What's the good word, Maish?

MAISH. [*Staring straight ahead.*] Blow. That's a good word. I don't want any.

MAN. How do you know what I'm selling?

MAISH. So pitch. I'm busy.

MAN. Mr. Henson sent me. [MAISH's *hand hits the ashtray nervously and knocks it off the table.* MAISH *bends down to pick it up.*]
Cut to
[*Tight close-up of the* MAN's *foot on* MAISH's *hand.* MAISH *looks up from the floor, his face dead white.*]

MAN. Now you pitch. Tell me when Mr. Henson can expect his dough.

MAISH. Soon.

MAN. How soon is soon?

MAISH. Three weeks.

MAN. You said two, didn't you? [MAISH *bites his lips. The* MAN's *foot remains on his hand.*]

MAISH. [*His voice a croak.*] Two weeks. [*The* MAN *lifts his foot, picks up the ashtray, sets it back on the table.*]

MAN. You dropped something, Mr. Loomis. I'll see you in two weeks.
[*He turns and walks away.* ARMY *stares across the table at* MAISH. MAISH *takes out a handkerchief and wipes his face. Then reaches for a half-smoked cigar he pulls out of his pocket. Then he pats around for a match.*]

MAISH. Got a match?

ARMY. You and a mouse. That's a match.

MAISH. Who am I, Atlas? These guys play for real, Army, you know that. This is no bank transaction. If I welsh, you can take a spoon, scoop what's left of me off the wall and put it in a cup. That's how serious they look on bets. And if they don't go to that trouble—they'll get my license so quick they'll blur the ink. I won't be able to sell peanuts at a fight, so I'm licked either way.

ARMY. Who told you to bet?

MAISH. Who told me I hadda eat?

ARMY. You picked the sport.

MAISH. This isn't a sport. If there was head room, they'd hold them in sewers. So what do I do?

ARMY. [*Very quietly.*] What does the Mountain do?

MAISH. You tell me. That's this precious business of ours. He gives them a million

dollars' worth of fighting for fourteen years. And then they're not interested in paying for the dump truck to cart 'em away. The sport. The sport and the precious crowd.

ARMY. *You* ever buy him a ticket back to Tennessee?

MAISH. Don't stick it on me. All I do is curry the horse. I'm one of the stable boys. I don't set up the rules. I get sucked in just like he does. [*He stares at the chair* MOUNTAIN *was sitting in.*] He asks me . . . He sits there and he asks me "What'll I do Maish?" He asks *me* what he's gonna do. Like I was the Book of Knowledge and I'm supposed to tell him. I don't know what to tell him. I'm so scared right now, Army, that . . .

ARMY. Stop it. You lost a bank roll and a meal ticket. But this poor beat-up kid—did you ever figure out what he lost tonight?

MAISH. You don't think I feel sorry for him. I don't want to hurt that kid, Army. I swear I don't want to hurt him. He thinks he's the only one that's got a memory. I got a memory too. I remember him like he was. Like the first day he comes into my office. All hands and feet and his mouth full of teeth and he talks like General Lee. [*He shakes his head.* MAISH *pats in his pocket again for a match.* ARMY *lights his cigar.*]

ARMY. Take one on me. [*Long pause.*] You talk about memories, Maish. Remember Christmas, 1945? Right at this table. We had six bucks between us. Four of it you spent on a beefsteak and a new tie for him. Remember that, Maish?

MAISH. [*Nods.*] Sure. That horrible-lookin' tie. He wore it until there wasn't anything left of it.

ARMY. I remember a lot of times like that. That time in Scranton when that big Swede knocked him out. Remember? We couldn't get him back on his feet. They took him to a hospital that night. I remember waiting outside in the corridor with you. [MAISH *nods.*] You cried that night, Maish.

MAISH. All right, knock it off.

ARMY. Okay. But you hear me out now, Maish. I'm telling you this now. I'm telling you that I love this guy like he was of my flesh. And I figure if I don't watch for him and weep for him—now nobody

else will, least of all you for some reason.
So be careful, Maish. That's what I'm telling you now. Be careful. [ARMY *rises,
leaves the table, goes across the room and
out the door,* MAISH *watches him for a
moment and then rises after him. He starts
to walk slowly toward the door.*]
*Dissolve to the alley outside of the
fight area.*
[*We see* MC CLINTOCK *very slowly
walking into the alley, aimlessly,
without direction. Once in the center
of the alley he leans against the wall,
his back touching one of the torn
fight posters. The crowd noise comes
up momentarily loud and sharp.*
MC CLINTOCK'S *head goes up. He
slowly turns so that he is face to face
with the picture of a boxer on the
poster with his hands up. And then
for no rhyme nor reason* MC CLINTOCK
*starts to spar with the picture. First
lightly as if he knew it were a joke,
then much more seriously until pretty
soon his hands flick out in short jabs.
They hit the wall and they hurt. He
suddenly draws back with his right as
if to smash at the poster when sud-*

*denly a hand comes down on his
shoulder. He stops. His head comes
down. We pull back to see* MAISH
standing near him.]
MAISH. Mountain, take it easy.
MC CLINTOCK. [*Nods slowly, numbly.*]
Yeah. Yeah, Maish. Take it easy.
MAISH. The world didn't end tonight.
Remember that. The world didn't end
because you left the ring. It didn't end for
you either.
MC CLINTOCK. Sure. Sure, Maish. Just
. . . just stick around for a little, will ya?
I could always depend on you, Maish. I
always . . . I always needed to depend on
you. [MAISH *nods slowly, pats his arm, but
as he does so his eyes travel down the wall
to another poster showing a big, stupid
Arabian prince in a wrestling costume.
And there is a big sign "Wrestling" over
the top of it.* MAISH'S *eyes slowly move
from the poster to* MC CLINTOCK, *who
stares up at him hopefully like a pet dog
desperately needing reassurance.*]
MAISH. [*Wets his lips.*] C'mon, let's get
out of here. [*The two men slowly walk
away and down the alley.*]
We take a slow fade to black

A C T   T W O

> *We dissolve to*
> An anteroom of a small office with a sign on the door: New York
> State Employment Office. Sitting on a bench are MC CLINTOCK
> and ARMY, the former appears nervous and fidgety. He is con-
> stantly running a finger through his collar that is much too tight,
> as is his suit, shirt and everything else that he wears. He looks
> helplessly at ARMY who pats his arm reassuringly.

ARMY. You look fine. Don't worry. You
look just great.
MC CLINTOCK. [*In a whisper.*] But what
do I say, Army?
ARMY. What d'ya mean what d'ya say?
Just tell her you want a job, that's all. It's
simple.
MC CLINTOCK. But what kind of a job?
ARMY. You don't have to worry about
that. You just tell her the sort of thing you
can do and it's up to them to find you one.
MC CLINTOCK. Army, in the past two
days I've been thirty-five places already.
Most of these jokers won't even let me in
the door.

ARMY. It's different here. This place is
official. They're here just to get people
jobs. People like you that can't find them
easy on their own. [*At this moment a
young woman appears at the door of the
inner office.*]
GRACE. Mr. McClintock, please. [MC
CLINTOCK *bolts to his feet, almost upsetting* ARMY.]
MC CLINTOCK. That's me! That's me!
GRACE. [*Smiles.*] In here please, Mr.
McClintock. [MC CLINTOCK *turns to* ARMY
and grabs his arm.]
ARMY. [*Firmly removes his fingers.*]
I'm right here at ringside but I can't go

in to fight for you. Go ahead. [MC CLIN-TOCK, *with another journey of his finger through his collar, walks hesitantly after the young woman. We pan with them into her office as the door closes. He turns around with a start at its closing.*]

GRACE. Sit down, Mr. McClintock. Right over here please near the desk.

MC CLINTOCK. Thanks. Thank you very much. [*He sits down with another eye toward the door. They both start to speak together.*]

MC CLINTOCK. I was . . .

GRACE. Now, Mr. McClintock . . .

MC CLINTOCK. I was just wondering if . . . Oh, I beg your pardon.

GRACE. You were going to say?

MC CLINTOCK. I was just wondering if my friend could come in.

GRACE. Is he looking for employment, too?

MC CLINTOCK. No. No, not exactly but—well, he's kind of my handler.

GRACE. I beg your pardon.

MC CLINTOCK. [*Wets his lips.*] It's okay, he'll stay out there. [*Then she looks at him and smiles, looks through a sheet of paper.*]

GRACE. Harlan McClintock. Your age is . . .

MC CLINTOCK. Thirty-three. [*She makes a little notation with a pencil.*]

GRACE. Place of birth?

MC CLINTOCK. Kenesaw, Tennessee.

GRACE. I see. Your education: [*She looks up at him.*] Mr. McClintock, you left that blank here.

MC CLINTOCK. My education? You mean school?

GRACE. That's right.

MC CLINTOCK. Ninth grade.

GRACE. Then you left, is that it?

MC CLINTOCK. [*Nods.*] Then I left.

GRACE. Now, field of interest.

MC CLINTOCK. I beg your pardon?

GRACE. Your field of interest. What do you like to do?

MC CLINTOCK. Most anything. I don't much care.

GRACE. [*Looks down at his sheet and frowns slightly.*] Past employment record, Mr. McClintock. You have nothing written down there. [*Then she looks up at him.*] Who've been your past employers?

MC CLINTOCK. Well . . . you see . . . I really haven't had past employers—I mean past employers like you mean down on that sheet. I've always been kind of on my own except you might say I've been working for Maish.

GRACE. Maish?

MC CLINTOCK. You see, all I've been doing the past fourteen years is fightin'.

GRACE. Fighting.

MC CLINTOCK. That's right. You know, in the ring.

GRACE. You mean a prize fighter.

MC CLINTOCK. [*Smiles.*] That's right. Prize fighter.

GRACE. A professional prize fighter.

MC CLINTOCK. [*Delightedly.*] Yeah, that's it. You catch on. A professional prize fighter. Heavyweight.

[GRACE *stares at him for a moment and we cut to a tight closeup of* MC CLINTOCK's *face as he becomes conscious of her stare. He almost unconsciously puts one hand across his face to hide the scar tissue. He turns his face away ever so slightly.* GRACE *notices this and turns away herself, and then looks down again at the paper.*]

GRACE. That sounds like interesting work, Mr. McClintock.

MC CLINTOCK. [*Looks up at her.*] Well, it's . . . it's a living. I don't want you to go to no trouble. Army says I should just tell you that . . . well, anything you got's jake with me. Dishwashing, anything. [*She looks at him again for a long moment.*]

GRACE. [*Kindly.*] Let's see if we can't examine something else, Mr. McClintock—something you might like even more. How about factory work?

MC CLINTOCK. [*Shakes his head.*] I never worked in a factory. I wouldn't know anything about it.

GRACE. No sort of assembly-line work, blueprint reading, anything like that? [*He shakes his head. She wets her lips.*] Anything in sales, Mr. McClintock. There's a lot of openings in that sort of thing now. Department-store work. Anything like that?

MC CLINTOCK. [*Shakes his head.*] I . . . couldn't do anything like that. I couldn't sell nothin'. [*Then with a kind of lopsided grin.*] With my face I'd scare away the customers. [*He laughs lightly at this and when he looks up she is staring at him, not*

laughing with him at all. He becomes embarrassed now and half rises to his feet.]
MC CLINTOCK. Look, Miss, I don't want to take up your time. [*And now in his hopelessness, the words come out; he forgets his embarrassment.*] The only reason I come is because Army said I should come. I've been answering all these ads like I told ya and I've been getting no place at all. Maish needs the dough real bad and I can't do nothin' for him any more, and I got to. I got to get some kind of a job. Don't make any difference what I do. Anything at all.
GRACE. Mr. McClintock . . .
MC CLINTOCK. [*Unaware of her now.*] A guy goes along fourteen years. All he does is fight. Once a week, twice a week, prelims, semi-finals, finals. He don't know nothin' but that. All he can do is fight. Then they tell him no more. And what's he do? What's he supposed to do? What's he supposed to know how to do besides fight? They got poor Maish tied up by the ears and I got to do somethin' for him . . . [*He looks down at his hands. Then he pauses for a moment, then sits down hesitantly in a chair.*]
GRACE. [*Quietly.*] Mr. McClintock, we handle a lot of placements here. I'm sure we can find you something . . .
MC CLINTOCK. I know you're going to do the best you can—but [*He points to the paper on her desk.*] I don't fit in any of the holes. I mean that question there. Why did you leave your last job? State reason.
GRACE. That's question nine. You see, Mr. McClintock . . .
MC CLINTOCK. I understand it but what do I write down? What do I write down that would make sense? I left my last job because I got hit so much that I was on my way to punchy land and I'd probably go blind. How would that read there?
GRACE. [*Her eyes narrow.*] Punchy land?
MC CLINTOCK. Sure. You fight so long and then you walk around on your heels listening to the bells. That's what happens to you. Doc looks at my eyes—says one or two more I might go blind.
GRACE. [*Very softly.*] I see.
MC CLINTOCK. [*Getting excited again.*] And that's not fair. It's a dirty break that's all. In 1948 they ranked me number five.

I'm not kidding ya. Number five. And that wasn't any easy year neither. There was Charles and Wolcott and Louis still around. And they had me up there at number five. Maish was sure that . . .
GRACE. Maish? Who's Maish, Mr. McClintock?
MC CLINTOCK. Maish is my manager. And where does it leave him? That's a nice thing to do to a guy who's kept you going for fourteen years. You stop cold on him. So it's a bum break. It ain't fair at all. [*Then he rises and he turns his back to her and he slowly subsides.*] I'm . . . I'm real sorry, Miss. I didn't mean to blow up like that. You ought to kick me out of here. Honest I'm real sorry.
GRACE. [*Again quietly.*] That's perfectly all right, Mr. McClintock. As long as you've got your address down here we'll contact you if anything comes up, and we'll . . . [*She stops, staring across the room at him. At the big shoulders that are slumped in front of her and the big hands down by his sides that clench and unclench. A certain softness shows in her face. A pitying look. She wets her lips and then forces a smile.*] Right after the war I did a lot of work with disabled veterans . . . [*As soon as she has said this she is sorry. His head jerks up and he turns slowly toward her.*]
MC CLINTOCK. Yeah? Go on.
GRACE. I meant . . . I meant you'd be surprised the . . . the different kinds of openings that come up for . . . [*She struggles for a word.*]
MC CLINTOCK. For cripples. For those kind of guys?
GRACE. I didn't mean just that. I meant for people who have special problems.
MC CLINTOCK. I've got no special problems. [*He takes a step toward her.*] There wasn't no place on that question sheet of yours. But I was almost the heavyweight champion of the world. I'm a big ugly slob and I look like a freak—but I was almost the heavyweight champion of the world. I'd like to put that down some place on that paper. This isn't just a punk. This was a guy who was almost the *heavyweight champion of the world.* [*He slams his fists on the desk. And then as quickly as the anger came it leaves. Very slowly he takes his hat from off the desk. He looks at it briefly, closes his eyes and turns away*

again. He looks down at his hand and feels the bruise over his eye, and stands there looking away from her. GRACE *is staring at him all the time.*]

GRACE. Did you hurt your hand, Mr. McClintock?

MC CLINTOCK. [*Looks at his hand.*] I guess I did. That's the . . . that's the thing of it. When you go for so long the hurt piles up and you don't even feel them. You get out of the ring and you go back to a dressing room and you look in the mirror. You look like somebody just ran over you with a tractor—but somehow it doesn't seem to hurt. There's always a reason for it. You know that . . . you know that you just took another step up. Then after the last one—when the wad's all shot, and you're over the hill and there aren't going to be any more—then suddenly you do start to hurt. The punches you got fourteen years ago—even them. And when Maish and the Doc and Army—they were all standing around me that night and I heard somebody say—he's wound up. Then it hurts. Then it hurts like you've got to scream. Like now. It hurts now. Before at least—before every little piece of skin they took off you—was part of the bill you had to pay. And then all of a sudden one night you have to throw all the fourteen years out into an alley and you know then that you've been paying that bill for nothing.

[*We cut to a very tight closeup of* GRACE'S *face as she comes around from behind her desk. She touches his arm tentatively.*]

GRACE. Mr. McClintock—I think—I think we can get you something you'll like. Just give us time.

MC CLINTOCK. [*Looks at her.*] Something I'll like? Do that, Miss. I don't want much. Just . . . the heavyweight championship of the world. That's all. [*He stares at her and you can see in his face that he wants to say something—wants to apologize—wants to explain to her that this is a bitterness directed at no one, but it can't come out. It can't be articulated. He turns slowly and walks out of the room. She stands there watching him through the open door. We see* ARMY *rise. The two men exchange words and then they both leave.* GRACE *slowly closes the door, goes back to her desk pensively. We take a low fade out on her face.*]

Fade on a shot of Maish's hotel room—night

[*In the semi-dark room* MAISH *and* ARMY *play cards.* MAISH *slaps down a card with tremendous vigor.*]

MAISH. Jack of spades. [ARMY *goes through a series of facial and body movements, shrugging left and right, opening and closing his mouth, drumming on the bridge of his nose with his fingers.*]

ARMY. That's good to know. That's very good to know. [*He draws a card, throws it down.* MAISH *draws another. He throws it down.*]

ARMY. Queen of spades.

MAISH. That's what it looks like, doesn't it?

ARMY. [*Nods.*] That's good to know. That's very good to know. [*He goes through the series of motions again.*] That's very good to know.

MAISH. [*Looks up at him.*] Army, would you not say that any more, please?

ARMY. Say what?

MAISH. "It's good to know. It's good to know." Everything is good to know with you. [ARMY *grins, draws a card, throws it down face down, lays out his hand, throws a single card across the table.*]

ARMY. I'll knock for two.

MAISH. You've got me. I've got a Jack and eight free. You've got me . . .

ARMY. That's good to know. [*Then he ducks away jokingly.* MAISH *rises and flings the cards at him across the table.*]

ARMY. C'mon I'll play you another hand.

MAISH. Don't do me any favors. [*He rises and pats around his pockets.*]

ARMY. [*Points to an ashtray.*] It's over here. [MAISH *walks across the room, takes a half-smoked cigar out of an ashtray, lights it.*]

ARMY. One inch shorter you'd be smoking your nose.

MAISH. So does it hurt you?

ARMY. Wanna watch television? There's a fight on.

MAISH. You don't get enough of that, huh?

ARMY. It's somethin' to do.

MAISH. If it's somethin' to do, go to a bar, will ya. I get my gut full of it nine, ten hours a day. I don't like it in my hotel room.

ARMY. Cards?

MAISH. How about ice skating? You bored, Army? [*He chomps nervously on the cigar.*] What am I going to do?

ARMY. [*Shrugs.*] Ask 'em for another week.

MAISH. Ask 'em, ask 'em, ask 'em! Do you think it'll cut ice with them. They want their money. [*The phone rings and* MAISH *nervously and quickly picks it up.*]

MAISH. [*On the phone.*] Hello. Yeah. [*A pause.*] Well, when he gets in tell him I want to talk to him, will ya? No, I can't talk to you. I want to talk to Parelli himself. Thanks. [*He puts down the receiver and finds* ARMY *staring at him.*] Well? You want to lodge a complaint? You look it.

ARMY. Parelli handles wrestling.

MAISH. Is that a secret?

ARMY. What do you want with a wrestling promoter?

MAISH. You got the longest nose in the business.

ARMY. You gonna answer, Maish?

MAISH. [*With an enforced matter-of-factness.*] For a kick, Army. We'll let the kid wrestle a few.

ARMY. Mountain?

MAISH. Why not? They pay good for that stuff, just like they pay actors or somethin'. I could work up a routine for him—ya know. We could make him something like . . . well, you know, like Gorgeous George and the Mad Baron—he'd be . . . he'd be Mountain McClintock the Mountaineer. We could dress him up in a coonskin hat and a . . . a . . . costume of some kind. And we could bill him as . . . [*He stops abruptly. He sees the other staring at him.*] So what's wrong with it? It's money, ain't it?

ARMY. It's money, sure, but what kind of money is it, Maish?

MAISH. What difference does it make what kind of money it is?

ARMY. A guy like him don't take getting laughed at.

MAISH. [*Whirls around at him.*] What're you talking about—a guy like him? So what is he? A prima donna? All of a sudden he's sensitive! All of a sudden he's very fragile like precious china or something. Since when does a guy like him get sensitive all of a sudden!

ARMY. Since when? Since we knowed

him! That's since when. You never see things like that, Maish.

MAISH. Maybe I got no time. Ever look at it that way? Maybe I'm too busy stitching him up so he can show the next week. Maybe I'm too busy on my hands and knees pleading with a promoter to use him so we can get groceries. Maybe I've got no time to hold these poor sensitive boys on my lap.

ARMY. Hey, Maish—you stink.

MAISH. Sure I stink. I'm a crummy selfish louse—because for fourteen years I nurse along a pug, and instead of three square meals for my old age, I got nothing but debts and a headache. You want to know who owes who? Okay. Just check the records. Look at the win and loss. The Mountain comes in at the short end. He owes me. I figure it's as simple as that. What do I ask of this guy? Stick on a costume and make a few people laugh a couple of minutes. Is that going to curdle his sensitive insides? [MAISH's *voice has a barely perceptible tremor in it.*]

ARMY. He's only got one thing left, Maish, that's his pride. You don't want to job that off . . . [MAISH *doesn't answer.* ARMY *walks over to him and grabs him.*] Leave something, will you? You talk about him when he was number five contender in *Ring Magazine.* You want to remember him that way. Leave it so that's the way he'll remember himself. Not a . . . not a clown. Not like somebody who takes a pie in the face so he can eat that day. He was a somebody, Maish. Let it go at that. Don't turn him into a geek. [MAISH *looks intensely at* ARMY. *He can't vocalize his frustration any more than he can put into words the sense of the truth that he gets from what* ARMY *has told him, and it is a truth that* MAISH *cannot answer. Finally he kicks at a table, upsetting a lamp.*]

MAISH. So I'm selling his soul on the street! So light a candle! So weep for him! So rip your clothes a little. So I may take an inch off his pride, but, by God, he and I'll have a full gut to show for it. You can starve to death, wise guy. [*He turns almost aimlessly, not knowing what to do, and finally goes out the door and slams it.*]
Dissolve out
Fade in
   [*With a shot of the Squared-Circle*

Bar as in Act One. It is mid-evening and the place is only partially filled. At the far end of the room the same group of old fighters stand in a semi-circle around one of the others. MC CLINTOCK *stands on their fringe, listening, and as the men talk* MC CLINTOCK *studies their faces. All of them are scarred, ring-battered and there's a kind of sameness in each face.*]

FIGHTER NUMBER ONE. That was Keister. Willie Keister. Used to fight out of Philly. Lightweight.

FIGHTER NUMBER TWO. He wasn't never no lightweight. He always fought middle. I remember him good.

FIGHTER NUMBER ONE. Middleweight, your bleeding ears—He never weighed more than 135 pounds in his life.

[*This talk continues underneath as the camera moves away to take in a shot of the bar and the archway that adjoins the lobby of the little hotel. From out of the lobby we see* GRACE *enter the bar. She looks around.*]

BARTENDER. Sorry, Miss, unescorted ladies ain't permitted.

GRACE. I was looking for Mr. McClintock. The man at the desk said he'd be in here.

BARTENDER. McClintock? The Mountain you mean. That's him. [*He points down toward the end of the room.*]

GRACE. Thank you. [*She walks very slowly toward the group of men in the rear and when she gets close we can then pick up what they are saying.*]

FIGHTER NUMBER ONE. So it's round four. He comes out real slow like he always does.

FIGHTER NUMBER TWO. Yeah. He always did come out slow.

FIGHTER NUMBER ONE. He jabs a couple of times. Remember how he used to do that? From way up high on the shoulder. You could hardly see it coming.

FIGHTER NUMBER TWO. You hardly ever could.

FIGHTER NUMBER ONE. He touches me a couple of times up on the forehead. I back off. He keeps coming after me. I want him to lead. Now this is a guy you got to let lead because he's the best counter puncher in the business.

FIGHTER NUMBER TWO. Yeah. He can

always counter punch. Man, could that boy counter punch. I remember one time in Chicago . . .

FIGHTER NUMBER THREE. Go ahead, Steve. Go ahead.

FIGHTER NUMBER ONE. So, we keep sparring like that right on through the round. He don't hurt me, I don't hurt him. [*He continues to speak underneath as* MC CLINTOCK *turns and sees* GRACE. *He reacts, leaves the group and walks over to see her hurriedly.*]

MC CLINTOCK. Miss Carrie, what're you doing here?

GRACE. Well, I . . . [*She is suddenly conscious of the rest of the men looking at her and* MC CLINTOCK *sees this too. He takes her arm.*]

MC CLINTOCK. Let's go over here and sit down. [*He takes her across to a booth and they sit down. The men move away chuckling with an occasional glance at them.*]

GRACE. A friend of mine and I had dinner over at McCleary's. It isn't very far from here. She got a headache and went on home, and I . . .

MC CLINTOCK. Yeah?

GRACE. And I remembered your giving me your hotel and . . .

MC CLINTOCK. It was real nice of you to look me up. [*She looks around the room and smiles a little embarrassedly.*]

GRACE. You know—I've never been around here before.

MOUNTAIN. [*Nods.*] No change. If you're here once, you've seen it all.

GRACE. [*Smiles.*] Atmosphere.

MC CLINTOCK. Yeah, you might call it atmosphere. [*She looks over his shoulder at the men in the back of the room. One fighter is going through the motions of a battle.* GRACE *looks questioningly at him and then at* MC CLINTOCK.]

MC CLINTOCK. That? That goes on all the time around here. Maish says this part of the room is the graveyard. And these guys spend their time dying in here. Fighting their lives away inside their heads. That's what Maish says.

GRACE. That's . . . that's kind of sad.

MC CLINTOCK. I suppose it is.

GRACE. [*With a smile leans toward him.*] I've got a confession to make. I didn't eat at McCleary's. I ate at home. I came on purpose. I asked for you at your hotel. I've been thinking about you a lot, Mr. McClintock. [*There is a long pause.*] I was just wondering . . .

MC CLINTOCK. Yeah? Go ahead.

GRACE. I was just wondering if you ever thought of working with children. [*There's a long pause.*]

MC CLINTOCK. What?

GRACE. Work with children. Like a summer camp. You know in athletics . . .

MC CLINTOCK. I—I never give it much thought.

GRACE. Do you like children?

MC CLINTOCK. Children? Well, I haven't had much to do with kids but I've always liked them. [*Then thoughtfully, going over it in his mind.*] Yeah, I like kids a lot. You were thinking of a summer camp or something . . .

GRACE. That's right. That sort of thing. In a month or so there'll be a lot of openings. I was thinking, well, perhaps you ought to give that some thought.

MC CLINTOCK. [*His hand goes to his face.*] But they'd have to see me and listen to me talk and . . .

GRACE. Why not? You've got to begin some place. You've got to give it a try.

MC CLINTOCK. Sure, I'm going to have to. [*Then he stares at her intently.*] Why did you come here tonight?

GRACE. [*Looks away.*] I've been thinking about you. I want to help—if I can. [*Then as if to dispel the seriousness of the mood she cocks her head, grins very girl-like.*] How about it, Mr. McClintock—could I have a beer?

MC CLINTOCK. A beer? You mean here?

GRACE. I kind of like it here.

MC CLINTOCK. [*Grins at her.*] Why, sure. [*He stands up and calls to the* BARTENDER *who is passing.*]

MC CLINTOCK. Hey, Charlie! Two beers, huh? [*The* BARTENDER *acknowledges with a wave, goes back toward the bar.* MC CLINTOCK *sits down again and looks across the table at her.*]

GRACE. [*Points to the juke box.*] How about music?

MC CLINTOCK. What?

GRACE. Don't you like to listen to music when you drink beer?

MC CLINTOCK. Music? Why . . . I never even gave it much thought. Sure. Sure we can play music. [*He rises, fishes in his*

pocket, takes out a coin, puts it in the juke box.*]

We cut to

[*A tight close-up of* FIGHTER NUMBER TWO *across the room—a toothless, terribly ugly little man.*]

FIGHTER NUMBER TWO. [*Smiles.*] Hey, Mountain—play "My Heart Tells Me."

[*There's laughter at this.* MC CLINTOCK *quickly turns his face away, shoves a coin in the slot, indiscriminately punches a few buttons, then returns to the booth.* BARTENDER *brings over two bottles of beer, slops them down in front of them.*]

MC CLINTOCK. How about a glass, Charlie, for the lady?

BARTENDER. [*Over his shoulder as he heads back to the bar.*] Fancy-shmancy. [*There's another moment's pause.*]

GRACE. Pretty.

MC CLINTOCK. [*Listens for a moment.*] Yeah. Yeah it is kind of pretty. Them are violins.

GRACE. [*Smiles.*] Beautiful.

MC CLINTOCK. I never paid much attention to music before. I never had much time.

GRACE. What's that?

MC CLINTOCK. Music. Just plain old music. [*He looks away thoughtfully for a moment.*] The only music I know by heart really is the national anthem because they play it before every fight. The national anthem. [GRACE *smiles at this.*] Oh, yeah—there was Smiley Collins, too.

GRACE. Who's Smiley Collins?

MC CLINTOCK. He was a fighter. He used to play a violin. [*A pause.*] That's funny, ain't it? He was a fighter but he used to play a violin. [*As* MC CLINTOCK *talks we can see him losing himself in the conversation and in the sheer delight of having a girl across from him.*]

GRACE. He used to play the violin? Seriously?

MC CLINTOCK. Real serious. Oh, I don't know nothin' about his violin playing—but, oh, man, did that boy have a right hand. Like dynamite. He could knock down a wall with it.

GRACE. What about his violin . . .

MC CLINTOCK. [*Interrupts her, not even hearing her.*] I remember his last fight. He fought a guy by the name of Willie Floyd. Floyd had twenty pounds on him. [*At this moment the* BARTENDER *brings a glass, puts it down in front of* GRACE, *then walks away.* MC CLINTOCK *picks up her bottle and pours the beer for her.*]

GRACE. [*Smiles.*] Thanks.

MC CLINTOCK. They don't have many ladies here—that's the reason he forgets to put glasses out. [*He holds up his bottle to her glass.*] Drink hearty. That's what Maish always says. Drink hearty.

GRACE. [*Smiles.*] Drink hearty. Drink hearty, Mr. McClintock. [*The two of them drink. His eyes never leave her face. She notices this, smiles again.*] You think a lot of Maish, don't you?

MC CLINTOCK. He's number one. They don't come like him.

GRACE. He was your—manager.

MC CLINTOCK. [*Nods.*] Yeah, for fourteen years. He's been a real great friend, not just a manager. In the old days—in the old days when I was just getting started—Maish would stake me to everything from clothes to chow. He's a real great guy. [*Then he stops abruptly and stares at her.*] Why ain't you married?

GRACE. [*Laughs.*] Should I be?

MC CLINTOCK. [*Nods.*] You're pretty. Not just pretty. you're beautiful.

GRACE. Thank you.

MC CLINTOCK. Pretty as a young colt. That's what my old man used to say.

GRACE. Your father?

MC CLINTOCK. [*Nods.*] Yeah. A girl's as pretty as a young colt, so he used to tell me.

GRACE. [*Very interested.*] Go ahead, Mountain . . .

MC CLINTOCK. About my father? Big guy. Nice old guy too. I remember once—I fought a guy named Jazzo. Elmer Jazzo. And he looked just like my old man. Spittin' image. And in the first round I didn't even want to hit him. Then in round two I shut my eyes and I . . .

GRACE. [*Interrupts.*] Mountain.

MC CLINTOCK. [*Looks at her.*] Yeah?

GRACE. There isn't much else is there—besides fighting?

MC CLINTOCK. [*Very thoughtfully looks away.*] No. No, there isn't I guess. I'm . . . I'm sorry . . .

GRACE. Don't be. It's just that there is so much more for you that you'll be able to find now. [*They look at each other and both smile. The music is playing and they*

are both aware of it suddenly.] Hey, Mountain . . .

MC CLINTOCK. Yeah?

GRACE. Them are violins.

[*They both laugh. The camera pulls away from them as they start to talk, lost in an awareness of each other and in the pleasantness of being together. We continue a slow dolly away from them, and then a slow fade out to black. We fade on with a shot of the alley outside the area.* GRACE *and* MC CLINTOCK *walk slowly away from the door toward the street. They walk slowly, looking around.*]

MC CLINTOCK. [*Kicks a can out of the way.*] A garden, ain't it?

GRACE. Where are the flowers?

MC CLINTOCK. [*Flicks his ear.*] Right here. [GRACE *smiles a little forcedly.*]

GRACE. It's late, Mountain. I've got to go home.

MC CLINTOCK. I'll get you a cab. [*She starts to walk off.*] Grace . . . [*She turns to him.*] I . . . I've had a good time.

GRACE. I have too.

MC CLINTOCK. You know when we came out of the bar I heard Charlie say that I had a pretty date.

GRACE. [*Smiles.*] Thank Charlie for me.

MC CLINTOCK. It wasn't just that he thought you were pretty. He said that I had a date. It's like with the music, I don't even think I ever had a real date in all this time. A real one. Not somebody I liked. Somebody I wanted to be with.

GRACE. I think that's a compliment.

MC CLINTOCK. One time . . . one time Army had a girl friend living in St. Louis. She had a friend. Army fixed me up. We were supposed to meet after the fight. These two girls were waitin' for us outside. This girl that I was supposed to go with—she takes one look at me and she . . . she . . .

GRACE. She what, Mountain?

MC CLINTOCK. She turned around and she ran away. She looked at my face and she turned around and ran away. [GRACE *instinctively touches his arm and holds it tightly.*] That shouldn't have hurt. I should have been used to it. I know what I look like. I know what I sound like, too. But it . . . it did hurt. I didn't want it to happen again so I never let it happen.

Cut to a tight close-up of Grace
[As she stares at him and she won-
deringly shakes her head, feeling that
acme of tenderness a woman can feel
for a man.]
GRACE. *[Softly.]* The cab, Mountain. It's
late.

MC CLINTOCK. Sure. *[The two start*
walking again toward the opening of the
alley.]

GRACE. Remember to think about what
I told you. I think you'd like working with
children.

MC CLINTOCK. I'll think about it. I'll
think about it a lot. Don't build me up
none, Miss Carrie. Don't say I'm anything
special. *[A pause.]* Tell 'em . . . tell 'em
I fought a hundred and eleven fights. Tell
'em I never took a dive. I'm proud of that.
[GRACE looks at him intently for a moment
and there's a continuing softness on her
face.]

GRACE. *[Whispers.]* Sure you are, Mountain. You must be very proud. *[She quickly*
kisses him on the side of his face, studies
him for a moment and hurriedly walks
away from him. He stands there touching
his face, looking after her.]

We take a slow dissolve out to a shot of
MAISH's *hotel room, the same night.*

[The door opens, MC CLINTOCK *enters.*
In the room are MAISH, ARMY *and a*
FAT MAN *who has been sitting in a*
corner of the room. FAT MAN *rises.]*

MAISH. It's about time. Army was lookin'
for ya. Somebody said you left the bar
with a girl.

MC CLINTOCK. *[Grins broadly.]* I want to
tell you all about it, Maish. No kiddin',
she's a wonderful girl. Her name is . . .

MAISH. Tell me later. We've got business
to attend to here.

MC CLINTOCK. *[Filled to overflowing.]*
Army, it's the girl from the employment
office. Miss Carrie.

ARMY. Pretty kid.

MC CLINTOCK. Beautiful. Beautiful girl.

PARELLI. How about it, Maish? I ain't
got all night.

MAISH. Right away, Mountain, I'd like
you to meet somebody. This is Mr. Parelli.
Mr. Parelli promotes wrestling matches at
Matthew's Arena.

MC CLINTOCK. I'm gladda know you.

PARELLI. Likewise. So get with it,
Maish.

MAISH. We've got ourselves a nice deal
here, kid. Want to tell him, Mr. Parelli?

PARELLI. There isn't much to tell. Maish
here thinks you might be a good draw.
Your name's pretty well known. I've seen
you fight a couple of times myself.
[MC CLINTOCK smiles.] Yeah I think I can
line you up with some matches. I think it
might be worth both our while.

MC CLINTOCK. *[His smile fades some-*
what.] Maish didn't tell ya. I'm not supposed to fight any more. I don't think I
can get my license back. *[PARELLI looks at*
MAISH *questioningly and* MAISH *forces a*
smile.]

MAISH. We're not talking about boxing
now, Kid. This is for wrestling. I told ya
Mr. Parelli promotes wrestling matches.

MC CLINTOCK. Wrestling matches? I
don't know how to wrestle.

PARELLI. *[Laughs.]* You don't have to
know how. Couple hours and you can
learn the holds. There's really only two
big things you've got to learn in my business, Kid. That's how to fake, make it look
real, and that's how to land without hurt-
ing yourself. That's about it.

MC CLINTOCK. I don't get it.

MAISH. What do you mean you don't
get it? He's laying it out for you. And
listen to what else, Mountain. I've got a
funny idea. We'll dress you up in a coonskin hat see, and you're going to be billed
as the Mountaineer. How about that, huh?
Just like old times. Even buy you some
kind of a long squirrel gun or something.
[Then there's a long dead silence as
MC CLINTOCK *turns away.]*

MAISH. Well?

PARELLI. I don't think he goes for it,
Maish.

MAISH. What're you talkin' about he
don't go for it? Mountain, what've you got
to say?

MC CLINTOCK. I'd lose you a fortune,
Maish. I can't wrestle. I don't think I
could win a match. *[PARELLI laughs.]*

MAISH. What do you mean win a match?
These are all set up, Kid. One night you
win, the next night the other guy wins.

PARELLI. It depends on who plays the
heavy.

MC CLINTOCK. A tank job.

MAISH. Will you talk sense? This is an
entirely different thing. Everybody knows

there's a fix on in these things. It's a part of the game.

MC CLINTOCK. I never took a dive for anybody. A hundred and eleven fights. I never took one single dive.

PARELLI. It's like Maish says. These aren't exactly dives . . . [*Then there's a long pause.*] Well, look I'll tell you what, you guys talk it over. Give me a call, Maish, by tomorrow. I've got to know by tomorrow.

MAISH. You get the contracts ready. We'll be ready to sign in the morning.

PARELLI. Sure. Nice meeting you, Mountain. [MC CLINTOCK *nods.* PARELLI *goes out. There is the off-stage sound of the door closing.* MC CLINTOCK *stares at* MAISH. MAISH *averts his glance.*]

MAISH. [*With his back to him.*] I figure you owe it to me. [*Then a pause.*] What do you figure?

MC CLINTOCK. [*Nods.*] I guess so.

MAISH. So there's nothing more to it then. [MC CLINTOCK *turns, his face shows an anguish we haven't seen before.*]

MC CLINTOCK. But Maish—I was almost heavyweight champion of the world. [MAISH *turns, walks over to him and grabs him tightly. His voice is fierce and intent.*]

MAISH. Then you remember just that. When I stick you in a silly costume you just remember you were almost heavyweight champion of the world. And I'll remember I was the guy who managed you. We'll do this one with our eyes closed. [*Then he releases him. He breathes a little heavily.*] Army, take him home. [*He turns his back to them.* ARMY *walks over to* MC CLINTOCK.]

MC CLINTOCK. Never mind, Army. I'll go home by myself. [MOUNTAIN *exits.*]

MAISH. He's upset—that's all. He just don't know.

ARMY. He knows. Believe me, he knows.

MAISH. But he'll come around.

ARMY. Sure he will. You'll fix it that way.

You gotta knack, Maish. You violin him to death. And if that don't work—squeeze a little. Back him up. Twist it up a little for him. What a knack you got! [*He turns to go.* MAISH's *voice is soft, pleading.*]

MAISH. Army, stick, will ya?

ARMY. Stick?

MAISH. Help me with him. Just stay alongside.

ARMY. [*Understanding now.*] Partners again, huh? If he sees me, he'll move faster—that the idea?

MAISH. He'll want both of us. It'll help him, Army. A lousy one-night stand.

ARMY. Stop it! You break him into a dummy harness once—he'll stay with it. [*Pounds his fists silently.*] It ain't enough I gotta watch him go down all these years. Now you want me in the pit. I gotta officiate at the burial.

MAISH. It don't have to be that way. [*And now desperately groping for the words and for the first time we're listening to the mind of this man.* ARMY *grabs him by the lapels and holds on to him very tightly.*]

ARMY. This is a slob to you, Maish. This is a hunk. This is a dead-weight—has-been. This is a cross you got to bear? I'll tell you what he is, Maish, this boy. This is a decent man. This is a man with a heart. This is somebody, flesh and blood, now, Maish. You can't sell this on the market by the pound, because if you do, if you do, you'll rot in hell for it. You understand me, Maish, you'll rot. [*He cries uncontrollably and then stops.*]

MAISH. Please, Army, for him at least. Don't leave him alone.

ARMY. Of course not. I can't leave him alone. He'll do it for you even if I'm not there. So I'll *be* there [*A pause.*] Why is it, Maish . . . tell me . . . why is it . . . so many people have to feed off one guy's misery? Tell me, Maish . . . doesn't it . . . doesn't it make you want to die?

Fade out

ACT THREE

Fade in
[*With a tight close-up of a suit of buckskin, the coonskin hat, an old relic of a muzzle-loading Long-Tom rifle, a powder horn and a few other accoutrements. Then we pull back for a cover*

shot of the room. It is a small dressing room very similar to the one in Act One. PARELLI *is looking over the costume and chuckling softly through his cigar. He picks up one of the legs of the trousers, examines it, laughs again, tosses it aside, then starts toward the door as it opens.* MAISH *enters.]*

PARELLI. [*Nods.*] Looks good. Where is he?

MAISH. He's coming.

PARELLI. The guy at the gym says he don't have those holds down at all. Didn't understand them.

MAISH. He will. Give him a little while.

PARELLI. He knows just what to do, doesn't he?

MAISH. Yeah. He's all zeroed in.

PARELLI. And this is important. When the other guy gets a lock on him or any kind of a hold—have him look in pain, you understand? That's important. He's got to look as if he's giving up the ghost. [*Then with a grimace.*] Pain, you understand, Maish. Real pain. Torture. Agony.

MAISH. [*Sardonically.*] He'll die out there for ya. [*Then he looks out toward the open door.*] How's the house?

PARELLI. The usual. Not good, not bad. They want action. It don't have to be good action, but it's got to be action. So tell your boy to move around.

MAISH. I told you he knows all about it.

PARELLI. Okay. [*He starts to walk by him and* MAISH *pinches his sleeve with two fingers.*]

MAISH. The dough, Parelli.

PARELLI. It'll be waiting for you after the fight. I don't know how you talked me into an advance. Most people can't.

MAISH. [*With a grin.*] With me, it's an art.

PARELLI. It must be. [*He looks at his watch.*] He better get here soon. [*Then with a grin.*] It's going to take him a long time to get into that outfit.

MAISH. He'll be right along. I just talked to him.

PARELLI. Okay. I'll see you later. [*He goes out of the room. He closes the door.* MAISH *walks over to the table that the costume is on. He picks up the pieces one by one and looks at them. He has a dull, emotionless look on his face. When he gets to the gun he picks it up, and the door opens.* ARMY *enters.*]

ARMY. What's the season—grouse? What you huntin', Maish?

MAISH. Right now I'm huntin' a wrestler named McClintock. Have you seen him?

ARMY. [*Shakes his head.*] Not since last night.

MAISH. [*Slams a fist against his palm.*] He's late.

ARMY. That's good to know. [*He kicks the door shut and walks over to* MAISH. *He looks down at the paraphernalia.*]

MAISH. [*Stares at him.*] Enough to make a fuss over? [*He points to the clothes.*] Is it, Army?

ARMY. [*Shrugs.*] I don't have to wear it.

MAISH. If you did—it would break your heart, huh? [*At this moment there's the sound of the crowd from up above and both men look up and then look at each other.*]

MAISH. Army.

ARMY. Go.

MAISH. You know me, Army.

ARMY. You bet I do.

MAISH. I don't mean just that way. I mean you know me inside. You know how I hate this. You know how it keeps me from sleeping. You know how it eats away my stomach, Army . . . [*At this moment* MC CLINTOCK *enters. He smiles at* ARMY.]

MC CLINTOCK. I looked for ya. I was afraid you wasn't gonna come.

MAISH. He's here. You better get into this thing.

MC CLINTOCK. Sure, Maish. Sure. [*Then suddenly his eyes fall on the coonskin cap and costume and the gun leaning against the wall. His face goes numb. He walks over to them, lifts them up one piece at a time. He stares down at them.*]

MAISH. [*Wets his lips, forces a smile.*] Ain't that a lark, Kid? It's gonna kill 'em. Gonna knock 'em dead. [MC CLINTOCK *nods dumbly.* MAISH, *continuing, hurriedly.*] You know you take it off when you get in. You walk around the ring a couple of times and you take it off. You don't have to wear it very long. [*His words tumble out in a torrent.*] And underneath you wear Long Johns and it isn't until after the bout you've got to put the stuff back.

on . . . [*He stops abruptly as* MC CLINTOCK *turns to him.*]

MC CLINTOCK. Clown.

MAISH. [*Points to* ARMY.] He called it that. You're taking it from him. Can't you think a thought for yourself?

MC CLINTOCK. [*Shakes his head.*] He called it that but I call it that too. [*He nods toward the hallway.*] And everybody out there will call it that, too. Clown. [*He puts the flat of both hands on the table, and bends his head far down so that his face cannot be seen.*] Maish—don't make me!

Cut to a very tight close-up of MAISH
[*What we see on his features is a look of pain—a kind of sudden, personal agony, and then he composes his features almost one by one and his voice comes out loud again and shrill, along with a laugh.*]

MAISH. What do you mean don't make you? What am I, your father? Don't make you. You don't do nothin' you don't want to do. If you don't think you owe it to me. Okay. [*There's a knock on the door.*]

MAISH. Yeah?
[*The door opens and* PARELLI *is standing there. Behind him a* PHOTOGRAPHER.]

PARELLI. [*Grins into the room.*] How about a couple of pictures, Maish? We ain't had any with the costume yet.

MC CLINTOCK. [*His head goes up.*] Pictures?

PARELLI. Part of the build-up, Kid. One picture is worth a million words. That's what the Greeks say. [*Then to* PHOTOGRAPHER.] How about it? You want 'em in here or out in the hall?

PHOTOGRAPHER. Out in the hall. I've got more room. [*There's a long pause.* PARELLI *waits expectantly.*]

PARELLI. So? What's he waiting for—a valet? Let's hurry it up. [*He goes out, closing the door.* MC CLINTOCK *rises, looks quickly at* ARMY *and then at* MAISH, *then turns back to the table and picks up the coonskin hat, puts it on his head. Then he puts his arms into the coat and slowly puts it on.* MAISH *turns away. We are looking from close up at him and at his face and features as they work, and a little of the agony returns. Over his shoulder we see* MC CLINTOCK *buttoning the jacket, then he takes the gun, looks at it.* MC

CLINTOCK *goes to the door, stops with his hand on the knob, stands there motionless, his eyes closed.*]

VOICE. McClintock's on next. Let's go!

MC CLINTOCK. [*Almost a whisper.*] Tell 'em to go away, Maish.

MAISH. What're you talking about? [*There's a loud knock on the door and this time* PARELLI'S *voice.*]

PARELLI. What's going on in there? What're you trying to pull off here, Maish? Get your boy out there. Photographer's waitin' for him and his match is on.

MAISH. [*Raises his voice but it still comes out weakly.*] He'll . . . he'll be right out, Parelli. He'll be right there. [*Then he turns to* MC CLINTOCK.] Mountain, you cross me now—and I'm dead. Understand? I'm dead. [MC CLINTOCK *shakes his head back and forth, back and forth.*]

MC CLINTOCK. Can't. Can't, Maish. Can't.

MAISH. [*Grabs him and holds him tightly by the shirt front.*] You got a debt, Mister. You owe me.

MC CLINTOCK. Maish . . .

MAISH. I mean it, Mountain. I've got my whole life on the line now. I can't afford to let you cross me. [MC CLINTOCK *shakes his head.* MAISH'S *voice desperate.*] I swear I'll beat you to a pulp myself! I wouldn't have been in this jam if it weren't for you.

MC CLINTOCK. [*Looks up.*] Maish, I'll do anything you want but . . .

MAISH. But it bothers you too much. Well, it didn't bother you last week to stand up in a ring with your hands down at your sides and let Gibbons beat you to a pulp. That didn't bother you a bit! *It didn't bother you that I had every nickel in the world tossed on a table to say that you wouldn't go three!* [*Then there's a long, long pause as* MC CLINTOCK'S *face shows a gradual understanding, and* MAISH *on the other hand looks like a man whose tongue has suddenly gotten red hot in his mouth.*]

MC CLINTOCK. Maish . . . Maish, you bet against me. [MAISH *doesn't answer him and there's another pause.* MC CLINTOCK *takes a step toward him.*]

MC CLINTOCK. Maish. Why'd you bet against me?

MAISH. Would it make any difference, Mountain, if I hocked my left foot to bet on you—would it have made any difference? You're not a winner any more, Mountain. And that means there's only one thing left—make a little off the losing. [MC CLINTOCK *takes another step toward him, and* MAISH, *whose back has been to him, turns to face him.* MC CLINTOCK *stares at him and his lips tremble.*]

MC CLINTOCK. [*Finally.*] You fink! You dirty fink, you, Maish! Dirty, lousy fink. [MAISH's *face goes white but he doesn't say anything.*]

MC CLINTOCK. And because I wouldn't go down—because I stood up and took it for ya—I've got to pay for it like this. [*He pulls at the costume.*] Like this, Maish, huh? [*He turns and walks away from him, shaking his head, trying to articulate, desperate to let something that he feels now come out without quite knowing how to let it come out.*] In all the dirty, crummy fourteen years I fought for you—I never felt ashamed. Not of a round—not of a minute. [*Then he turns to* MAISH, *looks down at himself, then across at* MAISH.] But now all of a sudden you make me feel ashamed. You understand, Maish? You make me feel ashamed. I'd have gone into any ring barehanded against a guy with a cleaver— and that wouldn't have hurt me near as much as this.

ARMY. Mountain. Listen to me . . . [MC CLINTOCK, *suddenly unable to control himself any more, raises his hand and with the flat of it smashes* ARMY *against the face.* ARMY *goes backward, falling against a table and winding up on his hands and knees.* MAISH *starts toward him.*]

ARMY. [*Picks up his head.*] Get away, Maish. Get away. [*Then very slowly he rises to his feet, rubs his jaw briefly, looks at* MC CLINTOCK.]

MC CLINTOCK. [*In a whisper.*] Army . . . Army—for the love of God . . .

ARMY. That's all right, Kid. I rated it. I shouldn't have been here. I had no reason to be here. I had it coming. [*He turns accusingly toward* MAISH.] Go on, Kid, go on and leave. Take what precious little you've got left and get out of here. [MC CLINTOCK *turns slowly and walks out of the room. After a few moments' pause,* ARMY *turns and goes to the door, looks down the corridor and says.*] Good night, Mountain. [*From down the hall at this moment comes a shouting, fuming, sweat-*ing PARELLI. *He arrives at the door almost too excited to speak.*]

PARELLI. He's walkin' out! The boy's walkin' out! What's with this? *What's with it?* [*Then* PARELLI *walks over to* MAISH, *sticks his finger in his chest and prods him.*]

PARELLI. You know what I'm gonna do to you for this, don't you? [MAISH *keeps his head down. Shouts.*] I'm gonna see to it that you don't get a license to walk a dog from now on. You don't think I will? You don't think I will, Maish? Well, let me tell ya . . .

[*The camera moves back over to* ARMY, *still standing by the door.*]

ARMY. [*Very quietly.*] Good-bye, Mountain—

Dissolve to the bar

[*Dolly down through it until we reach the rear and a group of men talking fight talk. All of them living in a little round-by-round dream world.* MC CLINTOCK *stands a few feet away from the fringes, staring at them and listening. Finally one of them says loudly enough to be heard.*]

FIGHTER NUMBER ONE. That wasn't his name, Stevie. His name was Hacker. Charles Hacker. And he never fought Louis. [*Then he looks up over the crowd and sees* MC CLINTOCK.] How about that Mountain? You know him. Hacker Charles Hacker. He never fought Louis did he? [*The crowd turns and stares toward* MC CLINTOCK *who takes a step toward them.*]

MC CLINTOCK. No, he never fought Louis. He fought me, though.

FIGHTER NUMBER TWO. No kiddin' Mountain. No kiddin'? How'd you do? [MC CLINTOCK *takes another step and the men make way for him until he is standing almost in their midst.*]

MC CLINTOCK. It went three rounds. He was always strong in the beginning.

FIGHTER NUMBER TWO. Yeah, yeah. He was always strong.

MC CLINTOCK. He come in at me and he don't box none. He never did . . . [*Then he stops abruptly and he stares around the circle of faces. We pan with his eye to take in a shot of each face, and the winding up on a tight close-up of his own as he suddenly slowly shakes his head.*]

MC CLINTOCK. I . . . I don't remember i

I'm sorry but I don't remember it. [*He turns, walks away from them and goes over to the bar.*] Give me a beer, will you?

BARTENDER. Sure, Mountain. Comin' up.

[*The camera pulls away from the shot of* MOUNTAIN *sitting at the bar until he is framed in the window. It continues to pull away until we pick up a shot of* ARMY *across the street staring toward the window. Then we see* GRACE *approaching him.*]

ARMY. [*Turns to her.*] I'm over here, Miss.

GRACE. [*Approaches him.*] You're . . . you're Army?

ARMY. That's right. Thanks for coming.

GRACE. Tell me what happened . . .

ARMY. What happened is that he walked out of a match. But I want to make sure he *keeps* walking. I didn't want him to stop at that graveyard over there.

GRACE. How can I help?

ARMY. You can help him by not conning him. He's been conned by experts. He's riddled. He'll listen to you. When he gets out of there head him toward Grand Central Station and give him this. [*He takes out an envelope and hands it to* GRACE.]

GRACE. What's that?

ARMY. That's a train ticket to Kenesaw, Tennessee.

GRACE. [*Studies the envelope for a moment.*] Is that home?

ARMY. [*Very quietly.*] It was once. Maybe it'll be again. [*Then there is a 'ong pause.*] Do you love him, Miss?

GRACE. I don't know. I feel so sorry for him though, I want to cry.

ARMY. [*Touches her arm gently.*] You :ell him that, Miss. Tell him you think he's a decent guy, and you like him. But tell him, for the time being, you don't come vith a kiss. He's been chasing a ghost too 'ong now—and the next thing he's got a hunger for—he oughta get. It's only fair. Thanks very much, Miss. [*Then there is a 'ong pause.*] You're a brick. [*He walks away. And as he does so* MOUNTAIN *comes 'ut of the bar.* GRACE *walks over across he street to him. The camera stays with* ARMY *looking at the two of them over his houlder. We can see them talking but :an't hear them. Then we see* GRACE *hand* MOUNTAIN *the envelope. He takes it in his hands, they exchange a few more unintelligible words, and then* MOUNTAIN *starts* to walk away. GRACE *turns, starts across the street and then stops.*]

Cut to close shot of GRACE *as she whirls around.*

Cut to

[*Very tight close-up of* MC CLINTOCK'S *face in the lamplight of the street. The broken nose, the misshapen ears, scar tissues, bruises that never healed and never will any more. The battered ugliness that is a legacy of the profession.*]

GRACE. Mountain!

[MOUNTAIN *stops, turns to her.* GRACE *runs over to him and very lightly kisses him.* MOUNTAIN *reaches up and touches his face wonderingly.*]

MOUNTAIN. Thanks for that. [*Then hesitantly, terribly unsure, he kisses her back.*] Thanks for not running away.

GRACE. When you get home, when you get settled—write me and tell me what's happened.

MOUNTAIN. When I get home? [*He looks down at the ticket.*] I'll go there—but . . . I don't know if it's home any more.

GRACE. Go find out. You look for it, Mountain. Because wherever home is— it's not over there. [*She points toward the bar. Then she hands him a slip of paper.*] It's my home address, Mountain. Write me. [*He very tentatively takes the paper and then slowly shakes his head. He crumples it in his fist. She grabs his hand and guides it into his pocket.*]

GRACE. Good-bye, Mountain. [*He turns and walks slowly away.* GRACE *watches him for a moment and then starts to cross the street toward the camera. Halfway across the street her head goes down and her hands are down at her side. She blinks her eyes and very quietly begins to cry.*]

Dissolve out on her face to cover shot of the dressing room in semi-darkness.

[MAISH *sits alone by the rubbing table. The only light comes from the bulbs out in the hall.* ARMY *appears at the door, peers inside, sees* MAISH *and enters.*]

ARMY. You gonna stay here all night?

MAISH. That's a thought.

ARMY. Fox is out there with some other guys.

MAISH. It comes, I figured.

ARMY. If it comes, it comes. Get it over

with, Maish. [MAISH *studies* ARMY *intently.*]

MAISH. Hey, Army, what are you going to do?

ARMY. [*Smiles.*] Tomorrow I'll be for hire. You know, Maish—you said so yourself—I'm the best cut man in the business. And after I patch up my millionth cut, maybe somebody'll give me a gold watch.

MAISH. You're needed, aren't you?

ARMY. [*Nods.*] A little bit. C'mon, take your lickin' and let's get out of here. [*The two men walk out into the hall.* FOX *and the two other men are waiting.*]

FOX. Maish— [MAISH *stops dead in his tracks, staring straight ahead.* FOX *comes up behind him.*] This ain't a payoff, Maish, relax.

MAISH. You here to give medal? [*Looks at the other two men.*] It must be very heavy.

FOX. We're here to give you a proposition. This is Mr. Arnold. [*A heavy-set man comes up alongside. He is the same man we saw in the bar.*]

MAISH. Mr. Arnold and I have met. You work for Henson?

MAN. Yeah.

FOX. Here's the proposition. Maish. It's a sweetie, a real sweetie.

[*With this he propels the other man to the front and into the light. He is a young fighter in his late teens. At a first sudden glance there is a striking resemblance between this boy and* MOUNTAIN—*as* MOUNTAIN *must have appeared very early in the game.* MAISH *looks at him briefly.*]

MAISH. What's he want—a haircut?

FOX. Mr. Henson would like him managed. Managed good.

MAN. Groomed—that's the word.

MAISH. Why me? That's the question.

FOX. He wants a nice dependable guy with know-how, Maish, and you're it. Some guy who knows his business—and who'll go along.

MAISH. I know my business . . .

MAN. And you'll go along.

MAISH. I've got a choice, huh?

MAN. Yeah, you've got a choice. You take this kid and make a fighter out of him—or the Commissioner gets a phone call that a certain manager's been making bets.

FOX. That's against the law, Maish.

MAISH. Is that a fact?

FOX. [*Seriously.*] You know it is. Parimutuels at race or harness tracks—that's the only place betting is permitted. They'd take away your license. Maish, It wouldn't be just a suspension, Maish—it'd be permanent. [MAISH *takes a step closer to the young fighter and studies his face in the light.*]

MAISH. Where're you from, Kid ?

FOX. [*Interjects.*] It's an amazing coincidence. It really is, Maish. He's from Kentucky. You could call him Mountain . . .

FIGHTER. Who is Mountain?

MAISH. [*His lip trembles perceptibly.*] He was a good, fast kid. All hands and feet with his mouth full of teeth and he talked like General Lee. Like you do—like you look. You better go back there and work in a drugstore. [*He turns away.*]

FIGHTER. To hell with the drugstore. I want to be a fighter. [MAISH *studies him very intently for a moment, looking him up and down.*]

MAISH. You want to be a fighter? All right, check this. There's eight champions in this business. Everybody else is an also-ran. There's the good and the bad in it The good's great—the bad stinks; so we'l give it a whirl. [*Then there's a long pause.*] Army—you're needed. [ARMY *who has been standing by the door sighs resignedly, joins* MAISH, *and the two of them walk down the corridor with the young* FIGHTER *in the middle.*]

We lap dissolve

[*To a film clip of a train and a section of a car.* MC CLINTOCK *sits across from a* WOMAN *and a little* BOY.]

BOY. [*Suddenly leans over to him.*] Hiya

MC CLINTOCK. [*Looks down in surprise.*] Hiya.

[BOY *picks up one of* MC CLINTOCK' *big hands and examines it.*]

BOY. You're a fighter, aren't you?

MC CLINTOCK. [*Looks down at him.*] Yeah. I was a fighter.

BOY. I can tell by your ears. You go big ears. [*There is a long pause and very slowly* MOUNTAIN *grins.*]

MOUNTAIN. Yeah, cauliflower ears. [*The BOY returns his grin and we can see* MOUNTAIN *relaxing for the first time.*]

BOY. How do you get ears like that I'd like ears like that.

WOMAN. Jeffrey, don't be rude . . .

MC CLINTOCK. That's all right, Ma'am.
[*The* BOY *goes over to sit next to* MC CLIN-TOCK.]
BOY. [*Suddenly assuming a fight position.*] Like this? This is the way you do it?
MC CLINTOCK. [*Straightens the* BOY's *hands.*] No, you hold your right down, keep that left up, hunch your shoulder like this. Okay. Now lead. No, no, no—with the left, and don't drop your right. Okay, now lead again. [*The* BOY *does all this, delighted.*]
WOMAN. I hope he's not bothering you . . .
MC CLINTOCK. Not a bit, Ma'am. I like it.
WOMAN. Where are you heading for?
[*There is a long pause.* MC CLINTOCK *reaches in his pocket and takes out the slip of paper that* GRACE *had given him. Unfolds it and smooths it out.*]

MC CLINTOCK. Home. I'm heading for home. I don't know fcr how long. Cause I . . . cause I'll probably be taking a job one of these days soon. Work with kids like Jeffrey here.
BOY. [*Impatiently.*] C'mon, Champ. Let's you and me spar.
MC CLINTOCK. Okay, Champ. Now lead again. That's right. Right from the shoulder. Okay, now cross with the right. No, no, no—don't drop your left. That's right.
[*The camera starts to pull away very slowly from them until their voices cannot be heard and all we can see is the pantomime of* MOUNTAIN MC CLINTOCK *and the little boy fighting the* MOUNTAIN's *greatest fight. We take a very slow dissolve to the film clip of the train as it disappears into the night.*]
A slow fade to black.

For Discussion and Writing

1. The television dramas of Rod Serling frequently gain distinction by his original treatment of a familiar theme. What is the unexpected twist in *Requiem for a Heavyweight* that distinguishes this play from the usual sentimental story about a "washed-up" fighter?

2. Characterization is simpler and more direct on television than in the theater. Because of outside interruptions and distractions, it is considered essential in TV writing to give each character a strong basic personality trait—an essential pattern of his own that audiences can easily recognize and follow.

Discuss the basic personality trait of each of the four main characters in *Requiem for a Heavyweight*.

Which, in your opinion, is the most complex of the characterizations? How are the subtleties in this character presented?

In what ways does Maish resemble Starbuck in "The Rainmaker"—another man who lives by his wits? What is the basic difference between the two?

3. Television writers call the TV camera close-up a magnificent instrument for the depiction of character. Why do you think this is so?

The camera can also advance action by focusing on objects.

Find examples of both these techniques in the script and discuss how they carry the story forward. What do they reveal that would be lost in a stage production?

4. In the final stage direction, what is the meaning of the words, ". . . and all we can see is the pantomime of Mountain McClintock and the little boy fighting the Mountain's greatest fight"? Do you think this play has an ambiguous ending?

5. In a comparison of *Requiem for a Heavyweight* to the other plays you have read in this book, what do you think are the essential differences between television plays and theater plays? Consider such points as:
   a. Subject matter
   b. Technical approach
   c. Pace
   d. Intimacy
   e. Scope

6. Plays from the theater are frequently adapted for television performance. Select any play in this text and do one of the following adaptations with it:
   a. Choose a scene and adapt it for TV by substituting the use of the camera for dialogue wherever possible. Make any changes required for the new medium.
   b. Choose an act for TV adaptation, and outline proposed changes to give this act greater visual variety in settings and action in order to hold the television audience.

Harvey

⟨1944⟩

MARY CHASE

CHARACTERS

(In Order of Appearance)

MYRTLE MAE SIMMONS	DUANE WILSON
VETA LOUISE SIMMONS	LYMAN SANDERSON, M.D.
ELWOOD P. DOWD	WILLIAM R. CHUMLEY, M.D.
MISS JOHNSON	BETTY CHUMLEY
MRS. ETHEL CHAUVENET	JUDGE OMAR GAFFNEY
RUTH KELLY, R.N.	E. J. LOFGREN

The action of the play takes place in a city in the Far West in the library of the old Dowd family mansion and the reception room of Chumley's Rest. Time is the present.

ACT ONE
SCENE 1: The library, late afternoon.
SCENE 2: Chumley's Rest, an hour later.

ACT TWO
SCENE 1: The library, an hour later.
SCENE 2: Chumley's Rest, four hours later.

ACT THREE
Chumley's Rest, a few minutes later.

$\mathcal{M}$ary Chase says that she got the idea for *Harvey* when she heard about a neighbor whose son had been killed in action shortly after Pearl Harbor. Miss Chase began to think about what play she could concoct that might cheer up not only the mother, but a whole world weary of war. She decided to write about the Pooka—that mischievous animal spirit of Irish folk tales.

After her play had gone through fifty rewrites and eighteen completely different versions, it opened on Broadway in 1944, received the Pulitzer Prize as the best American play of the season, ran for over four years and has been widely translated into other languages, including Japanese.

Harvey is called a "comic fantasy" because the humor arises out of a fanciful occurrence in an everyday environment in which only ordinary, realistic, everyday events are supposed to happen. Real or make-believe, the character Harvey has become an international celebrity and a household word the world over, for the play makes a compelling case for understanding and charity among human beings.

Harvey

ACT ONE

SCENE 1

*The time is mid-afternoon of a spring day.
The scene is the library of the old Dowd family mansion—a room
lined with books and set with heavy, old-fashioned furniture of
a faded grandeur. The most conspicuous item in the room is an
oil painting over a black marble Victorian mantelpiece. This is
the portrait of a lantern-jawed older woman. There are double
doors at right. These doors now pulled apart, lead to the hallway and across to the parlor, which is not seen. Telephone is on
small table at left. This afternoon there is a festive look to the
room—silver bowls with spring flowers set about. From the
parlor to the right comes the sound of a bad female voice singing,
"I'm Called Little Buttercup."*
AT RISE: MYRTLE MAE *is discovered coming through door from
parlor, and as telephone rings, she goes to it.*

MYRTLE. Mrs. Simmons? Mrs. Simmons is my mother, but she has guests this afternoon. Who wants her? [*Respectful change in tone after she hears who it is.*] Oh—wait just a minute. Hang on just a minute. [*Goes to doorway and calls.*] Psst—Mother! [*Cranes her neck more.*] Psst—Mother! [*Crooks her finger insistently several times. Singing continues.*]

VETA. [*Enters, humming "Buttercup."*] Yes, dear?

MYRTLE. Telephone.

VETA. [*Turning to go out again.*] Oh, no, dear. Not with all of them in there. Say I'm busy.

MYRTLE. But, Mother. It's the Society Editor of the Evening News Bee—

VETA. [*Turning.*] Oh—the Society Editor. She's very important. [*She fixes her hair and goes to phone. Her voice is very sweet. She throws out chest and assumes dignified pose.*] Good afternoon, Miss Ellerbe. This is Veta Simmons. Yes—a tea and reception for the members of the Wednesday Forum. You might say—pro-gram tea. My mother, you know—[*Waves hand toward portrait.*] the late Marcella Pinney Dowd, pioneer cultural leader. She came here by ox-team as a child and she founded the Wednesday Forum. [MYRTLE *is watching out door.*] Myrtle—how many would you say?

MYRTLE. Seventy-five, at least. Say a hundred.

VETA. [*On phone.*] Seventy-five. Miss Tewksbury is the soloist, accompanied by Wilda McCurdy, accompanist.

MYRTLE. Come on! Miss Tewksbury is almost finished with her number.

VETA. She'll do an encore.

MYRTLE. What if they don't give her a lot of applause?

VETA. I've known her for years. She'll do an encore. [MYRTLE *again starts to leave.*] You might say that I am entertain-ing, assisted by my daughter, Miss Myrtle Mae Simmons. [*To Myrtle—indicates her dress.*] What color would you call that?

MYRTLE. Rancho Rose, they told me.

VETA. [*Into phone.*] Miss Myrtle Mae Simmons looked charming in a modish Rancho Rose toned crepe, picked up at the girdle with a touch of magenta on emerald. I wish you could see her, Miss Ellerbe.

MYRTLE. [Looks through door.] Mother—please—she's almost finished and where's the cateress?

VETA. [To Myrtle.] Everything's ready. The minute she's finished singing we open the dining-room doors and we begin pouring. [Into phone.] The parlors and halls are festooned with smilax. Yes, festooned. [Makes motion in air with finger.] That's right. Yes, Miss Ellerbe, this is the first party we've had in years. There's a reason but I don't want it in the papers. We all have our troubles, Miss Ellerbe. The guest list? Oh, yes—

MYRTLE. Mother—come.

VETA. If you'll excuse me now, Miss Ellerbe. I'll call you later. [Hangs up.]

MYRTLE. Mother—Mrs. Chauvenet just came in!

VETA. [Arranging flowers on phone table.] Mrs. Eugene Chauvenet Senior! Her father was a scout with Buffalo Bill.

MYRTLE. So that's where she got that hat!

VETA. [As she and MYRTLE start to exit.] Myrtle, you must be nice to Mrs. Chauvenet. She has a grandson about your age.

MYRTLE. But what difference will it make, with Uncle Elwood?

VETA. Myrtle—remember! We agreed not to talk about that this afternoon. The point of this whole party is to get you started. We work through those older women to the younger group.

MYRTLE. We can't have anyone here in the evenings, and that's when men come to see you—in the evenings. The only reason we can even have a party this afternoon is because Uncle Elwood is playing pinochle at the Fourth Avenue Firehouse. Thank God for the firehouse!

VETA. I know—but they'll just have to invite you out and it won't hurt them one bit. Oh, Myrtle—you've got so much to offer. I don't care what anyone says, there's something sweet about every young girl. And a man takes that sweetness, and look what he does with it! [Crosses to mantel with flowers.] But you've got to meet somebody, Myrtle. That's all there is to it.

MYRTLE. If I do they say, That's Myrtle Mae Simmons! Her uncle is Elwood P.

Dowd—the biggest screwball in town. Elwood P. Dowd and his pal—

VETA. [Puts hand on her mouth.] You promised.

MYRTLE. [Crossing above table, sighs.] All right—let's get them into the dining-room.

VETA. Now when the members come in here and you make your little welcome speech on behalf of your grandmother—be sure to do this. [Gestures toward portrait on mantel.]

MYRTLE. [In fine disgust.] And then after that, I mention my Uncle Elwood and say a few words about his pal Harvey. Damn Harvey! [In front of table, as she squats.]

VETA. [The effect on her is electric. She runs over and closes doors.] Myrtle Mae—that's right! Let everybody in the Wednesday Forum hear you. You said that name. You promised you wouldn't say that name and you said it.

MYRTLE. [Rising.] I'm sorry, Mother. But how do you know Uncle Elwood won't come in and introduce Harvey to everybody? [To mantel. Places flowers on it.]

VETA. This is unkind of you, Myrtle Mae. Elwood is the biggest heartache I have. Even if people do call him peculiar he's still my brother, and he won't be home this afternoon.

MYRTLE. Are you sure?

VETA. Of course I'm sure.

MYRTLE. But Mother, why can't we live like other people?

VETA. Must I remind you again? Elwood is not living with us—we are living with him.

MYRTLE. Living with him and Harvey! Did Grandmother know about Harvey?

VETA. I've wondered and wondered about that. She never wrote me if she did.

MYRTLE. Why did she have to leave all her property to Uncle Elwood?

VETA. Well, I suppose it was because she died in his arms. People are sentimental about things like that.

MYRTLE. You always say that and it doesn't make sense. She couldn't make out her will after she died, could she?

VETA. Don't be didactic, Myrtle Mae. It's not becoming in a young girl, and men loathe it. Now don't forget to wave your hand.

MYRTLE. I'll do my best. [*Opens door.*]

VETA. Oh, dear—Miss Tewksbury's voice is certainly fading!

MYRTLE. But not fast enough. [*She exits.*]

VETA. [*Exits through door, clapping hands, pulling down girdle.*] Lovely, Miss Tewksbury—perfectly lovely. I loved it.

[*Through door at left enters* ELWOOD P. DOWD. *He is a man about 47 years old with a dignified bearing, and yet a dreamy expression in his eyes. His expression is benign, yet serious to the point of gravity. He wears an overcoat and a battered old hat. This hat, reminiscent of the Joe College era, sits on the top of his head. Over his arm he carries another hat and coat. As he enters, although he is alone, he seems to be ushering and bowing someone else in with him. He bows the invisible person over to a chair. His step is light, his movements quiet and his voice low-pitched.*]

ELWOOD. [*To invisible person.*] Excuse me a moment. I have to answer the phone. Make yourself comfortable, Harvey. [*Phone rings.*] Hello. Oh, you've got the wrong number. But how are you, anyway? This is Elwood P. Dowd speaking. I'll do? Well, thank you. And what is your name, my dear? Miss Elsie Greenawalt? [*To chair.*] Harvey, it's a Miss Elsie Greenawalt. How are you today, Miss Greenawalt? That's fine. Yes, my dear. I would be happy to join your club. I belong to several clubs now—the University Club, the Country Club and the Pinochle Club at the Fourth Avenue Firehouse. I spend a good deal of my time there, or at Charlie's Place, or over at Eddie's Bar. And what is your club, Miss Greenawalt? [*He listens—then turns to empty chair.*] Harvey, I get the Ladies Home Journal, Good Housekeeping and the Open Road for Boys for two years for six twenty-five. [*Back to phone.*] It sounds fine to me. I'll join it. [*To chair.*] How does it sound to you, Harvey? [*Back to phone.*] Harvey says it sounds fine to him also, Miss Greenawalt. He says he will join, too. Yes—two subscriptions. Mail everything to this address. . . . I hope I will have the pleasure of meeting you some time, my dear. Harvey, she says she would like to meet me. When? When would you like to meet me, Miss Greenawalt? Why

not right now? My sister seems to be having a few friends in and we would consider it an honor if you would come and join us. My sister will be delighted. 343 Temple Drive—I hope to see you in a very few minutes. Goodbye, my dear. [*Hangs up.*] She's coming right over. [*Moves to* HARVEY.] Harvey, don't you think we'd better freshen up? Yes, so do I. [*He takes up hats and coats and exits.*]

VETA. [*Enters, followed by* MAID.] I can't seem to remember where I put that guest list. I must read it to Miss Ellerbe . . . Have you seen it, Miss Johnson?

MAID. No, I haven't, Mrs. Simmons.

VETA. Look on my dresser. [MAID *exits.*]

MYRTLE. [*Enters.*] Mother—Mrs. Chauvenet—she's asking for you. [*Turning—speaking in oh-so-sweet tone to someone in hall.*] Here's Mother, Mrs. Chauvenet. Here she is. [*Enter* MRS. CHAUVENET. *She is a woman of about 65—heavy, dressed with the casual sumptuousness of a wealthy Western society woman—in silvery gold and plush, and mink scarf even though it is a spring day. She rushes over to* VETA.]

MRS. CHAUVENET. Veta Louise Simmons! I thought you were dead. [*Gets to her and takes hold of her.*]

VETA. [*Rushing to her, they kiss.*] Aunt Ethel! [*Motioning to* MYRTLE *to come forward and meet the great lady.*] Oh, no—I'm very much alive—thank you—

MRS. CHAUVENET. [*Turning to* MYRTLE.] —and this full-grown girl is your daughter—I've know you since you were a baby.

MYRTLE. I know.

MRS. CHAUVENET. What's your name, dear?

VETA. [*Proudly.*] This is Myrtle—Aunt Ethel. Myrtle Mae—for the two sisters of her father. He's dead. That's what confused you.

MRS. CHAUVENET. Where's Elwood?

VETA. [*With a nervous glance at* MYRTLE MAE.] He couldn't be here, Aunt Ethel—now let me get you some tea.

MRS. CHAUVENET. Elwood isn't here?

VETA. No—

MRS. CHAUVENET. Oh, shame on him. That was the main reason I came. [*Takes off scarf—puts it on chair.*] I want to see Elwood.

VETA. Come—there are loads of people anxious to speak to you.

MRS. CHAUVENET. Do you realize, Veta, it's been years since I've seen Elwood?

VETA. No—where does the time go?

MRS. CHAUVENET. But I don't understand it. I was saying to Mr. Chauvenet only the other night—what on earth do you suppose has happened to Elwood Dowd? He never comes to the club dances any more. I haven't seen him at a horse show in years. Does Elwood see anybody these days?

VETA. [And MYRTLE, with a glance at each other.] Oh, yes—Aunt Ethel. Elwood sees somebody.

MYRTLE. Oh, yes.

MRS. CHAUVENET. [To MYRTLE.] Your Uncle Elwood, child, is one of my favorite people. [VETA rises.] Always has been.

VETA. Yes, I remember.

MRS. CHAUVENET. Is Elwood happy, Veta?

VETA. Elwood's very happy, Aunt Ethel. You don't need to worry about Elwood— [Looks through doorway. She is anxious to get the subject on something else.] Why, there's Mrs. Frank Cummings—just came in. Don't you want to speak to her?

MRS. CHAUVENET. [Peers out.] My—but she looks ghastly! Hasn't she failed though?

VETA. If you think she looks badly— you should see him!

MRS. CHAUVENET. Is that so? I must have them over. [Looks again.] She looks frightful. I thought she was dead.

VETA. Oh, no.

MRS. CHAUVENET. Now—what about tea, Veta?

VETA. Certainly —[Starts forward to lead the way.] If you will forgive me, I will precede you —— [ELWOOD enters. MRS. CHAUVENET turns back to pick up her scarf from chair, and sees him.]

MRS. CHAUVENET. [Rushing forward.] Elwood! Elwood Dowd! Bless your heart.

ELWOOD. [Coming forward and bowing as he takes her hand.] Aunt Ethel! What a pleasure to come in and find a beautiful woman waiting for me!

MRS. CHAUVENET. [Looking at him fondly.] Elwood—you haven't changed.

VETA. [Moves forward quickly, takes hold of her.] Come along, Aunt Ethel— you mustn't miss the party.

MYRTLE. There's punch if you don't like tea.

MRS. CHAUVENET. But I do like tea. Stop pulling at me, you two. Elwood, what night next week can you come to dinner?

ELWOOD. Any night. Any night at all, Aunt Ethel—I would be delighted.

VETA. Elwood, there's some mail for you today. I took it up to your room.

ELWOOD. Did you, Veta? That was nice of you. Aunt Ethel—I want you to meet Harvey. As you can see he's a Pooka. [Turns toward air beside him.] Harvey, you've heard me speak of Mrs. Chauvenet? We always called her Aunt Ethel. She is one of my oldest and dearest friends. [Inclines head toward space and goes "Hmm!" and then listens as though not hearing first time. Nods as though having heard someone next to him speak.] Yes—yes— that's right. She's the one. This is the one. [To MRS. CHAUVENET.] He says he would have known you anywhere. [Then as a confused, bewildered look comes over MRS. CHAUVENET's face and as she looks to left and right of ELWOOD and cranes her neck to see behind him—ELWOOD not seeing her expression, crosses her towards VETA and MYRTLE MAE.] You both look lovely. [Turns to the air next to him.] Come on in with me, Harvey—We must say hello to all of our friends —— [Bows to MRS. CHAUVENET.] I beg your pardon, Aunt Ethel. If you'll excuse me for one moment —— [Puts his hand gently on her arm, trying to turn her.]

MRS. CHAUVENET. What?

ELWOOD. You are standing in his way —— [SHE gives a little—her eyes wide on him.] Come along, Harvey. [HE watches the invisible Harvey cross to door, then stops him.] Uh-uh! [ELWOOD goes over to door. He turns and pantomimes as he arranges the tie and brushes off the head of the invisible Harvey. Then he does the same thing to his own tie. They are ALL watching him, MRS. CHAUVENET in horrified fascination. The heads of VETA and MYRTLE, bowed in agony.] Go right on in, Harvey. I'll join you in a minute. [He pantomimes as though slapping him on the back, and ushers him out. Then turns and comes back to MRS. CHAUVENET.] Aunt Ethel, I can see you are disturbed about Harvey. Please don't be. He stares like that at everybody. It's his way. But he liked you. I could tell. He liked you very much. [Pats her arm reassuringly, smiles at her, then calmly and confidently goes

on out. After his exit—MRS. CHAUVENET, MYRTLE *and* VETA *are silent. Finally* VETA —*with a resigned tone*—*clears her throat.*]
VETA. [*Looking at* MRS. CHAUVENET.] Some tea—perhaps—?
MRS. CHAUVENET. Why, I—not right now —I—well—I think I'll be running along. [*Crosses back of table.*]
MYRTLE. But ——
VETA. [*Putting a hand over hers to quiet her.*] I'm so sorry ——
MRS. CHAUVENET. I'll—I'll be talking to you soon. Goodbye — goodbye —— [*She exits quickly.* VETA *stands stiffly—her anger paralyzing her.* MYRTLE *finally tiptoes over and closes one side of door—peeking over, but keeping herself out of sight.*]
MYRTLE. Oh, God —— [*Starts to run for doorway.*] Oh, my God!
VETA. Myrtle—where are you going?
MYRTLE. Up to my room. He's introducing Harvey to everybody. I can't face those people now. I wish I were dead.
VETA. Come back here. Stay with me. We'll get him out of there and upstairs to his room.
MYRTLE. I won't do it. I can't. I can't.
VETA. Myrtle Mae! [MYRTLE *stops.* VETA *goes over to her and pulls her to where they are directly in line with doorway.*] Now—pretend I'm fixing your corsage.
MYRTLE. [*Covering her face with her hands in shame.*] Oh, Mother!
VETA. We've got to. Pretend we're having a gay little chat. Keep looking. When you catch his eye, tell me. He always comes when I call him. Now, then—do you see him yet?
MYRTLE. No—not yet. How do you do, Mrs. Cummings.
VETA. Smile, can't you? Have you no pride? I'm smiling —— [*Waves and laughs.*] and he's my own brother!
MYRTLE. Oh, Mother—people get run over by trucks every day. Why can't something like that happen to Uncle Elwood?
VETA. Myrtle Mae Simmons, I'm ashamed of you. This thing is not your uncle's fault. [*Phone rings.*]
MYRTLE. Ouch! You're sticking me with that pin!
VETA. That's Miss Ellerbe. Keep looking. Keep smiling. [*She goes to phone.*]
MYRTLE. Mrs. Cummings is leaving. Uncle Elwood must have told her what Harvey is. Oh, God!

VETA. [*On phone.*] Hello—this is Mrs. Simmons. Should you come in the clothes you have on—What have you on? Who is this? But I don't know any Miss Greenawalt. Should you what?—May I ask who invited you? Mr. Dowd! Thank you just the same, but I believe there has been a mistake.—Well, I never!
MYRTLE. Never what?
VETA. One of your Uncle Elwood's friends. She asked me if she should bring a quart of gin to the Wednesday Forum!
MYRTLE. There he is—he's talking to Mrs. Halsey.
VETA. Is Harvey with him?
MYRTLE. What a thing to ask! How can I tell? How can anybody tell but Uncle Elwood?
VETA. [*Calls.*] Oh, Elwood, could I see you a moment, dear? [*To Myrtle.*] I promise you your Uncle Elwood has disgraced us for the last time in this house. I'm going to do something I've never done before.
MYRTLE. What did you mean just now when you said this was not Uncle Elwood's fault? If it's not his fault, whose fault is it?
VETA. Never you mind. I know whose fault it is. Now lift up your head and smile and go back in as though nothing had happened.
MYRTLE. You're no match for Uncle Elwood.
VETA. You'll see. [ELWOOD *is coming.*]
MYRTLE. [*As* THEY *pass at door.*] Mother's waiting for you. [*She exits.*]
VETA. Elwood! Could I see you for a moment, dear?
ELWOOD. Yes, sister. Excuse me, Harvey. [VETA *steps quickly over and pulls double doors together.*]
VETA. Elwood, would you mind sitting down in here and waiting for me until the party is over? I want to talk to you. It's very important.
ELWOOD. Of course, sister. I happen to have a little free time right now and you're welcome to all of it, Veta. Do you want Harvey to wait too?
VETA. [*Quite seriously—not in a pampering, humoring tone at all.*] Yes, Elwood. I certainly do. [*She steals out—watching him as she crosses through door. After she has gone out we see doors being pulled together from the outside and hear the click of a lock.* ELWOOD *goes calmly*

over to bookcase, peruses it carefully, and then when he has found the book he wants, takes it out and from behind it pulls a half-filled pint bottle of liquor.]

ELWOOD. [Looking at book he holds in one hand.] Ah—Jane Austen. [He gets one chair, pulls it down, facing front. Gets chair and pulls it right alongside. Sits down, sets bottle on floor between chairs.] Sit down, Harvey. Veta wants to talk to us. She said it was important. I think she wants to congratulate us on the impression we made at her party. [Reads. Turns to Harvey. Inclines head and listens, then looks at back of book and answers as though Harvey had asked what edition it is, who published it and what are those names on the fly leaf; turning head toward empty chair each time and twice saying "Hmm?"] Jane Austen—De Luxe Edition —Limited—Grosset and Dunlap—The usual acknowledgments. Chapter One ——

AND THE CURTAIN FALLS

SCENE 2

The scene is the office in the main building of Chumley's Rest—a sanitarium for mental patients. The wall at back is half plaster and half glass. There is a door up center. Through this we can see the corridor of the sanitarium itself. In the right wall is a door which is' lettered "Dr. Chumley." On right wall is a book-case, a small filing-case on top of it. Across the room is another door lettered "Dr. Sanderson." Down left is the door leading from the outside. There is a big desk at right angles with foot-lights, with chair either side of desk. At right is a table with chairs on either side.
The time is an hour after Scene 1.
At rise MISS RUTH KELLY, head nurse at Chumley's Rest, is seated left of desk, taking notes as she talks to VETA SIMMONS, who stands. MISS KELLY is a very pretty young woman of about twenty-four. She is wearing a starched white uniform and cap. As she talks to Veta she writes on a slip of paper with a pencil.

KELLY. [Writing.] Mrs. O. R. Simmons, 343 Temple Drive, is that right?

VETA. [Nodding, taking handkerchief from handbag.] We were born and raised there. It's old but we love it. It's our home. [Crosses to table, puts down handbag.]

KELLY. And you wish to enter your brother here at the sanitarium for treatment. Your brother's name?

VETA. [Coming back to desk—raising handkerchief to eyes and dabbing.] It's — oh ——

KELLY. Mrs. Simmons, what is your brother's name?

VETA. I'm sorry. Life is not easy for any of us. I'll have to hold my head up and go on just the same. That's what I keep telling Myrtle and that's what Myrtle Mae keeps telling me. She's heartbroken about her Uncle Elwood—Elwood P. Dowd. That's it. [Sits on chair beside desk.]

KELLY. [Writing.] Elwood P. Dowd. His age?

VETA. Forty-seven the 24th of last April. He's Taurus—Taurus—the bull. I'm Leo, and Myrtle is on a cusp.

KELLY. Forty-seven. Is he married?

VETA. No, Elwood has never married. He stayed with mother. He was always a great home boy. He loved his home.

KELLY. You have him with you now?

VETA. He's in a taxicab down in the driveway. [KELLY rings buzzer.] I gave the driver a dollar to watch him, but I didn't tell the man why. You can't tell these things to perfect strangers. [Enter WILSON. He is the sanitarium strongarm. He is a big burly attendant, black-browed, about 28. KELLY crosses in front of desk toward bookcase.]

KELLY. Mr. Wilson, would you step down to a taxi in the driveway and ask

a Mr. Dowd if he would be good enough
to step up to Room number 24–South
Wing G?

WILSON. [*Glaring.*] Ask him?

KELLY. [*With a warning glance toward
Veta.*] This is his sister, Mrs. Simmons.
[KELLY *crosses to cabinet for card.*]

WILSON. [*With a feeble grin.*] How do—
why, certainly—be glad to *escort* him.
[*Exits.*]

VETA. Thank you.

KELLY. [*Handing Veta printed slip.*] The
rates here, Mrs. Simmons—you'll find them
printed on this card.

VETA. [*Waving it away.*] That will all
be taken care of by my mother's estate.
The late Marcella Pinney Dowd. Judge
Gaffney is our attorney.

KELLY. Now I'll see if Dr. Sanderson
can see you. [*Starts toward office.*]

VETA. Dr. Sanderson? I want to see Dr.
Chumley himself.

KELLY. Oh, Mrs. Simmons, Dr. Sanderson is the one who sees everybody. Dr.
Chumley sees no one.

VETA. He's still head of this institution,
isn't he? He's still a psychiatrist, isn't he?

KELLY. [*Shocked at such heresy.*] Still a
psychiatrist! Dr. Chumley is more than
that. He is a psychiatrist with a national
reputation. Whenever people have mental
breakdowns they at once think of Dr.
Chumley.

VETA. [*Pointing.*] That's his office, isn't
it? Well, you march right in and tell him
I want to see him. If he knows who's in
here he'll come out here.

KELLY. I wouldn't dare disturb him,
Mrs. Simmons. I would be discharged if
I did.

VETA. Well, I don't like to be pushed
off onto any second fiddle.

KELLY. Dr. Sanderson is nobody's second fiddle. [*Crosses to back of desk, her
eyes aglow.*] He's young, of course, and
he hasn't been out of medical school very
long, but Dr. Chumley tried out twelve
and kept Dr. Sanderson. He's really wonderful — [*Catches herself.*] to the patients.

VETA. Very well. Tell him I'm here.

KELLY. [*Straightens her cap. As she
exits into door, primps.*] Right away.
[VETA *rises, takes off coat—puts it on back
of chair.*] Oh dear—oh dear. [WILSON *and*

ELWOOD *appear in corridor.* ELWOOD *pulls
over a little from* WILSON *and sees* VETA.]

ELWOOD. Veta—isn't this wonderful —!
[WILSON *takes him forcefully off up-stairs.*
VETA *is still jumpy and nervous from the
surprise, and her back to door as* — *enter*
DR. SANDERSON. LYMAN SANDERSON *is a
good-looking young man of 27 or 28. He
is wearing a starched white coat over dark
trousers. His eyes follow* MISS KELLY, *who
has walked out before him and gone out,
closing doors. Then he sees* VETA, *pulls
down his jacket and gets a professional
bearing.* VETA *has not heard him come in.
She is busy with compact.*]

SANDERSON. [*Looking at slip in his
hand.*] Mrs. Simmons?

VETA. [*Startled—she jumps.*] Oh—oh
dear—I didn't hear you come in. You
startled me. You're Dr. Sanderson?

SANDERSON. [*He nods.*] Yes. Will you
be seated, please?

VETA. [*Sits.*] Thank you. I hope you
don't think I'm jumpy like that all the
time, but I —

SANDERSON. Of course not. Miss Kelly
tells me you are concerned about your
brother. Dowd, is it? Elwood P. Dowd?

VETA. Yes, Doctor—he's—this isn't easy
for me, Doctor.

SANDERSON. [*Kindly.*] Naturally these
things aren't easy for the families of patients. I understand.

VETA. [*Twisting her handkerchief nervously.*] It's what Elwood's doing to himself, Doctor—that's the thing. Myrtle Mae
has a right to nice friends. She's young,
and her whole life is before her. That's
my daughter.

SANDERSON. Your daughter. How long
has it been since you began to notice any
peculiarity in your brother's actions?

VETA. I noticed it right away when
Mother died, and Myrtle Mae and I came
back home from Des Moines to live with
Elwood. I could see that he—that he —
[*Twists handkerchief—looks pleadingly at
Sanderson.*]

SANDERSON. That he—what? Take your
time, Mrs. Simmons. Don't strain. Let it
come. I'll wait for it.

VETA. Doctor—everything I say to you
is confidential? Isn't it?

SANDERSON. That's understood.

VETA. Because it's a slap in the face to

everything we've stood for in this community the way Elwood is acting now.

SANDERSON. I am not a gossip, Mrs. Simmons. I am a psychriatrist.

VETA. Well—for one thing—he drinks.

SANDERSON. To excess?

VETA. To excess? Well—don't you call it excess when a man never lets a day go by without stepping into one of those cheap taverns, sitting around with riffraff and people you never heard of? Inviting them to the house—playing cards with them—giving them food and money. And here I am trying to get Myrtle Mae started with a nice group of young people. If that isn't excess I'm sure I don't know what excess is.

SANDERSON. I didn't doubt your statement, Mrs. Simmons. I merely asked if your brother drinks.

VETA. Well, yes, I say definitely Elwood drinks and I want him committed out here permanently, because I cannot stand another day of that Harvey. Myrtle and I have to set a place at the table for Harvey. We have to move over on the sofa and make room for Harvey. We have to answer the telephone when Elwood calls and asks to speak to Harvey. Then at the party this afternoon with Mrs. Chauvenet there—We didn't even know anything about Harvey until we came back here. Doctor, don't you think it would have been a little bit kinder of Mother to have written and told me about Harvey? Be honest, now—don't you?

SANDERSON. I really couldn't answer that question, because I ——

VETA. I can. Yes—it certainly would have.

SANDERSON. This person you call Harvey—who is he?

VETA. He's a rabbit.

SANDERSON. Perhaps—but just who is he? Some companion—someone your brother has picked up in these bars, of whom you disapprove?

VETA. [Patiently.] Doctor—I've been telling you. Harvey is a rabbit—a big white rabbit—six feet high—or is it six feet and a half? Heavens knows I ought to know. He's been around the house long enough.

SANDERSON. [Regarding her narrowly.] Now, Mrs. Simmons, let me understand this —— you say ——

VETA. [Impatient.] Doctor—do I have to keep repeating myself? My brother insists that his closest friend is this big white rabbit. This rabbit is named Harvey. Harvey lives at our house. Don't you understand? He and Elwood go every place together. Elwood buys railroad tickets, theater tickets, for both of them. As I told Myrtle Mae—if your uncle was so lonesome he had to bring something home—why couldn't he bring something human? He has me, doesn't he? He has Myrtle Mae, doesn't he? [She leans forward.] Doctor—[She rises to him. HE inclines toward her.] I'm going to tell you something I've never told anybody in the world before. [Puts her hand on his shoulder.] Every once in a while I see that big white rabbit myself. Now isn't that terrible? I've never even told that to Myrtle Mae.

SANDERSON. [Now convinced. Starts to rise.] Mrs. Simmons—

VETA. [Straightening.] And what's more —he's every bit as big as Elwood says he is. Now don't ever tell that to anybody, Doctor. I'm ashamed of it.

SANDERSON. I can see that you have been under a great nervous strain recently.

VETA. Well— I certainly have.

SANDERSON. Grief over your mother's death depressed you considerably?

VETA. Nobody knows how much.

SANDERSON. Been losing sleep?

VETA. How could anybody sleep with that going on?

SANDERSON. Short-tempered over trifles?

VETA. You just try living with those two and see how your temper holds up.

SANDERSON. [Presses buzzer.] Loss of appetite?

VETA. No one could eat at a table with my brother and a big white rabbit. Well, I'm finished with it. I'll sell the house—be appointed conservator of Elwood's estate, and Myrtle Mae and I will be able to entertain our friends in peace. It's too much, Doctor. I just can't stand it.

SANDERSON. [He has been repeatedly pressing a buzzer on his desk. He looks with annoyance toward hall door. His answer now to VETA is gentle.] Of course, Mrs. Simmons. Of course it is. You're tired.

VETA. [She nods.] Oh, yes I am.

SANDERSON. You've been worrying a great deal.

VETA. [*Nods.*] Yes, I have. I can't help it.

SANDERSON. And now I'm going to help you.

VETA. Oh, Doctor . . .

SANDERSON. [*Goes cautiously to door—watching her.*] Just sit there quietly, Mrs. Simmons. I'll be right back. [*He exits.*]

VETA. [*Sighing with relief, rises and calls out as she takes coat.*] I'll just go down to the cab and get Elwood's things. [*She exits.* SANDERSON, KELLY *and* WILSON *come in.*]

SANDERSON. Why didn't someone answer the buzzer?

KELLY. I didn't hear you, Doctor —

SANDERSON. I rang and rang. [*Looks into his office. It is empty.*] Mrs. Simmons— [*Looks out door, shuts it, comes back.*] Sound the gong, Wilson. That poor woman must not leave the grounds.

WILSON. She's made with a getaway, huh, doc? [WILSON *presses a button on the wall and we hear a loud gong sounding.*]

SANDERSON. Her condition is serious. Go after her. [WILSON *exits.*]

KELLY. I can't believe it. [SANDERSON *picks up phone.*]

SANDERSON. Main gate. Henry, Dr. Sanderson. Allow no one out of the main gate. We're looking for a patient. [*Hangs up.*] I shouldn't have left her alone, but no one answered the buzzer.

KELLY. Wilson was in South, Doctor.

SANDERSON. [*Making out papers.*] What have we available, Miss Kelly?

KELLY. Number 13, upper West R., is ready, Doctor.

SANDERSON. Have her taken there immediately, and I will prescribe preliminary treatment. I must contact her brother. Dowd is the name. Elwood P. Dowd. Get him on the telephone for me, will you please, Miss Kelly?

KELLY. But Doctor—I didn't know it was the woman who needed the treatment. She said it was for her brother.

SANDERSON. Of course she did. It's the oldest dodge in the world—always used by a cunning type of psychopath. She apparently knew her brother was about to commit her, so she came out to discredit him. Get him on the telephone, please.

KELLY. But, Doctor—I thought the woman was all right, so I had Wilson take the brother up to No. 24 South Wing G. He's there now.

SANDERSON. [*Staring at her with horror.*] You had Wilson take the brother in? No gags, please Kelly. You're not serious, are you?

KELLY. Oh, I did, Doctor. I did. Oh, Doctor, I'm terribly sorry.

SANDERSON. Oh, well, then if you're sorry, that fixes everything. [*He starts to pick up house phone and finishes the curse under his breath.*] Oh — no! [*Buries his head in his hands.*]

KELLY. I'll do it, Doctor. I'll do it. [*She takes phone.*] Miss Dunphy—will you please unlock the door to Number 24— and give Mr. Dowd his clothes and—? [*Looks at Sanderson for direction.*]

SANDERSON. Ask him to step down to the office right away.

KELLY. [*Into phone.*] Ask him to step down to the office right away. There's been a terrible mistake and Dr. Sanderson wants to explain.

SANDERSON. Explain? Apologize!

KELLY. [*Hanging up.*] Thank heaven they hadn't put him in a hydro tub yet. She'll let him out.

SANDERSON. [*Staring at her.*] Beautiful— and dumb, too. It's almost too good to be true.

KELLY. Doctor—I feel terrible. I didn't know. Judge Gaffney called and said Mrs. Simmons and her brother would be out here, and when she came in here—you don't have to be sarcastic.

SANDERSON. Oh, don't I? Stop worrying. We'll squirm out of it some way. [*Thinking—starts toward right door.*]

KELLY. Where are you going?

SANDERSON. I've got to tell the chief about it, Kelly. He may want to handle this himself.

KELLY. He'll be furious. I know he will. He'll die. And then he'll terminate me.

SANDERSON. [*Catches her shoulders.*] The responsibility is all mine, Kelly.

KELLY. Oh, no—tell him it was all my fault, Doctor.

SANDERSON. I never mention your name. Except in my sleep.

KELLY. But this man Dowd—

SANDERSON. Don't let him get away. I'll be right back.

KELLY. But what shall I say to him? What shall I do? He'll be furious.

SANDERSON. Look, Kelly—he'll probably be fit to be tied—but he's a man, isn't he?

KELLY. I guess so—his name is Mister.

SANDERSON. Go into your old routine—you know—the eyes—the swish—the works. I'm immune—but I've seen it work with some people—some of the patients out here. Keep him here, Kelly—if you have to do a strip tease. [*He exits.*]

KELLY. [*Very angry. Speaks to closed door.*] Well, of all the—oh—you're wonderful, Dr. Sanderson! You're just about the most wonderful person I ever met in my life. [*Kicks chair.*]

WILSON. [*Has entered in time to hear last sentence.*] Yeah—but how about giving me a lift here just the same?

KELLY. What?

WILSON. That Simmons dame.

KELLY. Did you catch her?

WILSON. Slick as a whistle. She was comin' along the path hummin' a little tune. I jumped out at her from behind a tree. I says "Sister—there's a man wants to see you." Shoulda heard her yell! She's whacky, all right.

KELLY. Take her to No. 13 upper West R.

WILSON. She's there now. Brought her in through the diet kitchen. She's screamin' and kickin' like hell. I'll hold her if you'll come and undress her.

KELLY. Just a second, Wilson. Dr. Sanderson told me to stay here till her brother comes down—

WILSON. Make it snappy— [*Goes out. ELWOOD enters. KELLY rises.*]

KELLY. You're Mr. Dowd?

ELWOOD. [*Carrying other hat and coat over his arm. He bows.*] Elwood P.

KELLY. I'm Miss Kelly.

ELWOOD. Let me give you one of my cards. [*Fishes in vest pocket—pulls out card.*] If you should want to call me—call me at this number. Don't call me at that one. That's the old one.

KELLY. Thank you.

ELWOOD. Perfectly all right, and if you lose it—don't worry, my dear. I have plenty more.

KELLY. Won't you have a chair, please, Mr. Dowd?

ELWOOD. Thank you. I'll have two. Allow me. [*He brings another chair. Puts extra hat and coat on table. Motions Harvey to sit in chair. He stands waiting.*]

KELLY. Dr. Sanderson is very anxious to talk to you. He'll be here in a minute. Please be seated.

ELWOOD. [*Waving her toward chair.*] After you, my dear.

KELLY. Oh, I really can't, thank you. I'm in and out all the time. But you mustn't mind me. Please sit down.

ELWOOD. [*Bowing.*] After you.

KELLY. [*Sits. Elwood sits on chair he has just put in place.*] Could I get you a magazine to look at?

ELWOOD. I would much rather look at you, Miss Kelly, if you don't mind. You really are very lovely.

KELLY. Oh—well. Thank you. Some people don't seem to think so.

ELWOOD. Some people are blind. That is often brought to my attention. And now, Miss Kelly—I would like to have you meet— [*Enter SANDERSON. MISS KELLY rises and backs up to below desk. ELWOOD rises when she does, and he makes a motion to the invisible Harvey to rise, too.*]

SANDERSON. [*Going to him, extending hand.*] Mr. Dowd?

ELWOOD. Elwood P. Let me give you one of my cards. If you should want—

SANDERSON. Mr. Dowd—I am Dr. Lyman Sanderson, Dr. Chumley's assistant out here.

ELWOOD. Well, good for you! I'm happy to know you. How are you, Doctor?

SANDERSON. That's going to depend on you, I'm afraid. Please sit down. You've met Miss Kelly, Mr. Dowd?

ELWOOD. I have had that pleasure, and I want both of you to meet a very dear friend, of mine—

SANDERSON. Later on—be glad to. Won't you be seated, because first I want to say—

ELWOOD. After Miss Kelly—

SANDERSON. Sit down, Kelly— [*SHE sits, as does ELWOOD—who indicates to Harvey to sit also.*] Is that chair quite comfortable, Mr. Dowd?

ELWOOD. Yes, thank you. Would you care to try it? [*He takes out a cigarette.*]

SANDERSON. No, thank you. How about an ash tray there? Could we give Mr. Dowd an ash tray? [*KELLY gets it. ELWOOD and Harvey rise also. ELWOOD beams as he turns and watches her. KELLY puts ash tray by DOWD, who moves it to share with Harvey.*] Is it too warm in here for you, Mr. Dowd? Would you like me to open a window? [ELWOOD *hasn't heard. He is watching Miss Kelly.*]

KELLY. [*Turning, smiling at him.*] Mr. Dowd—Dr. Sanderson wants to know if he should open a window?

ELWOOD. That's entirely up to him. I wouldn't presume to live his life for him. [*During this dialogue* SANDERSON *is near window.* KELLY *has her eyes on his face.* ELWOOD *smiles at Harvey fondly.*]

SANDERSON. Now then, Mr. Dowd, I can see that you're not the type of person to be taken in by any high-flown phrases or beating about the bush.

ELWOOD. [*Politely.*] Is that so, Doctor?

SANDERSON. You have us at a disadvantage here. You know it. We know it. Let's lay the cards on the table.

ELWOOD. That certainly appeals to me, Doctor.

SANDERSON. Best way in the long run. People are people, no matter where you go.

ELWOOD. That is very often the case.

SANDERSON. And being human are therefore liable to mistakes. Miss Kelly and I have made a mistake here this afternoon, Mr. Dowd, and we'd like to explain it to you.

KELLY. It wasn't Doctor Sanderson's fault, Mr. Dowd. It was mine.

SANDERSON. A human failing—as I said.

ELWOOD. I find it very interesting, nevertheless. You and Miss Kelly here? [THEY *nod.*] This afternoon—you say? [THEY *nod.* ELWOOD *gives Harvey a knowing look.*]

KELLY. We do hope you'll understand, Mr. Dowd.

ELWOOD. Oh, yes. Yes. These things are often the basis of a long and warm friendship.

SANDERSON. And the responsibility is, of course, not hers—but mine.

ELWOOD. Your attitude may be old-fashioned, Doctor—but I like it.

SANDERSON. Now, if I had seen your sister first—that would have been an entirely different story.

ELWOOD. Now there you surprise me. I think the world and all of Veta—but I had supposed she had seen her day.

SANDERSON. You must not attach any blame to her. She is a very sick woman. Came in here insisting you were in need of treatment. That's perfectly ridiculous.

ELWOOD. Veta shouldn't be upset about me. I get along fine.

SANDERSON. Exactly—but your sister had already talked to Miss Kelly, and there had been a call from your family lawyer, Judge Gaffney—

ELWOOD. Oh, yes, I know him. Know his wife, too. Nice people. [*He turns to Harvey—cigarette business: he needs a match.*]

SANDERSON. Is there something I can get for you, Mr. Dowd?

ELWOOD. What did you have in mind?

SANDERSON. A light—here—let me give you a light. [*Crosses to* DOWD, *lights his cigarette.* ELWOOD *brushes smoke away from the rabbit.*] Your sister was extremely nervous and plunged right away into a heated tirade on your drinking.

ELWOOD. That was Veta.

SANDERSON. She became hysterical.

ELWOOD. I tell Veta not to worry about that. I'll take care of that.

SANDERSON. Exactly. Oh, I suppose you take a drink now and then—the same as the rest of us?

ELWOOD. Yes, I do. As a matter of fact, I would like one right now.

SANDERSON. Matter of fact, so would I, but your sister's reaction to the whole matter of drinking was entirely too intense. Does your sister drink, Mr. Dowd?

ELWOOD. Oh, no, Doctor. No. I don't believe Veta has ever taken a drink.

SANDERSON. Well, I'm going to surprise you. I think she has and does—constantly.

ELWOOD. I am certainly surprised.

SANDERSON. But it's not her alcoholism that's going to be the basis for my diagnosis of her case. It's much more serious than that. It was when she began talking so emotionally about this big white rabbit —Harvey—yes, I believe she called him Harvey—

ELWOOD. [*Nodding.*] Harvey is his name.

SANDERSON. She claimed you were persecuting her with this Harvey.

ELWOOD. I haven't been persecuting her with Harvey. Veta shouldn't feel that way. And now, Doctor, before we go any further I must insist you let me introduce— [*He starts to rise.*]

SANDERSON. Let me make my point first, Mr. Dowd. This trouble of your sister's didn't spring up overnight. Her condition stems from trauma.

ELWOOD. [*Sits down again.*] From what?

SANDERSON. From trauma.—Spelled T-R-A-U-M-A. It means shock. Nothing unusual about it. There is the birth trauma. The shock to the act of being born.

ELWOOD. [*Nodding.*] That's the one we never get over—

SANDERSON. You have a nice sense of humor, Dowd—hasn't he, Miss Kelly?

KELLY. Oh, yes, Doctor.

ELWOOD. May I say the same about both of you?

SANDERSON. To sum it all up—your sister's condition is serious, but I can help her. She must however remain out here temporarily.

ELWOOD. I've always wanted Veta to have everything she needs.

SANDERSON. Exactly.

ELWOOD. But I wouldn't want Veta to stay out here unless she liked it out here and wanted to stay here.

SANDERSON. Of course. [*To* KELLY.] Did Wilson get what he went after? [KELLY *nods.*]

KELLY. Yes, Doctor. [*She rises.*]

SANDERSON. What was Mrs. Simmons' attitude, Miss Kelly?

KELLY. Not unusual, Doctor.

SANDERSON. [*Rising.*] Mr. Dowd, if this were an ordinary delusion—something reflected on the memory picture—in other words, if she were seeing something she had seen once—that would be one thing. But this is more serious. It stands to reason nobody has ever seen a white rabbit six feet high.

ELWOOD. [*Smiles at Harvey.*] Not very often, Doctor.

SANDERSON. I like you, Dowd.

ELWOOD. I like you, too, Doctor. And Miss Kelly here. [*Looks for* MISS KELLY, *who is just crossing in front of window seat.* ELWOOD *springs to his feet.* KELLY *sits quickly.* ELWOOD *motions Harvey down and sits, himself.*] I like her, too.

SANDERSON. So she must be committed here temporarily. Under these circumstances I would commit my own grandmother. [*Goes to desk.*]

ELWOOD. Does your grandmother drink, too?

SANDERSON. It's just an expression. Now will you sign these temporary commit-ment papers as next-of-kin—just a formality?

ELWOOD. You'd better have Veta do that, Doctor. She always does all the signing and managing for the family. She's good at it.

SANDERSON. We can't disturb her now.

ELWOOD. Perhaps I'd better talk it over with Judge Gaffney?

SANDERSON. You can explain it all to him later. Tell him I advised it. And it isn't as if you couldn't drop in here any time and make inquiries. Glad to have you. I'll make out a full visitor's pass for you. When would you like to come back? Wednesday, say? Friday, say?

ELWOOD. You and Miss Kelly have been so pleasant I can come back right after dinner. About an hour.

SANDERSON. [*Taken aback.*] Well—we're pretty busy around here, but I guess that's all right.

ELWOOD. I don't really have to go now. I'm not very hungry.

SANDERSON. Delighted to have you stay—but Miss Kelly and I have to get on upstairs now. Plenty of work to do. But I tell you what you might like to do.

ELWOOD. What might I like to do?

SANDERSON. We don't usually do this—but just to make sure in your mind that your sister is in good hands—why don't you look around here? If you go through that door—[*Rises—points beyond stairway.*] and turn right just beyond the stairway you'll find the occupational therapy room down the hall, and beyond that the conservatory, the library and the diet kitchen.

ELWOOD. For Veta's sake I believe I'd better do that, Doctor.

SANDERSON. Very well, then. [*He is now anxious to terminate the interview. Rises, shakes hands.*] It's been a great pleasure to have this little talk with you, Mr. Dowd. [*Gives him pass.*]

ELWOOD. [*Walking toward him.*] I've enjoyed it too, Doctor—meeting you and Miss Kelly.

SANDERSON. And I will say that for a layman you show an unusually acute perception into psychiatric problems.

ELWOOD. Is that a fact? I never thought I knew anything about it. Nobody does, do you think?

SANDERSON. Well—the good psychiatrist is not found under every bush.

ELWOOD. You have to pick the right bush. Since we all seem to have enjoyed this so much, let us keep right on. I would like to invite you to come with me now down to Charlie's Place and have a drink. When I enjoy people I like to stay right with them.

SANDERSON. Sorry—we're on duty now. Give us a rain-check. Some other time be glad to.

ELWOOD. When?

SANDERSON. Oh—can't say right now. Miss Kelly and I don't go off duty till ten o'clock at night.

ELWOOD. Let us go to Charlie's at ten o'clock tonight.

SANDERSON. Well—

ELWOOD. And you, Miss Kelly?

KELLY. I—[Looks at Sanderson.]

SANDERSON. Dr. Chumley doesn't approve of members of the staff fraternizing, but since you've been so understanding perhaps we could manage it.

ELWOOD. I'll pick you up out here in a cab at ten o'clock tonight and the four of us will spend a happy evening. I want you both to become friends with a very dear friend of mine. You said later on—so later on it will be. Goodbye, now. [Motions goodbye to Harvey. Tips hat, exits.]

KELLY. Whew—now I can breathe again!

SANDERSON. Boy, that was a close shave all right, but he seemed to be a pretty reasonable sort of fellow. That man is proud—what he has to be proud of I don't know. I played up to that pride. You can get to almost anybody if you want to. Now I must look in on that Simmons woman.

KELLY. Dr. Sanderson—! [SANDERSON turns.] You say you can get to anybody if you want to. How can you do that?

SANDERSON. Takes study, Kelly. Years of specialized training. There's only one thing I don't like about this Dowd business.

KELLY. What's that?

SANDERSON. Having to make that date with him. Of course the man has left here as a good friend and booster of this sanitarium—so I guess I'll have to go with him tonight—but you don't have to go.

KELLY. Oh!

SANDERSON. No point in it. I'll have a drink with him, pat him on the back and leave. I've got a date tonight, anyway.

KELLY. [Freezing.] Oh, yes—by all means. I didn't intend to go, anyway. The idea bored me stiff. I wouldn't go if I never went anywhere again. I wouldn't go if my life depended on it.

SANDERSON. [Stepping back to her.] What's the matter with you, Kelly? What are you getting so emotional about?

KELLY. He may be a peculiar man with funny clothes, but he knows how to act. His manners were perfect.

SANDERSON. I saw you giving him the doll-puss stare. I didn't miss that.

KELLY. He wouldn't sit down till I sat down. He told me I was lovely and he called me dear. I'd go to have a drink with him if you weren't going.

SANDERSON. Sure you would. And look at him! All he does is hang around bars. He doesn't work. All that corny bowing and getting up out of his chair every time a woman makes a move. Why, he's as outdated as a cast-iron deer. But you'd sit with him in a bar and let him flatter you.— You're a wonderful girl, Kelly.

KELLY. Now let me tell you something— you— [Enter the great DR. WILLIAM CHUMLEY. DR. CHUMLEY is a large, handsome man of about 57. He has gray hair and wears rimless glasses which he removes now and then to tap on his hand for emphasis. He is smartly dressed. His manner is confident, pompous and lordly. He is good and he knows it.]

CHUMLEY. Dr. Sanderson! Miss Kelly! [THEY break apart and jump to attention like two buck privates before a c.o.]

KELLY AND SANDERSON. Yes, Doctor?

CHUMLEY. Tell the gardener to prune more carefully around my prize dahlias along the fence by the main road. They'll be ready for cutting next week. The difficulty of the woman who has the big white rabbit—has it been smoothed over?

SANDERSON. Yes, Doctor. I spoke to her brother and he was quite reasonable.

CHUMLEY. While I have had many patients out here who saw animals, I have never before had a patient with an animal that large. [Puts book in book-case.]

SANDERSON. Yet, Doctor. She called him Harvey.

CHUMLEY. Harvey. Unusual name for an animal of any kind. Harvey is a man's name. I have known several men in my day named Harvey, but I have never heard of any type of animal whatsoever with that name. The case has an interesting phase, Doctor. [*Finishes straightening books.*]

SANDERSON. Yes, Doctor.

CHUMLEY. I will now go upstairs with you and look in on this woman. It may be that we can use my formula 977 on her. I will give you my advice in prescribing the treatment, Doctor.

SANDERSON. Thank you, Doctor.

CHUMLEY. [*Starts to move across stage and stops, draws himself up sternly.*] And now—may I ask—what is that hat and coat doing on that table? Whose is it?

SANDERSON. I don't know. Do you know, Miss Kelly? Was it Dowd's?

KELLY. [*Above table, picking up hat and coat.*] He had his hat on, Doctor. Perhaps it belongs to a relative of one of the patients.

CHUMLEY. Hand me the hat. [KELLY *hands it. Looking inside.*] There may be some kind of identification—Here—what's this? [*Pushes two fingers up through the holes.*] Two holes cut in the crown of this hat. See!

KELLY. That's strange!

CHUMLEY. Some new fad—put them away. Hang them up—get them out of here. [KELLY *takes them into office and comes out again.* WILSON *comes in.*]

WILSON. [*Very impressed with Dr. Chumley and very fond of him.*] Hello, Dr. Chumley.

CHUMLEY. Oh, there you are.

WILSON. How is every little old thing? [DR. CHUMLEY *picks up pad of notes from desk.*]

CHUMLEY. Fair, thank you, Wilson, fair.

WILSON. Look—somebody's gonna have to give me a hand with this Simmons dame—order a restraining jacket or something. She's terrible. [*To Kelly.*] Forgot me, didn't you? Well, I got her corset off all by myself.

CHUMLEY. We're going up to see this patient right now, Wilson.

WILSON. She's in a hydro tub now—my God—I left the water running on her! [*Runs off upstairs, followed by* KELLY. BETTY CHUMLEY, *the Doctor's wife, enters. She is a good-natured, gay, bustling woman of about 55.*]

BETTY. Willie—remember your promise—. Hello, Dr. Sanderson. Willie, you

haven't forgotten Dr. McClure's cocktail party? We promised them faithfully.

CHUMLEY. That's right. I have to go upstairs now and look in on a patient. Be down shortly— [*Exits upstairs.*]

BETTY. [*Calling after him.*] Give a little quick diagnosis, Willie—we don't want to be late to the party. I'm dying to see the inside of that house. [*Enter* ELWOOD. *He doesn't see Betty at first. He looks around the room carefully.*] Good evening.

ELWOOD. [*Removing his hat and bowing.*] Good evening. [*Puts hat on desk. Walks over to her.*]

BETTY. I am Mrs. Chumley. Doctor Chumley's wife.

ELWOOD. I'm happy to know that. Dowd is my name. Elwood P. Let me give you one of my cards. [*Gives her one.*] If you should want to call me—call me at this one. Don't call me at that one, because that's—[*Points at card.*] the old one. [*Starts one step. Looking.*]

BETTY. Thank you. Is there something I can do for you?

ELWOOD. [*Turns to her.*] What did you have in mind?

BETTY. You seem to be looking for someone.

ELWOOD. [*Walking.*] Yes, I am. I'm looking for Harvey. I went off without him.

BETTY. Harvey? Is he a patient here?

ELWOOD. [*Turns.*] Oh, no. Nothing like that.

BETTY. Does he work here?

ELWOOD. [*Looking out door.*] Oh no. He is what you might call my best friend. He is also a pooka. He came out here with me and Veta this afternoon.

BETTY. Where was he when you last saw him?

ELWOOD. In that chair there—with his hat and coat on the table.

BETTY. There doesn't seem to be any hat and coat around here now. Perhaps he left?

ELWOOD. Apparently. I don't see him anywhere. [*Looks in* SANDERSON's *office.*]

BETTY. What was that word you just said—pooka?

ELWOOD. [*Looking in hallway.*] Yes—that's it.

BETTY. Is that something new? [*Looks in hallway.*]

ELWOOD. Oh, no. As I understand it. That's something very old.

BETTY. Oh, really? I had never happened to hear it before.

ELWOOD. I'm not too surprised at that. I hadn't myself, until I met him. I do hope you get an opportunity to meet him. I'm sure he would be quite taken with you.

BETTY. Oh, really? Well, that's very nice of you to say so, I'm sure.

ELWOOD. Not at all. If Harvey happens to take a liking to people he expresses himself quite definitely. If he's not particularly interested, he sits there like an empty chair or an empty space on the floor. Harvey takes his time making his mind up about people. Choosey, you see.

BETTY. That's not such a bad way to be in this day and age.

ELWOOD. Harvey is fond of my sister, Veta. That's because he is fond of me, and Veta and I come from the same family. Now you'd think that feeling would be mutual, wouldn't you? But Veta doesn't seem to care for Harvey. Dont you think that's rather too bad, Mrs. Chumley?

BETTY. Oh, I don't know, Mr. Dowd. I gave up a long time ago expecting my family to like my friends. It's useless.

ELWOOD. But we must keep on trying. [Sits.]

BETTY. Well, there's no harm in trying, I suppose.

ELWOOD. Because if Harvey has said to me once he has said a million times— "Mr. Dowd, I would do anything for you." Mrs. Chumley—

BETTY. Yes—

ELWOOD. Did you know that Mrs. McElhinney's Aunt Rose is going to drop in on her unexpectedly tonight from Cleveland?

BETTY. Why, no I didn't—

ELWOOD. Neither does she. That puts you both in the same boat, doesn't it?

BETTY. Well, I don't know anybody named—Mrs.—

ELWOOD. Mrs. McElhinney? Lives next door to us. She is a wonderful woman. Harvey told me about her Aunt Rose. That's an interesting little news item, and you are perfectly free to pass it around.

BETTY. Well, I—

ELWOOD. Would you care to come downtown with me now, my dear? I would be glad to buy you a drink.

BETTY. Thank you very much, but I am waiting for Dr. Chumley and if he came

down and found me gone he would be liable to raise—he would be irritated!

ELWOOD. We wouldn't want that, would we? Some other time, maybe? [He rises.]

BETTY. I'll tell you what I'll do, however.

ELWOOD. What will you do, however? I'm interested.

BETTY. If your friend comes in while I'm here I'd be glad to give him a message for you.

ELWOOD. [Gratefully.] Would you do that? I'd certainly appreciate that. [Goes to desk for his hat.]

BETTY. No trouble at all. I'll write it down on the back of this. [Holds up card. Takes pencil from purse.] What would you like me to tell him if he comes in while I'm still here?

ELWOOD. Ask him to meet me downtown—if he has no other plans.

BETTY. [Writing.] Meet Mr. Dowd downtown. Any particular place downtown?

ELWOOD. He knows where. Harvey knows this town like a book.

BETTY. [Writing.] Harvey—you know where. Harvey what?

ELWOOD. Just Harvey.

BETTY. I'll tell you what.

ELWOOD. What?

BETTY. Doctor and I are going right downtown—to 12th and Montview. Dr. McClure is having a cocktail party.

ELWOOD. [He writes that down on pad on desk.] A cocktail party at 12th and Montview.

BETTY. We're driving there in a few minutes. We could give your friend a lift into town.

ELWOOD. I hate to impose on you—but I would certainly appreciate that.

BETTY. No trouble at all. Dr. McClure is having this party for his sister from Wichita.

ELWOOD. I didn't know Dr. McClure had a sister in Wichita.

BETTY. Oh—you know Dr. McClure?

ELWOOD. No.

BETTY. [Puts Elwood's card down on desk.] But— [Sits.]

ELWOOD. You're quite sure you haven't time to come into town with me and have a drink?

BETTY. I really couldn't—but thank you just the same.

ELWOOD. Some other time, perhaps?

BETTY. Thank you.

ELWOOD. It's been very pleasant to meet you, and I hope to see you again.

BETTY. Yes, so do I.

ELWOOD. Goodnight, my dear. [*Tips hat—bows—goes to door, turns.*] You can't miss Harvey. He's very tall—[*Shows with hands.*] Like that—[*Exits.* CHUMLEY *enters, followed by* SANDERSON *and* KELLY. CHUMLEY *goes to desk.* KELLY *crosses to office for Chumley's hat and coat.*]

CHUMLEY. [*Working with pen on desk-pad.*] That Simmons woman is uncooperative, Doctor. She refused to admit to me that she has this big rabbit. Insists it's her brother. Give her two of these at nine—another at ten—if she continues to be so restless. Another trip to the hydro-room at eight, and one in the morning at seven. Then we'll see if she won't co-operate tomorrow, won't we, Doctor?

SANDERSON. Yes, Doctor.

CHUMLEY. You know where to call me if you need me. Ready, pet?

BETTY. Yes, Willie—and oh, Willie—

CHUMLEY. Yes—

BETTY. There was a man in here—a man named—let me see—[*Picks up card from desk.*] Oh, here is his card—Dowd—Elwood P. Dowd. [KELLY *enters. She has Dr. Chumley's hat.*]

SANDERSON. That's Mrs. Simmons' brother, Doctor. I told him he could look around and I gave him full visiting privileges.

CHUMLEY. She mustn't see anyone tonight. Not anyone at all. Tell him that.

SANDERSON. Yes, Doctor.

BETTY. He didn't ask to see her. He was looking for someone—some friend of his.

CHUMLEY. Who could that be, Dr. Sanderson?

SANDERSON. I don't know, Doctor.

BETTY. He said it was someone he came out here with this afternoon.

SANDERSON. Was there anyone with Dowd when you saw him, Miss Kelly?

KELLY. No, Doctor—not when I saw him.

BETTY. Well, he said there was. He said he last saw his friend sitting right in that chair there with his hat and coat. He seemed quite disappointed.

KELLY. [*A funny look is crossing her face.*] Dr. Sanderson—

BETTY. I told him if we located his friend we'd give him a lift into town. He could ride in the back seat. Was that all right, Willie?

CHUMLEY. Of course—of course—

BETTY. Oh here it is. I wrote it down on the back of this card. His friend's name was Harvey.

KELLY. Harvey!

BETTY. He didn't give me his last name. He mentioned something else about him—pooka—but I didn't quite get what that was.

SANDERSON *and* CHUMLEY. Harvey!

BETTY. [*Rises.*] He said his friend was very tall—. Well, why are you looking like that, Willie? This man was a very nice, polite man, and he merely asked that we give his friend a lift into town, and if we can't do a favor for someone, why are we living?

SANDERSON. [*Gasping.*] Where—where did he go, Mrs. Chumley? How long ago was he in here?

CHUMLEY. [*Thundering.*] Get me that hat! By George, we'll find out about this! [KELLY *goes out to get it.*]

BETTY. I don't know where he went. Just a second ago. [SANDERSON, *his face drawn, sits at desk and picks up house phone.* CHUMLEY, *with a terrible look on his face, has started to thumb through phone book.*]

SANDERSON. [*On house phone.*] Main gate—Henry—Dr. Sanderson—

CHUMLEY. [*Thumbing through book.*] Gaffney—Judge Gaffney —

SANDERSON. Henry—did a man in a brown suit go out through the gate a minute ago? He did? He's gone? [*Hangs up and looks stricken.* KELLY *enters with hat.*]

CHUMLEY. [*Has been dialing.*] Judge Gaffney—this is Dr. William Chumley—the psychiatrist. I'm making a routine checkup on the spelling of a name before entering it into our records. Judge—you telephoned out here this afternoon about having a client of yours committed? How is that name spelled? With a W, not a U —Mr. Elwood P. Dowd. Thank you, Judge —[*Hangs up—rises—pushes chair in to desk —takes hat from* KELLY. *Stands silently for a moment, contemplating* SANDERSON.] Dr. Sanderson—I believe your name is Sanderson?

SANDERSON. Yes, Doctor.

CHUMLEY. You know that much, do you? You went to medical school—you specialized in the study of psychiatry? You graduated—you went forth. [*Holds up hat and runs two fingers up through holes in it.*] Perhaps they neglected to tell you that a rabbit has large pointed ears! That a hat for a rabbit would have to be perforated to make room for those ears?

SANDERSON. Dowd seemed reasonable enough this afternoon, Doctor.

CHUMLEY. Doctor—the function of a psychiatrist is to tell the difference between those who are reasonable, and those who merely talk and act reasonably. [*Presses buzzer. Flings hat on desk.*] Do you realize what you have done to me? You don't answer. I'll tell you. You have permitted a psycopathic case to walk off these grounds and roam around with an overgrown white rabbit. You have subjected me—a psychiatrist—to the humiliation of having to call—of all things—a lawyer to find out who came out here to be committed—and who came out here to commit! [WILSON *enters.*]

SANDERSON. Dr. Chumley—I—

CHUMLEY. Just a minute, Wilson—I want you. [*Back to* SANDERSON.] I will now have to do something I haven't done in fifteen years. I will have to go out after this patient, Elwood P. Dowd, and I will have to bring him back, and when I do bring him back, your connection with this institution is ended—as of that moment! [*Turns to* WILSON—OTHERS *are standing frightened.*] Wilson, get the car. [*To* BETTY.] Pet, call the McClures and say we can't make it. Miss Kelly—come upstairs with me and we'll get that woman out of the tub— [*Starts upstairs on the run.*]

KELLY. [*Follows him upstairs.*] Yes—Doctor——[SANDERSON *turns on his heel, goes into his office.* WILSON *is getting into a coat in hall.*]

BETTY. I'll have to tell the cook we'll be home for dinner. She'll be furious. [*She turns.*] Wilson ——

WILSON. Yes, ma'am.

BETTY. What is a pooka?

WILSON. A what?

BETTY. A pooka.

WILSON. You can search me, Mrs. Chumley.

BETTY. I wonder if it would be in the Encyclopedia here? [*Goes to bookcase and takes out book.*] They have everything here. I wonder if it is a lodge, or what it is! [*Starts to look in it, then puts it on table open.*] Oh, I don't dare to stop to do this now. Dr. Chumley won't want to find me still here when he comes down. [*Starts to cross to door very fast.*] He'll raise—I mean—oh, dear! [*She exits.*]

WILSON. [*Picks up book, looks in it. Runs forefinger under words.*] P-o-o-k-a. "Pooka. From old Celtic mythology. A fairy spirit in animal form. Always very large. The pooka appears here and there, now and then, to this one and that one at his own caprice. A wise but mischievous creature. Very fond of rum-pots, crackpots," and how are you, Mr. Wilson. [*Looks at book startled—looks at doorway fearfully—then back to book.*] How are you, Mr. Wilson? [*Shakes book, looks at it in surprise.*] Who in the encyclopedia wants to know? [*Looks at book again, drops it on table.*] Oh—to hell with it! [*He exits quickly.*]

CURTAIN

ACT   TWO

SCENE 1

The Dowd library again, about an hour later.
AT RISE: *Doorbell is ringing and* MYRTLE *enters. She calls behind her.*

MYRTLE. That's right. The stairs at the end of the hall. It goes to the third floor. Go right up. I'll be with you in a minute.

[JUDGE OMAR GAFFNEY *enters, an elderly white-haired man. He looks displeased.*]

JUDGE. Well, where is she?

MYRTLE. Where is who? Whom do you mean, Judge Gaffney? Sit down, won't you?

JUDGE. I mean your mother. Where's Veta Louise?

MYRTLE. Why Judge Gaffney! You know where she is. She took Uncle Elwood out to the sanitarium.

JUDGE. I know that. But why was I called at the club with a lot of hysteria? Couldn't even get what she was talking about. Carrying on something fierce.

MYRTLE. Mother carrying on! What about?

JUDGE. I don't know. She was hysterical.

MYRTLE. That's strange! She took Uncle Elwood out to the sanitarium. All she had to do was put him in. [*Goes back, opens door and looks through, calling.*] Did you find it? I'll be right up. [*Waits. Turns to him.*] They found it.

JUDGE. Who? Found what? What are you talking about?

MYRTLE. When Mother left the house with Uncle Elwood I went over to the real estate office to put the house on the market. And what do you think I found there? [*She sits.*]

JUDGE. I'm not a quiz kid.

MYRTLE. Well, I found a man there who was looking for an old house just like this to cut up into buffet apartments. He's going through it now.

JUDGE. Now see here, Myrtle Mae. This house doesn't belong to you. It belongs to your Uncle Elwood.

MYRTLE. But now that Elwood is locked up, Mother controls the property, doesn't she?

JUDGE. Where is your mother? Where is Veta Louise?

MYRTLE. Judge, she went out to Chumley's Rest to tell them about Harvey and put Uncle Elwood in.

JUDGE. Why did she call me at the club when I was in the middle of a game, and scream at me to meet her here about something important?

MYRTLE. I don't know. I simply don't know. Have you got the deed to this house?

JUDGE. Certainly, it's in my safe. Myrtle, I feel pretty bad about this thing of locking Elwood up.

MYRTLE. Mother and I will be able to take a long trip now—out to Pasadena.

JUDGE. I always liked that boy. He could have done anything—been anything—made a place for himself in this community.

MYRTLE. And all he did was get a big rabbit.

JUDGE. He had everything. Brains, personality, friends. Men liked him. Women liked him. I liked him.

MYRTLE. Are you telling me that once Uncle Elwood was like other men—that women actually liked him—I mean in that way?

JUDGE. Oh, not since he started running around with this big rabbit. But they did once. Once that mail-box of your grandmother's was full of those little blue-scented envelopes for Elwood.

MYRTLE. I can't believe it.

JUDGE. Of course there was always something different about Elwood.

MYRTLE. I don't doubt that.

JUDGE. Yes—he was always so calm about any sudden change in plans. I used to admire it. I should have been suspicious. Take your average man looking up and seeing a big white rabbit. He'd do something about it. But not Elwood. He took that calmly, too. And look where it got him!

MYRTLE. You don't dream how far overboard he's gone on this rabbit.

JUDGE. Oh, yes I do. He's had that rabbit in my office many's the time. I'm old but I don't miss much. [*Noise from upstairs.*] What's that noise?

MYRTLE. The prospective buyer on the third floor. [*Looks up.* VETA *is standing in doorway, looking like something the cat dragged in. Shakes her head sadly; looks into the room and sighs; her hat is crooked.* MYRTLE *jumps up.*] Mother! Look, Judge—

JUDGE. [*Rising.*] Veta Louise—what's wrong, girl?

VETA. [*Shaking her head.*] I never thought I'd see either of you again. [MYRTLE *and* JUDGE *take* VETA *to chair.*]

MYRTLE. Take hold of her, Judge. She looks like she's going to faint. [JUDGE *gets hold of her on one side and* MYRTLE *on the other. They start to bring her into the room.*] Now, Mother—you're all right. You're going to be perfectly all right.

JUDGE. Steady—steady, girl, steady.

VETA. Please—not so fast.

JUDGE Don't rush her, Myrtle—Ease her in.

VETA. Let me sit down. Only get me some place where I can sit down.

JUDGE. [*Guiding her to a big chair.*] Here you are, girl. Easy, Myrtle—easy. [VETA *is about to lower herself into chair. She sighs. But before she can complete the lowering,* MYRTLE MAE *lets out a yelp and* VETA *straightens up quickly.*]

MYRTLE. Oh—[*She picks up envelope off chair. Holds it up.*] The gas bill.

VETA. [*Hand at head.*] Oh—oh, my—[*Sits.*]

JUDGE. Get her some tea. Myrtle. Do you want some tea, Veta?

MYRTLE. I'll get you some tea, Mother. Get her coat off, Judge.

JUDGE. Let Myrtle get your coat off, Veta. Get her coat off, Myrtle.

VETA. Leave me alone. Let me sit here. Let me get my breath.

MYRTLE. Let her get her breath, Judge.

VETA. Let me sit here a minute and then let me get upstairs to my own bed where I can let go.

MYRTLE. What happened to you, Mother?

VETA. Omar, I want you to sue them. They put me in and let Elwood out.

JUDGE. What's this?

MYRTLE. Mother!

VETA. [*Taking off hat.*] Just look at my hair.

MYRTLE. But why? What did you say? What did you do? [*Kneels at* VETA's *feet.*] You must have done something.

VETA. I didn't do one thing. I simply told them about Elwood and Harvey.

JUDGE. Then how could it happen to you? I don't understand it.

VETA. I told them about Elwood, and then I went down to the cab to get his things. As I was walking along the path —this awful man stepped out. He was a white slaver. I know he was. He had on one of those white suits. That's how they advertise.

MYRTLE. A man—what did he do, Mother?

VETA. What did he do? He took hold of me and took me in there and then he —— [*Bows her head.* MYRTLE *and* JUDGE *exchange a look.*]

JUDGE. [*Softly.*] Go on, Veta Louise. Go on, girl.

MYRTLE. [*Goes over, takes her hand.*] Poor Mother —— Was he a young man?

JUDGE. Myrtle Mae—perhaps you'd better leave the room.

MYRTLE. Now? I should say not! Go on, Mother.

JUDGE. [*Edging closer.*] What did he do, Veta?

VETA. He took me upstairs and tore my clothes off.

MYRTLE. [*Shrieking.*] Oh—did you hear that, Judge! Go on, Mother. [*She is all ears.*]

JUDGE. By God—I'll sue them for this!

VETA. And then he sat me down in a tub of water.

MYRTLE. [*Disappointed.*] Oh! For heaven's sake! [*Rises.*]

VETA. I always thought that what you were showed on your face. Don't you believe it, Judge! Don't you believe it, Myrtle. This man took hold of me like I was a woman of the streets—but I fought. I always said if a man jumped at me—I'd fight. Haven't I always said that, Myrtle?

MYRTLE. She's always said that, Judge. That's what Mother always told me to do.

VETA. And then he hustled me into that sanitarium and set me down in that tub of water and began treating me like I was a ——

MYRTLE. A what ——?

VETA. A crazy woman—but he did that just for spite.

JUDGE. Well, I'll be damned!

VETA. And those doctors came upstairs and asked me a lot of questions—all about sex-urges—and all that filthy stuff. That place ought to be cleaned up, Omar. You better get the authorities to clean it up. Myrtle, don't you ever go out there. You hear me?

JUDGE. This stinks to high heaven, Veta. By God, it stinks!

VETA. You've got to do something about it, Judge. You've got to sue them.

JUDGE. I will, girl. By God, I will! If Chumley thinks he can run an unsavory place like this on the outskirts of town he'll be publicly chastised. By God, I'll run him out of the State!

VETA. Tell me, Judge. Is that all those doctors do at places like that—think about sex?

JUDGE. I don't know.

VETA. Because if it is they ought to be

ashamed—of themselves. It's all in their head anyway. Why don't they get out and go for long walks in the fresh air? [*To* MYRTLE.] Judge Gaffney walked everywhere for years—didn't you, Judge?

JUDGE. Now let me take some notes on this. You said—these doctors came up to talk to you—Dr. Chumley and—What was the other doctor's name?

VETA. Sanderson —— [*Sits up straight—glances covertly at them and becomes very alert.*] But, Judge, don't you pay any attention to anything he tells you. He's a liar. Close-set eyes. They're always liars. Besides—I told him something in strictest confidence and he blabbed it.

MYRTLE. What did you tell him, Mother?

VETA. Oh, what difference does it make? Let's forget it. I don't even want to talk about it. You can't trust anybody.

JUDGE. Anything you told this Dr. Sanderson you can tell us, Veta Louise. This is your daughter and I am your lawyer.

VETA. I know which is which. I don't want to talk about it. I want to sue them and I want to get in my own bed. [JUDGE *rises.*]

MYRTLE. But, Mother—this is the important thing, anyway. Where is Uncle Elwood?

VETA. [*To herself.*] I should have known better than to try to do anything about him. Something protects him—that awful Pooka ——

MYRTLE. Where is Uncle Elwood? Answer me.

VETA. [*Trying to be casual.*] How should I know? They let him go. They're not interested in men at places like that. Don't act so naive, Myrtle Mae. [*Noise from upstairs.*] What's that noise?

MYRTLE. I've found a buyer for the house.

VETA. What?

MYRTLE. Listen, Mother, we've got to find Uncle Elwood—no matter who jumped at you we've still got to lock up Uncle Elwood.

VETA. I don't know where he is. The next time *you* take him, Judge. Wait until Elwood hears what they did to me. He won't stand for it. Don't forget to sue them, Judge —— Myrtle Mae, all I hope is that never, never as long as you live

a man pulls the clothes off you and dumps you down into a tub of water. [*She exits.*]

MYRTLE. [*Turning to* JUDGE.] Now, see —Mother muffed everything. No matter what happened out there—Uncle Elwood's still wandering around with Harvey.

JUDGE. [*Pondering.*] The thing for me to do is to take some more notes.

MYRTLE. It's all Uncle Elwood's fault. He found out what she was up to—and he had her put in. Then he ran.

JUDGE. Oh, no—don't talk like that. Your uncle thinks the world and all of your mother. Ever since he was a little boy he always wanted to share everything he had with her.

MYRTLE. I'm not giving up. We'll get detectives. We'll find him. And, besides—you'd better save some of that sympathy. for me and Mother—you don't realize what we have to put up with. Wait till I show you something he brought home about six months ago, and we hid it out in the garage. You just wait ——

JUDGE. I'm going up to talk to Veta. There's more in this than she's telling. I sense that.

MYRTLE. [*As she exits.*] Wait till I show you, Judge.

JUDGE. All right. I'll wait. [WILSON *enters.*]

WILSON. Okay—is he here?

JUDGE. What? What's this?

WILSON. That crackpot with the rabbit. Is he here?

JUDGE. No—and who, may I ask, are you?

WILSON. [*Stepping into hallway, calling.*] Not here, Doctor—okay—[*To* JUDGE.] Doctor Chumley's comin' in, anyway. What's your name?

JUDGE. Chumley—well, well, well—I've got something to say to him! [*Sits.*]

WILSON. What's your name? Let's have it.

JUDGE. I am Judge Gaffney—where is Chumley?

WILSON. The reason I asked your name is the Doctor always likes to know who he's talkin' to. [*Enter* CHUMLEY.] This guy says his name is Judge Gaffney, Doctor.

JUDGE. Well, well, Chumley ——

CHUMLEY. Good evening, Judge. Let's not waste time. Has he been here?

JUDGE. Who? Elwood—no—but see here, Doctor ——

WILSON. Sure he ain't been here? He's wise now. He's hidin'. It'll be an awful job to smoke him out.

CHUMLEY. It will be more difficult, but I'll do it. They're sly. They're cunning. But I get them. I always get them. Have you got the list of the places we've been, Wilson?

WILSON. [*Pulling paper out of his pocket.*] Right here, Doctor.

CHUMLEY. [*Sits.*] Read it.

WILSON. We've been to seventeen bars, Eddie's Place, Charlie's Place, Bessie's Barn-dance, the Fourth Avenue Firehouse, the Tenth and Twelfth and Ninth Avenue firehouses, just to make sure. The Union Station, the grain elevator—say, why does this guy go down to a grain elevator?

JUDGE. The foreman is a friend of his. He has many friends—many places.

CHUMLEY. I have stopped by here to ask Mrs. Simmons if she has any other suggestions as to where we might look for him.

JUDGE. Doctor Chumley, I have to inform you that Mrs. Simmons has retained me to file suit against you ——

DR. CHUMLEY. What?

JUDGE. —for what happened to her at the sanitarium this afternoon . . .

CHUMLEY. A suit!

JUDGE. And while we're on that subject ——

WILSON. That's pretty, ain't it, Doctor? After us draggin' your tail all over town trying to find that guy.

CHUMLEY. What happened this afternoon was an unfortunate mistake. I've discharged my assistant who made it. And I am prepared to take charge of this man's case personally. It interests me. And my interest in a case is something no amount of money can buy. You can ask any of them.

JUDGE. But this business this afternoon, Doctor ——

CHUMLEY. Water under the dam. This is how I see this thing. I see it this way —— [MYRTLE *has come into the room. She is carrying a big flat parcel, wrapped in brown paper. Stands it up against wall and listens.*] The important item now is to get this man and take him out to the sanitarium where he belongs.

MYRTLE. [*Coming forward.*] That's right, Judge—that's just what I think ——

JUDGE. Let me introduce Miss Myrtle Mae Simmons, Mr. Dowd's niece, Mrs. Simmons's daughter. [CHUMLEY *rises.*]

MYRTLE. How do you do, Dr. Chumley.

CHUMLEY. [*Giving her the careful scrutiny he gives all women.*] How do you do, Miss Simmons.

WILSON. Hello, Myrtle ——

MYRTLE. [*Now seeing him and looking at him with a mixture of horror and intense curiosity.*] What? Oh ——

CHUMLEY. Now, then—let me talk to Mrs. Simmons.

MYRTLE. Mother won't come down, Doctor. I know she won't. [*To* JUDGE.] You try to get Mother to talk to him, Judge. [*Puts package down.*]

JUDGE. But, see here; your mother was manhandled. She was—God knows what she was—the man's approach to her was not professional, it was personal. [*Looks at Wilson.*]

CHUMLEY. Wilson—this is a serious charge.

WILSON. Dr. Chumley, I've been with you for ten years. Are you gonna believe—what's your name again?

JUDGE. Gaffney. Judge Omar Gaffney.

WILSON. Thanks. You take the word of this old blister Gaffney ——

CHUMLEY. Wilson!

WILSON. Me! Me and a dame who sees a rabbit!

JUDGE. It's not Mrs. Simmons who sees a rabbit. It's her brother.

MYRTLE. Yes, it's Uncle Elwood.

JUDGE. If you'll come with me, Doctor ——

CHUMLEY. Very well, Judge. Wilson, I have a situation here. Wait for me. [HE *and* JUDGE *exit.*]

WILSON. O K, Doctor. [MYRTLE MAE *is fascinated by* WILSON. *She lingers and looks at him.* HE *comes over to her, grinning.*]

WILSON. So your name's Myrtle Mae?

MYRTLE. What? Oh—yes —— [*She backs up. He follows.*]

WILSON. If we grab your uncle you're liable to be comin' out to the sanitarium on visting days?

MYRTLE. Oh, I don't really know— I ——

WILSON. Well, if you do, I'll be there.

MYRTLE. You will? Oh ——

WILSON. And if you don't see me right

away—don't give up. Stick around. I'll
show up.

MYRTLE. You will—? Oh ——

WILSON. Sure. [*He is still following her.*]
You heard Dr. Chumley tell me to wait?

MYRTLE. Yeah ——

WILSON. Tell you what—while I'm waiting I sure could use a sandwich and a
cup of coffee.

MYRTLE. Certainly. If you'll forgive me
I'll precede you into the kitchen. [*She
tries to go. He traps her.*]

WILSON. Yessir—you're all right, Myrtle.

MYRTLE. What?

WILSON. Doctor Chumley noticed it right
away. He don't miss a trick. [*Crowds
closer; raises finger and pokes her arm for
emphasis.*] Tell you somethin' else, Myrtle ——

MYRTLE. What?

WILSON. You not only got a nice build—
but, kid, you got something else, too.

MYRTLE. What?

WILSON. You got the screwiest uncle that
ever stuck his puss inside our nuthouse.
*MYRTLE starts to exit in a huff, and WIL-
SON raises hand to give her a spank, but
he turns and so he puts up raised hand
to his hair. They exit. The stage is empty
for a half second and then ELWOOD comes
in, goes to phone, dials a number.*]

ELWOOD. Hello, Chumley's Rest? Is Doctor Chumley there? Oh—it's Mrs. Chumley!
This is Elwood P. Dowd speaking. How
are you tonight? Tell me, Mrs. Chumley,
were you able to locate Harvey?—Don't
worry about it. I'll find him. I'm sorry I
missed you at the McClure cocktail party.
The people were all charming and I was
able to leave quite a few of my cards. I
waited until you phoned and said you
couldn't come because a patient had escaped. Where am I? I'm here. But I'm
leaving right away. I must find Harvey.
Well, goodbye, Mrs. Chumley. My re-
gards to you and anybody else you happen to run into. Goodbye. [*Hangs up, then
he sees the big flat parcel against wall.
He gets an "Ah, there it is!" expression on
his face, goes over and takes off paper.
We see revealed a very strange thing. It is
a oil painting of ELWOOD seated on a
chair while behind him stands a large
white rabbit, in a blue polka-dot collar
and red necktie. ELWOOD holds it away
from him and surveys it proudly. Then*

looks *around for a place to put it. Takes it
over and sets it on mantel. It obscures
the picture of Marcella Pinney Dowd completely. He gathers up wrapping paper,
admires the rabbit again, tips his hat to
it and exits. Phone rings and VETA enters,
followed by DR. CHUMLEY.*]

VETA. Doctor, you might as well go
home and wait. I'm suing you for fifty
thousand dollars and that's final. [*Crosses
to phone—her back is to mantel, she hasn't
looked up.*]

CHUMLEY. [*Follows her.*] Mrs. Simmons ——

VETA. [*Into phone.*] Yes —— Well, all
right.

CHUMLEY. This picture over your mantel.

VETA. That portrait happens to be the
pride of this house.

CHUMLEY. [*Looking at her.*] Who
painted it?

VETA. Oh, some man. I forget his name.
He was around here for the sittings, and
then we paid him and he went away.
Hello—yes—No. This is Dexter 1567.
[*Hangs up.*]

CHUMLEY. I suppose if you have the
money to pay people, you can persuade
them to do anything.

VETA. Well, Dr. Chumley —— [*Walks
over and faces him.*] When you helped
me out of that tub at your place, what did
I say to you?

CHUMLEY. You expressed yourself. I
don't remember the words.

VETA. I said, "Dr. Chumley, this is a
belated civility." Isn't that what I said?

CHUMLEY. You said something of the
sort ——

VETA. You brought this up; you may as
well learn something quick. I took a course
in art last winter. The difference between
a fine oil painting and a mechanical thing
like a photograph is simply this: a photograph shows only the reality; a painting
shows not only the reality but the dream
behind it ——. It's our dreams that keep
us going. That separate us from the beasts.
I wouldn't even want to live if I thought
it was all just eating and sleeping and
taking off my clothes. Well—putting them
on again —— [*Turns—sees picture—screams
—totters—falls back.*] Oh—Doctor—oh—hold
me—oh ——

CHUMLEY. [*Taking hold of her.*] Steady

now—steady—don't get excited. Everything's all right. [*Seats her in chair.*] Now —what's the matter?

VETA. [*Pointing.*] Doctor—that is *not* my mother!

CHUMLEY. I'm glad to hear that.

VETA. Oh, Doctor. Elwood's been here. He's been here.

CHUMLEY. Better be quiet. [*Phone rings.*] I'll take it. [*He answers it.*] Hello. Yes, yes—who's calling? [*Drops his hand over mouthpiece quickly.*] Here he is. Mrs. Simmons, it's your brother!

VETA. [*Getting up. Weak no longer.*] Oh—let me talk to him!

CHUMLEY. Don't tell him I'm here. Be casual.

VETA. Hello, Elwood—[*Laughs.*] Where are you? What? Oh—just a minute. [*Covers phone.*] He won't say where he is. He wants to know if Harvey is here.

CHUMLEY. Tell him Harvey *is* here.

VETA. But he isn't.

CHUMLEY. Tell him. That will bring him here, perhaps. Humor him. We have to humor them.

VETA. Yes—Elwood. Yes, dear. Harvey is here. Why don't you come home? Oh, oh, oh—well—all right. [*Looks around uncomfortably. Covers phone again.*] It won't work. He says for me to call Harvey to the telephone.

CHUMLEY. Say Harvey is here, but can't come to the telephone. Say—he—say—he's in the bath-tub.

VETA. Bath-tub?

CHUMLEY. Say he's in the bath-tub, and you'll send him over there. That way we'll find out where he is.

VETA. Oh, Doctor!

CHUMLEY. Now, you've got to do it, Mrs. Simmons.

VETA. Hello, Elwood, Yes, dear. Harvey is here but he can't come to the telephone, he's in the bath-tub. I'll send him over as soon as he's dry. Where are you? Where, Elwood? [*Bangs phone.*]

CHUMLEY. Did he hang up?

VETA. Harvey just walked in the door! He told me to look in the bath-tub—it must be a stranger. But I know where he is. He's at Charlie's Place. That's a bar at 12th and Main.

CHUMLEY. [*Picking up his hat from table.*] 12th and Main. That's two blocks down and one over, isn't it?

VETA. Doctor—where are you going?

CHUMLEY. I'm going over there to get your brother and take him out to the sanitarium, where he belongs.

VETA. Oh, Dr. Chumley—don't do that. Send one of your attendants. I'm warning you.

CHUMLEY. But, Mrs. Simmons, if I am to help your brother ——

VETA. He can't be helped. [*Looks at picture.*] There is no help for him. He must be picked up and locked up and left.

CHUMLEY. You consider your brother a dangerous man?

VETA. Dangerous!

CHUMLEY. Why?

VETA. I won't tell you why, but if I didn't, why would I be asking for a permanent commitment for him?

CHUMLEY. Then I must observe this man. I must watch the expression on his face as he talks to this rabbit. He does talk to the rabbit, you say?

VETA. They tell each other everything.

CHUMLEY. What's that?

VETA. I said, of course he talks to him. But don't go after him, Doctor. You'll regret it if you do.

CHUMLEY. Nonsense. You underestimate me, Mrs. Simmons.

VETA. Oh, no, Doctor. You underestimate my brother.

CHUMLEY. Not at all. Don't worry now I can handle him! [*He exits.*]

VETA. [*After he has gone.*] You can handle him? That's what you think! [*Calls.*] Myrtle Mae! See who's in the bath-tub OH!

CURTAIN

SCENE 2

The main office at CHUMLEY'S REST *again, four hours later.*
AT RISE. KELLY *is on the phone.* WILSON *is helping* SANDERSON *carry boxes of books out of his office and onto table.*

KELLY. Thank you. I may call later. [*Hangs up.*]

WILSON. How about the stuff in your room, Doctor—upstairs?

SANDERSON. All packed—thanks—Wilson.

WILSON. Tough your gettin' bounced. I had you pegged for the one who'd make the grade.

SANDERSON. Those are the breaks.

WILSON. When you takin' off?

SANDERSON. As soon as Dr. Chumley gets back.

WILSON. [*To* KELLY.] Did you get a report back yet from the desk sergeant in the police accident bureau?

KELLY. Not yet. I just talked to the downtown dispensary. They haven't seen him.

WILSON. It's beginning to smell awful funny to me. Four hours he's been gone and not a word from him. [*Goes to* SANDERSON—*extends hand.*] I may not see you again, Doctor, so I want to say I wish you a lot of luck and I'm mighty sorry you got a kick in the atpray.

SANDERSON. Thanks, Wilson—good luck to you, too—

WILSON. [*Starts to exit, but stops at door, turns toward* KELLY.] Look, Kelly, let me know when you hear from the desk sergeant again. If there's no sign of the doctor, I'm goin' into town and look for him. He should know better'n to go after a psycho without me.

SANDERSON. I'd like to help look for the doctor, too, Wilson.

WILSON. That's swell of you, Doctor, right after he give you the brush.

SANDERSON. I've no resentment against Dr. Chumley. He was right. I was wrong. [*He rises.*] Chumley is the biggest man in his field. It's my loss not to be able to work with him.

WILSON. You're not so small yourself, Doctor —

SANDERSON. Thanks, Wilson.

WILSON. Don't mention it. [*Exits.*]

KELLY. [*Taking deep breath.*] Dr. Sanderson —

SANDERSON. [*Without looking up.*] Yes —

KELLY. [*Plunging in.*] Well, Doctor — [*Takes another deep breath.*] I'd like to say that *I* wish you a lot of luck, too, and I'm sorry to see you leave.

SANDERSON. [*Going on with his work.*] Are you sure you can spare these good wishes, Miss Kelly?

KELLY. [*She flushes.*] On second thought —I guess I can't. Forget it. [*Starts for below desk.*]

SANDERSON. [*Now looking up.*] Miss Kelly — This is for nothing—just a little advice. I'd be a little careful if I were you about the kind of company I kept.

KELLY. I beg your pardon, Doctor?

SANDERSON. You don't have to. I told you it was free. I saw you Saturday night —dancing with that drip in the Rose Room down at the Frontier Hotel.

KELLY. [*Putting books on desk.*] Oh, did you? I didn't notice you.

SANDERSON. I'd be a little careful of him, Kelly. He looked to me like a schizophrenic all the way across the floor.

KELLY. You really shouldn't have given him a thought, Doctor. He was my date— not yours. [*Hands book to* SANDERSON.]

SANDERSON. That was his mentality. The rest of him—well —

KELLY. But she was beautiful, though—

SANDERSON. Who?

KELLY. That girl you were with—

SANDERSON. I thought you didn't notice?

KELLY. You bumped into us twice. How could I help it?

SANDERSON. Not that it makes any difference to you, but that girl is a charming little lady. *She* has a sweet kind disposition and *she* knows how to conduct herself.

KELLY. Funny she couldn't rate a better date on a Saturday night!

SANDERSON. And she has an excellent mind.°

KELLY. Why doesn't she use it?

SANDERSON. Oh, I don't suppose you're to be censured for the flippant hard shell you have. You're probably compensating for something.

KELLY. I am not, and don't you use any of your psychiatry on me.

SANDERSON. Oh—if I could try something else on you—just once! Just to see if you'd melt under any circumstances. I doubt it.

KELLY. You'll never know, Doctor.

SANDERSON. Because you interest me as a case history—that's all. I'd like to know where you get that inflated ego—

KELLY. [*Now close to tears.*] If you

aren't the meanest person—inflated ego—case history! [*Turns and starts out.*]

SANDERSON. Don't run away. Let's finish it. [*Phone rings.*]

KELLY. Oh, leave me alone. [*Goes to answer it.*]

SANDERSON. Gladly. [*Exits.*]

KELLY. [*In angry, loud voice.*] Chumley's Rest. Yes—Sergeant. No accident report on him either in town or the suburbs. Look, Sergeant—maybe we better—[*Looks up as door opens and ELWOOD enters. He is carrying a bouquet of dahlias.*] Oh, never mind, Sergeant. They're here now. [*Hangs up. Goes toward ELWOOD.*] Mr. Dowd—!

ELWOOD. [*Handing her flowers.*] Good evening, my dear. These are for you.

KELLY. For me—oh, thank you!

ELWOOD. They're quite fresh, too. I just picked them outside.

KELLY. I hope Dr. Chumley didn't see you. They're his prize dahlias. Did he go upstairs?

ELWOOD. Not knowing, I cannot state. Those colors are lovely against your hair.

KELLY. I've never worn burnt orange. It's such a trying color.

ELWOOD. You would improve any color, my dear.

KELLY. Thank you. Did Dr. Chumley go over to his house?

ELWOOD. I don't know. Where is Dr. Sanderson?

KELLY. In his office there—I think.

ELWOOD. [*Going over to door and knocking.*] Thank you.

SANDERSON. [*Enters.*] Dowd! There you are!

ELWOOD. I have a cab outside, if it's possible for you and Miss Kelly to get away now.

SANDERSON. Where is Dr. Chumley?

ELWOOD. Is he coming with us? That's nice.

KELLY. [*Answering question on SANDERSON's face.*] I don't know, Doctor.

ELWOOD. I must apologize for being a few seconds late. I thought Miss Kelly should have some flowers. After what happened out here this afternoon the flowers really should be from you, Doctor. As you grow older and pretty women pass you by, you will think with deep gratitude of these generous girls of your youth. Shall we go now? [KELLY *exits.*]

SANDERSON. [*Pressing buzzer.*] Just a moment, Dowd —— The situation has changed since we met this afternoon. But I urge you to have no resentments. Dr. Chumley is your friend. He only wants to help you.

ELWOOD. That's very nice of him. I would like to help him, too.

SANDERSON. If you'll begin by taking a cooperative attitude—that's half the battle. We all have to face reality, Dowd—sooner or later.

ELWOOD. Doctor, I wrestled with reality for forty years, and I am happy to state that I finally won out over it. [KELLY *enters.*] Won't you and Miss Kelly join me—down at Charlie's? [*Enter WILSON.*]

WILSON. Here you are! [*Goes over to ELWOOD.*] Upstairs, buddy—we're going upstairs. Is the doctor O.K.? [*He asks SANDERSON this.*]

ELWOOD. There must be some mistake. Miss Kelly and Dr. Sanderson and I are going downtown for a drink. I'd be glad to have you come with us, Mr. ——

WILSON. Wilson.

ELWOOD. —Wilson. They have a wonderful floor show.

WILSON. Yeah? Well—wait'll you see the floor show we've got —— Upstairs, buddy!

SANDERSON. Just a minute, Wilson. Where did you say Dr. Chumley went, Dowd?

ELWOOD. As I said, he did not confide his plans in me.

WILSON. You mean the doctor ain't showed up yet?

KELLY. Not yet.

WILSON. Where is he?

SANDERSON. That's what we're trying to find out.

KELLY. Mr. Dowd walked in here by himself.

WILSON. Oh, he did, eh? Listen, you—talk fast or I'm workin' you over!

ELWOOD. I'd rather you didn't do that, and I'd rather you didn't even mention such a thing in the presence of a lovely young lady like Miss Kelly—

SANDERSON. Mr. Dowd, Dr. Chumley went into town to pick you up. That was four hours ago.

ELWOOD. Where has the evening gone to?

WILSON. Listen to that! Smart, eh?

SANDERSON. Just a minute, Wilson. Did you see Dr. Chumley tonight, Dowd?

ELWOOD. Yes, I did. He came into Charlie's Place at dinnertime. It is a cozy spot. Let's all go there and talk it over with a tall one.

WILSON. We're going no place—Now I'm askin' you a question, and if you don't button up your lip and give me some straight answers I'm gonna beat it out of you!

ELWOOD. What you suggest is impossible.

WILSON. What's that?

ELWOOD. You suggest that I button up my lip and give you some straight answers. It can't be done.

SANDERSON. Let me handle this, Wilson.

WILSON. Well, handle it, then. But find out where the Doctor is.

SANDERSON. Dr. Chumley *did* come into Charlie's Place, you say?

ELWOOD. He did, and I was very glad to see him.

WILSON. Go on ——

ELWOOD. He had asked for me, and naturally the proprietor brought him over and left him. We exchanged the conventional greetings. I said, "How do you do, Dr. Chumley," and he said, "How do you do, Mr. Dowd." I believe we said that at least once.

WILSON. Okay—okay—

ELWOOD. I am trying to be factual. I then introduced him to Harvey.

WILSON. To who?

KELLY. A white rabbit. Six feet tall.

WILSON. Six feet!

ELWOOD. Six feet one and a half!

WILSON. Okay—fool around with him, and the Doctor is probably some place bleedin' to death in a ditch.

ELWOOD. If those were his plans for the evening he did not tell me.

SANDERSON. Go on, Dowd.

ELWOOD. Dr. Chumley sat down in the booth with us. I was sitting on the outside like this. [*Shows.*] Harvey was on the inside near the wall, and Dr. Chumley was seated directly across from Harvey where he could look at him.

WILSON. That's right. Spend all night on the seatin' arrangements!

ELWOOD. Harvey then suggested that I buy him a drink. Knowing that he does not like to drink alone, I suggested to Dr. Chumley that we join him.

WILSON. And so?

ELWOOD. We joined him.

WILSON. Go on—go on.

ELWOOD. We joined him again.

WILSON. Then what?

ELWOOD. We kept right on joining him.

WILSON. Oh, skip all the joining!

ELWOOD. You are asking me to skip a large portion of the evening—

WILSON. Tell us what happened—come on—please ——

ELWOOD. Dr. Chumley and Harvey got into a conversation—quietly at first. Later it became rather heated and Dr. Chumley raised his voice.

WILSON. Yeah—why?

ELWOOD. Harvey seemed to feel that Dr. Chumley should assume part of the financial responsibility of the joining, but Dr. Chumley didn't seem to want to do that.

KELLY. [*It breaks out from her.*] I can believe *that* part of it!

WILSON. Let him talk. See how far he'll go. This guy's got guts.

ELWOOD. I agreed to take the whole thing because I did not want any trouble. We go down to Charlie's quite often—Harvey and I—and the proprietor is a fine man with an interesting approach to life. Then the other matter came up.

WILSON. Cut the damned double-talk and get on with it!

ELWOOD. Mr. Wilson, you are a sincere type of person, but I must ask you not to use that language in the presence of Miss Kelly. [*He makes a short bow to her.*]

SANDERSON. You're right, Dowd, and we're sorry. You say—the other matter came up?

ELWOOD. There was a beautiful blonde woman—a Mrs. Smethills—and her escort seated in the booth across from us. Dr. Chumley went over to sit next to her, explaining to her that they had once met. In Chicago. Her escort escorted Dr. Chumley back to me and Harvey and tried to point out that it would be better for Dr. Chumley to mind his own affairs. Does he have any?

WILSON. Does he have any what?

ELWOOD. Does he have any affairs?

WILSON. How would I know?

KELLY. Please hurry, Mr. Dowd—we're all so worried.

ELWOOD. Dr. Chumley then urged Harvey to go with him over to Blondie's Chicken Inn. Harvey wanted to go to Eddie's instead. While they were arguing about it I went to the bar to order another drink, and when I came back they were gone.

WILSON. Where did they go? I mean where did the Doctor go?

ELWOOD. I don't know—I had a date out here with Dr. Sanderson and Miss Kelly, and I came out to pick them up—hoping that later on we might run into Harvey and the Doctor and make a party of it.

WILSON. So—you satisfied? You got his story—[Goes over to ELWOOD, fists clenched.] O.K. You're lyin' and we know it!

ELWOOD. I never lie, Mr. Wilson.

WILSON. You've done somethin' with the Doctor and I'm findin' out what it is ——

SANDERSON. [Moving after him.] Don't touch him, Wilson ——

KELLY. Maybe he isn't lying, Wilson—

WILSON. [Turning on them. Furiously.] That's all this guy is, is a bunch of lies! You two don't believe this story he tells about the Doctor sittin' there talkin' to a big white rabbit, do you?

KELLY. Maybe Dr. Chumley did go to Charlie's Place.

WILSON. And saw a big rabbit, I suppose.

ELWOOD. And why not? Harvey was there. At first the Doctor seemed a little frightened of Harvey but that gave way to admiration as the evening wore on—. The evening wore on! That's a nice expression. With your permission I'll say it again. The evening wore on.

WILSON. [Lunging at him.] With your permission I'm gonna knock your teeth down your throat

ELWOOD. [Not moving an inch.] Mr. Wilson—haven't you some old friends you can go play with? [SANDERSON has grabbed WILSON and is struggling with him.]

WILSON. [He is being held. Glares fiercely at ELWOOD. KELLY dials phone.] The nerve of this guy! He couldn't come out here with an ordinary case of D.T.'s. No. He has to come out with a six-foot rabbit.

ELWOOD. Stimulating as all this is, I really must be getting downtown.

KELLY. [On phone.] Charlie's Place? Is Dr. Chumley anywhere around there? He was there with Mr. Dowd earlier in the evening. What? Well, don't bite my head off! [Hangs up.] My, that man was mad. He said Mr. Dowd was welcome any time, but his friend was not.

ELWOOD. That's Mr. McNulty the bartender. He thinks a lot of me. Now let's all go down and have a drink.

WILSON. Wait a minute ——

KELLY. Mr. Dowd —— [Goes over to him.]

ELWOOD. Yes, my dear—may I hold your hand?

KELLY. Yes—if you want to. [ELWOOD does.] Poor Mrs. Chumley is so worried. Something must have happened to the Doctor. Won't you please try and remember something—something else that might help her? Please ——

ELWOOD. For you I would do anything. I would almost be willing to live my life over again. Almost. But I've told it all.

KELLY. You're sure?

ELWOOD. Quite sure—but ask me again, anyway, won't you? I liked that warm tone you had in your voice just then.

SANDERSON. [Without realizing he is saying it.] So did I. [Looks at KELLY.]

WILSON. Oh, nuts!

ELWOOD. What?

WILSON. Nuts!

ELWOOD. Oh! I must be going. I have things to do.

KELLY. Mr. Dowd, what is it you do?

ELWOOD. [Sits, as KELLY sits at desk.] Harvey and I sit in the bars and we have a drink or two and play the jukebox. Soon the faces of the other people turn toward mine and smile. They are saying: "We don't know your name, Mister, but you're a lovely fellow." Harvey and I warm ourselves in all these golden moments. We have entered as strangers—soon we have friends. They come over. They sit with us. They drink with us. They talk to us. They tell about the big terrible things they have done. The big wonderful things they will do. Their hopes, their regrets, their loves, their hates. All very large because nobody ever brings anything small into a bar. Then I introduce them to Harvey. And he is bigger and grander than anything they offer me. When they leave, they leave impressed. The same people seldom come back—but that's envy, my dear. There's a little bit of envy in the best of us—too bad, isn't it?

SANDERSON. [*Leaning forward.*] How did you happen to call him Harvey?

ELWOOD. Harvey is his name.

SANDERSON. How do you know that?

ELWOOD. That was rather an interesting coincidence, Doctor. One night several years ago I was walking early in the evening along Fairfax Street—between 18th and 19th. You know that block?

SANDERSON. Yes, yes.

ELWOOD. I had just helped Ed Hickey into a taxi. Ed had been mixing his rye with his gin, and I felt he needed conveying. I started to walk down the street when I heard a voice saying: "Good evening, Mr. Dowd." I turned and there was this great white rabbit leaning against a lamp post. Well, I thought nothing of that, because when you have lived in a town as long as I have lived in this one, you get used to the fact that everybody knows your name. Naturally, I went over to chat with him. He said to me: "Ed Hickey is a little spiffed this evening, or could I be mistaken?" Well, of course he was not mistaken. I think the world and all of Ed but he was spiffed. Well, anyway, we stood there and talked, and finally I said—"You have the advantage of me. You know my name and I don't know yours." Right back at me he said: "What name do you like?" Well, I didn't even have to think a minute: Harvey has always been my favorite name. So I said, "Harvey," and this is the interesting part of the whole thing. He said—"What a coincidence! My name happens to be Harvey."

SANDERSON. What was your father's name, Dowd?

ELWOOD. John. John Frederick.

SANDERSON. Dowd, when you were a child you had a playmate, didn't you? Some one you were very fond of—with whom you spent many happy, carefree hours?

ELWOOD. Oh, yes, Doctor. Didn't you?

SANDERSON. What was his name?

ELWOOD. Verne. Verne McElhinney. Did you ever know the McElhinneys, Doctor?

SANDERSON. No.

ELWOOD. Too bad. There were a lot of them, and they circulated. Wonderful people.

SANDERSON. Think carefully, Dowd. Wasn't there someone, somewhere, some time, whom you knew—by the name of Harvey? Didn't you ever know anybody by that name?

ELWOOD. No, Doctor. No one. Maybe that's why I always had such hopes for it.

SANDERSON. Come on, Wilson, we'll take Mr. Dowd upstairs now.

WILSON. I'm taking him nowhere. You've made this your show—now run it. Lettin' him sit here—forgettin' all about Dr. Chumley! O.K. It's your show—you run it.

SANDERSON. Come on, Dowd— [*Pause. Putting out his hand.*] Come on, Elwood—

ELWOOD. [*Rises.*] Very well, Lyman. [SANDERSON *and* KELLY *take him to door.*] But I'm afraid I won't be able to visit with you for long. I have promised Harvey I will take him to the floor-show. [THEY *exit—*WILSON *is alone. Sits at desk, looks at his watch.*]

WILSON. Oh, boy! [*Puts head in arms on desk.* DR. CHUMLEY *enters.* WILSON *does not see him until he gets almost to the center of the room.*]

WILSON. [*Jumping up, going to him.*] Dr. Chumley—Are you all right?

CHUMLEY. All right? Of course I'm all right. I'm being followed. Lock that door.

WILSON. [*Goes to door, locks it.*] Who's following you?

CHUMLEY. None of your business. [*Exits into office, locks door behind him.* WILSON *stands a moment perplexed, then shrugs shoulders, turns off lights and exits. The stage is dimly lit. Then from door left comes the rattle of the doorknob. Door opens and shuts, and we hear locks opening and closing and see light from hall on stage. The invisible Harvey has come in. There is a count of eight while he crosses the stage, then door of* CHUMLEY'S *office opens and closes, with sound of locks clicking. Harvey has gone in—and then —*]

CURTAIN

ACT THREE

The sanitarium office at Chumley's Rest, a few minutes later. AT RISE: *Lights are still dim as at preceding curtain. There is a loud knocking and the sound of* CHUMLEY'S *voice calling, "Wilson! Wilson!"*

WILSON. [*Enters, opens outside door.* CHUMLEY *enters, white-faced.*] How didja get out here, Doctor? I just saw you go in there.

CHUMLEY. I went out through my window. Wilson—don't leave me!

WILSON. No, Doctor.

CHUMLEY. Get that man Dowd out of here.

WILSON. Yes, Doctor. [*Starts to exit.*]

CHUMLEY. No—don't leave me!

WILSON. [*Turning back—confused.*] But you said—

CHUMLEY. Dumphy—on the telephone.

WILSON. Yes, Doctor. [*Crosses to phone.*] Dumphy—give that guy Dowd his clothes and get him down here right away. [*A knock on the door.*]

CHUMLEY. Don't leave me!

WILSON. Just a minute, Doctor. [*Turns on lights. Opens door.*] Judge Gaffney.

JUDGE. I want to see Dr. Chumley. [*Enter* JUDGE *and* MYRTLE MAE.]

WILSON. Hiya, Myrtle.

MYRTLE. Hello.

JUDGE. Chumley, we've got to talk to you. This thing is serious.

MYRTLE. It certainly is.

GAFFNEY. More serious than you suspect. Where can we go to talk? [*Moves toward Chumley's office.*]

CHUMLEY. [*Blocking door.*] Not in there.

WILSON. The Doctor doesn't want you in his office.

CHUMLEY. No, sir.

JUDGE. Then sit down, Dr. Chumley. Sit down, Myrtle Mae.

CHUMLEY. [*Dazed.*] Sit down, Dr. Chumley. Sit down, Myrtle Mae. Don't go, Wilson. Don't leave me.

JUDGE. Now, Chumley, here are my notes—the facts. Can anybody hear me?

WILSON. Yeah, we can all hear you. Is that good?

JUDGE. [*Gives Wilson a look of reproof.*] Now, Chumley, has it ever occurred to you that possibly there might *be* something like this rabbit Harvey?

MYRTLE. Of course there isn't. And anybody who thinks so is crazy. [CHUMLEY *stares at her.*] Well, don't look at me like that. There's nothing funny about me. I'm like my father's family—they're all dead.

JUDGE. Now, then, my client, the plaintiff, Mrs. Veta Louise Simmons, under oath, swears that on the morning of November 2nd while standing in the kitchen of her home, hearing her name called, she turned and saw this great white rabbit, Harvey. He was staring at her. Resenting the intrusion, the plaintiff made certain remarks and drove the creature from the room. He went.

CHUMLEY. What did she say to him?

JUDGE. She was emphatic. The remarks are not important.

CHUMLEY. I want to know how she got this creature out of her sanitarium—I mean—her home.

MYRTLE. I hate to have you tell him, Judge. It isn't a bit like Mother.

WILSON. Quit stalling. Let's have it.

GAFFNEY. She looked him right in the eye and exclaimed in the heat of anger— "To hell with you!"

CHUMLEY. [*Looking at door.*] "To hell with you!" He left?

JUDGE. Yes, he left. But that's beside the point. The point is—is it perjury or is it something we can cope with? I ask for your opinion. [KELLY *enters from stairs;* SANDERSON *comes from diet kitchen.*]

SANDERSON. Ruthie! I've been looking all over for you.

CHUMLEY. Dr. Sanderson, disregard what I said this afternoon. I want you on my staff. You are a very astute young man.

KELLY. Oh, Lyman! Did you hear?

SANDERSON. Oh, baby!

KELLY. See you later. [*Exits, blowing him a kiss.* SANDERSON *exits into his office.*]

MYRTLE. You've just got to keep Uncle Elwood out here, Doctor.

CHUMLEY. No. I want this sanitarium the way it was before that man came out here this afternoon.

MYRTLE. I know what you mean.

CHUMLEY. You do?

MYRTLE. Well, it certainly gets on anyone's nerves the way Uncle Elwood knows what's going to happen before it happens. This morning, for instance, he told us that Harvey told him Mrs. McElhinney's Aunt Rose would drop in on her unexpectedly tonight from Cleveland.

CHUMLEY. And did she?

MYRTLE. Did she what?

CHUMLEY. Aunt Rose—did she come just as Harvey said she would?

MYRTLE. Oh, yes. Those things always turn out the way Uncle Elwood says they will—but what of it? What do we care about the McElhinneys?

CHUMLEY. You say this sort of thing happens often?

MYRTLE. Yes, and isn't it silly? Uncle Elwood says Harvey tells him everything. Harvey knows everything. How could he when there is no such thing as Harvey?

CHUMLEY. [Goes over, tries lock at door.] Fly-specks. I've been spending my life among fly-specks while miracles have been leaning on lamp posts on 18th and Fairfax.

VETA. [Enters. Looks around cautiously. Sighs with relief.] Good. Nobody here but people.

MYRTLE. Oh, Mother! You promised you wouldn't come out here.

VETA. Well, good evening. Now, Myrtle Mae, I brought Elwood's bathrobe. Well, why are you all just sitting here? I thought you'd be committing him.

JUDGE. Sit down there, girl. [Motioning to chair near Wilson.]

VETA. I will not sit down there.

WILSON. How about you and me stepping out Saturday night, Myrtle Mae?

VETA. Certainly not. Myrtle Mae, come here.

MYRTLE. I'm sorry.

VETA. Is everything settled?

CHUMLEY. It will be.

SANDERSON. [Enters from his office.] Doctor, may I give an opinion?

CHUMLEY. Yes, do. By all means.

VETA. [Sniffing.] His opinion! Omar— he's the doctor I told you about. The eyes!

SANDERSON. It's my opinion that Elwood P. Dowd is suffering from a third-degree hallucination and the—[Pointing at Veta's back.] other party concerned is the victim of auto-suggestion. I recommend shock formula number 977 for him and bedrest at home for—[Points again.]

CHUMLEY. You do?

SANDERSON. That's my diagnosis, Doctor. [To Veta.] Mr. Dowd will not see this rabbit any more after this injection. We've used it in hundreds of psychopathic cases.

VETA. Don't you call my brother a psychopathic case! There's never been anything like that in our family.

MYRTLE. If you didn't think Uncle Elwood was psychopathic, why did you bring him out here?

VETA. Where else could I take him, I couldn't take him to jail, could I? Besides, this is not your uncle's fault. Why did Harvey have to speak to him in the first place? With the town full of people, why did he have to bother Elwood?

JUDGE. Stop putting your oar in. Keep your oar out. If this shock formula brings people back to reality, give it to him. That's where we want Elwood.

CHUMLEY. I'm not sure that it would work in a case of this kind, Doctor.

SANDERSON. It always has.

VETA. Harvey always follows Elwood home.

CHUMLEY. He does?

VETA. Yes. But if you give him the formula and Elwood doesn't see Harvey, he won't let him in. Then when he comes to the door, I'll deal with him.

MYRTLE. Mother, won't you stop talking about Harvey as if there was such a thing?

VETA. Myrtle Mae, you've got a lot to learn and I hope you never learn it. [She starts up toward WILSON. ELWOOD is heard off stage humming.]

JUDGE. Sh! Here he is.

ELWOOD. [Enters.] Good evening, everybody.

VETA. Good evening, Elwood. I've brought you your bathrobe.

ELWOOD. Thank you, Veta.

JUDGE. Well, Chumley, what do we do? We've got to do something.

VETA. Oh, yes, we must.

MYRTLE. I should say so.

CHUMLEY. [Looking at door.] Yes, it's imperative.

ELWOOD. Well, while you're making up your minds, why don't we all go down to Charlie's and have a drink?

VETA. You're not going anywhere, Elwood. You're staying here.

MYRTLE. Yes, Uncle Elwood.

JUDGE. Stay here, son.

ELWOOD. I plan to leave. You want me to stay. An element of conflict in any discussion is a good thing. It means everybody is taking part and nobody is left out. I like that. Oh—how did you get along with Harvey, Doctor?

CHUMLEY. Sh-h!

JUDGE. We're waiting for your answer, Doctor.

CHUMLEY. What?

JUDGE. What is your decision?

CHUMLEY. I must be alone with this man. Will you all step into the other room? [MYRTLE exits.] I'll have my diagnosis in a moment.

VETA. Do hurry, Doctor.

CHUMLEY. I will.

VETA. You stay here, Elwood. [She and JUDGE GAFFNEY exit.]

CHUMLEY. Here, Mr. Dowd. Let me give you this chair. [Indicates chair.] Let me give you a cigar. [Does so.] Is there anything else I can get you?

ELWOOD. [Seated in chair.] What did you have in mind?

CHUMLEY. Mr. Dowd—[Lowers voice, looks toward office.] What kind of a man are you? Where do you come from?

ELWOOD. [Getting out card.] Didn't I give you one of my cards?

CHUMLEY. And where on the face of this tired old earth did you find a thing like him?

ELWOOD. Harvey the Pooka?

CHUMLEY. [Sits.] Is it true that he has a function—that he —— ?

ELWOOD. Gets advance notice? I'm happy to say it is. Harvey is versatile. Harvey can stop clocks.

CHUMLEY. What?

ELWOOD. You've heard that expression, "His face would stop a clock"?

CHUMLEY. Yes. But why? To what purpose?

ELWOOD. Harvey says that he can look at your clock and stop it and you can go away as long as you like with whomever you like and go as far as you like. And when you come back not one minute will have ticked by.

CHUMLEY. You mean that he actually —— ? [Looks toward office.]

ELWOOD. Einstein has overcome time and space. Harvey has overcome not only time and space—but any objections.

CHUMLEY. And does he do this for you?

ELWOOD. He is willing to at any time, but so far I've never been able to think of any place I'd rather be. I always have a wonderful time just where I am, whomever I'm with. I'm having a fine time right now with you, Doctor. [Holds up cigar.] Corona-Corona.

CHUMLEY. I know where I'd go.

ELWOOD. Where?

CHUMLEY. I'd go to Akron.

ELWOOD. Akron?

CHUMLEY. There's a cottage camp outside Akron in a grove of maple trees, cool, green, beautiful.

ELWOOD. My favorite tree.

CHUMLEY. I would go there with a pretty young woman, a strange woman, a quiet woman.

ELWOOD. Under a tree?

CHUMLEY. I wouldn't even want to know her name. I would be—just Mr. Brown.

ELWOOD. Why wouldn't you want to know her name? You might be acquainted with the same people.

CHUMLEY. I would send out for cold beer. I would talk to her. I would tell her things I have never told anyone—things that are locked in here. [Beats his breast. ELWOOD looks over at his chest with interest.] And then I would send out for more cold beer.

ELWOOD. No whiskey?

CHUMLEY. Beer is better.

ELWOOD. Maybe under a tree. But she might like a highball.

CHUMLEY. I wouldn't let her talk to me, but as I talked I would want her to reach out a soft white hand and stroke my head and say, "Poor thing! Oh, you poor, poor thing!"

ELWOOD. How long would you like that to go on?

CHUMLEY. Two weeks.

ELWOOD. Wouldn't that get monotonous? Just Akron, beer, and "poor, poor thing" for two weeks?

CHUMLEY. No. No, it would not. It would be wonderful.

ELWOOD. I can't help but feel you're making a mistake in not allowing that woman to talk. If she gets around at all, she may have picked up some very interesting little news items. And I'm sure you're making a mistake with all that beer and no whiskey. But it's your two weeks.

CHUMLEY. [*Dreamily.*] Cold beer at Akron and one last fling! God, man!

ELWOOD. Do you think you'd like to lie down for awhile?

CHUMLEY. No. No. Tell me Mr. Dowd, could he—would he do this for me?

ELWOOD. He could and he might. I have never heard Harvey say a word against Akron. By the way, Doctor, where is Harvey?

CHUMLEY. [*Rising. Very cautiously.*] Why, don't you know?

ELWOOD. The last time I saw him he was with you.

CHUMLEY. Ah!

ELWOOD. Oh! He's probably waiting for me down at Charlie's.

CHUMLEY. [*With a look of cunning toward his office.*] That's it! He's down at Charlie's.

ELWOOD. Excuse me, Doctor. [*Rises.*]

CHUMLEY. No, no Mr. Dowd. Not in there.

ELWOOD. I couldn't leave without saying good night to my friend, Dr. Sanderson.

CHUMLEY. Mr. Dowd, Dr. Sanderson is not your friend. None of those people are your friends. *I* am your friend.

ELWOOD. Thank you, Doctor. And I'm yours.

CHUMLEY. And this sister of yours—she is at the bottom of this conspiracy against you. She's trying to persuade me to lock you up. Today she had commitment papers drawn up. She's got your power of attorney and the key to your safety box. She brought you out here ——

ELWOOD. My sister did all that in one afternoon? Veta is certainly a whirlwind.

CHUMLEY. God, man, haven't you any righteous indignation?

ELWOOD. Dr. Chumley, my mother used to say to me, "In this world, Elwood"— she always called me Elwood—she'd say, "In this world, Elwood, you must be oh, so smart or oh, so pleasant." For years I was smart. I recommend pleasant. You may quote me.

CHUMLEY. Just the same, I will protect you if I have to commit her. Would you like me to do that?

ELWOOD. No, Doctor, not unless Veta wanted it that way. Oh, not that you don't

have a nice place out here, but I think Veta would be happier at home with me and Harvey and Myrtle Mae. [KELLY *enters with flower in hair, goes to put magazines on table.* ELWOOD *turns to her.*] Miss Kelly! "Diviner grace has never brightened this enchanting face!" [*To Chumley.*] Ovid's Fifth Elegy. [*To Miss Kelly.*] My dear, you will never look lovelier!

KELLY. I'll never feel happier, Mr. Dowd. I know it. [*Kisses him.*]

CHUMLEY. Well!

KELLY. Yes, Doctor. [WILSON *enters hall in time to see the kiss.*]

ELWOOD. I wonder if I would be able to remember any more of that poem?

WILSON. Say, maybe this rabbit gag is a good one. Kelly never kissed me.

ELWOOD. [*Looking at* WILSON.] Ovid has always been my favorite poet.

WILSON. O.K., pal—You're discharged. This way out—[*Takes him by arm down stage.*]

CHUMLEY. Wilson! Take your hands off that man!

WILSON. What?

CHUMLEY. Apologize to Mr. Dowd.

WILSON. Apologize to him—this guy with the rabbit?

CHUMLEY. [*Looking toward his office.*] Apologize! Apologize ——

WILSON. I apologize. This is the door.

ELWOOD. If I leave, I'll remember. [WILSON *exits.*]

CHUMLEY. Wait a minute, Dowd. Do women often come up to you and kiss you like Miss Kelly did just now?

ELWOOD. Every once in a while.

CHUMLEY. Yes?

ELWOOD. I encourage it, too.

CHUMLEY. [*To himself.*] To hell with decency! I've got to have that rabbit! Go ahead and knock. [ELWOOD *starts for Sanderson's door just as* SANDERSON *comes out.*]

ELWOOD. Dr. Sanderson, I couldn't leave without ——

SANDERSON. Just a minute, Dowd—[*To Chumley.*] Doctor, do you agree with my diagnosis?

CHUMLEY. Yes, yes! Call them all in.

SANDERSON. Thank you, Doctor. Mrs. Simmons—Judge Gaffney—will you step in here for a minute, please?

VETA. [*Enters.*] Is it settled? [MYRTLE *and* JUDGE *enter.*]

CHUMLEY. I find I concur with Dr. Sanderson.

SANDERSON. Thank you, Doctor.

MYRTLE. Oh, that's wonderful! What a relief!

JUDGE. Good boy!

ELWOOD. Well, let's celebrate—[*Takes little book out of his pocket.*] I've got some new bars listed in the back of this book.

CHUMLEY. [*Speaking to others in low tone.*] This injection carries a violent reaction. We can't give it to him without his consent. Will he give it?

VETA. Of course he will, if I ask him.

CHUMLEY. To give up this rabbit—I doubt it.

MYRTLE. Don't ask him. Just give it to him.

ELWOOD. "Bessie's Barn Dance. Blondie's Chicken Inn. Better Late Than Never— Bennie's Drive In" ——

VETA. Elwood!

ELWOOD. We'll go to Bennie's Drive In—. We should telephone for a table. How many of us will there be, Veta?

VETA. [*Starting to count, then catching herself.*] Oh—Elwood!

CHUMLEY. Mr. Dowd, I have a formula —977—that will be good for you. Will you take it?

JUDGE. Elwood, you won't see this rabbit any more.

SANDERSON. But you will see your responsibilities, your duties ——

ELWOOD. I'm sure if you thought of it, Doctor, it must be a very fine thing. And if I happen to run into anyone who needs it, I'll be glad to recommend it. For myself, I wouldn't care for it.

VETA. Hear that, Judge! Hear that, Doctor! That's what we have to put up with.

ELWOOD. [*Turning to look at her.*] Veta, do you want me to take this?

VETA. Elwood, I'm only thinking of you. You're my brother and I've known you for years. I'd do anything for you. That Harvey wouldn't do anything for you. He's making a fool out of you, Elwood. Don't be a fool.

ELWOOD. Oh, I won't.

VETA. Why, you could amount to something. You could be sitting on the Western Slope Water Board right now if you'd only go over and ask them.

ELWOOD. All right, Veta. If that's what you want, Harvey and I will go over and ask them tomorrow.

VETA. Tomorrow! I never want to see another tomorrow. Not if Myrtle Mae and I have to live in the house with that rabbit. Our friends never come to see us—we have no social life; we have no life at all. We're both miserable. I wish I were dead —but maybe you don't care!

ELWOOD. [*Slowly.*] I've always felt that Veta should have everything she wants. Veta, are you sure? [VETA *nods.*] I'll take it. Where do I go, Doctor?

CHUMLEY. In Dr. Sanderson's office, Dowd.

ELWOOD. Say goodbye to the old fellow for me, won't you? [*Exits.* CHUMLEY *exits.*]

JUDGE. How long will this take, Doctor?

SANDERSON. Only a few minutes. Why don't you wait? [*Exits.*]

JUDGE. We'll wait. [*Sits.*]

VETA. [*Sighs.*] Dr. Sanderson said it wouldn't take long.

MYRTLE. Now, Mother, don't fidget.

VETA. Oh, how can I help it?

MYRTLE. [*Picks up edge of draperies.*] How stunning! Mother, could you see me in a housecoat of this material?

VETA. [*To Myrtle—first looking at draperies. Sighs again.*] Yes, dear, but let me get a good night's sleep first. [*Loud knocking at door.*]

JUDGE. Come in. [*Enter* CAB DRIVER.]

JUDGE. What do you want?

CAB DRIVER. I'm lookin' for a little, short —— [*Seeing Veta.*] Oh, there you are! Lady, you jumped outta the cab without payin' me.

VETA. Oh, yes. I forgot. How much is it?

CAB DRIVER. All the way out here from town? $2.75.

VETA. [*Looking in purse.*] $2.75! I could have sworn I brought my coin purse—where is it? [*Gets up, goes to table, turns pocketbook upside down, in full view of audience. Nothing comes out of it but a compact and a handkerchief.*] Myrtle, do you have any money?

MYRTLE. I spent that money Uncle Elwood gave me for my new hair-do for the party.

VETA. Judge, do you have $2.75 I could give this man?

JUDGE. Sorry. Nothing but a check.

CAB DRIVER. We don't take checks.

JUDGE. I know.

VETA. Dr. Chumley, do you happen to have $2.75 I could borrow to pay this cab driver?

CHUMLEY. [*He has just entered, now wearing white starched jacket.*] Haven't got my wallet. No time to get it now. Have to get on with this injection. Sorry. [*Exits.*]

VETA. Well, I'll get it from my brother, but I can't get it right now. He's in there to get an injection. It won't be long. You'll have to wait.

CAB DRIVER. You're gonna get my money from your brother and he's in there to get some of that stuff they shoot out here?

VETA. Yes, it won't be but a few minutes.

CAB DRIVER. Lady, I want my money now.

VETA. But I told you it would only be a few minutes. I want you to drive us back to town, anyway.

CAB DRIVER. And I told you I want my money now or I'm nosin' the cab back to town, and you can wait for the bus—at six in the morning.

VETA. Well, of all the pig-headed, stubborn things—!

MYRTLE. I should say so.

JUDGE. What's the matter with you?

CAB DRIVER. Nothin' that $2.75 won't fix. You heard me. Take it or leave it.

VETA. [*Getting up.*] I never heard of anything so unreasonable in my life. [*Knocks.*] Dr. Chumley, will you let Elwood step out here a minute. This cab driver won't wait.

CHUMLEY. [*Off.*] Don't be too long. [*Enter* ELWOOD. CHUMLEY *follows.*]

VETA. Elwood, I came off without my coin purse. Will you give this man $2.75? But don't give him any more. He's been very rude.

ELWOOD. [*Extending his hand.*] How do you do? Dowd is my name. Elwood P.

CAB DRIVER. Lofgren's mine. E. J.

ELWOOD. I'm glad to meet you, Mr. Lofgren. This is my sister, Mrs. Simmons. My charming little niece, Myrtle Mae Simmons. Judge Gaffney and Dr. Chumley. [ALL *bow coldly.*]

CAB DRIVER. Hi—

ELWOOD. Have you lived around here long, Mr. Lofgren?

CAB DRIVER. Yeah, I've lived around here all my life.

ELWOOD. Do you enjoy your work?

CAB DRIVER. It's O.K. I been with the Apex Cabs fifteen years and my brother Joe's been drivin' for Brown Cabs pretty near twelve.

ELWOOD. You drive for Apex and your brother Joe for Brown's? That's interesting, isn't it, Veta? [VETA *reacts with a sniff.*] Mr. Lofgren—let me give you one of my cards. [*Gives him one.*]

CHUMLEY. Better get on with this, Mr. Dowd.

ELWOOD. Certainly. One minute. My sister and my charming little niece live here with me at this address. Won't you and your brother come and have dinner with us some time?

CAB DRIVER. Sure—be glad to.

ELWOOD. When—when would you be glad to?

CAB DRIVER. I couldn't come any night but Tuesday. I'm on duty all the rest of the week.

ELWOOD. You must come on Tuesday, then. We'll expect you and be delighted to see you, won't we, Veta?

VETA. Oh, Elwood, I'm sure this man has friends of his own.

ELWOOD. Veta, one can't have too many friends.

VETA. Elwood, don't keep Dr. Chumley waiting—that's rude.

ELWOOD. Of course. [*Gives him bill.*] Here you are—keep the change. I'm glad to have met you and I'll expect you Tuesday with your brother. Will you excuse me now?

CAB DRIVER. Sure. [ELWOOD *exits.* CHUMLEY *follows.*] A sweet guy.

VETA. Certainly. You could just as well have waited.

CAB DRIVER. Oh, no. Listen, lady. I've been drivin' this route fifteen years. I've brought 'em out here to get that stuff and drove 'em back after they had it. It changes 'em.

VETA. Well, I certainly hope so.

CAB DRIVER. And you ain't kiddin'. On the way out here they sit back and enjoy the ride. They talk to me. Sometimes we stop and watch the sunsets and look at the birds flyin'. Sometimes we stop and watch the birds when there ain't no birds and look at the sunsets when it's rainin'. We have a swell time and I always get a big tip. But afterward—oh—oh —— [*Starts to exit again.*]

VETA. Afterwards—oh—oh! What do you mean afterwards—oh—oh?

CAB DRIVER. They crab, crab, crab. They yell at me to watch the lights, watch the brakes, watch the intersections. They scream at me to hurry. They got no faith— in me or my buggy—yet it's the same cab —the same driver—and we're goin' back over the very same road. It's no fun—and no tips—[*Turns to door.*]

VETA. But my brother would have tipped you, anyway. He's very generous. Always has been.

CAB DRIVER. Not after this he won't be. Lady, after this, he'll be a perfectly normal human being and you know what bastards they are! Glad I met you. I'll wait. [*Exits.*]

VETA. [*Starts to run for door.*] Oh, Judge Gaffney—Myrtle Mae! Stop it—stop it— don't give it to him! Elwood, come out of there.

JUDGE. You can't do that. Dr. Chumley is giving the injection.

MYRTLE. Mother—stop this ——

VETA. [*Pounding on door.*] I don't want Elwood to have it! I don't want Elwood that way. I don't like people like that.

MYRTLE. Do something with her, Judge —Mother, stop it ——

VETA. [*Turning on her.*] You shut up! I've lived longer than you have. I remember my father. I remember your father. I remember ——

CHUMLEY. [*Opens door.*] What's this? What's all this commotion?

WILSON. [*Enters.*] What's the trouble, Doctor? She soundin' off again?

JUDGE. She wants to stop the injection.

VETA. You haven't—you haven't already given it to him, have you?

CHUMLEY. No, but we're ready. Take Mrs. Simmons away, Wilson.

VETA. Leave me alone. Take your hands off me, you white-slaver!

JUDGE. You don't know what you want. You didn't want that rabbit, either.

VETA. And what's wrong with Harvey? If Elwood and Myrtle Mae and I want to live with Harvey it's nothing to you! You don't even have to come around. It's our business. Elwood—Elwood! [ELWOOD enters. SHE throws herself weeping into his arms. HE pats her shoulder.]

ELWOOD. There, there, Veta. [*To others.*] Veta is all tired out. She's done a lot today.

JUDGE. Have it your own way. I'm not giving up my game at the club again, no matter how big the animal is. [*He exits.*]

VETA. Come on, Elwood—let's get out of here. I hate this place. I wish I'd never seen it!

CHUMLEY. But—see—here——

ELWOOD. It's whatever Veta says, Doctor.

VETA. Why, look at this! That's funny. [*It's her coin purse.*] It must have been there all the time. I could have paid that cab driver myself. Harvey!

VETA. Come on, Myrtle Mae. Come on, Elwood. Hurry up. [*She exits.* MYRTLE *follows.*]

ELWOOD. Good night, Doctor Chumley. Good night, Mr. Wilson.

VETA. [*Off stage.*] Come along Elwood.

ELWOOD. Doctor, for years I've known what my family thinks of Harvey. But I've often wondered what Harvey's family thinks of me. [*He looks beyond* CHUMLEY *to the door of his office.*] Oh—there you are! Doctor—do you mind? [*Gestures for him to step back.*] You're standing in his way. [*There is the sound of a lock clicking open and the door of* CHUMLEY'S *office opens wide. The invisible Harvey crosses to him and as they exit together.*] Where've you been? I've been looking all over for you ——

CURTAIN

For Discussion and Writing

1. Between the first and final versions of *Harvey*, Mary Chase made many revisions. Perhaps the three most interesting are these:

    a. The title changed from *The White Rabbit* to *Pooka* and finally to *Harvey*.

    b. At first the "pooka" or animal spirit took the form of a canary. By the final version, it had become a white rabbit.

    c. In the Boston tryout, Harvey appeared on stage as an eight-foot tall rabbit. On Broadway, he was invisible throughout the play.

Discuss the reasons the playwright may have had for making these changes. In your opinion, did they improve the play?

2. This play is called a comic fantasy because it blends comedy of character with elements of the supernatural. How do each of the characters contribute to the blend or add to the comedy?

3. Discuss how the following devices are used to create the comic situations in this play:

    a. Mistaken identity

    b. Satire (poking fun at or ridiculing a man's pomposity and follies)

    c. Element of surprise (the unexpected)

    d. Contradictions in human behavior

4. Elwood P. Dowd's ultimate triumph has satisfied audiences all over the world. Why do you think this is so?

5. Imagine you are Harvey. Write a soliloquy in which you reveal your opinion of the people who irritate you most in this play. In assuming Harvey's character, keep in mind that he is not a human being, or even actually a rabbit, but a pooka.

"The Hairy Ape"

{1922}

EUGENE O'NEILL

CHARACTERS
(In Order of Appearance)

ROBERT SMITH, "YANK"   SECOND ENGINEER
PADDY   A GUARD
LONG   A SECRETARY OF AN ORGANIZATION
MILDRED DOUGLAS   STOKERS, LADIES, GENTLEMEN, ETC.
HER AUNT

SCENES

SCENE 1: The firemen's forecastle of an ocean liner—an hour after sailing from New York.

SCENE 2: Section of promenade deck, two days out—morning.

SCENE 3: The stockade. A few minutes later.

SCENE 4: Same as Scene 1. Half an hour later.

SCENE 5: Fifth Avenue, New York. Three weeks later.

SCENE 6: An island near the city. The next night.

SCENE 7: In the city. About a month later.

SCENE 8: In the city. Twilight of the next day.

TIME: *The Modern.*

"*The Hairy Ape*" opened March 9, 1922, at the Playwright's Theater on Macdougal Street in Greenwich Village on a cramped stage to a small packed house. Despite the space restrictions, the stage settings for the eight scenes created, according to one critic, the "illusion of vast spaces and endless perspectives." Reported another observer, the audience was astounded by this "bitter, brutal, wildly fantastic play of nightmare hue and nightmare distortion." In spite of an unsuccessful attempt to close the play because of the "indecent" language used by the stokers, it ran for 127 performances. The play was produced in Paris the same year, in Moscow in 1923, and was revived in London in 1931 with Paul Robeson in the lead.

Like all O'Neill plays, "*The Hairy Ape*" became a center of critical controversy. Though the work was subtitled "A Comedy of Ancient and Modern Life," a storm of questions broke: Was the play really tragedy? Or was it, perhaps, more irony than tragedy? Or was it, as one critic claimed, merely a "savage joke"? Even the language of the playwright polarized audiences—was the play poetically eloquent, "a sort of wild organ music," or was it "choked and thwarted and inarticulate"? Was the style realism, symbolism, or expressionism? Was the hero frustrated by the forces of society or by his own limitations of intellect, education, and opportunity? Or was he not a hero at all, but a human derelict and failure, one of O'Neill's non-heroes who "yammer and yearn, curse and are—lost"? Was O'Neill "the only American playwright willing to confront and wrestle with ideas," or was he just an emotionalist and not a thinker at all?

The answers to these questions—after half a century—are still dividing readers and audiences. But winner of four Pultizer awards and the only American playwright ever to receive the Nobel Prize for Literature, O'Neill occupies a unique place among the world's giants of drama. He rescued the American theater from melodrama by experimenting with unorthodox form. He gave it substance with his rejection of the traditional values of Victorianism, Puritanism, and the Protestant Ethic. By challenging the materialism and opportunism of our culture, O'Neill helped the American theater to come of age.

O'Neill never dealt with "neat" little themes. His plays spill over with tension, torment, frustration, excesses—and lack of finesse, for he is not a tidy writer. Power, honesty, courage, passion—these are facets of his genius that place him among the all-time "greats" of the theater.

"The Hairy Ape"

SCENE 1

The firemen's forecastle of a transatlantic liner an hour after sailing from New York for the voyage across. Tiers of narrow, steel bunks, three deep, on all sides. An entrance in rear. Benches on the floor before the bunks. The room is crowded with men, shouting, cursing, laughing, singing—a confused, inchoate uproar swelling into a sort of unity, a meaning—the bewildered, furious, baffled defiance of a beast in a cage. Nearly all the men are drunk. Many bottles are passed from hand to hand. All are dressed in dungaree pants, heavy ugly shoes. Some wear singlets, but the majority are stripped to the waist.

The treatment of this scene, or of any other scene in the play, should by no means be naturalistic. The effect sought after is a cramped space in the bowels of a ship, imprisoned by white steel. The lines of bunks, the uprights supporting them, cross each other like the steel framework of a cage. The ceiling crushes down upon the men's heads. They cannot stand upright. This accentuates the natural stooping posture which shoveling coal and the resultant over-development of back and shoulder muscles have given them. The men themselves should resemble those pictures in which the appearance of Neanderthal Man is guessed at. All are hairy-chested, with long arms of tremendous power, and low, receding brows above their small, fierce, resentful eyes. All the civilized white races are represented, but except for the slight differentiation in color of hair, skin, eyes, all these men are alike.

[The curtain rises on a tumult of sound. YANK is seated in the foreground. He seems broader, fiercer, more truculent, more powerful, more sure of himself than the rest. They respect his superior strength—the grudging respect of fear. Then, too, he represents to them a self-expression, the very last word in what they are, their most highly developed individual.]

VOICES. Gif me trink dere, you!
'Ave a wet!
Salute!
Gesundheit!
Skoal!
Drunk as a lord, God stiffen you!
Here's how!
Luck!
Pass back that bottle, damn you!
Pourin' it down his neck!
Ho, Groggy! Where the devil have you been?
La Touraine.
I hit him smash in yaw, py Gott!
Jenkins—the First—he's a rotten swine—

And the coppers nabbed him—and I run—
I like peer better. It don't pig head gif you.
A slut, I'm sayin'! She robbed me aslape—
To hell with 'em all!
You're a bloody liar!
Say dot again! *[Commotion. Two men about to fight are pulled apart.]*
No scrappin' now!
Tonight—
See who's the best man!
Bloody Dutchman!
Tonight on the for'ard square.
I'll bet on Dutchy.
He packa da wallop, I tella you!

Shut up, Wop!

No fightin', maties. We're all chums, ain't we?

[*A voice starts bawling a song.*]

"Beer, beer, glorious beer!
Fill yourselves right up to here."

YANK. [*For the first time seeming to take notice of the uproar about him, turns around threateningly—in a tone of contemptuous authority.*] Choke off dat noise! Where d'yuh get dat beer stuff? Beer, hell! Beer's for goils—and Dutchmen. Me for somep'n wit a kick to it! Gimme a drink, one of youse guys. [*Several bottles are eagerly offered. He takes a tremendous gulp at one of them; then, keeping the bottle in his hand, glares belligerently at the* OWNER, *who hastens to acquiesce in this robbery by saying:*] All righto, Yank. Keep it and have another.

[YANK *contemptuously turns his back on the crowd again. For a second there is an embarrassed silence. Then:*]

VOICES. We must be passing the Hook.

She's beginning to roll to it.

Six days in hell—and then Southampton.

Py Yesus, I vish somepody take my first vatch for me!

Gittin' seasick, Square-head?

Drink up and forget it!

What's in your bottle?

Gin.

Dot's nigger trink.

Absinthe? It's doped. You'll go off your chump, Froggy!

Cochon!

Whisky, that's the ticket!

Where's Paddy?

Going asleep.

Sing us that whisky song, Paddy.

[*They all turn to an old, wizened* IRISHMAN *who is dozing, very drunk, on the benches forward. His face is extremely monkey-like with all the sad, patient pathos of that animal in his small eyes.*]

Singa da song, Caruso Pat!

He's getting old. The drink is too much for him.

He's too drunk.

PADDY. [*Blinking about him, starts to his feet resentfully, swaying, holding on to the edge of a bunk.*] I'm never too drunk to sing. 'Tis only when I'm dead to the world I'd be wishful to sing at all.

[*With a sort of sad contempt.*] "Whisky Johnny," ye want? A chanty, ye want? Now that's a queer wish from the ugly like of you, God help you. But no matther.

[*He starts to sing in a thin, nasal, doleful tone.*]

Oh, whisky is the life of man!
    Whisky! O Johnny! [*They all join in on this.*]
Oh, whisky is the life of man!
    Whisky for my Johnny! [*Again chorus.*]
Oh, whisky drove my old man mad!
    Whisky! O Johnny!
Oh, whisky drove my old man mad!
    Whisky for my Johnny!

YANK. [*Again turning around scornfully.*] Aw hell! Nix on dat old sailing ship stuff! All dat bull's dead, see? And you're dead, too, yuh damned old Harp, on'y yuh don't know it. Take it easy, see? Give us a rest. Nix on de loud noise. [*With a cynical grin.*] Can't' youse see I'm tryin' to t'ink?

ALL. [*Repeating the word after him, as one, with the same cynical amused mockery.*] Think!

[*The chorused word has a brazen metalic quality as if their throats were phonograph horns. It is followed by a general uproar of hard, barking laughter.*]

VOICES. Don't be cracking your head wit ut, Yank.

You gat headache, py yingo!

One thing about it—it rhymes with drink!

Ha, ha, ha!

Drink, don't think!

Drink, don't think!

Drink, don't think!

[*A whole chorus of voices has taken up this refrain stamping on the floor, pounding on the benches with fists.*]

YANK. [*Taking a gulp from his bottle—good-naturedly:*] Aw right. Can de noise. I got yuh de foist time.

[*The uproar subsides. A very drunken sentimental* TENOR *begins to sing.*]

"Far away in Canada,
    Far across the sea,
There's a lass who fondly waits
    Making a home for me—"

YANK. [*Fiercely contemptuous.*] Shut up, yuh lousy boob! Where d'yuh get dat tripe? Home? Home, hell! I'll make a home for yuh! I'll knock yuh dead. Home!

T'hell wit home! Where d'yuh get dat tripe? Dis is home, see? What d'yuh want wit home? [*Proudly.*] I runned away from mine when I was a kid. On'y too glad to beat it, dat was me. Home was lickings for me, dat's all. But yuh can bet your shoit no one ain't never licked me since! Wanter try it, any of youse? Huh! I guess not. [*In a more placated but still contemptuous tone.*] Goils waitin' for yuh, huh? Aw, hell! Dat's all tripe. Dey don't wait for no one. Dey'd double-cross yuh for a nickel. Dey're all tarts, get me? Treat 'em rough, dat's me. To hell wit 'em. Tarts, dat's what, de whole bunch of 'em.

LONG. [*Very drunk, jumps on a bench excitedly, gesticulating with a bottle in his hand.*] Listen 'ere, Comrades; Yank 'ere is right. 'E says this 'ere stinkin' ship is our 'ome. And 'e says as 'ome is 'ell. And 'e's right! This is 'ell. We lives in 'ell, Comrades—and right enough we'll die in it. [*Raging.*] And who's ter blame, I arsks yer. We ain't. We wasn't born this rotten way. All men is born free and ekal. That's in the bleedin' Bible, maties. But what d'they care for the Bible—them lazy, bloated swine what travels first cabin? Them's the ones. They dragged us down 'til we're on'y wage slaves in the bowels of a bloody ship, sweatin,' burnin' up, eatin' coal dust! Hit's them's ter blame— the damned Capitalist clarss!

[*There had been a gradual murmur of contemptuous resentment rising among the* MEN *until now he is interrupted by a storm of catcalls, hisses, boos, hard laughter.*]

VOICES. Turn it off!
Shut up!
Sit down!
Closa da face!
Tamn fool! [*Etc.*]

YANK. [*Standing up and glaring at* LONG.] Sit down before I knock yuh down! [LONG *makes haste to efface himself.* YANK *goes on contemptuously.*] De Bible, huh? De Cap'tlist class, huh? Aw, nix on dat Salvation Army-Socialist bull. Git a soapbox! Hire a hall! Come and be saved, huh? Jerk us to Jesus, huh? Aw g'wan! I've listened to lots of guys like you, see? Yuh're all wrong. Wanter know what I t'ink? Yuh ain't no good for no one. Yuh're de bunk. Yuh ain't got no noive, get me?

Yuh're yellow, dat's what. Yellow, dat's you. Say! What's dem slobs in de foist cabin got to do wit us? We're better men dan dey are, ain't we? Sure! One of us guys could clean up de whole mob wit one mit. Put one of 'em down here for one watch in de stokehole, what'd happen? Dey'd carry him off on a stretcher. Dem boids don't amount to nothin'. Dey're just baggage. Who makes dis old tub run? Ain't it us guys? Well den, we belong, don't we? We belong and dey don't. Dat's all. [*A loud chorus of approval.* YANK *goes on.*] As for dis bein' hell—aw, nuts! Yuh lost your noive, dat's what. Dis is a man's job, get me? It belongs. It runs dis tub. No stiffs need apply. But yuh're a stiff, see? Yuh're yellow, dat's you.

VOICES. [*With a great hard pride in them.*]
Righto!
A man's job!
Talk is cheap, Long.
He never could hold up his end.
Divil take him!
Yank's right. We make it go.
Py Gott, Yank say right ting!
We don't need no one cryin' over us.
Makin' speeches.
Throw him out!
Yellow!
Chuck him overboard!
I'll break his jaw for him!
[*They crowd around* LONG *threateningly.*]

YANK. [*Half good-natured again—contemptuously.*] Aw, take it easy. Leave him alone. He ain't woith a punch. Drink up. Here's how, whoever owns dis.

[*He takes a long swallow from his bottle. All drink with him. In a flash all is hilarious amiability again, back-slapping, loud talk, etc.*]

PADDY. [*Who has been sitting in a blinking, melancholy daze—suddenly cries out in a voice full of old sorrow.*] We belong to this, you're saying? We make the ship to go, you're saying? Yerra then, that Almighty God have pity on us! [*His voice runs into the wail of a keen; he rocks back and forth on his bench. The men stare at him, startled and impressed in spite of themselves.*] Oh, to be back in the fine days of my youth, ochone! Oh, there was fine beautiful ships them days—clippers wid tall masts touching the sky—fine strong men in them—men that was sons of the sea as if 'twas the mother that bore them. Oh, the clean skins of them, and the clear eyes, the straight backs and full chests of them! Brave men they was, and bold men surely! We'd be sailing out, bound down round the Horn maybe. We'd be making sail in the dawn, with a fair breeze, singing a chanty song wid no care to it. And astern the land would be sinking low and dying out, but we'd give it no heed but a laugh, and never a look behind. For the day that was, was enough, for we was free men—and I'm thinking 'tis only slaves do be giving heed to the day that's gone or the day to come—until they're old like me. [*With a sort of religious exaltation.*] Oh, to be scudding south again wid the power of the Trade Wind driving her on steady through the nights and the days! Full sail on her! Nights and days! Nights when the foam of the wake would be flaming wid fire, when the sky'd be blazing and winking wid stars. Or the full of the moon maybe. Then you'd see her driving through the gray night, her sails stretching aloft all silver and white, not a sound on the deck, the lot of us dreaming dreams, till you'd believe 'twas no real ship at all you was on but a ghost ship like the *Flying Dutchman* they says does be roaming the seas forevermore widout touching a port. And there was the days, too. A warm sun on the clean decks. Sun warming the blood of you, and wind over the miles of shiny green ocean like strong drink to your lungs. Work—aye, hard work —but who'd mind that at all? Sure, you worked under the sky and 'twas work wid skill and daring to it. And wid the day done, in the dog watch, smoking me pipe at ease, the lookout would be raising land maybe, and we'd see the mountains of South Americy wid the red fire of the setting sun painting their white tops and the clouds floating by them! [*His tone of exaltation ceases. He goes on mournfully.*] Yerra, what's the use of talking? 'Tis a dead man's whisper. [*To* YANK *resentfully.*] 'Twas them days a ship was part of the sea, and a man was part of a ship, and the sea joined all together and made it one. [*Scornfully.*] Is it one wid this you'd be, Yank—black smoke from the funnels smudging the sea, smudging the decks— the bloody engines pounding and throb-bing and shaking—wid divil a sight of sun or a breath of clean air—choking our lungs wid coal dust—breaking our backs and hearts in the hell of the stokehole— feeding the bloody furnace—feeding our lives along wid the coal, I'm thinking— caged in by steel from a sight of the sky like bloody apes in the zoo! [*With a harsh laugh.*] Ho-ho, divil mend you! Is it to belong to that you're wishing? Is it a flesh and blood wheel of the engines you'd be?

YANK. [*Who has been listening with a contemptuous sneer, barks out the answer.*] Sure ting! Dat's me. What about it?

PADDY. [*As if to himself—with great sorrow:*] Me time is past due. That a great wave wid sun in the heart of it may sweep me over the side sometime I'd be dreaming of the days that's gone!

YANK. Aw, yuh crazy Mick! [*He springs to his feet and advances on* PADDY *threateningly—then stops, fighting some queer struggle within himself—lets his hands fall to his sides—contemptuously:*] Aw, take it easy. Yuh're aw right, at dat. Yuh're bugs, dat's all—nutty as a cuckoo. All dat tripe yuh been pullin'—Aw, dat's all right. On'y it's dead, get me? Yuh don't belong no more, see. Yuh don't get de stuff. Yuh're too old. [*Disgustedly.*] But aw say, come up for air onct in a while, can't yuh? See what's happened since yuh croaked. [*He suddenly bursts forth vehemently, growing more and more excited.*] Say! Sure! Sure I meant it! What de hell—Say, lemme talk! Hey! Hey, you old Harp! Hey, youse guys! Say, listen to me—wait a moment— I gotter talk, see? I belong and he don't. He's dead but I'm livin'. Listen to me! Sure I'm part of de engines! Why de hell not! Dey move, don't they? Dey're speed, ain't dey? Dey smash trou, don't dey? Twenty-five knots a hour! Dat's goin' some! Dat's new stuff! Dat belongs! But him, he's too old. He gets dizzy. Say, listen. All dat crazy tripe about nights and days; all dat crazy tripe about stars and moons; all dat crazy tripe about suns and winds, fresh air and de rest of it— Aw hell, dat's all a dope dream! Hittin' de pipe of de past, dat's what he's doin'. He's old and he don't belong no more. But me, I'm young! I'm in de pink! I move wit it! It, get me! I mean de ting dat's de guts of all dis. It ploughs trou all de tripe he's been sayin'. It blows dat up! It knocks dat dead! It slams dat offen de face of de oith! It, get me! De engines and de coal and de smoke and all de rest of it! He can't breathe and swallow coal dust, but I kin, see? Dat's fresh air for me! Dat's food for me! I'm new, get me? Hell in de stokehole? Sure! It takes a man to work in hell. Hell, sure, dat's my fav'rite climate. I eat it up! I git fat on it! It's me makes it hot! It's me makes it roar! It's me makes it move! Sure, on'y for me everything stops. It all goes dead, get me? De noise and smoke and all de engines movin' de woild, dey stop. Dere ain't nothin' no more! Dat's what I'm sayin'. Everyting else dat makes de woild move, somep'n makes it move. It can't move witout somep'n else, see? Den yuh get down to me. I'm at de bottom, get me! Dere ain't nothin' foither. I'm de end! I'm de start! I start somep'n and de woild moves! It—dat's me!—de new dat's moiderin' de old! I'm de ting in coal dat makes it boin; I'm steam and oil for de engines; I'm de ting in noise dat makes yuh hear it; I'm smoke and express trains and steamers and factory whistles; I'm de ting in gold dat makes it money! And I'm what makes iron into steel! Steel, dat stands for de whole ting! And I'm steel—steel—steel! I'm de muscles in steel, de punch behind it! [*As he says this he pounds with his fist against the steel bunks. All the* MEN, *roused to a pitch of frenzied self-glorification by his speech, do likewise. There is a deafening metallic roar, through which* YANK's *voice can be heard bellowing:*] Slaves, hell! We run de whole woiks. All de rich guys dat tink dey're somep'n, dey ain't nothin'! Dey don't belong. But us guys, we're in de move, we're at de bottom, de whole ting is us! [PADDY *from the start of* YANK's *speech has been taking one gulp after another from his bottle, at first frightenedly, as if he were afraid to listen, then desperately, as if to drown his senses, but finally has achieved complete indifferent, even amused, drunkenness.* YANK *sees his lips moving. He quells the uproar with a shout.*] Hey, youse guys,

take it easy! Wait a moment! De nutty Harp is sayin' somep'n.

PADDY. [*Is heard now—throws his head back with a mocking burst of laughter.*] Ho-ho-ho-ho-ho——

YANK. [*Drawing back his fist, with a snarl.*] Aw! Look out who yuh're givin' the bark!

PADDY. [*Begins to sing the "Miller of Dee" with enormous good nature.*]
   "I care for nobody, no, not I,
      And nobody cares for me."

YANK. [*Good-natured himself in a flash, interrupts* PADDY *with a slap on the bare back like a report.*] Dat's de stuff! Now yuh're gettin' wise to somep'n. Care for nobody, dat's de dope! To hell wit 'em all! And nix on nobody else carin'. I kin care for myself, get me! [*Eight bells sound, muffled, vibrating through the steel walls as if some enormous brazen gong were imbedded in the heart of the ship. All the men jump up mechanically, file through the door silently, close upon each other's heels in what is very like a prisoners' lock-step.* YANK *slaps* PADDY *on the back.*] Our watch, yuh old Harp! [*Mockingly.*] Come on down in hell. Eat up de coal dust. Drink in de heat. It's it, see! Act like yuh liked it, yuh better—or croak yuhself.

PADDY. [*With jovial defiance.*] To the divil wid it! I'll not report this watch. Let them log me and be damned. I'm no slave the like of you. I'll be settin' here at me ease, and drinking, and thinking, and dreaming dreams.

YANK. [*Contemptuously.*] Tinkin' and dreamin', what'll that get yuh? What's tinkin' got to do wit it? We move, don't we? Speed, ain't it? Fog, dat's all you stand for. But we drive trou dat, don't we? We split dat up and smash trou—twenty-five knots a hour! [*Turns his back on* PADDY *scornfully.*] Aw, yuh make me sick! Yuh don't belong!

[*He strides out the door in rear.* PADDY *hums to himself, blinking drowsily.*]

CURTAIN

SCENE 2

Two days out. A section of the promenade deck.
[MILDRED DOUGLAS *and her* AUNT *are discovered reclining in deck chairs. The former is a girl of twenty, slender, delicate, with a pale, pretty face marred by a self-conscious expression of disdainful superiority. She looks fretful, nervous, and discontented, bored by her own anemia. Her* AUNT *is a pompous and proud—and fat—old lady. She is a type even to the point of a double chin and lorgnettes. She is dressed pretentiously, as if afraid her face alone would never indicate her position in life.* MILDRED *is dressed all in white.*
The impression to be conveyed by this scene is one of the beautiful, vivid life of the sea all about—sunshine on the deck in a great flood, the fresh sea wind blowing across it. In the midst of this, these two incongruous, artificial figures, inert and disharmonious, the elder like a gray lump of dough touched up with rouge, the younger looking as if the vitality of her stock had been sapped before she was conceived, so that she is the expression not of its life energy but merely of the artificialities that energy had won for itself in the spending.]

MILDRED. [*Looking up with affected dreaminess.*] How the black smoke swirls back against the sky! Is it not beautiful?
AUNT. [*Without looking up.*] I dislike smoke of any kind.
MILDRED. My great-grandmother smoked a pipe—a clay pipe.
AUNT. [*Ruffling.*] Vulgar!
MILDRED. She was too distant a relative to be vulgar. Time mellows pipes.
AUNT. [*Pretending boredom but irritated.*] Did the sociology you took up at college teach you that—to play the ghoul on every possible occasion, excavating old bones? Why not let your great-grandmother rest in her grave?
MILDRED. [*Dreamily.*] With her pipe beside her—puffing in Paradise.
AUNT. [*With spite.*] Yes, you are a natural born ghoul. You are even getting to look like one, my dear.
MILDRED. [*In a passionless tone.*] I detest you, Aunt. [*Looking at her critically.*] Do you know what you remind me of? Of a cold pork pudding against a background of linoleum tablecloth in the kitchen of a—but the possibilities are wearisome. [*She closes her eyes.*]
AUNT. [*With a bitter laugh.*] Merci for your candor. But since I am and must be your chaperon—in appearance, at least—let us patch up some sort of armed truce.

For my part you are quite free to indulge any pose of eccentricity that beguiles you —as long as you observe the amenities—
MILDRED. [*Drawling.*] The inanities?
AUNT. [*Going on as if she hadn't heard.*] After exhausting the morbid thrills of social service work on New York's East Side —how they must have hated you, by the way, the poor that you made so much poorer in their own eyes!—you are now bent on making your slumming international. Well, I hope Whitechapel will provide the needed nerve tonic. Do not ask me to chaperon you there, however. I told your father I would not. I loathe deformity. We will hire an army of detectives and you may investigate everything—they allow you to see.
MILDRED. [*Protesting with a trace of genuine earnestness.*] Please do not mock at my attempts to discover how the other half lives. Give me credit for some sort of groping sincerity in that at least. I would like to help them. I would like to be some use in the world. Is it my fault I don't know how? I would like to be sincere, to touch life somewhere. [*With weary bitterness.*] But I'm afraid I have neither the vitality nor integrity. All that was burnt out in our stock before I was born. Grandfather's blast furnaces, flaming to the sky, melting steel, making mil-

lions—then father keeping those home fires burning, making more millions—and little me at the tail-end of it all. I'm a waste product in the Bessemer process—like the millions. Or rather, I inherit the acquired trait of the by-product, wealth, but none of the energy, none of the strength of the steel that made it. I am sired by gold and dammed by it, as they say at the race track—damned in more ways than one.

[She laughs mirthlessly.]

AUNT. [Unimpressed — superciliously:] You seem to be going in for sincerity today. It isn't becoming to you, really— except as an obvious pose. Be as artificial as you are, I advise. There's a sort of sincerity in that, you know. And, after all, you must confess you like that better.

MILDRED. [Again affected and bored.] Yes, I suppose I do. Pardon me for my outburst. When a leopard complains of its spots, it must sound rather grotesque. [In a mocking tone.] Purr, little leopard. Purr, scratch, tear, kill, gorge yourself and be happy—only stay in the jungle where your spots are camouflage. In a cage they make you conspicuous.

AUNT. I don't know what you are talking about.

MILDRED. It would be rude to talk about anything to you. Let's just talk. [She looks at her wrist watch.] Well, thank goodness, it's about time for them to come for me. That ought to give me a new thrill, Aunt.

AUNT. [Affectedly troubled.] You don't mean to say you're really going? The dirt —the heat must be frightful—

MILDRED. Grandfather started as a puddler. I should have inherited an immunity to heat that would make a salamander shiver. It will be fun to put it to the test.

AUNT. But don't you have to have the captain's—or someone's—permission to visit the stokehole?

MILDRED. [With a triumphant smile.] I have it—both his and the chief engineer's. Oh, they didn't want to at first, in spite of my social service credentials. They didn't seem a bit anxious that I should investigate how the other half lives and works on a ship. So I had to tell them that my father, the president of Nazareth Steel, chairman of the board of directors of this line, had told me it would be all right.

AUNT. He didn't.

MILDRED. How naïve age makes one! But I said he did, Aunt. I even said he had given me a letter to them—which I had lost. And they were afraid to take the chance that I might be lying. [Excitedly.] So it's ho! for the stokehole. The second engineer is to escort me. [Looking at her watch again.] It's time. And here he comes, I think.

[The SECOND ENGINEER enters. He is a husky, fine-looking man of thirty-five or so. He stops before the two and tips his cap, visibly embarrassed and ill-at-ease.]

SECOND ENGINEER. Miss Douglas?

MILDRED. Yes. [Throwing off her rugs and getting to her feet.] Are we all ready to start?

SECOND ENGINEER. In just a second, ma'am. I'm waiting for the Fourth. He's coming along.

MILDRED. [With a scornful smile.] You don't care to shoulder this responsibility alone, is that it?

SECOND ENGINEER. [Forcing a smile.] Two are better than one. [Disturbed by her eyes, glances out to sea—blurts out:] A fine day we're having.

MILDRED. Is it?

SECOND ENGINEER. A nice warm breeze—

MILDRED. It feels cold to me.

SECOND ENGINEER. But it's hot enough in the sun—

MILDRED. Not hot enough for me. I don't like Nature. I was never athletic.

SECOND ENGINEER. [Forcing a smile.] Well, you'll find it hot enough where you're going.

MILDRED. Do you mean hell?

SECOND ENGINEER. [Flabbergasted, decides to laugh.] Ho-ho! No, I mean the stokehole.

MILDRED. My grandfather was a puddler. He played with boiling steel.

SECOND ENGINEER. [All at sea—uneasily:] Is that so? Hum, you'll excuse me, ma'am, but are you intending to wear that dress?

MILDRED. Why not?

SECOND ENGINEER. You'll likely rub against oil and dirt. It can't be helped.

MILDRED. It doesn't matter. I have lots of white dresses.

SECOND ENGINEER. I have an old coat you might throw over—

MILDRED. I have fifty dresses like this. I will throw this one into the sea when I come back. That ought to wash it clean, don't you think?

SECOND ENGINEER. [*Doggedly.*] There's ladders to climb down that are none too clean—and dark alleyways—

MILDRED. I will wear this dress and none other.

SECOND ENGINEER. No offense meant. It's none of my business. I was only warning you—

MILDRED. Warning? That sounds thrilling.

SECOND ENGINEER. [*Looking down the deck—with a sigh of relief:*] There's the Fourth now. He's waiting for us. If you'll come—

MILDRED. Go on. I'll follow you. [*He goes.* MILDRED *turns a mocking smile on her* AUNT.] An oaf—but a handsome, virile oaf.

AUNT. [*Scornfully.*] Poser!

MILDRED. Take care. He said there were dark alleyways—

AUNT. [*In the same tone.*] Poser!

MILDRED. [*Biting her lips angrily.*] You are right. But would that my millions were not so anemically chaste!

AUNT. Yes, for a fresh pose I have no doubt you would drag the name of Douglas in the gutter!

MILDRED. From which it sprang. Goodby, Aunt. Don't pray too hard that I may fall into the fiery furnace.

AUNT. Poser!

MILDRED. [*Viciously.*] Old hag!

[*She slaps her* AUNT *insultingly across the face and walks off, laughing gaily.*]

AUNT. [*Screams after her:*] I said poser!

CURTAIN

SCENE 3

The stokehole. In the rear, the dimly-outlined bulks of the furnaces and boilers. High overhead one hanging electric bulb sheds just enough light through the murky air laden with coal dust to pile up masses of shadows everywhere. A line of men, stripped to the waist, is before the furnace doors. They bend over, looking neither to right nor left, handling their shovels as if they were part of their bodies, with a strange, awkward, swinging rhythm. They use the shovels to throw open the furnace doors. Then from these fiery round holes in the black a flood of terrific light and heat pours full upon the men who are outlined in silhouette in the crouching, inhuman attitudes of chained gorillas. The men shovel with a rhythmic motion, swinging as on a pivot from the coal which lies in heaps on the floor behind to hurl it into the flaming mouths before them. There is a tumult of noise—the brazen clang of the furnace doors as they are flung open or slammed shut, the grating, teeth-gritting grind of steel against steel, and of crunching coal. This clash of sounds stuns one's ears with its rending dissonance. But there is order in it, rhythm, a mechanical, regulated recurrence, a tempo. And rising above all, making the air hum with the quiver of liberated energy, the roar of leaping flames in the furnaces, the monotonous throbbing beat of the engines.
[*As the curtain rises, the furnace doors are shut. The* MEN *are taking a breathing spell. One or two are arranging the coal behind them, pulling it into more accessible heaps. The others can be dimly made out leaning on their shovels in relaxed attitudes of exhaustion.*]

PADDY. [*From somewhere in the line—plaintively:*] Yerra, will this divil's own watch nivir end? Me back is broke. I'm destroyed entirely.

YANK. [*From the center of the line—with exuberant scorn:*] Aw, yuh make me sick! Lie down and croak, why don't yuh? Always beefin', dat's you! Say, dis is a cinch! Dis was made for me! It's my meat, get me! [*A whistle is blown—a thin, shrill note from somewhere overhead in the darkness.* YANK *curses without resentment.*] Dere's de damn engineer crackin' de whip. He tinks we're loafin'.

PADDY. [*Vindictively.*] God stiffen him!

YANK. [*In an exultant tone of command.*] Come on, youse guys! Git into de game! She's gittin' hungry! Pile some grub in her. Trow it into her belly! Come on now, all of youse! Open her up!

[*At this last all the* MEN, *who have followed his movements of getting into position, throw open their furnace doors with a deafening clang. The fiery light floods over their shoulders as they bend round for the coal. Rivulets of sooty sweat have traced maps on their backs. The enlarged muscles form bunches of high light and shadow.*]

YANK. [*Chanting a count as he shovels without seeming effort.*] One-two-three—[*His voice rising exultantly in the joy of battle.*] Dat's de stuff! Let her have it! All togedder now! Sling it into her! Let her ride! Shoot de piece now! Call de toin on her! Drive her into it! Feel her move! Watch her smoke! Speed, dat's her middle name! Give her coal, youse guys! Coal, dat's her booze! Drink it up, baby! Let's see yuh sprint! Dig in and gain a lap! Dere she go-o-es.

[*This last in the chanting formula of the gallery gods at the six-day bike race. He slams his furnace door shut. The others do likewise with as much unison as their wearied bodies will permit. The effect is of one fiery eye after another being blotted out with a series of accompanying bangs.*]

PADDY. [*Groaning.*] Me back is broke. I'm bate out—bate—

[*There is a pause. Then the inexorable whistle sounds again from the dim regions above the electric light. There is a growl of cursing rage from all sides.*]

YANK. [*Shaking his fist upward—contemptuously.*] Take it easy dere, you! Who d'yuh tink's runnin' dis game, me or you?

When I git ready, we move, Not before! When I git ready, get me!

VOICES. [*Approvingly.*] That's the stuff! Yank tal him, py golly! Yank ain't affeerd. Goot poy, Yank! Give him hell! Tell 'im 'e's a bloody swine! Bloody slave-driver!

YANK. [*Contemptuously.*] He ain't got no noive. He's yellow, get me? All de engineers is yellow. Dey got streaks a mile wide. Aw, to hell wit him! Let's move, youse guys. We had a rest. Come on, she needs it! Give her pep! It ain't for him. Him and his whistle, dey don't belong. But we belong, see! We gotter feed de baby! Come on!

[*He turns and flings his furnace door open. They all follow his lead. At this instant the* SECOND *and* FOURTH ENGINEERS *enter from the darkness on the left with* MILDRED *between them. She starts, turns paler, her pose is crumbling, she shivers with fright in spite of the blazing heat, but forces herself to leave the* ENGINEERS *and take a few steps nearer the men. She is right behind* YANK. *All this happens quickly while the men have their backs turned.*]

YANK. Come on, youse guys!

[*He is turning to get coal when the whistle sounds again in a peremptory, irritating note. This drives* YANK *into a sudden fury. While the other* MEN *have turned full around and stopped dumbfounded by the spectacle of* MILDRED *standing there in her white dress,* YANK *does not turn far enough to see her. Besides, his head is thrown back, he blinks upward through the murk trying to find the owner of the whistle, he brandishes his shovel murderously over his head in one hand, pounding on his chest, gorilla-like, with the other, shouting.*]

YANK. Toin off dat whistle! Come down outa dere, yuh yellow, brass-buttoned, Belfast bum, yuh! Come down and I'll knock yer brains out! Yuh lousy, stinkin', yellow mut of a Catholic-moiderin' bastard! Come down and I'll moider yuh! Pullin' dat whistle on me, huh? I'll show yuh! I'll crash yer skull in! I'll drive yer teet' down yer troat! I'll slam yer nose

trou de back of yer head! I'll cut yer guts out for a nickel, yuh lousy boob, yuh dirty, crummy, muckeatin' son of a—
[*Suddenly he becomes conscious of all the other* MEN *staring at something directly behind his back. He whirls defensively with a snarling, murderous growl, crouching to spring, his lips drawn back over his teeth, his small eyes gleaming ferociously. He sees* MILDRED, *like a white apparition in the full light from the open furnace doors. He glares into her eyes, turned to stone. As for her, during his speech she has listened, paralyzed with horror, terror, her whole personality crushed, beaten in, collapsed, by the terrific impact of this unknown, abysmal brutality, naked and shameless. As she looks at his gorilla face, as his eyes bore into hers, she utters a low, choking cry and shrinks away from him, putting both hands up before her eyes to shut out the sight of his face, to protect her own.*

This startles YANK *to a reaction. His mouth falls open, his eyes grow bewildered.*]
MILDRED. [*About to faint—to the* ENGINEERS, *who now have her one by each arm—whimperingly:*] Take me away! Oh, the filthy beast!
[*She faints. They carry her quickly back, disappearing in the darkness at the left, rear. An iron door clangs shut. Rage and bewildered fury rush back on* YANK. *He feels himself insulted in some unknown fashion in the very heart of his pride. He roars.*]
YANK. God damn yuh!
[*And hurls his shovel after them at the door which has just closed. It hits the steel bulkhead with a clang and falls clattering on the steel floor. From overhead the whistle sounds again in a long, angry, insistent command.*]

CURTAIN

SCENE 4

The firemen's forecastle. YANK's *watch has just come off duty and had dinner. Their faces and bodies shine from a soap and water scrubbing but around their eyes, where a hasty dousing does not touch, the coal dust sticks like black make-up, giving them a queer, sinister expression.*
[YANK *has not washed either face or body. He stands out in contrast to them, a blackened, brooding figure. He is seated forward on a bench in the exact attitude of Rodin's "The Thinker." The others, most of them smoking pipes, are staring at* YANK *half-apprehensively, as if fearing an outburst; half-amusedly, as if they saw a joke somewhere that tickled them.*]

VOICES. He ain't ate nothin'.
Py golly, a fallar gat to gat grub in him.
Divil a lie.
Yank feeda da fire, no feeda da face.
Ha-ha.
He ain't even washed hisself.
He's forgot.
Hey, Yank, you forgot to wash.
YANK. [*Sullenly.*] Forgot nothin'! To hell wit washin'.
VOICES. It'll stick to you.
It'll get under your skin.
Give yer the bleedin' itch, that's wot.
It makes spots on you—like a leopard.
Like a piebald nigger, you mean.
Better wash up, Yank.
You sleep better.
Wash up, Yank.
Wash up! Wash up!
YANK. [*Resentfully.*] Aw say, youse guys. Lemme alone. Can't youse see I'm tryin' to tink?
ALL. [*Repeating the word after him, as one, with cynical mockery.*] Think!
[*The word has a brazen, metallic quality as if their throats were phonograph horns. It is followed by a chorus of hard, barking laughter.*]

YANK. [*Springing to his feet and glaring at them belligerently.*] Yes, tink! Tink, dat's what I said! What about it? [*They are silent, puzzled by his sudden resentment at what used to be one of his jokes.* YANK *sits down again in the same attitude of "The Thinker."*]

VOICES. Leave him alone.
He's got a grouch on.
Why wouldn't he?

PADDY. [*With a wink at the others.*] Sure I know what's the matther. 'Tis aisy to see. He's fallen in love, I'm telling you.

ALL. [*Repeating the word after him, as one, with cynical mockery.*] Love! [*The word has a brazen, metallic quality as if their throats were phonograph horns. It is followed by a chorus of hard, barking laughter.*]

YANK. [*With a contemptuous snort.*] Love, hell! Hate, dat's what. I've fallen in hate, get me?

PADDY. [*Philosophically.*] 'Twould take a wise man to tell one from the other. [*With a bitter, ironical scorn, increasing as he goes on.*] But I'm telling you it's love that's in it. Sure what else but love for us poor bastes in the stokehole would be bringing a fine lady, dressed like a white quane, down a mile of ladders and steps to be havin' a look at us? [*A growl of anger goes up from all sides.*]

LONG. [*Jumping on a bench—hecticly:*] Hinsultin' us! Hinsultin' us the bloody cow! And them bloody engineers! What right 'as they got to be exhibitin' us 's if we was bleedin' monkeys in a menagerie? Did we sign for hinsults to our dignity as 'onest workers? Is that in the ship's articles? You kin bloody well bet it ain't! But I knows why they done it. I arsked a deck steward 'oo she was and 'e told me. 'Er old man's a bleedin' millionaire, a bloody Capitalist! 'E's got enuf bloody gold to sink this bleedin' ship! 'E makes arf the bloody steel in the world! 'E owns this bloody boat! And you and me, Comrades, we're 'is slaves! And the skipper and mates and engineers, they're 'is slaves! And she's 'is bloody daughter and we're all 'er slaves, too! And she gives 'er orders as 'ow she wants to see the bloody animals below decks and down they takes 'er! [*There is a roar of rage from all sides.*]

YANK. [*Blinking at him bewilderedly.*] Say! Wait a moment! Is all dat straight goods?

LONG. Straight as string! The bleedin' steward as waits on 'em, 'e told me about 'er. And what're we goin' ter do. I arsks yer? 'Ave we got ter swaller 'er hinsults like dogs? It ain't in the ship's articles. I tell yer we got a case. We kin go to law——

YANK. [*With abysmal contempt.*] Hell! Law!

ALL. [*Repeating the word after him, as one, with cynical mockery.*] Law! [*The word has a brazen metallic quality as if their throats were phonograph horns. It is followed by a chorus of hard, barking laughter.*]

LONG. [*Feeling the ground slipping from under his feet—desperately:*] As voters and citizens we kin force the bloody governments——

YANK. [*With abysmal contempt.*] Hell! Governments!

ALL. [*Repeating the word after him, as one, with cynical mockery.*] Governments! [*The word has a brazen metallic quality as if their throats were phonograph horns. It is followed by a chorus of hard, barking laughter.*]

LONG. [*Hysterically.*] We're free and equal in the sight of God——

YANK. [*With abysmal contempt.*] Hell! God!

ALL. [*Repeating the word after him, as one, with cynical mockery.*] God! [*The word has a brazen metallic quality as if their throats were phonograph horns. It is followed by a chorus of hard, barking laughter.*]

YANK. [*Witheringly.*] Aw, join de Salvation Army!

ALL. Sit down! Shut up! Damn fool! Sea-lawyer! [LONG *slinks back out of sight.*]

PADDY. [*Continuing the trend of his thoughts as if he had never been interrupted—bitterly:*] And there she was standing behind us, and the Second pointing at us like a man you'd hear in a circus would be saying: In this cage is a queerer kind of baboon than ever you'd find in darkest Africy. We roast them in their own sweat—and be damned if you won't hear some of thim saying they like it! [*He glances scornfully at* YANK.]

YANK. [*With a bewildered uncertain growl.*] Aw!

PADDY. And there was Yank roarin' curses and turning round wid his shovel to brain her—and she looked at him, and him at her—

YANK. [*Slowly.*] She was all white. I tought she was a ghost. Sure.

PADDY. [*With heavy, biting sarcasm.*] 'Twas love at first sight, divil a doubt of it! If you'd seen the endearin' look on her pale mug when she shriveled away with her hands over her eyes to shut out the sight of him! Sure, 'twas as if she'd seen a great hairy ape escaped from the Zoo!

YANK. [*Stung—with a growl of rage:*] Aw!

PADDY. And the loving way Yank heaved his shovel at the skull of her, only she was out the door! [*A grin breaking over his face.*] 'Twas touching, I'm telling you! It put the touch of home, swate home in the stokehole.

[*There is a roar of laughter from all.*]

YANK. [*Glaring at PADDY menacingly.*] Aw, choke dat off, see!

PADDY. [*Not heeding him—to the others:*] And her grabbin' at the Second's arm for protection. [*With a grotesque imitation of a woman's voice.*] Kiss me, Engineer dear, for it's dark down here and me old man's in Wall Street making money! Hug me tight, darlin', for I'm afeerd in the dark and me mother's on deck makin' eyes at the skipper!

[*Another roar of laughter.*]

YANK. [*Threateningly.*] Say! What yuh tryin' to do, kid me, yuh old Harp?

PADDY. Divil a bit! Ain't I wishin' myself you'd brained her?

YANK. [*Fiercely.*] I'll brain her! I'll brain her yet, wait 'n' see! [*Coming over to PADDY—slowly:*] Say, is dat what she called me—a hairy ape?

PADDY. She looked it at you if she didn't say the word itself.

YANK. [*Grinning horribly.*] Hairy ape, huh? Sure! Dat's de way she looked at me, aw right. Hairy ape! So dat's me, huh? [*Bursting into rage—as if she were still in front of him.*] Yuh skinny tart! Yuh white-faced bum, yuh! I'll show yuh who's a ape! [*Turning to the others, bewilderment seizing him again.*] Say, youse guys. I was bawlin' him out for pullin' de whistle on us. You heard me. And den I seen youse lookin' at somep'n and I tought he'd sneaked down to come up in back of me, and I hopped round to knock him dead

wit de shovel. And dere she was wit de light on her! Christ, yuh coulda pushed me over wit a finger! I was scared, get me? Sure! I tought she was a ghost, see? She was all in white like dey wrap around stiffs. You seen her. Kin yuh blame me? She didn't belong, dat's what. And den when I come to and seen it was a real skoit and seen de way she was lookin' at me—like Paddy said—Christ, I was sore, get me? I don't stand for dat stuff from nobody. And I flung de shovel —on'y she'd beat it. [*Furiously.*] I wished it'd banged her! I wished it'd knocked her block off!

LONG. And be 'anged for murder or 'lectrocuted? She ain't bleedin' well worth it.

YANK. I don't give a damn what! I'd be square wit her, wouldn't I? Tink I wanter let her put somep'n over on me? Tink I'm goin' to let her git away wit dat stuff? Yuh don't know me! No one ain't never put nothin' over on me and got away wit it, see!—not dat kind of stuff—no guy and no skoit neither! I'll fix her! Maybe she'll come down again—

VOICE. No chance, Yank. You scared her out of a year's growth.

YANK. I scared her? Why de hell should I scare her? Who de hell is she? Ain't she de same as me? Hairy ape, huh? [*With his old confident bravado.*] I'll show her I'm better'n her, if she on'y knew it. I belong and she don't, see! I move and she's dead! Twenty-five knots a hour, dat's me! Dat carries her but I make dat. She's on'y baggage. Sure! [*Again bewilderedly.*] But, Christ, she was funny lookin'! Did yuh pipe her hands? White and skinny. Yuh could see de bones through 'em. And her mush, dat was dead white, too. And her eyes, dey was like dey'd seen a ghost. Me, dat was! Sure! Hairy ape! Ghost, huh? Look at dat arm! [*He extends his right arm, swelling out the great muscles.*] I coulda took her wit dat, wit just my little finger even, and broke her in two. [*Again bewilderedly.*] Say, who is dat skoit, huh? What is she? What's she come from? Who made her? Who give her de noive to look at me like dat? Dis ting's got my goat right. I don't get her. She's new to me. What does a skoit like her mean, huh? She don't belong, get me! I can't see her. [*With growing anger.*] But one ting I'm wise to, aw right, aw right! Youse all kin

bet your shoits I'll git even wit her. I'll
show her if she tinks she— She grinds de
organ and I'm on de string, huh? I'll fix
her! Let her come down again and I'll
fling her in de furnace! She'll move den!
She won't shiver at nothin', den! Speed,
dat'll be her! She'll belong den!
[*He grins horribly.*]
PADDY. She'll never come. She's had her
belly-full, I'm telling you. She'll be in bed
now, I'm thinking, wid ten doctors and
nurses feedin' her salts to clean the fear
out of her.
YANK. [*Enraged.*] Yuh tink I made her
sick, too, do yuh? Just lookin' at me, huh?
Hairy ape, huh? [*In a frenzy of rage.*] I'll
fix her! I'll tell her where to git off! She'll
git down on her knees and take it back or
I'll bust de face offen her! [*Shaking one
fist upward and beating on his chest with
the other.*] I'll find yuh! I'm comin', d'yuh
hear? I'll fix yuh, God damn yuh!
[*He makes a rush for the door.*]
VOICES. Stop him!
He'll get shot!

He'll murder her!
Trip him up!
Hold him!
He's gone crazy!
Gott, he's strong!
Hold him down!
Look out for a kick!
Pin his arms!
[*They have all piled on him and,
after a fierce struggle, by sheer
weight of numbers have borne him
to the floor just inside the door.*]
PADDY. [*Who has remained detached.*]
Kape him down till he's cooled off.
[*Scornfully.*] Yerra, Yank, you're a great
fool. Is it payin' attention at all you are
to the like of that skinny sow widout one
drop of rale blood in her?
YANK. [*Frenziedly, from the bottom of
the heap.*] She done me doit! She done me
doit, didn't she? I'll git square wit her! I'll
get her some way! Git offen me, youse
guys! Lemme up! I'll show her who's
a ape!
CURTAIN

SCENE 5

*Three weeks later. A corner of Fifth Avenue in the Fifties
on a fine Sunday morning. A general atmosphere of clean, well-
tidied, wide street; a flood of mellow, tempered sunshine; gentle,
genteel breezes. In the rear, the show windows of two shops, a
jewelry establishment on the corner, a furrier's next to it. Here
the adornments of extreme wealth are tantalizingly displayed.
The jeweler's window is gaudy with glittering diamonds,
emeralds, rubies, pearls, etc., fashioned in ornate tiaras, crowns,
necklaces, collars, etc. From each piece hangs an enormous tag
from which a dollar sign and numerals in intermittent electric
lights wink out the incredible prices. The same in the furrier's.
Rich furs of all varieties hang there bathed in a downpour of
artificial light. The general effect is of a background of mag-
nificence cheapened and made grotesque by commercialism, a
background in tawdry disharmony with the clear light and
sunshine on the street itself.
[Up the side street YANK and LONG come swaggering. LONG is
dressed in shore clothes, wears a black Windsor tie, cloth cap.
YANK is in his dirty dungarees. A fireman's cap with black peak
is cocked defiantly on the side of his head. He has not shaved for
days and around his fierce, resentful eyes—as around those of
LONG to a lesser degree—the black smudge of coal dust still
sticks like make-up. They hesitate and stand together at the
corner, swaggering, looking about them with a forced, defiant
contempt.*]

LONG. [*Indicating it all with an oratori-
cal gesture.*] Well, 'ere we are. Fif' Avenoo. This 'ere's their bleedin' private lane,

as yer might say. [*Bitterly.*] We're tres-
passers 'ere. Proletarians keep orf the
grass!

YANK. [*Dully.*] I don't see no grass, yuh boob. [*Staring at the sidewalk.*] Clean, ain't it? Yuh could eat a fried egg offen it. The white wings got some job sweepin' dis up. [*Looking up and down the avenue—surlily:*] Where's all de white-collar stiffs yuh said was here—and de skoits—*her* kind?

LONG. In church, blarst 'em! Arskin' Jesus to give 'em more money.

YANK. Choich, huh? I useter go to choich onct—sure—when I was a kid. Me old man and woman, dey made me. Dey never went demselves, dough. Always got too big a head on Sunday mornin', dat was dem. [*With a grin.*] Dey was scrappers for fair, bot' of dem. On Satiday nights when dey bot' got a skinful dey could put up a bout oughter been staged at de Garden. When dey got trough dere wasn't a chair or table wit a leg under it. Or else dey bot' jumped on me for somep'n. Dat was where I loined to take punishment. [*With a grin and a swagger.*] I'm a chip offen de old block, get me?

LONG. Did yer old man follow the sea?

YANK. Naw. Worked along shore. I runned away when me old lady croaked wit de tremens. I helped at truckin' and in de market. Den I shipped in de stoke-hole. Sure. Dat belongs. De rest was nothin'. [*Looking around him.*] I ain't never seen dis before. De Brooklyn water-front, dat was where I was dragged up. [*Taking a deep breath.*] Dis ain't so bad at dat, huh?

LONG. Not bad? Well, we pays for it wiv our bloody sweat, if yer wants to know!

YANK. [*With sudden angry disgust.*] Aw, hell! I don't see no one, see—like her. All dis gives me a pain. It don't belong. Say, ain't dere a back room around dis dump? Let's go shoot a ball. All dis is too clean and quiet and dolled-up, get me? It gives me a pain.

LONG. Wait and yer'll bloody well see—

YANK. I don't wait for no one. I keep on de move. Say, what yuh drag me up here for, anyway? Tryin' to kid me, yuh simp, yuh?

LONG. Yer wants to get back at 'er, don't er? That's what yer been sayin' every bloomin' hour since she hinsulted yer.

YANK. [*Vehemently.*] Sure ting I do! Didn't I try to get even wit her in South-ampton? Didn't I sneak on de deck and wait for her by de gangplank? I was goin' to spit in her pale mug, see! Sure, right in her pop-eyes! Dat woulda made me even, see? But no chanct. Dere was a whole army of plainclothes bulls around. Dey spotted me and gimme de bum's rush. I never seen her. But I'll git square wit her yet, you watch! [*Furiously.*] De lousy tart! She tinks she kin get away wit moider—but not wit me! I'll fix her! I'll tink of a way!

LONG. [*As disgusted as he dares to be.*] Ain't that why I brought yer up 'ere—to show yer? Yer been lookin' at this 'ere 'ole affair wrong. Yer been actin' an' talkin' 's if it was all a bleedin' personal matter between yer and that bloody cow. I wants to convince yer she was on'y a representa-tive of 'er clarss. I wants to awaken yer bloody clarss consciousness. Then yer'll see it's 'er clarss ye've got to fight, not 'er alone. There's a 'ole mob of 'em like 'er, Gawd blind 'em!

YANK. [*Spitting on his hands—belliger-ently:*] De more de merrier when I gits started. Bring on de gang!

LONG. Yer'll see 'em in arf a mo', when that church lets out. [*He turns and sees the window display in the two stores for the first time.*] Blimey! Look at that, will yer? [*They both walk back and stand looking in the jeweler's.* LONG *flies into a fury.*] Just look at this 'ere bloomin' mess! Just look at it! Look at the bleedin' prices on 'em—more'n our 'ole bloody stokehole makes in ten voyages sweatin' in 'ell! And they—'er and 'er bloody clarss—buys 'em for toys to dangle on 'em! One of these 'ere would buy scoff for a starvin' family for a year!

YANK. Aw, cut de sob stuff! T' hell wit de starvin' family! Yuh'll be passin' de hat to me next. [*With naïve admiration.*] Say, dem tings is pretty, huh? Bet yuh dey'd hock for a piece of change aw right. [*Then turning away, bored.*] But, aw hell, what good are dey? Let her have 'em. Dey don't belong no more'n she does. [*With a ges-ture of sweeping the jeweler's into obli-vion.*] All dat don't count, get me?

LONG. [*Who has moved to the furrier's—indignantly:*] And I s'pose this 'ere don't count neither—skins of poor, 'armless ani-mals slaughtered so as 'er and 'ers can keep their bleedin' noses warm!

YANK. [*Who has been staring at something inside—with queer excitement:*] Take a slant at dat! Give it de once-over! Monkey fur—two t'ousand bucks! [*Bewilderedly.*] Is dat straight goods—monkey fur? What de hell—?

LONG. [*Bitterly.*] It's straight enuf. [*With grim humor.*] They wouldn't bloody well pay that for a 'airy ape's skin—no, nor for the 'ole livin' ape with all 'is 'ead, and body, and soul thrown in!

YANK. [*Clenching his fists, his face growing pale with rage as if the skin in the window were a personal insult.*] Trowin' it up in my face! Christ! I'll fix her!

LONG. [*Excitedly.*] Church is out. 'Ere they come, the bleedin' swine. [*After a glance at* YANK's *lowering face—uneasily:*] Easy goes, Comrade. Keep yer bloomin' temper. Remember force defeats itself. It ain't our weapon. We must impress our demands through peaceful means—the votes of the on-marching proletarians of the bloody world!

YANK. [*With abysmal contempt.*] Votes, hell! Votes is a joke, see? Votes for women! Let dem do it!

LONG. [*Still more uneasily.*] Calm, now. Treat 'em wiv the proper contempt. Observe the bleedin' parasites but 'old yer 'orses.

YANK. [*Angrily.*] Git away from me! Yuh're yellow, dat's what. Force, dat's me! De punch, dat's me every time, see!

[*The* CROWD *from church enter from the right, sauntering slowly and affectedly, their heads held stiffly up, looking neither to right nor left, talking in toneless, simpering voices. The* WOMEN *are rouged, calcimined, dyed, over-dressed to the nth degree. The* MEN *are in Prince Alberts, high hats, spats, canes, etc. A procession of gaudy marionettes, yet with something of the relentless horror of Frankensteins in their detached, mechanical unawareness.*]

VOICES. Dear Doctor Caiaphas! He is so sincere!

What was the sermon? I dozed off.

About the radicals, my dear—and the false doctrines that are being preached.

We must organize a hundred per cent American bazaar.

And let everyone contribute one one-hundredth per cent of their income tax. What an original idea!

We can devote the proceeds to rehabilitating the veil of the temple.

But that has been done so many times.

YANK. [*Glaring from one to the other of them—with an insulting snort of scorn:*] Huh! Huh!

[*Without seeming to see him, they make wide detours to avoid the spot where he stands in the middle of the sidewalk.*]

LONG. [*Frightenedly.*] Keep yer bloomin' mouth shut, I tells yer.

YANK. [*Viciously.*] G'wan! Tell it to Sweeney! [*He swaggers away and deliberately lurches into a top-hatted* GENTLEMAN, *then glares at him pugnaciously.*] Say, who d'yuh tink yuh're bumpin'? Tink yuh own de oith?

GENTLEMAN. [*Coldly and affectedly.*] I beg your pardon.

[*He has not looked at* YANK *and passes on without a glance, leaving him bewildered.*]

LONG. [*Rushing up and grabbing* YANK's *arm.*] 'Ere! Come away! This wasn't what I meant. Yer'll 'ave the bloody coppers down on us.

YANK. [*Savagely—giving him a push that sends him sprawling.*] G'wan!

LONG. [*Picks himself up—hysterically:*] I'll pop orf then. This ain't what I meant. And whatever 'appens yer can't blame me. [*He slinks off left.*]

YANK. T' hell wit youse! [*He approaches a* LADY—*with a vicious grin and a smirking wink:*] Hello, Kiddo. How's every little ting? Got anything on for tonight? I know an old boiler down to de docks we kin crawl into. [*The* LADY *stalks by without a look, without a change of pace.* YANK *turns to others—insultingly.*] Holy smokes, what a mug! Go hide yuhself before de horses shy at yuh. Gee, pipe de heinie on dat one! Say, youse, yuh look like de stoin of a ferryboat. Paint and powder! All dolled up to kill! Yuh look like stiffs laid out for de boneyard! Aw, g'wan, de lot of youse! Yuh give me de eye-ache. Yuh don't belong, get me! Look at me, why don't youse dare? I belong, dat's me! [*Pointing to a skyscraper across the street which is in process of construction—with bravado:*] See dat building goin' up dere? See de steel work? Steel, dat's me! Youse guys live on it and tink yuh're somep'n. But I'm *in* it, see! I'm de hoistin' engine dat makes it go up! I'm it—de inside and bottom of it! Sure! I'm steel and steam and smoke and de rest of it! It moves—speed—twenty-five stories up—and me at de top and bottom—movin'! Youse simps don't move. Yuh're on'y dolls I winds up to see 'm spin. Yuh're de garbage, get me —de leavins—de ashes we dump over de side! Now, what 'a' yuh gotta say? [*But as they seem neither to see nor hear him, he flies into a fury.*] Bums! Pigs! Tarts! Bitches! [*He turns in a rage on the* MEN, *bumping viciously into them but not jarring them the least bit. Rather it is he who recoils after each collision. He keeps growling.*] Git off de oith! G'wan, yuh bum! Look where yuh're goin', can't yuh? Git outa here! Fight, why don't yuh? Put up yer mits! Don't be a dog! Fight or I'll knock yuh dead! [*But, without seeming to see him, they all answer with mechanical affected politeness:*] I beg your pardon.

[*Then, at a cry from one of the* WOMEN, *they all scurry to the furrier's window.*]

THE WOMAN. [*Ecstatically, with a gasp of delight.*] Monkey fur! [*The whole crowd of* MEN *and* WOMEN *chorus after her in the same tone of affected delight.*] Monkey fur!

YANK. [*With a jerk of his head back on his shoulders, as if he had received a punch full in the face—raging:*] I see yuh, all in white! I see yuh, yuh white-faced tart, yuh! Hairy ape, huh? I'll hairy ape yuh!

[*He bends down and grips at the street curbing as if to pluck it out and hurl it. Foiled in this, snarling with passion, he leaps to the lamp-post on the corner and tries to pull it up for a club. Just at that moment a bus is heard rumbling up. A fat, high-hatted, spatted* GENTLEMAN *runs out from the side street. He calls out plaintively:*]

GENTLEMAN. Bus! Bus! Stop there!

[*And runs full tilt into the bending, straining* YANK, *who is bowled off his balance.*]

YANK. [*Seeing a fight—with a roar of joy as he springs to his feet:*] At last! Bus, huh? I'll bust yuh!

[*He lets drive a terrific swing, his fist landing full on the fat* GENTLEMAN'S *face. But the* GENTLEMAN *stands unmoved as if nothing had happened.*]

GENTLEMAN. I beg your pardon. [*Then irritably.*] You have made me lose my bus. [*He claps his hands and begins to scream:*] Officer! Officer!

[*Many police whistles shrill out on the instant and a whole platoon of* POLICEMEN *rush in on* YANK *from all sides. He tries to fight but is clubbed to the pavement and fallen upon. The* CROWD *at the window have not moved or noticed this disturbance. The clanging gong of the patrol wagon approaches with a clamoring din.*]

CURTAIN

SCENE 6

Night of the following day. A row of cells in the prison on Blackwell's Island. The cells extend back diagonally from right front to left rear. They do not stop, but disappear in the dark background as if they ran on, numberless, into infinity. One electric bulb from the low ceiling of the narrow corridor sheds its light through the heavy steel bars of the cell at the extreme front and reveals part of the interior.

[YANK *can be seen within, crouched on the edge of his cot in the attitude of Rodin's "The Thinker." His face is spotted with black and blue bruises. A blood-stained bandage is wrapped around his head.*]

YANK. [*Suddenly starting as if awakening from a dream, reaches out and shakes* the bars—aloud to himself, wonderingly:] Steel. Dis is de Zoo, huh?

[A *burst of hard, barking laughter comes from the unseen* OCCUPANTS *of the cells, runs back down the tier, and abruptly ceases.*]

VOICES. [*Mockingly.*] The Zoo? That's a new name for this coop—a damn good name!

Steel, eh? You said a mouthful. This is the old iron house.

Who is that boob talkin'?

He's the bloke they brung in out of his head. The bulls had beat him up fierce.

YANK. [*Dully.*] I musta been dreamin'. I tought I was in a cage at de Zoo—but de apes don't talk, do dey?

VOICES. [*With mocking laughter.*] You're in a cage aw right.

A coop!

A pen!

A sty!

A kennel!

[*Hard laughter—a pause.*]

Say, guy! Who are you? No, never mind lying. What are you?

Yes, tell us your sad story. What's your game?

What did they jug yuh for?

YANK. [*Dully.*] I was a fireman—stokin' on de liners. [*Then with sudden rage, rattling his cell bars.*] I'm a hairy ape, get me? And I'll bust youse all in de jaw if yuh don't lay off kiddin' me.

VOICES. Huh! You're a hard boiled duck, ain't youse!

When you spit, it bounces!

[*Laughter.*]

Aw, can it. He's a regular guy. Ain't you?

What did he say he was—a ape?

YANK. [*Defiantly.*] Sure ting! Ain't dat what youse all are—apes?

[*A silence. Then a furious rattling of bars from down the corridor.*

A VOICE. [*Thick with rage.*] I'll show yuh who's a ape, yuh bum!

VOICES. Ssshh! Nix!

Can de noise!

Piano!

You'll have the guard down on us!

YANK. [*Scornfully.*] De guard? Yuh mean de keeper, don't yuh?

[*Angry exclamations from all the cells.*]

VOICE. [*Placatingly.*] Aw, don't pay no attention to him. He's off his nut from the beatin'-up he got. Say, you guy! We're waitin' to hear what they landed you for —or ain't yuh tellin'?

YANK. Sure, I'll tell youse. Sure! Why de hell not? On'y—youse won't get me. Nobody gets me but me, see? I started to tell de Judge and all he says was: "Toity days to tink it over." Tink it over! Christ, dat's all I been doin' for weeks! [*After a pause.*] I was tryin' to git even wit someone, see?—someone dat done me doit.

VOICES. [*Cynically.*] De old stuff, I bet. Your goil, huh?

Give yuh the double-cross, huh?

That's them every time!

Did yuh beat up de odder guy?

YANK. [*Disgustedly.*] Aw, yuh're all wrong! Sure dere was a skoit in it—but not what youse mean, not dat old tripe. Dis was a new kind of skoit. She was dolled up all in white—in de stokehole. I tought she was a ghost. Sure. [*A pause.*]

VOICES. [*Whispering.*] Gee, he's still nutty.

Let him rave. It's fun listenin'.

YANK. [*Unheeding — groping in his thoughts.*] Her hands—dey was skinny and white like dey wasn't real but painted on somep'n. Dere was a million miles from me to her—twenty-five knots a hour. She was like some dead ting de cat brung in. Sure, dat's what. She didn't belong. She belonged in de window of a toy store, or on de top of a garbage can, see! Sure! [*He breaks out angrily.*] But would yuh believe it, she had de noive to do me doit. She lamped me like she was seein' somep'n broke loose from de menagerie. Christ, yuh'd oughter seen her eyes! [*He rattles the bars of his cell furiously.*] But I'll get back at her yet, you watch! And if I can't find her I'll take it out on de gang she runs wit. I'm wise to where dey hangs out now. I'll show her who belongs! I'll show her who's in de move and who ain't. You watch my smoke!

VOICES. [*Serious and joking.*] Dat's de talkin'!

Take her for all she's got!

What was this dame, anyway? Who was she, eh?

YANK. I dunno. First cabin stiff. Her old man's a millionaire, dey says—name of Douglas.

VOICES. Douglas? That's the president of the Steel Trust, I bet.

Sure. I seen his mug in de papers.

He's filthy with dough.

VOICE. Hey, feller, take a tip from me. If you want to get back at that dame, you better join the Wobblies. You'll get some action then.

YANK. Wobblies? What de hell's dat?

VOICE. Ain't you ever heard of the I. W. W.?

YANK. Naw. What is it?

VOICE. A gang of blokes—a tough gang. I been readin' about 'em today in the paper. The guard give me the *Sunday Times*. There's a long spiel about 'em. It's from a speech made in the Senate by a guy named Senator Queen. [*He is in the cell next to* YANK's. *There is a rustling of paper.*] Wait'll I see if I got light enough and I'll read you. Listen. [*He reads:*] "There is a menace existing in this country today which threatens the vitals of our fair Republic—as foul a menace against the very life-blood of the American Eagle as was the foul conspiracy of Catiline against the eagles of ancient Rome!"

VOICE. [*Disgustedly.*] Aw, hell! Tell him to salt de tail of dat eagle!

VOICE. [*Reading:*] "I refer to that devil's brew of rascals, jailbirds, murderers, and cutthroats who libel all honest working men by calling themselves the Industrial Workers of the World; but in the light of their nefarious plots, I call them the Industrious *Wreckers* of the World!"

YANK. [*With vengeful satisfaction.*] Wreckers, dat's de right dope! Dat belongs! Me for dem!

VOICE. Ssshh! [*Reading:*] "This fiendish organization is a foul ulcer on the fair body of our Democracy—"

VOICE. Democracy, hell! Give him the boid, fellers—the raspberry! [*They do.*]

VOICE. Ssshh! [*Reading:*] "Like Cato I say to this Senate, the I. W. W. must be destroyed! For they represent an ever-present dagger pointed at the heart of the greatest nation the world has ever known, where all men are born free and equal, with equal opportunities to all, where the Founding Fathers have guaranteed to each one happiness, where Truth, Honor, Liberty, Justice, and the Brotherhood of Man are a religion absorbed with one's mother's milk, taught at our father's knee, sealed, signed, and stamped in the glorious Constitution of these United States!"

[*A perfect storm of hisses, catcalls, boos, and hard laughter.*]

VOICES. [*Scornfully.*] Hurrah for de Fort' of July!
Pass de hat!
Liberty!
Justice!
Honor!
Opportunity!
Brotherhood!

ALL. [*With abysmal scorn.*] Aw, hell!

VOICE. Give the Queen Senator guy the bark! All togedder now—one—two—three—

[*A terrific chorus of barking and yapping.*]

GUARD. [*From a distance.*] Quiet there, youse—or I'll git the hose.

[*The noise subsides.*]

YANK. [*With growling rage.*] I'd like to catch dat senator guy alone for a second. I'd loin him some trute!

VOICE. Ssshh! Here's where he gits down to cases on the Wobblies. [*Reads:*] "They plot with fire in one hand and dynamite in the other. They stop not before murder to gain their ends, nor at the outraging of defenseless womanhood. They would tear down society, put the lowest scum in the seats of the mighty, turn Almighty God's revealed plan for the world topsy-turvy, and make of our sweet and lovely civilization a shambles, a desolation where man, God's masterpiece, would soon degenerate back to the ape!"

VOICE. [*To* YANK.] Hey, you guy. There's your ape stuff again.

YANK. [*With a growl of fury.*] I got him. So dey blow up tings, do they? Dey turn tings round, do dey? Hey, lend me dat paper, will yuh?

VOICE. Sure. Give it to him. On'y keep it to yourself, see? We don't wanter listen to no more of that slop.

VOICE. Here you are. Hide it under your mattress.

YANK. [*Reaching out.*] Tanks. I can't read much but I kin manage. [*He sits, the paper in the hand at his side, in the attitude of Rodin's "The Thinker." A pause. Several snores from down the corridor. Suddenly* YANK *jumps to his feet with a furious groan as if some appalling thought had crashed on him—bewilderedly.*] Sure —her old man—president of de Steel Trust —makes half de steel in de world—steel— where I thought I belonged—drivin' trou —movin'—in dat—to make *her*—and cage me in for her to spit on! Christ! [*He shakes the bars of his cell door till the whole tier trembles. Irritated, protesting exclamations from those awakened or trying to get to sleep.] He made dis—dis cage! Steel! It don't belong, dat's what! Cages, cells, locks, bolts, bars—dat's what it means!—holdin' me down with him at de top! But I'll drive trou! Fire, dat melts it! I'll be fire—under de heap—fire dat never goes out—hat as hell—breakin' out in de night—

[While he has been saying this last he has shaken his cell door to a clanging accompaniment. As he comes to the "breakin' out" he seizes one bar with both hands and, putting his two feet up against the others so that his position is parallel to the floor like a monkey's, he gives a great wrench backwards. The bar bends like a licorice stick under his tremendous strength. Just at this moment the

PRISON GUARD rushes in, dragging a hose behind him.]

GUARD. [Angrily.] I'll loin youse bums to wake me up! [Sees YANK.] Hello, it's you, huh? Got the D. Ts., hey? Well, I'll cure 'em. I'll drown your snakes for yuh! [Noticing the bar.] Hell, look at dat bar bended! On'y a bug is strong enough for dat!

YANK. [Glaring at him.] Or a hairy ape, yuh big yellow bum! Look out! Here I come!

[He grabs another bar.]

GUARD. [Scared now—yelling off left.] Toin de hose on, Ben!—full pressure! And call de others—and a straitjacket!

[The curtain is falling. As it hides YANK from view, there is a splattering smash as the stream of water hits the steel of YANK's cell.]

CURTAIN

SCENE 7

Nearly a month later. An I. W. W. local near the waterfront, showing the interior of a front room on the ground floor, and the street outside. Moonlight on the narrow street, buildings massed in black shadow. The interior of the room, which is general assembly room, office, and reading room, resembles some dingy settlement boys' club. A desk and high stool are in one corner. A table with paper, stacks of pamphlets, chairs about it, is at center. The whole is decidedly cheap, banal, commonplace, and unmysterious as a room could well be. [The SECRETARY is perched on the stool making entries in a large ledger. An eye shade casts his face into shadows. Eight or ten MEN, LONGSHOREMEN, IRON WORKERS, and the like, are grouped about the table. Two are playing checkers. One is writing a letter. Most of them are smoking pipes. A big signboard is on the wall at the rear, "Industrial Workers of the World—Local No. 57." YANK comes down the street outside. He is dressed as in Scene Five. He moves cautiously, mysteriously. He comes to a point opposite the door; tip-toes softly up to it, listens, is impressed by the silence within, knocks carefully, as if he were guessing at the password to some secret rite. Listens. No answer. Knocks again a bit louder. No answer. Knocks impatiently, much louder.]

SECRETARY. [Turning around on his stool.] What the hell is that—someone knocking? [Shouts:] Come in, why don't you?

[All the MEN in the room look up. YANK opens the door slowly, gingerly, as if afraid of an ambush. He

looks around for the secret doors, mystery, is taken aback by the commonplaceness of the room and the MEN in it, thinks he may have gotten in the wrong place, then sees the signboard on the wall and is reassured.]

YANK. [Blurts out:] Hello.

MEN. [Reservedly.] Hello.

YANK. [More easily.] I thought I'd bumped into de wrong dump.

SECRETARY. [Scrutinizing him carefully.] Maybe you have. Are you a member?

YANK. Naw, not yet. Dat's what I come for—to join.

SECRETARY. That's easy. What's your job—longshore?

YANK. Naw. Fireman—stoker on de liners.

SECRETARY. [With satisfaction.] Welcome to our city. Glad to know you people are waking up at last. We haven't got many members in your line.

YANK. Naw, Dey're all dead to de woild.

SECRETARY. Well, you can help to wake 'em. What's your name? I'll make out your card.

YANK. [Confused.] Name? Lemme tink.

SECRETARY. [Sharply.] Don't you know your own name?

YANK. Sure; but I been just Yank for so long—Bob, dat's it—Bob Smith.

SECRETARY. [Writing.] Robert Smith. [Fills out the rest of card.] Here you are. Cost you half a dollar.

YANK. Is dat all—four bits? Dat's easy. [Gives the SECRETARY the money.]

SECRETARY. [Throwing it in drawer.] Thanks. Well, make yourself at home. No introductions needed. There's literature on the table. Take some of those pamphlets with you to distribute aboard ship. They may bring results. Sow the seed, only go about it right. Don't get caught and fired. We got plenty out of work. What we need is men who can hold their jobs—and work for us at the same time.

YANK. Sure.
[But he still stands, embarrassed and uneasy.]

SECRETARY. [Looking at him—curiously:] What did you knock for? Think we had a coon in uniform to open doors?

YANK. Naw. I tought it was locked—and dat yuh'd wanter give me the once-over trou a peep-hole or somep'n to see if I was right.

SECRETARY. [Alert and suspicious but with an easy laugh.] Think we were running a crap game? That door is never locked. What put that in your nut?

YANK. [With a knowing grin, convinced that this is all camouflage, a part of the secrecy.] Dis burg is full of bulls, ain't it?

SECRETARY. [Sharply.] What have the cops got to do with us? We're breaking no laws.

YANK. [With a knowing wink.] Sure. Youse wouldn't for woilds. Sure. I'm wise to dat.

SECRETARY. You seem to be wise to a lot of stuff none of us knows about.

YANK. [With another wink.] Aw, dat's aw right, see? [Then made a bit resentful by the suspicious glances from all sides.] Aw, can it! Youse needn't' put me trou de toid degree. Can't youse see I belong? Sure! I'm reg'lar. I'll stick, get me? I'll shoot de woiks for youse. Dat's why I wanted to join in.

Secretary. [Breezily, feeling him out.] That's the right spirit. Only are you sure you understand what you've joined? It's all plain and above board; still, some guys get a wrong slant on us. [Sharply.] What's your notion of the purpose of the I. W. W.?

YANK. Aw, I know all about it.

SECRETARY. [Sarcastically.] Well, give us some of your valuable information.

YANK. [Cunningly.] I know enough not to speak outa my toin. [Then resentfully again.] Aw, say! I'm reg'lar. I'm wise to de game. I know yuh got to watch your step with a stranger. For all youse know, I might be a plain-clothes dick, or somep'n, dat's what yuh're thinkin', huh? Aw, forget it! I belong, see? Ask any guy down to de docks if I don't.

SERETARY. Who said you didn't?

YANK After I'm 'nitiated, I'll show yuh.

SECRETARY. [Astounded.] Initiated? There's no initiation.

YANK. [Disappointed.] Ain't there no password—no grip nor nothin'?

SECRETARY. What'd you think this is— the Elks—or the Black Hand?

YANK. De Elks, hell! De Black Hand, dey're a lot of yellow backstickin' Ginees. Naw. Dis is a man's gang, ain't it?

SECRETARY. You said it! That's why we stand on two feet in the open. We got no secrets.

YANK. [Surprised but admiringly.] Yuh mean to say yuh always run wide open— like dis?

SECRETARY. Exactly.

YANK. Den yuh sure got your noive wit youse!

SECRETARY. [*Sharply.*] Just what was it made you want to join us? Come out with that straight.

YANK. Yuh call me? Well, I got noive, too! Here's my hand. Yuh wanter blow tings up, don't yuh? Well, dat's me! I belong!

SECRETARY. [*With pretended carelessness.*] You mean change the unequal conditions of society by legitimate direct action—or with dynamite?

YANK. Dynamite! Blow it offen de oith —steel—all de cages—all de factories, steamers, buildings, jails—de Steel Trust and all dat makes it go.

SECRETARY. So—that's your idea, eh? And did you have any special job in that line you wanted to propose to us?

[*He makes a sign to the* MEN, *who get up cautiously one by one and group behind* YANK.]

YANK. [*Boldly.*] Sure, I'll come out wit it. I'll show youse I'm one of de gang. Dere's dat millionaire guy, Douglas—

SECRETARY. President of the Steel Trust, you mean? Do you want to assassinate him?

YANK. Naw, dat don't get yuh nothin'. I mean blow up de factory, de woiks, where he makes de steel. Dat's what I'm after— to blow up steel, knock all de steel in de woild up to de moon. Dat'll fix tings! [*Eagerly, with a touch of bravado.*] I'll do it by me lonesome! I'll show yuh! Tell me where his woiks is, how to git there, all de dope. Gimme de stuff, de old butter—and watch me do de rest! Watch de smoke and see it move! I don't give a damn if dey nab me—long as it's done! I'll soive life for it—and give 'em de laugh! [*Half to himself.*] And I'll write her a letter and tell her de hairy ape done it. Dat'll square tings.

SECRETARY. [*Stepping away from* YANK.] Very interesting.

[*He gives a signal. The* MEN, *huskies all, throw themselves on* YANK, *and before he knows it they have his legs and arms pinioned. But he is too flabbergasted to make a struggle, anyway. They feel him over for weapons.*]

MAN. No gat, no knife. Shall we give him what's what and put the boots to him?

SECRETARY. No. He isn't worth the trouble we'd get into. He's too stupid. [*He comes closer and laughs mockingly in* YANK's *face.*] Ho-ho! By God, this is the biggest joke they've put up on us yet. Hey, you Joke! Who sent you—Burns or Pinkerton? No, by God, you're such a bonehead I'll bet you're in the Secret Service! Well, you dirty spy, you rotten agent provocateur, you can go back and tell whatever skunk is paying you blood-money for betraying your brothers that he's wasting his coin. You couldn't catch a cold. And tell him that all he'll ever get on us, or ever has got, is just his own sneaking plots that he's framed up to put us in jail. We are what our manifesto says we are, neither more nor less—and we'll give him a copy of that any time he calls. And as for you— [*He glares scornfully at* YANK, *who is sunk in an oblivious stupor.*] Oh, hell, what's the use talking? You're a brainless ape.

YANK. [*Aroused by the word to fierce but futile struggles.*] What's dat, yuh Sheeny bum, yuh!

SECRETARY. Throw him out, boys.

[*In spite of his struggles, this is done with gusto and éclat. Propelled by several parting kicks,* YANK *lands sprawling in the middle of the narrow cobbled street. With a growl he starts to get up and storm the closed door, but stops bewildeded by the confusion in his brain, pathetically impotent. He sits there, brooding, in as near to the attitude of Rodin's "Thinker" as he can get in his position.*]

YANK. [*Bitterly.*] So dem boids don't tink I belong, neider. Aw, to hell wit 'em! Dey're in de wrong pew—de same old bull—soap-boxes and Salvation Army—no guts! Cut out an hour offen de job a day and make me happy! Gimme a dollar more a day and make me happy! Tree squares a day, and cauliflowers in de front yard—ekal rights—a woman and kids —a lousy vote—and I'm all fixed for Jesus, huh? Aw, hell! What does dat get yuh? Dis ting's in your inside, but it ain't your belly. Feedin your face—sinkers and coffee —dat don't touch it. It's way down—at de bottom. Yuh can't grab it, and yuh can't stop it. It moves, and everything moves. It stops and de whole woild stops. Dat's me now—I don't tick, see?—I'm a busted Ingersoll, dat's what. Steel was me, and I owned de woild. Now I ain't steel, and de woild owns me. Aw, hell! I can't see—it's all dark, get me? It's all wrong! [*He turns a bitter mocking face up like an ape gibbering at the moon.*] Say, youse up dere, Man in de Moon, yuh look so wise, gimme de answer, huh? Slip me de inside dope, de information right from de stable—where do I get off at, huh?

A POLICEMAN. [*Who has come up the street in time to hear this last—with grim humor:*] You'll get off at the station, you boob, if you don't get up out of that and keep movin'.

YANK. [*Looking up at him—with a hard, bitter laugh:*] Sure! Lock me up! Put me in a cage! Dat's de on'y answer yuh know. G'wan, lock me up!

POLICEMAN. What you been doin'?

YANK. Enuf to gimme life for! I was born, see? Sure, dat's de charge. Write it in de blotter. I was born, get me?

POLICEMAN. [*Jocosely.*] God pity your old woman! [*Then matter-of-fact.*] But I've no time for kidding. You're soused. I'd run you in but it's too long a walk to the station. Come on now, get up, or I'll fan your ears with this club. Beat it now!

[*He hauls* YANK *to his feet.*]

YANK. [*In a vague mocking tone.*] Say, where do I go from here?

POLICEMAN. [*Giving him a push—with a grin, indifferently:*] Go to hell.

CURTAIN

SCENE 8

Twilight of the next day. The monkey house at the Zoo. One spot of clear gray light falls on the front of one cage so that the interior can be seen. The other cages are vague, shrouded in shadow from which chatterings pitched in a conversational tone can be heard. On the one cage a sign from which the word "gorilla" stands out. The gigantic ANIMAL *himself is seen squatting on his haunches on a bench in much the same attitude as Rodin's "Thinker."*

[YANK *enters from the left. Immediately a chorus of angry chattering and screeching breaks out. The* GORILLA *turns his eyes but makes no sound or move.*]

YANK. [*With a hard, bitter laugh.*] Welcome to your city, huh? Hail, hail, de gang's all here! [*At the sound of his voice the chattering dies away into an attentive silence.* YANK *walks up to the* GORILLA'S *cage and, leaning over the railing, stares in at its occupant, who stares back at him, silent and motionless. There is a pause of dead stillness. Then* YANK *begins to talk in a friendly confidential tone, half-mockingly, but with a deep undercurrent of sympathy.*] Say, yuh're some hard-lookin' guy, ain't yuh? I seen lots of tough nuts dat de gang called gorillas, but yuh're de foist real one I ever seen. Some chest yuh got, and shoulders, and dem arms and mits! I bet yuh got a punch in eider fist dat'd knock 'em all silly! [*This with genuine admiration. The* GORILLA, *as if he understood, stands upright, swelling out* his chest and pounding on it with his fist. YANK *grins sympathetically.*] Sure, I get yuh. Yuh challenge de whole woild, huh? Yuh got what I was sayin' even if yuh muffed de woids. [*Then bitterness creeping in.*] And why wouldn't yuh get me? Ain't we both members of de same club—de Hairy Apes? [*They stare at each other—a pause—then* YANK *goes on slowly and bitterly.*] So yuh're what she seen when she looked at me, de white-faced tart! I was you to her, get me? On'y outa de cage—broke out—free to moider her, see? Sure! Dat's what she tought. She wasn't wise dat I was in a cage, too—worser'n yours—sure—a damn sight—'cause you got some chanct to bust loose—but me—— [*He grows confused.*] Aw, hell! It's wrong, ain't it? [*A pause.*] I s'pose yuh wanter know what I'm doin' here, huh? I been warmin' a bench down to de Battery—ever since last night. Sure. I seen de sun come up. Dat was pretty, too—all red and pink and green. I was lookin' at de skyscrapers—steel—and all de ships comin' in, sailin' out, all over de oith—and dey was steel, too. De sun was warm, dey wasn't no clouds, and dere was a breeze blowin'. Sure, it was great stuff. I got it aw right—what Paddy said about dat bein' de right dope—on'y I couldn't get *in* it, see? I couldn't belong in dat. It was over my head. And I kept tinkin'— and den I beat it up here to see what youse was like. And I waited till dey was all gone to git yuh alone. Say, how d'yuh feel sittin' in dat pen all de time, havin' to stand for 'em comin' and starin' at yuh —de white-faced, skinny tarts and de boobs what marry 'em—makin' fun of yuh, laughin' at yuh, gittin' scared of yuh—damn 'em! [*He pounds on the rail with his fist. The* GORILLA *rattles the bars of his cage and snarls. All the other monkeys set up an angry chattering in the darkness.* YANK *goes on excitedly.*] Sure! Dat's de way it hits me, too. On'y yuh're lucky, see? Yuh don't belong wit 'em and yuh know it. But me, I belong wit 'em—but I don't, see? Dey don't belong wit me, dat's what. Get me? Tinkin' is hard—— [*He passes one hand across his forehead with a painful gesture. The* GORILLA *growls impatiently.* YANK *goes on gropingly.*] It's dis way, what I'm drivin' at. Youse can sit and dope dream in de past, green woods, de jungle, and de rest of it. Den yuh belong and dey don't. Den yuh kin laugh at 'em, see? Yuh're de champ of de woild. But me—I ain't got no past to tink in, nor nothin' dat's comin', on'y what's now—and dat don't belong. Sure, you're de best off! Yuh can't tink, can yuh? Yuh can't talk neider. But I kin make a bluff at talkin' and tinkin'—a'most git away wit it— a'most!—and dat's where de joker comes in. [*He laughs.*] I ain't on oith and I ain't in heaven, get me? I'm in de middle tryin' to separate 'em, takin' all de woist punches from bot' of 'em. Maybe dat's what dey call hell, huh? But you, yuh're at de bottom. You belong! Sure! Yuh're de on'y one in de woild dat does, yuh lucky stiff! [*The* GORILLA *growls proudly.*] And dat's why dey gotter put yuh in a cage, see? [*The* GORILLA *roars angrily.*]

Sure! Yuh get me. It beats it when you try to tink it or talk it—it's way down— deep—behind—you 'n' me we feel it. Sure! Bot' members of dis club! [*He laughs— then in a savage tone:*] What de hell! T' hell wit it! A little action, dat's our meat! Dat belongs! Knock 'em down and keep bustin' 'em till dey croaks yuh wit a gat— wit steel! Sure! Are yuh game? Dey've looked at youse, ain't dey—in a cage? Wanter git even? Wanter wind up like a sport 'stead of croakin' slow in dere? [*The* GORILLLA *roars an emphatic affirmative.* YANK *goes on with a sort of furious exaltation.*] Sure! Yuh're reg'lar! Yuh'll stick to de finish! Me 'n' you, huh?—bot' members of this club! We'll put up one last star bout dat'll knock 'em offen deir seats! Dey'll have to make de cages stronger after we're trou! [*The* GORILLA *is straining at his bars, growling, hopping from one foot to the other.* YANK *takes a jimmy from under his coat and forces the lock on the cage door. He throws this open.*] Pardon from de governor! Step out and shake hands! I'll take yuh for a walk down Fif' Avenoo. We'll knock 'em offen de oith and croak wit de band playin'. Come on, Brother. [*The* GORILLA *scrambles gingerly out of his cage. Goes to* YANK *and stands looking at him.* YANK *keeps his mocking tone—holds out his hand.*] Shake—de secret grip of our order. [*Something, the tone of mockery, perhaps, suddenly enrages the* ANIMAL. *With a spring he wraps his huge arms around* YANK *in a murderous hug. There is a crackling snap of crushed ribs—a gasping cry, still mocking, from* YANK.] Hey, I didn't say kiss me! [*The* GORILLA *lets the crushed body slip to the floor; stands over it uncertainly, considering; then picks it up, throws it in the cage, shuts the door, and shuffles off menacingly into the darkness at left. A great uproar of frightened chattering and whimpering comes from the other cages. Then* YANK *moves, groaning, opening his eyes, and there is silence. He mutters painfully:*] Say—dey oughter match him—wit Zybszko. He got me, aw right. I'm trou. Even him didn't tink I belonged. [*Then, with sudden passionate despair.*] Christ, where do I get off at? Where do I fit in? [*Checking himself as suddenly.*] Aw, what de hell! No squawkin', see! No quittin', get me! Croak wit your boots on! [*He grabs hold of the bars of the cage and hauls himself painfully to his feet—looks around him bewilderedly —forces a mocking laugh.*] In de cage, huh? [*In the strident tones of a circus barker.*] Ladies and gents, step forward and take a slant at de one and only—[*His voice weakening*]—one and original—Hairy Ape from de wilds of——

[*He slips in a heap on the floor and dies. The monkeys set up a chattering, whimpering wail. And, perhaps, the Hairy Ape at last belongs.*]

CURTAIN

For Discussion and Writing

1. For the first two scenes of this play, Yank, the protagonist, lives unde the illusion that he plays a vital part in society. Why does he think soi In what way do Paddy and Long disagree about their roles in the social order? In your opinion, which of the three comes closest to fact?

2. Why, in Scene Three, is Yank's illusion about his importance in the world shaken by Mildred Douglas? In your opinion, can a man's faith in himself be shaken by such a brief encounter? O'Neill has been criticized for dropping Mildred Douglas from the play after this scene. Do you agree with the playwright or with his critics?

3. In reaction to Mildred and her visit to the stokehole, Yank, in a succession of scenes, tries to

shove church-goers off the sidewalk on Fifth Avenue;
break through the steel bars of his jail cell;
join the I.W.W. as a volunteer bomber;
communicate with a caged gorilla in the zoo.

In each of these attempts, what does he hope to achieve and why does he fail each time? At the beginning of the play Yank considered himself a "successful" coal-stoker, proud of his importance to the operation of the ship. Does he learn anything from his defeats? What is the real tragedy of Yank's life? Do you believe that, in one form or another, all of us are threatened by a similar tragedy?

4. What were your reactions to the final scene where Yank is not only rejected but destroyed when he tries to communicate with a caged gorilla in the zoo? Did this bizarre close strike you as a natural, inevitable ending to Yank's life? If the manner of Yank's final destructrion is symbolic, how do you explain it in terms of the rest of mankind? Are caged gorillas "better off" than the Yanks in this world?

5. Throughout the play, O'Neill uses a cage—either suggested or real— as a symbol. When staged in the theater, the opening scene in the forecastle, with its low ceilings, bars of light, and other stage effects suggests a cage, as does the staging for the stokehole in a later scene, as does the jail scene, which could be either cell or cage. Finally, Yank's life and the play end in a real cage in a zoo. What is the playwright's purpose in using the idea of a cage as the central symbol of his play? Is he implying something about all of our lives as well as Yank's?

6. About the turn of the century, writers began to distrust "realism" as a mode for disclosing the "truth" about life. By the end of the first World War, in an attempt to dramatize the tensions in the sub-conscious mind of the protagonist, playwrights resorted to "expressionistic" distortion of sets, costumes, and all of the other characters. The external world was nc longer depicted objectively or realistically, but subjectively from the poin'

of view of the main character. The more upset by events he became, the more distorted or "expressionistic" became his view of life.

Discuss the scenes and incidents in which O'Neill uses distortion or "expressionism." Does this technique tell us more about Yank than we could learn from a realistic reporting of his experiences?

7. Write a script of the dialogue that might take place between Yank and Mildred if O'Neill had brought them face to face on deck the day after their confrontation in the stokehole.

Or, as an alternative, assume that animals can think, and record the thoughts of the gorilla in the final scene of the play from the time Yank approaches the cage until the two change places and the gorilla shuffles off into the darkness.

The Glass Menagerie

⟨1945⟩

TENNESSEE WILLIAMS

NOBODY, NOT EVEN THE RAIN, HAS SUCH SMALL HANDS.

e. e. cummings

CHARACTERS

AMANDA WINGFIELD [*the mother*]: A little woman of great but confused vitality clinging frantically to another time and place. Her characterization must be carefully created, not copied from type. She is not paranoiac, but her life is paranoia. There is much to admire in Amanda, and as much to love and pity as there is to laugh at. Certainly she has endurance and a kind of heroism, and though her foolishness makes her unwittingly cruel at times, there is tenderness in her slight person.

LAURA WINGFIELD [*her daughter*]: Amanda, having failed to establish contact with reality, continues to live vitally in her illusions, but Laura's situation is even graver. A childhood illness has left her crippled, one leg slightly shorter than the other, and held in a brace. This defect need not be more than suggested on the stage. Stemming from this, Laura's separation increases till she is like a piece of her own glass collection, too exquisitely fragile to move from the shelf.

TOM WINGFIELD [*her son*]: And the narrator of the play. A poet with a job in a warehouse. His nature is not remorseless, but to escape from a trap he has to act without pity.

JIM O'CONNOR [*the gentleman caller*]: A nice, ordinary, young man.

SCENE: *An Alley in St. Louis*

PART I. Preparation for a Gentleman Caller. PART II. The Gentleman calls.

Time: Now and the Past.

*T*he *Glass Menagerie*, first produced in 1945, established the reputation of Tennessee Williams as an important new playwright. In this play he draws each of his characters with accuracy and realism. At the same time, he makes imaginative use of all the devices of the theater—sound, music, lights, movement, symbols to show that theater transcends written language.

The Glass Menagerie, based partially on people and incidents in his own life, was written first as a short story called "Portrait of a Girl in Glass," then as a screenplay called "The Gentleman Caller," which Hollywood turned down. Two years later, as the stage play *The Glass Menagerie*, it won the Drama Critics Circle Award for the best play of the year.

Williams has become one of the most important and controversial writers in the American theater. He is widely produced in Europe and in American universities, where his plays—particularly *The Glass Menagerie*—are part of the curriculum.

Production Notes

Being a "memory play," *The Glass Menagerie* can be presented with unusual freedom of convention. Because of its considerable delicate or tenuous material, atmospheric touches and subtleties of direction play a particularly important part. Expressionism and all other unconventional techniques in drama have only one valid aim, and that is a closer approach to truth. When a play employs unconventional techniques, it is not, or certainly shouldn't be, trying to escape its responsibility of dealing with reality, or interpreting experience, but is actually or should be attempting to find a closer approach, a more penetrating and vivid expression of things as they are. The straight realistic play with its genuine frigidaire and authentic ice-cubes, its characters that speak exactly as its audience speaks, corresponds to the academic landscape and has the same virtue of a photographic likeness. Everyone should know nowadays the unimportance of the photographic in art: that truth, life, or reality is an organic thing which the poetic imagination can represent or suggest, in essence, only through transformation, through changing into other forms than those which were merely present in appearance.

These remarks are not meant as a preface only to this particular play. They have to do with a conception of a new, plastic theatre which must take the place of the exhausted theatre of realistic conventions if the theatre is to resume vitality as a part of our culture.

THE SCREEN DEVICE

There is *only one important difference between the original and acting version of the play* and that is the *omission* in the latter of the device which I tentatively included in my *original* script. This device was the use of a screen on which were projected magic-lantern slides bearing images or titles. I do not regret the omission of this device from the present Broadway production. The extraordinary power of Miss Taylor's performance made it suitable to have the utmost simplicity in the physical production. But I think it may be interesting to some readers to see how this device was conceived. So I am putting it into the published manuscript. These images and legends, projected from behind, were cast on a section of wall between the front-room and dining-room areas, which should be indistinguishable from the rest when not in use.

The purpose of this will probably be apparent. It is to give accent to certain values in each scene. Each scene contains a particular point (or several) which is structurally the most important. In an episodic play, such as this, the basic structure or narrative line may be obscured from the audience; the effect may seem fragmentary rather than architectural. This may not be the fault of the play so much as a lack of attention in the audience. The legend or image upon the screen will strengthen the effect of what is merely allusion in the writing and allow the primary point to be made more simply and lightly than if the entire responsibility were on the spoken lines.

Aside from this structural value, I think the screen will have a definite emotional appeal, less definable but just as important. An imaginative producer or director may invent many other uses for this device than those indicated in the present script. In fact the possibilities of the device seem much larger to me than the instance of this play can possibly utilize.

THE MUSIC

Another extra-literary accent in this play is provided by the use of music. A single recurring tune, "The Glass Menagerie," is used to give emotional emphasis to suitable passages. This tune is like circus music, not when you are on the grounds or in the immediate vicinity of the parade, but when you are at some distance and very likely thinking of something else. It seems under those circumstances to continue almost interminably and it weaves in and out of your preoccupied consciousness; then it is the lightest, most delicate music in the world and perhaps the saddest. It expresses the surface vivacity of life with the underlying strain of immutable and inexpressible sorrow. When you look at a piece of delicately spun glass you think of two things: how beautiful it is and how easily it can be broken. Both of those ideas should be woven into the recurring tune, which dips in and out of the play as if it were carried on a wind that changes. It serves as a thread of connection and allusion between the narrator with his separate point in time and space and the subject of his story. Between each episode it returns as reference to the emotion, nostalgia, which is the first condition of the play. It is primarily LAURA's music and therefore comes out most clearly when the play focuses upon her and the lovely fragility of glass which is her image.

THE LIGHTING

The lighting in the play is not realistic. In keeping with the atmosphere of memory, the stage is dim. Shafts of light are focused on selected areas or actors, sometimes in contradistinction to what is the apparent center. For instance, in the quarrel scene between TOM and AMANDA, in which LAURA has no active part, the clearest pool of light is on her figure. This is also true of the supper scene, when her silent figure on the sofa should remain the visual center. The light upon LAURA should be distinct from the others, having a peculiar pristine clarity such as light used in early religious portraits of female saints or madonnas. A certain correspondence to light in religious paintings, such as El Greco's, where the figures are radiant in atmosphere that is relatively dusky, could be effectively used throughout the play. [It will also permit a more effective use of the screen.] A free, imaginative use of light can be of enormous value in giving a mobile, plastic quality to plays of a more or less static nature.

T. W.

The Glass Menagerie

The *Wingfield apartment is in the rear of the building, one of those vast hive-like conglomerations of cellular living-units that flower as warty growths in overcrowded urban centers of lower middle-class population and are symptomatic of the impulse of this largest and fundamentally enslaved section of American society to avoid fluidity and differentiation and to exist and function as one interfused mass of automatism.*

The apartment faces an alley and is entered by a fire-escape, a structure whose name is a touch of accidental poetic truth, for all of these huge buildings are always burning with the slow and implacable fires of human desperation. The fire-escape is included in the set—that is, the landing of it and steps descending from it.

The scene is memory and is therefore nonrealistic. Memory takes a lot of poetic license. It omits some details; others are exaggerated, according to the emotional value of the articles it touches, for memory is seated predominantly in the heart. The interior is therefore rather dim and poetic.

At the rise of the curtain, the audience is faced with the dark, grim rear wall of the Wingfield tenement. This building, which runs parallel to the footlight, is flanked on both sides by dark, narrow alleys which run into murky canyons of tangled clotheslines, garbage cans and the sinister latticework of neighboring fire-escapes. It is up and down these side alleys that exterior entrances and exits are made, during the play. At the end of TOM's *opening commentary, the dark tenement wall slowly reveals (by means of a transparency) the interior of the ground floor Wingfield apartment.*

Downstage is the living room, which also serves as a sleeping room for LAURA, *the sofa unfolding to make her bed. Upstage, center, and divided by a wide arch or second proscenium with transparent faded portieres (or second curtain), is the dining room. In an old-fashioned what-not in the living room are seen scores of transparent glass animals. A blown-up photograph of the father hangs on the wall of the living room, facing the audience, to the left of the archway. It is the face of a very handsome young man in a doughboy's First World War cap. He is gallantly smiling, ineluctably smiling, as if to say, "I will be smiling forever."*

The audience hears and sees the opening scene in the dining room through both the transparent fourth wall of the building and the transparent gauze portieres of the dining-room arch. It is during this revealing scene that the fourth wall slowly ascends, out of sight. This transparent exterior wall is not brought down again until the very end of the play, during TOM's *final speech. The narrator is an undisguised convention of the play. He takes whatever license with dramatic convention as is convenient to his purposes.*

TOM *enters dressed as a merchant sailor from alley, stage left, and strolls across the front of the stage to the fire-escape. There he stops and lights a cigarette. He addresses the audience.*

TOM. Yes, I have tricks in my pocket, I have things up my sleeve. But I am the opposite of a stage magician. He gives you illusion that has the appearance of truth. I give you truth in the pleasant disguise of illusion.

To begin with, I turn back time. I reverse it to that quaint period, the thirties, when the huge middle class of America was matriculating in a school for the blind. Their eyes had failed them, or they had failed their eyes, and so they were having their fingers pressed forcibly down on the fiery Braille alphabet of a dissolving economy.

In Spain there was revolution. Here there was only shouting and confusion.

In Spain there was Guernica. Here there were disturbances of labor, sometimes pretty violent, in otherwise peaceful cities such as Chicago, Cleveland, Saint Louis . . .

This is the social background of the play.

[MUSIC.]

The play is memory.

Being a memory play, it is dimly lighted, it is sentimental, it is not realistic.

In memory everything seems to happen to music. That explains the fiddle in the wings.

I am the narrator of the play, and also a character in it.

The other characters are my mother, Amanda, my sister, Laura, and a gentleman caller who appears in the final scenes. He is the most realistic character in the play, being an emissary from a world of reality that we were somehow set apart from.

But since I have a poet's weakness for symbols, I am using this character also as a symbol; he is the long delayed but always expected something that we live for.

There is a fifth character in the play who doesn't appear except in this larger-than-life-size photograph over the mantel.

This is our father who left us a long time ago.

He was a telephone man who fell in love with long distances; he gave up his job with the telephone company and skipped the light fantastic out of town . . .

The last we heard of him was a picture post-card from Mazatlan, on the Pacific coast of Mexico, containing a message of two words—

"Hello— Good-bye!" and no address.

I think the rest of the play will explain itself. . . .

[AMANDA's *voice becomes audible through the portieres.*]

[LEGEND ON SCREEN: "OU SONT LES NEIGES."]

[*He divides the portieres and enters the upstage area.*]

[AMANDA *and* LAURA *are seated at a drop-leaf table. Eating is indicated by gestures without food or utensils.* AMANDA *faces the audience.* TOM *and* LAURA *are seated in profile.*]

[*The interior has lit up softly and through the scrim we see* AMANDA *and* LAURA *seated at the table in the upstage area.*]

AMANDA. [*Calling.*] Tom?

TOM. Yes, Mother.

AMANDA. We can't say grace until you come to the table!

TOM. Coming, Mother. [*He bows slightly and withdraws, reappearing a few moments later in his place at the table.*]

AMANDA. [*To her son.*] Honey, don't push with your fingers. If you have to push with something, the thing to push with is a crust of bread. And chew—chew! Animals have sections in their stomachs which enable them to digest food without mastication, but human beings are supposed to chew their food before they swallow it down. Eat food leisurely, son, and really enjoy it. A well-cooked meal has lots of delicate flavors that have to be held in the mouth for appreciation. So chew your food and give your salivary glands a chance to function!

[TOM *deliberately lays his imaginary fork down and pushes his chair back from the table.*]

TOM. I haven't enjoyed one bite of this dinner because of your constant directions on how to eat it. It's you that make me rush through meals with your hawk-like attention to every bite I take. Sickening—spoils my appetite—all this discussion of—animals' secretion—salivary glands—mastication!

AMANDA. [*Lightly.*] Temperament like a Metropolitan star! [*He rises and crosses downstage.*] You're not excused from the table.

TOM. I'm getting a cigarette.

AMANDA. You smoke too much.

[LAURA *rises.*]

LAURA. I'll bring in the blanc mange.

[*He remains standing with his cigarette by the portieres during the following.*]

AMANDA. [*Rising.*] No, sister, no, sister —you be the lady this time and I'll be the darky.

LAURA. I'm already up.

AMANDA. Resume your seat, little sister —I want you to stay fresh and pretty—for gentlemen callers!

LAURA. I'm not expecting any gentlemen callers.

AMANDA. [*Crossing out to kitchenette. Airily.*] Sometimes they come when they are least expected! Why, I remember one Sunday afternoon in Blue Mountain— [*Enters kitchenette.*]

TOM. I know what's coming!

LAURA. Yes. But let her tell it.

TOM. Again?

LAURA. She loves to tell it.

[AMANDA *returns with bowl of dessert.*]

AMANDA. One Sunday afternoon in Blue Mountain—your mother received—*seventeen!*—gentlemen callers! Why, sometimes there weren't chairs enough to accommodate them all. We had to send the nigger over to bring in folding chairs from the parish house.

TOM. [*Remaining at portieres.*] How did you entertain those gentlemen callers?

AMANDA. I understood the art of conversation!

TOM. I bet you could talk.

AMANDA. Girls in those days *knew* how to talk, I can tell you.

TOM. Yes?

IMAGE: AMANDA AS A GIRL ON A PORCH, GREETING CALLERS.]

AMANDA. They knew how to entertain their gentlemen callers. It wasn't enough for a girl to be possessed of a pretty face and a graceful figure—although I wasn't slighted in either respect. She also needed to have a nimble wit and a tongue to meet all occasions.

TOM. What did you talk about?

AMANDA. Things of importance going on in the world! Never anything coarse or common or vulgar. [*She addresses* TOM *as though he were seated in the vacant chair at the table though he remains by portieres. He plays this scene as though he held the book.*] My callers were gentlemen—all! Among my callers were some of the most prominent young planters of the Mississippi Delta—planters and sons of planters!

[TOM *motions for music and a spot of light on* AMANDA.]

]*Her eyes lift, her face glows, her voice becomes rich and elegiac.*]

[SCREEN LEGEND: "OU SONT LES NEIGES."]

There was young Champ Laughlin who later became vice-president of the Delta Planters Bank.

Hadley Stevenson who was drowned in Moon Lake and left his widow one hundred and fifty thousand in Government bonds.

There were the Cutrere brothers, Wesley and Bates. Bates was one of my bright particular beaux! He got in a quarrel with that wild Wainwright boy. They shot it out on the floor of Moon Lake Casino. Bates was shot through the stomach. Died in the ambulance on his way to Memphis. His widow was also well-provided for, came into eight or ten thousand acres, that's all. She married him on the rebound —never loved her—carried my picture on him the night he died!

And there was that boy that every girl in the Delta had set her cap for! That beautiful, brilliant young Fitzhugh boy from Greene County!

TOM. What did he leave his widow?

AMANDA. He never married! Gracious,

you talk as though all of my old admirers had turned up their toes to the daisies!

TOM. Isn't this the first you've mentioned that still survives?

AMANDA. That Fitzhugh boy went North and made a fortune—came to be known as the Wolf of Wall Street! He had the Midas touch, whatever he touched turned to gold! And I could have been Mrs. Duncan J. Fitzhugh, mind you! But—I picked your *father!*

LAURA. [*Rising.*] Mother, let me clear the table.

AMANDA. No, dear, you go in front and study your typewriter chart. Or practice your shorthand a little. Stay fresh and pretty!—It's almost time for our gentlemen callers to start arriving. [*She flounces girlishly toward the kitchenette.*] How many do you suppose we're going to entertain this afternoon?

[TOM *throws down the paper and jumps up with a groan.*]

LAURA. [*Alone in the dining room.*]

I don't believe we're going to receive any, Mother.

AMANDA. [*Reappearing, airily.*] What? No one—not one? You must be joking! [LAURA *nervously echoes her laugh. She slips in a fugitive manner through the half-open portieres and draws them gently behind her. A shaft of very clear light is thrown on her face against the faded tapestry of the curtains.* MUSIC: "THE GLASS MENAGERIE" UNDER FAINTLY. *Lightly.*] Not one gentleman caller? It can't be true! There must be a flood, there must have been a tornado!

LAURA. It isn't a flood, it's not a tornado, Mother. I'm just not popular like you were in Blue Mountain. . . . [TOM *utters another groan.* LAURA *glances at him with a faint, apologetic smile. Her voice catching a little.*] Mother's afraid I'm going to be an old maid.

THE SCENE DIMS OUT WITH "GLASS MENAGERIE" MUSIC

SCENE 2

"Laura, Haven't You Ever Liked Some Boy?"
On the dark stage the screen is lighted with the image of blue roses.
Gradually LAURA'S *figure becomes apparent and the screen goes out.*
The music subsides.
LAURA *is seated in the delicate ivory chair at the small claw-foot table.*
She wears a dress of soft violet material for a kimono—her hair tied back from her forehead with a ribbon.
She is washing and polishing her collection of glass.
AMANDA *appears on the fire-escape steps. At the sound of her ascent,* LAURA *catches her breath, thrusts the bowl of ornaments away and seats herself stiffly before the diagram of the typewriter keyboard as though it held her spellbound.*
Something has happened to AMANDA. *It is written in her face as she climbs to the landing: a look that is grim and hopeless and a little absurd.*
She has on one of those cheap or imitation velvety-looking cloth coats with imitation fur collar. Her hat is five or six years old, one of those dreadful cloche hats that were worn in the late twenties and she is clasping an enormous black patent-leather pocketbook with nickel clasps and initials. This is her full-dress outfit, the one she usually wears to the D.A.R.
Before entering she looks through the door.
She purses her lips, opens her eyes very wide, rolls them upward and shakes her head.

408 TENNESSEE WILLIAMS

Then she slowly lets herself in the door. Seeing her mother's expression LAURA *touches her lips with a nervous gesture.*

LAURA. Hello, Mother, I was— [*She makes a nervous gesture toward the chart on the wall.* AMANDA *leans against the shut door and stares at* LAURA *with a martyred look.*]

AMANDA. Deception? Deception? [*She slowly removes her hat and gloves, continuing the sweet suffering stare. She lets the hat and gloves fall on the floor—a bit of acting.*]

LAURA. [*Shakily.*] How was the D.A.R. meeting? [AMANDA *slowly opens her purse and removes a dainty white handkerchief which she shakes out delicately and delicately touches to her lips and nostrils.*] Didn't you go to the D.A.R. meeting, Mother?

AMANDA. [*Faintly, almost inaudibly.*] —No.—No. [*Then more forcibly.*] I did not have the strength—to go to the D.A.R. In fact, I did not have the courage! I wanted to find a hole in the ground and hide myself in it forever! [*She crosses slowly to the wall and removes the diagram of the typewriter keyboard. She holds it in front of her for a second, staring at it sweetly and sorrowfully—then bites her lips and tears it in two pieces.*]

LAURA. [*Faintly.*] Why did you do that, Mother? [AMANDA *repeats the same procedure with the chart of the Gregg Alphabet.*] Why are you—

AMANDA. Why? Why? How old are you, Laura?

LAURA. Mother, you know my age.

AMANDA. I thought that you were an adult; it seems that I was mistaken. [*She crosses slowly to the sofa and sinks down and stares at* LAURA.]

LAURA. Please don't stare at me, Mother. [AMANDA *closes her eyes and lowers her head. Count ten.*]

AMANDA. What are we going to do, what is going to become of us, what is the future?

[*Count ten.*]

LAURA. Has something happened, Mother? [AMANDA *draws a long breath and takes out the handkerchief again. Dabbing process.*] Mother, has—something happened?

AMANDA. I'll be all right in a minute, I'm just bewildered—[*Count five.*]—by life. . . .

LAURA. Mother, I wish that you would tell me what's happened!

AMANDA. As you know, I was supposed to be inducted into my office at the D.A.R. this afternoon. [IMAGE: A SWARM OF TYPE-WRITERS.] But I stopped off at Rubicam's business college to speak to your teachers about your having a cold and ask them what progress they thought you were making down there.

LAURA. Oh. . . .

AMANDA. I went to the typing instructor and introduced myself as your mother. She didn't know who you were. Wingfield, she said. We don't have any such student enrolled at the school!

I assured her she did, that you had been going to classes since early in January.

"I wonder," she said, "if you could be talking about that terribly shy little girl who dropped out of school after only a few days' attendance?"

"No," I said, "Laura, my daughter, has been going to school every day for the past six weeks!"

"Excuse me," she said. She took the attendance book out and there was your name, unmistakably printed, and all the dates you were absent until they decided that you had dropped out of school.

I still said, "No, there must have been some mistake! There must have been some mix-up in the records!"

And she said, "No—I remember her perfectly now. Her hands shook so that she couldn't hit the right keys! The first time we gave a speed-test, she broke down completely—was sick at the stomach and almost had to be carried into the wash-room! After that morning she never showed up any more. We phoned the house but never got any answer—while I was working at Famous and Barr, I suppose, demonstrating those— Oh!"

I felt so weak I could barely keep on my feet!

I had to sit down while they got me a glass of water!

Fifty dollars' tuition, all of our plans—my hopes and ambitions for you—just gone up the spout, just gone up the spout like that. [LAURA *draws a long breath and gets awkwardly to her feet. She crosses to the victrola and winds it up.*] What are you doing?

LAURA. Oh! [*She releases the handle and returns to her seat.*]

AMANDA. Laura, where have you been going when you've gone out pretending that you were going to business college?

LAURA. I've just been going out walking.

AMANDA. That's not true.

LAURA. It is. I just went walking.

AMANDA. Walking? Walking? In winter? Deliberately courting pneumonia in that light coat Where did you walk to, Laura?

LAURA. All sorts of places—mostly in the park.

AMANDA. Even after you'd started catching that cold?

LAURA. It was the lesser of two evils, Mother. [IMAGE: WINTER SCENE IN PARK.] I couldn't go back up. I—threw up—on the floor!

AMANDA. From half past seven till after five every day you mean to tell me you walked around in the park, because you wanted to make me think that you were still going to Rubicam's Business College?

LAURA. It wasn't as bad as it sounds. I went inside places to get warmed up.

AMANDA. Inside where?

LAURA. I went in the art museum and the bird-houses at the Zoo. I visited the penguins every day! Sometimes I did without lunch and went to the movies. Lately I've been spending most of my afternoons in the Jewel-box, that big glass house where they raise the tropical flowers.

AMANDA. You did all this to deceive me, just for deception? [LAURA *looks down.*] Why?

LAURA. Mother, when you're disappointed, you get that awful suffering look on your face, like the picture of Jesus' mother in the museum!

AMANDA. Hush!

LAURA. I couldn't face it.

[*Pause. A whisper of strings.*]

[LEGEND: "THE CRUST OF HUMILITY."]

AMANDA. [*Hopelessly fingering the huge pocketbook.*] So what are we going to do the rest of our lives? Stay home and watch the parades go by? Amuse ourselves with the glass menagerie, darling? Eternally play those worn-out phonograph records

your father left as a painful reminder of him?

We won't have a business career—we've given that up because it gave us nervous indigestion! [*Laughs wearily.*] What is there left but dependency all our lives? I know so well what becomes of unmarried women who aren't prepared to occupy a position. I've seen such pitiful cases in the South—barely tolerated spinsters living upon the grudging patronage of sister's husband or brother's wife!—stuck away in some little mousetrap of a room—encouraged by one in-law to visit another—little birdlike women without any nest—eating the crust of humility all their life!

Is that the future that we've mapped out for ourselves?

I swear it's the only alternative I can think of!

It isn't a very pleasant alternative, is it? Of course—some girls do *marry*.

[LAURA *twists her hands nervously.*]

Haven't you ever liked some boy?

LAURA. Yes. I liked one once. [*Rises.*] I came across his picture a while ago.

AMANDA. [*With some interest.*] He gave you his picture?

LAURA. No, it's in the year-book.

AMANDA. [*Disappointed.*] Oh—a high-school boy.

[SCREEN IMAGE: JIM AS HIGH-SCHOOL HERO BEARING A SILVER CUP.]

LAURA. Yes. His name was Jim. [LAURA *lifts the heavy annual from the claw-foot table.*] Here he is in the The Pirates of Penzance.

AMANDA. [*Absently.*] The what?

LAURA. The operetta the senior class put on. He had a wonderful voice and we sat across the aisle from each other Mondays, Wednesdays and Fridays in the Aud. Here he is with the silver cup for debating! See his grin?

AMANDA. [*Absently.*] He must have had a jolly disposition.

LAURA. He used to call me—Blue Roses.

[IMAGE: BLUE ROSES.]

AMANDA. Why did he call you such a name as that?

LAURA. When I had that attack of pleurosis—he asked me what was the matter when I came back. I said pleurosis—he thought that I said Blue Roses! So that's what he always called me after that.

Whenever he saw me, he'd holler, "Hello, Blue Roses!" I didn't care for the girl that he went out with. Emily Meisenbach. Emily was the best-dressed girl at Soldan. She never struck me, though, as being sincere . . . It says in the Personal Section —they're engaged. That's—six years ago! They must be married by now.

AMANDA. Girls that aren't cut out for business careers usually wind up married to some nice man. [*Gets up with a spark of revival.*] Sister, that's what you'll do!

[LAURA *utters a startled, doubtful laugh. She reaches quickly for a piece of glass.*]

LAURA. But, Mother—

AMANDA. Yes? [*Crossing to photograph.*]

LAURA. [*In a tone of frightened apology.*] I'm —cripped!

[IMAGE: SCREEN.]

AMANDA. Nonsense! Laura, I've told you never, never to use that word. Why, you're not crippled, you just have a little defect —hardly noticeable, even! When people have some slight disadvantage like that, they cultivate other things to make up for it—develop charm—and vivacity—and—charm! That's all you have to do! [*She turns again to the photograph.*] One thing your father had *plenty of*—was *charm!*

[TOM *motions to the fiddle in the wings.*]

THE SCENE FADES OUT WITH MUSIC

SCENE 3

LEGEND ON SCREEN: "AFTER THE FIASCO—"
TOM *speaks from the fire-escape landing.*

TOM. After the fiasco at Rubicam's Business College, the idea of getting a gentleman caller for Laura began to play a more and more important part in Mother's calculations.

It became an obsession. Like some archetype of the universal unconscious, the image of the gentleman caller haunted our small apartment. . . .

(IMAGE: YOUNG MAN AT DOOR WITH FLOWERS.]

An evening at home rarely passed without some allusion to this image, this spectre, this hope. . . .

Even when he wasn't mentioned, his presence hung in Mother's preoccupied look and in my sister's frightened, apologetic manner—hung like a sentence passed upon the Wingfields!

Mother was a woman of action as well as words.

She began to take logical steps in the planned direction.

Late that winter and in the early spring —realizing that extra money would be needed to properly feather the nest and plume the bird—she conducted a vigorous campaign on the telephone, roping in subscribers to one of those magazines for matrons called *The Home-maker's Companion*, the type of journal that features

the serialized sublimations of ladies of letters who think in terms of delicate cup-like breasts, slim, tapering waists, rich, creamy thighs, eyes like wood-smoke in autumn, fingers that soothe and caress like strains of music, bodies as powerful as Etruscan sculpture.

[SCREEN IMAGE: GLAMOR MAGAZINE COVER.]

[AMANDA *enters with phone on long extension cord. She is spotted in the dim stage.*]

AMANDA. Ida Scott? This is Amanda Wingfield!

We *missed* you at the D.A.R. last Monday!

I said to myself: She's probably suffering with that sinus condition! How is that sinus condition?

Horrors! Heavens have mercy—You're a Christian martyr, yes, that's what you are, a Christian martyr!

Well, I just now happened to notice that your subscription to the *Companion's* about to expire! Yes, it expires with the next issue, honey!—just when that wonderful new serial by Bessie Mae Hopper is getting off to such an exciting start. Oh, honey, it's something that you can't miss! You remember how *Gone With the Wind* took everybody by storm? You simply couldn't go out if you hadn't read it. All everybody *talked* was Scarlet O'Hara. Well, this is a book that critics already compare to *Gone With the Wind*. It's the *Gone With the Wind* of the post-World War generation!—What?—Burning?—Oh, honey, don't let them burn, go take a look in the oven and I'll hold the wire! Heavens —I think she's hung up!

DIM OUT

[LEGEND ON SCREEN: "YOU THINK I'M IN LOVE WITH CONTINENTAL SHOE-MAKERS?"]

[Before the stage is lighted, the violent voices of TOM and AMANDA are heard.]

[They are quarreling behind the portieres. In front of them stands LAURA with clenched hands and panicky expression.]

[A clear pool of light on her figure throughout this scene.]

TOM. What in Christ's name am I—

AMANDA. [Shrilly.] Don't you use that—

TOM. Supposed to do!

AMANDA. Expression! Not in my—

TOM. Ohhh!

AMANDA. Presence! Have you gone out of your senses?

TOM. I have, that's true, *driven* out!

AMANDA. What is matter with you, you —big—big—IDIOT!

TOM. Look!—I've got *no thing*, no single thing—

AMANDA. Lower your voice!

TOM. In my life here that I can call my OWN! Everything is—

AMANDA. Stop that shouting!

TOM. Yesterday you confiscated my books! You had the nerve to—

AMANDA. I took that horrible novel back to the library—yes! That hideous book by that insane Mr. Lawrence. [TOM *laughs wildly.*] I cannot control the output of diseased minds or people who cater to them— [TOM *laughs still more wildly.*] BUT I WON'T ALLOW SUCH FILTH BROUGHT INTO MY HOUSE! No, no, no, no, no!

TOM. House, house! Who pays rent on it, who makes a slave of himself to—

AMANDA. [Fairly screeching.] Don't you DARE to—

TOM. No, no, *I* mustn't say things! *I've* got to just—

AMANDA. Let me tell you—

TOM. I don't want to hear any more!

[He tears the portieres open. The up-stage area is lit with a turgid smoky red glow.]

[AMANDA's *hair is in metal curlers and she wears a very old bathrobe, much too large for her slight figure, a relic of the faithless Mr. Wingfield.*]

[An upright typewriter and a wild disarray of manuscripts are on the drop-leaf table. The quarrel was probably precipitated by AMANDA's interruption of his creative labor. A chair lying overthrown on the floor.]

[Their gesticulating shadows are cast on the ceiling by the fiery glow.]

AMANDA. You *will* hear more, you—

TOM. No, I won't hear more, I'm going out!

AMANDA. You come right back in—

TOM. Out, out, out! Because I'm—

AMANDA. Come back here, Tom Wingfield! I'm not through talking to you!

TOM. Oh, go—

LAURA. [Desperately.]—Tom!

AMANDA. You're going to listen, and no more insolence from you! I'm at the end of my patience!

[He comes back toward her.]

TOM. What do you think I'm at? Aren't I supposed to have any patience to reach the end of, Mother? I know, I know. It seems unimportant to you, what I'm *doing* —what I *want* to do—having a little *difference* between them! You don't think that—

AMANDA. I think you've been doing things that you're ashamed of. That's why you act like this. I don't believe that you go every night to the movies. Nobody goes to the movies night after night. Nobody in their right mind goes to the movies as often as you pretend to. People don't go to the movies at nearly midnight, and movies don't let out at two A.M. Come in stumbling. Muttering to yourself like a maniac! You get three hours' sleep and then go to work. Oh, I can picture the way you're doing down there. Moping, doping, because you're in no condition.

TOM. [Wildly.] No, I'm in no condition!

AMANDA. What right have you got to jeopardize your job? Jeopardize the security of us all? How do you think we'd manage if you were—

TOM. Listen! You think I'm crazy *about* the *warehouse*? [He bends fiercely toward her slight figure.] You think I'm in love with the Continental Shoemakers? You think I want to spend fifty-five *years* down there in that—*celotex interior!* with—*fluorescent—tubes!* Look! I'd rather somebody picked up a crowbar and battered out my brains—than go back mornings! I *go!* Every time you come in yelling that God damn "*Rise and Shine!*" "*Rise and Shine!*" I say to myself, "How *lucky dead* people are!" But I get up. I *go!* For sixty-five dollars a month I give up all that I dream of doing and being *ever!* And you say self—*self's* all I ever think of. Why, listen, if self is what I thought of, Mother, I'd be where he is—GONE! [*Pointing to father's picture.*] As far as the system of transportation reaches! [*He starts past her. She grabs his arm.*] Don't grab at me, Mother!

AMANDA. Where are you going?

TOM. I'm going to the *movies!*

AMANDA. I don't believe that lie!

TOM. [*Crouching toward her, overtowering her tiny figure. She backs away, gasping.*] I'm going to opium dens! Yes, opium dens, dens of vice and criminals' hangouts, Mother. I've joined the Hogan gang, I'm a hired assassin, I carry a tommy-gun in a violin case! I run a string of cat-houses in the Valley! They call me Killer, Killer Wingfield, I'm leading a double-life, a simple, honest warehouse worker by day, by night a dynamic *czar* of the *underworld,* Mother. I go to gambling casinos, I spin away fortunes on the roulette table! I wear a patch over one eye and a false mustache, sometimes I put on green whiskers. On those occasions they call me—*El Diablo!* Oh, I could tell you things to make you sleepless! My enemies plan to dynamite this place. They're going to blow us all sky-high some night! I'll be glad, very happy, and so will you! You'll go up, on a broomstick, over Blue Mountain with seventeen gentlemen callers! You ugly—babbling old—*witch.* . . . [*He goes through a series of violent, clumsy movements, seizing his overcoat, lunging to the door, pulling it fiercely open. The women watch him, aghast. His arm catches in the sleeve of the coat as he struggles to pull it on. For a moment he is pinioned by the bulky garment. With an outraged groan he tears the coat off again, splitting the shoulder of it, and hurls it across the room. It strikes against the shelf of* LAURA's *glass collection, there is a tinkle of shattering glass.* LAURA *cries out as if wounded.*]

[MUSIC. LEGEND: "THE GLASS MENAGERIE."]

LAURA. [*Shrilly.*] My glass!—menagerie. . . . [*She covers her face and turns away.*]

[*But* AMANDA *is still stunned and stupefied by the "ugly witch" so that she barely notices this occurrence. Now she recovers her speech.*]

AMANDA. [*In an awful voice.*] I won't speak to you—until you apologize! [*She crosses through portieres and draws them together behind her.* TOM *is left with* LAURA. LAURA *clings weakly to the mantel with her face averted.* TOM *stares at her stupidly for a moment. Then he crosses to shelf. Drops awkwardly on his knees to collect the fallen glass, glancing at* LAURA *as if he would speak but couldn't.*]

"The Glass Menagerie" steals in as

THE SCENE DIMS OUT

SCENE 4

The interior is dark. Faint light in the alley.
A deep-voiced bell in a church is tolling the hour of five as the scene commences.
TOM *appears at the top of the alley. After each solemn boom of the bell in the tower, he shakes a little noise-maker or rattle as if to express the tiny spasm of man in contrast to the sustained power and dignity of the Almighty. This and the unsteadiness of his advance make it evident that he has been drinking.*
As he climbs the few steps to the fire-escape landing light steals up inside. LAURA *appears in night-dress, observing* TOM's *empty bed in the front room.*

TOM *fishes in his pockets for door-key, removing a motley assortment of articles in the search, including a perfect shower of movie-ticket stubs and an empty bottle. At last he finds the key, but just as he is about to insert it, it slips from his fingers. He strikes a match and crouches below the door.*

TOM. [*Bitterly.*] One crack—and it falls through!

[LAURA *opens the door.*]

LAURA. Tom! Tom, what are you doing?

TOM. Looking for a door-key.

LAURA. Where have you been all this time?

TOM. I have been to the movies.

LAURA. All this time at the movies?

TOM. There was a very long program. There was a Garbo picture and a Mickey Mouse and a travelogue and a newsreel and a preview of coming attractions. And there was an organ solo and a collection for the milk-fund — simultaneously — which ended up in a terrible fight between a fat lady and an usher!

LAURA. [*Innocently.*] Did you have to stay through everything?

TOM. Of course! And, oh, I forgot! There was a big stage show! The headliner on this stage show was Malvolio the Magician. He performed wonderful tricks, many of them, such as pouring water back and forth between pitchers. First it turned to wine and then it turned to beer and then it turned to whiskey. I know it was whiskey it finally turned into because he needed somebody to come up out of the audience to help him, and I came up—both shows! It was Kentucky Straight Bourbon. A very generous fellow, he gave souvenirs. [*He pulls from his pack pocket a shimmering rainbow-colored scarf.*] He gave me this. This is his magic scarf. You can have it, Laura. You wave it over a canary cage and you get a bowl of gold-fish. You wave it over the gold-fish bowl and they fly away canaries. . . . But the wonderfullest trick of all was the coffin trick. We nailed him into a coffin and he got out of the coffin without removing one nail. [*He has come inside.*] There is a trick that would come in handy for me—get me out of this 2 by 4 situation! [*Flops onto bed and starts removing shoes.*]

LAURA. Tom—Shhh!

TOM. What're you shushing me for?

LAURA. You'll wake Mother.

TOM. Goody, goody! Pay 'er back for all those "Rise an' Shines." [*Lies down, groaning.*] You know it don't take much intelligence to get yourself into a nailed-up coffin, Laura. But who in hell ever got himself out of one without removing one nail?

[*As if in answer, the father's grinning photograph lights up.*]

SCENE DIMS OUT

[*Immediately following: The church bell is heard striking six. At the sixth stroke the alarm clock goes off in* AMANDA'S *room, and after a few moments we hear her calling: "Rise and Shine! Rise and Shine! Laura, go tell your brother to rise and shine!"*]

TOM. [*Sitting up slowly.*] I'll rise—but I won't shine.

[*The light increases.*]

AMANDA. Laura, tell your brother his coffee is ready.

[LAURA *slips into front room.*]

LAURA. Tom!—It's nearly seven. Don't make Mother nervous. [*He stares at her stupidly. Beseechingly.*] Tom, speak to Mother this morning. Make up with her, apologize, speak to her!

TOM. She won't to me. It's her that started not speaking.

LAURA. If you just say you're sorry she'll start speaking.

TOM. Her not speaking—is that such a tragedy?

LAURA. Please—please!

AMANDA. [*Calling from kitchenette.*] Laura, are you going to do what I asked you to do, or do I have to get dressed and go out myself?

LAURA. Going, going—soon as I get on my coat! [*She pulls on a shapeless felt hat with nervous, jerky movement, pleadingly glancing at* TOM. *Rushes awkwardly for coat. The coat is one of* AMANDA'S *inaccurately made-over, the sleeves too short for* LAURA.] Butter and what else?

AMANDA. [*Entering upstage.*] Just butter. Tell them to charge it.

LAURA. Mother, they make such faces when I do that.

AMANDA. Sticks and stones can break

our bones, but the expression on Mr. Garfinkel's face won't harm us! Tell your brother his coffee is getting cold.

LAURA. [*At door.*] Do what I asked you, will you, will you, Tom?

[*He looks sullenly away.*]

AMANDA. Laura, go now or just don't go at all!

LAURA. [*Rushing out.*] Going—going! [*A second later she cries out.* TOM *springs up and crosses to door.* AMANDA *rushes anxiously in.* TOM *opens the door.*]

TOM. Laura?

LAURA. I'm all right. I slipped, but I'm all right.

AMANDA. [*Peering anxiously after her.*] If anyone breaks a leg on those fire-escape steps, the landlord ought to be sued for every cent he possesses! [*She shuts door. Remembers she isn't speaking and returns to other room.*]

[*As* TOM *enters listlessly for his coffee, she turns her back to him and stands rigidly facing the window on the gloomy gray vault of the areaway. Its light on her face with its aged but childish features is cruelly sharp, satirical as a Daumier print.*]

[MUSIC UNDER: "AVE MARIA."]

[TOM *glances sheepishly but sullenly at her averted figure and slumps at the table. The coffee is scalding hot; he sips it and gasps and spits it back in the cup. At his gasp,* AMANDA *catches her breath and half turns. Then catches herself and turns back to window.*]

[TOM *blows on his coffee, glancing sidewise at his mother. She clears her throat.* TOM *clears his. He starts to rise. Sinks back down again, scratches his head, clears his throat again.* AMANDA *coughs.* TOM *raises his cup in both hands to blow on it, his eyes staring over the rim of it at his mother for several moments. Then he slowly sets the cup down and awkwardly and hesitantly rises from the chair.*]

TOM. [*Hoarsely.*] Mother. I—I apologize, Mother. [AMANDA *draws a quick, shuddering breath. Her face works grotesquely. She breaks into childlike tears.*] I'm sorry for what I said, for everything that I said, I didn't mean it.

AMANDA. [*Sobbingly.*] My devotion has made me a witch and so I make myself hateful to my children!

TOM. *No,* you *don't.*

AMANDA. I worry so much, don't sleep, it makes me nervous!

TOM. [*Gently.*] I understand that.

AMANDA. I've had to put up a solitary battle all these years. But you're my right-hand bower! Don't fall down, don't fail!

TOM. [*Gently.*] I try, Mother.

AMANDA. [*With great enthusiasm.*] Try and you will SUCCEED! [*The notion makes her breathless.*] Why, you—you're just *full* of natural endowments! Both of my children—they're *unusual* children! Don't you think I know it? I'm so—*proud!* Happy and —feel I've—so much to be thankful for but— Promise me one thing, Son!

TOM. What, Mother?

AMANDA. Promise, son, you'll—never be a drunkard!

TOM. [*Turns to her grinning.*] I will never be a drunkard, Mother.

AMANDA. That's what frightened me so, that you'd be drinking! Eat a bowl of Purina!

TOM. Just coffee, Mother.

AMANDA. Shredded wheat biscuit?

TOM. No. No, Mother, just coffee.

AMANDA. You can't put in a day's work on an empty stomach. You've got ten minutes—don't gulp! Drinking too-hot liquids makes cancer of the stomach. . . . Put cream in.

TOM. No, thank you.

AMANDA. To cool it.

TOM. No! No, thank you, I want it black.

AMANDA. I know, but it's not good for you. We have to do all that we can to build ourselves up. In these trying times we live in, all that we have to cling to is —each other. . . . That's why it's so important to— Tom, I— I sent out your sister so I could discuss something with you. If you hadn't spoken I would have spoken to you. [*Sits down.*]

TOM. [*Gently.*] What is it, Mother, that you want to discuss?

AMANDA. *Laura!*

[TOM *puts his cup down slowly.*]

[LEGEND ON SCREEN: "LAURA."]

[MUSIC: "THE GLASS MENAGERIE."]

TOM. —Oh.—Laura . . .

AMANDA. [*Touching his sleeve.*] You know how Laura is. So quiet but—still water runs deep! She notices things and I think she—broods about them. [TOM *looks up.*] A few days ago I came in and she was crying.

TOM. What about?

AMANDA. You.

TOM. Me?

AMANDA. She has an idea that you're not happy here.

TOM. What gave her that idea?

AMANDA. What gives her any idea? However, you do act strangely. I—I'm not criticizing, understand *that!* I know your ambitions do not lie in the warehouse, that like everybody in the whole wide world —you've had to—make sacrifices, but—Tom —Tom—life's not easy, it calls for—Spartan endurance! There's so many things in my heart that I cannot describe to you! I've never told you but I—*loved* your father. . . .

TOM. [*Gently.*] I know that, Mother.

AMANDA. And you—when I see you taking after his ways! Staying out late—and— well, you *had* been drinking the night you were in that—terrifying condition! Laura says that you hate the apartment and that you go out nights to get away from it! Is that true, Tom?

TOM. No. You say there's so much in your heart that you can't describe to me. That's true of me, too. There's so much in my heart that I can't describe to *you!* So let's respect each other's—

AMANDA. But, why—*why,* Tom—are you always so *restless?* Where do you *go* to, nights?

TOM. I—go to the movies.

AMANDA. Why do you go to the movies so much, Tom?

TOM. I go to the movies because—I like adventure. Adventure is something I don't have much of at work, so I go to the movies.

AMANDA. But, Tom, you go to the movies *entirely* too *much!*

TOM. I like a lot of adventure.

[AMANDA *looks baffled, then hurt. As the familiar inquisition resumes he becomes hard and impatient again.* AMANDA *slips back into her querulous attitude toward him.*]

[IMAGE ON SCREEN: SAILING VESSEL WITH JOLLY ROGER.]

AMANDA. Most young men find adventure in their careers.

TOM. Then most young men are not employed in a warehouse.

AMANDA. The world is full of young men employed in warehouses and offices and factories.

TOM. Do all of them find adventure in their careers?

AMANDA. They do or they do without it! Not everybody has a craze for adventure.

TOM. Man is by instinct a lover, a hunter, a fighter, and none of those instincts are given much play at the warehouse!

AMANDA. Man is by instinct! Don't quote instinct to me! Instinct is something that people have got away from! It belongs to animals! Christian adults don't want it!

TOM. What do Christian adults want, then, Mother?

AMANDA. Superior things! Things of the mind and the spirit! Only animals have to satisfy instincts! Surely your aims are somewhat higher than theirs! Than monkeys—pigs—

TOM. I reckon they're not.

AMANDA. You're joking. However, that isn't what I wanted to discuss.

TOM. [*Rising.*] I haven't much time.

AMANDA. [*Pushing his shoulders.*] Sit down.

TOM. You want me to punch in red at the warehouse, Mother?

AMANDA. You have five minutes. I want to talk about Laura.

[LEGEND: "PLANS AND PROVISIONS."]

TOM. All right! What about Laura?

AMANDA. We have to be making some plans and provisions for her. She's older than you, two years, and nothing has happened. She just drifts along doing nothing. It frightens me terribly how she just drifts along.

TOM. I guess she's the type that people call home girls.

AMANDA. There's no such type, and if there is, it's a pity! That is unless the home is hers, with a husband!

TOM. What?

AMANDA. Oh, I can see the handwriting on the wall as plain as I see the nose in front of my face! It's terrifying! More and more you remind me of your father! He was out all hours without explanation!—Then *left!* Good-bye!

And me with the bag to hold. I saw that letter you got from the Merchant Marine. I know what you're dreaming of. I'm not standing here blindfolded.

Very well, then. Then *do* it!
But not till there's somebody to take your place.

TOM. What do you mean?

AMANDA. I mean that as soon as Laura has got somebody to take care of her, married, a home of her own, independent— why, then you'll be free to go wherever you please, on land, on sea, whichever way the wind blows you!
But until that time you've got to look out for your sister. I don't say me because I'm old and don't matter! I say for your sister because she's young and dependent.
I put her in business college—a dismal failure! Frightened her so it made her sick at the stomach.
I took her over to the Young People's League at the church. Another fiasco. She spoke to nobody, nobody spoke to her. Now all she does is fool with those pieces of glass and play those worn-out records. What kind of a life is that for a girl to lead?

TOM. What can I do about it?

AMANDA. Overcome selfishness!
Self, self, self is all that you ever think of!

[TOM *springs up and crosses to get his coat. It is ugly and bulky. He pulls on a cap with earmuffs.*]

Where is your muffler? Put your wool muffler on! [*He snatches it angrily from the closet and tosses it around his neck and pulls both ends tight.*] Tom! I haven't said what I had in mind to ask you.

TOM. I'm too late to—

AMANDA. [*Catching his arm—very importunately. Then shyly.*] Down at the warehouse, aren't there some—nice young men?

TOM. No!

AMANDA. There *must* be—*some* . . .

TOM. Mother—
[*Gesture.*]

AMANDA. Find out one that's clean-living—doesn't drink and—ask him out for sister!

TOM. What?

AMANDA. For *sister!* To *meet!* Get acquainted!

TOM. [*Stamping to door.*] Oh, my go-osh!

AMANDA. Will you? [*He opens door. Imploringly.*] Will you? [*He starts down.*] Will you? *Will* you, dear?

TOM. [*Calling back.*] YES!

[AMANDA *closes the door hesitantly and with a troubled but faintly hopeful expression.*]

[SCREEN IMAGE: GLAMOR MAGAZINE COVER.]

[*Spot* AMANDA *at phone.*]

AMANDA. Ella Cartwright? This is Amanda Wingfield!
How are you, honey?
How is that kidney condition?
[*Count five.*]
Horrors!
[*Count five.*]
You're a Christian martyr, yes, honey, that's what you are, a Christian martyr!
Well, I just now happened to notice in my little red book that your subscription to the *Companion* has just run out! I knew that you wouldn't want to miss out on the wonderful serial starting in this new issue. It's by Bessie Mae Hopper, the first thing she's written since *Honeymoon for Three.*
Wasn't that a strange and interesting story? Well, this one is even lovelier, I believe. It has a sophisticated, society background. It's all about the horsey set on Long Island!

FADE OUT

SCENE 5

LEGEND ON SCREEN: "ANNUNCIATION." *Fade with music.*
It is early dusk of a spring evening. Supper has just been finished in the Wingfield apartment. AMANDA *and* LAURA *in light-colored dresses are removing dishes from the table, in the upstage area, which is shadowy, their movements formalized almost as a dance or ritual, their moving forms as pale and silent as moths.*

TOM, *in white shirt and trousers, rises from the table and crosses toward the fire-escape.*

AMANDA. [*As he passes her.*] Son, will you do me a favor?

TOM. What?

AMANDA. Comb your hair! You look so pretty when your hair is combed! [TOM *slouches on sofa with evening paper. Enormous caption 'Franco Triumphs."*] There is only one respect in which I would like you to emulate your father.

TOM. What respect is that?

AMANDA. The care he always took of his appearance. He never allowed himself to look untidy. [*He throws down the paper and crosses to fire-escape.*] Where are you going?

TOM. I'm going out to smoke.

AMANDA. You smoke too much. A pack a day at fifteen cents a pack. How much would that amount to in a month? Thirty times fifteen is how much. Tom? Figure it out and you will be astounded at what you could save. Enough to give you a night-school course in accounting at Washington U! Just think what a wonderful thing that would be for you, Son! [TOM *is unmoved by the thought.*]

TOM. I'd rather smoke. [*He steps out on landing, letting the screen door slam.*]

AMANDA. [*Sharply.*] I know! That's the tragedy of it . . . [*Alone, she turns to look at her husband's picture.*]

[DANCE MUSIC: "ALL THE WORLD IS WAITING FOR THE SUNRISE!"]

TOM. [*To the audience.*] Across the alley from us was Paradise Dance Hall. On evenings in spring the windows and doors were open and the music came outdoors. Sometimes the lights were turned out except for a large glass sphere that hung from the ceiling. It would turn slowly about and filter the dusk with delicate rainbow colors. Then the orchestra played a waltz or a tango, something that had a slow and sensuous rhythm. Couples would come outside, to the relative privacy of the alley. You could see them kissing behind ash-pits and telephone poles. This was the compensation for lives that passed like mine, without any change or adventure.

Adventure and change were imminent in this year. They were waiting around the corner for all these kids.

Suspended in the mist over Berchtesgaden, caught in the folds of Chamberlain's umbrella—

In Spain there was Guernica!

But here there was only hot swing music and liquor, dance halls, bars, and movies, and sex that hung in the gloom like a chandelier and flooded the world with brief, deceptive rainbows. . . .

All the world was waiting for bombardments!

[AMANDA *turns from the picture and comes outside.*]

AMANDA. [*Sighing.*] A fire-escape landing's a poor excuse for a porch. [*She spreads a newspaper on a step and sits down, gracefully and demurely as if she were settling into a swing on a Mississippi veranda.*] What are you looking at?

TOM. The moon.

AMANDA. Is there a moon this evening?

TOM. It's rising over Garfinkel's Delicatessen.

AMANDA. So it is! A little silver slipper of a moon. Have you made a wish on it yet?

TOM. Um-hum.

AMANDA. What did you wish for?

TOM. That's a secret.

AMANDA. A secret, huh? Well, I won't tell mine either. I will be just as mysterious as you.

TOM. I bet I can guess what yours is.

AMANDA. Is my head so transparent?

TOM. You're not a sphinx.

AMANDA. No, I don't have secrets. I'll tell you what I wish for on the moon. Success and happiness for my precious children! I wish for that whenever there's a moon, and when there isn't a moon, I wish for it, too.

TOM. I thought perhaps you wished for a gentleman caller.

AMANDA. Why do you say that?

TOM. Don't you remember asking me to fetch one?

AMANDA. I remember suggesting that it would be nice for your sister if you brought home some nice young man from the warehouse. I think that I've made that suggestion more than once.

TOM. Yes, you have made it repeatedly.

AMANDA. Well?

TOM. We are going to have one.

AMANDA. *What?*

TOM. A gentleman caller!

[THE ANNUNCIATION IS CELEBRATED WITH MUSIC.]

[AMANDA *rises.*]

[IMAGE ON SCREEN: CALLER WITH BOUQUET.]

AMANDA. You mean you have asked some nice young man to come over?

TOM. Yep. I've asked him to dinner.

AMANDA. You really did?

TOM. I did!

AMANDA. You did, and did he—*accept?*

TOM. He did!

AMANDA. Well, well—well, well! That's —lovely!

TOM. I thought that you would be pleased.

AMANDA. It's definite, then?

TOM. Very definite.

AMANDA. Soon?

TOM. Very soon.

AMANDA. For heaven's sake, stop putting on and tell me some things, will you?

TOM. What things do you want me to tell you?

AMANDA. *Naturally* I would like to know when he's *coming!*

TOM. He's coming tomorrow.

AMANDA. *Tomorrow?*

TOM. Yep. Tomorrow.

AMANDA. But, Tom!

TOM. Yes, Mother?

AMANDA. Tomorrow gives me no time!

TOM. Time for what?

AMANDA. Preparations! Why didn't you phone me at once, as soon as you asked him, the minute that he accepted? Then, don't you see, I could have been getting ready!

TOM. You don't have to make any fuss.

AMANDA. Oh, Tom, Tom, Tom, of course I have to make a fuss! I want things nice, not sloppy! Not thrown together. I'll certainly have to do some fast thinking, won't I?

TOM. I don't see why you have to think at all.

AMANDA. You just don't know. We can't have a gentleman caller in a pig-sty! All my wedding silver has to be polished, the monogrammed table linen ought to be laundered! The windows have to be washed and fresh curtains put up. And how about clothes? We have to *wear* something, don't we?

TOM. Mother, this boy is no one to make a fuss over!

AMANDA. Do you realize he's the first young man we've introduced to your sister?

It's terrible, dreadful, disgraceful that poor little sister has never received a single gentleman caller! Tom, come inside! [*She opens the screen door.*]

TOM. What for?

AMANDA. I want to ask you some things.

TOM. If you're going to make such a fuss, I'll call it off, I'll tell him not to come!

AMANDA. You certainly won't do anything of the kind. Nothing offends people worse than broken engagements. It simply means I'll have to work like a Turk! We won't be brilliant, but we will pass inspection. Come on inside. [TOM *follows, groaning.*] Sit down.

TOM. Any particular place you would like me to sit?

AMANDA. Thank heavens I've got that new sofa! I'm also making payments on a floor lamp I'll have sent out! And put the chintz covers on, they'll brighten things up! Of course I'd hoped to have these wall re-papered. . . . What is the young man's name?

TOM. His name is O'Connor.

AMANDA. That, of course, means fish— tomorrow is Friday! I'll have that salmon loaf—with Durkee's dressing! What does he do? He works at the warehouse?

TOM. Of course! How ever would I—

AMANDA. Tom, he—doesn't drink?

TOM. Why do you ask me that?

AMANDA. Your father *did!*

TOM. Don't get started on that!

AMANDA. He *does* drink, then?

TOM. Not that I know of!

AMANDA. Make sure, be certain! The last thing I want for my daughter's a boy who drinks!

TOM. Aren't you being a little bit premature? Mr. O'Connor has not yet appeared on the scene!

AMANDA. But will tomorrow. To meet your sister, and what do I know about his character? Nothing! Old maids are better off than wives of drunkards!

TOM. Oh, my God!

AMANDA. Be still!

TOM. [*Leaning forward to whisper.*] Lots of fellows meet girls whom they don't marry!

AMANDA. Oh, talk sensibly, Tom—and don't be sarcastic! [*She has gotten a hairbrush.*]

TOM. What are you doing?

AMANDA. I'm brushing that cow-lick down!

What is this young man's position at the warehouse?

TOM. [*Submitting grimly to the brush and the interrogation.*] This young man's position is that of a shipping clerk, Mother.

AMANDA. Sounds to me like a fairly responsible job, the sort of a job *you* would be in if you just had more *get-up*.

What is his salary? Have you any idea?

TOM. I would judge it to be approximately eighty-five dollars a month.

AMANDA. Well—not princely, but—

TOM. Twenty more than I make.

AMANDA. Yes, how well I know! But for a family man, eighty-five dollars a month is not much more than you can just get by on. . . .

TOM. Yes, but Mr. O'Connor is not a family man.

AMANDA. He might be, mightn't he? Some time in the future?

TOM. I see. Plans and provisions.

AMANDA. You are the only young man that I know of who ignores the fact that the future becomes the present, the present the past, and the past turns into everlasting regret if you don't plan for it!

TOM. I will think that over and see what I can make of it.

AMANDA. Don't be supercilious with your mother! Tell me some more about this—what do you call him?

TOM. James D. O'Connor. The D. is for Delaney.

AMANDA. Irish on *both* sides! *Gracious!* And doesn't drink?

TOM. Shall I call him up and ask him right this minute?

AMANDA. The only way to find out about those things is to make discreet inquiries at the proper moment. When I was a girl in Blue Mountain and it was suspected that a young man drank, the girl whose attentions he had been receiving, if any girl *was*, would sometimes speak to

the minister of his church, or rather her father would if her father was living, and sort of feel him out on the young man's character. That is the way such things are discreetly handled to keep a young woman from making a tragic mistake!

TOM. Then how did you happen to make a tragic mistake?

AMANDA. That innocent look of your father's had everyone fooled!

He *smiled*—the world was *enchanted!* No girl can do worse than put herself at the mercy of a handsome appearance!

I hope that Mr. O'Connor is not too good-looking.

TOM. No, he's not too good-looking. He's covered with freckles and hasn't too much of a nose.

AMANDA. He's not right-down homely, though?

TOM. Not right-down homely. Just medium homely, I'd say.

AMANDA. Character's what to look for in a man.

TOM. That's what I've always said, Mother.

AMANDA. You've never said anything of the kind and I suspect you would never give it a thought.

TOM. Don't be so suspicious of me.

AMANDA. At least I hope he's the type that's up and coming.

TOM. I think he really goes in for self-improvement.

AMANDA. What reason have you to think so?

TOM. He goes to night school.

AMANDA. [*Beaming.*] Splendid! What does he do, I mean study?

TOM. Radio engineering and public speaking!

AMANDA. Then he has visions of being advanced in the world!

Any young man who studies public speaking is aiming to have an executive job some day!

And radio engineering? A thing for the future!

Both of these facts are very illuminating. Those are the sort of things that a mother should know concerning any young man who comes to call on her daughter. Seriously or—not.

TOM. One little warning. He doesn't know about Laura. I didn't let on that we had dark ulterior motives. I just said, why don't you come and have dinner with us? He said okay and that was the whole conversation.

AMANDA. I bet it was! You're eloquent as an oyster.

However, he'll know about Laura when he gets here. When he sees how lovely and sweet and pretty she is, he'll thank his lucky stars he was asked to dinner.

TOM. Mother, you mustn't expect too much of Laura.

AMANDA. What do you mean?

TOM. Laura seems all those things to you and me because she's ours and we love her. We don't even notice she's crippled any more.

AMANDA. Don't say crippled! You know that I never allow that word to be used!

TOM. But face facts, Mother. She is and —that's not all—

AMANDA. What do you mean "not all"?

TOM. Laura is very different from other girls.

AMANDA. I think the difference is all to her advantage.

TOM. Not quite all—in the eyes of others —strangers—she's terribly shy and lives in a world of her own and those things make her seem a little peculiar to people outside the house.

AMANDA. Don't say peculiar.

TOM. Face the facts. She is.

[THE DANCE-HALL MUSIC CHANGES TO A TANGO THAT HAS A MINOR AND OMINOUS TONE.]

AMANDA. In what way is she peculiar— may I ask?

TOM. [Gently.] She lives in a world of her own—a world of—little glass ornaments, Mother. ˙. . . [Gets up. AMANDA remains holding brush, looking at him, troubled.]

She plays old phonograph records and— that's about all— [He glances at himself in the mirror and crosses to door.]

AMANDA. [Sharply.] Where are you going?

TOM. I'm going to the movies. [Out screen door.]

AMANDA. Not to the movies, every night to the movies! [Follows quickly to screen door.] I don't believe you always go to the movies! [He is gone. AMANDA looks worriedly after him for a moment. Then vitality and optimism return and she turns from the door. Crossing to portieres.] Laura! Laura! [LAURA answers from kitchenette.]

LAURA. Yes, Mother.

AMADA. Let those dishes go and come in front! [LAURA appears with dish towel. Gaily.] Laura, come here and make a wish on the moon!

[SCREEN IMAGE: MOON.]

LAURA. [Entering.] Moon—moon?

AMANDA. A little silver slipper of a moon. Look over your left shoulder, Laura, and make a wish!

[LAURA looks faintly puzzled as if called out of sleep. AMANDA seizes her shoulders and turns her at an angle by the door.]

Now!

Now, darling, wish!

LAURA. What shall I wish for, Mother?

AMANDA. [Her voice trembling and her eyes suddenly filling with tears.] Happiness! Good fortune!

[The violin rises and the stage dims out.]

CURTAIN

SCENE 6

IMAGE: HIGH SCHOOL HERO.

TOM. And so the following evening I brought Jim home to dinner. I had known Jim slightly in high school. In high school Jim was a hero. He had tremendous Irish good nature and vitality with the scrubbed and polished look of white chinaware. He seemed to move in a continual spotlight. He was a star in basketball, captain of the debating club, president of the senior class

and the glee club and he sang the male lead in the annual light operas. He was always running or bounding, never just walking. He seemed always at the point of defeating the law of gravity. He was shooting with such velocity through his adolescence that you would logically expect him to arrive at nothing short of the White House by the time he was thirty. But Jim apparently ran into more interference after his graduation from Soldan. His speed had definitely slowed. Six years after he left high school he was holding a job that wasn't much better than mine.

[IMAGE: CLERK.]

He was the only one at the warehouse with whom I was on friendly terms. I was valuable to him as someone who could remember his former glory, who had seen him win basketball games and the silver cup in debating. He knew of my secret practice of retiring to a cabinet of the wash-room to work on poems when business was slack in the warehouse. He called me Shakespeare. And while the other boys in the warehouse regarded me with suspicious hostility, Jim took a humorous attitude toward me. Gradually his attitude affected the others, their hostility wore off and they also began to smile at me as people smile at an oddly fashioned dog who trots across their path at some distance.

I knew that Jim and Laura had known each other at Soldan, and I had heard Laura speak admiringly of his voice. I didn't know if Jim remembered her or not. In high school Laura had been as unobtrusive as Jim had been astonishing. If he did remember her, it was not as my sister, for when I asked him to dinner, he grinned and said, "You know, Shakespeare, I never thought of you as having folks!"

He was about to discover that I did. . . .

[LIGHT UPSTAGE.]

[LEGEND ON SCREEN: "THE ACCENT OF A COMING FOOT."]

[*Friday evening. It is about five o'clock of a late spring evening which comes "scattering poems in the sky."*]

[*A delicate lemony light is in the Wingfield apartment.*]

[AMANDA *has worked like a Turk in preparation for the gentleman caller. The results are astonishing. The new floor lamp with its rose-silk shade is in place, a colored paper lantern conceals the broken light fixture in the ceiling, new billowing white curtains are at the windows, chintz covers are on chairs and sofa, a pair of new sofa pillows make their initial appearance.*]

[*Open boxes and tissue paper are scattered on the floor.*]

[LAURA *stands in the middle with lifted arms while* AMANDA *crouches*

before her, adjusting the hem of the new dress, devout and ritualistic. The dress is colored and designed by memory. The arrangement of LAURA's *hair is changed; it is softer and more becoming. A fragile, unearthly prettiness has come out in* LAURA: *she is like a piece of translucent glass touched by light, given a momentary radiance, not actual, not lasting.*]

AMANDA. [*Impatiently.*] Why are you trembling?

LAURA. Mother, you've made me so nervous!

AMANDA. How have I made you nervous?

LAURA. By all this fuss! You make it seem so important!

AMANDA. I don't understand you, Laura. You couldn't be satisfied with just sitting home, and yet whenever I try to arrange something for you, you seem to resist it. [*She gets up.*] Now take a look at yourself. No, wait! Wait just a moment—I have an idea!

LAURA. What is it now?

[AMANDA *produces two powder puffs which she wraps in handkerchiefs and stuffs in* LAURA's *bosom.*]

LAURA. Mother, what are you doing?

AMANDA. They call them "Gay Deceivers"!

LAURA. I won't wear them!

AMANDA. You will!

LAURA. Why should I?

AMANDA. Because, to be painfully honest, your chest is flat.

LAURA. You make it seem like we were setting a trap.

AMANDA. All pretty girls are a trap, a pretty trap, and men expect them to be.

[LEGEND: "A PRETTY TRAP."]

Now look at yourself, young lady. This is the prettiest you will ever be! I've got to fix myself now! You're going to be surprised by your mother's appearance! [*She crosses through portieres, humming gaily.*]

[LAURA *moves slowly to the long mirror and stares solemnly at herself.*]

[*A wind blows the white curtains inward in a slow, graceful motion and with a faint, sorrowful sighing.*]

AMANDA. [*Off stage.*] It isn't dark

enough yet. [LAURA *turns slowly before the mirror with a troubled look.*]

[LEGEND ON SCREEN: "THIS IS MY SISTER: CELEBRATE HER WITH STRINGS!" MUSIC.]

AMANDA. [*Laughing off.*] I'm going to show you something. I'm going to make a spectacular appearance!

LAURA. What is it, Mother?

AMANDA. Possess your soul in patience —you will see!

Something I've resurrected from that old trunk! Styles haven't changed so terribly much after all. . . .

[*She parts the portieres.*]

Now look at your mother!

[*She wears a girlish frock of yellowed voile with a blue silk sash. She carries a bunch of jonquils—the legend of her youth is nearly revived. Feverishly.*]

This is the dress in which I led the cotillion. Won the cakewalk twice at Sunset Hill, wore one spring to the Governor's ball in Jackson!

See how I sashayed around the ballroom, Laura?

[*She raises her skirt and does a mincing step around the room.*]

I wore it on Sundays for my gentlemen callers! I had it on the day I met your father—

I had malaria fever all that spring. The change of climate from East Tennessee to the Delta—weakened resistance—I had a little temperature all the time—not enough to be serious—just enough to make me restless and giddy!—Invitations poured in —parties all over the Delta!—"Stay in bed," said Mother, "you have fever!"—but I just wouldn't.—I took quinine but kept on going, going!—Evenings, dances!—Afternoons, long, long rides! Picnics—lovely!—So lovely, that country in May,—All lacy with dogwood, literally flooded with jonquils!—That was the spring I had the craze for jonquils. Jonquils became an absolute obsession. Mother said, "Honey, there's no more room for jonquils." And still I kept on bringing in more jonquils. Whenever, wherever I saw them, I'd say, "Stop! Stop! I see jonquils!" I made the young men help me gather the jonquils! It was a joke, Amanda and her jonquils! Finally there were no more vases to hold them, every available space was filled with jonquils. No vases to hold them? All right, I'll hold them myself! And then I—[*She stops in front of the picture.* MUSIC.] met your father!

Malaria fever and jonquils and then— this—boy. . . .

[*She switches on the rose-colored lamp.*]

I hope they get here before it starts to rain.

[*She crosses upstage and places the jonquils in bowl on table.*]

I gave your brother a little change so he and Mr. O'Connor could take the service car home.

LAURA. [*With altered look.*] What did you say his name was?

AMANDA. O'Connor.

LAURA. What is his first name?

AMANDA. I don't remember. Oh, yes, I do. It was—Jim!

[LAURA *sways slightly and catches hold of a chair.*]

[LEGEND ON SCREEN: "NOT JIM!"]

LAURA. [*Faintly.*] Not—Jim!

AMANDA. Yes, that was it, it was Jim! I've never known a Jim that wasn't nice!

[MUSIC: OMINOUS.]

LAURA. Are you sure his name is Jim O'Connor?

AMANDA. Yes. Why?

LAURA. Is he the one that Tom used to know in high school?

AMANDA. He didn't say so. I think he just got to know him at the warehouse.

LAURA. There was a Jim O'Connor we both knew in high school—[*Then, with effort.*] If that is the one that Tom is bringing to dinner—you'll have to excuse me, I won't come to the table.

AMANDA. What sort of nonsense is this?

LAURA. You asked me once if I'd ever liked a boy. Don't you remember I showed you this boy's picture?

AMANDA. You mean the boy you showed me in the year book?

LAURA. Yes, that boy.

AMANDA. Laura, Laura, were you in love with that boy?

LAURA. I don't know, Mother. All I know is I couldn't sit at the table if it was him!

AMANDA. It won't be him! It isn't the least bit likely. But whether it is or not, you will come to the table. You will not be excused.

LAURA. I'll have to be, Mother.

AMANDA. I don't intend to humor your

silliness, Laura. I've had too much from you and your brother, both!

So just sit down and compose yourself till they come. Tom has forgotten his key so you'll have to let them in, when they arrive.

LAURA. [*Panicky.*] Oh, Mother—*you* answer the door!

AMANDA. [*Lightly.*] I'll be in the kitchen —busy!

LAURA. Oh, Mother, please answer the door, don't make me do it!

AMANDA. [*Crossing into kitchenette.*] I've got to fix the dressing for the salmon. Fuss, fuss — silliness! — over a gentleman caller!

[*Door swings shut.* LAURA *is left alone.*]

[LEGEND: "TERROR!"]

[*She utters a low moan and turns off the lamp—sits stiffly on the edge of the sofa knotting her fingers together.*]

[LEGEND ON SCREEN: "THE OPENING OF A DOOR!"]

[*TOM and* JIM *appear on the fire-escape steps and climb to landing. Hearing their approach,* LAURA *rises with a panicky gesture. She retreats to the portieres.*]

[*The doorbell.* LAURA *catches her breath and touches her throat. Low drums.*]

AMANDA. [*Calling.*] Laura, sweetheart! The door!

[LAURA *stares at it without moving.*]

JIM. I think we just beat the rain.

TOM. Uh-huh. [*He rings again, nervously.* JIM *whistles and fishes for a cigarette.*]

AMANDA. [*Very, very gaily.*] Laura, that is your brother and Mr. O'Connor! Will you let them in, darling?

[LAURA *crosses toward kitchenette door.*]

LAURA. [*Breathlessly.*] Mother—you go to the door!

[AMANDA *steps out of kitchenette and stares furiously at* LAURA. [*She points imperiously at the door.*]

LAURA. Please, please!

AMANDA. [*In a fierce whisper.*] What is the matter with you, you silly thing?

LAURA. [*Desperately.*] Please, you answer it, *please!*

AMANDA. I told you I wasn't going to

humor you, Laura. Why have you chosen this moment to lose your mind?

LAURA. Please, please, please, you go!

AMANDA. You'll have to go to the door because I can't!

LAURA. [*Despairingly.*] I can't either!

AMANDA. *Why?*

LAURA. I'm *sick!*

AMANDA. I'm sick, too—of your nonsense! Why can't you and your brother be normal people? Fantastic whims and behavior!

[TOM *gives a long ring.*]

Preposterous goings on! Can you give me one reason—[*Calls out lyrically.*] COMING! JUST ONE SECOND!—why you should be afraid to open a door? Now you answer it, Laura!

LAURA. Oh, oh, oh . . . [*She returns through the portieres. Darts to the victrola and winds it frantically and turns it on.*]

AMANDA. Laura Wingfield, you march right to that door!

LAURA. Yes—yes, Mother!

[*A faraway, scratchy rendition of "Dardanella" softens the air and gives her strength to move through it. She slips to the door and draws it cautiously open.*]

[*TOM enters with the caller,* JIM O'CONNOR.]

TOM. Laura, this is Jim. Jim, this is my sister, Laura.

JIM. [*Stepping inside.*] I didn't know that Shakespeare had a sister!

LAURA. [*Retreating stiff and trembling from the door.*] How—how do you do?

JIM. [*Heartily extending his hand.*] Okay!

[LAURA *touches it hesitantly with hers.*]

JIM. Your hand's *cold*, Laura!

LAURA. Yes, well—I've been playing the victrola. . . .

JIM. Must have been playing classical music on it! You ought to play a little hot music to warm you up!

LAURA. Excuse me—I haven't finished playing the victrola. . . . [*She turns awkwardly and hurries into the front room. She pauses a second by the victrola. Then catches her breath and darts through the portieres like a frightened deer.*]

JIM. [*Grinning.*] What was the matter?

TOM. Oh—with Laura? Laura is—terribly shy.

JIM. Shy, huh? It's unusual to meet a shy girl nowadays. I don't believe you ever mentioned you had a sister.

TOM. Well, now you know. I have one. Here is the *Post Dispatch*. You want a piece of it?

JIM. Uh-huh.

TOM. What piece? The comics?

JIM. Sports! [*Glances at it.*] Ole Dizzy Dean is on his bad behavior.

TOM. [*Disinterest.*] Yeah. [*Lights cigarette and crosses back to fire-escape door.*]

JIM. Where are *you* going?

TOM. I'm going out on the terrace.

JIM. [*Goes after him.*] You know, Shakespeare—I'm going to sell you a bill of goods!

TOM. What goods?

JIM. A course I'm taking.

TOM. Huh?

JIM. In public speaking! You and me, we're not the warehouse type.

TOM. Thanks—that's good news. But what has public speaking got to do with it?

JIM. It fits you for—executive positions!

TOM. Awww.

JIM. I tell it's done a helluva lot for me.

[IMAGE: EXECUTIVE AT DESK.]

TOM. In what respect?

JIM. In every! Ask yourself what is the difference between you an' me and men in the office down front? Brains?—no!—Ability?—No! Then what? Just one little thing—

TOM. What is that one little thing?

JIM. Primarily it amounts to—social poise! Being able to square up to people and hold your own on any social level!

AMANDA. [*Offstage.*] Tom?

TOM. Yes, Mother?

AMANDA. Is that you and Mr. O'Connor?

TOM. Yes, Mother.

AMANDA. Well, you just make yourselves comfortable in there.

TOM. Yes, Mother.

AMANDA. Ask Mr. O'Connor if he would like to wash his hands.

JIM. Aw, no—no—thank you—I took care of that at the warehouse. Tom—

TOM. Yes?

JIM. Mr. Mendoza was speaking to me about you.

TOM. Favorably?

JIM. What do you think?

TOM. Well—

JIM. You're going to be out of a job if you don't wake up.

TOM. I am waking up—

JIM. You show no signs.

TOM. The signs are interior.

[IMAGE ON SCREEN: THE SAILING VESSEL WITH JOLLY ROGER AGAIN.]

TOM. I'm planning to change. [*He leans over the rail speaking with quiet exhilaration. The incandescent marquees and signs of the first-run movie houses light his face from across the alley. He looks like a voyager.*] I'm right at the point of committing myself to a future that doesn't include the warehouse and Mr. Mendoza or even a night-school course in public speaking.

JIM. What are you gassing about?

TOM. I'm tired of the movies.

JIM. Movies!

TOM. Yes, movies! Look at them— [*A wave toward the marvels of Grand Avenue.*] All of those glamorous people—having adventures—hogging it all, gobbling the whole thing up! You know what happens? People go to the *movies* instead of *moving!* Hollywood characters are supposed to have all the adventures for everybody in America, while everybody in America sits in a dark room and watches them have them! Yes, until there's a war. That's when adventure becomes available to the masses! *Everyone's* dish, not only Gable's! Then the people in the dark room come out of the dark room to have some adventures themselves—Goody, goody!—It's our turn now, to go to the South Sea Islands—to make a safari—to be exotic, far-off!—But I'm not patient. I don't want to wait till then. I'm tired of the *movies* and I am *about* to *move!*

JIM. [*Incredulously.*] Move?

TOM. Yes.

JIM. When?

TOM. Soon!

JIM. Where? Where?

[THEME THREE MUSIC SEEMS TO ANSWER THE QUESTION, WHILE TOM THINKS IT OVER. HE SEARCHES AMONG HIS POCKETS.]

TOM. I'm starting to boil inside. I know I seem dreamy, but inside—well, I'm boiling!—Whenever I pick up a shoe, I shudder a little thinking how short life is and what I am doing!—Whatever that means, I know it doesn't mean shoes—except as

something to wear on a traveler's feet!
[*Finds paper.*] Look—

JIM. What?

TOM. I'm a member.

JIM. [*Reading.*] The Union of Merchant Seamen.

TOM. I paid my dues this month, instead of the light bill.

JIM. You will regret it when they turn the lights off.

TOM. I won't be here.

JIM. How about your mother?

TOM. I'm like my father. The bastard son of a bastard! See how he grins? And he's been absent going on sixteen years!

JIM. You're just talking, you drip. How does your mother feel about it?

TOM. Shhh! — Here comes Mother! Mother is not acquainted with my plans!

AMANDA. [*Enters portieres.*] Where are you all?

TOM. On the terrace, Mother.

[*They start inside. She advances to them.* TOM *is distinctly shocked at her appearance. Even* JIM *blinks a little. He is making his first contact with girlish Southern vivacity and in spite of the night-school course in public speaking is somewhat thrown off the beam by the unexpected outlay of social charm.*]

[*Certain responses are attempted by* JIM *but are swept aside by* AMANDA's *gay laughter and chatter.* TOM *is embarrassed but after the first shock* JIM *reacts very warmly. Grins and chuckles, is altogether won over.*]

[IMAGE: AMANDA AS A GIRL.]

AMANDA. [*Coyly smiling, shaking her girlish ringlets.*] Well, well, well, so this is Mr. O'Connor. Introductions entirely unnecessary. I've heard so much about you from my boy. I finally said to him, Tom—good gracious!—why don't you bring this paragon to supper? I'd like to meet this nice young man at the warehouse!—Instead of just hearing you sing his praises so much!

I don't know why my son is so standoffish—that's not Southern behavior!

Let's sit down and—I think we could stand a little more air in here! Tom, leave the door open. I felt a nice fresh breeze a moment ago. Where has it gone to?

Mmm, so warm already! And not quite summer, even. We're going to burn up when summer really gets started.

However, we're having—we're having a very light supper. I think light things are better fo' this time of year. The same as light clothes are. Light clothes an' light food are what warm weather calls fo'. You know our blood gets so thick during th' winter—it takes a while fo' us to *adjust* ou'selves—when the season changes . . .

It's come so quick this year. I wasn't prepared. All of a sudden—heavens! Already summer!—I ran to the trunk an' pulled out this light dress—Terribly old! Historical almost! But feels so good—so good an' co-ol, y' know. . . .

TOM. Mother—

AMANDA. Yes, honey?

TOM. How about—supper?

AMANDA. Honey, you go ask Sister if supper is ready! You know that Sister is in full charge of supper!

Tell her you hungry boys are waiting for it.

[*To* JIM.]

Have you met Laura?

JIM. She—

AMANDA. Let you in? Oh, good, you've met already! It's rare for a girl as sweet an' pretty as Laura to be domestic! But Laura is, thank heavens, not only pretty but also very domestic. I'm not at all. I never was a bit. I never could make a thing but angel-food cake. Well, in the South we had so many servants. Gone, gone, gone. All vestige of gracious living! Gone completely! I wasn't prepared for what the future brought me. All of my gentlemen callers were sons of planters and so of course I assumed that I would be married to one and raise my family on a large piece of land with plenty of servants. But man proposes—and woman accepts the proposal!—To vary that old, old saying a little bit—I married no planter! I married a man who worked for the telephone company!—That gallantly smiling gentleman over there! [*Points to the picture.*] A telephone man who—fell in love with long distance!—Now he travels and I don't even know where!—But what am I going on for about my—tribulations?

Tell me yours—I hope you don't have any!

Tom?

TOM. [*Returning.*] Yes, Mother?

AMANDA. Is supper nearly ready?

TOM. It looks to me like supper is on the table.

AMANDA. Let me look— [*She rises prettily and looks through portieres.*] Oh, lovely!—But where is Sister?

TOM. Laura is not feeling well and she says that she thinks she'd better not come to the table.

AMANDA. What? — Nonsense! — Laura? Oh, Laura!

LAURA. [*Off stage, faintly.*] Yes, Mother.

AMANDA. You really must come to the table. We won't be seated until you come to the table!

Come in, Mr. O'Connor. You sit over there, and I'll—

Laura? Laura Wingfield!

You're keeping us waiting, honey! We can't say grace until you come to the table!

[*The back door is pushed weakly open and* LAURA *comes in. She is obviously quite faint, her lips trembling, her eyes wide and staring. She moves unsteadily toward the table.*]

[LEGEND: "TERROR!"]

[*Outside a summer storm is coming abruptly. The white curtains billow inward at the windows and there is a sorrowful murmur and deep blue dusk.*]

[LAURA *suddenly stumbles — she catches at a chair with a faint moan.*]

TOM. Laura!

AMANDA. Laura!

[*There is a clap of thunder.*]

[LEGEND: "AH!"]

[*Despairingly.*]

Why, Laura, you *are* sick, darling! Tom, help your sister into the living room, dear! Sit in the living room, Laura—rest on the sofa.

Well!

[*To the gentleman caller.*]

Standing over the hot stove made her ill!—I told her that was just too warm this evening, but—

[TOM *comes back in.* LAURA *is on the sofa.*]

Is Laura all right now?

TOM. Yes.

AMANDA. What *is* that? Rain? A nice cool rain has come up!

[*She gives the gentleman caller a frightened look.*]

I think we may—have grace—now . . .

[TOM *looks at her stupidly.*]

Tom, honey—you say grace!

TOM. Oh . . .

"For these and all thy mercies—"

[*They bow their heads,* AMANDA *stealing a nervous glance at* JIM. *In the living room* LAURA, *stretched on the sofa, clenches her hand to her lips, to hold back a shuddering sob.*] God's Holy Name be praised—

THE SCENE DIMS OUT

SCENE 7

A SOUVENIR.

Half an hour later. Dinner is just being finished in the upstage area which is concealed by the drawn portieres.

As the curtain rises LAURA *is still huddled upon the sofa, her feet drawn under her, her head resting on a pale blue pillow, her eyes wide and mysteriously watchful. The new floor lamp with its shade of rose-colored silk gives a soft, becoming light to her face, bringing out the fragile, unearthly prettiness which usually escapes attention. There is a steady murmur of rain, but it is slackening and stops soon after the scene begins; the air outside becomes pale and luminous as the moon breaks out.*

A moment after the curtain rises, the lights in both rooms flicker and go out.

JIM. Hey, there, Mr. Light Bulb!

[AMANDA *laughs nervously.*]

[LEGEND: "SUSPENSION OF A PUBLIC SERVICE."]

AMANA. Where was Moses when the lights went out? Ha-ha. Do you know the answer to that one, Mr. O'Connor?

JIM. No, Ma'am, what's the answer?

AMANDA. In the dark!

[JIM *laughs appreciatively.*]

Everybody sit still. I'll light the candles. Isn't it lucky we have them on the table? Where's a match? Which of you gentlemen can provide a match?

JIM. Here.

AMANDA. Thank you, sir.

JIM. Not at all, Ma'am.

AMANDA. I guess the fuse has burnt out. Mr. O'Connor, can you tell a burnt-out fuse? I know I can't and Tom is a total loss when it comes to mechanics.

[SOUND: GETTING UP: VOICES RECEDE A LITTLE TO KITCHENETTE.]

Oh, be careful you don't bump into something. We don't want our gentleman caller to break his neck. Now wouldn't that be a fine howdy-do?

JIM. Ha-ha!

Where is the fuse-box?

AMANDA. Right here next to the stove. Can you see anything?

JIM. Just a minute.

AMANDA. Isn't electricity a mysterious thing?

Wasn't it Benjamin Franklin who tied a key to a kite?

We live in such a mysterious universe, don't we? Some people say that science clears up all the mysteries for us. In my opinion it only creates more!

Have you found it yet?

JIM. No, Ma'am. All these fuses look okay to me.

AMANDA. Tom!

TOM. Yes, Mother?

AMANDA. That light bill I gave you several days ago. The one I told you we got the notices about?

[LEGEND: "HA!"]

TOM. Oh.—Yeah.

AMANDA. You didn't neglect to pay it by any chance?

TOM. Why, I—

AMANDA. Didn't! I might have know it!

JIM. Shakespeare probably wrote a poem on that light bill, Mrs. Wingfield.

AMANDA. I might have known better than to trust him with it! There's such a high price for negligence in this world!

JIM. Maybe the poem will win a ten-dollar prize.

AMANDA. We'll just have to spend the remainder of the evening in the nineteenth century, before Mr. Edison made the Mazda lamp!

JIM. Candlelight is my favorite kind of light.

AMANDA. That shows you're romantic! But that's no excuse for Tom.

Well, we got through dinner. Very considerate of them to let us get through dinner before they plunged us into everlasting darkness, wasn't it, Mr. O'Connor?

JIM. Ha-ha!

AMANDA. Tom, as a penalty for your carelessness you can help me with the dishes.

JIM. Let me give you a hand.

AMANDA. Indeed you will not!

JIM. I ought to be good for something.

AMANDA. Good for something? [*Her tone is rhapsodic.*]

You? Why, Mr. O'Connor, nobody, *nobody's* given me this much entertainment in years—as you have!

JIM. Aw, now, Mrs. Wingfield!

AMANDA. I'm not exaggerating, not one bit! But Sister is all by her lonesome. You keep her company in the parlor!

I'll give you this lovely old candelabrum that used to be on the altar at the church of the Heavenly Rest. It was melted a little out of shape when the church burnt down. Lightning struck it one spring. Gypsy Jones was holding a revival at the time and he intimated that the church was destroyed because the Episcopalians gave card parties.

JIM. Ha-ha.

AMANDA. And how about you coaxing Sister to drink a little wine? I think it would be good for her! Can you carry both at once?

JIM. Sure. I'm Superman!

AMANDA. Now, Thomas, get into this apron!

[*The door of kitchenette swings closed on* AMANDA's *gay laughter; the flickering light approaches the portieres.*]

[LAURA *sits up nervously as he enters. Her speech at first is low and breathless from the almost intolerable strain of being alone with a stranger.*]

[THE LEGEND: "I DON'T SUPPOSE YOU REMEMBER ME AT ALL!"]

[*In her first speeches in this scene, before* JIM's *warmth overcomes her paralyzing shyness,* LAURA's *voice is thin and breathless as though she has run up a steep flight of stairs.*]

[JIM's *attitude is gently humorous. In playing this scene it should be stressed that while the incident is apparently unimportant, it is to* LAURA *the climax of her secret life.*]

JIM. Hello, there, Laura.

LAURA. [*Faintly.*] Hello. [*She clears her throat.*]

JIM. How are you feeling now? Better?

LAURA. Yes. Yes, thank you.

JIM. This is for you. A little dandelion wine. [*He extends it toward her with extravagant gallantry.*]

LAURA. Thank you.

JIM. Drink it—but don't get drunk!

[*He laughs heartily.* LAURA *takes the glass uncertainly; laughs shyly.*] Where shall I set the candles?

LAURA. Oh—oh, anywhere . . .

JIM. How about here on the floor? Any objections?

LAURA. No.

JIM. I'll spread a newspaper under to catch the drippings. I like to sit on the floor. Mind if I do?

LAURA. Oh, no.

JIM. Give me a pillow?

LAURA. What?

JIM. A pillow!

LAURA. Oh . . . [*Hands him one quickly.*]

JIM. How about you? Don't you like to sit on the floor?

LAURA. Oh—yes.

JIM. Why don't you, then?

LAURA. I—will.

JIM. Take a pillow! [LAURA *does. Sits on the other side of the candelabrum.* JIM *crosses his legs and smiles engagingly at her.*] I can't hardly see you sitting way over there.

LAURA. I can—see you.

JIM. I know, but that's not fair, I'm in the limelight. [LAURA *moves her pillow closer.*] Good! Now I can see you! Comfortable?

LAURA. Yes.

JIM. So am I. Comfortable as a cow! Will you have some gum?

LAURA. No, thank you.

JIM. I think that I will indulge, with your permission. [*Musingly unwraps it and holds it up.*] Think of the fortune made by the guy that invented the first piece of chewing gum. Amazing, huh? The Wrigley Building is one of the sights of Chicago.—I saw it summer before last when I went up to the Century of Progress. Did you take in the Century of Progress?

LAURA. No, I didn't.

JIM. Well, it was quite a wonderful exposition. What impressed me most was the Hall of Science. Gives you an idea of what the future will be in America, even more wonderful than the present time is! [*Pause. Smiling at her.*] Your brother tells me you're shy. Is that right, Laura?

LAURA. I—don't know.

JIM. I judge you to be an old-fashioned type of girl. Well, I think that's a pretty good type to be. Hope you don't think I'm being too personal—do you?

LAURA. [*Hastily, out of embarrassment.*] I believe I *will* take a piece of gum, if you —don't mind. [*Clearing her throat.*] Mr. O'Connor, have you—kept up with your singing?

JIM. Singing? Me?

LAURA. Yes. I remember what a beautiful voice you had.

JIM. When did you hear me sing?

[VOICE OFF STAGE IN THE PAUSE.]

VOICE. [*Off stage.*]

O blow, ye winds, heigh-ho,
A-roving I will go!
I'm off to my love
With a boxing glove—
Ten thousand miles away!

JIM. You say you've heard me sing?

LAURA. Oh, yes! Yes, very often . . . I don't suppose—you remember me—at all?

JIM. [*Smiling doubtfully.*] You know I have an idea I've seen you before. I had that idea soon as you opened the door. It seemed almost like I was about to remember your name. But the name that I started to call you—wasn't a name! And so I stopped myself before I said it.

LAURA. Wasn't it—Blue Roses?

JIM. [*Springs up. Grinning.*] Blue Roses! —My gosh, yes—Blue Roses! That's what I had on my tongue when you opened the door! Isn't it funny what tricks your memory plays? I didn't connect you with high school somehow or other. But that's where it was; it was high school. I didn't even know you were Shakespeare's sister!

Gosh, I'm sorry.

LAURA. I didn't expect you to. You—barely knew me!

JIM. But we did have a speaking acquaintance, huh?

LAURA. Yes, we—spoke to each other.

JIM. When did you recognize me?

LAURA. Oh, right away!

JIM. Soon as I came in the door?

LAURA. When I heard your name I thought it was probably you. I knew that Tom used to know you a little in high school. So when you came in the door— Well, then I was—sure.

JIM. Why didn't you *say* something, then?

LAURA. [*Breathlessly.*] I didn't know what to say, I was—too surprised!

JIM. For goodness' sakes! You know, this sure is funny!

LAURA. Yes! Yes, isn't it, though . . .

JIM. Didn't we have a class in something together?

LAURA. Yes, we did.

JIM. What class was that?

LAURA. It was—singing—Chorus!

JIM. Aw!

LAURA. I sat across the aisle from you in the Aud.

JIM. Aw.

LAURA. Mondays, Wednesdays and Fridays.

JIM. Now I remember—you always came in late.

LAURA. Yes, it was so hard for me, getting upstairs. I had that brace on my leg —it clumped so loud!

JIM. I never heard any clumping.

LAURA. [*Wincing at the recollection.*] To me it sounded like—thunder!

JIM. Well, well, well, I never even noticed.

LAURA. And everybody was seated before I came in. I had to walk in front of all those people. My seat was in the back row. I had to go clumping all the way up the aisle with everyone watching!

JIM. You shouldn't have been self-conscious.

LAURA. I know, but I was. It was always such a relief when the singing started.

JIM. Aw, yes, I've placed you now! I used to call you Blue Roses. How was it that I got started calling you that?

LAURA. I was out of school a little while with pleurosis. When I came back you asked me what was the matter. I said I had pleurosis—you thought I said Blue Roses. That's what you always called me after that!

JIM. I hope you didn't mind.

LAURA. Oh, no—I liked it. You see, I wasn't acquainted with many—people. . . .

JIM. As I remember you sort of stuck by yourself.

LAURA. I—I—never have had much luck at—making friends.

JIM. I don't see why you wouldn't.

LAURA. Well, I—started out badly.

JIM. You mean being—

LAURA. Yes, it sort of—stood between me—

JIM. You shouldn't have let it!

LAURA. I know, but it did, and—

JIM. You were shy with people!

LAURA. I tried not to be but never could—

JIM. Overcome it?

LAURA. No, I—I never could!

JIM. I guess being shy is something you have to work out of kind of gradually.

LAURA. [*Sorrowfully.*] Yes—I guess it—

JIM. Takes time!

LAURA. Yes—

JIM. People are not so dreadful when you know them. That's what you have to remember! And everybody has problems, not just you, but practically everybody has got some problems. You think of yourself as having the only problems, as being the only one who is disappointed. But just look around you and you will see lots of people as disappointed as you are. For instance, I hoped when I was going to high school that I would be further along at this time, six years later, than I am now—You remember that wonderful write-up I had in *The Torch?*

LAURA. Yes! [*She rises and crosses to table.*]

JIM. It said I was bound to succeed in anything I went into! [LAURA *returns with the annual.*] Holy Jeez! *The Torch!* [*He accepts it reverently. They smile across it with mutual wonder.* LAURA *crouches beside him and they begin to turn through it.* LAURA's *shyness is dissolving in his warmth.*]

LAURA. Here you are in *The Pirates of Penzance!*

JIM. [*Wistfully.*] I sang the baritone lead in that operetta.

LAURA. [*Raptly.*] So—*beautifully!*

JIM. [*Protesting.*] Aw—

LAURA. Yes, yes—beautifully—beautifully!

JIM. You heard me?

LAURA. All three times!

JIM. No!

LAURA. Yes!

JIM. All three performances?

LAURA. [*Looking down.*] Yes.

JIM. Why?

LAURA. I—wanted to ask you to—autograph my program.

JIM. Why didn't you ask me to?

LAURA. You were always surrounded by your own friends so much that I never had a chance to.

JIM. You should have just—

LAURA. Well, I—thought you might think I was—

JIM. Thought I might think you was—what?

LAURA. Oh—

JIM. [*With reflective relish.*] I was beleaguered by females in those days.

LAURA. You were terribly popular!

JIM. Yeah—

LAURA. You had such a—friendly way—

JIM. I was spoiled in high school.

LAURA. Everybody—liked you!

JIM. Including you?

LAURA. I—yes, I—I did, too— [*She gently closes the book in her lap.*]

JIM. Well, well, well!—Give me that program, Laura. [*She hands it to him. He signs it with a flourish.*] There you are—better late than never!

LAURA. Oh, I—what a—surprise!

JIM. My signature isn't worth very much right now.

But some day—maybe—it will increase in value!

Being disappointed is one thing and being discouraged is something else. I am disappointed but I am not discouraged.

I'm twenty-three years old.

How old are you?

LAURA. I'll be twenty-four in June.

JIM. That's not old age!

LAURA. No, but—

JIM. You finished high school?

LAURA. [*With difficulty.*] I didn't go back.

JIM. You mean you dropped out?

LAURA. I made bad grades in my final examinations. [*She rises and replaces the book and the program. Her voice strained.*] How is—Emily Meisenbach getting along?

JIM. Oh, that kraut-head!

LAURA. Why do you call her that?

JIM. That's what she was.

LAURA. You're not still—going with her?

JIM. I never see her.

LAURA. It said in the Personal Section that you were—engaged!

JIM. I know, but I wasn't impressed by that—propaganda!

LAURA. It wasn't—the truth?

JIM. Only in Emily's optimistic opinion!

LAURA. Oh—

[LEGEND: "WHAT HAVE YOU DONE SINCE HIGH SCHOOL?"]

[JIM *lights a cigarette and leans indolently back on his elbows smiling at* LAURA *with a warmth and charm which lights her inwardly with altar candles. She remains by the table and turns in her hands a piece of glass to cover her tumult.*]

JIM. [*After several reflective puffs on a cigarette.*] What have you done since high school? [*She seems not to hear him.*] Huh? [*Laura looks up.*] I said what have you done since high school, Laura?

LAURA. Nothing much.

JIM. You must have been doing something these six long years.

LAURA. Yes.

JIM. Well, then, such as what?

LAURA. I took a business course at business college—

JIM. How did that work out?

LAURA. Well, not very—well—I had to drop out, it gave me—indigestion—

[JIM *laughs gently.*]

JIM. What are you doing now?

LAURA. I don't do anything—much. Oh, please don't think I sit around doing nothing! My glass collection takes up a good deal of time. Glass is something you have to take good care of.

JIM. What did you say—about glass?

LAURA. Collection I said—I have one— [*She clears her throat and turns away again, shy.*]

JIM. [*Abruptly.*] You know what I judge to be the trouble with you?

Inferiority complex! Know what that is? That's what they call it when someone low-rates himself!

I understand it because I had it, too. Although my case was not so aggravated as yours seems to be. I had it until I took up public speaking, developed my voice, and learned that I had an aptitude for science. Before that time I never thought of myself as being outstanding in any way whatsoever!

Now I've never made a regular study of it, but I have a friend who says I can analyze people better than doctors that make a profession of it. I don't claim that to be necessarily true, but I can sure guess a person's psychology, Laura! [*Takes out his gum.*] Excuse me, Laura. I always take it out when the flavor is gone. I'll use this scrap of paper to wrap it in. I know how it is to get it stuck on a shoe.

Yep—that's what I judge to be your principal trouble. A lack of confidence in yourself as a person. You don't have the proper amount of faith in yourself. I'm basing that fact on a number of your remarks and also on certain observations I've made. For instance that clumping you thought was so awful in high school. You say that you even dreaded to walk into class. You see what you did? You dropped out of school, you gave up an education because of a clump, which as far as I know was practically non-existent. A little physical defect is what you have. Hardly noticeable even! Magnified thousands of times by imagination.

You know what my strong advice to you is? Think of yourself as *superior* in some way!

LAURA. In what way would I think?

JIM. Why, man alive, Laura! Just look about you a little. What do you see? A world full of common people! All of 'em born and all of 'em going to die!

Which of them has one-tenth of your good points! Or mine! Or anyone else's, as far as that goes—Gosh!

Everybody excels in some one thing. Some in many!

[*Unconsciously glances at himself in the mirror.*]

All you've got to do is discover in *what!* Take me, for instance.

[*He adjusts his tie at the mirror.*]

My interest happens to lie in electro-dynamics. I'm taking a course in radio engineering at night school, Laura, on top of a fairly responsible job at the warehouse. I'm taking that course and studying public speaking.

LAURA. Ohhhh.

JIM. Because I believe in the future of television!

[*Turning back to her.*]

I wish to be ready to go up right along with it. Therefore I'm planning to get in on the ground floor. In fact I've already made the right connections and all that remains is for the industry itself to get under way! Full steam—

[*His eyes are starry.*]

Knowledge—Zzzzzp! Money—Zzzzzzp!— Power!

That's the cycle democracy is built on!

[*His attitude is convincingly dynamic. LAURA stares at him, even her shyness eclipsed in her absolute wonder. He suddenly grins.*]

I guess you think I think a lot of myself!

LAURA. No—o-o-o, I—

JIM. Now how about you? Isn't there something you take more interest in than anything else?

LAURA. Well, I do—as I said—have my— glass collection—

[*A peal of girlish laughter from the kitchen.*]

JIM. I'm not right sure I know what you're talking about.

What kind of glass is it?

LAURA. Little articles of it, they're ornaments mostly!

Most of them are little animals made out of glass, the tiniest little animals in the world. Mother calls them a glass menagerie!

Here's an example of one, if you'd like to see it!

This is one of the oldest. It's nearly thirteen.

[MUSIC: "THE GLASS MENAGERIE."]

[*He stretches out his hand.*]

Oh, be careful—if you breathe, it breaks!

JIM. I'd better not take it. I'm pretty clumsy with things.

LAURA. Go on, I trust you with him!

[*Places it in his palm.*]

There now—you're holding him gently!

Hold him over the light, he loves the light! You see how the light shines through him?

JIM. It sure does shine!

LAURA. I shouldn't be partial, but he is my favorite one.

JIM. What kind of a thing is this one supposed to be?

LAURA. Haven't you noticed the single horn on his forehead?

JIM. A unicorn, huh?

LAURA. Mmm-hmmm!

JIM. Unicorns, aren't they extinct in the modern world?

LAURA. I know!

JIM. Poor little fellow, he must feel sort of lonesome.

LAURA. [Smiling.] Well, if he does he doesn't complain about it. He stays on a shelf with some horses that don't have horns and all of them seem to get along nicely together.

JIM. How do you know?

LAURA. [Lightly.] I haven't heard any arguments among them!

JIM. [Grinning.] No arguments, huh? Well, that's a pretty good sign! Where shall I set him?

LAURA. Put him on the table. They all like a change of scenery once in a while!

JIM. [Stretching.] Well, well, well, well—

Look how big my shadow is when I stretch!

LAURA. Oh, oh, yes—it stretches across the ceiling!

JIM. [Crossing to door.] I think it's stopped raining. [Opens fire-escape door.] Where does the music come from?

LAURA. From the Paradise Dance Hall across the alley.

JIM. How about cutting the rug a little, Miss Wingfield?

LAURA. Oh, I—

JIM. Or is your program filled up? Let me have a look at it. [Grasps imaginary card.] Why, every dance is taken! I'll just have to scratch some out. [WALTZ MUSIC: "LA GOLONDRINA."] Ahhh, a waltz! [He executes some sweeping turns by himself then hold his arms toward LAURA.]

LAURA. [Breathlessly.] I—can't dance!

JIM. There you go, that inferiority stuff!

LAURA. I've never danced in my life!

JIM. Come on, try!

LAURA. Oh, but I'd step on you!

JIM. I'm not made out of glass.

LAURA. How—how—how do we start?

JIM. Just leave it to me. You hold your arms out a little .

LAURA. Like this?

JIM. A little bit higher. Right. Now don't tighten up, that's the main thing about it—relax.

LAURA. [Laughing breathlessly.] It's hard not to.

JIM. Okay.

LAURA. I'm afraid you can't budge me.

JIM. What do you bet I can't? [He swings her into motion.]

LAURA. Goodness, yes, you can!

JIM. Let yourself go, now, Laura, just let yourself go.

LAURA. I'm—

JIM. Come on!

LAURA. Trying!

JIM. Not so stiff— Easy does it!

LAURA. I know but I'm—

JIM. Loosen th' backbone! There now, that's a lot better.

LAURA. Am I?

JIM. Lots, lots better! [He moves her about the room in a clumsy waltz.]

LAURA. Oh, my!

JIM. Ha-ha!

LAURA. Oh, my goodness!

JIM. Ha-ha-ha! [They suddenly bump into the table. JIM stops.] What did we hit on?

LAURA. Table.

JIM. Did something fall off it? I think—

LAURA. Yes.

JIM. I hope that it wasn't the little glass horse with the horn!

LAURA. Yes.

JIM. Aw, aw, aw. Is it broken?

LAURA. Now it is just like all the other horses.

JIM. It's lost its—

LAURA. Horn!

It doesn't matter. Maybe it's a blessing in disguise.

JIM. You'll never forgive me. I bet that that was your favorite piece of glass.

LAURA. I don't have favorites much. It's no tragedy, Freckles. Glass breaks so easily. No matter how careful you are. The traffic jars the shelves and things fall off them.

JIM. Still I'm awfully sorry that I was the cause.

LAURA. [Smiling.] I'll just imagine he had an operation.

The horn was removed to make him feel less—freakish!

[*They both laugh.*]

Now he will feel more at home with the other horses, the ones that don't have horns. . . .

JIM. Ha-ha, that's very funny!

[*Suddenly serious.*]

I'm glad to see that you have a sense of humor.

You know—you're—well—very different! Surprisingly different from anyone else I know!

[*His voice becomes soft and hesitant with a genuine feeling.*]

Do you mind me telling you that?

[LAURA *is abashed beyond speech.*]

I mean it in a nice way . . .

[LAURA *nods shyly, looking away.*]

You make me feel sort of—I don't know how to put it!

I'm usually pretty good at expressing things, but—

This is something that I don't know how to say!

[LAURA *touches her throat and clears it—turns the broken unicorn in her hands.*]

[*Even softer.*]

Has anyone ever told you that you were pretty?

[PAUSE: MUSIC.]

[LAURA *looks up slowly, with wonder, and shakes her head.*]

Well, you are! In a very different way from anyone else.

And all the nicer because of the difference, too.

[*His voice becomes low and husky.* LAURA *turns away, nearly faint with the novelty of her emotions.*]

I wish that you were my sister. I'd teach you to have some confidence in yourself. The different people are not like other people, but being different is nothing to be ashamed of. Because other people are not such wonderful people. They're one hundred times one thousand. You're one times one! They walk all over the earth. You just stay here. They're common as—weeds, but—you—well, you're—*Blue Roses!*

[IMAGE ON SCREEN: BLUE ROSES.]

[MUSIC CHANGES.]

LAURA. But blue is wrong for—roses . . .

JIM. It's right for you!—You're—pretty!

LAURA. In what respect am I pretty?

JIM. In all respects—believe me! Your eyes—your hair—are pretty! Your hands are pretty!

[*He catches hold of her hand.*]

You think I'm making this up because I'm invited to dinner and have to be nice. Oh, I could do that! I could put on an act for you, Laura, and say lots of things without being very sincere. But this time I am. I'm talking to you sincerely. I happened to notice you had this inferiority complex that keeps you from feeling comfortable with people. Somebody needs to build your confidence up and make you feel proud instead of shy and turning away and—blushing—

Somebody—ought to—

Ought to—*kiss* you, Laura!

[*His hand slips slowly up her arm to her shoulder.*]

[MUSIC SWELLS TUMULTUOUSLY.]

[*He suddenly turns her about and kisses her on the lips.*]

[*When he releases her.* LAURA *sinks on sofa with a bright, dazed look.*]

[JIM *backs away and fishes in his pocket for a cigarette.*]

[LEGEND ON SCREEN: "SOUVENIR."]

Stumble-john!

[*He lights the cigarette, avoiding her look.*]

[*There is a peal of girlish laughter from* AMANDA *in the kitchen.*]

[LAURA *slowly raises and opens her hand. It still contains the little broken glass animal. She looks at it with a tender, bewildered expression.*]

Stumble-john!

I shouldn't have done that—That was way off the beam.

You don't smoke, do you?

[*She looks up, smiling, not hearing the question.*]

[*He sits beside her a little gingerly. She looks at him speechlessly—waiting.*]

[*He coughs decorously and moves a little farther aside as he considers the situation and senses her feelings, dimly, with perturbation.*]

[*Gently.*]

Would you—care for a—mint?

[*She doesn't seem to hear him but her look grows brighter even.*]

Peppermint—Life-Saver?

My pocket's a regular drug store—wherever I go . . .

[*He pops a mint in his mouth. Then gulps and decides to make a clean breast of it. He speaks slowly and gingerly.*]

Laura, you know, if I had a sister like you, I'd do the same thing as Tom. I'd bring out fellows and—introduce her to them. The right type of boys of a type to —appreciate her.

Only—well—he made a mistake about me.

Maybe I've got no call to be saying this. That may not have been the idea in having me over. But what if it was?

There's nothing wrong about that. The only trouble is that in my case—I'm not in a situation to—do the right thing.

I can't take down your number and say I'll phone.

I can't call up next week and—ask for a date.

I thought I had better explain the situation in case you—misunderstood it and—hurt your feelings. . . .

[*Pause.*]

[*Slowly, very slowly, LAURA's look changes, her eyes returning slowly from his to the ornament in her palm.*]

[AMANDA *utters another gay laugh in the kitchen.*]

LAURA. [*Faintly.*] You — won't — call again?

JIM. No, Laura, I can't.

[*He rises from the sofa.*]

As I was just explaining, I've—got strings on me.

Laura, I've—been going steady!

I go out all of the time with a girl named Betty. She's a home-girl like you, and Catholic, and Irish, and in a great many ways we—get along fine.

I met her last summer on a moonlight boat trip up the river to Alton, on the *Majestic.*

Well—right away from the start it was —love!

[LEGEND: LOVE!]

[LAURA *sways slightly forward and grips the arm of the sofa. He fails to notice, now enrapt in his own comfortable being.*]

Being in love has made a new man of me!

[*Leaning stiffly forward, clutching the arm of the sofa,* LAURA *struggles visibly with her storm. But* JIM *is oblivious, she is a long way off.*]

The power of love is really pretty tremendous!

Love is something that—changes the whole world, Laura!

[*The storm abates a little and* LAURA *leans back. He notices her again.*]

It happened that Betty's aunt took sick, she got a wire and had to go to Centralia. So Tom—when he asked me to dinner— I naturally just accepted the invitation, not knowing that you—that he—that I—

[*He stops awkwardly.*]

Huh—I'm a stumble-john!

[*He flops on the sofa.*]

[*The holy candles in the altar of* LAURA's *face have been snuffed out. There is a look of almost infinite desolation.*]

[JIM *glances at her uneasily.*]

I wish that you would—say something.

[*She bites her lip which was trembling and then bravely smiles. She opens her hand again on the broken glass ornament. Then she gently takes his hand and raises it level with her own. She carefully places the unicorn in the palm of his hand, then pushes his fingers closed upon it.*] What are you—doing that for? You want me to have him?—Laura? [*She nods.*] What for?

LAURA. A—souvenir . . .

[*She rises unsteadily and crouches beside the victrola to wind it up.*]

[LEGEND ON SCREEN: "THINGS HAVE A WAY OF TURNING OUT SO BADLY!"]

[OR IMAGE: "GENTLEMAN CALLER WAVING GOOD-BYE!—GAILY."]

[*At this moment,* AMANDA *rushes brightly back in the front room. She bears a pitcher of fruit punch in an old-fashioned cut-glass pitcher and a plate of macaroons. The plate has a gold border and poppies on it.*]

AMANDA. Well, well, well! Isn't the air delightful after the shower? I've made you children a little liquid refreshment.

[*Turns gaily to the gentleman caller.*]

Jim, do you know that song about lemonade?

"Lemondade, lemonade
    Made in the shade and stirred with
        a spade—
    Good enough for any old maid!"

JIM. [*Uneasily.*] Ha-ha! No—I never heard it.

AMANDA. Why, Laura! You look so serious!

JIM. We were having a serious conversation.

AMANDA. Good! Now you're better acquainted!

JIM. [Uncertainly.] Ha-ha! Yes.

AMANDA. You modern young people are much more serious-minded than my generation. I was so gay as a girl!

JIM. You haven't changed, Mrs. Wingfield.

AMANDA. Tonight I'm rejuvenated! The gaiety of the occasion, Mr. O'Connor!

[She tosses her head with a peal of laughter. Spills lemonade.]

Oooo! I'm baptizing myself!

JIM. Here—let me—

AMANDA. [Setting the pitcher down.] There now. I discovered we had some maraschino cherries. I dumped them in, juice and all.

JIM. You shouldn't have gone to that trouble, Mrs. Wingfield.

AMANDA. Trouble, trouble? Why, it was loads of fun!

Didn't you hear me cutting up in the kitchen? I bet your ears were burning! I told Tom how outdone with him I was for keeping you to himself so long a time! He should have brought you over much, much sooner! Well, now that you've found your way, I want you to be a very frequent caller! Not just occasional but all the time.

Oh, we're going to have a lot of gay times together! I see them coming!

Mmm, just breathe that air! So fresh, and the moon's so pretty!

I'll skip back out—I know where my place is when young folks are having a —serious conversation!

JIM. Oh, don't go out, Mrs. Wingfield. The fact of the matter is I've got to be going.

AMANDA. Going, now? You're joking! Why, it's only the shank of the evening, Mr. O'Connor!

JIM. Well, you know how it is.

AMANDA. You mean you're a young workingman and have to keep workingmen's hours. We'll let you off early tonight. But only on the condition that next time you stay later.

What's the best night for you? Isn't Saturday night the best night for you workingmen?

JIM. I have a couple of time-clocks to punch, Mrs. Wingfield. One at morning, another one at night!

AMANDA. My, but you are ambitious! You work at night, too?

JIM. No, Ma'am, not work but—Betty! [He crosses deliberately to pick up his hat. The band at the Paradise Dance Hall goes into a tender waltz.]

AMANDA. Betty? Betty? Who's—Betty! [There is an ominous cracking sound in the sky.]

JIM. Oh, just a girl. The girl I go steady with! [He smiles charmingly. The sky falls.]

[LEGEND: "THE SKY FALLS."]

AMANDA. [A long-drawn exhalation.] Ohhhh . . . Is it a serious romance, Mr. O'Connor?

JIM. We're going to be married the second Sunday in June.

AMANDA. Ohhh—how nice!

Tom didn't mention that you were engaged to be married.

JIM. The cat's not out of the bag at the warehouse yet.

You know how they are. They call you Romeo and stuff like that.

[He stops at the oval mirror to put on his hat. He carefully shapes the brim and the crown to give a discreetly dashing effect.]

It's been a wonderful evening, Mrs. Wingfield. I guess this is what they mean by Southern hospitality.

AMANDA. It really wasn't anything at all.

JIM. I hope it don't seem like I'm rushing off. But I promised Betty I'd pick her up at the Wabash depot, an' by the time I get my jalopy down there her train'll be in. Some women are pretty upset if you keep 'em waiting.

AMANDA. Yes, I know—The tyranny of women!

[Extends her hand.]

Good-bye, Mr. O'Connor.

I wish you luck—and happiness—and success! All three of them, and so does Laura!—Don't you, Laura?

LAURA. Yes!

JIM. [Taking her hand.] Good-bye, Laura. I'm certainly going to treasure that souvenir. And don't you forget the good advice I gave you.

[Raises his voice to a cheery shout.]

So long, Shakespeare!

Thanks again, ladies— Good night!

[*He grins and ducks jauntily out.*]

[*Still bravely grimacing,* AMANDA *closes the door on the gentleman caller. Then she turns back to the room with a puzzled expression. She and* LAURA *don't dare to face each other.* LAURA *crouches beside the victrola to wind it.*]

AMANDA. [*Faintly.*] Things have a way of turning out so badly.

I don't believe that I would play the victrola.

Well, well—well—

Our gentleman caller was engaged to be married!

Tom!

TOM. [*From back.*] Yes, Mother?

AMANDA. Come in here a minute. I want to tell you something awfully funny.

TOM. [*Enters with macaroon and a glass of lemonade.*] Has the gentleman caller gotten away already?

AMANDA. The gentleman caller has made an early departure.

What a wonderful joke you played on us!

TOM. How do you mean?

AMANDA. You didn't mention that he was engaged to be married.

TOM. Jim? Engaged?

AMANDA. That's what he just informed us.

TOM. I'll be jiggered! I didn't know about that.

AMANDA. That seems very peculiar.

TOM. What's peculiar about it?

AMANDA. Didn't you call him your best friend down at the warehouse?

TOM. He is, but how did I know?

AMANDA. It seems extremely peculiar that you wouldn't know your best friend was going to be married!

TOM. The warehouse is where I work, not where I know things about people!

AMANDA. You don't know things anywhere! You live in a dream; you manufacture illusions!

[*He crosses to door.*]

Where are you going?

TOM. I'm going to the movies.

AMANDA. That's right, now that you've had us make such fools of ourselves. The effort, the preparations, all the expense! The new floor lamp, the rug, the clothes for Laura! All for what? To entertain some other girl's fiancé!

Go to the movies, go! Don't think about us, a mother deserted, an unmarried sister who's crippled and has no job! Don't let anything interfere with your selfish pleasure! Just go, go, go—to the movies!

TOM. All right, I will! The more you shout about my selfishness to me the quicker I'll go, and I won't go to the movies!

AMANDA. Go, then! Then go to the moon —you selfish dreamer!

[TOM *smashes his glass on the floor. He plunges out on the fire-escape, slamming the door.* LAURA *screams— cut by door.*]

[*Dance-hall music up.* TOM *goes to the rail and grips it desperately, lifting his face in the chill white moonlight penetrating the narrow abyss of the alley.*]

[LEGEND ON SCREEN: "AND SO GOODBYE . . ."]

[TOM'S *closing speech is timed with the interior pantomime. The interior scene is played as though viewed through soundproof glass.* AMANDA *appears to be making a comforting speech to* LAURA *who is huddled upon the sofa. Now that we cannot hear the mother's speech, her silliness is gone and she has dignity and tragic beauty.* LAURA'S *dark hair hides her face until at the end of the speech she lifts it to smile at her mother.* AMANDA'S *gestures are slow and graceful, almost dancelike, as she comforts the daughter. At the end of her speech she glances a moment at the father's picture—then withdraws through the portieres. At the close of* TOM'S *speech,* LAURA *blows out the candles, ending the play.*]

TOM. I didn't go to the moon, I went much further—for time is the longest distance between two places—

Not long after that I was fired for writing a poem on the lid of a shoe-box.

I left Saint Louis. I descended the steps of this fire-escape for a last time and followed, from then on, in my father's footsteps, attempting to find in motion what was lost in space—

I traveled around a great deal. The cities swept about me like dead leaves,

leaves that were brightly colored but torn away from the branches.

I would have stopped, but I was pursued by something.

It always came upon me unawares, taking me altogether by surprise. Perhaps it was a familiar bit of music. Perhaps it was only a piece of transparent glass—

Perhaps I am walking along a street at night, in some strange city, before I have found companions. I pass the lighted window of a shop where perfume is sold. The window is filled with pieces of colored glass, tiny transparent bottles in delicate colors, like bits of a shattered rainbow.

Then all at once my sister touches my shoulder. I turn around and look into her eyes . . .

Oh, Laura, Laura, I tried to leave you behind me, but I am more faithful than I intended to be!

I reach for a cigarette, I cross the street, I run into the movies or a bar, I buy a drink, I speak to the nearest stranger—anything that can blow your candles out!

[LAURA *bends over the candles.*]

—for nowadays the world is lit by lightning! Blow out your candles, Laura—and so good-bye. . . .

[*She blows the candles out.*]

THE SCENE DISSOLVES

For Discussion and Writing

1. Critic John Gassner says Tennessee Williams is concerned always with "unfortunate characters who try to create and preserve ideal images of themselves as pathetic defenses against the frustration or shipwreck of their lives."

For each of the four characters in *The Glass Menagerie*, compare the image the character seeks to create for himself, with the actual reality of his or her life.

2. Tennessee William's production notes on page ooo suggest that the truth of life is approached more closely in the theater through the use of unconventional, anti-realistic techniques than through a photographic realistic copying of life. Do you agree or disagree with the playwright's viewpoint? Refer to scenes from *The Glass Menagerie* in your discussion.

3. Williams, who makes extensive use of symbolism, says, "Symbols are nothing but the natural speech of drama . . . a symbol in a play has only one legitimate purpose which is to say a thing more directly and simply and beautifully than it could be said in words."

Identify the symbols used in this play and discuss what you think the playwright means each of them to stand for.

4. The playwright calls *The Glass Menagerie* a memory play. Discuss what he means by this and what moods this device helps to create.

5. The device of the narrator is used in three of the plays in this book: *The Glass Menagerie, Our Town,* and *Teahouse of the August Moon.*

How is the use of the narrator different for each of the plays?

6. Both *The Little Foxes* and *The Glass Menagerie* have a female character who lives very largely in the romantic past of the South. Compare these two characters.

7. Write one of the following as Tennessee Williams might have done it:

The diary Laura could have kept during this play.

The dialogue between Tom and the Gentleman Caller when Tom invites him to dinner.

The dialogue between the Gentleman Caller and his fiancé when he tells her the story of where he has spent the evening.

The poem Tom wrote on the shoebox which lost him his job at the warehouse.

Day of Absence
A Satirical Fantasy

{1965}

DOUGLAS TURNER WARD

CHARACTERS
(In Order of Appearance)

CLEM	INDUSTRIALIST
LUKE	BUSINESSMAN
JOHN	CLUBWOMAN
MARY	COURIER
FIRST OPERATOR	ANNOUNCER
SECOND OPERATOR	CLAN
THIRD OPERATOR	AIDE
SUPERVISOR	PIOUS
JACKSON	DOLL WOMAN
MARY	BRUSH MAN
FIRST CITIZEN	MOP MAN
SECOND CITIZEN	RASTUS
THIRD CITIZEN	

The time is now. Play opens in unnamed Southern town of medium population on a somnolent cracker morning— meaning no matter the early temperature, it's gonna get hot. The hamlet is just beginning to rouse itself from the sleepy lassitude of night.

Day of Absence—New York production

$\mathcal{A}$ doublebill of one-act plays by Douglas Turner Ward, *Happy Ending* and *Day of Absence,* opened off-Broadway at the St. Mark's Playhouse in New York City on November 15, 1965. The plays were sharp, exceedingly funny satires from the black point of view on black-white relationships, and it had taken five years to raise funds for their production. They opened to a prolonged subway strike that reduced attendance, but those who did come were rewarded by seeing the playwright (under the name Douglas Turner) play the important role of the Mayor and the producer, Robert Hooks, the major role of John. Both men also doubled in minor roles.

Critical recognition, after a slow start, began to mount. In the spring of 1966, Douglas Turner Ward was honored by an Obie award for his acting and a Vernon Rice award for the writing in his first two produced plays. The plays ran for fourteen months and have since been produced on television, in black community theaters, in England, on college campuses, and in high schools.

In a program note for the 1969 London season of his Negro Ensemble Company, Mr. Ward said, "I've always felt that those Black plays which seem to be so clenched-fist-and-teeth, almost shrill, in their attack against Whitey emerge out of the Black writer's knowledge that he's talking to white people who don't hear him, don't understand him. He's got to sock it—scream." Despite criticism of his "racial conservatism" by both ethnic separatists and dogmatists, Mr. Ward has found perhaps a more effective weapon in the laugh. And although the laugh may be at the expense of the whites in the audience, they hear him—and they understand him— "loud and clear."

NOTES ON PRODUCTION

No scenery is necessary—only actors shifting in and out on an almost bare stage and freezing into immobility as focuses change or blackouts occur.

Play is conceived for performance by a Negro cast, a reverse minstrel show done in white-face. Logically, it might also be performed by whites —at their own risk. If any producer is faced with choosing between opposite hues, author strongly suggests: "Go 'long wit' the blacks—besides all else, they need the work more."

If acted by the latter, race members are urged to go for broke, yet cautioned not to ham it up too broadly. In fact—it just might be more effective if they aspire to serious tragedy. Only qualification needed for Caucasian casting is that the company fit a uniform pattern—insipid white.

Before any horrifying discrimination doubts arise, I hasten to add that a bonafide white actor should be cast as the Announcer in all productions; likewise a Negro thespian in pure native black as Rastus. This will truly subvert any charge that the production is unintegrated.

All props, except essential items (chairs, brooms, rags, mop, debris) should be imaginary (phones, switchboard, mikes, eating utensils, food, etc.). Actors should indicate their presence through mime.

The cast of characters develops as the play progresses. In the interest of economical casting, actors should double or triple in roles wherever possible.

PRODUCTION CONCEPT

This is a red-white-and-blue play—meaning the entire production should be designed around the basic color scheme of our patriotic trinity. *Lighting* should illustrate, highlight and detail time, action and mood. Opening scenes stage-lit with white rays of morning, transforming to panic reds of afternoon, flowing into ominous blues of evening. *Costuming* should be orchestrated around the same color scheme. In addition, subsidiary usage of grays, khakis, yellows, pinks, and combined patterns of stars-and-bars should be employed. Some actors (Announcer and Rastus excepted, of course) might wear white shoes or sneakers, and some women characters clothed in knee-length frocks might wear white stockings. Blonde wigs, both for males and females, can be used in selected instances. *Makeup* should have uniform consistency, with individual touches thrown in to enhance personal identity.

SAMPLE MODELS OF MAKEUP AND COSTUMING

Mary: Kewpie-doll face, ruby-red lips painted to valentine-pursing, moon-shaped rouge circles implanted on each cheek, blond wig of fat-flowing ringlets, dazzling ankle-length snow-white nightie.

Mayor: Seersucker white ensemble, ten-gallon hat, red string-tie and blue belt.

Clem: Khaki pants, bare headed, and blond.

Luke: Blue work-jeans, strawhatted.

Club Woman: Yellow dress patterned with *symbols of Dixie, gray hat*.

Clan: A veritable, riotous advertisement of red-white-and-blue combinations with stars-and-bars tossed in.

Pious: White ministerial garb with *black* cleric's collar topping his snow-white shirt.

Operators: All in red with different color wigs.

All other characters should be carefully defined through costuming which typifies their identity.

Day of Absence

SCENE: *Street.*

TIME: *Early morning.*

CLEM. [*Sitting under a sign suspended by invisible wires and bold-printed with the lettering: "STORE."*] 'Morning, Luke. . . .

LUKE. [*Sitting a few paces away under an identical sign.*] 'Morning, Clem. . . .

CLEM. Go'n' be a hot day

LUKE. Looks that way. . . .

CLEM. Might rain though. . . .

LUKE. Might.

CLEM. Hope it does. . . .

LUKE. Me, too. . . .

CLEM. Farmers could use a little wet spell for a change. . . . How's the Missis?

LUKE. Same.

CLEM. 'N' the kids?

LUKE. Them, too. . . . How's yourns?

CLEM. Fine, thank you. . . .

[*They both lapse into drowsy silence waving lethargically from time to time at imaginary passersby.*] Hi, Joe. . . .

LUKE. Joe. . . .

CLEM. . . . How'd it go yesterday, Luke?

LUKE. Fair.

CLEM. Same wit' me. . . . Business don't seem to git no better or no worse. Guess we in a rut, Luke, don't it 'pear that way to you?—Morning, ma'am.

LUKE. Morning. . . .

CLEM. Tried display, sales, advertisement, stamps—everything, yet merchandising stumbles 'round in the same old groove. . . . But—that's better than plunging downwards, I reckon.

LUKE. Guess it is.

CLEM. Morning, Bret. How's the family? . . . That's good.

LUKE. Bret—

CLEM. Morning, Sue.

LUKE. How do, Sue.

CLEM. [*Staring after her.*] . . . . Fine hunk of woman.

LUKE. Sure is.

CLEM. Wonder if it's any good?

LUKE. Bet it is.

CLEM. Sure like to find out!

LUKE. So would I.

CLEM. You ever try?

LUKE. Never did. . . .

CLEM. Morning, Gus. . . .

LUKE. Howdy, Gus.

CLEM. Fine, thank you.

[*They lapse into silence again.* CLEM *rouses himself slowly, begins to look around quizzically.*]

Luke . . . ?

LUKE. Huh?

CLEM. Do you . . . er, er—feel anything —funny . . . ?

LUKE. Like what?

CLEM. Like . . . er—something—strange?

LUKE. I dunno . . . haven't thought about it.

CLEM. I mean . . . like something's wrong—outta place, unusual?

LUKE. I don't know. . . . What you got in mind?

CLEM. Nothing . . . just that—just that— like somp'ums outta kilter. I got a funny feeling somp'ums not up to snuff. Can't figger out what it is . . .

LUKE. Maybe it's in your haid?

CLEM. No, not like that. . . . Like somp'ums happened—or happening—gone haywire, loony.

LUKE. Well, don't worry 'bout it, it'll pass.

CLEM. Guess you right. [*Attempts return to somnolence but doesn't succeed.*] . . . I'm sorry, Luke, but you sure you don't feel nothing peculiar . . . ?

LUKE. [*Slightly irked.*] Toss it out your mind, Clem! We got a long day ahead of us. If something's wrong, you'll know 'bout it in due time. No use worrying about it 'till it comes and if it's coming, it will. Now, relax!

CLEM. All right, you right. . . . Hi, Margie. . . .

LUKE. Marge.

CLEM. [*Unable to control himself.*]

Luke, I don't give a damn what you say. Somp'ums topsy-turvy, I just know it!

LUKE. [*Increasingly irritated.*] Now look here, Clem—it's a bright day, it looks like it's go'n' git hotter. You say the wife and kids are fine and the business is no better or no worse? Well, what else could be wrong? . . . If somp'ums go'n' happen, it's go'n' happen anyway and there ain't a damn fool thing you kin do to stop it! So you ain't helping me, yourself or nobody else by thinking 'bout it. It's not go'n' be no better or no worse when it gits here. It'll come to you when it gits ready to come and it's go'n' be the same whether you worry about it or not. So stop letting it upset you!

[LUKE *settles back in his chair.* CLEM *does likewise.* LUKE *shuts his eyes. After a few moments, they reopen. He forces them shut again. They reopen in greater curiosity. Finally, he rises slowly to an upright position in the chair, looks around frowningly. Turns slowly to* CLEM.]

. . . Clem? . . . You know something? . . . Somp'um is peculiar. . . .

CLEM. [*Vindicated.*] I knew it, Luke! I just knew it! Ever since we been sitting here, I been having that feeling!

[*Scene is blacked out abruptly. Lights rise on another section of the stage where a young couple lie in bed under an invisible-wire-suspension-sign lettered: "HOME." Loud insistent sounds of baby yells are heard.* JOHN, *the husband, turns over trying to ignore the cries;* MARY, *the wife, is undisturbed.* JOHN's *efforts are futile, the cries continue until they cannot be denied. He bolts upright, jumps out of bed and disappears off-stage. Returns quickly and tries to rouse* MARY.]

JOHN. Mary . . . [*Nudges her, pushes her, yells into her ear, but she fails to respond.*] Mary, get up. . . Get up!

MARY. Ummm . . . [*Shrugs away, still sleeping.*]

JOHN. GET UP!

MARY. UMMMMMMMMM!

JOHN. Don't you hear the baby bawling! . . . NOW GET UP!

MARY. [*Mumbling drowsily.*] . . . What baby . . . whose baby . . . ?

JOHN. Yours!

MARY. Mine? That's ridiculous. . . . what'd you say . . . ? Somebody's baby bawling? . . . How could that be so? [*Hearing screams.*] Who's crying? Somebody's crying! . . . What's crying? . . . WHERE'S LULA?

JOHN. I don't know. You better get up.

MARY. That's outrageous! . . . What time is it?

JOHN. Late 'nuff! Now rise up!

MARY. You must be joking. . . . I'm sure I still have four or five hours sleep in store—even more after that head-splittin' blow-out last night . . . [*Tumbles back under covers.*]

JOHN. Nobody told you to gulp those last six bourbons—

MARY. Don't tell me how many bourbons to swallow, not after you guzzled the whole stinking bar! . . . Get up? . . . You must be cracked. . . . Where's Lula? She must be here, she always is . . .

JOHN. Well, she ain't here yet, so get up and muzzle that brat before she does drive me cuckoo!

MARY. [*Springing upright, finally realizing gravity of situation.*] Whaddaya mean Lula's not here? She's always here, she must be here. . . . Where else kin she be? She supposed to be. . . . She just can't *not* be here— CALL HER!

[*Blackout as* JOHN *rushes offstage. Scene shifts to a trio of Telephone Operators perched on stools before imaginary switchboards. Chaos and bedlam are taking place to the sound of buzzes.* PRODUCTION NOTE: *Effect of following dialogue should simulate rising pandemonium.*]

FIRST OPERATOR. The line is busy—

SECOND OPERATOR. Line is busy—

THIRD OPERATOR. Is busy—

FIRST OPERATOR. Doing best we can—

SECOND OPERATOR. Having difficulty—

THIRD OPERATOR. Soon as possible—

FIRST OPERATOR. Just one moment—

SECOND OPERATOR. Would you hold on—

THIRD OPERATOR. Awful sorry, madam—

FIRST OPERATOR. Would you hold on, please—

SECOND OPERATOR. Just a second, please—

THIRD OPERATOR. Please hold on, please—

FIRST OPERATOR. The line is busy—

SECOND OPERATOR. The line is busy—

THIRD OPERATOR. The line is busy—
FIRST OPERATOR. Doing best we can—
SECOND OPERATOR. Hold on please—
THIRD OPERATOR. Can't make connections—
FIRST OPERATOR. Unable to put it in—
SECOND OPERATOR. Won't plug through—
THIRD OPERATOR. Sorry madam—
FIRST OPERATOR. If you wait a moment—
SECOND OPERATOR. Doing best we can—
THIRD OPERATOR. Sorry—
FIRST OPERATOR. One moment—
SECOND OPERATOR. Just a second—
THIRD OPERATOR. Hold on—
FIRST OPERATOR. Yes—
SECOND OPERATOR. STOP IT!—
THIRD OPERATOR. HOW DO I KNOW—
FIRST OPERATOR. YOU ANOTHER ONE!
SECOND OPERATOR. HOLD ON DAMMIT!
THIRD OPERATOR. UP YOURS, TOO!
FIRST OPERATOR. THE LINE IS BUSY—
SECOND OPERATOR. THE LINE IS BUSY—
THIRD OPERATOR. THE LINE IS BUSY—
[*The switchboard clamors a cacophony of buzzes as* OPERATORS *plug connections with the frenzy of a Chaplin movie. Their replies degenerate into a babble of gibberish. At the height of frenzy, the* SUPERVISOR *appears.*]
SUPERVISOR. WHAT'S THE SNARL-UP?
FIRST OPERATOR. Everybody calling at the same time, ma'am!
SECOND OPERATOR. Board can't handle it!
THIRD OPERATOR. Like everybody in big New York City is trying to squeeze a call through to li'l' ole us!
SUPERVISOR. God! . . . Somp'um terrible musta happened! . . . Buzz the emergency frequency hookup to the Mayor's office and find out what the hell's going on!
[*Scene blacks out quickly to* CLEM *and* LUKE.]
CLEM. [*Something slowly dawning on him.*] Luke . . . ?
LUKE. Yes, Clem?
CLEM. [*Eyes roving around in puzzlement.*] Luke . . . ?
LUKE. [*Irked.*] I said what, Clem!
CLEM. Luke . . . ? Where—where is—the—the—?

LUKE. THE WHAT?!
CLEM. Nigras . . . ?
LUKE. What . . . ?
CLEM. Nigras. . . . Where is the Nigras, where is they, Luke . . . ? ALL THE NIGRAS! . . . I don't see no Nigras . . . !
LUKE. Whatcha mean . . . ?
CLEM. [*Agitatedly.*] Luke, there ain't a darky in sight. . . . And if you remember, we ain't spied a nappy hair all morning. . . . The Nigras, Luke! We ain't laid eyes on nary a coon this whole morning!!!
LUKE. You must be crazy or something, Clem!
CLEM. Think about it, Luke, we been sitting here for an hour or more—try and recollect if you remember seeing jist *one* go by!
LUKE. [*Confused.*] . . . I don't recall . . . But . . . but there musta been some. . . . The heat musta got you, Clem! How in hell could that be so?
CLEM. [*Triumphantly.*] Just think, Luke! . . . Look around ya. . . . Now, every morning mosta people walkin' 'long this street is colored. They's strolling by going to work, they's waiting for the buses, they's sweeping sidewalks, cleaning stores, starting to shine shoes and wetting the mops—right? . . . Well, look around you, Luke—where is they? [*Luke paces up and down, checking.*] I told you, Luke, they ain't nowheres to be seen.
LUKE. . . . This . . . this . . . some kind of holiday for 'em—or something?
CLEM. I don't know, Luke . . . but . . . but what I do know is they ain't here 'n' we haven't seen a solitary one. . . . It's scaryfying. Luke . . . !
LUKE. Well . . . maybe they's jist standing 'n' walking and shining on other streets.—Let's go look!
[*Scene blacks out to* JOHN *and* MARY. *Baby cries are as insistent as ever.*]
MARY. [*At end of patience.*] SMOTHER IT!
JOHN. [*Beyond his.*] That's a hell of a thing to say 'bout your own child! You should know what to do to hush her up!
MARY. Why don't you try?
JOHN. You had her!
MARY. You shared in borning her!
JOHN. Possibly not!
MARY. Why, you lousy—!
JOHN. What good is a mother who can't shut up her own daughter?

MARY. I told you she yells louder every time I try to lay hands on her.— Where's Lula? Didn't you call her?!

JOHN. I told you I can't get the call through!

MARY. Try ag'in—

JOHN. It's no use! I tried numerous times and can't even git through to the switchboard. You've got to quiet her down yourself. [*Firmly.*] Now, go in there and clam her up 'fore I lose my patience!

[MARY *exits. Soon, we hear the yells increase. She rushes back in.*]

MARY. She won't let me touch her, just screams louder!

JOHN. Probably wet 'n' soppy!

MARY. Yes! Stinks something awful! Phooooey! I can't stand that filth and odor!

JOHN. That's why she's screaming! Needs her didee changed.—Go change it!

MARY. How you 'spect me to when I don't know how? Suppose I faint?

JOHN. Well let her blast away. I'm getting outta here.

MARY. You can't leave me here like this!

JOHN. Just watch me! . . . See this nice split-level cottage, peachy furniture, multi-colored teevee, hi-fi set 'n' the rest? . . . Well, how you think I scraped 'em together while you curled up on your fat li'l' fanny? . . . By gitting outta here—not only *on time* . . . but EARLIER!—Beating a frantic crew of nice young executives to the punch—gitting there fustest with the mostest brown-nosing you ever saw! Now if I goof one day—just ONE DAY!—You reckon I'd stay ahead? NO! . . . There'd be a wolf-pack trampling over my prostrate body, racing to replace my smiling face against the boss' left rump! . . . NO, MAM! I'm zooming outta here on time, just as I always have and what's more— you go'n' fix me some breakfast. I'M HUNGRY!

MARY. But—

JOHN. No buts about it! [*Flash blackout as he gags on a mouthful of coffee.*] What you trying to do, STRANGLE ME! [*Jumps up and starts putting on jacket.*]

MARY. [*Sarcastically.*] What did you expect?

JOHN. [*In biting fury.*] That you could possibly boil a pot of water, toast a few slices of bread and fry a coupler eggs! . . . It was a mistaken assumption!

MARY. So they aren't as good as Lula's!

JOHN. That is an overstatement. Your efforts don't result in anything that could possibly be digested by man, mammal, or insect! . . . When I married you, I thought I was fairly acquainted with your faults and weaknesses—I chalked em up to human imperfection. . . . But now I know I was being extremely generous, over-optimistic and phenomenally deluded!— You have no idea how useless you really are!

MARY. Then why'd you marry me?

JOHN. Decoration!

MARY. You shoulda married Lula!

JOHN. I might've if it wasn't 'gainst the segregaton law! . . . But for the sake of my home, my child and my sanity, I will even take a chance in sacrificing my slippery grip on the status pole and drive by her shanty to find out whether she or someone like her kin come over here and prevent some ultimate disaster. [*Storms toward door, stopping abruptly at exit.*] Are you sure you kin make it to the bath-room wit'out Lula backing you up?

[*Blackout. Scene shifts to* MAYOR's *office where a cluttered desk stands center amid papered debris.*]

MAYOR. [*Striding determinedly toward desk, stopping midways, bellowing.*] WOODFENCE! . . . WOODFENCE! . . . WOODFENCE! [*Receiving no reply, completes distance to desk.*] JACKSON! . . . JACKSON!

JACKSON. [*Entering worriedly.*] Yes, sir . . . ?

MAYOR. Where's Vice-Mayor Wood-fence, that no-good brother-in-law of mine?

JACKSON. Hasn't come in yet, sir.

MAYOR. HASN'T COME IN? . . . Damn bastard! Knows we have a crucial confer-ence. Soon as he staggers through that door, tell him to shoot in here! [*Angrily focusing on his disorderly desk and littered surroundings.*] And git Mandy here to straighten up this mess—Rufus too! You know he shoulda been waiting to knock dust off my shoes soon as I step in. Get 'em in here! . . . What's the matter wit' them lazy Nigras? . . . Already had to dress myself because of JC, fix my own coffee without MayBelle, drive myself to work 'counta Bubber, feel my old Hag's tits after Sapphi—NEVER MIND!—Git 'em in here—QUICK!

JACKSON. [*Meekly.*] They aren't . . . they aren't here, sir . . .

MAYOR. Whaddaya mean they aren't here? Find out where they at. We got important business, man! You can't run a town wit' laxity like this. Can't allow things to git snafued jist because a bunch of lazy Nigras been out gitting drunk and living it up all night! Discipline, man, discipline!

JACKSON. That's what I'm trying to tell you, sir . . . they didn't come in, can't be found . . . none of 'em.

MAYOR. Ridiculous, boy! Scare 'em up and tell 'em scoot here in a hurry befo' I git mad and fire the whole goddamn lot of 'em!

JACKSON. But we can't find 'em, sir.

MAYOR. Hogwash! Can't nobody in this office do anything right?! Do I hafta handle every piddling little matter myself? Git me their numbers, I'll have 'em here befo' you kin shout to—

[*Three men burst into room in various states of undress.*]

ONE. Henry—they vanished!

TWO. Disappeared into thin air!

THREE. Gone wit'out a trace!

TWO. Not a one on the street!

THREE. In the house!

ONE. On the job!

MAYOR. Wait a minute! . . . Hold your water! Calm down—!

ONE. But they've gone, Henry—GONE! All of 'em!

MAYOR. What the hell you talking 'bout? Who's gone—?

ONE. The Nigras, Henry! They gone!

MAYOR. Gone? . . . Gone where?

TWO. That's what we trying to tell ya—they just disappeared! The Nigras have disappeared, swallowed up, vanished! All of 'em! Every last one!

MAYOR. Have everybody 'round here gone batty? . . . That's impossible, how could the Nigras vanish?

THREE. Beats me, but it's happened!

MAYOR. You mean a whole town of Nigras just evaporate like this—poof!—Overnight?

ONE. Right!

MAYOR. Y'all must be drunk! Why, half this town is colored. How could they just sneak out!

TWO. Don't ask me, but there ain't one in sight!

MAYOR. Simmer down 'n' put it to me easy-like.

ONE. Well . . . I first suspected somp'um smelly when Sarah Jo didn't show up this morning and I couldn't reach her—

TWO. Dorothy Jane didn't 'rive at my house—

THREE. Georgia Mae wasn't at mine neither—and SHE sleeps in!

ONE. When I reached the office, I realized I hadn't seen nary one Nigra all morning! Nobody else had either—wait a minute—Henry, have you?!

MAYOR. Now that you mention it . . . no, I haven't . . .

ONE. They gone, Henry. . . . Not a one on the street, not a one in our homes, not a single, last living one to be found nowheres in town. What we gon' do!

MAYOR. [*Thinking.*] Keep heads on your shoulders 'n' put clothes on your back. . . . They can't be far. . . . Must be 'round somewheres. . . . Probably playing hide 'n' seek, that's it! . . . JACKSON!

JACKSON. Yessir?

MAYOR. Immediately mobilize our Citizens Emergency Distress Committee!—Order a fleet of sound trucks to patrol streets urging the population to remain calm—situation's not as bad as it looks—everything's under control! Then have another squadron of squawk buggies drive slowly through all Nigra alleys, ordering them to come out wherever they are. If that don't git 'em organize a vigilante search-squad to flush 'em outta hiding! But most important of all, track down that lazy goldbricker, Woodfence, and tell him to git on top of the situation! By God, we'll find 'em even if we hafta dig 'em outta the ground!

[*Blackout. Scene shifts back to* JOHN *and* MARY *a few hours later. A funeral solemnity pervades their mood.* JOHN *stands behind* MARY *who sits, in a scene duplicating the famous "American Gothic" painting.*]

JOHN. . . . Walked up to the shack, knocked on door, didn't git no answer. Hollered "LULA? LULA . . . ?—Not a thing. Went 'round the side, peeped in window—nobody stirred. Next door—nobody there. Crossed other side of street and banged on five or six other doors—not a colored person could be found! Not a man, neither woman or child—not even a little black dog could be seen, smelt or heard for blocks around. . . . They've gone, Mary.

MARY. What does it all mean, John?

JOHN. I don't know, Mary . . .

MARY. I always had Lula, John. She never missed a day at my side. . . . That's why I couldn't accept your wedding proposal until I was sure you'd welcome me and her together as a package. How am I gonna git through the day? My baby don't know *me*, I ain't acquainted wit' *it*. I've never lifted cover off pot, swung a mop or broom, dunked a dish or even pushed a dustrag. I'm lost wit'out Lula, I need her, John, I need her. [*Begins to weep softly.* JOHN *pats her consolingly.*]

JOHN. Courage, honey. . . . Everybody in town is facing the same dilemma. We mustn't crack up . . .

[*Blackout. Scene shifts back to* MAYOR's *office later in day. Atmosphere and tone resembles a wartime headquarters at the front.* MAYOR *is poring over huge map.*]

INDUSTRIALIST. Half the day is gone already, Henry. On behalf of the factory owners of this town, you've got to bail us out! Seventy-five percent of all production is paralyzed. With the Nigra absent, men are waiting for machines to be cleaned, floors to be swept, crates lifted, equipment delivered and bathrooms to be deodorized. Why, restrooms and toilets are so filthy until they not only cannot be sat in, but it's virtually impossible to get within hailing distance because of the stench!

MAYOR. Keep your shirt on, Jeb—

BUSINESSMAN. Business is even in worse condition, Henry. The volume of goods moving 'cross counters has slowed down to a trickle—almost negligible. Customers are not only not purchasing—but the absence of handymen, porters, sweepers, stock-movers, deliverers and miscellaneous dirty-work doers is disrupting the smooth harmony of marketing!

CLUB WOMAN. Food poisoning, severe indigestitis, chronic diarrhea, advanced diaper chafings and a plethora of unsanitary household disasters dangerous to life, limb and property! . . . As a representative of the Federation of Ladies' Clubs, I must sadly report that unless the trend is reversed, a complete breakdown in family unity is imminent. . . . Just as homosexuality and debauchery signalled the fall of Greece and Rome, the downgrading of Southern Bellesdom might very well prophesy the collapse of our indigenous institutions. . . . Remember—it has always been pure, delicate, lily-white images of Dixie femininity which provided backbone, inspiration and ideology for our male warriors in their defense against the on-rushing black horde. If our gallant men are drained of this worship and idolatry—God knows! The cause won't be worth a Confederate nickel!

MAYOR. Stop this panicky defeatism, y'all hear me! All machinery at my disposal is being utilized. I assure you wit' great confidence the damage will soon repair itself.—Cheerful progress reports are expected any moment now.—Wait! See, here's Jackson. . . . Well, Jackson?

JACKSON. [*Entering.*] As of now, sir, all efforts are fruitless. Neither hide nor hair of them has been located. We have not unearthed a single one in our shack-to-shack search. Not a single one has heeded our appeal. Scoured every crick and cranny inside their hovels, turning furniture upside down and inside out, breaking down walls and tearing through ceilings. We made determined efforts to discover where 'bouts of our faithful uncle Toms and informers—but even they have vanished without a trace. \ . . . Searching squads are on the verge of panic and hysteria, sir, wit' hotheads among 'em campaigning for scorched earth policies. Nigras on a whole lack cellars, but there's rising sentiment favoring burning to find out whether they're underground—DUG IN!

MAYOR. Absolutely counter such foolhardy suggestions! Suppose they are tombed in? We'd only accelerate the gravity of the situation using incendiary tactics! Besides, when they're rounded up where will we put 'em if we've already burned up their shacks—IN OUR OWN BEDROOMS?

JACKSON. I agree, sir, but the mood of the crowd is becoming irrational. In anger and frustration, they's forgetting their original purpose was to FIND the Nigras!

MAYOR. At all costs! Stamp out all burning proposals! Must prevent extremist no-tions from gaining ascendancy. Git wit' it. . . . Wait—'n' for Jehovah's sake, find out where the hell is that trifling slacker, WOODFENCE!

COURIER. [*Rushing in.*] Mr. Mayor! Mr. Mayor! . . . We've found some! We've found some!

MAYOR. [*Excitedly.*] Where?!

COURIER. In the—in the—[*Can't catch breath.*]

MAYOR. [*Impatiently.*] Where, man? Where?

COURIER. In the colored wing of the city hospital!

MAYOR. The hos—? The hospital! I shoulda known! How could those helpless, crippled, cut and shot Nigras disappear from a hospital! Shoulda thought of that! . . . Tell me more, man!

COURIER. I—I didn't wait, sir. . . . I—I ran in to report soon as I heard—

MAYOR. WELL GIT BACK ON THE PHONE, YOU IDIOT, DON'T YOU KNOW WHAT THIS MEANS!

COURIER. Yes, sir. [*Races out.*]

MAYOR. Now we gitting somewhere! . . . Gentlemen, if one sole Nigra is among us, we're well on the road to re-habilitation! Those Nigras in the hospital must know somp'um 'bout the others where'bouts. . . . Scat back to your colleagues, boost up their morale and inform 'em that things will zip back to normal in a jiffy!

[*They start to file out, then pause to observe the* COURIER *reentering dazedly.*]

Well . . . ? Well, man . . . ? WHAT'S THE MATTER WIT' YOU, NINNY, TELL ME WHAT ELSE WAS SAID?

COURIER. They all . . . they all . . . they all in a—in a—a coma, sir . . .

MAYOR. They all in a what . . . ?

COURIER. In a coma, sir . . .

MAYOR. Talk sense, man! . . . Whaddaya mean, they all in a coma?

COURIER. Doctor says every last one of the Nigras are jist laying in bed . . . STILL . . . not moving . . . neither live or dead . . . laying up there in a coma . . . every last one of 'em . . .

MAYOR. [*Sputters, then grabs phone.*] Get me Confederate Memorial. . . . Put me through to the Staff Chief. . . . YES, this is the Mayor. . . . Sam? . . . What's this I hear? . . . But how could they be in a coma, Sam? . . . You don't know! Well, what the hell you think the city's paying you for! . . . You've got 'nuff damn hacks and quacks there to find out! . . . How could it be somp'um unknown? You mean Nigras know somp'um 'bout drugs your damn butchers don't?! . . . Well, what the crap good are they! . . . All right, all right, I'll be calm. . . . Now, tell me. . . . Uh huh, uh huh. . . . Well, can't you give 'em some injections or somp'um . . . ?—You did . . . uh huh . . . DID YOU TRY A LI'L' ROUGH TREATMENT?—that too, huh. . . . All right, Sam, keep trying. . . . [*Puts phone down delicately, continuing absently.*] Can't wake 'em up. Just lay there. Them that's sick won't git no sicker, them that's half-well won't git no better, babies that's due won't be born and them that's come won't show no life. Nigras wit' cuts won't bleed and them which need blood won't be transfused. . . . He say dying Nigras is even refusing to pass away! [*Is silently perplexed for a moment, then suddenly breaks into action.*] JACKSON?! . . . Call up the police—THE JAIL! Find out what's going on there! Them Nigras are captives! If there's one place we got darkies under control, it's there! Them sonsabitches too onery to act right either for colored or white!

[JACKSON *exits. The* COURIER *follows.*] Keep your fingers crossed, citizens, them Nigras in jail are the most important Nigras we got!

[*All hands are raised conspicuously aloft, fingers prominently ex-ed. Seconds tick by. Soon* JACKSON *returns crestfallen.*]

JACKSON. Sheriff Bull says they don't know whether they still on premises or not. When they went to rouse Nigra jail-birds this morning, cell-block doors refused to swing open. Tried everything—even exploded dynamite charges—but it just wouldn't budge. . . . Then they hoisted guards up to peep through barred windows, but couldn't see good 'nuff to tell whether Nigras was inside or not. Finally, gitting desperate, they power-hosed the cells wit' water but had to cease 'cause Sheriff Bull said he didn't wanta jeopardize drowning the Nigras since it might spoil his chance of shipping a record load of cotton pickers to the State Penitentiary for cotton-snatching jubilee. . . . Anyway —they ain't heard a Nigra-squeak all day.

MAYOR. That so . . . ? WHAT 'BOUT TRAINS 'N' BUSSES PASSING THROUGH? There must be some dinges riding through?

JACKSON. We checked . . . not a one on board.

MAYOR. Did you hear whether any other towns lost their Nigras?

JACKSON. Things are status-quo everywhere else.

MAYOR. [Angrily.] Then what the hell they picking on us for!

COURIER. [Rushing in.] MR. MAYOR! Your sister jist called—HYSTERICAL! She says Vice-Mayor Woodfence went to bed wit her last night, but when she woke up this morning he was gone! Been missing all day!

MAYOR. Could Nigras be holding brother-in-law Woodfence hostage?

COURIER. No, sir. Besides him—investigations reveal that dozens of more prominent citizens—two City Council members, the chairman of the Junior Chamber of Commerce, our City College All-Southern half-back, the chairlady of the Daughters of the Confederate Rebellion, Miss Cotton-Sack Festival of the Year and numerous other miscellaneous nobodies—are all absent wit'out leave. Dangerous evidence points to the conclusion that they have been infiltrating!

MAYOR. Infiltrating?

COURIER. Passing all along!

MAYOR. PASSING ALL ALONG?

COURIER. Secret Nigras all the while!

MAYOR. NAW!

[CLUB WOMAN keels over in faint. JACKSON, BUSINESSMAN and INDUSTRIALIST begin to eye each other suspiciously.]

COURIER. Yessir!

MAYOR. PASSING?

COURIER. Yessir!

MAYOR. SECRET NIG—?

COURIER. Yessir!

MAYOR. [Momentarily stunned to silence.] The dirty mongrelizers! . . . Gentlemen, this is a grave predicament indeed. . . . It pains me to surrender priority to our states' right credo, but it is my solemn task and frightening duty to inform you that we have no other re-course but to seek outside help for deliverance.

[Blackout. Lights re-rise on Huntley-Brinkley-Murrow-Sevareid-Cronkite-Reasoner-type ANNOUNCER grasping a hand-held microphone [imaginary] a few hours later. He is vigorously, excitedly mouthing his commentary, but no sound escapes his lips. . . . During this dumb, wordless section of his broadcast, a bedraggled assortment of figures marching with picket signs occupy his attention. On their picket signs are inscribed various appeals and slogans. "CINDY LOU UNFAIR TO BABY JOE" . . . "CAP'N SAM MISS BIG BOY" . . . "RETURN LI'L' BLUE TO MARSE JIM" . . . "INFORMATION REQUESTED 'BOUT MAMMY GAIL" . . . "BOSS NATHAN PROTEST TO FAST LEROY." Trailing behind the marchers, forcibly isolated, is a woman dressed in widow-black holding a placard which reads: "WHY DIDN'T YOU TELL US—YOUR DEFILED WIFE AND TWO ABSENT MONGRELS."]

ANNOUNCER. [Who has been silently mouthing his delivery during the picketing procession, is suddenly heard as if caught in the midst of commentary.] . . . Factories standing idle from the loss of non-essential workers. Stores shuttered from the absconding of uncrucial personnel. Uncollected garbage threatening pestilence and pollution. . . . Also, each second somewheres in this former utopia below the Mason and Dixon, dozens of decrepit old men and women usually tended by faithful nurses and servants are popping off like flies—abandoned by sons, daughters and grandchildren whose refusal to provide their doddering relatives with bedpans and other soothing necessities results in their hasty, nasty, messy corpus delicties. . . . But most critically affected of all by this complete drought of Afro-American resources are policemen and other public safety guardians denied their daily quota of Negro arrests. One officer known affectionately as "TWO-A-DAY-PETE" because of his unblemished record of TWO Negro head-whippings per day has already been carted off to the County Insane Asylum—straight-jacketed, screaming and biting, unable to withstand the shock of having his spotless slate sullied by interruption. . . . It is feared that similar attacks are soon expected among municipal judges prevented for the first time in years of distinguished bench-sitting from sentencing one single Negro to a hoosegow or pokey. . . . Ladies and gentlemen, as you trudge in from the joys and headaches of workday chores and dusk begins to descend on this sleepy Southern hamlet, we REPEAT—today—before early morning dew had dried upon magnolia blossoms, your comrade citizens of this lovely Dixie village awoke to the realization that some—pardon me! Not some—but ALL OF THEIR NEGROES were missing. . . . Absent, vamoosed, departed, at bay, fugitive, away, gone and so-far unretrieved. . . . In order to dispel your incredulity, gauge the temper of your suffering compatriots and just possibly prepare you for the likelihood of an equally nightmarish eventuality, we have gathered a cross-section of this city's most distinguished leaders for exclusive interviews. . . . First, Mr. Council Clan, grand-dragoon of this area's most active civic organizations and staunch bell-wether of the political opposition. . . . Mr. Clan, how do you ACCOUNT for this incredible disappearance?

CLAN. A PLOT, plain and simple, that's what it is, as plain as the corns on your feet!

ANNOUNCER. Whom would you consider responsible?

CLAN. I could go on all night.

ANNOUNCER. Cite a few?

CLAN. Too numerous.

ANNOUNCER. Just one?

CLAN. Name names when time comes.

ANNOUNCER. Could you be referring to native Negroes?

CLAN. Ever try quaranteening lepers from their spots?

ANNOUNCER. Their organizations?

CLAN. Could you slice a nose off a mouth and still keep a face?

ANNOUNCER. Commies?

CLAN. Would you lop off a titty from a chest and still have a breast?

ANNOUNCER. Your city government?

CLAN. Now you talkin'!

ANNOUNCER. State administration?

CLAN. Warming up!

ANNOUNCER. Federal?

CLAN. Kin a blind man see?

ANNOUNCER. The Court?

CLAN. Is a pig clean?

ANNOUNCER. Clergy?

CLAN. Do a polecat stink?

ANNOUNCER. Well, Mr. Clan, with this massive complicity, how do you think the plot could've been prevented from succeeding?

CLAN. If I'da been in office, it never woulda happened.

ANNOUNCER. Then you're laying major blame at the doorstep of the present administration?

CLAN. Damn tooting!

ANNOUNCER. But from your oft-expressed views, Mr. Clan, shouldn't you and your followers be delighted at the turn of events? After all—isn't it one of the main policies of your society to *drive* Negroes away? *Drive* 'em back where they came from?

CLAN. DRIVVVE, BOY! DRIIIIVVVE! That's right! . . . When we say so and not befo'. Ain't supposed to do nothing 'til we tell 'em. Got to stay put until we exercise our God-given right to tell 'em when to git!

ANNOUNCER. But why argue if they've merely jumped the gun? Why not rejoice at this premature purging of undesirables?

CLAN. The time ain't ripe yet, boy. . . . The time ain't ripe yet.

ANNOUNCER. Thank you for being so informative, Mr. Clan—Mrs. Aide? Mrs. Aide? Over here, Mrs. Aide. . . . Ladies and gentlemen, this city's Social Welfare Commissioner, Mrs. Handy Anna Aide. . . . Mrs. Aide, with all your Negroes AWOL, haven't developments alleviated the staggering demands made upon your Welfare Department? Reduction of relief requests, elimination of case loads, removal of chronic welfare dependents, et cetera?

AIDE. Quite the contrary. Disruption of our pilot projects among Nigras saddles our white community with extreme hardship. . . . You see, historically, our agencies have always been foremost contributors to the Nigra Git-A-Job movement. We pioneered in enforcing social welfare theories which oppose coddling the fakers. We strenuously believe in helping Nigras help themselves by participating in meaningful labor. "Relief is Out, Work is In," is our motto. We place them as maids, cooks, butlers, and breast-feeders, cesspool-diggers, wash-basin maintainers, shoe-shine boys, and so on—mostly on a volunteer self-work basis.

ANNOUNCER. Hired at prevailing salaried rates, of course?

AIDE. God forbid! Money is unimportant. Would only make 'em worse. Our main goal is to improve their ethical behavior. "Rehabilitation Through Positive Participation" is another motto of ours. All unwed mothers, loose-living malingering fathers, bastard children and shiftless grandparents are kept occupied through constructive muscle-therapy. This provides the Nigra with less opportunity to indulge his pleasure-loving amoral inclinations.

ANNOUNCER. They volunteer to participate in these pilot projects?

AIDE. Heavens no! They're notorious shirkers. When I said the program is voluntary, I meant white citizens in overwhelming majorities do the volunteering. Placing their homes, offices, appliances and persons at our disposal for use in "Operation Uplift." . . . We would never dare place such a decision in the hands of the Nigra. It would never get off the ground! . . . No, they have no choice in the matter. "Work or Starve" is the slogan we use to stimulate Nigra awareness of what's good for survival.

ANNOUNCER. Thank you, Mrs. Aide, and good luck. . . . Rev? . . . Rev? . . . Ladies and gentlemen, this city's foremost spiritual guidance counselor, Reverend Reb Pious. . . . How does it look to you, Reb Pious?

PIOUS. [Continuing to gaze skyward.] It's in His hands, son, it's in His hands.

ANNOUNCER. How would you assess the disappearance, from a moral standpoint?

PIOUS. An immoral act, son, morally wrong and ethically indefensible. A perversion of Christian principles to be condemned from every pulpit of this nation.

ANNOUNCER. Can you account for its occurrence after the many decades of the Church's missionary activity among them?

PIOUS. It's basically a reversion of the Nigra to his deep-rooted primitivism. . . .

Now, at last, you can inderstand the difficulties of the Church in attempting to anchor God's kingdom among ungratefuls. It's a constant, unrelenting, no-holds-barred struggle against Satan to wrestle away souls locked in his possession for countless centuries! Despite all our aid, guidance, solace and protection, Old BeezleBub still retains tenacious grips upon the Nigras, childish loyalty—comparable to the lure of bright flames to an infant.

ANNOUNCER. But actual physical departure, Reb Pious? How do you explain that?

PIOUS. Voodoo, my son, voodoo. . . . With Satan's assist, they have probably employed some heathen magic which we cultivated, sophisticated Christians know absolutely nothing about. However, before long we are confident about counteracting this evil witch-doctory and triumphing in our Holy Savior's name. At this perilous juncture, true believers of all denominations are participating in joint, 'round-the-clock observances, offering prayers for our Master's swiftest intercession. I'm optimistic about the outcome of his intervention. . . . Which prompts me—if I may, sir—to offer these words of counsel to our delinquent Nigras. . . . I say to you without rancor or vengeance, quoting a phrase of one of your greatest prophets, Booker T. Washington: "Return your buckets to where they lay and all will be forgiven."

ANNOUNCER. A very inspirational appeal, Reb Pious. I'm certain they will find the tug of its magnetic sincerity irresistible. Thank you, Reb Pious. . . . All in all—as you have witnessed, ladies and gentlemen—this town symbolizes the face of disaster. Suffering as severe a prostration as any city wrecked, ravaged, and devastated by the holocaust of war. A vital, lively, throbbing organism brought to a screeching halt by the strange enigma of the missing Negroes. . . . We take you now to offices of the one man into whose hands has been thrust the final responsibility of rescuing this shuddering metropolis from the precipice of destruction. . . . We give you the honorable Mayor, Henry R. E. Lee. . . . Hello, Mayor Lee.

MAYOR. [Jovially.] Hello, Jack.

ANNOUNCER. Mayor Lee, we have just concluded interviews with some of your city's leading spokesmen. If I may say so, sir, they don't sound too encouraging about the situation.

MAYOR. Nonsense, Jack! The situation's as well-in-hand as it could be under the circumstances. Couldn't be better in hand. Underneath every dark cloud, Jack, there's always a ray of sunlight, ha, ha, ha.

ANNOUNCER. Have you discovered one, sir?

MAYOR. Well, Jack, I'll tell you. . . . Of course we've been faced wit' a little crisis, but look at it like this—we've faced 'em befo': Sherman marched through Georgia—ONCE! Lincoln freed the slaves —MOMENTARILY! Carpetbaggers even put Nigras in the Governor's mansion, state legislature, Congress and the Senate of the United States. But what happened? —Ole Dixie bounced right on back up. . . . At this moment the Supreme Court's trying to put Nigras in our schools and the Nigra has got it in his haid to put hisself everywhere. . . . But what you 'spect go'n' happen?—Ole Dixie will kangaroo back even higher. Southern courage, fortitude, chivalry and superiority always wins out. . . . SHUCKS! We'll have us some Nigras befo' daylight is gone!

ANNOUNCER. Mr. Mayor, I hate to introduce this note, but in an earlier interview, one of your chief opponents, Mr. Clan, hinted at your own complicity in the affair—

MAYOR. A LOT OF POPPYCOCK! Clan is politicking! I've beaten him four times outta four and I'll beat him four more times outta four! This is no time for partisan politics! What we need now is level-headedness and across-the-board unity. This typical, rash, mealy-mouth, shooting-off-at-the-lip of Clan and his ilk proves their insincerity and voters will remember that in the next election! Won't you, voters? [Has risen to the height of his campaign oratory.]

ANNOUNCER. Mr. Mayor! . . . Mr. Mayor! . . . Please—

MAYOR. . . . I tell you, I promise you—

ANNOUNCER. PLEASE, MR. MAYOR!

MAYOR. Huh? . . . Oh—yes, carry on.

ANNOUNCER. Mr. Mayor, your cheerfulness and infectious good spirits lead me to conclude that startling new developments warrant fresh-found optimism.

What concrete, declassified information do you have to support your claim that Negroes will reappear before nightfall?

MAYOR. Because we are presently awaiting the pay-off of a masterful five-point supra-recovery program which can't help but reap us a bonanza of Nigras 'fore sundown! . . . First: Exhaustive efforts to pinpoint the where'bouts of our own missing darkies continue to zero in on the bullseye. . . . Second: The President of the United States, following an emergency cabinet meeting, has designated us the prime disaster area of the century—National Guard is already on the way. . . . Third: In an unusual, but bold maneuver, we have appealed to the NAACP 'n' all other Nigra conspirators to help us git to the bottom of the vanishing act. . . . Fourth: We have exercised our nonreciprocal option and requested that all fraternal southern states express their solidarity by lending us some of their Nigras temporarily on credit. . . . Fifth and foremost: We have already gotten consent of the Governor to round up all stray, excess and incorrigible Nigras to be shipped to us under escort of the State Militia. . . . That's why we've stifled pessimism and are brimming wit' confidence that this full-scale concerted mobilization will ring down a jackpot of jigaboos 'fore light vanishes from sky!—

ANNOUNCER. Congratulations! What happens if it fails?

MAYOR. Don't even think THAT! Absolutely no reason to suspect it will. . . . [Peers over shoulder, then whispers confidentially while placing hand over mouth by ANNOUNCER's imaginary mike.] . . . But speculating on the dark side of your question—if we don't turn up some by nightfall, it may be all over. The harm has already been done. You see the South has always been glued together by the uninterrupted presence of its darkies. No telling how unstuck we might git if things keep on like they have.—Wait a minute, it musta paid off already! Mission accomplished 'cause here's Jackson head a time wit' the word. . . . Well, Jackson, what's new?

JACKSON. Situation on the home front remains static, sir—can't uncover scent or shadow. The NAACP and all other Nigra front groups 'n' plotters deny any knowledge or connection wit' the missing

Nigras. Maintained this even after appearing befo' a Senate Emergency Investigating Committee which subpoenaed 'em to Washington post haste and threw 'em in jail for contempt. A handful of Nigras who agreed to make spectacular appeals for ours to come back to us, have themselves mysteriously disappeared. But, worst news of all, sir, is our sister cities and counties, inside and outside the state, have changed their minds, fallen back on their promises and refused to lend us any Nigras, claiming they don't have 'nuff for themselves.

MAYOR. What 'bout Nigras promised by the Governor?

JACKSON. Jailbirds and vagrants escorted here from chain-gangs and other reservations either revolted and escaped enroute or else vanished mysteriously on approaching our city limits. . . . Deterioration rapidly escalates, sir. Estimates predict we kin hold out only one more hour before overtaken by anarchistic turmoil. . . . Some citizens seeking haven elsewheres have already fled, but on last report were being forcibly turned back by armed sentinels in other cities who wanted no parts of 'em—claiming they carried a jinx.

MAYOR. That bad, huh?

JACKSON. Worse, sir . . . we've received at least five reports of plots on your life.

MAYOR. What?!—We've gotta act quickly then!

JACKSON. Run out of ideas, sir.

MAYOR. Think harder, boy!

JACKSON. Don't have much time, sir. One measly hour, then all hell go'n' break loose.

MAYOR. Gotta think of something drastic, Jackson!

JACKSON. I'm dry, sir.

MAYOR. Jackson! Is there any planes outta here in the next hour?

JACKSON. All transportation's been knocked out, sir.

MAYOR. I thought so!

JACKSON. What were you contemplating, sir?

MAYOR. Don't ask me what I was contemplating! I'm still boss 'round here! Don't forget it!

JACKSON. Sorry, sir.

MAYOR. . . . Hold the wire! . . . Wait a minute . . . ! Waaaaait a minute—

GODAMNIT! All this time crapping 'round, diddling and fotsing wit' puny li'l' solutions—all the while neglecting our ace in the hole, our trump card! Most potent weapon for digging Nigras outta the woodpile! All the while right befo' our eyes! . . . Ass! Why didn't you remind me?

JACKSON. What is it, sir?

MAYOR. . . . ME—THAT'S WHAT! ME! A personal appeal from ME! *Directly to them!* . . . Although we wouldn't let 'em march to the polls and express their affection for me through the ballot box, we've always known I'm held highest in their esteem. A direct address from their beloved Mayor! . . . If they's anywheres close within the sound of my voice, they'll shape up! Or let us know by a sign they's ready to!

JACKSON. You sure *that'll* turn the trick, sir?

MAYOR. As sure as my ancestors befo' me who knew that when they puckered their lips to whistle, ole Sambo was gonna come a-lickety-splitting to answer the call! . . . That same chips-down blood courses through these Confederate gray veins of Henry R. E. Lee!

ANNOUNCER. I'm delighted to offer our network's facilities for such a crucial public interest address, sir. We'll arrange immediately for your appearance on an international hookup, placing you in the widest proximity to contact them wherever they may be.

MAYOR. Thank you, I'm very grateful. . . . Jackson, re-grease the machinery and set wheels in motion. Inform townspeople what's being done. Tell 'em we're all in this together. The next hour is countdown. I demand absolute cooperation, city-wide silence and inactivity. I don't want the Nigras frightened if they's nearby. This is the most important hour in town's history. Tell 'em if one single Nigra shows up during hour of decision, victory is within sight. I'm gonna git 'em that one—maybe all! Hurry and crack to it!

[ANNOUNCER *rushes out, followed by* JACKSON. *Blackout. Scene re-opens, with* MAYOR *seated, eyes front, spotlight illuminating him in semi-darkness. Shadowy figures stand in the background, prepared to answer*

phones or aid in any other manner.
MAYOR *waits patiently until "GO!"*
signal is given. Then begins, his voice
combining elements of confidence,
tremolo and gravity.]
Good evening. . . . Despite the fact that
millions of you wonderful people throughout the nation are viewing and listening
to this momentous broadcast—and I thank
you for your concern and sympathy in
this hour of our peril—I primarily want
to concentrate my attention and address
these remarks solely for the benefit of our
departed Nigra friends who may be listening somewhere in our far-flung land
to the sound of my voice. . . . If you are
—it is with heart-felt emotion and fond
memories of our happy association that I
ask—"Where are you . . . ?" Your absence
has left a void in the bosom of every
single man, woman and child of our
great city. I tell you—you don't know
what it means for us to wake up in the
morning and discover that your cheerful,
grinning, happy-go-lucky faces are missing! . . . From the depths of my heart, I
can only meekly, humbly suggest what it
means to me personally. . . . You see—the
one face I will never be able to erase
from my memory is the face—not of my
Ma, not of Pa, neither wife or child—but
the image of the first woman I came to
love so well when just a wee lad—the
vision of the first human I laid clear sight
on at childbirth—the profile—better yet,
the full face of my dear old . . . Jemimah
—God rest her soul. . . . Yes! My dear ole
mammy, wit' her round ebony moonbeam
gleaming down upon me in the crib, teeth
shining, blood-red bandana standing
starched, peaked and proud, gazing down
upon me affectionately as she crooned me
a Southern lullaby. . . . OH! It's a memorable picture I will eternally cherish in
permanent treasure chambers of my heart,
now and forever always. . . . Well, if
this radiant image can remain so infinitely
vivid to me all these many years after her
unfortunate demise in the Po' folks home
—THINK of the misery the rest of us
must be suffering after being *freshly* denied your soothing presence?! We need
ya. If you kin hear me, just contact this
station 'n' I will welcome you back personally. Let me just tell you that since
you eloped, nothing has been the same.

How could it? You're part of us, you belong to us. Just give us a sign and we'll
be contented that all is well. . . . Now if
you've skipped away on a little fun-fest,
we understand, ha, ha. We know you like
a good time and we don't begrudge it to
ya. Hell—er, er, we like a good time ourselves—who doesn't? . . . In fact, think of
all the good times we've had together,
huh? We've had some real fun, you and
us, yesiree! . . . Nobody knows better
than you and I what fun we've had together. You singing us those old Southern
coon songs and dancing those Nigra jigs
and us clapping, prodding 'n' spurring you
on! Lots of fun, huh? . . . OH BOY! The
times we've had together. . . . If you've
snucked away for a bit of fun by yourself,
we'll go 'long wit' ya—long as you let us
know where you at so we won't be worried about you. . . . We'll go 'long wit'
you long as you don't take the joke too
far. I'll admit a joke is a joke and you've
played a LULU! . . . I'm warning you,
we can't stand much more horsing 'round
from you! Business is business 'n' fun is
fun! You've had your fun so now let's get
down to business! Come on back, YOU
HEAR ME! . . . . If you been hood-
winked by agents of some foreign government, I've been authorized by the
President of these United States to inform
you that this liberty-loving Republic is
prepared to rescue you from their clutches.
Don't pay no 'tention to their sireen songs
and atheistic promises! You better off
under our control and you know it! . . .
If you been bamboozled by rabble-rousing
nonsense of your own so-called leaders,
we prepared to offer some protection. Just
call us up! Just give us a sign! . . . Come
on, give us a sign . . . give us a sign—
even a teeny-weeny one . . . ? [*Glances*
around checking on possible communica-
tions. A bevy of headshakes indicate no
success. MAYOR *returns to address with*
desperate fervor.] Now look—you don't
know what you doing! If you persist in
this disobedience, you know all too well
the consequences! We'll track you to the
end of the earth, beyond the galaxy,
across the stars! We'll capture you and
chastise you with all the vengeance we
command! 'N' you know only too well
how stern we kin be when double-crossed!
The city, the state and the entire nation

will crucify you for this unpardonable defiance! [*Checks again.*] No call . . . ? No sign . . . ? Time is running out! Deadline slipping past! They gotta respond! They gotta! [*Resuming.*] Listen to me! I'm begging y'all, you've gotta come back . . . ! LOOK, GEORGE! [*Waves dirty rag aloft.*] I brought the rag you wax the car wit'. . . . Don't this bring back memories, George, of all the days you spent shining that automobile to shimmering perfection . . . ? And you, Rufus?! . . . Here's the shoe polisher and the brush! . . . 'Member, Rufus? . . . Remember the happy mornings you spent popping this rag and whisking this brush so furiously 'till it created music that was sympho-nee to the ear . . . ? And you—MANDY? . . . Here's the waste-basket you didn't dump this morning. I saved it just for you! . . . LOOK, all y'all out there . . . ?

[*Signals and a three-person procession parades one after the other before the imaginary camera.*]

DOLL WOMAN. [*Brandishing a crying baby [doll] as she strolls past and exits.*] She's been crying ever since you left, Caldonia . . .

MOP MAN. [*Flashing mop.*] It's been waiting in the same corner, Buster . . .

BRUSH MAN. [*Flagging toilet brush in one hand and toilet plunger in other.*] It's been dry ever since you left, Washington . . .

MAYOR. [*Jumping in on the heels of the last exit.*] Don't these things mean anything to y'all? By God! Are your memories so short?! Is there nothing sacred to ya? . . . Please come back, for my sake, please! All of you—even you questionable ones! I promise no harm will be done to you! Revenge is disallowed! We'll forgive everything! Just come on back and I'll git down on my knees— [*Immediately drops to knees.*] I'll be kneeling in the middle of Dixie Avenue to kiss the first shoe of the first one 'a you to show up. . . . *I'll smooch any other spot you request.* . . . Erase this nightmare 'n' we'll concede any demand you make, just come on back—please? . . . PLEEEEEEEZE?

VOICE. [*Shouting.*] TIME!

MAYOR. [*Remaining on knees, frozen in a pose of supplication. After a brief,*

deadly silence, he whispers almost inaudibly.] They wouldn't answer . . . they wouldn't answer . . .

[*Blackout as bedlam erupts offstage. Total blackness holds during a sufficient interval where offstage sound-effects create the illusion of complete pandemonium, followed by a diminution which trails off into an expressionistic simulation of a city coming to a stricken standstill: industrial machinery clanks to halt, traffic blares to silence, etc. . . . The stage remains dark and silent for a long moment, then lights re-arise on the* ANNOUNCER.]

ANNOUNCER. A pitiful sight, ladies and gentlemen. Soon after his unsuccessful appeal Mayor Lee suffered a vicious pummeling from the mob and barely escaped with his life. National Guardsmen and State Militia were impotent in quelling the fury of a town venting its frustration in an orgy of destruction—a frenzy of rioting, looting and all other aberrations of a town gone berserk. . . . Then—suddenly—as if a magic wand had been waved, madness evaporated and something more frightening replaced it: Submission. . . . Even whimperings ceased. The city: exhausted, benumbed.—Slowly its occupants slinked off into shadows, and by midnight, the town was occupied exclusively by zombies. The fight and life had been drained out. . . . Pooped. . . . Hope ebbed away as completely as the beloved, absent Negroes. . . . As our crew packed gear and crept away silently, we treaded softly—as if we were stealing away from a mausoleum. . . . The Face Of A Defeated City.

[*Blackout. Lights rise slowly at the sound of rooster-crowing, signalling the approach of a new day, the next morning. Scene is same as opening of play.* CLEM *and* LUKE *are huddled over dazedly, trancelike. They remain so for a long count. Finally, a figure drifts on stage, shuffling slowly.*]

LUKE. [*Gazing in silent fascination at the approaching figure.*] Clem . . . ? Do you see what I see or am I dreaming . . . ?

CLEM. It's a . . . a Nigra, ain't it, Luke . . . ?

LUKE. Sure looks like one, Clem—but we better make sure—eyes could be playing tricks on us. ... Does he still look like one to you, Clem?

CLEM. He still does, Luke—but I'm scared to believe—

LUKE. Why ... ? It looks like Rastus, Clem!

CLEM. Sure does, Luke . . . but we better not jump to no hasty conclusion . . .

LUKE. [*In timid softness.*] That you, Rastus ... ?

RASTUS. [*Stepin Fetchit, Willie Best, Nicodemus, B. McQueen and all the rest rolled into one.*] Why . . . howdy . . . Mr. Luke . . . Mr. Clem . . .

CLEM. It is him, Luke! It is him!

LUKE. Rastus?

RASTUS. Yas . . . sah?

LUKE. Where was you yesterday?

RASTUS. [*Very, very puzzled.*] Yes . . . ter . . . day? . . . Yester . . . day . . . ? Why . . . right . . . here . . . Mr. Luke . . .

LUKE. No you warn't, Rastus, don't lie to me! Where was you yestiddy?

RASTUS. Why . . . I'm sure I was . . . Mr. Luke . . . Remember . . . I made . . . that . . . delivery for you . . .

LUKE. That was MONDAY, Rastus, yestiddy was TUESDAY.

RASTUS. Tues . . . day . . . ? You don't say. . . . Well . . . well . . . well . . .

LUKE. Where was you 'n' all the other Nigras yesterday, Rastus?

RASTUS. I . . . thought . . . yestiddy . . . was Monday, Mr. Luke—I coulda swore it . . . ! . . . See how . . . things . . . kin git all mixed up? . . . I coulda swore it . . .

LUKE. TODAY is WEDNESDAY, Rastus. Where was you TUESDAY?

RASTUS. Tuesday . . . huh? That's somp'um . . . I . . . don't . . . remember . . . missing . . . a day . . . Mr. Luke . . . but I guess you right . . .

LUKE. Then where was you?

RASTUS. Don't rightly know, Mr. Luke. I didn't know I had skipped a day—But that jist goes to show you how time kin fly, don't it, Mr. Luke. . . . Uuh, uuh, uuh . . .

[*He starts shuffling off, scratching head, a flicker of a smile playing across his lips.* CLEM *and* LUKE *gaze dumbfoundedly as he disappears.*]

LUKE. [*Eyes sweeping around in all directions.*] Well. . . . There's the others, Clem. . . . Back jist like they useta be. . . . Everything's same as always . . .

CLEM. Is it . . . Luke?

[*Slow fade.*]

CURTAIN

For Discussion and Writing

1. Although the playwright indicates that this play can be performed either by blacks or whites, why do you think he prefers a negro cast acting in white face like "a reverse minstrel show"? In your opinion, would more be gained by using a black or a white cast? Why must the Announcer be a "bona fide white actor" in either case? And why must Rastus be a black?

2. Read the "Production Concept" of a red-white-and-blue play with its directions for both lighting and costuming. Discuss what the playwright is trying to accomplish by this color scheme and whether or not you think such a scheme will strengthen the total effect of the play.

3. Ward calls *Day of Absence* a satirical fantasy—perhaps because, through the introduction of supernatural elements, the play holds human vices and follies up to ridicule. Point out instances in which the playwright satirizes such attitudes and behavior in our society.
   Besides the sudden and unexplained disappearance of all blacks, what other elements of fantasy and the supernatural appear in the play?

4. Critics say that *Day of Absence* contains many elements of the Theater of the Absurd. How many of the following characteristics of Theater of the Absurd apply to *Day of Absence* and in what way?

   Presents a shocking situation (often visual) which is not to be taken literally but rather as a symbol of some human condition or conflict.

   The situation forces us to see with new understanding the absurdity of some of our present-day values.

   The characters are one-dimensional and subjectively drawn.

   Action is often a pattern of images rather than a plotted story.

   Language is treated as a hindrance to "real" communication.

5. Where do you think Rastus has been? Why does the playwright never tell us where the black people were on their "day of absence"? Discuss whether you would have enjoyed the play more—or less—if the writer had somehow let the audience in on the secret of the blacks' disappearance.

6. What are the implications of the last two lines of the play? What have the whites learned from this experience? What have the blacks learned?

7. Imagine a "day of absence" of your own during which some essential factor (human or otherwise) disappears from our society. Write a script for a roving television news reporter who is excitedly explaining to his audience the effects of what has happened.
   Or, as an alternative, write a script for the dialogue that takes place between Mary and Lula upon Lula's return.

Notes on the Playwrights

Notes on the Playwrights

MARY CHASE (1907–   )

Mary Chase was born Mary Coyle in 1907 in Denver, Colorado to an Irish family with four uncles from whom she acquired her taste for Celtic pookas, and a feeling for literature.

At fifteen, she became a summer apprentice reporter for the *Rocky Mountain News*, enrolling at the same time in the University of Denver. After two years there and another year at the University of Colorado, she left college to become a full time reporter. She married Robert Chase, a fellow reporter on the *Rocky Mountain News*, and retired to be a housewife. In the next few years, she bore three sons, wrote five plays, and engaged in a variety of other occupations.

Mary Chase seems never to have lost her understanding of the world of the child. Her sympathy for the young is the core of the fantasy in each of her Broadway successes—*Harvey, Mrs. McThing,* and *Bernadine.*

LILLIAN HELLMAN (1905–   )

America's foremost woman playwright was born in New Orleans in 1905. Shuttled back and forth between New Orleans and New York from the time manent New Yorker. She took courses both at New York University and she was five until she was sixteen, Miss Hellman finally became a per- Columbia University, and then worked for a New York publisher, did book reviewing, wrote short stories which didn't sell, and worked for a brief period as a Hollywood manuscript reader. She took a job later as playreader in the office of Herman Shumlin, a theatrical producer. The plays she read were so bad she decided to write her own, most of which were produced and directed on Broadway by Mr. Shumlin, and later adapted to films in Hollywood.

Her first play, *The Children's Hour*, produced in 1934, was an instant success. Her best known plays are *The Little Foxes* (1939), *Watch on the Rhine* (1941), which won the Drama Critics Circle Award, *Another Part of the Forest* (1946), *Autumn Garden* (1951), and *Toys in the Attic* (1960).

All her plays show concern for social problems and the eternal human battle between good and evil.

JOSEPH KESSELRING (1902–1967)

Nothing in Joseph Kesslering's background indicated that he would one day write what many consider the world's funniest play about murder— unless it was the fact that he collected weapons for a hobby.

Born in New York in 1902, he made his stage debut as a singer and an actor at the age of eight in a musical play performed by the boys' choir of a New York church and became at twenty years of age a professor of music at Bethel College in Newton, Kansas. At the age of twenty-four, his career took a sudden turn with his appearance as a professional actor in the Chicago company of *Gentlemen Prefer Blondes.*

Shortly thereafter he began to experiment with the writing of vaudeville sketches and short stories, turning his attention at last to the writing of plays. Over a period of thirty years, Kesselring wrote more than a dozen plays of which only four reached Broadway, and among these only *Arsenic and Old Lace* proved a "hit."

RICHARD NASH (1913–   )

Although many critics agree that the Western locale adds greatly to the appeal of *The Rainmaker*, its author is an out-and-out "easterner," a native of Philadelphia where he attended high school and graduated in 1934 from the University of Pennsylvania.

Six years later, he won the Maxwell Anderson Verse Drama Award for *Parting at Imsdorf*, and by 1958 six of his plays had been produced on Broadway, among them *The Young and Fair*. He also wrote the librettos for the musicals *Wildcat*, which starred Lucille Ball, and *The Happy Time*, which opened on Broadway in 1968.

Between plays, Nash headed the theater department at Bryn Mawr College, wrote film scripts (including a screen version of *Porgy and Bess*) and contributed seven television plays to the early Philco Playhouse. He has received a number of international drama awards for his plays.

EUGENE O'NEILL (1888–1953)

Eugene O'Neill's life was haunted by tragedy. Son of the famous matinee idol, James O'Neill, he spent his unstable childhood backstage and in hotel rooms with a mother who suffered from drug addiction and an older brother, James, an alcoholic. Restless and rebellious, his only roots were in the family summer home in New London, Connecticut. O'Neill left home after his suspension from Princeton University in 1907 to follow a bohemian existence including an annulled marriage, gold prospecting, acting and stage managing, shipping out to sea, newspaper reporting, malaria and eventually tuberculosis. Hospitalized for six months, he turned his attention to playwriting, and enrolled finally in George Pierce Baker's "Workshop 47" for playwrights at Harvard University. In 1916, his one-act sea plays were produced by the Provincetown Players at the Wharf Theater in Provincetown, Massachusetts.

O'Neill established his Broadway reputation with *The Emperor Jones*, 1920, "*The Hairy Ape*," 1922, and *Desire Under the Elms*, 1924. In 1931 came *Mourning Becomes Electra*, in 1933, *Ah Wilderness*, and *The Iceman Cometh*, 1946.

In 1943, stricken by palsy and no longer able to hold a pencil, O'Neill stopped writing. After ten years of intense physical and mental suffering, he died in 1953, a lonely, embittered man, his work mocked by the new critics.

After his death, the Broadway openings of his previously unproduced work made him the most celebrated dramatist of the 1950's. He gained new stature with *Long Day's Journey Into Night*, 1956, *A Moon for the Misbegotten*, 1957, *A Touch of the Poet*, 1958. *More Stately Mansions*, unsuccessful in an earlier production, opened on Broadway in 1967.

O'Neill won three Pulitzer Prizes in his lifetime: *Beyond the Horizon*, 1920, *Anna Christie*, 1921, *Strange Interlude*, 1928; a fourth Pultizer Prize was awarded posthumously in 1957 for *A Long Day's Journey Into Night*, an autobiographical play. An exciting innovator, he became in 1936 the only American playwright ever to receive the Nobel Prize for literature.

JOHN PATRICK (1906–   )

John Patrick, was born in Louisville, Kentucky, was separated from his parents in early childhood, and cared for by aunts who sent him to a succession of boarding schools which he remembers with pain. He later attended Holy Cross College in New Orleans, and Columbia and Harvard Universities.

After a brief career as a radio script writer, Patrick became a produced playwright in 1935 with a play described by critics as one of the worst plays they had ever seen. He next spent two years in Hollywood as a screen writer. Three months after Pearl Harbor, he joined the American Field Service and served overseas as driver with a British Ambulance Unit in Egypt, Syria, India and Burma.

He came home with the rank of captain and the script of *The Hasty Heart*, written in longhand in just twelve days on a transport ship. Finally produced in 1945 this play was his first Broadway success. Among his better known screen plays are *Three Coins in a Fountain, Love Is a Many-Splendoured Thing, The World of Suzie Wong,* and *Les Girls.*

RICHARD RODGERS, composer (1902–   )
OSCAR HAMMERSTEIN II, lyricist (1895–1960)

These collaborators, who changed the whole character of the American musical theater, seemed destined to cross paths from the beginning. Born in New York City only seven years apart, both were educated at Columbia University and both wrote material for student productions. But though they worked together on an insertion number for the 1920 Varsity show, thirty-two years passed before they joined their talents professionally to create *Oklahoma.*

Richard Rodgers left Columbia at the end of his sophomore year to work with Lorenz Hart and to study music under Walter Damrosch. The collaboration of Rodgers and Hart, which lasted for twenty-four years, resulted in such Broadway musical successes as *A Connecticut Yankee, I'd Rather Be Right, The Boys from Syracuse* (adapted from Shakespeare's *Comedy of Errors*), and *Pal Joey* (from John O'Hara's novel).

Oscar Hammerstein finished his B.A. at Columbia and two years later received a degree from Columbia Law School. Instead of practicing law, he entered the theatrical profession as a stage manager. By the time he joined forces with Rodgers in 1942, he had written the lyrics and librettos for such hits as *The Desert Song, Show Boat,* and *Carmen Jones* (a modernized version of the opera Carmen).

Rodgers and Hammerstein together wrote nine musical plays, four of which are landmarks in the American theater: *Oklahoma,* 1943 (Pulitzer Prize), *Carousel,* 1945 (Drama Critics Award), *South Pacific,* 1949 (both Pulitzer Prize and Drama Critics Award), and *The King and I* in 1951. Their final collaboration, before Hammerstein's death, was on *Sound of Music* in 1959.

ROD SERLING (1924–   )

Rod Serling, once called television's angry young man, was born in Syracuse, New York. After high school, he enlisted in World War II as a paratrooper, and was wounded in the Philippines. Along the way, he proved to be an able amateur boxer. Under the G.I. Bill of Rights, he enrolled in Antioch College, Ohio, where he met his wife, began to write radio dramas, and won second prize in a CBS script contest.

He sold his first TV script in 1951, and by 1955, he had sold ninety scripts to major television networks and was one of the most discussed writers in the business. Some of his successful television dramas are *Patterns, The Rock, Requiem for a Heavyweight,* and *Old MacDonald Had a Curve* (all collected in a book called *Patterns*), and *The Comedian* written in 1957. He then turned in 1959 to fantasy in a science-fiction series for CBS-TV, entitled *Twilight Zone.*

Serling has won many awards for his TV dramas, including three "Emmies" and two Sylvania "Best Drama" awards.

ROBERT E. SHERWOOD (1896–1955)

Born in New Rochelle, New York, into a well-to-do family, Robert Sherwood gave voice to the conflicts of his generation. He left Harvard in his senior year to join the Canadian Black Watch in World War I. Severely wounded, Sherwood returned to America a confirmed pacifist. He served as film critic and then as editor of two influential magazines, a connection terminated in each case because of his insistence on the right to absolutely free speech.

Sherwood's reputation as a playwright was established by such plays as *The Road to Rome* (1927), *Reunion in Vienna* (1931), *The Petrified Forest* (1935), and *Idiot's Delight* (1936). Then in the face of the rising tide of Fascism and Naziism, he searched American history for a renewal of faith and wrote in 1938 *Abe Lincoln in Illinois,* which prepared the way for *There Shall Be No Night.*

Sherwood won three Pulitzer Prizes in drama, became the Director of the Overseas Branch of the Office of War Information and assisted in the writing of President Franklin D. Roosevelt's speeches. In 1949, his biography of *Roosevelt and Hopkins* won him a fourth Pulitzer Prize. He later won an Oscar for his film script *The Best Years of Our Lives.*

DOUGLAS TURNER WARD (1931–   )

Born on a plantation in Louisiana and raised in New Orleans, Douglas Turner Ward moved in 1948 to New York, where he spent three years as a journalist and studied acting in Paul Mann's Actors' Workshop. Turning to the theater, he became a working actor in such off-Broadway productions as *The Iceman Cometh* at the Circle-in-the-Square, *The Blacks,* and *Blood Knot.* Jose Quintero featured him in the New York City Center production of *Lost in the Stars;* he understudied Sidney Poitier in Lorraine Hansbury's *Raisin in the Sun* and played the leading role in the cross-country tour. His other credits include *One Flew Over the Cuckoo's Nest* on Broadway, *Coriolanus* for the New York Shakespeare Festival, and frequent television appearances on leading network shows.

The next step was playwriting, and since 1965, Ward has had three one-act plays successfully produced off Broadway: *Happy Ending, Day of Absence,* and *Brotherhood.* As a result of his August 1966 *New York Times* article on "American Theater: For Whites Only?" in which he pleaded for the establishment of a permanent Negro repertory company, a substantial grant from the Ford Foundation enabled him to found the Negro Ensemble Company. As its Artistic Director, Ward is committed to producing quality plays "concentrating primarily on themes of Negro life."

THORNTON WILDER (1897–)

Considered by some to be America's "foremost man of letters," Thornton Wilder was born in Madison, Wisconsin, where his father was the editor of a small-town newspaper. Educated in California and China, Wilder spent a year in the Coast Guard in World War I, received his B.A. from Yale in 1920 and his M.A. from Princeton in 1925. He has since followed a dual career of teacher-lecturer and writer-playwright, and he has been a professor both at the University of Chicago and Harvard University.

He has written many distinguished novels, including *The Bridge of San Luis Rey* which received the Pulitzer Prize in 1928 and *The Eighth Day* which received the National Book Award for fiction in 1968. He has written four full-length plays: *Our Town*, 1938, *Skin of Our Teeth*, 1942 (both Pulitzer Prize winners), *The Merchant of Yonkers*, 1938, *The Matchmaker*, 1955 (a rewrite of *The Merchant of Yonkers*) on which the musical, *Hello Dolly*, is based.

TENNESSEE WILLIAMS (1911–)

Tennessee Williams, born Thomas Lanier Williams in Columbus, Mississippi in 1911, was later dubbed "Tennessee'" because of his Indian-fighting Tennessee ancestors. When Williams was seven, his father, formerly a traveling salesman, brought his family to St. Louis to live. Neither Williams nor his sister ever made the adjustment from the gentle, rural Southern existence to the confined life of a city. When he graduated from the University of Iowa in 1938, his one act plays were already being produced by a St. Louis theatrical group.

Williams received the Drama Critics Circle Award for *The Glass Menagerie*, 1945, *A Streetcar Named Desire*, 1947, *Cat on a Hot Tin Roof*, 1955, and *Night of the Iguana*, 1961. *A Streetcar Named Desire* and *Cat on a Hot Tin Roof* also received Pulitzer Prizes.

Williams has also written film adaptations, short stories, poetry, and a novel, and has received wide international acclaim.

Glossary of Theater Terms

Glossary of Theater Terms

Antagonist: The character in conflict with the main character or hero of the play. Sometimes referred to as "the villain."

Anti-climax: A point after the climax in a dramatic piece. Frequently lessens the effect of the crisis.

Aside: Usually a brief remark by a character to the audience which the other characters are not supposed to hear. Can also be a monologue to convey a character's thoughts.

Avant-garde: New movements and experiments in the theater.

Backdrop: A curtain sometimes dropped at the back of the stage and painted to represent the sky or some other background.

Backstage: The area of the theater behind the curtain of the prosenium arch. When the curtain is up, backstage is behind the back wall of the set.

Book: The libretto, text or story of a musical comedy. Does not include the lyrics.

Climax: A high point of interest in a play. The moment of crisis when audience suspense is greatest.

Comedy: A play, usually light and humorous, with a happy ending.

Complication: An added difficulty for the protagonist in the development of the rising action or suspense of a play.

Conflict: The struggle out of which the dramatic action develops.

Crisis: A decisive turning point in dramatic action.

Cross (abbreviated as "X"): To go from one place to another on stage.

Denouement: The unraveling of the complications of the plot at the end of a play. In tragedy, it is called "catastrophe."

Downstage: The front part of the stage, nearest to the audience. Down center (DC) is downstage center, down left (DL) is downstage left (the actor's left and the audience's right), and down right (DR) is downstage right (the actor's right and the audience's left).

Exposition: The explanation early in the play of anything the audience needs to know that happened before the play began.

Falling action: The dramatic action coming after the climax.

Fantasy: A play stressing the imaginative or fanciful rather than the realistic.

Farce: A broadly exaggerated comedy based on improbable situations, fast physical action, and characterizations bordering on the ludicrous.

Left stage (or "left," abbreviation "L"): Left side of the stage (the actor's left, the audience's right).

Libretto (see Book)

Live drama: Drama performed on a stage before an audience, as opposed to motion pictures. In television, drama broadcast directly from a performance as opposed to filmed drama.

Lyrics: The words of the songs in musical plays and musical comedies.

Melodrama: A play aiming at thrills and featuring implausible characterization, dialogue, and situation; generally exaggerated heroic and villainous figures with a happy ending and virtue triumphant.

Off-Broadway: Small New York theaters operating on lower budgets than the larger Broadway theaters.

Offstage: The area of the stage which is not visible to the audience.

Presentational theater: Anti-realistic theater. Direct and open use of theatrical devices instead of attempting to represent life realistically.

Property (or "Prop"): Any object used on the stage as part of the action of the play (like a telephone or a letter).

Proscenium (or "proscenium arch"): The rectangular stage opening framing the play, through which the audience sees the action.

Protagonist: The main character or hero of a play.

Recognition scene: A scene near the end of a play (especially a tragedy) in which the principal character learns the truth about himself.

Representational theater: Realistic theater representing life.

Reprise: In musical comedy, a repetition of a song or dance performed with variations.

Resolution: The final solution to the complication in the play.

Right Stage (or "right," abbreviation "R"): Right side of the stage (the actor's right, the audience's left).

Rising action: The dramatic action up to the climax or turning point of a play.

Score: The music for a musical play.

Scrim: A thin, transparent drop curtain which, when lighted from behind, gives an unreal effect of dream, mist, imagination.

Set: (short for "Setting"): The arrangement of scenery, props, and light effects which make up the background for the scene.

Social drama: Plays dealing with man in relation to his social environment and social problems.

Stage business (or "Business"): Actions performed by an actor to make his characterization more lifelike. May or may not be in the script.

Stage left (see "Left stage")

Stage right (see "Right stage")

Sub-plot (subordinate plot): A minor or secondary story line in a play.

Suspense (or "Dramatic suspense"): Audience uncertainty about the outcome of the crisis in the play.

Up stage: The back half of the stage, away from the audience.

Other Important American Plays

Other Important American Plays

1920 The Emperor Jones–EUGENE O'NEILL

1923 The Adding Machine–ELMER RICE

1924 The Show-Off–GEORGE KELLY
    What Price Glory?–LAURENCE STALLINGS AND MAXWELL ANDERSON
    Desire Under the Elms–EUGENE O'NEILL

1925 Craig's Wife–GEORGE KELLY

1926 The Great God Brown–EUGENE O'NEILL
    The Silver Cord–SIDNEY HOWARD

1928 The Front Page–BEN HECHT AND CHARLES MACARTHUR
    Strange Interlude–EUGENE O'NEILL

1929 Street Scene–ELMER RICE
    Berkeley Square–JOHN S. BALDERSTON

1930 Green Pastures–MARC CONNELLY
    Elizabeth the Queen–MAXWELL ANDERSON

1931 Mourning Becomes Electra–EUGENE O'NEILL
    Of Thee I Sing (musical comedy)–KAUFMAN AND RYSKIND

1932 Biography–S. N. BEHRMAN
    The Animal Kingdom–PHILIP BARRY

1933 Ah Wilderness–EUGENE O'NEILL
    Men in White–SIDNEY KINGSLEY

1934 The Children's Hour–LILLIAN HELLMAN
    Yellow Jack–SIDNEY HOWARD
    Dodsworth–SIDNEY HOWARD

1935 Waiting for Lefty–CLIFFORD ODETS
    Awake and Sing–CLIFFORD ODETS
    The Petrified Forest–ROBERT SHERWOOD
    Winterset–MAXWELL ANDERSON
    Dead End–SIDNEY KINGSLEY
    Porgy and Bess (musical play)–GEORGE GERSHWIN & THE HEYWARDS

1936 Idiot's Delight–ROBERT SHERWOOD
    Bury the Dead–IRWIN SHAW
    You Can't Take It With You–GEORGE S. KAUFMAN & MOSS HART
    The Women–CLARE BOOTH

1937 The Cradle Will Rock (musical drama)–MARC BLITZSTEIN

1938 Abe Lincoln in Illinois–ROBERT SHERWOOD
    Here Come the Clowns–PHILIP BARRY

1939   Life With Father–LINDSAY AND CROUSE
        The Man Who Came to Dinner–KAUFMAN AND HART
        The Time of Your Life–WILLIAM SAROYAN
        My Heart's in the Highlands–WILLIAM SAROYAN

1940   The Male Animal–JAMES THURBER & ELLIOTT NUGENT
        Pal Joey (musical drama)–RICHARD RODGERS & LORENZ HART

1941   Watch on the Rhine–LILLIAN HELLMAN
        Lady in the Dark (musical drama)–MOSS HART

1942   The Skin of Our Teeth–THORNTON WILDER

1944   I Remember Mama–JOHN VAN DRUTEN

1945   The Hasty Heart–JOHN PATRICK
        Carousel (musical drama)–RODGERS & HAMMERSTEIN

1946   Born Yesterday–GARSON KANIN
        The Iceman Cometh–EUGENE O'NEILL

1947   All My Sons–ARTHUR MILLER
        A Streetcar Named Desire–TENNESSEE WILLIAMS

1948   Mister Roberts–JOSHUA LOGAN & THOMAS HEGGEN
        Summer and Smoke–TENNESSEE WILLIAMS

1949   Death of a Salesman–ARTHUR MILLER
        South Pacific (musical drama)–RODGERS & HAMMERSTEIN

1950   Come Back, Little Sheba–WILLIAM INGE
        The Member of the Wedding–CARSON MCCULLERS

1951   Billy Budd (adapted from Melville)–LOUIS COXE & ROBERT
        CHAPMAN
        I Am A Camera–JOHN VAN DRUTEN
        Darkness at Noon–SIDNEY KINGSLEY

1953   The Crucible–ARTHUR MILLER
        Picnic–WILLIAM INGE
        Camino Real–TENNESSEE WILLIAMS

1954   The Caine Mutiny Court Martial–HERMAN WOUK

1955   The Diary of Anne Frank–FRANCES GOODRICH & ALBERT HACKETT
        Bus Stop–WILLIAM INGE

1956   Long Day's Journey Into Night–EUGENE O'NEILL
        My Fair Lady (musical play based on Shaw's *Pygmalion*)–
        LERNER & LOEWE

1957   West Side Story (musical drama)–LAURENTS, SONDHEIM, AND
        LEONARD BERNSTEIN

1959   A Raisin in the Sun–LORRAINE HANSBERRY
        The Andersonville Trial–SAUL LEVITT

1960   Toys in the Attic–LILLIAN HELLMAN
        The Zoo Story; The Sandbox (one act plays)–EDWARD ALBEE

1961   The Connection–JACK GELBER
        The American Dream (one-act play)–EDWARD ALBEE

1962   Who's Afraid of Virginia Woolf?–EDWARD ALBEE
        Oh Dad, Poor Dad, Mamma's Hung You in the Closet and I'm
        Feelin' So Sad–ARTHUR KOPIT

1963   Hughie (one-act play)–EUGENE O'NEILL

1964   The Old Glory (three short plays)–ROBERT LOWELL
        Fiddler on the Roof (musical drama based on Sholem Alei-
        cheim's stories)–JOSEPH STEIN, SHELDON HARNICH, JERRY BOCK
        The Toilet; Dutchman (one-act plays)–LE ROI JONES

1965   Man of La Mancha (musical drama)–DALE WASSERMAN, JOE
        DARION, MITCH LEIGH
        The Odd Couple–NEIL SIMON
        America Hurrah (three one-act plays)–JEAN CLAUDE VAN ITALLIE

1966   The Lion in Winter–JAMES GOLDMAN

1968   The Price–ARTHUR MILLER
        The Great White Hope–HOWARD SACKLER

1969   1776 (musical drama)–PETER STONE, SHERMAN EDWARDS

1971   Basic Training of Pavlo Hummel–DAVID RABE
        Sticks and Bones–DAVID RABE

1972   That Championship Season–JASON MILLER

SCRIBNER STUDENT PAPERBACKS

SSP 2   Fitzgerald, The GREAT GATSBY

SSP 6   Hemingway, THE OLD MAN AND THE SEA

SSP 7   Paton, CRY, THE BELOVED COUNTRY

SSP 8   Rawlings, THE YEARLING

SSP 10   Wharton, ETHAN FROME

SSP 11   Schweitzer, A VARIETY OF SHORT PLAYS

SSP 12   Kirkpatrick and Goodfellow, POETRY WITH PLEASURE

SSP 13   Schweitzer, DISCOVERING SHORT STORIES

SSP 14   Schweitzer, A VARIETY OF SHORT STORIES

SSP 15   Ridout and Stuart, SHORT STORIES FOR DISCUSSION

SSP 16   Poulakis, AMERICAN FOLKLORE

SSP 17   Massey, THE COMIC SPIRIT IN AMERICA

SSP 18   Bogart, THE JAZZ AGE

SSP 19   THE AMERICAN DREAM

SSP 20   Mintz, AMERICA, THE MELTING POT

SSP 21   Pappas, HEROES OF THE AMERICAN WEST

SSP 22   Goodman, AMERICANS TODAY

SSP 23   Hemingway, A FAREWELL TO ARMS

SSP 24   Cleary, THE SUNDOWNERS

SSP 25   Marqués, THE OXCART

SSP 28   Sheffy and Collier, IMPRESSIONS IN ASPHALT

SSP 29   Bogart, THE BITTER YEARS

SSP 30   Brown, TWICE FIFTEEN

SSP 31   Harrison and Pugner, A SCIENCE FICTION READER

SSP 32   Corbin and Balf, TWELVE AMERICAN PLAYS, Alternate Edition

SCRIBNER STUDENT PAPERBACKS